1809: Thunder on the Danube

1809

Thunder on the Danube: Napoleon's Defeat of the Habsburgs

VOLUME I: ABENSBERG

JOHN H. GILL

FRONTLINE BOOKS, LONDON

This volume is dedicated to

John R. Elting
Colonel, US Army
(1912–2000)

Friend, Guide, Soldier

FRONTLINE BOOKS, LONDON

1809 Thunder on the Danube: Napoleon's Defeat of the Habsburgs

This edition published in 2008 by Frontline Books, an imprint of Pen and Sword Books Ltd, 47 Church Street, Barnsley, S. Yorkshire, S70 2AS
www.frontline-books.com

Copyright © John H. Gill, 2008

ISBN: 978-184415-713-6

CIP data records for this title are available from the British Library and the Library of Congress

For more information on our books, please visit www.frontline-books.com, email info@frontline-books.com or write to us at the above address.

Typeset and designed by JCS Publishing Services Ltd, www.jcs-publishing.co.uk
Printed and bound in Great Britain by Biddles Ltd, King's Lynn

Contents

Maps, Charts and Tables

MAPS

CHARTS

TABLES

Key to Map Symbols

John H. Gill © 2006, all rights reserved

Units types are indicated by the following symbols. As in the text, units known by their proprietors' or commanders' names are printed in italics.

Sample cavalry unit: Austrian *Liechtenstein* Hussars No. 7 =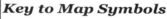
Liechtenstein

Sample infantry unit: Austrian *Hiller* Infantry No. 2 = *Hiller*

Sample artillery (all sides): ▮▮▮

Nationality is shown by colour: white for Austrians, black for French, and grey for Napoleon's German allies.

Bavarian 3rd Division = 3 Div   **French 1st Cavalry Division =** 1

Austrian movements (advance and retreat) are shown with dashed lines, while those of the French and allied German troops are solid.

Austrian movement = ······▶   **Allied movement =** ───────▶

Where helpful for clarity, the following units size symbols have been used.

Regiment   **Battalion or Squadron**   **Company**

Illustrations

Except where noted in the plate section, all illustrations are from the author's collection

Acknowledgements

Historical works are always team products in one sense or another and this is no exception. I would therefore like to take a few lines to thank some of the many who have helped nudge this project in its extended development. Errors and interpretations, of course, will come knocking at my door, but I could never have come so far without the kind assistance of a host of others, some of whom I would like to acknowledge.

In Austria, the scholars and staff at the Haus-, Hof-, und Staatsarchiv and the Kriegsarchiv were courteous and friendly, their support invaluable, particularly Dr Broucek and Dr Gaisbauer. The library team at the Kriegsarchiv deserves special thanks for patience and helpfulness. At an individual level, I am indebted to Dr Manfried Rauchensteiner, Mag Michael Wenzel, and Herr Ferdi Wöber for their tremendous thoughtfulness and *Gastfreundlichkeit*. Just across the border, Dr Laszlo Ottovay and Dr Eva Nyulaszi-Straub were instrumental in providing me a host of recondite Hungarian sources across long distances and several years.

Among German archives, I had the pleasure of working with helpful professionals at the Generallandesarchiv in Karlsruhe (Dr Brüning), the Sächsisches Hauptstaatsarchiv Dresden (Archivrat Schirok), the Militärgeschichtliches Forschungsamt (Frau R. Stang), the Hauptstaatsarchiv Stuttgart (wonderfully accessible and very prompt service), and, above all, with the extremely supportive Dr A. Fuchs and staff at the Kriegsabteilung of the Bayerisches Hauptstaatsarchiv. Dr Fuchs, now retired, deserves particular mention for many years of assistance on a variety of projects. Dr Thomas Hemmann, whose excellent website is worth a look (www. napoleonzeit.de), Herr Uwe Wild, and Herr Alfred Umhey have been very considerate in helping in a number of cases.

On the French side, the Archives de la Guerre in Vincennes have been the source of much of my background material and have always proven helpful, the staff truly going out of its way on at least one occasion. The Archives Nationales and the Archives of the Ministry of Foreign Affairs have also been prompt and professional.

Among my American and British friends, I would like to thank Dr Mike Leggiere, Dr Sam Mustafa, Dr Mike Pavkovic, and Dr Rick Schneid for unstinting support and comradeship. All four deserve tribute, in addition to sharing their insights and resources, often going above and beyond the call to rescue me. Dr Roger Harrison and Dr Michael Yaffe of the Near East–South Asia Center for Strategic Studies generously gave editorial comment and larger wisdom. Dr Ashley J. Tellis toured Regensburg with me recently and kindly supplied the author photograph. Mr Dave Hollins in the UK, a font of knowledge on matters Austrian, has pointed the way to a number of interesting details. Herr Mark van Hattem of the small but superb Dutch Army Museum (Legermuseum) in Delft offered insightful observations on Austrian thinking. Mr Peter Harrington, Curator of the Anne S. K. Brown Collection (John Hay Library, Brown University), the world resource for military iconography, helped locate and supply many of the images in this volume.

It is fitting as well to pass a fond thought towards those whose friendship we treasured and whose passing we regret: Dr David G. Chandler, Col John R. Elting, Mrs Anne Elting, and Dr Gunther E. Rothenberg.

I must also offer heartfelt thanks to Frontline Books. From conversations in Washington to wandering the stacks of libraries in London, it has been a cherished pleasure to enjoy the friendship, consideration, and professional understanding that Lionel Leventhal, Michael Leventhal, Kate Baker, and the entire Frontline staff display as a matter of course. Special mention must go to Jessica Cuthbert-Smith for thorough and thoughtful editing.

Finally, my deepest gratitude goes to Anne Rieman, Grant Gill, and Hunter Gill. Anne, who has indulged my quirky hours, who has read and re-read draft chapters, and who sacrificed part of a trip to Paris to help me make photocopies in Vincennes, is beyond all praise. She and the boys have tolerated long hours of absence, endless discussions of early nineteenth-century European political-military affairs, and short (or long) diversions from otherwise sensible routes of travel to halt at battle sites famous and obscure: pausing on the banks of the Traun (where the Young Guard Grenadiers enacted their own skirmish), for example, or driving through snow squalls to Znaim. Their patience, understanding, and assistance fill one's heart.

Preface

> Under such circumstances, when the spring is wound so tight, a war can become desirable, if only to resolve matters. Thus in the physical world, the painfully tense condition of Nature at the approach of a storm awakes a desire for the thunder to break loose . . .
>
> Emperor Napoleon to the Austrian Ambassador, 15 August 1808[1]

It was a campaign framed in thunder. At Hausen on 19 April, the first major engagement of the war, a sudden, furious deluge brought the sanguinary struggle to a halt and sent soldiers of both sides scurrying for the sheltering woods. Three months later at Znaim, a similar downpour punctuated the war's final clash and ushered in the armistice that concluded the conflict. Lightning, thunder and torrential rain also preceded the titanic Battle of Wagram, pummelling the 150,000 French and German soldiers who waited, shivering in knee-deep water, to cross the last remaining arm of the Danube. Even the tiny encounter at Gefrees was interrupted when the hot July skies burst and lashed the combatants with pelting, pounding, wind-driven rain. Storms of uncommon violence were thus the overture, coda and finale to the conflict, a theme of natural cataclysm to accompany humankind's destructive endeavours.

The brutal drama of battle matched these spectacles of nature. When Archduke Charles led the Austrian Main Army into Bavaria on 10 April, for example, he stood on the threshold of a rare opportunity to destroy the French army in detail. Napoleon was still in Paris, directing his scattered forces at long distance through his chief of staff, Marshal Alexander Berthier. Berthier, however, was unequal to the task and the tense opening phases of the war thus saw the emperor hastening to the Danube valley to correct the manifold errors of his faithful lieutenant. His success in completely reversing the dire strategic situation, seizing the initiative from the lumbering Austrians, and gaining a series of five stunning victories in as many days has seldom been equalled in the annals of military history. Napoleon himself considered these manoeuvres his finest achievement. Likewise, his concentration of the army in early July and his detailed preparations for the second crossing of the Danube stand as masterpieces of strategy and operational art.

The ensuing Battle of Wagram was, by any standard, a struggle of awesome proportions, in scale and duration second only during the Napoleonic era to the climactic Battle of Nations at Leipzig in 1813. For two long, hot July days the French and Austrian armies, totalling more than 320,000 men with 900 guns, battered each other along a 22-kilometre firing line. These gigantic dimensions, however, were easily within the compass of Napoleon's capabilities, and the French army, in the words of one participant, manoeuvred 'like a regiment responding to the voice of its commander'.[2] As French military historian Edmond Buat has observed: 'On the French side, a single will, in effect, directed the general and specific movements of a mass of almost 200,000 men ... in the brilliant period of the imperial epic, one is unlikely to find a more vivid and striking example of the preponderant influence exercised in battle by a supreme commander.'[3]

Nor was this 'preponderant influence' confined to one battlefield or theatre of war. It extended across the entire bloody panorama of vicious battles and bold manoeuvres, a driving, unifying force that orchestrated operations from the Baltic to the Adriatic, from the Rhine to the Vistula. Simultaneously, of course, a host of other issues clamoured for Napoleon's attention. From his various headquarters along the Danube, he directed the distant war in Spain, managed the manifold affairs of empire and busied himself with the engrossing minutiae of military matters, all the while propelling the present campaign to its victorious conclusion. As a surgeon in the Baden brigade noted: 'the entire enterprise showed careful thought, proper consideration of all circumstances and sure control of all forces: everything hung from a single thread, sprang from a single vision or was the expression of a well thought out plan.'[4] Though strained by these competing and incessant demands, in 1809 Napoloeon was still the master of the situation, his broad vision, iron will and astonishing energy overpowering all obstacles to garner yet another triumph.

But this was also Napoleon's last successful campaign.[5] It brought his first serious repulse when the desperate Battle of Aspern-Essling ended his initial attempt to carry his army across the Danube, and even the hard-fought victory at Wagram did not result in a crushing, irremediable defeat for the Austrians. No Austerlitz, no Jena, no Friedland crowned this campaign, and the triumph, when won, was dearly purchased. Indeed, this was the beginning of Imperial France's military decline. The army that took the field in 1809, for instance, was hastily assembled and distinctly inferior to its famous predecessors of 1805 and 1806. It was still capable of remarkable martial feats, still characterised by impetuous energy and spirit, but a great influx of conscripts had diluted its strength, leaving it somewhat cumbersome, inefficient, and fragile. There were simply too many veterans in the wilds of Spain and too few in Germany. Moreover, Napoleon himself was beginning to show signs of the pernicious weaknesses that would grow more serious in the coming years: overestimation of his own abilities, contempt for the enemy, a certain carelessness and imprecision in orders and execution, even simple physical fatigue. He was still the 'Emperor of Battles', but the sharp edge of his skills was corroding.[6] The war of 1809 thus represents a watershed in the military history of the Napoleonic epoch, the turning point where his blazing star begins to falter.

While Napoleon and his army were showing these symptoms of decay, their foes were improving. Reorganised and modernised after the catastrophe of 1805, the Austrian army of 1809 was arguably one of the best ever fielded by the Habsburgs, and its chief, Archduke Charles, was a man of considerable military talent. Its courage and resilience at Aspern and Wagram were undeniable and certainly impressed Napoleon. Sometime later, when fawning courtiers sought to gain imperial favour by denigrating the Austrians, Napoleon responded with pointed scorn: 'It is obvious that you were not at Wagram.'[7] Measured against Napoleon's legions they were inadequate but the margin of French superiority had narrowed noticeably as compared to previous campaigns.

A key ingredient of Napoleon's earlier successes was thus absent in 1809. With an army only marginally superior to his adversary's, Napoleon's personal skills as a commander assumed even greater significance. Despite the decline in the quality of his instrument, despite the scale of operations, despite the nascent erosion of his own skills, his implacable will compensated, driving large armies across vast distances, infusing them with the 'sacred fire' and aiming them at a single purpose.[8] Archduke Charles and the rest of Austria's senior leaders, on the other hand, were still mired in the eighteenth century, their conceptions of strategy and the relationship of military operations to political goals hardly changed since the time of Maria Theresa and Field Marshal von Daun. Unable to adapt to the devastating nature of Napoleonic warfare, they were incapable of devising a modern strategy for their reformed army. Napoleon's genius towered over their limited horizons. While we may question some of his strategic decisions, he pursued his goals relentlessly, retaining the strategic initiative and never losing sight of the principal theatre of war. Nothing could contrast more dramatically with the dissolute, hesitant efforts of the Habsburg hierarchy.

For Austria, this war, begun with such high hopes, became another in a long string of costly and humiliating failures against Revolutionary and Imperial France. Despite the courage of the army and the best efforts of its commander, the military means were incapable of achieving the political end. Indeed, it can be argued that the Habsburg court was unable to devise a military strategy relevant to its constrained circumstances. Napoleon once again occupied the Schönbrunn Palace and French soldiers once more bore their proud eagles through the streets of Vienna. For the second time in four years, the eradication of the Habsburg monarchy seemed a real possibility and Kaiser Franz was fortunate to escape the war with the mere loss of territory and treasure.

Beyond the fate of empires, however, beyond the grandeur of high strategy and the glory of bright banners snapping in the wind, this is also a poignant human story. Napoleon loses one of his few true friends when Marshal Jean Lannes is mortally wounded at Aspern. General St Hilaire, promised a marshal's baton after his brilliant performance in April, is killed before he can receive this honour. General Lasalle, the quintessential hussar, falls to an Austrian bullet in the closing hours of Wagram after presentiments of death. Archduke Charles, forced to open the conflict before he and his army are ready, is relieved of command and dismissed in disgrace by his suspicious brother for accepting an armistice that probably saved the Habsburg monarchy.[9] There are ordinary soldiers too, of course, passing for our review in their thousands: the French lieutenant elevated to the nobility for his bravery, the ardent Viennese volunteers who gave their all at Ebelsberg, the Baden artillery captain who calmly smoked his pipe while his leg was amputated at Wagram.

This book then, is a military history of the war of 1809, Napoleon's last successful war, Archduke Charles's last command. In the pages that follow the reader will find a detailed account of the decisions, manoeuvres, battles, soldiers, and commanders that made up this conflict's constituent campaigns. In presenting this chronicle, I hope to establish a framework for analysing the difficult operational problems faced by the French emperor and his Habsburg adversaries, as well as the political considerations that influenced their strategic planning and battlefield actions. In particular, I want to highlight the importance of leadership and the moral dimension of war. For it is principally these factors, operating between the deafening crashes of thunder, that determined victory and defeat in 1809.

Sources and Conventions

First, complete source citations are included in the endnotes, and there is also a bibliographic note for this volume; for reasons of space a full bibliography will appear at the end of this series. Second, to deliver a clear and accurate account while retaining something of the flavour of the age, I have adopted the following conventions:

- French, German, and Austrian rank titles are preserved in so far as this is feasible and convenient, a table at the end of the volume relates these to current US and British ranks and lists abbreviations;
- 'Ligne' and 'Léger' refer respectively to French line and light infantry;
- I have also followed contemporary practice in designating Austrian regiments, using the titles derived from their *Inhaber* ('patrons' or 'proprietors') rather than their numbers (*Kaiser* Cuirassiers No. 1, not the 1st Cuirassier Regiment), although numbers are included where appropriate for clarity ('EH' abbreviates 'Erzherzog' as in Infantry Regiment *EH Ludwig* No. 8);
- To minimise confusion between individuals and units, units known by the names of their *Inhaber* or their commanders are presented in italics (Württemberg Oberst Karl von Neuffer commanded Jäger-Bataillon *von Neuffer*);
- I have used Arabic numerals for the French corps d'armée (Davout's 3rd Corps) and Roman numerals for the Austrians (Bellegarde's I Corps);
- Battalions or squadrons of a regiment are designated by Roman numerals (II/*Jordis* indicates the 2nd Battalion of *Jordis* Infantry Regiment No. 59);
- The term 'Rheinbund' refers to the Confederation of the Rhine;
- The terms 'Allied' and 'Allies', when capitalised, refer to the French and their German confederates, while 'German' refers to the host of small states between the Rhine and the Prussian border;

+ In most cases, modern German/Austrian, Italian, and Polish spellings have been used for geographical names so the reader can locate these on a present-day map or road sign (e.g. Eggmühl instead of Eckmühl). However, conventional Austrian names have been retained for terrain features and towns in the Czech Republic, Slovakia, and Hungary to minimise confusion;

+ All dates are given according to the Gregorian calendar rather than the Julian calendar then in use in Russia.

This work has been a long labour, aimed at several audiences and completed with the kind assistance of many others. I hope you will enjoy reading it as much as I enjoyed writing it.

CHAPTER I

War Is Unavoidable

The roots of the Franco-Austrian War of 1809 can be traced back to the rise of Republican and Imperial France and the collapse of the old international order in Europe. Though spattered with the blood of innumerable brutal battles, this old order had been founded on a set of shared assumptions that placed limits on the behaviour of states. This was the age of cabinet wars and small, expensive, professional armies. Influence might be gained or lost, baronies exchanged or fortresses conquered, but a certain balance was maintained among the major powers: Austria, Russia, Prussia, France, and Great Britain. The precise position each of these states occupied in the constellation of powers could shift, and frequently did (Prussia, for instance, had been a second-rate power until the mid-eighteenth century), but their status as Great Powers was fairly stable, their legitimacy as hereditary monarchies unquestioned.

As the eighteenth century became the nineteenth, however, events in France fundamentally altered the equations of power on the continent. Rising from the violence and dark chaos of its political and social upheaval, the new France was a revolutionary state, inherently threatening to the existence as well as the interests of the established dynasties.[1] This did not mean that every eye in every capital was focused on Paris. In the first years following the Revolution, Russia, Prussia, and Austria were far more concerned with the partitions of Poland than they were with events beyond the Rhine.[2] Indeed most governments made some effort to incorporate the new France into the European system. As time went on, however, most European rulers, particularly the court in Vienna, came to find France abhorrent and incomprehensible, a regicide nation ruled by zealots that proceeded to accept an upstart commoner as its emperor. It was dangerous and unpredictable, capable of anything.

Furthermore, Revolutionary France proved as difficult to combat as it was to comprehend. As the various regimes in Paris were challenging the very foundations of the international system, their armies were forging new ways of war, casting aside old patterns and inflicting a series of diplomatic humiliations and military reverses upon their numerous opponents. Shaped by the exigencies of France's confused and desperate situation, the size, composition, organisation, tactics, logistics, and spirit of these armies were unprecedented on the European scene, and the old, dynastic militaries, trammelled by the linear norms of the Frederickian era, were left to grope for adequate responses to a phenomenon they only dimly understood. This process accelerated with the growing prominence of Napoleon Bonaparte and assumed terrifying proportions as he began to combine military genius with political power.

The hammer blows fell most heavily on the ancient House of Habsburg. Bitter military defeats of 1797, 1800, and 1805 stunned the Danube monarchy and left it powerless to resist French demands. The treaties that concluded these campaigns, signed at Campo Formio (17 October 1797), Lunéville (9 February 1801), and Pressburg (26 December 1805) respectively, not only cost Vienna prestige, territory, and treasure, but also resulted in a general retreat of Austrian power from Germany and Italy. The erosion of Habsburg influence in central Germany, the principal arena of Franco-Austrian rivalry, was especially alarming to Vienna. Here French successes gradually demolished the ramshackle framework of the Holy Roman Empire, the ossified institution through which the dynasty had for centuries influenced events in Germany. The Treaty of Lunéville, for example, was followed by the Imperial Recess of 25 February 1803 that legitimised French possession of all German lands on the left (west) bank of the Rhine and drastically reorganised the smaller states of the decrepit empire in accordance with Napoleon's wishes. The consequences of Austerlitz and the Treaty of Pressburg were even more devastating for Habsburg interests. Having broken Austrian military power on the battlefield, Napoleon solidified his hold on Germany by forming the Confederation of the Rhine (Rheinbund) on 12 July 1806 with himself as its protector. He then dissolved the old empire, forcing Kaiser Franz of Habsburg, simultaneously 'Holy Roman Emperor of the German Nation' and Emperor of Austria, to surrender the imperial title that had been virtually hereditary to the Habsburg family since 1438.[3] Though Prussia still remained to challenge French hegemony, Napoleon had effectively assumed

Austria's place as the arbiter of political affairs between the Rhine and the Elbe.

The Austrian position in Italy was also crumbling. Annexing some territories outright and bringing others under his control by crowning himself the King of Italy in May 1805, Napoleon exploited his repeated military victories to effect a dramatic expansion of French influence in Italy at Vienna's expense. As a consequence, Austria, once the dominant factor in the northern half of the peninsula, was gradually pushed back over the Alps and the Isonzo; its sole remaining outlet to the sea, Trieste, existed at Napoleon's pleasure and Vienna had to grant French troops unrestricted free passage through Istria. Franz was equally helpless when Napoleon evicted the Bourbons from Naples and installed his elder brother Joseph as king in their stead. By the late summer of 1806, therefore, France had replaced Austria as the pre-eminent power in both central Germany and the Italian peninsula. Its armies demoralised, its treasury exhausted, and its foreign policy in ruins, the Habsburg monarchy stood on the margins of European affairs, its Great Power status no longer assured.

Austria's situation deteriorated further that autumn when Prussia, which had observed from the sidelines during the Ulm-Austerlitz campaign, decided to take up arms against the Grande Armée. Napoleon's double victory at Jena-Auerstädt and the relentless pursuit that followed, deepened the pall of gloom hanging over Vienna. Although some of Franz's ministers advised armed intervention on the side of Prussia and Russia, Archduke Charles, the army commander, declared that the Habsburg military was hopelessly unprepared for combat and the Kaiser would not be moved. Even after Napoleon was checked in the gruesome affray at Eylau on 7 February 1807, Franz reportedly told a Russian emissary: 'Beat the French a second time and I will declare myself!'[4] But there were no more dubious victories for Napoleon. In the spring, his army recovered, he struck out at the Russians, caught their principal force at Friedland and smashed it. Alexander I, Tsar of all the Russias, sued for peace and met the Emperor of the French on a raft in the river Neman at Tilsit to decide the fate of Europe. Friedrich Wilhelm III, the hapless King of Prussia, whose misguided policies had started the war, could only wait in the wings, trusting that the tsar's munificence would preserve his realm from Napoleon's wrath. The Austrians were not even invited.

Although he had excluded them from the Tilsit negotiations, Napoleon was generally well disposed towards the Austrians in the late summer of 1807. For many in Vienna, however, the situation was worse than it had been after Pressburg. 'Of all evil results, the evilest has come to pass,' lamented Kaiser Franz's new foreign minister, Graf Johann Philipp Stadion.[5] With the Holy Roman Empire destroyed, Prussia crushed, and Russia allied to France, Austria was isolated in Europe, nearly bankrupt, and threatened from every quarter: the French in Italy, Germany and Silesia, the Russians on the borders of Galicia. Napoleon had even resurrected a Polish entity in the Grand Duchy of Warsaw, lighting a distant lamp for the ethnic Poles under the Habsburg sceptre.[6] With its army only beginning to recover from the cataclysm of 1805, and with no prospect of alliance, Austria was hardly able to influence its own destiny. It could only bide its time, build its strength, and wait for an opportunity.

This enforced delay in seeking vengeance against Napoleon deeply frustrated Stadion and, more than any other individual, he would be the architect of the coming conflict. Eldest son of the first minister at the court of the Elector of Mainz, Philipp Stadion grew up within the comfortable confines of the Holy Roman Empire, imbued with a deep respect for its institutions and the balance it seemed to maintain among the interests of states great and small. His family's privileged position among the minor imperial nobility also brought power, status, and considerable revenue derived from large estates in Schwaben (Swabia). Napoleon destroyed this predictable old world and it is hardly surprising that Stadion bore an implacable hatred for the French emperor.[7] As he told the former Hanoverian ambassador in Vienna: 'Austria cannot view the Peace of Pressburg as anything other than a ceasefire; it has not renounced the hope and desire to take its revenge for all its humiliations.'[8] From December 1805, when he assumed office in place of the discredited Graf Ludwig Cobenzl, he thus strove to set the conditions for a new contest with France, a struggle that would lead to the eviction of France from central Germany and the restoration of some institution similar to the Holy Roman Empire with Austria as its leading power.[9] This extraordinarily ambitious goal implied two immediate tasks.[10] First, he had to preclude any further erosion of Austria's current position. Indeed, convinced as he was of Napoleon's malevolent intentions towards Vienna, Stadion firmly believed he had to forestall another French war of conquest that might eradicate the Habsburg monarchy entirely. Thus, as early as July 1807, he wrote: 'We must not deceive ourselves, any day we could find ourselves in circumstances where we will have to risk everything, where our very existence, one way or another, could be extinguished.'[11] This sense of desperate crisis, this notion of an imminent, all-or-nothing struggle for the 'very existence' of the monarchy would continue to inform his judgements throughout the coming two years.

With Austrian power at a low ebb in the wake of Pressburg, however, his ability even to guarantee the empire's continued existence was questionable and he recognised that, for the moment at least, war was an unacceptable policy option. The other extreme alternative, alliance with France, he found repugnant, as it would place Austria in the ranks of 'tributary lands groaning under the French yoke'.[12] Biding his time, then, Stadion worked to preserve Austria's independence, attempting to retain its freedom to manoeuvre diplomatically on the European stage while exerting himself to strengthen the monarchy morally and materially for the coming test. None the less, he chafed impatiently under the delay and eagerly examined every new development in the hope of discovering an opportunity for Austria to strike at Napoleon.

Stadion's second task was the establishment of a domestic consensus that would actively support a new war in Germany. Fortunately for him, Vienna was awash with dispossessed nobles, defeated generals, distraught courtiers, and other disgruntled individuals who had lost their old dispensations in the storm of war and revolution since 1792. They provided the foreign minister with a receptive audience for his interpretation of events. Forced from their lands and lives by Napoleon's conquests, they shared Stadion's sense of loss and outrage at the destruction of the old order, his experience as an exile, his hatred of Napoleon and the French Revolution, and his desire for vengeance. They also shared—and stoked—his sense of crisis.[13] A loose collection of individuals rather than a cohesive interest group, they nonetheless formed a dedicated and vocal 'war party' ('Kriegspartei') at the heart of the Habsburg Empire. Their passionate urgings for a new contest with France charged the air with tension and helped push the hesitant Kaiser down the road to war. The existence of a vague war faction can be traced back to the campaign of 1806–7, when some prominent Austrians had called for Franz to join Prussia, and, by early 1808, its members had acquired considerable influence. Especially important among those who advocated confrontation with the 'Corsican ogre' were the expatriate Germans and Italians who filled the ranks of Stadion's foreign ministry. Among these, the foreign minister's ardent elder brother, Friedrich Lothar Stadion, Austria's ambassador to Bavaria, would play a critical role as war approached. More noticeable and influential, however, were members of the Kaiser's family, particularly his younger brother Johann and a clutch of displaced imperial relations who had gained access to the throne when Franz married their sister, Maria Ludovica Habsburg-d'Este, in January 1808. Driven from their Italian home by the brash General Bonaparte, the d'Este family yearned for the downfall of the minatory Emperor Napoleon. Two of them, the Archdukes Ferdinand and Maximilian, had acquired important military responsibilities and, together with their cousin Johann, they toured the Habsburg lands, issuing inflammatory proclamations and causing Napoleon to complain.[14] The charming and determined Maria Ludovica herself was a key member of the war party, exerting her not inconsiderable influence on her doting husband.

On the other hand, Stadion's task was greatly complicated by the diverse and disordered nature of the war faction. While Stadion and others aimed to turn back the clock, to restore the 'old order of things', Maria Ludovica and most of the Habsburgs were primarily concerned with dynastic security; the principal interest of the d'Este brothers, for example, was a return to their Italian possessions and status. Others, such as Archduke Johann, were motivated by romantic nationalist notions of a pan-Teutonic battle with Gaul as well as pragmatic desires to strengthen the Austrian state and to regain the lost Tyrol.[15] Only loathing for Napoleon united these disparate elements.[16] The credibility of the war party was also sapped somewhat by the general lack of military experience among its members and the fact that many of them were court creatures who would not be in the ranks trading lead with Napoleon's veterans.[17] Furthermore, an influential 'peace party' centred around the Archdukes Rainer and Joseph also had the Kaiser's ear. These men advocated accommodation with France and a reduction in military expenditures to preserve peace and save the empire from its grave financial woes. The peace party drew important support from Archduke Charles. As the Habsburg generalissimus, Charles's noble rank, military prestige, and adamant refusal to hurl his slowly reforming army into a new struggle proved insurmountable hurdles to the war party's passionate calls for confrontation.

At the centre of this policy controversy was Kaiser Franz.[18] Indecisive and uncertain, he was, as Napoleon said, easily swayed by the last person to brief him and was more comfortable meddling in bureaucratic minutiae than guiding his huge and complex realm through the troubled waters of early nineteenth-century Europe.[19] Principally concerned with securing his dynasty's future, he vacillated, resisting Stadion's efforts to energise the empire for war, but also spurning the reform initiatives of the peace party. For Franz, the danger seemed neither imminent nor deadly enough to overcome his distaste for major decisions. This state of affairs—the Kaiser temporising, the war party relegated to a noisy but marginal role, Stadion frustrated by his inability to effect dramatic alterations in imperial policy—might have continued indefinitely in Vienna had Napoleon not seized an opportunity to interfere in the affairs of Spain.

SPRING 1808: RELATIVES, CREATURES, AND GENERALS

Events on the Iberian Peninsula in 1808 had a sensational impact in Vienna, sharply accentuating Stadion's fears but also seeming to open the door for Austrian action. Since Tilsit, Napoleon had been manoeuvring to tighten the grip of his Continental System in Spain and Portugal. Although Spain, an ally of France since 1796, nominally participated in the embargo of British goods, Madrid's enforcement was lax, and Portugal, closely aligned with Britain, remained completely outside the system. Furthermore, Spain's behaviour during the opening phases of the Prussian campaign had been virtually treacherous from the French point of view, and concern for his strategic rear had nagged Napoleon throughout the war with Prussia and Russia.[20] Beginning in late 1807, therefore, he began deploying significant forces to the peninsula: sending Général de Division (GD) Andoche Junot to Lisbon with a corps of 25,000 and gradually finding reasons to move over 70,000 additional men across the Pyrenees. By early March, these troops were in control of key fortresses throughout northern Spain, and Marshal Joachim Murat, Napoleon's brother-in-law, was en route to Madrid to assume his post as the emperor's 'Lieutenant General in Spain'. When he reached the Spanish capital on 24 March 1808, Murat found the court in the throes of a series of byzantine intrigues that ended with the vapid King Charles IV abdicating in favour of his son, the inept and obdurate Ferdinand VII, only to recant his decision several days later and plead for French assistance in restoring his throne. Murat, however, refused to recognise either claimant and, with the crown of Spain in dispute, Napoleon lured the entire Bourbon clan to Bayonne to 'discuss' the matter. Disgusted with the weakness, incompetence, and venality of the Spanish court, Napoleon intervened in the family's dynastic politics and cajoled the pathetic Charles IV into a second abdication on 6 May, this time in favour of a Bonaparte.[21] By June, the emperor had transferred his pliant brother Joseph from Naples to Madrid, leaving all Europe aghast at his high-handed treatment of a putative ally and one of the continent's oldest ruling houses.[22]

Stadion and others in Vienna, appalled by the news from Iberia, saw the fate of the Spanish Bourbons as their own future: 'Spain's present ruin is a warning from Providence', he told the Kaiser.[23] For Stadion, the French seizure of Spain's northern bastions in February and the internecine dynastic clashes among the Bourbons in March were clear evidence of Napoleon's malign intent. Conspicuously absent from his analysis was the extension of the Continental System that lay at the heart of Napoleon's actions beyond the Pyrenees.[24] In his first report on the Spanish situation (30 March 1808), the Habsburg ambassador in Paris, Graf Clemens von Metternich-Winneburg, reinforced Stadion's assessment, opining that the fall of the Spanish Bourbons had been the result of long planning and preparation by Napoleon. The French emperor's next goal, Metternich believed, would be the doddering Ottoman Empire.[25] Stadion, however, drawing selectively on Metternich's dispatches, assumed that Napoleon would strike at Austria immediately after crushing the Spanish: 'what conceivable cause would restrain Napoleon from falling on Austria as soon as he comes to see such an enterprise as feasible or indeed easily executed?' He further assumed that Spanish resistance would collapse in a matter of weeks and that Austria had at worst two and at best five months to prepare for the coming conflict. Before poor Charles and Ferdinand had even reached Bayonne, therefore, and well before Joseph Bonaparte had been declared the new King of Spain, the Habsburg foreign minister had concluded that Austria had entered a dire crisis and that an Austrian war with France in 1808 was unavoidable. On 13 and 15 April, he made urgent presentations to Kaiser Franz, emphasising the inevitability of confrontation, the particular threat to the House of Habsburg, and the need for immediate measures to strengthen the realm.[26] Otherwise, he told his master, Napoleon would 'subjugate the Austrian imperial house, break up the monarchy and finally divide it among his relatives, creatures, and generals.'[27]

Stadion's forceful and persuasive presentations, supported by a memorandum from Archduke Charles, had a dramatic effect on Kaiser Franz.[28] With uncharacteristic speed, he issued a flurry of decrees, and Vienna's cumbersome governmental machinery lurched into action. The Kaiser's decisions, promulgated through May and June, provided for an expansion of the monarchy's military establishment through the raising of reserve battalions for the line infantry regiments and the creation of a broadly recruited national militia, the Landwehr.[29] Although they served to augment the standing army, these measures were basically defensive in nature, an initial reaction to events in Iberia and Stadion's alarming assertion that Napoleon might turn his deadly attention towards Austria by mid-summer. They demonstrated, however, the Habsburgs' pervasive feeling of vulnerability as well as the extent to which Stadion was able to exploit the family's dynastic fears to conjure up a sense of imminent and ineluctable danger within Franz's court.[30]

In addition to enlisting the support of the Kaiser and the court for his war policy, Stadion sought to mobilise public opinion behind his cause. A host of writers, poets, composers, and dramatists echoed the sentiments of the war party, particularly the nascent stirrings of Germanic nationalism, and these supplied Stadion with a willing pool of earnest, often heatedly fervent, propagandists. He did not hesitate to employ them to stir the popular imagination. The result was 'a unique, if short-lived, popular enthusiasm for war', at least in the German-speaking regions of the empire, that gradually grew through the latter half of 1808 to reach a crescendo in early 1809.[31] This enthusiasm at home was important for Stadion, who was convinced that Napoleon could be defeated if the people of Germany and Italy could be induced to rise against the French in a massive movement under Austrian control: 'It seems equally essential to me that we make the war a national war not only for all Austrian provinces but also for the peoples of Germany and all other lands which have been conquered by French usurpation.'[32] Stadion thus cast his depiction of the coming war to fit his audience: for the common man, it was presented as a German struggle for liberation from French dominance; for the Kaiser, it was the only hope of preserving the dynasty; and for Stadion and his fellow expatriates, it represented a chance to reverse the presumed injustices of the preceding seventeen years and restore the old order of affairs in Germany. For all, however, it was unavoidable, a 'looming danger' that Austria must 'either delay, eliminate utterly, or at least resist to the greatest possible extent'.[33] In this atmosphere of anxious emergency, a desperate pressure to act built up in the minds of Austria's leaders and it was not be long before Vienna's actions assumed a decidedly offensive complexion.

SUMMER–AUTUMN 1808:
THESE MOST PROMISING CIRCUMSTANCES

The transition from defensive to offensive war evolved during the summer and autumn of 1808 as the contours of the war in Spain became clearer. First, that summer saw three major French defeats in the Iberian Peninsula. In addition to the failed first siege of Saragossa (15 June to 17 August), Junot was badly beaten by newly arrived British troops at Vimiero in Portugal (21 August), and, to Napoleon's shock and fury, GD Pierre Dupont surrendered his corps of over 20,000 to a hotchpotch Spanish army at Bailen on 21 July.

Where previous setbacks or questionable victories (such as Eylau) could be veiled and soon forgotten, the Capitulation of Bailen was impossible to hide. It sent shock waves throughout Europe, cracking the image of French invincibility. The only saving grace from the French perspective was that Napoleon himself had not been in Spain at the time of the disaster. Second, the growth of the guerrilla conflict in Spain and increasing British assistance for it gave rise to a burgeoning anti-French propaganda effort. Public tracts and private communications began to seep into central Europe as the various Spanish juntas and their English supporters endeavoured to influence the rest of the continent.[34] The version of events on the peninsula in these documents was decidedly coloured, but, avidly read in Vienna and elsewhere, these tracts provided powerful symbols (in particular Saragossa's stand) to inspire Napoleon's Austrian and German opponents.[35] Unfortunately for Austria, central European audiences often overlooked the prevailing exaggeration of these communications and likewise tended to ignore the many differences between Germany and Spain. As a result, unrealistic expectations gained ground in the minds of fervent German nationalists, and Stadion found ample reinforcement for his own preconceptions of popular uprisings.[36]

Most important for Stadion, however, it quickly became apparent that the Iberian conflict would be different from Napoleon's previous lightning conquests. Although the French disposed of the Spanish regular troops with relative ease, the obstinate resistance of local irregulars, epitomised by Saragossa's successful defiance of its besiegers, left little doubt that significant French forces would be in Spain well beyond the two- to five-month time frame Stadion had initially envisaged. Most observers still assumed that Napoleon would eventually triumph, but it now seemed obvious that the victory would be neither swift nor easy. These developments spurred dramatic growth in the strength, numbers, activity, and influence of the war party and also led Stadion to a new assessment of Austria's situation. Where previously he had feared an imminent French invasion, now he thought to perceive an irresistible opportunity in Napoleon's apparent preoccupation with Spain. As early as 30 June, persuaded that the threat was not as immediate as he had feared in April, he wrote to Metternich that 'our current efforts must demonstrate to you that we are as convinced as you that the danger exists but that it is not so near as to hinder the completion of our projects.'[37] An offensive war thus came to seem an increasingly attractive option as the summer progressed: 'We will do everything to avoid war if it is avoidable, but if it is not, we must begin it and not wait.'[38] Given Stadion's conviction that the destruction of the Habsburg Empire was 'the sole goal of

Napoleon', however, the inevitability of conflict was hardly in question.[39] For him, Austria could only escape its supposedly desperate circumstances by taking advantage of 'these most favourable circumstances, which will perhaps never again offer themselves' and striking Napoleon while he was embroiled in Iberia. The monarchy, however, would have to move soon to 'anticipate the danger and, without waiting for the eruption of Napoleon's plans, to choose the most advantageous moment to bring our tense political relations with France to a quick and permanent decision'.[40] GD Antoine François Count Andréossy, the French ambassador, reported that Austria appeared 'to see its salvation in our situation in that country [Spain]'.[41] What had seemed like emergency measures to stave off imminent assault in the spring thus became the first steps in preparation for an Austrian offensive as summer turned to autumn.

By September 1808, Stadion,[42] backed by the war faction, had made considerable progress in pushing the monarchy towards renewed conflict with France, but two major domestic obstacles remained: the Archduke Charles and the Kaiser himself.[43] As the Austrian generalissimus, Charles's support was essential to any conceivable war effort.[44] Stadion, however, had grave doubts concerning the archduke's 'dreadful lack of commitment' to the cause.[45]

Stadion's apprehensions were not groundless. Although he had acknowledged the threat posed by Napoleon's ambition in April ('There can be no more doubt as to what he [Napoleon] wants—he wants everything!'), Charles disagreed with Stadion on the Austrian response.[46] He saw the monarch as 'a consumptive man', whose 'red and puffy cheeks' were 'the true signs of approaching death'.[47]

Charles wanted more time to prepare the army and was not convinced that an offensive war would bring the old empire any lasting benefit.[48] In a late September memorandum, he attacked Stadion's most cherished notions, minimising the immediacy of the threat, disparaging the sense of urgency prevalent in Vienna, and questioning the wisdom of provoking any war with France, let alone one founded on an offensive strategy.[49] Stadion was 'devastated' by the tone of this note and several others he received in a heated correspondence with one of Charles's most trusted staff officers, Feldmarschall-Leutnant (FML) Philipp Graf Grünne, between 27 September and 3 October. Instead of greeting the possibility of war with 'calmness and hope for success', Stadion lamented, Charles was manifesting 'desperation, indeed the darkest desperation'.[50] Other observers in Vienna bluntly accused him of cowardice: 'above all, it is the pusillanimity of the Archduke

Charles which paralyses everything here', wrote the Prussian ambassador.[51] Nonetheless, convinced that war was unavoidable—more owing to Austria's actions than Napoleon's—Charles gradually abandoned his resistance to Stadion's plans. His motivations are obscure. Writing in the third person several years later, he recalled that 'the archduke had delayed the decision for war for a long time by his opposition. However, rather than hold on at all costs, even at the loss of his position, he eventually gave his assent.'[52] Maria Ludovica's influence probably contributed to the softening of his stance, but he also seems to have simply grown weary of the endless pressure and intriguing.[53] These factors, combined with his belief that 'sooner or later war is unavoidable', led him to conclude that 'there remains no alternative for us but to pre-empt the plans of our adversary or allow ourselves to be destroyed'. He stressed, however, that 'only the impossibility of avoiding war can permit us to begin it'.[54] As he wrote afterward, 'the archduke recognised that the ministry [Stadion] had brought things to a state where war was inevitable, and concerned himself from then on with the requisite preparations in order to contribute as much as possible to success.'[55] Charles's acquiescence in the question of war—and offensive war at that—left only the Kaiser as a major domestic challenge to the furtherance of Stadion's policies.

WINTER 1808: THERE REMAINS NO ALTERNATIVE

Franz I, Emperor of Austria, did not want war.[56] In particular, he evinced little interest for a risky enterprise to restore the defunct Holy Roman Empire. On the other hand, he 'took no serious measures to preserve the peace' and, by the autumn of 1808, he, like his brother Charles, found it increasingly difficult to resist the 'atmosphere of sustained psychological and administrative pressure' manufactured by Stadion.[57] Sensitive to Stadion's repeated warnings that the existence of the Habsburg dynasty itself was in immediate peril and surrounded by relatives, advisers, and sycophants who saw conflict as inevitable, Franz wavered, inclining towards war with Napoleon. 'By every indication,' he wrote in August, 'the storm will break over us sooner or later'; and 'for here we are concerned with the very existence of the monarchy.'[58] But though he wavered, he did not commit.

To drive the Kaiser to a firm decision, Stadion brought Metternich back from Paris in November for consultations and conferences. Adroit manipulation of Metternich's reports had been invaluable to Stadion's bureaucratic strategy ('Your reports ... are like gold') and he now sought to employ the ambassador's talents to apply further direct pressure on the vacillating Franz.[59] Metternich had opposed Stadion's war policy from his vantage point in Paris, but he was convinced that permanent peace with Napoleon was impossible and, taken out of context, quotations from his lengthy letters had provided the foreign minister with a wealth of apparently inflammatory reportage from Vienna's 'man on the scene'.[60] The effect of Metternich's reports may be gauged from Archduke Johann's comment: 'it was these which actually raised the question of whether we should not anticipate Napoleon.'[61] Likewise, Charles's foster father Herzog Albert of Sachsen-Teschen recorded that 'the reports arriving in Vienna ... above all those from the minister resident in Paris [Metternich], suddenly changed the tone which had previously reigned in the capital of Austria.'[62]

Stadion's slanting of his reports notwithstanding, through the summer, Metternich had advised Vienna to seek a *modus vivendi* with Napoleon while preparing for a future rupture; on at least three occasions, for example, he wrote that 'it would be insanity to provoke a war with France'.[63] Arriving in Vienna on 12 November, however, he was surprised by the extent of Austria's preparations. In addition to all the military activity and the extensive political manoeuvring within the capital, the Habsburg court seemed to have secured a significant victory on the domestic front by holding formal conclaves of the Hungarian Diet between September and November to crown the popular Maria Ludovica as Queen of Hungary and to grant Franz unprecedented power to mobilise the Hungarian militia, or Noble Insurrection, on his own authority without convening the Diet for approval. The atmosphere throughout the dense pomp and ceremony of these meetings had been heady and emotionally nationalistic, the talk threaded through with discussion of the 'next war' being a 'national war'.[64] If some observers regarded these sessions as 'a Diet of Illusions' whose results would be 'costly and of little utility', for Metternich, the decision for war appeared irreversible.[65] Opposition to the coming conflict would be not only pointless but possibly against his own interest as well as Austria's. He thus quickly changed his mind and lent his support to Stadion's policies, lamenting later in life that 'the cabinet was not open and candid with me'.[66]

By the time Metternich reached Vienna, however, the question of war, offensive war, had been, tacitly if not explicitly, decided. Stadion was, as one historian portrays him, 'already a captive of his war policy'. This policy had developed a powerful inertia of its own and only a radical change in Austrian behaviour, including a retreat from the fervid public agitation could have averted war at this stage.[67] Such a change or retreat was unthinkable in Vienna's byzantine workings without some dramatic external stimulus.

Those who 'held to pacific principles' were seen as traitors and 'could not fight against the torrent'.[68] As Stadion exclaimed to the Russian chargé, Ivan O. Anstett, in late November: 'We have established a system from which we will never depart'.[69]

If war was indeed unavoidable, however, the question of timing remained. In a series of December meetings, Metternich, now effectively a member of the war faction, joined his voice to those of Stadion, Maria Ludovica, and others urging the Kaiser to launch the war against France in early 1809. By mid-month, the decision had been made: Austria would invade Germany in March with the aim of evicting Napoleon's legions and re-establishing Habsburg primacy in central Europe.[70] As Stadion portrayed the concept to the Kaiser, 'our troops will simultaneously cross the borders of the monarchy into Germany and Italy in force, using our momentary superiority to make rapid progress and, so far as possible, to cripple all of Napoleon's tributary sovereigns, depriving France of their resources, and exploiting them ourselves'.[71]

Several considerations contributed to this decision for an Austrian offensive. In the first place, Stadion forcefully reiterated his assessment of Napoleon's hostile intentions; citing the deadly threat the French emperor posed to the Habsburg monarchy, he claimed that 'Napoleon's vast superiority cannot co-exist with Austria in its present state', and Austria 'must seize the moment which offers us the best advantages against him'.[72] Metternich composed three lengthy memoranda that seemed to support Stadion, each addressing a key dimension of Austria's policy vis-à-vis France. Relying heavily on information from the lubricious Charles-Maurice de Talleyrand-Périgord, the first of these notes discussed France's internal situation in the wake of the invasion of Spain, portraying Napoleon as utterly alienated from his people ('he is no longer the father of his people, he is the chief of his army') and opposed by a cohesive and powerful 'opposition party' under the leadership of Talleyrand and Joseph Fouché, France's minister of police. In the second paper, the ambassador hopefully stated his conviction that 'an intimate relationship between Austria and Russia' would result in 'a complete neutrality of Russia' towards Austria. The final memorandum was Metternich's intelligence estimate. Calculating the impact of the Iberian imbroglio on France's military power, he argued that Napoleon could field no more than approximately 206,000 men against Austria in the early stages of a conflict, that nearly half of these (99,000) would be supposedly unreliable Rheinbund troops, and that French reserves would be composed of 'conscripts below proper age for service'. Austria's forces, therefore, 'would be at least equal to those of France initially'. Factually, Metternich's assessments may not have been overly optimistic, but they left eager readers with the impression that France was internally weak, that the tsar could well remain neutral in a Franco-Austrian war, and that Napoleon's forces in Germany and France were poorly prepared to face the Austrian army.[73] Though not in themselves decisive, or even directly focused on the question of whether and when Austria should go to war, these notes thus coloured the thinking of senior Habsburg leaders as they evaluated their options in December 1808.[74] Napoleon himself heightened the state of alarm in Vienna with a 7 December proclamation to the Spanish that threatened to remove King Joseph to a different throne if Spain did not accept its new monarch. For key leaders in anxious Vienna, this could only mean that Joseph was destined for the Habsburg family's palaces.[75]

Second, Charles delivered a military assessment on 26 November that stated that the Austrian army could be ready for war by the end of March.[76] Moreover, Stadion and Metternich concluded that Napoleon would be unable to generate significant reinforcements for his forces in Germany until at least summer and perhaps not before autumn. Based on this assumption, Austria had a brief window encompassing the spring and early summer in which to act.[77] Finally, the finance minister Graf Joseph O'Donnell informed his colleagues that the pitiful condition of the monarchy's exchequer would not allow Franz to maintain his army in its present state of readiness beyond the following spring.[78] In Vienna's superheated atmosphere, these political, military, and fiscal factors seemed to leave no alternative but war, and war at the earliest possible moment in 1809. Some time would be required to negotiate subsidies from Britain, but Stadion was confident these could be secured by spring. Indeed, advancing Charles's schedule, the foreign minister set 1 March as the deadline for completion of all political, military, and financial preparations.[79] In a dramatic concluding touch, an all-night meeting was convened at Stadion's bedside (he was suffering a severe attack of gout) on 23 December to determine final instructions for Metternich prior to his return to Paris. Propelled by Stadion's energy, the Habsburg monarchy picked up momentum in its desperate rush towards conflict with Napoleon.

The year 1808 thus came to a close with the third of three critical decisions by Austria.[80] First, in April and May, Stadion had skilfully used Napoleon's Spanish meddling to convince the Kaiser that war with France was indeed ineluctable; further, he translated this gain into a series of concrete actions as Franz approved uncharacteristically rapid and far-reaching defensive preparations for a conflict that was presumed to be imminent. These defensive measures, however, soon developed a momentum of their own, building on and compounding the prevailing sense of exasperation. Moreover, they roused French suspicions and, being public, were difficult to retract. In short, they and Austria's growing propaganda campaign ('the most infamous vociferations', reported Andréossy, 'it is the rage of impotence') contributed to the long slide towards confrontation.[81] This, however, hardly disappointed Stadion. Indeed, French setbacks in Iberia not only reinforced the impulse to take up arms, but also seemed to offer the House of Habsburg a fleeting opportunity to challenge Napoleon's dominance of Italy and central Europe. It was an opportunity Stadion intended to exploit, and his second success was to achieve a gradual shift from a defensive to an offensive outlook within Vienna's ruling circles. This shift was accomplished by October and the foreign minister then turned his attention to the timing of the coming war. This question of timing, the third major Austrian decision, was settled in December. Given Stadion's evaluation of Napoleon's aggressive intentions and military capabilities, Charles's assessment of the army's readiness, and O'Donell's financial worries, the outcome seemed inescapable: the Austrian sword would be unsheathed in March of 1809. Though none of these decisions was irreversible, though the Kaiser continued to vacillate, only a drastic, and thus highly unlikely, change in Austrian policy could have halted or altered the march of Stadion's plans. The Habsburg Empire was therefore firmly on the road to war as 1808 came to an end.

1809: THE RUIN OF BOTH OUR STATES

As Austria prepared for war, however, the diplomatic component of its policy was gravely weak. But, to many in Vienna, this critical problem was not immediately apparent. Indeed, that January, Stadion assumed that Prussia would ally itself to Austria outright, that Russia would remain neutral, and that Great Britain would not only supply important subsidies but would also create diversions by landing a substantial army in northern Germany and by raiding the Italian coastline. Unfortunately for the Austrian war effort, none of these assumptions was to prove valid.

In April 1808, immediately following his initial presentations to the Kaiser on Napoleon's Spanish intervention, Stadion began to cast about quietly for external allies. Although Prussia was 'without an army, without income, and almost without territory', it was perhaps the most important target of his foreign policy attention and covert intriguing during the summer and autumn of 1808.[82] He began in May by sending an Austrian representative with friendly overtures to the Prussian court at Königsberg, and an active, informal interchange was soon underway between Prussian and Austrian officers in the border districts.[83] By late July, these officers were discussing a possible common response should France decide to occupy certain key Silesian fortresses, and, one month later, the governor general of that province, Oberst Graf Friedrich Wilhelm von Goetzen, sent the first of several Prussian army officers to the Habsburg capital.[84]

Goetzen, a fiery patriot, was one of Stadion's principal channels to the Prussian government, but a host of other, more influential personalities also supported the renewal of the struggle with France. Chief among these were the royal minister, Heinrich Friedrich Karl von und zum Stein, and leading Prussian military figures, such as Gebhardt Leberecht von Blücher, Gerhardt von Scharnhorst, and August von Gneisenau. These men and their allies formed an active war faction within the Hohenzollern court, repeatedly urging their hesitant king to join Austria in the coming war. Like their Austrian counterparts, they viewed their country's situation in the starkest terms and interpreted all of Napoleon's actions in the most dire and dangerous light. They were convinced that a new war would decide the monarchy's fate and argued that Prussia could not remain neutral, it must either incur unbearable humiliation by submitting to France or prepare to risk all in a terrible struggle: 'it is more glorious for the king and his nation to fall with weapons in hand than patiently to allow ourselves to be clapped in chains' wrote Stein.[85] King Friedrich Wilhelm III, on the other hand, harboured no love for Napoleonic France but favoured a more cautious course: 'a political existence, be it ever so small, is still better than none'.[86] In September, he thus ratified a new convention with Napoleon that reduced the proud Prussian army to a mere 42,000 men and obligated the kingdom to support France with 12,000 troops should war erupt with Austria.

Above all, however, Friedrich Wilhelm relied on Russia. 'The liberation of my state depends upon him alone', he wrote, and Scharnhorst recorded after an audience with his king in August 1808: '(1) for the preservation of his crown and state, he relies on Russia and not the outcome of the war between France and Austria; (2) that he therefore does not think it good to begin the war in alliance with Austria, in case Austria should not win.'[87] Indeed, as he told the tsar, Friedrich Wilhelm feared a new Franco-Austrian war, a war that could result in 'the ruin of both our states'. Alexander agreed: 'I believe, Sire, that a war between Austria and France would be one of the greatest evils that could befall Europe as I can see here nothing but the destruction of

Austria.'[88] Lacking the tsar's acquiescence, then, and in the absence of a nearly guaranteed Habsburg victory, the King of Prussia refused to commit himself and his kingdom to what seemed to him a very risky venture indeed.[89]

Emanating from sources with fundamentally different intentions, however, Prussia's contradictory actions and equivocal answers were often open to interpretation by a mind, such as Stadion's, that was actively searching for affirmation of the Austrian war policy.[90] The attitude of Friedrich Wilhelm's foreign minister, Graf August Friedrich von der Goltz, for instance, reinforced Stadion's preconceptions: 'The French army is busy in Spain, France is at odds with the Porte, it has enemies in Italy and is hated in Germany; a single victory and the universe will rise against Napoleon.'[91] Goetzen went farther, assuring Austrian General-Major (GM) Ferdinand Graf Bubna in October, among other things, that he was empowered to support Austria as soon as hostilities opened, that within twenty days Prussia could field 80,000 men above and beyond its regular army, and that Friedrich Wilhelm intended to blockade French-occupied Danzig.[92] Goetzen may have been extreme, but the presence—albeit unofficial—of two Prussian staff officers in Vienna that autumn seemed to substantiate Königsberg's intent to side with Austria in the coming war.[93] These two met with Charles, Johann, and other military leaders, and concocted some vague plans for joint Austro-Prussian operations, but the principal effect of their prolonged stay in the Habsburg capital was to bolster hopes that the two German powers would co-operate militarily against France. For Stadion and others in Vienna, this impression of Prussian support was confirmed by December reports from Karl Ritter von Hruby, the Austrian representative at Friedrich Wilhelm's court.[94]

Stadion's optimistic view of circumstances and the repeated importunities of his own zealous advisers notwithstanding, Friedrich Wilhelm had by no means concluded that the time was right to side openly with Austria. Tsar Alexander's attitude, not the hopes of the Austrian and Prussian war factions, would determine the actions of Prussia's king.[95] During a trip to St Petersburg in January 1809, he received the answer that would decide his policy for the next several months: the tsar was distinctly opposed to a renewal of war in central Europe and encouraged Prussia to 'attach itself invariably to France'.[96] When Friedrich Wilhelm encountered FML Prince Karl zu Schwarzenberg, Vienna's new ambassador to Russia, he thus cautioned the Austrian that he had come to the firm conviction that Austria, if she was the aggressor, must count on Russia's forces taking the field against her. In the name of 'the good cause', he [Friedrich Wilhelm] must ask Kaiser

Franz to consider 'that the smallest premature step would lead unfailingly and irrevocably to Europe's ruin'. The king repeated this warning to Hruby when he returned to Königsberg on 10 February.[97]

Reflecting Stadion's preconceptions, Vienna was initially pleased that the Prussian king was going to Russia. Although Schwarzenberg's departure from Vienna was hastened in an effort to put a representative of ambassadorial rank in the Russian capital while Friedrich Wilhelm was there, Franz and Stadion mistakenly saw the journey as a Prussian attempt to wean the tsar away from France.[98] The arrival of yet another Prussian officer in Vienna contributed to this Austrian optimism. Major Graf Heinrich von der Goltz, a cousin of the foreign minister, reached the Austrian capital on the night of 13/14 January and soon met with Charles, Stadion, and the Kaiser. Franz personally told the Prussian on the 19th that Austria had decided to attack, Stadion indicated that hostilities could begin as early as April, and Charles reviewed some generalities of Austrian military planning. Further operational discussions with Charles's staff officers occurred in early February, but Goltz's principal purpose in the Habsburg capital was to discover the extent of Austrian preparations without 'doing anything which could compromise the future decisions of the king'.[99] He was not empowered to conclude any agreements and, in the end, his mission achieved little of substance, as even Stadion realised.[100] This shallowness notwithstanding, Stadion reported to Kaiser Franz on 17 January that Goltz had provided 'repeated assurances that his king would join us in the event of a break with France'.[101] Goltz also delivered a letter to Franz from Friedrich Wilhelm III. Franz, seeking to exploit what appeared to be a propitious moment, responded with an enthusiastic letter of his own: 'It is not without a lively satisfaction that I find here reiterated assurance of that amity and that confidence of which it has given me the most convincing proofs.'[102] The following month, therefore, Stadion advised the new Habsburg ambassador to Prussia, Johann Freiherr von Wessenberg, that

> the king's recent confidential disclosures are . . . of such a nature as to permit no doubt regarding the sincerity of his sentiments, and Graf Goltz's visit has confirmed these sentiments. One can hardly imagine that the Prussian cabinet will decide on a contrary course of action after such steps, as these steps themselves have left them no alternative.[103]

Prussia certainly seethed with discontent. 'The mood of the local populace and especially the military is totally for war', wrote Wessenberg when he arrived in Berlin at the end of February. A French staff officer passing through the Prussian capital a month later agreed. His report to Marshal Louis Nicholas Davout read 'There is not one of them [the Prussian officer corps] who would not like to resume the war with France. This bellicose mood, which meets well with the hatred for the French, is pleasing to some townsmen and the greater part of the common people, and thus influences popular opinion.'[104] Friedrich Wilhelm, however, for all the censure heaped upon his head, had his own mind regarding this question.[105] He wanted peace to rebuild his shattered realm and was worried that his 1808 agreement with Napoleon would drag him into an unwanted war. He was equally apprehensive, however, that Austrian military activity in northern Germany or Poland might force him to join the Habsburg cause.[106] He was also alive to the danger that intemperate action by his emotional subordinates or restive elements of his population would undermine his efforts at neutrality and spark a harsh French reaction.[107] Determined to keep his kingdom out of any Franco-Austrian conflict, he thus refused the impassioned entreaties of his pro-war subordinates and proposed instead a utopian Austrian–Prussian–Russian defensive alliance to assuage Vienna's security concerns and protect his own interests.

By mid-February, Hruby's reports from Königsberg were beginning to sound pessimistic and, more disturbing, the Prussians refused to allow Wessenberg to travel beyond Berlin.[108] A 13 March note from foreign minister Goltz finally destroyed all reasonable expectation that Prussian troops would play an active role in opening operations. On the contrary, Friedrich Wilhelm advised Franz to avoid war or, if a rupture was truly inescapable, to maintain a defensive posture. In any event, he announced, Prussia's situation and its obligations towards France and Russia made an immediate decision impossible. To the Austrians, the Prussian statements in February and March seemed to be a retraction of their previous promises, and Stadion told Wessenberg 'I cannot hide from you, Baron, that H. M. could not suppress a shock of surprise as he read the Prussian court's latest declarations.'[109] Although the Prussians held out the hope of further negotiations, talks between Goltz and Wessenberg at the end of March produced no results.[110] If Austria were to begin a new war with Napoleon, therefore, it would do so without Prussian assistance, hoping that a quick success or two would bring a change in Königsberg's policies.[111] In the meantime, however, Austria's initial war plans had been formulated based on an assumption of active Prussian participation.

Russia's behaviour also entered into Austrian pre-war planning assumptions and, while he opened covert channels to Prussia, Stadion considered how he could effect a change in Tsar Alexander's foreign policy. Given the Franco-Russian alliance codified in the Treaty of Tilsit and Alexander's personality, however, Stadion believed direct appeals to St Petersburg would only harden the tsar's resistance. Instead, he favoured an indirect approach to erode Alexander's ties to Napoleon and slowly move him into the Austrian camp.[112] Unfortunately for Stadion, his initial overtures in the mid-summer of 1808 were in vain. While not unfriendly, the tsar's responses were cool and unequivocal: Austria should not incite war, should 'do nothing to change the tableau of my [Alexander's] most intimate political relationships' with Vienna and Paris. Specifically, he urged Franz not to take sides in the Spanish imbroglio as this would spare Russia the pain of making common cause with France against the Habsburg Empire.[113] Maximilian Graf Merveldt, the Austrian ambassador in St Petersburg, reinforced this gloomy assessment, but Stadion and other optimists in Vienna did not abandon their efforts to secure Russia's open support or, as a minimum, its neutrality in the coming struggle.[114]

Indeed, Tsar Alexander was remarkably consistent in his attitude towards Austria. This policy had two chief components: the preservation of peace and the continued integrity of the Habsburg monarchy.[115] Though no longer in Napoleon's thrall as he had been at Tilsit, Alexander repeatedly urged Vienna to avoid disturbing the central European equilibrium: 'It seems to me the most sage course for Austria is to remain a tranquil spectator to the struggle Napoleon has undertaken in Spain.'[116] During the glittering September to October summit meeting with Napoleon at Erfurt, he unintentionally encouraged Vienna by treating Austria's emissary with conspicuous grace and seeming understanding. In the aftermath of Erfurt, however, his warning was especially sharp when he detected unwarranted Austrian hopes: a new coalition against France would be 'easily erased' and a new war 'would mean disaster for Austria, if not its complete ruin'.[117] Like many in Vienna and Königsberg, the tsar expected an eventual confrontation with Napoleonic France—but not yet. Russia, he wrote to his mother, 'must build up her material and her forces . . . The wisest of all policies is to await the right moment to act.'[118] In the meantime, 'Napoleon and his army are invincible'; Austria, 'by every reasonable calculation', would 'necessarily succumb'.[119] Instead, Alexander intended to maintain his freedom of action, exploiting his alliance with the French emperor and his ally's entanglements in Spain to advance his own interests. Chief among these were the successful prosecution of his simultaneous wars with Sweden and the Ottoman Empire, and subsequent expansion of his realm to the north and south. A new Franco-Austrian war would, he was convinced, almost certainly result in the expungement of the Habsburg monarchy. By eradicating the last remaining buffer between his empire and Napoleon's, and by placing a strengthened French power on Russia's very borders, such a conflict would throw all the tsar's plans into disarray, destroy the Franco-Russian balance, and threaten the independence of his throne.[120] It could not be permitted, and short of breaking relations with Vienna, he sincerely exerted himself to avert the coming storm: 'the goal we want to attain', he told his foreign minister on 10 February 1809, 'is the maintenance of the peace.'[121]

Alexander's desires and intentions notwithstanding, the Habsburg court lent his words a decidedly optimistic interpretation.[122] Stadion knew that the tsar was inclined towards Austria and he counted on the Russian aristocracy's loathing for Napoleon to restrain their ruler or even compel him to change camps.[123] Furthermore, he was well aware that Austria played a critical role in the tsar's foreign policy as a buffer between Russia and France: Austria's continued existence was thus in Russia's interest. Statements by Russian diplomats ('... the will of my master [the tsar], his desire, and his wishes for the conservation of Austria seem to me beyond doubt ...') and the obvious friendliness of the Russian ambassador, Prince Alexander Kurakin, reinforced Stadion's assessment and allowed him to conclude that Russia would act to prevent Austria's destruction in some Napoleonic maelstrom if the coming war went poorly.[124] 'The interests of Russia will be tied to our conservation,' he told the tsar's chargé in November, 'If we fall, she will not be able to resist on her own.'[125]

The new Habsburg ambassador in St Petersburg also contributed to Stadion's hopeful outlook. Fürst Schwarzenberg, though not the ideal candidate in Stadion's eyes, was known to the tsar and was invested with sufficient social and military rank to demonstrate Vienna's interest in good relations.[126] Arriving on 4 February, he was 'noticeably well received'.[127] His reports certainly relayed Alexander's warnings and admonitions to Vienna, but he emphasised the Russian court's opposition to the alliance with Napoleon and the tsar's personal regret at the prospect of taking up arms against Austria. 'It seems', he concluded in one note, 'that we have nothing to fear from this country' if Austria could move quickly.[128] As the tsar's hysterically anti-Napoleon mother told him: 'A march combined with calm and sagacity, but executed with rapidity and the greatest energy in every detail, will soon have the most salutary effect here.'[129] Stadion thus felt confident when he informed his Kaiser in late February that 'Tsar Alexander will undertake nothing against us if we advance down our chosen path with celerity.'[130] Unfortunately for Schwarzenberg, the Russians moved with ponderous slowness. Nonetheless, the major achievement of his mission was a 21 April letter to Franz that contained a set of key assurances from the tsar. 'Although his situation imposed on him an obligation to send his troops into Galicia', Alexander told Schwarzenberg, he would retard their entry as much as possible and would instruct his commanders to 'avoid every collision and every act of hostility' with Austrian forces.[131]

This success notwithstanding, Austria could not prevent Russia from fulfilling the outward form of its obligations, and even this restrained action by the tsar's forces would later prove gravely detrimental to Austria's strategic situation. Moreover, at the time that Schwarzenberg set quill to paper, no one in St Petersburg knew that the Franco-Austrian War of 1809 was already eleven days old; twelve more days would pass before his missive reached the now desolate Stadion. As late as 5 April, Anstett told Stadion that Alexander was 'allied with Napoleon for war and peace'.[132] When Charles's hopeful battalions crossed the river Inn into Bavaria on 10 April, therefore, Vienna had no solid promise of Russian assistance or even neutrality. Stadion and others, however, appeared 'convinced that the Russians will confine themselves to menaces and that if Matters take a favourable turn it is not impossible that they may be persuaded to extend their goodwill to this Court beyond the limits of a strict Neutrality'. The French chargé, on the other hand, gave Austrian attitudes a very different interpretation: 'It seems therefore that the Court in Vienna is fooling itself in the hope it founds on Russia. This is not the only error it commits in its blindness, in its delirium.'[133]

1809: RED COATS AND POUNDS STERLING

While endeavouring to enlist Prussia and Russia as allies, Stadion also approached Britain. As with the two major land powers, however, Austrian overtures toward the great maritime power of the age were characterised by unreasonably high expectations and ultimately ended in disappointment.

Official relations between Vienna and London had been broken in January 1808 at Napoleon's insistence, but the two former coalition partners maintained an irregular contact through several informal and covert channels. Both had something to gain from co-operation. For Britain, the Habsburg Empire was a key central European ally, a continental power capable of fielding a large army to divert Napoleon's attentions and battalions from the growing struggle in Spain. As foreign secretary George Canning told the House of Commons in June: 'any nation of Europe that starts up with a determination to oppose a power that is the common enemy of all nations ... becomes instantly our essential ally.' The 'Flames' of resistance, he hoped, would continue to spread 'in the South from Spain to Italy and thence perhaps to Austria.'[134] Austria, on the other hand, wanted two critical things from Britain for the coming war: substantial subsidies to shore up its chronically precarious financial situation and a major military diversion in northern Germany to distract the French and underwrite insurrection. Additionally, Vienna planned to request British support in Italy and hoped London would reinvigorate the Russo-Swedish and Russo-Turkish conflicts to draw the tsar's troops away from Habsburg territory.

Though both governments stood to benefit, communications between the two capitals were seriously hampered by distance and the need for extreme circumspection in the face of zealous French surveillance.[135] Moreover, both sides were cautious. London was unwilling to commit its exchequer to uncertain projects and even more chary regarding the employment of its small and already over-stretched army.[136] In Vienna, Stadion did not want to appeal to Great Britain until he was assured of Archduke Charles's support for his war policy. Although Britain made tentative approaches during the summer, therefore, it was October before Stadion, now fairly certain Charles would not oppose him, sent a formal and detailed request to London.[137]

The Austrian appeal, dated 11 October, shocked the British Cabinet when it arrived in London on 1 December 1808.[138] It was a remarkable document. In return for fielding some 400,000 men in the coming spring, Austria expected Britain to supply £2.5 million immediately for pre-war preparations with an additional £5 million to be provided during the course of the year. London's response was predictable. Writing to Robert Adair in Constantinople on 2 December, Canning expressed himself frankly: 'it is hardly necessary to apprize you, that the amount of the pecuniary Demands of Austria as stated in this paper, is beyond all possibility of Compliance.'[139] Three weeks later, in a 24 December letter, he provided an official reply to Stadion's request, welcoming renewed contact with the Austrian government but rejecting the wildly unrealistic proposal for subsidies and offering no specific promises for English military assistance. Stadion would have to content himself with a general statement that Britain would make every effort to support Austria's enterprise as soon as war actually began. Wishing to avoid the appearance of inciting war, however, Canning made it quite clear that nothing could be done until hostilities actually opened.[140] Compounding his reluctance was Canning's evident scepticism regarding Vienna's sincerity and a sense in London that Austria had insulted King George III by breaking relations in January 1808.[141]

In Vienna, the weeks rolled by with no word from London. The extreme difficulty of exchanging confidential correspondence between the two prospective allies meant that one month after Canning had signed his disappointing reply, it still had not reached Stadion. The Austrian foreign minister did receive encouraging news during the first week of January when the Sicilian envoy in Vienna delivered an indirect message from Canning through Prince Fabrizio Castelcicala, the Sicilian representative in London. With Canning's authorisation, Castelcicala wrote that Britain 'not only wants to restore its friendly relations with His Majesty the Emperor, but also to give him all possible assistance in case His Imperial Majesty judges it appropriate to break with France'. The letter, however, was dated 1 November 1808 and had clearly been written before Stadion's request of 11 October had arrived in London. It offered no specific proposals either monetary or military and left the Austrian foreign minister with little more than a general statement of good will and a vague promise of future help.[142]

At the end of January, still lacking a direct answer to his 11 October letter, Stadion evidently believed he could wait no longer and he dispatched two secret emissaries to Britain to plead the Habsburg case in person. One of these two, Leutnant August Wagner, travelled by the more dangerous but faster route overland through Germany and Holland. His mission was to explicate Austria's intentions to the British leadership and suggest specific military operations.[143] The other agent, FML Graf Ludwig von Wallmoden, took the safer but longer route through Trieste and the Mediterranean. Travelling under the name Jean Simon, he was empowered to conclude a treaty of alliance and subsidies. The two men reached London in March and, though Canning was still unwilling to accept Vienna's extravagant demands, by 7 April, the British foreign secretary had released £250,000 in silver to establish a war chest for Austria on Malta and expressed the hope that this could be expanded to as much as £1 million. Not a shilling, however, was to be paid out until hostilities actually commenced. On 24 April, when it became known that Austria had indeed invaded Bavaria, Canning and Wallmoden quickly concluded a general treaty of alliance, leaving the details of subsidies to be arranged later. Wallmoden departed for Vienna the following day.[144]

In the meantime, Canning's 24 December letter finally reached Stadion on 10 March 1809. The tone and content of the 'very unsatisfactory'

British reply annoyed the foreign minister and placed him in considerable embarrassment.[145] It had been he, after all, who had argued that beginning the war in March would allow time to secure English subsidies and it had been he who had virtually promised those subsidies—on no solid evidence—in order to help convince Charles and others that an offensive war was financially feasible. To maintain the momentum of his policies, he thus suppressed the details of Canning's note and only passed on 'the general substance' to the Kaiser and his advisers.[146] As a result, Austria entered the war with no guarantee of English subsidies to underwrite its fragile domestic finances.[147]

Similarly, there was little reason for Austria to expect direct British military support, particularly in the invasion of northern Germany that Stadion hoped would ignite widespread rebellion against French domination. Leutnant Wagner had discussed Austria's operational plans during his sojourn in London, but he did not return to Austria until May, so Stadion could hardly have relied on his interactions with the British government during the final weeks before the war.[148] The two principal British representatives in Vienna that spring, Charles Stuart and Benjamin Bathurst, only arrived in April, (respectively just before and well after the invasion had begun), and neither of them brought a promise of military intervention. Indeed, London chose the youthful Bathurst in part because he would neither attract undue attention nor signal unconditional British commitment; his mission was considered 'merely temporary' and his authority strictly limited.[149] Charles Stuart, whose journey to Vienna was completely unauthorised, had no instructions whatsoever and was recalled when he seemed to be encouraging Stadion's demands for subsidies.[150] As one Austrian sympathiser feared, therefore, 'the cabinet in Vienna has been very late in explicating its plans with the government of His Britannic Majesty and remains ignorant of the degree of assistance upon which it can rely.'[151]

The outlook for British assistance in Italy was barely better. With 16,000 men on Sicily, a large fleet in the western Mediterranean, and significant political influence over the Sicilian and Sardinian courts, Britain was capable of playing an important role in and around the Italian Peninsula. Indeed, in December 1808, the British army commander in Sicily, Major General Sir John Stuart, had, like Canning, used indirect Sicilian channels to indicate that he had discretionary authority from London to provide military assistance to Austria in the event of war.[152] But again the British promise was vague, and Stadion exaggerated in April when he told the new Austrian ambassador to Britain, Ludwig Fürst Starhemberg, that 'the court in London has agreed to support a landing of Sicilian troops in Calabria.' He had little solid basis for entertaining such a hope. Furthermore, Vienna did not even respond to General Stuart's tentative overture, leaving the British commander to complain of 'the total want of any official communication'.[153] Nor was any attempt made to contact the local British naval commander, Vice-Admiral Lord Cuthbert Collingwood, until the war was already ten days old. As a consequence of this poor Austrian preparation, there was nothing for the admiral to co-ordinate when he visited Palermo in mid-February, and Stuart was unprepared to act when Habsburg battalions crossed into the Kingdom of Italy on 10 April.[154]

Likewise, Austria did not dispatch envoys to the rulers of Sicily and Sardinia until March. Both insular courts were receptive to the Austrian plans for restoration of their mainland territories, but neither could act without British assistance. Vienna expected considerable support from the Sicilian court in particular, but the Austrian emissary to Sicily, Oberstleutnant Victor Graf Sallier de La Tour, seemed remarkably misinformed regarding the state of affairs in the island kingdom when he arrived on 26 March.[155] Reflecting Vienna's ignorance, de La Tour believed the British troops were an auxiliary force of only 5,000 men under Sicilian command, and thus expected more effective assistance from the weak armies of Sicily and Sardinia than from Great Britain's substantial Mediterranean resources. Equally strange, de La Tour was unaware of Stuart's December offer of support for Austrian operations in Italy.[156] Stuart soon learned of de La Tour's mission and the two men corresponded, but two weeks passed before they actually met. In any event, lacking definitive guidance from London, the hesitant and cautious Stuart would not use his discretionary authority to satisfy the Austrian's urgent pleas: 'Every diversion is useful; the moment presses; and it is the last.' Even direct orders to Stuart, however, would have availed Austria little in the opening phases of the conflict: although Vienna wanted a diversion in southern Italy to coincide with its drive across the Alps, de La Tour reached the Sicilian capital far too late to orchestrate Anglo-Sicilian operations in support of the opening of Johann's offensive.[157] Similarly, Leutnant Wagner had also requested British assistance in the Mediterranean, but his extensive demands (naval support in the Adriatic and amphibious operations against Calabria, Genoa, and Tuscany) reached Canning's desk only two weeks before de La Tour's arrival in Palermo, hardly enough time to inform Stuart and Collingwood, let alone arrange complex, multinational expeditions in concert with Johann's operations.[158] Although Stadion's desire to maintain secrecy until the last possible moment is understandable, this long delay in entering into communications with London and its Mediterranean friends effectively precluded any hope of obtaining outside help in Italy during the opening phases of the campaign.

Vienna's tentative contacts with Britain's other Mediterranean ally, the fragmented Spanish resistance, proved equally unproductive. Stadion had not neglected Spain in his search for allies, but he seems to have made a realistic appraisal of the limited scope for diplomatic links with the various Spanish juntas.[159] Instead, he looked for military action and hoped to excite greater Iberian efforts by Britain and Spain to entangle Napoleon's armies in an interminable struggle as far as possible from Austria's borders. In December 1808, he thus dispatched an army officer, Major Jean Baptiste Baron de Crossard, to Spain to provide the central junta with general assurances of Vienna's support and to gather information on Spanish intentions. Crossard, however, quickly enmeshed himself in pointless intrigues that only served to undermine the position of the Habsburg diplomatic representative. His mission achieved nothing of consequence. The prevailing confusion in Spain, combined with the difficulties of communicating across the Mediterranean, made dramatic success highly unlikely, and Stadion does not appear to have placed much hope in significant support from this quarter. Overall, however, the Austrian approach to the Mediterranean theatre was uninformed, overconfident, and too late to influence the early stages of the war.[160]

1809: ALL EYES ARE TURNED TOWARDS AUSTRIA

Unfounded optimism also characterised Stadion's efforts to foment popular insurrection in Napoleonic Germany. Stadion expected that German uprisings would play a significant role in the coming war and his attempts to build contacts with the established states thus coincided with sweeping plans to generate support for the Austrian cause among the populations of the Rheinbund monarchies. As early as 1807, he had hinted at the importance of the 'people' (Volk), outlining partisan movements that could have a direct military effect 'not by fighting with the army, rather by disturbing the enemy on his flanks'. Moreover, by involving the entire nation in the struggle, one could overcome the individual subject's 'debilitating sense of personal neutrality and inactivity' while binding him 'more closely and warmly to the cause of his sovereign and the army'.[161] A year later, he expanded this concept beyond Austria's borders to embrace foreign populations as well: 'Though Bavaria and Württemberg are bound to the French by ties of avarice and slavishness, in many parts of the land the subjects are of a completely different mind. Discontent dominates northern Germany. Clear signs of dissatisfaction are even evident in the Duchy of Warsaw.' As his vision of the coming war evolved, he placed increasing emphasis on the importance of popular uprisings, and by early 1809 he was telling the Kaiser that 'The people themselves must become our allies.' Indeed, Stadion claimed to prefer alliances with the Volk over diplomatic bonds which 'can be dissolved at any moment'. In the development of his concept of national resistance, he drew inspiration from the Spanish example that proved to his satisfaction 'that Napoleon's generals are not invincible'. The strength of the Volk would thus supplement the army like 'a new ... allied power' and pave the way for the re-establishment of Austrian pre-eminence in Germany. He therefore urged Austria's military leadership to 'build centres of resistance in the discontented regions, to establish contact with them, [and] to support their efforts with the activities of our forces'.[162]

Undergirding Stadion's hopeful phrases were innumerable reports that seemed to confirm his preconceptions concerning popular rebellion. From Prussia's fervent patriots came promises that '100,000 former soldiers can be placed under arms in a matter of days' to rally around three Westphalian regiments composed of officers who had previously served the exiled Prince-Elector of Hesse-Kassel. 'The plan is solid and purposefully prepared by the best men,' Oberst Goetzen told Stadion in December, 'They only await the signal from me, namely that Austria has declared itself.' In Bohemia, information gathered by furtive Austrian police officials seemed to indicate that the secretive Tugendbund, or 'League of Virtue', with branches all across Germany and ties to the highest levels of the Prussian government, would be an important source of influence and support. From Munich, Friedrich Stadion reported that all northern Germany was in ferment, that the Bavarian crown prince was inclined towards Austria, and that 'all classes most ardently wish for ... a change and a return to a German existence ... All eyes are turned towards Austria and towards the heroes who have saved Germany many times, and every hand is ready to assist us if we arrive in force.' The elder Stadion portrayed similar sentiments in much of Württemberg, particularly Swabia, where many 'are ready to co-operate with the Austrian army when it inaugurates the general liberation'.[163] Fervid correspondence with a host of German nationalists—including an actual plan for local rebellion submitted by a prominent Westphalian colonel named Wilhelm von Dörnberg—gave further credence to this image of widespread, barely contained insurrection.

Even Metternich in Paris seemed to contribute to this enticing tableau, quoting Talleyrand as saying 'All Germany is for you.'[164]

Evaluating all this information in increasingly bellicose Vienna, Stadion concluded that Hesse-Kassel, Braunschweig, Hanover, and the patchwork of former Prussian provinces across northern Germany 'deserve the greatest attention'. He thus promoted an active propaganda campaign designed to stoke the fires of rebellion and advance the interests of the Habsburg monarchy. To lend additional weight to the propaganda, Austrian diplomats and agents provided covert funds and encouragement to prospective German rebels.[165] Stadion opposed, however, any significant advance planning or organisation. Furthermore, he was adamant that Austrian generals should closely control all rebellious activity rather than 'dealing with some form of junta or central committee' that would represent 'a power with which one must negotiate as with an allied court'.[166]

Reinforcing its vague attempts to 'control' the many conflicting strands of German discontent, the Habsburg court signed treaties with the exiled monarchs of Braunschweig and Hesse-Kassel in early 1809. Their states erased by Napoleon's reordering of Germany, Duke Friedrich Wilhelm of Braunschweig and Prince-Elector Wilhelm I of Hesse had taken refuge in Bohemia and now agreed to recruit tiny armies and lead them to their former lands in the hopes of regaining their thrones in the wake of an Austrian victory. For his part, Stadion hoped these princes would raise their former subjects against the French, create disorder in Napoleon's rear areas, and provide additional battalions to supplement Austria's forces—Wilhelm alone was expected to increase his ill-disciplined band from about 1,000 to more than 12,000 in a matter of weeks.[167]

Support for anti-French movements, however, went beyond efforts to enlist prospective rebels and quickly became a key element in Austria's foreign policy and military planning. It was a central theme in Stadion's communications with both Königsberg and London, for example. In Austrian planning, Prussia was expected to excite unrest in its former territories while Great Britain was to contribute arms, equipment, and the all-important subsidies; both were also seen as sources of regular troops to incite and strengthen popular uprisings across northern Germany. Communications flowed in both directions, of course, and Stadion's correspondence with fervent Prussian and German interlocutors fed his own preconceptions regarding Germany's willingness and readiness to oppose Napoleon. These considerations also exerted an important influence on Austrian operational planning, with Stadion suggesting the disposition of army corps to provide tangible support to local insurrectionists and to ensure that Austrian power would dominate in the territories those armies were expected to 'liberate'. As Friedrich Stadion wrote in March 1809 upon his appointment as the army's chief political adviser (Armeekomissar): 'In this great affair of the liberation of Germany, His Imperial and Royal Highness is the overlord; the generalissimus of the Imperial and Royal Army is the commander; and his headquarters is the headquarters of Germany and the capital of the German nation.'[168]

On the ground, these nationalistic sentiments and Austrian encouragement of them manifested themselves in the often hare-brained plots of zealous and excitable junior officers. In February 1809, for instance, a former Prussian lieutenant named Eugen von Hirschfeld proposed the abduction of Napoleon's youngest brother, King Jerome of Westphalia; only the urgent protestations of his Westphalian contact and several days of house arrest restrained the hot-headed lieutenant. As early as the autumn of 1808, however, plans for a general uprising in conjunction with an Austrian offensive were being considered by German nationalists in Berlin and elsewhere. That autumn, another former Prussian officer, Friedrich von Katte, thus received a visitor from Berlin who sought to recruit him for the coming rebellion in the name of a murky 'insurrectionary committee'. After some hesitation, Katte agreed, along with Hirschfeld, to undertake a *coup de main* against the important fortress city and arsenal of Magdeburg. Another agent appeared in March 1809 to warn that hostilities could begin at any moment and to urge immediate action with the aim of proving to Austria that northern Germany was ready to fight and simultaneously to preclude undisputed Austrian control of Magdeburg should Habsburg arms achieve a rapid success.[169] At the same time, a former Prussian major named Ludwig Kleist appeared in London, demanding British assistance for a German uprising and extravagantly promising that he and other patriotic luminaries could raise over 100,000 men between the Rhine and the Elbe in a matter of weeks if properly supported.[170]

These little episodes and others at the execution level highlight several interesting points about the German resistance movements in 1809. First, reliable information on the specific goals and plans of the rebels (to say nothing of the Austrians) was generally not available to men like Katte who were expected to carry out the uprising. Nor do they seem to have known the dispositions of the French and their allies in any detail. Moreover, although there were tenuous links between different prospective rebel leaders, co-ordination regarding timing, objectives, and future plans was nearly nonexistent. One activist recorded that 'our connections [to Königsberg and elsewhere] could in no wise be called an organised group.'[171] On the other hand, it is also clear from these incidents that Stadion's programme of nationalistic propaganda and covert contacts had had some effect: the rebel German officers recognised that support from regular troops—that only Austria could provide in sufficient numbers—was critical to their success. Acknowledgement of Austria's military importance, however, was balanced by a strong undercurrent of distrust regarding Vienna's ultimate designs. Furthermore, non-Prussians were very wary of Königsberg's intentions. Most important, all parties, German, Prussian, and Austrian alike, grossly overestimated the potential impact of their proposed actions. French dominance certainly generated murmurs of discontent and occasional outbursts between the Rhine and the Elbe, but these did not yet translate into a willingness to oppose Napoleon openly. A desperate foray against Magdeburg would not spark a wider rebellion.

Rolling rhetoric and vague plans notwithstanding, Austrian appeals to Germany's citizens thus found little echo in 1809. Germany was not ready. The passionate words of Stein, Goetzen, Friedrich Stadion, and a plethora of poets did not reflect the sentiments of the common man or his sovereign prince. Unfortunately for Austria, Stadion had formed his impression from contact with a limited number of dedicated nationalists and misread the situation in Germany badly. The information the foreign minister received in his office in Vienna only represented the aspirations of a 'thin layer of patriots who were strongly lacking in recognition of what was possible in the political realm'.[172] In the absence of the widespread German nationalistic sentiment that Stadion thought to perceive, the unformed, haphazard plans of scattered resistance groups offered little promise for effective co-operation with Austrian regular forces. Raising, organising, and equipping 100,000 or more German troops was completely beyond the realm of reality. Only in the Tyrol, ceded to Bavaria in 1805, did Habsburg propaganda resonate with effect. The active plotting for a Tyrolian uprising, the fiery enthusiasm of these former Habsburg subjects, and the comings and goings of their clandestine emissaries probably served to fuel expectations that other Germanic peoples were equally eager to oppose France and its allies. The Tyrol, however, remained an exception. As one contemporary observed: 'For Austria, the uprising of a few mountain folk was no substitute for its deluded expectations.'[173] In Germany proper, Vienna's hopes of supporting its own military operations through popular insurrection would soon prove illusory. A bitter Austrian officer recorded his thoughts in the aftermath of the war:

With our usual bonhomie, wrapped up this time with a bit too much frivolous vanity, we believed that we Austrians had only to show ourselves on the border and all Bavarians, Hessians, Württembergers, Saxons, indeed the entire Confederation of the Rhine would join us with joy, because we thought to appear as their rescuers, their saviours ... Did he [Stadion] not recognise that no king renounces a crown just to accept, at best, an unstylish imperial elector's cap? That no king who believes himself to be a sovereign lord (even if he is only a subject of the Corsican), that no such independent sovereign would again allow himself to be confined in the muddle of an utterly defective imperial constitution?[174]

Moreover, as a Bavarian remarked at the time, the recent history of Habsburg military endeavours did not inspire much confidence: 'Did the previous political system, the potential and intelligence of the Austrian government in war arouse such faith that one would blindly throw oneself into their arms?'[175]

Thus stood Austria in the late winter and early spring of 1809. As March slid into April and white-coated regiments marched through the cold rain towards the borders that separated Franz's empire from Napoleon's, the Habsburg generals could take but small satisfaction in the efforts of their statesmen. Austrian diplomacy had accomplished almost nothing in terms of providing concrete support to the forthcoming efforts of the army.[176] Prussia was uncommitted, Britain interested but cautious, Spain, Sicily, and Sardinia militarily irrelevant to the immediate outcome of a Franco-Austrian contest in central Europe. Even with Russia, the one relatively bright spot on the diplomatic horizon, Austrian success was limited: the best Schwarzenberg could win was a sort of meddling neutrality and that only became clear three weeks after Charles's troops had entered Bavaria. Vienna's greatest error, however, may have been its misappreciation of the potential for popular uprisings in Germany and elsewhere. By relying on a small coterie of emotional nationalists, Stadion reinforced his own preconceptions and attributed to the German populations qualities and capabilities that were not based on reality.[177] These serious problems notwithstanding, Stadion continued to press for war, interpreting events in the most favourable possible light and transferring the failures of diplomacy to the army's shoulders: if only Charles could gain a few quick military victories, all Austria's political defeats would be redeemed. His was a foreign policy founded on unsubstantiated hopes and optimistic desperation. The reality was that Austria, rushing to face Europe's greatest military power and one of history's greatest generals, would stand alone.

CHAPTER 2

What Do They Intend?

While searching for external allies, Austria continued its internal preparations for the coming war. Indeed, the confrontation with Napoleon dominated increasingly bellicose Vienna.[1] 'The war, the war, one hears no other word,' recorded one diarist in late January, 'One speaks only of departure, promotion, regiments and armies.'[2] Fanned by literature, press, music, and theatre, popular enthusiasm was unprecedented in the Austrian experience, as Claude Dodun, the French chargé d'affaires, reported in March: 'In 1805, the war was the government's, not the army's nor the people's; in 1809, it is desired by the government, by the army, and by the people.'[3] A bureaucrat in the Austrian Army Ministry agreed: 'Enthusiasm and excitement prevailed in Vienna. The war was popular to a high degree.'[4] 'The cry for war had become general' and 'Oesterreich über Alles' was the capital's favourite song.[5] These sentiments could not fail to have an effect on the Habsburg soldiery, and Grünne believed the army was 'grander, prouder, stronger than ever before, and imbued with a spirit and enthusiasm hitherto unknown within its ranks'.[6] By the end of March, however, the emotion of the moment had carried many in Vienna beyond the pale of reason. The Prussian ambassador thus remarked to his king that 'many persons believe the French armies will withdraw over the Rhine without risking a battle on this side of the Rhine. But with or without a battle, the successes of the first campaign will certainly all be Austrian, and it is clear that they will quickly be masters of all Germany up to the Rhine.'[7] A Bavarian observer noted that 'some Austrian officers even disdained Rhine wine because they hoped to drink the same on the banks of the Rhine itself within fourteen days.'[8] To Dodun, the citizens of Vienna seemed 'electrified to the point where they envisage this contest of arms as a triumphal march which will restore to Austria its ancient splendour ... They believe themselves capable of overcoming all obstacles; they believe their generals to be invincible, their soldiers invulnerable, their treasury inexhaustible.'[9] The Habsburg monarch would soon have cause to rue the dangerous overconfidence prevalent among so many of his subjects.

Much of this optimism, however, was forced. The sense of desperate urgency remained, an unremitting foreboding that seemed to demand action. 'War is seen as the sole means of salvation', wrote the French ambassador on 13 February.[10] One day earlier, in far St Petersburg, Schwarzenberg had summarised the tension in Vienna during his first audience with the tsar, arguing that Kaiser Franz was

> persuaded that the Emperor Napoleon will attack as soon as his affairs in Spain are terminated; this apprehension obligates Austria to put itself in a respectable state of defence, and it cannot maintain this attitude for long except by extraordinary efforts, which will necessarily exhaust it over the long term; and which put in question whether it might not be better to run the chances of a new war rather than remain in this state of crisis and anxiety.[11]

He might have noted that this 'state of crisis and anxiety' was largely self-generated. At the same time, Stadion was lecturing the tsar's chargé, Anstett, about Austrian concerns: 'I will explicate everything in a nutshell,' he told the Russian, 'The Emperor Napoleon has declared to Count Rumiantsev and Prince Kurakin that he will be in Vienna in 40 days and we will do what we can to prevent this.'[12]

It was in this charged atmosphere that the monarchy's principal leaders gathered on 8 February to deliberate once more the question of war. Stadion apparently dominated this conference, painting Austria's situation in brightly optimistic colours and again persuading the Kaiser and Charles that Napoleon's preoccupation with Spain presented a brilliant but fleeting opportunity for success. Austrian assumptions of active Prussian participation in the conflict—seemingly substantiated by a meeting between Major Goltz and Charles's staff on the 5 February—supported Stadion's arguments and the empire's tenuous financial situation lent the decision additional urgency: at best, the exchequer would suffice to maintain the army through the spring; after that Charles's troops would have to sustain themselves on foreign soil or demobilise.[13] Given the impulse of the preceding several months, there was little question of how the conference would conclude, and it duly produced concrete, military decisions to underwrite Stadion's plans for confrontation with Napoleon: the Kaiser reaffirmed the December decision for war and agreed to place the army on a war footing immediately. Charles, armed with an operations plan that his chief of staff, GM Anton Mayer von Heldensfeld, had submitted that very day, accepted the Kaiser's decision. Deep in one of his pessimistic moods, however, he was resigned rather than enthusiastic, declaring gloomily that 'I did not vote for war. Let those who made the decision assume the responsibility.'[14]

As a consequence of the 8 February conference, a series of military actions now followed each other in rapid succession.[15] On the 11th, Charles told GM Mayer that the Kaiser expected the army corps to assemble without delay; on the 12th, all furloughed soldiers were recalled; and on the 13th, Franz directed Feldmarschall Archduke Joseph, the Palatine of Hungary, to provide more than 5,000 horses and 2,000 drivers as supplements for the army's logistics trains.[16] The 12th also saw the Kaiser appoint Charles supreme commander of all Habsburg forces and chief of the entire military administrative apparatus, with broad authority over these and over all parts of the realm that might be touched by the war. As an American military historian has commented, 'Charles now had authority such as no servant of the dynasty had held since the days of Wallenstein.'[17] Mayer submitted march tables for the assembly of the army and a planning memoir for co-operation with Prussia on 15 February, and the following day instructions were issued for the raising of supplementary artillery and train personnel.[18] More importantly, the 16th also brought the promulgation of orders for the concentration of the army and its division into nine standard and two reserve corps, with the 25th set as the day most units were to depart their garrisons. Finally, on 17 February, Kaiser Franz directed the establishment of Freikorps, the traditional Austrian method of supplying light troops for its field armies. By mid-February then, the Kaiser had finally put in motion the substantive military measures that would lead irrevocably to war.

In the diplomatic arena, on the other hand, there was little activity between Vienna and Paris. Metternich, adhering to his 23 December instructions, maintained the façade of pacific intentions when he returned to Paris on 1 January 1809.[19] On the first day of March, however, he received instructions to change his tone and promptly informed Napoleon's foreign minister, Jean Baptiste de Nompère de Champagny, that Austria was assembling its forces on its western borders 'in response' to French and Rheinbund troops' movements.[20] This announcement notwithstanding, Stadion still hoped to mask Austria's final preparations for war, and Metternich never received directions to deliver 'a declaration of war, an ultimatum, or even an appropriate diplomatic note.'[21] Indications that 'decisive explications' would arrive in late March remained unfulfilled and his final letter from Stadion contained nothing definitive.[22] Although Metternich provided a wealth of excellent military intelligence and reinforced Vienna's preconceptions with Talleyrand's ominous pronouncements ('Napoleon definitely wants war'), Stadion kept him rather in the dark, and the ambassador was reduced to conducting relatively pointless discussions with his French interlocutors.[23] There was no Austrian effort to negotiate with Napoleon, nor was there even a serious attempt to fabricate a pretext for the war or force Napoleon into the role of the aggressor.[24] Stadion contented himself with sanctimonious declarations that Napoleon's malefic designs left Vienna no alternative but pre-emptive war.

THE GOAL OF THE COMING WAR

As Austria's soldiers girded themselves for war, Stadion formulated the goals for which they would fight. Unfortunately for the Habsburg monarchy, the definition of these war aims and their translation into a coherent military strategy proved insurmountable obstacles for Vienna's leaders in 1809. Moreover, owing to the gradual shift from a defensive to an offensive posture, Austria's war aims were slow to evolve; it was only in January 1809—after the decision for war had been made—that the specifics began to appear in written form.[25] These difficulties were apparent to some contemporaries even before the war began. Reviewing the monarchy's situation early in the year, for example, former Austrian foreign minister Franz Freiherr von Thugut commented:

> I do not understand what they intend. When I wanted war, I had allies and the hope of gaining more . . . Now they are advancing to the battlefield without allies, without hope of gaining any, and in the wake of a war as unhappy as the last one was! My friend, the level of courage that requires would be beyond me. I am certainly stubborn enough, but this responsibility would make me quake![26]

Thugut's insights would prove as trenchant as they were acerbic.

Despite the former minister's scorn, in some respects, Austria's goals were quite clear. In the broadest sense, Stadion wanted to portray Austria's cause as a noble crusade to 'deliver itself and Europe from the despotic yoke and invasive politics of Napoleon'. He thus assured potential allies and the public at large that the Habsburg monarchy was not making war on France, rather it was directing its efforts against 'the power of Napoleon'. Moreover, Austria purportedly did 'not wish to conduct a war of conquest', it merely wanted to 'assure its proper existence on stable and solid foundations' and would thus 'limit its desires to that which seems necessary to its internal stability and the security of its frontiers'.[27] As Stadion told the Kaiser on 22 January, the aim was: 'An increase in the state's population and income which is commensurate with our military status and the position we should hold in the European political order, [and] a secure, defensible border'.[28]

Stadion had a liberal definition of 'limited', however, and he aimed to attain dramatic results: 'The goal of the coming war is to set Napoleon's oppressive power in more narrow bounds, to destroy his tributary system, especially in Germany and Italy, and to establish the security and stability of our own monarchy on a firm basis'.[29] In the foreign minister's mind, the dramatic changes wrought by the French Revolution and Napoleon constituted crimes against the international order, and he saw the war as a means to achieve 'the restoration of the old order of things', returning Europe, above all Germany, to the way it had been 'before and after the Peace of Pressburg, up to the introduction of the Rheinbund act'.[30] Indeed, the Rheinbund was a particular target of Austrian policy. To be treated 'as if it did not exist', the Confederation was regarded as 'that act of the French regime whose destruction is an especial goal of the war'.[31] French influence in Germany therefore was to be eliminated and replaced by Austrian dominance.[32]

Within these general guidelines, Austria claimed to desire a peace under which 'every legitimate sovereign is re-established in the possessions which appertained to him prior to the usurpations of Napoleon'. This astonishing principle was to be 'applicable in Spain; in Italy, for King Ferdinand of Naples, the Pope, the King of Sardinia; in Germany and in the Duchy of Warsaw, for the King of Prussia, for the Elector of Hesse [Kassel], for the Duke of Braunschweig, for the ruling house of England'. Detailing specific goals in Germany, Stadion called for the return of the Tyrol and the Vorarlberg under Franz's sceptre, and left open the possibility of other border 'adjustments' to Austria's advantage during the peace process. As for the Rheinbund, the 'artificial' Napoleonic states of Berg and Westphalia were to be eradicated, while Bavaria, Württemberg, and Baden, Napoleon's staunchest German allies, were to suffer drastic reductions. The two Stadions planned similar rearrangements for the other German states to eliminate rivals to Austrian influence and to provide compensation for the dispossessed members of the Habsburg and d'Este families.[33] Belgium and Holland were also slated for 'liberation.' Away to the south, on Austria's Italian frontier, Istria and Dalmatia would find their way back to the Habsburg fold, and the monarchy's borders would be extended to the rivers Po and Chiesa. France's Italian possessions and Napoleon's Kingdom of Italy were to be dismantled, and the Kingdom of Sardinia enlarged so that it could serve as a buffer against French power for the future.[34]

These grandiose aims, as problematic as they were ambitious, deserve closer scrutiny because they relate to Vienna's military strategy. First, the goals expressed by Stadion were remarkable in scope. Although couched in terms of restored legitimacy and aversion to conquest, they represented in sum a complete overthrow of at least twenty years of European history. Evicted from Germany and Italy, France even stood to lose some of its territories on the west bank of the Rhine. Austria would become the dominant power between the Rhine and the Elbe, and would reassert itself in northern Italy, assuring its position by restoring the panoply of tiny states that had speckled the landscape of both regions in previous centuries. Their very scope, however, clearly placed these aims beyond the capability of Austria if she were forced to act alone. Achievement of Vienna's goals thus demanded the early and unstinting support of powerful allies in all three major theatres of war.

Second, much was left unclear in the Austrian conception of the war, and even those aims that had been committed to writing were not thought through to their logical conclusions. Stadion recognised that definition of the monarchy's security requirements 'must serve as the foundation of all military and political operations', and that this definition of the desired end-state of the conflict was central to deciding whether Austria should enter into war at all. Moreover, he saw this issue as the key factor in determining when to depart the battlefield and move to the peace table.[35] This insight notwithstanding, and despite the seeming specificity of his aims, Stadion's concept for the conflict was open-ended, imprecise, and incomplete, a list of unconstrained desires rather than a studied, well-crafted attempt to develop realistically achievable objectives. He and the other architects of the war policy seem to have assumed Austrian arms would conquer state after state until a concatenation of imaginary triumphs laid all of Germany and Italy at their feet.

The steps between the presumed initial victories and Stadion's vague picture of the desired political and strategic end-state, however, were undefined. Assuming Austrian power sufficed to evict Napoleon from Germany and Italy, these sweeping goals implied requirements (1) for Vienna to protect its presumed conquests from the inevitable French counterstroke, and (2) for a plan that would force France to accept these territorial gains as part of a lasting political settlement. As Napoleon was unlikely to acquiesce in Austria's proposed victories, from a 'modern' (*vice* a 'cabinet war') perspective, it followed that the Habsburg monarchy could only attain its aims by carrying the war into France to accomplish the utter overthrow of Napoleon's power, if not of the emperor himself.[36] This conclusion seems to have eluded many in Vienna. Austria's goals described a war of limited objectives: not an overthrow of Napoleon, but an old-style, eighteenth-century war of provinces within the European international system. Austria's leaders, however, addressed neither France's role in their future European order nor the fate of Napoleon and his nascent dynasty. Although Metternich had hinted that Austria might exploit internal dissension in France, Stadion evidently viewed any potential succession to Napoleon as a domestic matter for the French themselves to resolve and gave Metternich no instructions to pursue this issue.[37] There was no discussion of attacking into France itself from Germany or Italy, no planning for assistance from allies in this phase of the war. Most importantly, few other than the generalissimus seem to have considered whether a war of limited objectives was at all possible where Napoleon was involved. It seems highly improbable.[38] Such key lacunae in Austria's overarching political goals left Charles in a nearly impossible strategic situation, forcing him to prepare plans for a conflict with uncertain objectives and no clear terminus. These war aims, then, are simply further evidence that Stadion and much of Austria's leadership had no idea what they were undertaking in provoking war with Napoleon in 1809.

A third aspect of Vienna's war aims in 1809 is the question of whether this conflict was, as one American historian argues, a 'war to restore the Reich' (that is, the Holy Roman Empire).[39] Although there was no definitive statement to this effect, the conclusion indeed seems 'inescapable' that Stadion planned to reconstruct the old Reich on the ruins of the Rheinbund.[40] As one contemporary remarked in March 1809, Austria 'will be victorious and we will certainly see, very shortly, the Holy Roman Empire rise from its ashes'.[41] In most respects, for example, Austria's goals describe a return to the past, a restoration of the 'old order of things' with the important difference, of course, that Austria was to hold a position of unquestioned dominance. The writings of the two Stadions insisted on the 'illegitimacy' of Napoleon's arrangements and correspondingly rejected even the treaties signed since the Revolution.[42] For them, this would be a 'war of retribution', as the younger brother told the British envoy Stuart.[43] Raised in the comfort of the old imperial nobility, they were outraged by the dissolution of the old imperial constitution and preoccupied with associated issues such as the return of deposed princes and the compensation to be doled out to junior members of the Habsburg clan. As for the Rheinbund sovereigns, they had betrayed the old Reich and were to be treated accordingly, their resources exploited mercilessly on behalf of the Habsburg cause. But there is also a personal angle to consider, and the brothers singled out the King of Württemberg, who had sequestered the hereditary Stadion lands, for especially harsh treatment. Other German monarchs, however, could hope to ameliorate their fates by aligning themselves with Austria at the onset of hostilities.[44]

It is not surprising that this goal of re-establishing the Reich was left unstated in Austrian planning documents and manifestos. Hoping to convince Prussia and the Rheinbund states that 'with Austria Germany had been independent and happy' and that Austria's current intentions were just and selfless, the Stadions were unlikely to stress the restoration of an institution that would severely circumscribe the power and status of its supposed beneficiaries.[45] In the King of Bavaria's case, for instance, an Austrian victory would almost certainly result in a drastic reduction of his territory, would probably diminish his authority within his own borders, and could cost him his claim to a royal title as well. Other Rheinbund princes who had acquired larger territories and grander titles as a result of their affiliation with Napoleon faced similar consequences. Likewise, Prussia, Austria's German-speaking rival for leadership of the states between the Rhine and the Elbe, would have been even more reluctant to harness itself to the Austrian cause if the declared aim were a revived Reich under Vienna's leadership. Even Kaiser Franz had little interest in restoring the old imperial institution; explicit announcement of such an intention would have aroused his suspicion rather than his enthusiasm. This apparent desire to cloak their intentions vis-à-vis the Reich lent the Stadions' writings a certain air of evasiveness in 1809. Nonetheless, without explicitly saying so, Stadion prepared Austria's war aims so that the restoration of the old Reich would seem a natural consequence of the battlefield successes he expected the Habsburg armies to achieve.[46]

UNPARALLELED CONFUSION

After considerable effort, therefore, Stadion was able to articulate a sweeping set of objectives for the coming war. Translating these into a concrete political–military strategy to defeat France, however, proved to be a far more difficult problem, one that neither the foreign minister nor the army commander ever resolved satisfactorily. Charles and Stadion were consciously aware of the need to derive military actions from political goals, but the linkage between these two aspects of policy was often tenuous or absent.[47] As an Austrian historian has noted, 'the prelude to the military events of 1809 is characterised by unparalleled confusion' because 'the mutual interaction of politics and military strategy was grossly inadequate.'[48] Furthermore, by early March 1809, it had become apparent that the diplomatic half of the political–military equation had failed. Stadion's tangled web of international intrigue and covert contacts had not produced a single solid alliance.[49] The entire burden of Austria's war effort thus fell upon the shoulders of the army, with the foreign minister continuing to believe that a few signal military successes would compensate for Austria's political failures.

For Stadion, however, simple battlefield victories were not enough; Austria must also support its German friends.[50] The broad guidance he provided to the military for the development of operations plans thus contained an inherent contradiction: 'Begin in such a way as to occupy large regions and exploit the resources of these lands; but these initial eccentric operations must only be undertaken with the goal of uniting as much as possible all forces at some decisive point to carry forward a successful offensive war.'[51] An attempt to adhere to this guidance would require the army to disperse and concentrate at the same time, sending major detachments in all directions to flood the countryside from Saxony to Bavaria while simultaneously retaining the ability to concentrate rapidly to defeat the main French army in a full-scale engagement. As a further complication, of course, Stadion required important military victories early in the campaign to convert neutral countries to allies and to inspire the expected rebellion in Germany.

Attempting to divine Stadion's concept for the further execution of the war, however, we find few concrete pieces of evidence and are left to speculate that he envisaged events unfolding along the following lines. The conflict would open with Austria winning several significant, if not decisive, battles in both the German and Italian theatres. These victories, suitably embellished and broadcast, would spark popular uprisings under close Austrian direction. They would also push Prussia to join the growing coalition, perhaps prompted by the presence of an Austrian corps in Poland, and would encourage support from London; indeed, the uprisings in Germany and Italy would likely occur in response to British assistance. Furthermore, Russia would either affirm its strict neutrality or perhaps throw itself into the fray on Vienna's side. With allies assured and active, Austrian forces would establish themselves in the fortresses along the Rhine and in northern Italy while Vienna's political hegemony was secured in the 'liberated' territories.

As for the enemy, Stadion decided that Napoleon would be unable to mount a credible counter-offensive until some time during the summer. When the French emperor did attack, he would thus face a powerful coalition of regular Austrian troops reinforced by rapidly growing numbers of German recruits and supporting itself from the resources of the newly liberated Germany. If Austria began the campaign in March or early April, therefore, Stadion calculated that it would have at least 'the spring and part of the summer' to win several initial victories, organise its allies and prepare itself for Napoleon's counter-attack. Discussing Austria's ability to create a new army and a new popular enthusiasm for war within its own borders, Stadion wrote that 'Successful application of the same methods in Germany should in three or four months produce an equally terrible power and an equally admirable spirit in the German lands, and transform Germany, under the protection of the Austrian Army, into an unassailable bulwark of the Austrian monarchy.'[52] By engaging in this fantastically wishful thinking, particularly the gross underestimation of Napoleon's ability to respond, Stadion was able to convince himself and others that the coming war could conclude with some vaguely defined Austrian triumph.[53]

Charles's assessment of Austria's prospects was considerably less sanguine. In a key presentation to the Kaiser, he addressed the question of whether 'a war against France would be expedient at the present moment'. Opening this prescient document with a reminder to Franz that war is a dangerous enterprise in which 'the result is always uncertain', he methodically sketched the likely course of a new war with Napoleon to outline his serious concerns and advocate caution. He acknowledged that Austria's strategic situation had improved and opined that the initial phase of a campaign could go well 'if it begins after the complete redeployment of those French corps that are still on the road [towards Spain], if everything is well prepared and conducted with energy'. Under these circumstances, he thought, 'it is not impossible that the French armies will be forced to vacate the southern portions of Germany and withdraw behind the Rhine'. Despite the disadvantages that such a setback would have for Napoleon, however, 'France will not have suffered, it will still stand more powerful than Austria, unassailable behind the shield of the Rhine and a double row of fortresses'. Napoleon would thus gather his forces and counter-attack across the Rhine, where a 'decisive victory would take him into the heart of Austria' and possibly lead to 'the dissolution of the Austrian state'. Summing up, Charles wrote: 'In the best case, the result of a war can thus bring the liberation of Germany from the French, but will not be so disadvantageous for France that it will become weaker than Austria or incapable of posing a danger to us; in the worst case, on the other hand, it will mean the destruction of the Austrian monarchy.' He concluded his pessimistic but penetrating remarks by observing rhetorically that the present tension with France imposed severe political and financial stress on Austria, but that even throwing Napoleon across the Rhine would do nothing to decrease either the strain or the expense.[54]

In the eyes of the Austrian generalissimus, therefore, a war with France in 1809 threatened to place the existence of the monarchy at risk while offering few tangible or enduring benefits. Although Charles vacillated on the war question during the months leading up to the conflict, the disparity he perceived between Austria's military means and its desired political ends remained a consistent theme in his thinking. Once he came to believe that war was indeed ineluctable, he occasionally adopted a more optimistic tone,[55] but the extremely negative outlook that dominated his presentation to the Kaiser was never far below the surface. He thus entered into the war with more resignation than enthusiasm, writing later that, the requirements of the Iberian war notwithstanding, France was still superior to all other continental powers when hostilities opened: 'Herein lies the key to Austria's misfortunes in 1809.'[56]

ALL STRENGTH AT THE DECISIVE POINT

The foundation of Austrian operational planning for the coming war was thus a curious combination of Stadion's laputan optimism and Charles's sceptical pessimism. On the one hand, Stadion's incomplete and grandiose war aims presented the army with an unachievable strategic task. The requirement for rapid movements and dramatic victories early in the war illustrates this problem. Although the Habsburg army had improved markedly since 1805, it was still a cumbersome instrument, the command, mobility, and logistical demands implied in Stadion's vision were beyond its abilities. In GM Josef Radetzky's words, 'the means were not in proportion with the ends'.[57] This general strategic problem was compounded by Stadion's specific requirements. The goal of conquering Italy, for example, diverted at least one corps from the principal theatre of war in Germany, while Austrian forces in Bohemia and along the Danube were presented with conflicting aims that simultaneously demanded dispersion and concentration.[58] The foreign minister, however, unfamiliar with military matters, was incapable of judging the army's readiness and did not understand what he was asking Charles to undertake. Moreover, he did not trust Charles and his generals (nor they him) and feared that the military hierarchy would lose the war through lethargy.[59] On the other hand, Charles's support for the war was temporary, a thin veneer that threatened to crack at the first setback. He entered into actual operational planning with the conviction that he could only do his best on behalf of a cause that probably could not be won.[60] Given this dissonance between political and military authorities and the gap between goals and resources, it is hardly surprising that Radetzky concluded 'the campaign of 1809 was lost before it began'.[61]

Despite the misgivings, Charles and his staff accelerated their efforts to craft a concept for the Austrian offensive. Military planning for the war had been proceeding very slowly. Charles had provided chief of staff Mayer some vague guidance for offensive and defensive operations on 25 December 1808 after that month's series of decision conferences, but there was still no solid plan for assembling the army and invading Napoleonic Germany when Mayer submitted his defensive concept on 16 January. Mayer, frustrated at the lack of definition in Charles's guidance, was particularly irritated by the absence of a clear political framework for his formulations and complained that he was being forced to work 'like a blind man discussing colours'.[62] It was 3 February before Charles provided additional instructions and directed Mayer to prepare a plan for the army's offensive operations. As sketched for Mayer, the goal of the army's initial actions in the principal theatre of operations was the defeat of the French forces in middle and north-west Germany, specifically Marshal Davout's army of the Rhine.[63] French and Rheinbund troops in southern Germany were also to be attacked and all operations undertaken with an eye to supporting rebellion in those states assessed to be particularly restive and inclined toward Austria. If all went well, initial operations would conclude with Davout soundly defeated and the Austrian army ensconced in a central position along the Neckar and the southern stretches of the Rhine before Napoleon could organise and transport significant reinforcements out of France. A separate corps would secure Saxony, establish contact with an allied Prussian corps, observe or blockade Magdeburg and push into northern Germany.[64] To the east, Poland was targeted for invasion to knock the Grand Duchy of Warsaw's army out of the conflict and to pressure Prussia to join the Habsburg cause, while Austrian forces along the monarchy's southern borders 'could have no other object but to secure Italy and the Tyrol'.[65]

As for political considerations, Mayer was to assume: (1) that Prussia would provide active assistance from the onset of hostilities in the form of 40,000 men with another 40,000 to follow after several weeks; (2) that Russia would remain neutral; (3) that significant popular forces were ready to raise the flag of rebellion in Germany; and (4) that Great Britain would help with military and naval diversions as well as subsidies. The key military–strategic assumptions were that Napoleon's involvement in Spain would give Austria a dramatic numerical superiority in the early stages of the war and that the French emperor would be unable to mount a major counter-stroke until some time in the summer.[66] As previously discussed, none of these assumptions proved to be viable.

Turning to the enemy, the Austrian high command assessed French and Allied forces in Germany at approximately 200,000 with 16,000 more Frenchmen at Lyons who would probably be deployed across the Rhine in the event of war. On the strategic flanks, the Austrians estimated that they would have to cope with 20,000 Poles and 6,000 Saxons in the Duchy of Warsaw, and 77,800 French, Italians, and Neapolitans in the Italian peninsula and Dalmatia. After deducting fortress garrisons and occupation troops in Naples from this latter number, however, Mayer and his colleagues calculated that only some 30,000 French would be available for mobile operations in northern Italy.[67] Mayer thus arrived at a total French strength of approximately 230,000 men for the opening phases of the coming campaign (curiously, his calculations did not include the Polish and Saxon forces in the Grand Duchy of Warsaw). Comparing this reasonably accurate figure with a Habsburg host of 283,000 regulars supported by 40,000 Prussians, he concluded that Austria and its presumed ally could hope to begin the war with a considerable numerical advantage.[68] Furthermore, plans called for the raising of 310,000 second-line Austrian troops, perhaps as many as 35,000–50,000 infantry and cavalry from various national militias (the Hungarian, Croatian, and Slovenian Insurrections), and, after a few weeks of mobilisation, an additional 40,000 Prussians.[69]

Beyond this assumed overall quantitative superiority, the Austrians expected to enjoy several other advantages. In the first place, the component pieces of Davout's army were scattered all across Germany from the Rhine to the North Sea coast and the Prussian fortresses along the Oder. The Habsburg generals could thus hope to catch the French in the process of assembling and defeat them in detail. Secondly, they hoped that the composition of Napoleon's forces in Germany would give them a qualitative edge, or at least minimise and localise French tactical superiority. In Germany,

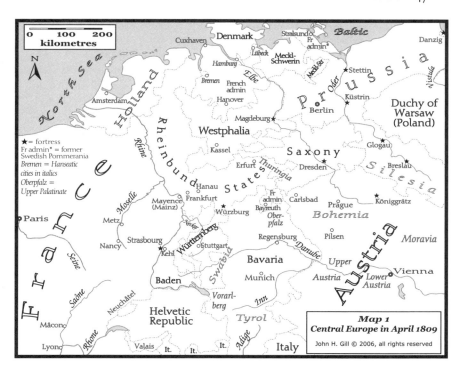

Map 1
Central Europe in April 1809

John H. Gill © 2006, all rights reserved

the main theatre of operations, some 91,000 of Napoleon's 200,000 men were Dutch or Rheinbund Germans, troops that the Austrians considered distinctly inferior to the French. There was even room to hope that some of these would abandon Napoleon as soon as Austria had secured a victory or two. Third, the French troops themselves were believed to have declined significantly as compared with earlier campaigns. Metternich had argued that 'Napoleon has but one army—*his Grande Armée*', this now found itself entangled in the Iberian affair, leaving the emperor with a reserve 'which could only be composed of conscripts below the age of service', conscripts who 'were no better than the new recruits of any other nation when not amalgamated with veteran soldiers'.[70] Fourth, Mayer evidently assumed that the French forces in Italy and Dalmatia, with only 30,000 available for offensive operations, were too weak to constitute a serious threat—a judgement that would have interesting implications for his initial plan.[71] As with most of their political–military assumptions, the conclusions the Austrians drew from their intelligence reports provided a false sense of their

Table 1: The Prussian Army in Early 1809

The following units were divided into six brigades

12	Infantry regiments
2	Jäger battalions
1	Schützen battalion
1	Model or training battalion ('Normal-Bataillon')
19	Cavalry regiments
1	Guard uhlan squadron
1	Model or training squadron ('Normal-Eskadron')
36	Foot artillery companies
9	Horse artillery companies

Approximate strengths by arm

Line infantry:	22,000
Line cavalry:	8,000
Artillery:	6,000
Guard infantry:	4,400
Guard cavalry:	1,600

Source: Rudolf Vaupel (ed), *Das Preussische Heer von Tilsiter Frieden bis zur Befreiung*, Leipzig: Hirzel, 1938, vol. I, p. 10.

prospects for success. Although the estimates of French strength were fairly accurate, in other respects the analysis was overly optimistic. The low value assigned to the fighting qualities of the French forces in Germany and their German allies, for example, was terribly misleading. Above all, however, the Austrian leadership dangerously underestimated Napoleon's ability to mobilise reinforcements, push them to the theatre of war, and react to Austrian moves with deadly speed and precision.

In addition to the enemy situation, Mayer's planning had to account for Austria's difficult geographic position. Surrounded on three sides by French satellites, he and Charles believed Austria had no choice but to act in divergent directions, and Mayer identified eight key 'strategic points' that would define upcoming operations: Warsaw, Dresden, Bamberg, Donauwörth, Munich, Innsbruck, Brixen, and Verona. Simultaneous movements against all these 'points' implied an undesirable dispersion of Austrian strength and would represent a violation of Charles's own strategic principle—opening a campaign 'with all strength at the decisive point'—but they were considered necessary to anticipate French threats and inspire rebellion.[72] These distant diversions notwithstanding, Mayer kept the chief object of the Austrian offensive, Davout's army, firmly in focus and crafted his plan to place as many Habsburg troops as possible in a central position in the principal theatre of operations. He therefore proposed to mass five of Austria's nine regular corps (I through V) and both of its reserve corps in Bohemia, prepared to advance towards the Elbe, the Main, or the Danube as the situation required. Two more regular corps were to assemble south of the Danube, on the Inn (VI) and at Salzburg (VIII), while the Prussians were expected to concentrate at Berlin and Krossen on the Oder.[73] In all, the plan provided for a total of nine Austrian corps (between 170,000 and 200,000 men) and 40,000 Prussians who could contribute to the decisive campaign in Germany.[74] It is important to note, however, that even in the best case, the combined Austro-Prussian force would only be roughly equal in numbers to the total French forces in Germany. To attain a significant advantage, therefore, the Austrians would have to remain concentrated and hope to catch the French in relatively isolated packets. Speed was essential.[75] Curiously, Mayer's concept of operations in Germany was almost entirely predicated upon the actions of the French. Rather than dictating to the enemy, Mayer and the other Habsburg generals started from the assumption that Davout's manoeuvres would determine Austrian courses of action in the deciding arena. As for the other theatres, Mayer detailed one corps to join Prussian troops for an offensive strike into Poland (VII Corps at Krakow) and another to the monarchy's southern borders (IX Corps at Klagenfurt and Laibach) where it could contribute to the conquest of the southern portions of the Tyrol. While operations in Poland occupied much of the plan, however, it contained no specific mention of invading Napoleon's Italian kingdom, indeed it made almost no reference to Italy whatsoever.[76]

In the event, Mayer's initial concept proved short-lived. Only three days after receiving it, Charles issued orders that affirmed most of plan but shifted VIII Corps from Salzburg to Klagenfurt and moved the small II Reserve Corps from Bohemia to Wels in the Danube valley in its place.[77] This change was almost certainly the result of Archduke Johann's personal influence with his brother, the Generalissimus. Stadion and Johann had assumed that Italy would be a theatre of offensive operations and Mayer's initial dispositions probably came as an unpleasantly annoying shock. By transferring VIII Corps, Charles not only made possible the invasion of

Italy that both the foreign minister and the young archduke had expected, but also satisfied his sibling's desire for a truly independent command with a substantial mission.[78] At the same time, however, the move deprived the Main Army (Hauptarmee) of over 20,000 men and sixty-two guns without contributing anything to the operations in Germany where the fate of the Habsburg monarchy would be decided. Charles evidently had second thoughts regarding this decision as war approached. He issued an order on 10 March, for example, recalling most of VIII Corps to Salzburg, and Johann had to hurry to Vienna to have the directive rescinded.[79] Again, at the end of the month, Charles wrote to Johann that VIII Corps had only been shifted to Klagenfurt with the 'definitive assurance' that the entire corps and part of IX Corps would advance up the Drava valley into the Tyrol to be in a position to co-operate with the Main Army. In his memoirs, Johann protested that he knew nothing of any such 'definitive assurances', but in any case, the end of March was far too late to effect a major change in plans for an invasion that was to commence on 10 April.[80] By that time, both of Johann's corps were fully committed to the advance into Italy and only a detachment of some 13,500 (a mere half of whom were regulars) was allotted to the Drava valley. The Main Army was thus significantly diminished to support 'an offensive into upper Italy which was irrelevant to the principal decision and which later actually proved disastrous'.[81]

While Charles and Johann were debating the merits of operations in Italy, the men who would make up their armies were beginning to move. Army headquarters had designated 25 February as the day most regiments would depart their garrisons to join the corps on the frontiers, but the long distances many units had to cover and the routine friction of military mobilisation and movement meant repeated delays and disruptions. The process proceeded, but not as smoothly as desired. Even had the army been able to adhere strictly to its detailed march tables, however, some of the troops allocated to the Main Army (at least 10,000 men) were not scheduled to arrive in their cantonment areas in Bohemia until 31 March. Worse, the last Grenz regiment was not slated to reach Pisek until 11 April. Volunteer formations and support troops posed additional problems. If the army were to be complete, then, Charles would have to wait until at least mid-April before crossing the border—hardly what Stadion had in mind when he had optimistically spoken of attacking on 1 March. At the very earliest, Charles could open his offensive between 20 and 22 March with the forces then available in Bohemia: 155,200 men, or some 54,000 short of what he could hope to gather by waiting another three weeks or so.[82]

The regiments had hardly taken the road, however, when new orders began to arrive that completely reoriented the thrust into Germany. Initial indications came when instructions issued on 25 and 28 February shifted several of the Main Army's corps slightly south and east of their original destinations. Two weeks later, on 11 March, an officer of the General Staff unexpectedly arrived in Linz to arrange quarters for army headquarters, and on the 12th and 13th, new orders directed the bulk of the Main Army to assembly areas south of the Danube. In accordance with these new instructions, V Corps started moving on 20 March with III, I Reserve, and IV Corps following in succession. Marching via Linz, all were to be in place along the Inn between 7 and 9 April, prepared to cross that river and initiate hostilities on the 10th. Instead of debouching into central Germany from

Table 2: Austrian Main Army Strengths, March–April 1809

Infantry and cavalry effectives only

	20 March	9 April	approx. 20 April*
I Corps	25,500	25,700	27,500
II Corps	26,100	28,340	28,340
III Corps	20,400	23,600	31,100
IV Corps	13,500	15,000	29,080
V Corps	23,500	24,190	29,900
VI Corps	28,500	31,790	34,790
(VIII Corps)	(21,300)	(26,500)	(26,500)
I Reserve Corps	13,700	15,920	15,920
II Reserve Corps	3,900	6,690	6,690
Main Army Total	153,300	171,230	203,320
(incl. VIII Corps)	(174,600)	(197,730)	(229,820)

Note: These figures are approximate and are compiled based on original corps organisations, that is, Vécsey's brigade (6,190) remains with II Corps, and Rottermund's brigade (1,550) remains with I Reserve Corps. This permits analysis of Austrian options, such as attacking out of Bohemia with the bulk of the Main Army. Additionally, VIII Corps is included to show the approximate strength of the Main Army had Charles retained the initial troop dispositions.
* Assuming Austria decided to wait an extra ten days before opening hostilities.
Sources: Krieg 1809, prepared by the staff of the k. und k. Kriegsarchiv, Vienna: Seidel & Sohn, 1907–10, vol. I, Annexes XIII, XIV, and XVII; Johann, Archduke of Austria, Erzherzog Johanns 'Feldzugserzählung' 1809, ed. Alois Veltzé, Vienna: Seidel & Sohn, 1909, pp. 50–3.

Bohemia, therefore, the army's main effort would now be an invasion of Bavaria along the Danube valley.[83]

This dramatic alteration in the Austrian plan for the Main Army has been one of the most enduring controversies of the 1809 war, puzzling to both contemporaries and subsequent historians. Unfortunately, as the authors of the Austrian official history point out, 'because the causes of these changes in the deployment cannot be determined, we are left with speculations.'[84] Nonetheless, it is clear that intelligence regarding French troop movements played a key role in the reconsideration. Up to early February, the Austrian General Staff had correctly placed most French forces in northern and central Germany, generally on a line stretching from Nuremberg to Hamburg. Around the time that Mayer was presenting his plan to Charles, however, new intelligence began to indicate that the Napoleon was adjusting his deployments, specifically, that he was shifting troops to the south.[85] Evidence of a major French concentration in Bavaria mounted as February turned to March and, by the middle of the month, the Austrians had reports that at least 70,000–90,000 men (Massena, Oudinot, parts of the Guard) were en route to Augsburg and other cities along the Danube. Many of the Rheinbund troops were also expected to assemble on the Danube and most French reinforcements appeared to be passing through Strasbourg. All this intelligence led Charles's staff to the conclusion that Napoleon was directing his army to gather around the great cities of the Danube rather than in Thuringia as initially assumed. It also convinced them that Regensburg (Ratisbonne) should be the initial object of their advance if the Austrian Main Army was to divide the French and make itself master of both banks of the Danube.[86]

A second key consideration for the planners in Vienna was Prussia. As late as mid-February, Austria was still counting on Friedrich Wilhelm's forces taking the field at the onset of hostilities, but, as previously mentioned, a 13 March note from the Prussian foreign minister destroyed all hope that Habsburg and Hohenzollern troops would march together when the campaign opened. The absence of Prussian participation need not have forced a change in the Austrian base of operations, but for many in the Habsburg capital, it removed the most cogent reason for launching the offensive from Bohemia.[87]

Intelligence about French forces along the Danube and the evaporation of the Prussian mirage thus caused a complete re-evaluation of Austrian planning and created room for doubt and anxiety to enter. During discussions that began in the latter part of February, the Bohemian plan was generally characterised as bolder, quicker to execute, and more decisive, but also fraught with uncertainty and danger. An advance from the Danube, on the other hand, was considered slower but more secure. As more and more reports confirming a massive French concentration in Bavaria reached Vienna, the Austrian leadership became concerned that the Main Army, coming from Bohemia, might not be able to capture Regensburg without conducting an opposed crossing of the Danube, that Napoleon might take the Habsburg forces in their left flank as they emerged from the Bohemian mountain passes and cut them off from their support base, or that the two relatively isolated corps along the Inn would be swallowed up by the bulk of the French emperor's command while a French observation corps held off the Austrian Main Army. There was also apprehension for the safety of the monarchy overall: if the Danube valley were not protected, Napoleon might use it as an avenue to strike into the heart of the realm as the French had in 1800 and 1805. Additionally, the advance from Bohemia now came to be seen as too distant from Archduke Johann's forces in Italy: the two armies would be unable to co-operate strategically and the French might cut communications between them. The Danube option would also offer the best chance of knocking Napoleon's largest Rheinbund ally, Bavaria, out of the war at an early stage. Finally, proponents of the Danube plan highlighted the topographic difficulties associated with operations out of Bohemia: rugged mountains and a poor road network in the rainy spring months could make an advance into Germany problematic and could endanger the army's ability to supply itself from its Bohemian bases. In all these respects, the Danube valley was considered to represent a superior line of operations. Above all, a concentration along the Inn offered the best opportunity of shielding the Austrian Empire from French invasion.

Arguing against the Danube plan were the delay in beginning the offensive (estimated by Stadion's protégé GM Karl von Stutterheim as twelve to fourteen days), the requirement to conduct numerous river crossings 'whereby an equal number of battles will be necessary', the good positions available to the enemy, and the resulting slowness of the overall operation. Furthermore, a drive up the Danube would effectively preclude any significant advance into the more sympathetic areas of Germany during the early stages of the campaign. Instead, the Austrians would find themselves invading one of Napoleon's most committed allies where the population was decidedly unreceptive to Habsburg blandishments.[88]

Consistent with Austria's traditionally cautious approach to military endeavours, Charles decided on the more conservative plan and ordered the shift to the Danube valley. In the words of one insightful historian, Christian Binder von Kriegelstein, 'at the first news that French forces were assembling in Bavaria, the [Austrian] plan for a sudden strike collapsed into an effort to "cover" the monarchy.' Binder's scorn at what he called Austria's 'strategic anxiety' may seem unfair, but it is clear that Charles, mistrusting his own army's mobility and painfully aware of Napoleon's capabilities, selected the more prudent but less decisive course of action because he was unwilling to hazard the bolder plan.[89]

The consequences of the change in plan are difficult to judge. Many commentators, contemporary and later, have criticised the move to the Danube on the grounds that it delayed the Austrian offensive by as much as three weeks, arguing that the Austrian army could have initiated the invasion as early as 20 March had it moved from Bohemia.[90] This is an unrealistic assessment. Even had Charles proceeded with the original plan, the army could hardly have launched itself across the border before the beginning of April. If the corps had begun departing their scattered cantonments on 20 March (only 155,200-strong even on that date, the army was too unready to contemplate an earlier move) and marched no faster than they did en route to the Inn, they could not have concentrated on the frontier before the end of the month, and possibly several days into April. Although three weeks is too extreme, therefore, it seems reasonable to calculate that the shift postponed the Austrian offensive for some seven to ten days, an important, if perhaps not decisive period. Moreover, the slowness with which the corps were transferred south of the Danube exacerbated the delay. A quick calculation shows that the four deploying corps undertook completely unremarkable marches on the move south. With the greatest distance to traverse, III Corps made an average of only fifteen kilometres per day and rested for five of its twenty-one days on the road. Similar figures apply to IV Corps, and the other two (V and I Reserve Corps) averaged only nine to eleven kilometres a day. Although there was good cause for Charles to husband his army's strength before the war, these daily march distances were inappropriate to the seriousness of the situation and the crucial importance of striking the French as early as possible.[91]

In addition to delaying the initial offensive, the move disrupted logistical arrangements. Depots and hospitals had, of course, all been established on the basis of the Bohemian plan, and reorienting lines of communication (not to mention operational thinking) in the context of the Austrian army 'was an enormous task'.[92] The long march also had a damaging effect on much of the army's equipment. Nor should one ignore the psychological impact on the soldiery. Wearing marches in miserable weather were hardly beneficial for morale, especially when 'the troops might ask in vain why they had been sent to Bohemia in quick and exhausting marches ... .only to be shifted, often just arrived, to Upper Austria' south of the Danube. The fact that all this marching did not result in any advance towards the army's objectives only made matters worse. Oberleutnant Heinrich von Hess, an officer on the army's operations staff, doubtless reflected the opinions of many others when he wrote that the army could have accomplished the new concentration on the Danube 'just as easily by marching through Bavaria itself as behind our own borders'.[93]

In sum, the move to the Danube valley was an operational error. One can only agree with Johann's observation that 'it delayed the outbreak [of the war] and gave rise to much confusion' and with Mayer's caustic 'much time for offensive operations was lost which the enemy used for his assembly and organisation'.[94] Continuing with the original plan to attack out of Bohemia would *not* have guaranteed victory, but it would have afforded the Austrians a *higher probability* of catching the French off guard and in detail. The shift south, on the other hand, granted Napoleon an additional week to prepare and strained the Austrian army for little appreciable gain.[95] The redeployment thus did not cause Austria to lose the opening campaign in Germany or the war, but, by shifting the bulk of his forces at the last moment, Charles significantly reduced his chances, however slight, of gaining a major success early in the conflict. It would not be Austria's last lost opportunity.[96]

Discussion of Charles's operational choices (Bohemia or the Danube), however, must not be allowed to obscure the larger, more serious problem: that the army was simply unprepared for war before early April.[97] In the latter half of March, logistical arrangements were incomplete, numerous regiments lacked significant numbers of replacements (in many cases entire battalions), most of the light troops and some of the artillery had not yet arrived, and ammunition was not at authorised levels.[98] In short, as the army's operations journal noted in late March: 'most branches of the army are not yet ready for combat.'[99] Well before the whitecoats marched south toward Linz, therefore, Austria had already lost much of the advantage it had hoped to gain from the dispersion, numerical inferiority, and presumed unpreparedness of the French. To meet Stadion's sanguine time line of 1 March and to strike before the French were concentrated and reinforced, the Habsburg leadership should have initiated mobilisation and significant troop movements at least a month earlier.[100] The redeployment to the Inn certainly postponed the opening of the offensive by a week or so, but it represented an additional delay, compounding the larger one. Austria had already forfeited its greatest chance for early victories by delaying mobilisation until mid-February. As one

Austrian sympathiser noted on 3 March: 'The most formidable preparations continue, but the time to conquer Bavaria and Saxony before the French are ready has already passed.'[101] For Vienna's purposes, the 8 February meeting should have been convened on 8 January.[102]

Before leaving this analysis of Austrian preparations, we must address one further issue: the dismissal of GM Mayer on 19 February. Full of his own importance and nearly insolent toward Charles at times, Mayer was a difficult subordinate and colleague, but he was also a thorough and intelligent soldier with considerable combat experience. Unfortunately, he and Grünne heartily detested one another, a situation that hardly augured well for unity of effort as Austria prepared for war. Indeed, the period preceding the outbreak of hostilities was one of intrigue upon intrigue, a tangled web of ambition, deceit, and acid malice that ended with Grünne, supported by another member of the generalissimus' staff, Oberst Maximilian Freiherr von Wimpffen, engineering Mayer's ousting and his replacement by 'one of the most mediocre officers of the army', GM Johann von Prochaska.[103] Mayer, exiled to a distant Balkan frontier as fortress commandant in Brod, had to plead for time to sell his horses and pack his belongings.[104] The immediate and obvious result of this 'pure power struggle' was that Charles, incapable or unwilling to assert himself over his immediate staff, lost his chief strategist— the architect of the army's operations plan—just as earnest preparations for imminent war were beginning.[105] The whole sordid affair thus sowed confusion and uncertainty in the army and society at large (currency rates on the stock exchange fell at the news of Mayer's dismissal) and removed the principal proponent of the Bohemian plan. Although it appears that Mayer's fall was not directly related to the change in offensive plans, it is not idle to wonder whether his energy and determination might not have sufficed to persuade Charles to retain the Bohemian option and to execute it with vigour once the army crossed the border.[106]

THIS MAGNIFICENT ARMY

Mayer's disgrace notwithstanding, the Austrian army slowly assembled on the frontiers of the monarchy. It was in some respects very different from the Austrian armies that had faced the French across the previous seventeen years, and was arguably one of the best ever fielded by the Habsburg monarchy. It was also a large force, representing a major exertion for the lethargic old empire. Planning for the war, Mayer had used a figure of 598,200 combatants (including 36,935 cavalry). The field forces comprised 283,400 of this impressive total and were divided into forty-six 'German' and fifteen Hungarian line regiments, seventeen Grenz regiments from the monarchy's Slavic borderlands, nine of the new Jäger battalions, and thirty-five cavalry regiments (Appendix 1).[107] These were to be supplemented by sedentary troops numbering some 314,810 and consisting of line unit depots, four garrison battalions, reserves, and the Landwehr. It was hoped that the Hungarian militia, the 'Noble Insurrection', would provide a further 50,000 infantry and cavalry, raising the total forces available some time after the start of hostilities to over 650,000 men under arms.[108] Additional 'Insurrection' troops from other border regions would be added as mobilisation proceeded.

This large army was the product of eight years of reform, the Habsburg answer to the challenge of militant France and the changing nature of land warfare.[109] These reforms were often tentative half-measures, and progress was by no means steady or consistent. Nor were they even guided by a clear vision or by a definitive, well-considered, and generally accepted plan. Nonetheless, in several areas, the army's capabilities slowly improved under Charles's guidance.

Of particular importance for the coming war were changes in Austrian organisation and tactics. Organisationally, the field army was for the first time arranged in French-style *corps d'armée* in an attempt to enhance its mobility, flexibility, and logistical sustainability. The nine standard or line corps were very similar to one another, each consisting of two line divisions, an advance guard division, and supporting elements for a total of approximately 30,000 men in twenty-five to thirty battalions and sixteen squadrons. While line divisions consisted of two or three brigades, with two three-battalion line regiments per brigade, the corps's light troops were combined in the advance guard division, usually four to six battalions of supposedly 'light' infantry (Jäger, Grenzer, or volunteers) and two light horse regiments (chevaulegers, hussars, or uhlans). Each corps commander had sixty-four to ninety-six guns at his disposal, organised (another innovation) into permanent batteries. The corps were thus potentially powerful, self-contained combat formations, each of which could train, march, and fight as an integrated entity with resulting benefits for combat effectiveness and unit cohesion. As agile, all-arms manoeuvre elements, they should have eased the command and control burden for the army commander while increasing his range of operational and tactical options; that is, they should have helped Austria move away from the ad hoc 'wings', 'lines' (*Treffen* or 'battles'), and 'columns' of the linear era when armies had no permanent structure above the regimental level and when guns were distributed individually across the battlefield.

The two reserve corps did not fit this pattern. Serving as command and control headquarters for the army's elite grenadiers and heavy cavalry, each was unique. By far the larger, I Reserve Corps consisted of twelve grenadier battalions and thirty-six squadrons, while II Reserve counted only five battalions and twenty-four squadrons in its order of battle. This peculiar arrangement, however, did not last: shortly after the opening battles in Bavaria, the two corps were amalgamated into one, with separate grenadier and cavalry components. Although some guns were attached to the reserve's grenadier and heavy cavalry brigades, it is important to note that there was no army-level artillery reserve. This arrangement had several drawbacks. In the first place, it tended to burden the corps with too many heavy guns and support vehicles, degrading speed and flexibility during the war of manoeuvre that characterised the actions in April. Second, by distributing all of the guns to the corps Charles deprived himself of a crucial tactical tool. Committed to the firing line with their corps, the various batteries found themselves engaged, exhausted, and short of ammunition relatively early in battle and Charles thus had no pool of fresh guns upon which he could call to influence the outcome at decisive moments. The batteries assigned to the reserve corps did not prove an effective substitute.[110]

In addition to these organisational changes in the regular army, imperial decrees in the late spring of 1808 created two new institutions to increase the monarchy's pool of trained, or at least partially trained, military manpower. In the first instance, two reserve battalions were established in May 1808 for each of the 'German' line infantry regiments to serve as a source of replacements in time of war. While these reserve battalions were intended solely to support the regular army, the second innovation was a step, albeit tentative, towards a true popular or national military. This was the Landwehr, or national militia, of the empire's 'German' provinces (Bohemia, Moravia-Silesia and the various Habsburg hereditary lands), which optimists hoped would supply 152,000 or more men to relieve the regular army of garrison and home defence requirements while harnessing national energies to support the war effort.

In the tactical arena, Austria made some limited efforts to adapt to the new techniques of continental warfare. The cavalry was largely unaffected, but the infantry acquired a new set of regulations in 1807 that were supposed to improve its ability to counter the French, especially the skirmishing tactics and battlefield mobility that had become the hallmark of the French army since the Revolution. Instead of streamlining and simplifying infantry manoeuvres, however, these regulations were even more complicated than their 1769 predecessors and 'incorporated all the artifices of Frederickian drill'.[111] Skirmishing, an art that placed a premium on individual initiative and tactical adaptability at the lowest levels, was stifled by the oppressive formality of the 1807 drill books, another expression of the officious bureaucratic climate that pervaded the entire Habsburg state. Other problems also hampered Austrian adaptation to the new tactical forms. The Grenzer, the quintessential light infantry in Maria Theresa's day, had been regularised in subsequent years, losing much of their independence and aggressiveness in the process. Volunteer units, another traditional source of light troops, had only recently been hammered together from levies on the Landwehr and could scarcely be expected to meet the demands of skirmishing over rugged terrain against Napoleon's veterans. Even the new Jäger battalions, specifically raised in 1808 as light infantry, had no manual to instruct them in their duties. Lacking formal guidance from above, each individual battalion developed its own tactics, hardly a situation conducive to integrated effort on the battlefield.[112] Furthermore, rather than using them as elite light troops to cover a corps or division front in battle, Austrian commanders routinely squandered Jägers by assigning them positions in the corps's order of battle as they would any other infantry battalion.[113] Major Georg Freiherr von Valentini, a Prussian officer who volunteered to serve the Habsburgs in 1809, concluded that 'In the Austrian army there is no body of troops exclusively dedicated to fighting in open order.'[114] The Austrian infantry thus enhanced its skirmishing capabilities in a limited fashion, but could in no way compare itself to its French opponents and their more advanced Rheinbund allies.

More important to the Austrian foot soldiers was the introduction of two unique infantry formations: the 'division mass' and 'battalion mass'. These were essentially variations on the standard square, but placed the individual infantrymen in tight, rectangular blocks, lacking the hollow centre of a conventional square. The 'division mass' was not well liked and was seldom employed, but the 'battalion mass' was, in Valentini's opinion, the Austrian army's 'favourite battle formation'. It was used to good effect in the open field fighting at Aspern and apparently became so popular that it nearly replaced the traditional square (which Austrian battalions still practised) as a defence against cavalry.[115] These formations, however, were difficult to manoeuvre, and away from flat, uncluttered terrain such as that along the banks of the Danube across from Vienna, they were of marginal utility. Moreover, the dense concentration of soldiers in the mass made it an unforgettable artillery target, allowing enemy gunners the opportunity to incapacitate many men with each ball or shell. The battalion mass was thus a useful innovation, but by no means decisive, an interesting and occasionally valuable tactical curiosity that is often overrated.[116]

The key reform in the artillery was the improvement in command, administration, and tactical employment of guns through the establishment of permanent battery organisations with their own train personnel. In addition, the train troops were militarised and their officers given equal status with their colleagues in the other arms. Finally, a special corps of *Handlanger* was formed to provide non-specialist manpower for the artillery. Problems with the train units and the *Handlanger*, however, proved the greatest obstacles to the rapid mobilisation of the army's artillery assets.[117]

Charles also attempted to introduce reforms to enhance the quality, competence, and spirit of the army's officers and men. For the ordinary soldier in the ranks, the *generalissimus* reduced terms of service and promulgated a new service regulation to ameliorate some of the wretchedness and brutality normally suffered by the rank and file. In place of beatings and degradation, he insisted that the soldiers were to be treated with a modicum of respect,

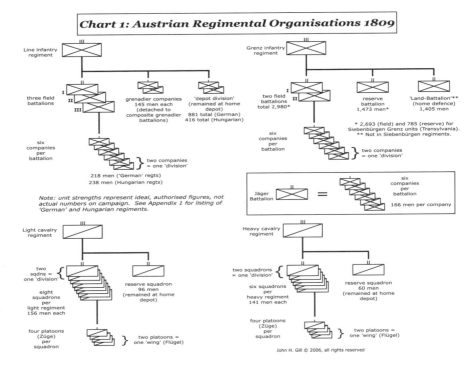

Chart 1: Austrian Regimental Organisations 1809

that the men were to be motivated by sincere attachment to their monarch, their regiment, and noble ideals of martial virtue.[118] If not an army of free citizens, the men at least were to be regarded as honourable servants of their emperor, not social misfits or convicts in uniform.

Physical punishment and abuse, however, were not so easily removed from the Austrian army's repertoire. A Bavarian who frequented the Habsburg encampments around Munich in April reported that he saw beatings administered several times. He concluded that 'corporals's sticks are still one of the most important items of field equipment in the Austrian army.' The same observer also commented on the state of morale in the units he observed: 'One had often read in the newspapers that the army's poets had written special songs for the Austrian troops and for the goals of this war; I was in their bivouacs often and at all hours of the day, but never heard one of these songs being sung and generally noticed little joy among the men.'[119]

These comments notwithstanding, Grünne was not wrong in noting the army's 'spirit and enthusiasm'. In the opening phases of this campaign at least, a strong sense of national purpose motivated large parts of the army and many of Charles's men indeed felt confident of success. 'Everything he [Charles] did was intended to raise the spirit of the army,' wrote Radetzky, 'and in this he succeeded.'[120] Oberleutnant Karl von Grueber of the *Albert* Cuirassiers thus recalled that: 'Anyone who had seen the enthusiasm of this magnificent army advancing towards Bavaria could hardly have doubted that our brows would be encircled by victory's green laurels.'[121]

Charles's dogged efforts at reform and Grueber's proud confidence notwithstanding, the Austrian army of 1809 suffered from a number of serious problems. In the first place, the infantry had to contend with a significant shortage of trained manpower. Under peacetime manning strictures, regiments kept only a small percentage of their men on active service, and the new reserve battalions, less than a year old, had not been in place long enough to generate a pool of trained or even partially trained replacements. As a result, few battalions were at full strength when they departed their garrisons in February and many had to incorporate large numbers of hastily collected recruits during the march to their assembly areas on the borders. Over half the troops in the 9th Jäger Battalion were new to the uniform in 1809, for example, and 40 per cent of the *Davidovitch* Infantry Regiment No. 34 were 'half-trained recruits' who had only joined the ranks in late February. The quantitative situation slowly improved during March, but many regiments were still incomplete when war opened on 10 April. As home to most of the raw recruits, the third battalions of the line

regiments tended to be the least effective, some being completely unprepared
for combat of any variety. The lack of training was compounded in some
instances by political unreliability, especially among the regiments drawn
from Galicia. Ethnic Poles who harboured little sympathy for Habsburg
dynastic concerns, these men displayed a distressing tendency to desert,
often moving directly into the ranks of their former enemies. But desertion
was not confined to Polish units. The *Vogelsang* Infantry No. 47, a Bohemian
regiment, also suffered from this malady, complaining that 257 men recruited
from former Austrian lands in Germany fled its ranks during the first ten
days of the war.[122]

The regular army's difficulties, however, utterly paled in comparison with
the problems associated with putting the Landwehr in the field. Subsequently
glorified to mythic proportions, in fact the Landwehr was an enormously
troublesome institution. The raising of the new battalions did generate
considerable patriotic exultation in many instances, particularly around
Vienna, where Kaiserin Maria Ludovica put in inspiring appearances and
often distributed the freshly sewn battle standards personally. 'How festive,
how moving, how uplifting!' remembered one new Landwehr soldier.[123] After
patriotic addresses and clerical blessings 'one heard, from a thousand voices at
once: Long live Kaiser Franz! Long live Archduke Charles!'[124] These inspiring
memories remained with veterans and witnesses for years afterwards.
Unfortunately for Austria, much of this immediate spirit was ephemeral
and, in districts away from the capital, it was often wholly absent.

Beyond questions of morale and the manifold challenges to be expected
in mobilising a national militia for the first time, the Landwehr was grossly
deficient in all aspects of military preparedness. Officers and NCOs were in
short supply and often totally unsuited to active service: 'Major von X has
been service with Koburg for forty-three years and approaches incapacity
as a result of continual fatigues ...' read the report on one battalion
commander.[125] One of the Vienna Volunteers battalions had an Oberleutnant
who was sixty-five and in his fiftieth year of military service. The 2nd Graz
Landwehr was commanded by a major who had also reached that age.
Some of these ageing leaders proved hardy and could at least claim practical
military backgrounds.[126] Many others, however, had little or no military
experience and were chosen simply on the basis of their status in their local
communities. Nor was the situation any better in regard to the common
soldiers: the men accepted into the ranks were frequently overage, physically
handicapped, or otherwise unfit for field duty. Equipment and training were
poor and many units showed minimal enthusiasm for the Habsburg cause.

As a Landwehr brigade commander in Bohemia reported in early May: 'all of the battalions are poorly clothed and equipped ... many battalions have seriously resisted mobilisation and order has only been restored through the intervention of regular troops.'[127] There were manifold instances of indiscipline and insubordination: the 2nd Chrudim Battalion mutinied and wounded its commander; the 1st Prachin fired on its officers; the 2nd Königgrätz rebelled, so did the 1st Chrudim and 1st Budweis; the 3rd and 5th Ober dem Manhartsberg (OMB) Battalions at first refused to march; and two companies of the 2nd Klattau simply went home.[128] A key problem was the firm conviction among many of the Landwehr men that they were not required to serve outside Austria; indeed, some felt that their duties should be restricted to their home provinces. On the other hand, the Vienna city Landwehr (Vienna Volunteers) and the Inner Austrian battalions agreed to serve beyond the borders of the Habsburg lands, as did the *Freibataillone* ('free battalions' hereafter referred to as 'volunteers'). For many of the others, in traditional Austrian regions as well as in Bohemia, this issue loomed large and curtailed their employment.

The Landwehr therefore was capable of assuming some limited responsibilities, but the late start in Austria's mobilisation meant that few battalions were formed and truly ready when war broke out. Subsequently, the rapid advance of Napoleon's forces further undermined the institution, overrunning recruiting areas and depriving many units of any reasonable chance to put themselves on a war footing. Consequently, dozens of battalions either never achieved formation, or, caught up in the hasty withdrawal from Bavaria, simply disintegrated and disappeared from the Austrian order of battle during late April and early May. Although several Landwehr units performed well enough in later stages of the conflict, therefore, it is hardly surprising that Charles concluded 'The Landwehr did nothing in the first phases of the war.'[129]

The quality of personnel in the Landwehr also suffered when Charles decided to form sixteen *Freibataillone* from the best of the Landwehr and other volunteers. As an attempt to speed mobilisation and increase the army's light troops in the weeks immediately preceding the war, this step was partially successful, and three of the battalions thus formed reached the army in time to participate in the opening of the invasion. Several others— in addition to the six Vienna Volunteer Battalions—arrived in time to play a role in the retreat to Vienna in early May and the later battles of the war.[130] Composed of true volunteers and led by more qualified officers, these units generally performed better and demonstrated a higher degree of durability when compared with the regular Landwehr. The Habsburg authorities also endeavoured to strengthen the volunteer battalions by arming, clothing, and equipping them ahead of their sister units.[131] Nonetheless, by drawing the best men from a weak institution, Charles hampered overall Landwehr mobilisation and robbed the ordinary Landwehr battalions of crucial leadership cadres.[132]

There was no Landwehr in Hungary. Instead, that kingdom offered up a feudal militia known as the 'Noble Insurrection', supposedly a 'raising' of nobles and their households who owed military service to Kaiser Franz in his guise as King of Hungary. Archduke Joseph, as the Palatine of Hungary, was responsible for calling up and preparing the Insurrection. He reported favourably on the spirit of the Hungarian aristocrats that he encountered during inspection trips in March, but the problems he faced in attempting to organise and field this relic as an effective fighting force were nearly overwhelming.[133] The Insurrection suffered from all of the manifold deficiencies of the Landwehr—weak leadership, poor or absent equipment,

Table 3: Sixteen Austrian Freibataillone (Volunteers), April 1809

1st through 6th Erzherzog Karl Legion (1st Battalion known as the 'Prager Jäger')

1st through 4th Inner Austrian Volunteers (2nd Battalion known as the 'Salzburger Jäger')

1st and 2nd Moravian-Silesian Volunteers

Combined Moravian Volunteers (from volunteers of the 2nd Brünn and 2nd Iglau Landwehr)

1st East Galician Volunteers

2nd West Galician Volunteers

3rd East Galician Volunteers

Smaller volunteer units in April
Dalmatian Freikorps (infantry)
Freikorps Schill (infantry and hussars)
Freikorps Carneville (two infantry companies and one hussar squadron)

Sources: Krieg 1809, prepared by the staff of the k. und k. Kriegsarchiv, Vienna: Seidel & Sohn, 1907–10, vol. I, pp. 86–7; Alphons Freiherr von Wrede, Geschichte der K. und K. Wehrmacht, Vienna: Seidel & Sohn, 1898, vol. II, pp. 459–60.

utterly inadequate training, slow mobilisation, and a crippling paucity of funds—all compounded by a notable ambivalence towards the war among important elements of Hungary's elite groups.[134] The result was a large, clumsy institution that required an enormous amount of administrative effort on the part of the Habsburg monarchy but offered very little military value in return. It was far from ready when the war began.[135] The small Insurrection forces of Croatia, Slovenia, and Transylvania were even less useful—the latter was not even authorised until the middle of June.

Leadership was one of the most serious weaknesses of these second-line forces, but the regular army also suffered from significant deficiencies in its officers. While Charles could decree more humane treatment of the Habsburg soldiery, improving the overall quality of the officer corps proved a far more daunting task. As a group, the officers of the Habsburg Empire were backward, conservative, and hesitant. Though brave enough, they clung tenaciously to the linear tactical and operational norms of the previous century, seldom exhibited initiative, shunned responsibility, and lacked the urgent energy of their French counterparts. Officers with an aggressive, offensive outlook were rare exceptions; the majority were tentative, defensive in orientation, obsessed with reserves, and excessively cautious. The longer they served, the more they were fettered by these negative qualities. During the course of the conflict, many would seem more concerned with avoiding defeat than with gaining victory. In an assessment prepared just after the war, an Austrian observer commented that 'the Austrian general is completely satisfied and content if he has followed his orders exactly, can demonstrate this, with extensive evidence if necessary, before a court martial, and thus have proof that no responsibility falls on him, regardless of whether success was achieved or not.'[136] Officers who displayed admirable courage in the face of the enemy were thus often unwilling to risk censure or dismissal by deviating from orders or acting on their own.

These common weaknesses were especially evident in the Austrian corps commanders. An undistinguished lot, they were uncomfortable with the demands of semi-independent corps command and required constant guidance and prodding from Charles. One eminent Austrian historian refers to them as 'mere overseers' rather than true leaders or commanders of whom one could expect initiative and enterprise.[137] Only FML Johann Freiherr von Hiller, VI Corps commander, rose above the common standard of mediocrity, and his talents were hardly extraordinary. Moreover, he proved a difficult subordinate who sought to evade Charles's authority. Even more problematic for Charles was the clutch of Habsburg archdukes whose desire for command was not matched by any conspicuous military ability. Ferdinand and Johann were at best very ordinary leaders, while Joseph, Ludwig, and Maximilian had only their titles and ambitions to recommend them. Almost all of these men at times chose to disregard their brother's orders or found ways to interpret his instructions in accord with their own desires and conceits. In title-conscious Austria, however, sons of the House of Habsburg could not be denied senior positions and Charles had no choice but to find commands for the various members of his extended family.

Indicative of the absence of initiative, lack of confidence, and fear of responsibility common among Austrian generals was their tendency to defer to their General Staff corps officers. It was not uncommon for commanding generals to happily abrogate their duties to men far junior in rank by placing the burden of battlefield decisions on the captains, majors, and colonels who brought the painfully detailed orders from headquarters and led the troops to their assigned positions. In later years, Charles complained bitterly of these 'incompetent generals' who 'regarded the officers of the General Staff not as subordinate, helpful instruments, rather as superior beings and as their saviours in embarrassment'.[138] Unfortunately for Austria, these General Staff corps officers frequently lacked the training and experience that would have justified this sacred trust of command. These deficiencies on both sides of the command and staff equation meant that Austria achieved none of the critical complementarity between commanders and staff officers that Napoleon sought to nurture in his subordinate headquarters.[139]

Charles was painfully aware of the limitations of the army's leaders, and he introduced doctrinal publications and a military journal in an effort to raise the level of professionalism within the officer corps.[140] What the army really needed, however, was more extensive training, especially exercises at the level of brigade, division, and corps. In Austria's prevailing penury, however, peacetime military manoeuvres were considered an unaffordable luxury, so the army's leaders entered the war of 1809 with no practical experience in organising, moving, and controlling their new commands. In combat, the brigade and division organisational structure often became almost meaningless as corps commanders tended to view their commands as miniature linear armies of the Frederickian era rather than integral but independent elements of a modern force.[141]

In particular, the lack of training and experience with higher formations, the obsession with reserves, and the reliance on outmoded linear norms meant that the Austrian army was nearly incapable of large-scale, multi-regimental attacks on the battlefield. Charles commented that 'the effectiveness of most generals seldom exceeded that of a regimental commander, with the result that they only understood how to employ and only actually employed isolated regiments, not the larger units with which they had been entrusted.[142] This problem was especially evident in the mounted arm. 'The Austrians have no idea how to use cavalry', Napoleon once remarked.[143] In the coming war, individual infantry or cavalry regiments, committed to costly assaults again and again, would suffer repeated repulses, despite all their valour.

The weaknesses in the army's senior commanders thus obviated many of the advantages of the recently adopted corps system, especially in fluid operational situations that demanded independence and initiative on the part of subordinate leaders. The pernicious result of these leadership problems was to reinforce the Austrian army's traditional penchant for tedious bureaucracy and operational minutiae. Throughout the war, army headquarters persisted in writing long and intricately detailed 'dispositions' and worrying about matters that were the proper purview of the corps or division commanders.[144] This pattern of command and control absorbed an enormous amount of time and administrative effort, delaying the implementation of orders, and exacerbating the army's inherent clumsiness. It also placed a great burden on Charles and diverted his attention from broader concerns, a problem he claimed to recognise too late in the war.[145] Furthermore, as one Austrian sympathiser recorded, 'The organisation and force of the Austrian army would have inspired great confidence if one did not recall that it was commanded by the same generals who have already been beaten so frequently.'[146]

Charles, then, was able to institute immediate changes on the margins of tactical performance but the more fundamental innovations required more time to take effect. Amelioration of the enlisted man's lot, reinvigoration of the officer corps, facility with the corps system, incorporation of a 'national' militia and a 'national' spirit could only be accomplished over an extended period of steady, persistent effort. In the absence of such a period, the army's utility as an offensive instrument remained minimal. Stadion, with little understanding of these military subtleties and convinced that Napoleon would soon turn his imperial attention towards the Habsburg realm, believed that a pre-emptive invasion of Germany was Austria's only option. He therefore encouraged early entry into an offensive campaign that the army was ill-equipped to execute.[147] Fortunately for Kaiser Franz's dynasty, the true significance of Charles's reforms lay in the improved *defensive* capability and robustness of the army, improvements that would ultimately help to limit the scope and extent of Napoleon's victory over Austria in 1809.

RAPID DECISION AND BOLD ENTERPRISES

This was the army that now found itself on the borders of Napoleon's empire, on the threshold of a new war with France. This was the army charged with striking with 'rapid decision' and 'bold enterprises' as Charles exhorted his I Corps commander, General der Kavallerie (GdK) Heinrich Graf Bellegarde, on 27 March.[148] The army's character, however, made swift and bold actions difficult. Nor were its dispositions particularly felicitous. As Mayer noted: 'In typical Austrian fashion, the forces were scattered from the Erzgebirge to the Adriatic Sea.'[149]

Convinced that the Danube valley was 'the key to the theatre of war and to the Austrian monarchy',[150] Charles assigned the bulk of the regular troops, approximately two-thirds of the 258,400 men available (171 of the 243 line, Grenz, and Jäger battalions), to the eight corps of the Main Army on the border with Germany.[151] Numbering 171,000 infantry and cavalry with 518 guns, the Main Army was intended to defeat the key French forces in Germany and push west to the sources of the Rhine and the area of the Neckar before Napoleon could introduce substantial reinforcements from France.[152] The bulk of the Main Army was concentrated under his immediate command along the Inn: six corps (III through VI and the two reserve corps) numbering about 127,000 combatants. Certain that the war would 'undoubtedly begin with a battle in Bavaria' and that the war's success or failure would be decided by the opening engagement, Charles considered using this force to strike a damaging blow against Marshal André Massena's troops along the Lech River before turning to seek Davout near Eger or Regensburg.[153] This proposed advance against Davout would then be undertaken in conjunction with the 49,000 men of I and II Corps debouching from Bohemia.[154] These two corps were part of the Main Army organisationally, and were supposed to drive rapidly across the border, defeat whatever enemy forces they encountered and then operate north of the Danube in support of the Main Army. As the senior corps commander, Bellegarde would direct the movements of both. He was to keep his command within a few marches of the great river to facilitate swift union if necessary, but his initial mission was essentially independent, and he was not required to join Charles immediately. Given his separation from Charles, routine Austrian caution, and the quotidian challenges of early nineteenth-century command and control techniques, however, Bellegarde's ability to contribute to the generalissimus' initial operations was practically nil. As a result, only the 127,000 men on the Inn—less than 50 per cent of the monarchy's total of available regular forces—would embark on the campaign concentrated under Charles's immediate command.

On the southern frontiers, GdK Archduke Johann's Army of Inner Austria was to conduct operations in Italy, the Tyrol, and Dalmatia. In the 'General Disposition for the Advance of the Imperial and Royal Army', Charles stressed to his brother the importance of the Tyrol and supporting the Main Army

> ... a strong force will push through the Pustertal to Brixen in the Tyrol to interrupt the shortest line of communications between the two enemy armies in Germany and Italy, to inspire the Tyrolians with confidence and to support the operations of the Main Army either by a further advance over the Brenner towards Bavaria or towards the valley of the Adige. The remaining troops will be used to cover the border toward Friaul through defensive or possibly through offensive operations.[155]

Johann, on the other hand, was determined to come to grips with the 'main force of the enemy' and thus focused his attention on Italy.[156] The total number of troops at his disposal, however, was hardly consistent with his view of his command's importance and the rather grand offensive operations implied in his thinking. Even with the addition of VIII Corps, he had only 60,430 regulars and 27,770 Landwehr to employ in his initial advance.[157] Nonetheless, Johann planned a full-scale offensive to 'clear the Tyrol, seek out and defeat the enemy before he is assembled, quickly gain the Adige and ... cover Carinthia and the Austrian border'.[158] On reaching the Adige, he would concern himself with 'establishing an advantageous defensive line before the enemy can gather up new reinforcements from Spain or the interior of his state'.[159] He would then 'await the outcome of events in Germany' as it was 'not possible and would be pointless' to prescribe further operations until the campaign began.[160]

While Johann marched south, FML Jean Gabriel Marquis de Chasteler-Courcelles, a French émigré, would lead a mixed group of 13,500 regulars and Landwehr into the Tyrol via the Drava valley. Although the size of Chasteler's command hardly approached the offensive force Charles had envisaged in the Tyrol, Johann hoped its advance would both liberate the region and outflank potential French defensive positions in northern Italy, thereby compelling his immediate opponents to retire. It was an ambitious set of operational objectives, but, with luck, Johann hoped that fourteen days would suffice to reach the Adige and have all the Tyrol in his possession.

Operations in Dalmatia also fell under Johann's purview. Here, GM Andreas Stoichevich with a hotchpotch force of 7,000 men was to 'take the offensive to achieve a better defensive line and activate the population', thereby covering Johann's left.[161] Misreading French intentions, however, Johann concluded that Napoleon would remove all his field forces from Dalmatia to upper Italy, leaving only fortress garrisons behind. Stoichevich's detachment, therefore, would be 'as weak as possible . . . to instigate rebellion among the populace and, over time, to seize the fortified places'.[162]

In distant Poland, the second most important theatre in Mayer's original concept, GdK Archduke Ferdinand d'Este commanded the 31,500 men of VII Corps. While Charles and Johann moved against their respective opponents, Ferdinand was to strike north from Cracow, knock the Grand Duchy of Warsaw out of the war and thus remove the threat Polish troops posed to Charles's strategic rear. He would then march west to the Elbe where he could act in concert with the Main Army, possibly inspiring unrest along the way. This rather extravagant military mission also had important political dimensions. In the first place, it was thought that the arrival of a strong Austrian corps in Poland would compel Friedrich Wilhelm III to ally himself with Austria either by bribing him with Polish territory or by approaching his borders and forcing him to choose sides—a choice which Vienna believed could only result in allegiance to the Austrian cause.[163] Second, Vienna hoped an Austrian victory in Poland would reverberate in St Petersburg, boosting the influence of the anti-French faction and weakening the tsar's attachment to his French alliance. Charles's instructions to Ferdinand reflected Vienna's belief that a swift, decisive stroke against the duchy could have dramatic repercussions to Austria's advantage:

> Russia, Prussia, and Galicia are waiting to see what the outcome of Your Grace's enterprises will be; it is therefore of the greatest importance to establish from the very start a bias in favour of our arms, as the slightest misfortune would have the most negative influence on the decisions of our neighbours and, from the political viewpoint, would be perhaps as damaging as a defeat on the Danube.

Finally, there was a domestic consideration. A dramatic Habsburg victory in the duchy could be expected to restrain the restive ethnic Polish population of Austrian Galicia, dousing any sparks of rebellion before they could endanger Vienna's control of its eastern-most province. To achieve the desired political impact, Ferdinand was told that his operations 'must imitate a rushing torrent, they must be quick, surprising, and decisive' and his strategic goals were specified with exemplary clarity: 'Your objective is to take Warsaw and neutralize the Poles ... then, leaving behind few or no detachments, to direct your operations towards Silesia.'[164]

While the regular Habsburg troops carried the war into Germany, Italy and Poland, the defence of the monarchy's long borders, the garrisoning of its fortresses, and other ancillary duties fell to a variety of second-line formations, primarily depot units of the regular army, and the newly raised Landwehr. The border from Salzburg to Neufelden just north of the Danube was the responsibility of nineteen Landwehr battalions from Salzburg and the various districts of Upper Austria, while the nineteen Lower Austrian battalions were scattered in varying degrees of readiness up and down the Danube valley from Linz to Vienna. Bohemia supplied fifty-five Landwehr battalions. Eighteen of these and one regular cavalry squadron were to screen the border immediately behind Bellegarde's two corps, support the investment of the Bavarian fortress at Oberhaus near Passau, and cover the gap between Bellegarde's force and Charles's. A mixed force of thirteen Landwehr battalions, two regular battalions, and a cavalry squadron was to protect Bohemia's border with Saxony, while depot troops and twenty-four other Landwehr battalions manned the fortresses and provided something of a reserve in the interior.[165] In Moravia and Silesia, seven battalions stood along the border with Prussia and seventeen in the local fortresses.

Further east, Vienna relied almost entirely on presumptions of Russian neutrality to protect its strategic rear, the long Galician border with the tsar's empire, while Ferdinand's VII Corps carried the war into Poland. The few border guards and depot troops in those distant districts numbered less than 8,000.[166] They would barely suffice to give notice of a Russian advance should Alexander decide to honour his commitments to Napoleon. On the monarchy's southern borders, Archduke Johann's command included thirty-three Landwehr battalions. In addition to rear area duties, a number of these were to play a role in the invasion and occupation of Italy. Many, however, were in such poor condition that Johann considered them completely unsuitable for any kind of combat operations. The various Insurrection forces, slowly assembling in Hungary and Croatia, were intended to support Johann, to guard the crossings over the March River, to occupy the passes through the Carpathian Mountains and, if needed, to assist in the defence of Vienna.[167]

Sodden and cold from spring's nasty mixture of rain, frozen rain, and snow, the last Austrian march columns found their way into their bivouacs along

Table 4: Austrian Sedentary Formations, April 1809

	Landwehr Battalions	Depot Companies	Depot Squadrons	Garrison Regiments	Kordon Companies	Other
Bohemia	55	26	6	–	6	III/10, III/42 2 sqdns/ Uhlans No. 2
Moravia/Silesia	24	14	3	–	4	–
Austria/Salzburg	38	14	7	–	10	–
Inner Austria	33	12	1	–	12	–
Galicia	–	36	2	1st	–	–
Hungary	–	26	15	2nd, 3rd, 4th	–	6 1/3 Grenz Res Bns
Transylvania	–	4	–	–	–	4 Grenz Res Bns 1 Grenz Res Sqdn

the Bavarian border on 9 April. As the men sought shelter from the weather, all seemed ready for the coming clash. The possibility of Habsburg success in what its leaders saw as a desperate, life-and-death struggle, however, was seriously reduced by the grave flaws in the monarchy's approach to the conflict. At the national strategic level, Stadion's ill-considered and unrealistic conception of the war proved a poor basis for military planning and left the army with an almost impossible mission. False assumptions and vague, visionary war aims created additional complications and, in some cases, nearly insurmountable obstacles to the development of a viable plan of campaign. The army's leadership contributed little to crafting a coherent political-military solution to its strategic challenge and compounded its problems by diffusing its efforts and squandering an irreplaceable seven to ten days. Moreover, the Austrian army of 1809, despite its undeniable strengths, retained many of the weaknesses of its predecessors, debilitating frailties that crippled it operationally and tactically, making it an unwieldy and uncertain offensive weapon poorly suited to Stadion's ambitious purposes. Fast marching, decisive strokes, and a sizable share of good luck could still bring an early victory, but Habsburg prospects were slim and growing slimmer with each passing day.

CHAPTER 3

Austria Would Not Be So Foolish

Napoleon did not want a war with Austria in 1809. Nor is there any evidence to indicate that he intended to turn on Austria as soon as he had solved his Iberian problem.[1] Austria may be excused for harbouring such fears, but its leaders consistently ignored or misunderstood the centrality of the long-term struggle against Great Britain in Napoleon's strategic view and thus overestimated what the tsar termed their 'perhaps imaginary dangers'.[2] Instead of Austria, Napoleon's focus from April 1808 through to April 1809 was on achieving the submission of Spain and Portugal in order to prosecute the continental blockade against his cross-channel foe more effectively. A new war in central Europe, even a victorious one, would only divert his resources from this all-important contest with Great Britain. Moreover, it would further alienate him from the war-weary population at home and would create possibly unbearable friction between him and his Russian ally.[3] As a result, containing Austria and maintaining peace in central Europe were key components of French foreign policy during these twelve months. Champagny neatly summarised his master's position in a 20 August 1808 letter to the French ambassador in Russia, GD Armand Caulaincourt: 'The emperor does not desire this [a war with the Habsburgs], he prefers peace because he wants above all to arrange the affairs of Spain, which he regards as a terrible blow delivered against England.'[4] The need to restore the lustre of French arms after the several defeats suffered during the summer of 1808 gave this grand strategic move against British interests particular urgency.[5] As Champagny's letter made its way north-east to St Petersburg, therefore, more than 100,000 French and German soldiers were marching toward the Pyrenees to quash the Spanish rebellion and avenge the surrender at Bailen.

SUMMER CRISIS AND AUTUMN GLITTER

Napoleon had first learned of Austria's plans to re-arm during May 1808, when reports from Andréossy in Vienna and Otto in Munich began to reach him at the Chateau de Marracq near Bayonne.[6] For the French leadership, the creation of the Landwehr and reserve battalions seemed 'to indicate either inquietude, which is without any real foundation, or secret designs' on the part of Vienna.[7] Commenting on Andréossy's reports, Champagny told the ambassador that 'the emperor has many other indications of the Austrian Court's unfriendly disposition'. Andréossy was therefore instructed to approach Stadion and seek explications for actions Napoleon viewed as undeniably directed against France and completely inconsistent with Austria's repeated statements of pacific intent.[8] Stadion attempted to mollify Andréossy by claiming that all of Austria's measures were defensive in nature, but the mounting volume of intelligence arriving at the Chateau de Marracq clearly contradicted Stadion's statements.[9] Though mystified as to why Austria would behave so belligerently at a time when, from the French perspective, circumstances were so unfavourable for the Habsburgs, the emperor could not ignore the potential threat.[10] With the evidence of Austrian activity piling up, he attempted to employ the diplomatic and military tools at his disposal to secure his strategic rear against Austria as he dealt with Spain.[11]

On the military front, Napoleon took advantage of the huge French troop presence in Poland, Germany, and Italy. By concentrating dispersed garrisons in field encampments, ordering unexpected manoeuvres, having his officers spread ominous rumours, and visibly reviving work on fortifications, he reminded Vienna that Austria was vulnerable to attack from three directions by an army of veterans with an almost unbroken history of victories.[12] Napoleon, unwilling 'to suffer its [Austria's] armaments without raising the entire Confederation of the Rhine',[13] brought additional pressure to bear on Austria by mobilising the Rheinbund contingents and hinting at the call-up of 160,000 new conscripts in France (above and beyond some 95,000 levied earlier in the year).[14]

The induction of the new French conscripts would not be officially decreed until September, but the call to the German princes put thousands of France's allies in the field for manoeuvres by the end of August. Bavaria, for example, assembled its three divisions of nearly 30,000 men in three widely separated training camps and made good use of the opportunity to conduct intensive drill. The armies of Baden, Hesse-Darmstadt, Saxony, and Württemberg also gathered for a season of training and reviews. Additionally, the emperor halted Marshal Adolphe Mortier's 5th Corps, on its way from Silesia to Spain, at Bayreuth pending the resolution of the situation. These actions were all bluff and bluster, however, designed to lend substance to the verbal warnings Champagny had given to Metternich that 'we do not fear a war, but we do not want one'.[15] The emperor remained focused on Iberia. Thus the departure of other French troops from Germany continued unabated and thousands of France's German allies were preparing to cross the Rhine for Spain even as their compatriots were encamped in their home countries to intimidate Vienna. Taken together with Austria's re-armament, however, Napoleon's measures generated a brief European crisis in the late summer of 1808 so that 'in Paris and in Germany all rumour is of the coming war with Austria'.[16]

On the diplomatic side, Napoleon supplemented his military moves with a mixture of threats and blandishments intended to assure the Habsburg court that he had no designs on the old empire, while simultaneously promising dreadful retribution should Austria break the peace. As he mobilised the Rheinbund and threatened to call up new French levies, for example, he also instructed Andréossy to use 'agreeable and conciliatory language to dissipate the Austrian fears or at least not to augment them'. Champagny followed a similar line in corresponding with Metternich, telling the Austrian ambassador that 'it is important to the interests of France that Austria retain the power that it has'.[17]

Threats and conciliation were also the principal themes in the public lecture Napoleon delivered to Metternich in front of the assembled diplomatic corps on 15 August. Using carefully measured tones, the emperor complained of Austria's military measures, challenging Metternich to explain why Vienna was draining its weak exchequer by increasing its reserves, raising a militia, provisioning fortresses, and purchasing horses. Napoleon was particularly provoked by the publication of patriotic but anti-French proclamations that were exciting the Austrian population. He rejected Metternich's claims that Austria's actions were purely defensive and calmly argued that France and its allies would overmatch any military exertion Austria could attempt even as he withdrew 100,000 men from Germany for Spain. 'If you are counting on the affairs of Spain', he warned, 'You are fooling yourselves.'[18] He argued that the new Austrian steps were not only unnecessary but also dangerous for Europe and particularly for the Habsburg monarchy. In these parlous circumstances, he charged, a small spark could ignite a general conflagration, indeed a short, violent war might be preferable to what he termed 'prolonged suffering'.[19] He concluded with a renewed appeal for peace and amicable relations, but left no doubt that he was prepared for war: 'a war to the death, where the Emperor of Austria will come into the centre of France or I will go to the farthest frontiers of the Austrian lands.'[20] But neither did he want to leave any question of which side he expected to emerge triumphant: 'You will be beaten.'[21]

The 15 August interview was splendid theatre, but it was aimed more at the rest of Europe than it was at Metternich, who had already heard the key points in several exchanges with Champagny and who would have a long private audience with Napoleon on 25 August. Theatrics aside, the occasion provided Napoleon an opportunity to elucidate his position for other courts, allied, vassal, and neutral. He was thus careful to paint Austria as an irresponsibly aggressive power while reiterating his own desire for peace and his ability to cope with simultaneous wars in Spain and central Europe.

As summer waned, Vienna seemed to respond to Napoleon's efforts and suddenly appeared interested in reducing tensions. Austria was not yet ready for war in any event, so Stadion could take an apparently conciliatory approach. During his 25 August audience, therefore, Metternich duly informed Napoleon that the new reserve and Landwehr formations would be demobilised on 1 September and that five regiments concentrated near Cracow would return to their garrisons. He did not tell the emperor that his instructions from Stadion proscribed entry into any agreement that would involve 'a revocation of the measures we have executed or a diminution or dispersion of our line troops'.[22] The day after the interview with Metternich, on the other hand, Napoleon felt confident enough to write to Pierre Daru, his Intendant General in Germany, that 'I have good relations with Austria and even better with Russia'.[23] He remained cautious, telling his brother, King Jerome of Westphalia, the following week: 'I will continue my armaments until I see that Vienna's promises to return things to where they were before the summer are realised.' Nonetheless, he continued, 'Since my last letter to Your Majesty, all the discussions have been very pacific, and I flatter myself that, by the beginning of October, I will be able to send Your Majesty a letter that will reassure you entirely . . . It is the conduct of Austria which guides us.'[24]

In fact, the promised Austrian moves were pre-planned and their timing had nothing to do with Napoleon's demands. Vienna, however, could portray them as concessions to the French just as Napoleon described his withdrawals from Germany as acquiescence to the wishes of Austria, Russia, and Prussia rather than the pragmatic redeployment of veteran units to Iberia. Both sides thus used the momentary circumstances to explain what they had intended to do in any case. The fundamental difference was that Napoleon's steps not only genuinely fulfilled his agreements with Russia and Prussia, they were also more sweeping in scope and would be impossible to reverse once implemented. Austria, on the other hand, was simply standing down from a heightened readiness posture; its forces would be able to mobilise rapidly as soon as a favourable opportunity presented itself.

The centrepiece of Napoleon's Austrian policy in 1808–9, however, was the intimate co-operation of his principal ally, Tsar Alexander.[25] In his approaches to St Petersburg, Napoleon sought to use Russia to restrain Austria while simultaneously precluding any inclination on the tsar's part to participate in or even tolerate another coalition aimed against France or to march on Constantinople to exploit the turmoil caused by the overthrow of the reigning sultan.[26] The French emperor thus made a concerted effort to reinvigorate his ties to the Russian imperial court and to use those ties to influence and intimidate Vienna. From the summer of 1808, as details of Austria's defensive measures reached Paris and tensions rose, Napoleon's communications with Russia consistently touched on the need to deter the Habsburgs. In early July 1808, he mentioned Austria's preparations in a personal letter to the tsar and instructed Caulaincourt to

> start from the principle that I do not know what Austria wants; it is greatly increasing its armaments; it is greatly exciting the departments; it is constructing fortifications in Hungary ... Up to now, I have regarded all this with pity ... Nonetheless, if this annoys the emperor [Alexander], we can tell them [Austria] jointly through Andréossy and through Prince Kurakin to disarm and to leave the world in peace.[27]

For Napoleon, the necessity of securing Russian assistance in moderating Austrian behaviour and averting the formation of a new anti-French coalition thus became one of the prime goals of the summit meeting between the two emperors held in Erfurt from 27 September to 14 October. 'The attitude of the Petersburg government', he told Caulaincourt one morning, 'was the sole arbiter of peace during [my] absence in Spain.'[28] This public display of alliance would serve to compliment the private assurances he believed he had already received from the tsar. Writing to Champagny, he asserted that 'Tsar Alexander has informed me that if I have a war with Austria, he will make common cause with me, and he showed me much solicitude regarding the affairs of Spain.'[29]

Despite Napoleon's careful political preparations and all the extravagant pomp he could arrange, the sparkling Erfurt event was only a partial success.

Alexander, advised by Talleyrand, tacked carefully between his desire to prevent war in central Europe and his reluctance to exert extraordinary pressure on Austria to attain this end.[30] Napoleon urged a joint démarche to Vienna. In his mind, the Austrian government 'only wants to cause anxiety, and the result is armament, threats, expenditure of money, bad temper, and in the end—gunfire'.[31] The tsar, however, repeatedly demurred, and the most the French emperor could extract after two weeks of talks and lavish entertainments was a promise that 'in case Austria goes to war against France, the Emperor of Russia engages to declare against Austria and to make common cause with France'.[32] Still, Napoleon felt confident that he had acquired the tsar's unstinting support and he convinced himself that this support would be instrumental in dissuading Austria from undertaking any military adventure for the foreseeable future. Even prior to the summit, he had been 'sure of the sentiments of Russia' and had believed that a conciliatory gesture to Vienna 'supported by the menace of a Russian army of one hundred thousand men, would not fail to have its effect'.[33] Now, with the Russian alliance at least outwardly renewed, he believed himself secure in the east and once again turned his full attention to Iberia. On 12 October, the same day that the French and Russian foreign ministers set their quills to the Erfurt treaty, he issued a decree that formally dissolved the Grande Armée and set many of its remaining regiments on the road to the Pyrenees.[34]

Austria was not invited to Erfurt, but Stadion sent FML Karl Freiherr von Vincent to the summit site with personal greetings from Kaiser Franz for each of the emperors. Vincent delivered his message in separate audiences with the two sovereigns on 1 October. Napoleon treated the Austrian general, who had been Vienna's emissary to French headquarters in Poland in 1807, to the same speech Metternich had heard on 15 August. This time, however, the tone was completely different. A French courier had ridden into Erfurt a few days in advance of Vincent, bearing a letter from Andréossy in which the ambassador reported that Austria had not changed its behaviour: it continued to arm, it maintained its efforts to incite anti-French patriotism, its officials harassed French messengers, and it refused to recognise Joseph Bonaparte as King of Spain or Marshal Joachim Murat as King of Naples.[35] Andréossy also indicated that Austria persisted in intrigues with France's enemies in Sicily, Turkey, Spain, and Britain. As a consequence of this report, Vincent found himself facing a wrathful Napoleon.[36] The emperor again expressed his desire to live in peace with Austria, but sharpened to a keen edge the warning he had issued to Metternich in August: 'Well then, it is war you seek; I have prepared for it, and I will be terrible … Under these conditions is it propitious for you to attack me?'[37]

Vincent then took his leave of Napoleon, no doubt gratefully, and went to call upon Alexander. The tsar received him with grace, spoke of his 'personal interest' in the maintenance of Austria's integrity, and pledged never to assist Napoleon against Austria as long as Austria did not initiate hostilities. He said nothing of Austrian disarmament except to note that 'no one has the authority to interfere in the affairs of a foreign sovereign'.[38] Eleven days later, as he was preparing to depart Erfurt, the tsar repeated these broad sentiments in his reply to the Austrian emperor's personal greeting: 'I wish you to be persuaded of the interest I take in Your Majesty and in the integrity of your empire'. He hoped thereby to 'calm Mr Stadion's worries about the meeting at Erfurt'.[39]

Napoleon's response to Franz, on the other hand, echoed the interview with Vincent, mixing a desire for peace with scarcely veiled threats: 'I will never do anything against the principal interests of your state,' he wrote, 'But Your Majesty must not bring into question that which has been settled by fifteen years of war'.[40] As he had with Metternich and Vincent, Napoleon also reminded Franz of the Franco-Russian alliance and the larger confrontation with Britain, but offered an indication of his desire to reduce tensions by stating that he intended to return the Rheinbund troops to their home garrisons.

Those German troops were now heartily sick of sitting in the rain. They had provided an earnest martial backdrop to the royal pomp and glitter in Erfurt, but September 1808 had brought incessant, torrential autumn rains that forced an end to active training. By the end of the month, as the two emperors were beginning their round of discussions and amusements, living conditions for the Bavarian troops, for instance, were wretched: straw bedding was soaked through and stinking, tents were flooded, and the 1st Infantry Regiment complained about an intolerable invasion of mice! King Maximilian I Joseph ordered his soldiers into billets on 1 October to escape the inclement weather, but the army had to wait for the conclusion of the imperial conclave before it could return to garrison.[41] By mid-October, however, the Bavarians and other Germans were headed home, as Napoleon issued a spate of orders upon the conclusion of the Erfurt meeting. Between 12 and 14 October, in addition to dissolving the Grande Armée, he signed the treaty of alliance with Alexander, wrote a joint appeal to King George III with the tsar, issued instructions to his brother Joseph in Madrid, made arrangements for logistical and financial matters in Germany, replied to Kaiser Franz, reduced the Prussia indemnity as a token to the tsar, and addressed innumerable other issues.[42] As indicated in the missive to Franz, his flood of immediate directives also encompassed the troops of the Confederation. 'The assurances given by the court of Vienna', he wrote, led him to the conclusion that 'the states of the Confederation are no longer menaced in any way'. The various German monarchs could therefore 'close their camps and return their troops to their quarters'.[43]

As these new orders were making their way to the various Rheinbund contingents on 14 October, the two emperors took leave of one another and of Erfurt. The tsar was content with the results of the conference, believing he had precluded a new Franco-Austrian confrontation without giving away too much to either of his fellow monarchs. He had also improved the security of his borders by achieving a small amelioration of Prussia's indemnity to France and a dramatic reduction in French forces in Silesia and Poland. At the same time, the situation in central Europe was not so calm that Paris and Vienna were likely to overcome the significant tension that remained in their bilateral relations; they were thus unlikely to combine against Russia to thwart its aspirations vis-à-vis the tottering Ottoman Empire. Privately, Alexander 'maintained that Austria would never be so foolish as to make herself the aggressor and enter the lists alone'.[44]

His treatment of Vincent and his personal note to Franz, however, threatened to undermine his careful calculations by allowing Stadion and others in Vienna to conclude that Russia was offering indirect support of Austria's opposition to Napoleon or that it would, at a minimum, follow a neutral policy if France and Austria came to blows. The tsar, however, had not changed his policy and hastened to remind Vienna of his position when he detected 'contradictions' in Austria's behaviour. Worried, he directed Kurakin in Vienna to seek clarifications:

> You will attempt to bring him [Stadion] to understand that if we demand the recognition of King Joseph, it is only to provide the court of Vienna with a means to calm those on its borders who have a right to be alarmed about its armaments, and that this means seems much simpler than demanding clear and categorical explications of such disproportionate augmentation of its forces.[45]

Napoleon, on the other hand, persuaded himself that he had subdued Austria and renewed his Russian alliance: 'All is well with Russia, I have nothing to fear from Austria.'[46] If not wholly satisfied by the outcome of the proceedings at Erfurt, he felt sufficiently secure to accelerate preparations for the campaign in Spain. Marshal Mortier's 5th Corps therefore resumed its march from Bayreuth towards the Rhine, as did Marshal Nicholas Soult and about half of his old 4th Corps. As for Napoleon himself, he left Erfurt on 14 October to arrive at Saint Cloud outside Paris on the night of the 18th. He did not tarry long. After ten days of frenetic work, he departed for the Pyrenees. On the evening of 4 November he was in Spain, taking a few moments in the pre-dawn hours the following morning to pen a note to Josephine: 'I hope that all this will soon be finished'.[47]

SCOUTS, SPIES AND DIPLOMATS

If Napoleon felt sufficiently secure to take himself south of the Pyrenees after Erfurt, he in no way relaxed his vigilance along his extended frontiers with the Habsburg monarchy.[48] He had already enjoined his subordinates to increase their intelligence collection activities during the summer of 1808 as Austria began to re-arm.[49] Although there was no formal intelligence 'system' in the modern sense to respond to these imperial demands, from Warsaw to Venice, Napoleon's diplomats, generals, and allies acted with care and alacrity to supply him with an ever-increasing flow of information. Their efforts allowed him to follow Austria's continuing preparations during the last quarter of 1808 and, by April 1809, supplied him with a fairly accurate and coherent picture of the enemy's strengths and dispositions.

Napoleon gathered intelligence from every quarter of the compass, but his primary sources were French embassies and his military commanders. In general, they performed their intelligence functions admirably. French embassies, for example, in addition to supplying a steady stream of newspapers, official proclamations, and reports on interaction with their host governments, collected information from a broad spectrum of sources and funnelled it back to Paris. Aristocrats and draymen, way-worn travellers, and soldiers of every rank all contributed, knowingly or not, to the French intelligence effort, supplementing local spy networks and personal observations by embassy personnel.[50] Moreover, French collection efforts were guided to satisfy the emperor's critical intelligence needs. A captain of the 9th Dragoons named Lagrange was thus posted in the French embassy in Vienna for the express purpose of monitoring military movements, and reports from the chargé carefully noted which regiments had passed through the Austrian capital, along with the condition of men, horses, and equipment.[51] In addition, they forwarded reports from diplomatic and military sources in the countries where they were posted. Louis Guillaume

Otto, the French ambassador in Munich, for example, assiduously reported information provided by the Bavarian representative in Vienna as well as news collected by Bavarian military officers and civilian officials along the frontiers with Austria.

The French army and its administrative functionaries also supplied Napoleon with precise, comprehensive military information. Davout had spent nearly a year establishing an extraordinarily thorough and efficient intelligence-gathering network in Germany, Prussia, and Bohemia. Metternich, recognising and fearing the marshal's energy and abilities, claimed that he was known as 'the grand inquisitor'.[52] Ably assisted by Daru, Davout sifted the mails, dispatched spies, invented excuses for Saxon officers to travel through Bohemia, collected deserters, and co-ordinated closely with French envoys in Vienna, Dresden, Berlin, Warsaw, and a host of minor German capitals. With a talent for grasping the finest detail, he arranged mobile 'reviewing offices' to garner intelligence from the public post, provided his subordinates with sample questionnaires to use with informants, and distributed charts depicting the colour scheme of each Austrian regiment.[53] Napoleon himself contributed to the development of the intelligence picture by ensuring all interested agencies received copies of key reports, by funding and co-ordinating resources, and occasionally by directing one post to verify the information supplied by another.[54] If the welter of material from this multitude of sources was at times confusing and contradictory, the larger result was a picture at once deeper, broader, and less encumbered by bias than that available to Austrian decision makers.[55] Consequently, Napoleon's intelligence on diplomatic and military developments was generally accurate and provided a sound foundation for his decisions.

Most of the intelligence amassed by this widespread, if ad hoc, network during late 1808 did not suggest that an invasion was imminent, but the picture that gradually emerged in the closing months of the year was still worrisome. Reports from Bavarian officers in the Tyrol and those who made their way into Bohemia spoke of unceasing work on fortifications, progress in the training of the Landwehr, and a high level of readiness among the regular regiments.[56] Davout reached similar conclusions concerning military activity based on his extensive contacts,[57] while French and Rheinbund ambassadors in Vienna described the Habsburg monarchy as 'nothing but a vast encampment' where the fortresses were being re-armed, the arsenals replenished and the cavalry remounted.[58]

Napoleon, of course, was most alert to all this reporting and it played a major role in his decision to leave Spain in January 1809. 'Austria', he told

Champagny shortly before departing, 'seems to have lost its head.'[59] Even more important as a proximate cause for his return to France, however, was news he received concerning possible plots against his throne in Paris.

By late December, the French had gained several signal victories over the inept Spanish armies and were pursuing Sir John Moore's small British expeditionary force through miserable weather into northeastern Spain. Driving at a brisk pace through the cold and snow towards Astorga on the afternoon of 1 January 1809, the emperor was informed that a courier out of France was approaching. He stopped his coach, had a fire lit, and paced back and forth in its warmth for a time before the messenger pounded up out of the grey gloom with a thick packet of dispatches. Napoleon's features disclosed nothing of his thinking as he read through the letters, but his concern was evident when he finished. He was silent for the remainder of the slow journey to Astorga. Night had fallen by the time the imperial cavalcade reached the town and made its way through streets jammed with other vehicles. Locating Soult, Napoleon directed the marshal to take over the pursuit of the British and announced his intention to remain in Astorga for a few days. In little more than two weeks he would be on his way back to France.[60]

In addition to the steadily accumulating evidence of Austria's aggressive intentions, the news Napoleon received from his capital concerned troubling moves by Talleyrand and Fouché. These two enemies, claiming to be worried that the emperor would not return alive from Spain, overcame their mutual enmity in a highly public reconciliation in December and began to consider alternative occupants for the French throne. Their choice fell upon Marshal Joachim Murat, the King of Naples, whom they considered easy to manipulate or replace as required. It was soon common knowledge in Paris that the two renowned foes had embraced and conducted an extended, intense, and cordial conversation. Antoine Chamans, Count de Lavalette, one of Napoleon's most loyal followers, immediately wrote to inform his imperial master. Furthermore, Lavalette, whose office as director general of the post included the secret 'black chamber' that monitored the mails, apprised Viceroy Eugene of the nascent conspiracy and alerted him to watch the correspondence destined for Murat. As a result, when Talleyrand and Fouché indeed wrote to Murat, their missive was intercepted and forwarded to a furious Napoleon in Spain.[61] The potential conspiracy was not entirely unexpected. Napoleon had held some suspicions before embarking on the Iberian campaign and had apparently received several disturbing dispatches during the last days of December. The letters that caught up with the imperial carriage on the cold road to Astorga, therefore, were not the sole cause of his return. They did, however, push him to make a decision he had probably been considering for several days.[62]

With both external and internal threats spurring him on, Napoleon transferred his headquarters to Valladolid, whence he could better communicate with Paris, Madrid, and his various commanders in Spain. From there, he poured all his prodigious energy into setting his Iberian affairs in order. He 'appeared more taken up with what was preparing in Germany, than the occurrences in the Peninsula' and delayed no longer than absolutely necessary.[63] Finally, after receiving the submission of a delegation of Madrid notables on 16 January, he concluded that all was sufficiently secure on the Spanish front.[64] The following morning, he departed Valladolid on horseback 'at a full gallop', as two trusted staff officers, his Mameluke Roustam and a tiny escort struggled to keep up. He made Burgos in five or six hours, switched to a coach and continued on towards Paris, covering the 1,100 or so kilometres to the capital in six days. 'No sovereign has ever covered such a stretch of road so rapidly on horseback', recorded GD Anne Jean Marie René Savary, one of his companions on this ride.[65]

Clattering into Paris at 8 a.m. on 23 January, Napoleon wasted no time in getting to work. That very afternoon, he visited civic construction projects in the city, the following day he received the diplomatic corps, and on the 28th he stripped Talleyrand of the title of Grand Chamberlain after a famously tempestuous interview.[66] Beyond this disgrace, however, no further punishment was visited upon the former foreign minister. He retained his title, albeit hollow, as Vice-Grand Elector and remained at court, all the while providing Metternich with intelligence, stoking Stadion's preconceptions about Napoleon, and plotting to remain in contact with Vienna from Paris should war eventuate.[67] Fouché escaped unscathed for the moment.

While attending to these domestic matters, of course, Napoleon also addressed other affairs of state, focusing especially on crafting diplomatic and military responses to Austria's increasingly worrisome behaviour. He had already begun to turn his attention from the Tagus towards the Danube while in Valladolid, receiving intelligence reports and issuing a stream of preliminary orders between 7 January and his departure on the 17th. His activity peaked on the 14th and 15th. During those two days alone at least twenty-five letters bearing on the Austrian problem left Valladolid under his signature, destined for diplomats, allies, marshals, and ministers from Paris to St Petersburg.[68]

An examination of this flood of correspondence reveals several interesting points. First, based on his own analysis and on the intelligence he had received, Napoleon was confident that two or three months would elapse before Austria could be ready for war. He therefore had at least the remainder of January, all of February, and probably most of March in which to make his preparations 'if it [Austria] wants to stir'.[69]

Second, he clearly believed that Austria could still be deterred. Although Andréossy reported great 'fermentation' in Vienna and continual discussion of attacking France, the ambassador also expressed the opinion that Napoleon's successes in Spain would 'if not calm the exasperated spirits here ... at least temper the bellicose zeal'.[70] As during the previous summer and autumn, the emperor turned to a combination of diplomatic palliatives and military threats to forestall this war that he did not want. This time, however, he saw a need for more forceful measures. In addition to the comprehensive steps he was already taking to bring the Army of Italy and the Army of the Rhine up to full strength, he ordered GD Nicholas Charles Oudinot's corps (from Hanau) and GD Jean Louis d'Espagne's division of cuirassiers (from Erlangen) south to Augsburg with the expressed intention of reassuring nervous Bavaria and intimidating Austria. 'The arrival of this corps', he told Otto, 'coincident with my return to Paris, will make Austria see that this is no jest.'[71] This desire to shock the potential enemy, to make an impression, helps explain the speed and secrecy of his journey from Valladolid to his capital. However, the impact of his appearance in Paris was vitiated in leading Habsburg circles by earlier reports from Metternich in which he passed on Talleyrand's belief that Napoleon was likely to depart Spain in the near future.[72]

To reinforce the image of French power, an image that would not achieve reality for some months, he used public media and diplomatic channels to exaggerate the strength of his forces already available in Germany and Italy, to magnify French victories in Spain, and to denigrate Habsburg martial prowess. In at least one case, he personally edited an article on Austrian military actions intended for placement in French and European newspapers.[73] More quietly, he pressed the movement of replacements to the corps on Austria's borders, meticulously directed the refurbishment of Bavarian and Italian fortresses, alerted two divisions in reserve between Lyons and Mâcon, halted the transfer of two other divisions from Metz to Paris, and issued secret orders for the defence of Italy and Dalmatia.[74] Napoleon, however, did not want his measures to incite conflict. He thus instructed Viceroy Eugene not to undertake anything that might provoke Austria and told his arch-chancellor, Jean-Jacques-Régis Cambacérès, to 'disavow' the notion that Austria desired war.[75]

Napoleon also mobilised the Rheinbund. In a series of letters from Valladolid on 15 January, he advised his German allies that 'the conduct of Austria raises the fear that this power is embarking on follies which will bring about its ruin' and told each to place his contingent on a war footing.[76] At the same time, to alleviate their concerns, he recounted the recent French victories in Iberia, assured them of his close ties with Russia, apprised them of his impending return to Paris, and described the vast force he was prepared to array in Italy and Germany without reducing his troops in Spain. He had every reason to expect that these instructions would quickly come to the attention of Habsburg agents and hoped that his measures would increase the pressure on Vienna to back down.

On the diplomatic front, the emperor also returned to the tactics of 1808, attempting to calm Austrian anxiety while enlisting the tsar's assistance. In addition to sending Alexander a personal note of friendship delivered by a special courier, Napoleon instructed Caulaincourt to impress upon the tsar the importance of taking decisive diplomatic action.[77] Simultaneously, Napoleon sought to conciliate Austria. In instructions sent to Andréossy on 17 January, Champagny stressed that 'the desire of the emperor is to conserve peace with Austria'. Two days after Napoleon's return from Valladolid, however, Champagny dispatched a letter recalling Andréossy from his post under the pretext of dealing with his personal affairs. 'The object of your recall is not to provoke a war, which His Majesty, on the contrary, wants to avoid,' wrote the foreign minister, explaining that, 'His sole aim is to return Austria to more sane thinking.' Although Andréossy was to avoid any word or action that could cause the Habsburg court to take umbrage, his recall was intended as a signal and the ambassador was enjoined to 'observe and note with exactitude' the impression produced when he announced his plans to Stadion.[78]

Andréossy's return to France did make an impression on the authorities in Vienna. Unfortunately for Napoleon's purposes, the effect on what Dodun termed 'the belligerent types' was transitory. It was not long before enthusiasm was once again in full bloom and 'war was regarded as certain by the public'.[79] Moreover, by the time the ambassador left for France on 1 March, the Habsburg decision for war had already been taken. The measures approved at the 8 February conference were well underway, and, as Chargé Dodun noted, the Austrians were now 'too far advanced to turn back'.[80] In the prevailing atmosphere of self-delusion and blind determination in the

Austrian capital, the withdrawal of Napoleon's ambassador appeared to the authorities in Vienna as yet another indication of his hostile intentions. Rather than serving as deterrents to war as the French emperor had hoped, his various initiatives became convenient justifications for Austria's aggressive strategy. In late February, as Habsburg troop movements were becoming increasingly visible, Stadion moved to exploit French military activity as a pretext for the steps Austria was in the process of implementing.[81] Metternich was therefore instructed to cite several of these points in explaining Austria's decision to place its forces on a war footing and move them towards the borders with France's allies.[82] Metternich dutifully held rather sterile talks with Champagny on 2 March,[83] but, in the words of one diplomatic historian: 'the role of diplomacy was now decidedly finished'.[84] As the tsar had warned in July: 'Reserve will be succeeded by confidence, suspicion will produce explications, and these explications will lead to war which it is in everyone's interest to avoid.'[85]

Andréossy followed a carefully specified route on his return to Paris so that he could observe Austrian military preparations and examine the readiness of key Bavarian fortifications.[86] His mission, of course, was only one small piece of the extensive French intelligence collection apparatus. The Bavarians remained active, other Rheinbund courts exploited their contacts in Vienna,[87] Eugene watched the Italian frontier, and Dodun's reporting from Vienna was exemplary in its thoroughness, detail, and sourcing.[88] In particular, Davout's investment in reconnaissance and espionage paid enormous dividends. As commander of the Army of the Rhine, his ambit included Poland as well as central and eastern Germany. From these vantage points he monitored Austrian mobilisation, sedulously preparing comprehensive orders of battle, observing fortresses, and even tracking individual regiments.[89] By interrogating travellers and themselves riding over the border, Saxon officers and members of the French legation in Dresden supplied a wealth of data on troop movements, unit strengths, logistics, public spirit, and mundane but important matters such as the date on which Austrian officers were to begin receiving their war-time pay supplements (1 March).[90] A similar stream of information flowed into Davout's headquarters from Poland.[91] As January turned to February, and February to March, these streams of intelligence became a flood. Not all of the information was accurate, but most of the individual reports were solid and the overall picture was unmistakable.[92]

In part, the amount of available intelligence burgeoned because there was simply more Austrian activity to report as the Habsburg hosts began to assemble, but the increase also resulted from the application of greater French resources and focused imperial guidance. On 23 February, for instance, Napoleon directed Champagny to place 10,000 francs per month at Otto's disposal so he would be 'truly informed of all the movements of the Austrians'.[93] Other orders directed reconnaissance along the frontiers of Italy, the preparation of maps from the Rhine to the Vistula, reconnaissance in Croatia, the collection of Austrian newspapers, and an array of other measures designed to place the French army and its emperor in readiness should war eventuate.[94] It was time and money well spent. In addition to a host of other useful facts, by the middle of March, Napoleon had in his hands a complete picture of Austrian dispositions along the borders with Germany and an enemy order of battle that was 95 per cent accurate: a remarkable achievement by any standard.[95]

What Napoleon did not have was a clear picture of Austrian intentions. From the beginning of the Austrian crisis, that is to say from the early summer of 1808, the emperor had expressed bafflement regarding Vienna's intentions: 'I do not know what it [Austria] wants'.[96] He concluded that Austrian behaviour was 'insolent' and 'ridiculous', that its armaments resulted from 'panicky fear' but that 'Austria is far from wanting war'.[97] He found it hard to believe that a power that had eschewed belligerence during the tense days after Eylau in 1807 would contemplate aggressive designs a mere two years later when circumstances seemed so unfavourable.[98] Through the Erfurt summit on into December 1808, he consistently repeated his conviction that 'excessive dread' was the only motivation for Habsburg activity and confidently commented that 'in reality there is nothing to fear from Austria'.[99]

Although his hopes of an early return to quiescence were dispelled by the intelligence that reached him in Spain during late December and early January, Napoleon maintained his conviction that Austria would not attack: 'when Austria sees the French and Russian armies ready to invade its territory, it will accept the guarantee [of its territorial integrity] ... and disarm'.[100] He continued to find Vienna's 'extravagant conduct' puzzling and 'mysterious', asking the Rheinbund princes rhetorically if the waters of the Danube 'had acquired the properties of the Lethe' (the river of forgetfulness in Greek mythology).[101] To the tsar, Napoleon complained that 'Austria's ridiculous armaments' were draining France's exchequer and, above all, paralysing his plans against Great Britain.[102] He persisted in his belief, however, that Austria would 'return to reasonable thinking'.[103] 'I do not think that they are so foolish as to commence operations having the Russian army on their flanks', he told

Otto on 4 March, adding that 'the Austrians will not be long in recognising that there are more troops in Germany and Italy than they can imagine.' If 'extraordinary events' arrived, however, he promised to be in Munich 'like a lightning bolt'.[104] Despite this confident tone and his desire to avoid war, he was clearly annoyed by Vienna's behaviour, his frustration manifesting itself in increasingly dire warnings that the Habsburg dynasty was 'rushing to its own ruin'. He had no intention of launching an offensive himself, he stated, but Franz would 'cease to reign' if Austria moved to war: 'I can dismember Austria'.[105] Nonetheless, as late as 22 March, we still find Napoleon in doubt regarding Vienna's intentions, hopeful that Austria would not attack and fairly certain that, even in the worst case, nothing would happen before the end of April at the earliest.[106]

MORE TROOPS THAN THEY CAN IMAGINE

Although still unsure of his foe's intentions, as intelligence on Austria's actions and potential capabilities accumulated, Napoleon took steps to enhance the defensive posture of his forces in Germany and Italy. He faced three serious obstacles in this endeavour: dispositions, numbers, and quality. The first two were susceptible to rapid improvement, but the last required more time than would be immediately available.

In the first place, although he had been endeavouring to concentrate his units in Germany since the autumn of 1808, in January 1809 his regiments were still scattered from the Rhine to the Vistula. After ordering the move of Oudinot's corps and Espagne's 3rd Heavy Cavalry Division to Augsburg on 15 January, Napoleon had the three large infantry divisions, two heavy cavalry divisions and three light cavalry regiments of Davout's Army of the Rhine stretched across central Germany between Bayreuth and Hanover. Further east, GD Louis Vincent LeBlond, Comte de St Hilaire's infantry division and five light cavalry regiments, also part of Davout's command, held the line of the Oder River and bolstered the Polish and Saxon garrisons in the Grand Duchy of Warsaw, including Danzig. Marshal Jean Baptiste Bernadotte garrisoned the Hanseatic cities with two small mixed divisions, one Dutch and the other French. The Rheinbund contingents had not yet begun to mobilise and the only other trained French troops immediately available were the two weak divisions that Napoleon had halted at Metz and Nancy. An additional two small divisions and four light cavalry regiments were clustered between Lyons and Mâcon, but the emperor initially envisaged employing these in the Italian theatre.

Napoleon was content with these arrangements for about one month following his return from Spain. Towards the middle of February, however, as intelligence of Austrian activity mounted, he began to pull his more distant troops back to south-central Germany. The French units in Danzig and Warsaw were ordered to Bayreuth on 13 February, and one week later St Hilaire's division and the remaining three light cavalry regiments were put on the road to Magdeburg, leaving only one French regiment (22nd Ligne) to garrison the Oder fortresses with a mixture of Polish and Saxon units.[107] During the same period, the emperor also directed the return of the Imperial Guard from Spain to Paris and called into existence a new corps composed of the four small divisions in eastern and south-eastern France. To be commanded by Massena, this new organisation was to assemble at Strasbourg. It would later become 4th Corps of the Army of Germany, but for deception purposes it initially laboured under the burdensome title 'Observation Corps of the Army of the Rhine'.[108]

Early March saw dramatic changes. On the 4th Davout, who was in Paris awaiting the birth of his fifth child, received instructions to assemble the forces under his command: his three veteran divisions at Bamberg, the two Saxon divisions near Dresden, the Poles at Warsaw, and the smaller German contingents at Würzburg. St Hilaire would maintain his course to Magdeburg. Furthermore, orders to Bernadotte called GD Pierre Louis Dupas's small mixed division south to Hanover, and Massena was directed to hasten the formation of his corps, with two of his divisions now to head for Ulm deep inside Germany.[109] The same day Berthier was appointed the 'major general' (chief of staff) of the forces gathering in Germany. With these orders of 4 March and expanded on the 11th, Napoleon sketched the outlines of a strategic concept to defend Germany against a possible Austrian offensive out of Bohemia, a concept that, in its general contours, would remain at the heart of his planning until the invasion actually occurred: his strategic right anchored by Massena, Oudinot, and the Bavarians south of the Danube near Ulm and Augsburg; his centre held by Davout's large corps with substantial German reserves forming behind; his left comprised of the Saxon army at Dresden. Farther east, a Polish corps would assemble around Warsaw.[110]

South of the Alps, similar preparatory measures were underway. Napoleon reinforced the Army of Italy with troops from Rome and from the Army of Naples. A total of twenty infantry battalions and six cavalry regiments were transferred to Eugene between late January and early April, severely depleting the French forces available elsewhere on the peninsula, especially those under GD Sextius Alexander François Miollis entrusted with the security of Rome, Tuscany, and the Adriatic coast.[111] Napoleon, however, calculated that the British, already embroiled in Spain and likely to attack the German coast in the event of a new war in central Europe, would not have enough forces to mount a serious threat to southern Italy.[112]

These new troops were accompanied by precise instructions to Eugene for the army's reorganisation. Napoleon also supplied his step-son with extraordinarily thorough guidance for the defence of Italy, a set of lengthy missives that afford significant insight into his strategic and organisational thinking.[113] As for precautions further east, he directed GD Auguste Marmont, through Eugene, to leave garrisons in the key coastal towns, but to concentrate the French troops of his small Army of Dalmatia in a defensive position on the Croatian frontier inland from Zara.[114] Marmont was thus well situated when the war began. The Army of Italy, on the other hand, was still strewn across northern Italy some distance from the border in early April, because Napoleon wanted to keep his troops dispersed in the lowlands to ease the logistical burden on the countryside. Furthermore, he was concerned that deploying to the mountainous border regions in the inclement spring weather would bring sickness and thus seriously weaken his Italian units before the war began.[115]

In addition to preparing his front-line forces for the coming struggle with Austria's principal armies, Napoleon initiated steps to cover his strategic rear against the danger of amphibious action by the British or local insurrection. His concepts embraced every corner of the probable theatre of operations. The garrison at Magdeburg, combined with those in Breslau, Glogau, and Stettin, would keep a wary eye on Prussia; these garrisons would consist principally of allied troops, but each would be based on a battalion of the 22nd Ligne, even though the regiment's fourth battalion, destined for Magdeburg, was still being established. Other allied formations would watch the northern coastline: Saxons and Poles in Danzig, the Mecklenburg contingents in Swedish Pomerania, Danes on the North Sea coast, the division of Dutch in the Hanseatic cities. In addition to this division committed to Germany, King Louis Bonaparte of Holland was to have a further 20,000 Dutch troops at hand to repel any British incursions along the shores of his own kingdom.[116] The Westphalian army, supplemented by a small Berg contingent, was to operate in central and northern Germany to preclude unrest and respond to rear area threats without diverting French battalions.[117] In the south where the war would open, Bavaria was asked to raise twelve new militia battalions to bolster its fortress garrisons and to maintain its hold on the Tyrol where a rebellion was expected.[118] As for French troops, Napoleon ordered the establishment of seventeen 'demi-brigades de réserve' to be formed from the depot battalions of his line and light infantry regiments. With a planned strength of some 45,000–55,000 men, these reserve demi-brigades were intended to protect the coast in France and the Low Countries and to serve as a general reserve for Germany and Italy. In early April, Napoleon refined his plan for the supplementary forces along the Rhine by designating six of the reserve demi-brigades as the nucleus of a 'corps d'armée de réserve' with a division of three brigades at Strasbourg and another at Mainz.[119] The defence of Italy, on the other hand, would gain additional strength from the utilisation of Italian depot troops and the creation of ad hoc 'mobile columns' of gendarmes to keep endemic banditry and general unrest in check in Tuscany.[120]

Despite his determination to generate adequate reserves, Napoleon kept his priorities clear, telling minister of war GD Henry Clarke that 'at present the matters of greatest importance are the Army of the Rhine and that of Italy'.[121] While assembling his various armies and disposing them more advantageously, therefore, he also addressed his second major challenge: filling all of these formations with troops. He was tireless in his efforts. From the time he left Astorga for Valladolid through the early days of April, he bombarded his field commanders, his allies, his minister of war administration, his director general of reviews and conscription and, most especially, the much-burdened Clarke with countless pages of detailed instructions on everything from conscription and remounts to shoes and pioneer tools.[122]

The emperor's thirst for information and his attention to detail were daunting. He scrutinised unit status reports with an uncompromising eye, demanding explanations for inaccuracies and swift rectification of any deficiency in strength or readiness. He personally annotated the Army of Italy's 1 March strength return, for example, to calculate the anticipated strengths of sixteen different battalions once they had incorporated conscript detachments varying in size from eighty to 545 men. The total number of recruits involved in this little exercise was only 5,433 out of an army total of some 94,600 soldiers.[123]

The army's personnel situation was made all the more challenging and complex by the sweeping reorganisation of French infantry that the emperor had instituted with a decree issued on 8 February 1808. Where there had previously been considerable disparity in the number of battalions per regiment, this document stipulated that each line or light infantry regiment was to consist of at least five battalions: four 'war' or field battalions (numbered one to four) and one depot battalion (the fifth battalion of each

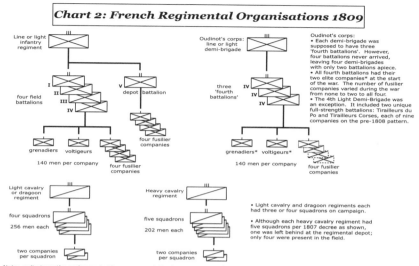

Chart 2: French Regimental Organisations 1809

Oudinot's corps:
• Each demi-brigade was supposed to have three 'fourth battalions'. However, four battalions never arrived, leaving four demi-brigades with only two battalions apiece.
• All fourth battalions had their two elite companies* at the start of the war. The number of fusilier companies varied during the war from none to two to all four.
• The 4th Light Demi-Brigade was an exception. It included two unique full-strength battalions: Tirailleurs du Po and Tirailleurs Corses, each of nine companies on the pre-1808 pattern.

• Light cavalry and dragoon regiments each had three or four squadrons on campaign.

• Although each heavy cavalry regiment had five squadrons per 1807 decree as shown, one was left behind at the regimental depot; only four were present in the field.

Note: unit strengths and organisations represent ideals, not necessarily the actual situation on campaign. Many infantry regiments had one or more battalions in Spain; some were still organising their fourth battalions; some fourth battalions remained in Germany. Also, although all regiments were often well under authorised manpower, cavalry units not infrequently exceeded nominal strength.

regiment). In part, this was to be accomplished by reducing the number of companies per battalion from nine to six (only four companies for each fifth or depot battalion) and utilising the excess personnel as cadres for the new battalions. During the summer and autumn of 1808, however, just as the army was beginning to implement the February directive, Napoleon ordered the massive redeployment of troops from Germany to Spain. As a result, the regimental reorganisation was badly disrupted and delayed. Moreover, many regiments never had a chance to assemble all four field battalions in one location: some were scooped up to fill ad hoc commands in Spain, some remained in Germany and yet others were in the process of forming in depots or training camps. The 2nd Ligne provides an extreme example of this phenomenon: the regiment's 1st and 2nd Battalions were with GD Gabriel Molitor's division near Mâcon, the 3rd Battalion was being established in northern Italy, and the 4th Battalion was serving with 7th Corps in Spain.[124] The 2nd Ligne may have been extreme, but it was not unique and many other regiments found themselves trying to manage the needs of a battalion at one end of the empire and three battalions at the other end, all the while creating a new depot battalion inside France.[125]

There was much to be done. Like the 19th Ligne of GD Dupas's division, which was 700 men below its authorised manpower establishment, many of the units in Germany were badly under strength. Oudinot's two divisions were especially weak, but every regiment needed replacements, and there were widespread shortages of vehicles and horses. As early as 5 December 1808, Napoleon had announced his intention to bring Davout's Army of the Rhine up to strength and add the fourth field battalion to each infantry regiment, but his plans assumed dramatically increased urgency and scope as the seriousness of Austria's preparations became apparent in early 1809.[126] By mid-February, therefore, as he was issuing orders for the withdrawal of almost all French units from Poland and the Oder River fortresses, he also promulgated astonishingly comprehensive directives for the transfer of thousands of replacements and reinforcements across the Rhine to Germany. Oudinot's corps, weakest of the major formations, received special attention, but Davout, Bernadotte, and the various cavalry units were also allotted their share of new recruits.[127] The decree that established Massena's Observation Corps highlighted another method of making up for the troops absent in Iberia—utilisation of Napoleon's Rheinbund allies. In the initial concept, each of Massena's four divisions was to include a German contingent to give these slender divisions additional depth.[128] Of course, Napoleon did not ignore the needs of Massena's French units and he gave Clarke thorough instructions on raising these to full strength. In addition to relying on the Rheinbund and new recruits joining from the depots of his own regiments, Massena's corps was to be bolstered by drafts from depots belonging to several regiments in Spain. Colonel Louis Léger Boyeldieu's 4th Ligne, for instance, received 300 men from the 44th Ligne and 200 from his own depot on 13 April while cantoned west of the Lech River.[129] Napoleon cautioned Clarke not to tell the depot commanders that their men were destined for other regiments: he was concerned that the depots would then 'strip the conscripts they are to send and have them depart naked'.[130] Recruit Joachim Delmarche, who felt himself 'content to be useful to my country' as he marched off to the 14th Ligne and presumably Spain, was thus quite surprised upon reaching Metz that he and several hundred of his fellow conscripts were to be incorporated in the 18th Ligne of Massena's corps.[131]

In addition, Napoleon assembled several new units. Only one of these, a weak Portuguese contingent of cavalry and infantry, would contribute to the corps already gathering in Germany, but six new Imperial Guard battalions drawn from the best of the conscripts would strengthen that institution and a provisional chasseur-à-cheval regiment thrown together from depots across the country would perform crucial services for the army staff.[132] He also planned to cobble together six provisional dragoon regiments from regimental depots and drafts from Spain in order to create an additional division for the Cavalry Reserve.[133]

All these measures to alleviate weaknesses in French dispositions and numbers led to great to-ing and fro-ing across Germany and Italy in the first three months of 1809. The simultaneous mobilisations undertaken by the German states, the Grand Duchy of Warsaw, and the Kingdom of Italy (whose army was undergoing a reorganisation similar to that of the French infantry) added to the urgent bustle of activity. 'The constant military movement gave the little city of Kassel a totally warlike appearance', noted the Bavarian ambassador to Westphalia, and comparable images were evident across the continent.[134] Despite the inevitable haste and confusion in which these emergency steps were implemented, by approximately 21 March, the emperor's forces in Germany had largely arrived in their initial positions and had achieved a substantial degree of organisation. Napoleon could thus be fairly well satisfied with the results of his efforts so far. The area where progress remained elusive, however, was troop quality.

The French army of 1809 was not at the same pinnacle of excellence as its famous predecessors of 1805 and 1806. In his previous imperial wars, Napoleon had been able to rely upon an army that he had assiduously trained on the Channel coast and then honed in the fire of combat over the course of three campaigns. Major elements of that army were still in Germany and eastern France as 1809 began, but a significant proportion had marched away over the Pyrenees during the latter half of 1808: 1st, 5th, and 6th Corps as well as a great deal of light cavalry and most of the dragoons. Of the forces left behind in Germany, all were in need of replacements to offset the attrition of the previous campaigns. Moreover, Soult's 4th Corps had been broken up, so that only Davout's 3rd Corps retained its pre-1808 configuration; the remainder had no identity above division or brigade and thus lost much of the benefit of the unit cohesion that they had developed during their earlier wars.[135]

This situation posed quality problems for Napoleon at both the individual and collective levels. In the first place, there was little time to train the individual soldiers in basic skills such as musketry and drill. Nor was there sufficient time to inure them to the hardships of extended marches, living off the land, and other routine campaign privations. Many of the conscripts called up by the September 1808 decrees only reached their depots in November or December. When they joined their regiments in the Armies of Germany and Italy, therefore, they had only been in uniform for three or four months. Even the men drafted according to the decrees of February and April 1808 did not start to arrive in the regimental depots until May, so they had, at best, less than one year of service time, little or no military experience outside their depots, and no combat seasoning whatsoever when they reached the banks of the Rhine or the Po.

The second aspect of the quality problem relates to collective training and unit cohesion. Because the men arrived only a few days or weeks before hostilities commenced, there was no time for adequate training in battalion, regimental, brigade, or higher echelon manoeuvres. The time available for integrating the new recruits and junior officers into their battalions and squadrons was similarly unsatisfactory in many cases. This was especially true in the fourth battalions, many of which had been freshly stitched together from the rawest of materials.

Davout's and Oudinot's commands illustrate the army's challenges as it responded to the problems of individual experience and unit organisation. At one end of the spectrum, the soldiers in Davout's 3rd Corps were very good indeed. In all but three of the infantry regiments, at least 70 per cent of the men were veterans, so the units absorbed conscript contingents with relative ease. Furthermore, as noted above, Davout's corps had experienced no major changes in organisation or senior commanders since the end of the 1807 campaign. As a consequence, its officers and men knew their commander and each other thoroughly, and could rely on time-tested habits of formal and informal co-operation to support them in combat. Oudinot's corps was another matter. Gutted during the reorganisations that followed upon the closure of the 1807 campaign, Oudinot's once elite combined grenadier division was now heavily diluted with raw recruits and counted at best perhaps 35 to 40 per cent veterans in scattered companies throughout its ranks. In the autumn of 1808, for instance, IV/69th Ligne was awaiting the arrival of 500 to 600 new conscripts, some 70 per cent of its strength.[136] Organisationally, too, 2nd Corps' state was far from ideal. Undergoing a complete reconfiguration in early 1809 as it grew from a division to a shallow corps, it was hastily thrown together, full of new officers who were as unfamiliar with their men as they were with one another. They would have no opportunity to establish bonds of loyalty, mutual trust, and expectation before being thrust rudely into battle in April.[137]

Overall, then, the army had less depth than it had enjoyed in the immediate past. There were fewer French battalions east of the Rhine and many of those that were available in Germany contained a substantial percentage of conscripts with little training and no experience. The operational impact of this situation was threefold. First, it meant that there were few veteran soldiers and fewer veteran units to replace losses during the course of the war. Second, the army as a whole was less flexible than in previous campaigns. With fewer first-rate troops at hand, Napoleon could not afford to divert any of his experienced French and German units from the principal operational tasks; he had to concentrate all or most of them to achieve desired results. The corollary was that he had to rely upon conscripts, poorly trained allies, and deception to protect his rear areas. Third, individual units were likely to be more fragile compared with the immediate past because many of the troops found themselves in unfamiliar surroundings without a robust framework of veteran comrades and well-known officers to shore up the new recruits during the horror and uncertainty of combat.

Lest too much attention accrue to the weaknesses of the French army in 1809, it must be stressed that this was fundamentally a sound force. If overall quality had declined somewhat when compared with the Grande Armée of the initial imperial wars, in aggregate the army of 1809 remained far superior to the courageous but raw conscript masses who marched into the 1813 campaign in Saxony. Most of the new soldiers were young men between the ages of 20 and 24. They might lack training and experience, but they had greater stamina than the youths who often filled Napoleon's ranks in the final desperate campaigns.[138] Despite the high numbers of conscripts in some units, therefore, the Austrians erred badly in concluding that the French army consisted entirely of untried soldiers. Sitting in Paris, Metternich could only observe the newly slapped together battalions Napoleon brought to his capital to review. It is hardly surprising that the Austrian ambassador wrote of these green formations in the most disparaging terms. What Metternich did not see were the thousands of cursing, confident veterans calmly eating up the muddy miles as they made their way across Germany to their assembly areas on the Austrian frontier. They would soon make their presence felt.

In addition to the solid core of veterans in most regiments, the French army also benefited from a superb cadre of leaders at all levels. There was certainly no lack of green young officers gathered up from military schools or superannuated retirees drafted back into active service, many of whom gave their new commanders occasion for complaint. Oudinot received a number of these men with large replacement detachments in mid-May at Vienna. Many were also concentrated in the hurriedly assembling fourth and fifth battalions slated for rear area duties. In contrast, the officer corps of most front-line units was composed of men who had attained their promotions through courage and competence during many years of service and multiple campaigns. Compared to their Austrian counterparts, they were youthful but experienced, skilled, energetic, and bold, often to the point of impetuosity. They had tremendous confidence in themselves and their leaders, Napoleon above all. 'Everyone viewed these preparations for war with pleasure,' remarked one junior officer, 'We were quite disposed to open the ball at any time, too bad for those who could not keep the measure.'[139]

Moreover, these men understood that they were expected to take the initiative and to operate with a minimum of guidance. No opportunity was to be missed, no exertion left untried. In the words of one young French staff officer, this enterprising spirit manifested itself in a 'manner of regarding nothing as impossible' and a 'limitless confidence in success.'[140] A postwar Austrian assessment offered:

> He who has the opportunity to observe the eager, restless, and anxious striving of everyone without exception, from first to last, from highest to lowest, how each endeavours to do everything that is at all possible, indeed to deduce what is not specifically stated, to exceed that which is expected, he who observes this must share the full conviction that no sovereign in all Europe can be considered better served, more closely obeyed or more wholly satisfied than Napoleon.[141]

Carl von Clausewitz assessed Napoleon's officers and men in this way:

> One has to have seen the steadfastness of one of the forces trained and led by Bonaparte in the course of his conquests—seen them under fierce and unrelenting fire—to get some sense of what can be accomplished by troops steeled by long experience of danger, in whom a proud record of victories has instilled a noble principle of placing the highest demands on themselves. As an idea alone it is unbelievable.[142]

Victory, not cautious adherence to meticulously written orders, was the measure of success.

Imbued with this spirit of independent intrepidity and with complete faith in their imperial master, French officers could be entrusted with orders that specified their missions, Napoleon's intentions, and the general operational context. The details of execution were left up to the subordinate. Napoleon could and did tailor his instructions to match his assessment of a commander's capabilities, so that some letters to Eugene, whom he was trying to tutor in a fond but exacting fashion, are extraordinarily comprehensive. In most cases, however, orders were spare and simple, starting with the phrase 'it is the intention of the emperor' to state Napoleon's general goals, sketch in the requisite situational details, and outline what was expected of the subordinate commander. They were also freighted with Napoleon's own tremendous will and energy. The drive and decision still speak across the years: 'Activity! Activity! Speed! I rely upon you!'[143] Or 'pursue the enemy with your sword in his back ... keep St Germain's brigade of cuirassiers at hand to spread terror among the cavalry of the enemy's rear guard.'[144] The contrast with the pedantic Austrian style of drafting 'dispositions' could hardly be more stark.

In tactics too, French speed and adaptability contrasted strongly with the Austrian emphasis on stiff formality and the minutiae of the drill book. Flexibility, drive, and an uncanny skill at deriving every possible advantage of terrain were especially prevalent in the French infantry. These qualities gave Napoleon's foot soldiers a significant superiority over most of their continental foes in broken terrain or village fighting, which placed a premium on the agility, open order tactics, and individual initiative that characterised the French infantry. Off the battlefield, the French army enjoyed a well-deserved renown for its marching ability. Combining this mobility, boldness, energy, and initiative with a general disregard for march formalities and an almost heedless determination to match the emperor's expectations, the French could conduct rapid, consecutive marches over long distances. Napoleon cultivated this capability and relied on it to surprise and confound his opponents. By concentrating his forces with unanticipated speed or falling suddenly on an unprotected flank with great force, he multiplied the kinetic power of the army with the psychological shock of rapid and relentless violence so that the enemy had no respite to recover physically or mentally.

The French mounted arm exhibited the initiative, flexibility, and zeal that were so prominent among their infantry compatriots, but man for man, or squadron for squadron, the French cavalry was in many cases inferior to the Austrian horse. More important than the qualities of individuals or of small units in the coming war, however, was the marked French superiority in co-ordinating the actions of multiple regiments to achieve tactical battlefield goals. Where the Austrians tended to employ their regiments as isolated, separate entities with little co-ordination above the regimental level, French commanders were adept at combining their formations for large orchestrated attacks of brigade or division size. They could thus overwhelm their opponents and had the potential to have a decisive influence on the outcome of any particular battle. On the other hand, Napoleon's mounted arm was often weakened by hard marches and the notoriously poor level of equine care in the French army.[145]

The artillery arm also suffered from serious shortfalls in March and April 1809. By employing many pieces captured in earlier conflicts, the French managed to have adequate guns on hand in each infantry and heavy cavalry division by the time the war began, but horses, harnesses, and support vehicles were in short supply. Similarly, most artillery companies were well below authorised strength and many of the men seem to have been lacking in experience as compared with their predecessors.[146] There were also shortages in staff officers, train personnel, and artillery artisans. The army's artillery chief, GD Nicolas Songis des Courbons, for example, told Berthier on 21 March that the units in Germany lacked 1,800 artillery train troops, 100 staff officers, nearly 400 vehicles, and 5,000 horses.[147] As a consequence, the corps artillery parks were weak, and the army's park existed 'in concept only'.[148] Davout's command, as usual, was in better condition than the others, but Massena and Oudinot had good reason to be concerned.[149] Despite its many problems, the French artillery maintained its traditional superiority in mobility and rapid action on the battlefield and left a very favourable impression with contemporaries.[150]

Napoleon's subordinates also scrambled to make up shortages in almost every other specialty area: medical personnel, engineers, pioneers, pontooneers, transport equipment. Their urgent efforts to scour the empire for surgeons, draft animals, wagons, harness, and tools were partially successful, but many important gaps remained when the war began.[151]

To bolster his bridging and logistics capabilities in a region of many watercourses, Napoleon turned to an unusual resource, issuing a decree on 17 March that called for two battalions of naval personnel from Antwerp to join the army in Germany. They would assist in river-crossing operations and facilitate the use of the Danube as an inexpensive highway for supplies. In response to this decree, the 44th Naval Battalion and a newly created Battalion of Naval Artificers found themselves on the road to the Danube valley in early April under Navy Captain Pierre Baste.[152] Although they arrived too late to participate in the initial phases of the war, Napoleon's foresight ensured that these sailors-turned-soldiers would be on hand to play a key role in mastering the Danube prior to the Battle of Wagram.

In addition to his French troops, Napoleon relied heavily on allied contingents in 1809, particularly in the opening weeks of the war. Germans represented the most numerous component, furnishing four entire corps, an independent division, and a significant proportion of Massena's command. They were crucially important to the outcome of the conflict both in the Danube valley and in Napoleon's strategic rear. The Dutch army and a

Danish 'division' contributed to countering rear area threats in Germany and along the North Sea coast. Allies were also important on the strategic flanks: troops of the Kingdom of Italy provided two divisions to the Army of Italy and the new Polish army carried the burden of the campaign in the Duchy of Warsaw almost entirely alone. Some of these forces, such as the armies of Poland, Italy, and several German states, were constructed after the French model and featured similar organisation and tactics. Others maintained their own organisational structures and followed tactical procedures that were not completely congruent with French practice. These differences, compounded by political frictions and language problems, presented a considerable challenge to Napoleon as he endeavoured to incorporate his allied contingents into the French command structure. The variations among the myriad of allied contingents, however, also highlight the importance of examining each army as a distinct entity. Though generalisations can be helpful, a great deal of historical fidelity is lost if all non-French units are thrown together in an undifferentiated group.

WAR SEEMS IMMINENT

Problems notwithstanding, by the middle of March Napoleon was well on his way to establishing a large army in southern Germany. He was still not persuaded that Austria truly meant to open a new war, but his comprehensive precautions proved their value, when, on the 23rd, he learned that the Austrians had arrested a French courier in Braunau on the Inn River. The courier, a retired French officer with the unlikely name of Sherlock, was not strictly official, but he had been carrying dispatches in a sealed diplomatic pouch, which the Austrians seized as he tried to cross into Bavaria.[153] To the French, this act was an egregious violation of diplomatic norms and Napoleon immediately re-examined his assumptions concerning Austria's probable behaviour. In addition to protests aimed at Metternich, he directed his generals in Germany to accelerate the march of their troops as much as possible 'without fatiguing them'.[154] He told Clarke to have all officers destined for the Army of Germany depart at once and wrote to his brother Joseph in Madrid: 'War seems imminent; I am dispatching my equipment.' Napoleon continued to believe that 'things will remain the same for the entire month of April', but the die now seemed cast, war more likely than not.[155]

Deeming that the situation was dangerous enough to warrant closer control, but not wanting to provoke Austria by leaving Paris himself, Napoleon decided to send Berthier to Strasbourg. In that key fortress city, the marshal would not only be ideally located to transmit imperial directives for the forces in Germany, he would also be able to manage the flow of reinforcements and equipment across the Rhine. Moreover, communications with Paris were excellent: good roads allowed swift movement of letters by courier and telegraphic messages could be passed in a few hours as long as weather conditions permitted.[156] Politically, by staying inside France, Berthier's displacement toward the theatre of war was less provocative than it would have been had he gone as far forward as the principal alternative, Augsburg. With these considerations as backdrop, Berthier departed Paris at 8 p.m. on 31 March, arriving in Strasbourg at 3 a.m. on 4 April.

Berthier had already taken steps to prepare for this forward deployment. In addition to managing the construction and movement of the army, he was careful to preposition the army's headquarters elements. On 21 March he had drafted orders for GD Martin Vignolle to go Strasbourg to 'establish a bureau of my headquarters' and for GB François Gédéon Bailly de Monthion to travel to Ulm.[157] At the same time, the Major General sent the army's newly designated chief engineer, GD Henri Gatien Bertrand, to Strasbourg to assemble a staff and oversee this essential branch of service. GD Songis, in charge of artillery, had been in the city, hard at work, for several days. Monthion soon moved his operation to Donauwörth to be closer to the presumed scene of action.[158] Thanks to Berthier's practical precautions, therefore, many of the quotidian but crucial pieces of the army's command and control system were in place and functioning when the Austrians invaded, easing Napoleon's assumption of command when he arrived in Donauwörth on 17 April.

Napoleon's plans for the coming conflict had evolved during March, and by the end of the month, he had settled on a broad strategy based on the intelligence he had at the time. At the heart of his thinking was his recognition that he would have to begin the war on the defensive. Though inconsistent with his preference for the offence, his initial defensive posture offered two significant advantages: it granted him time to strengthen and organise his new army while allowing the Austrians to tarnish their cause by adopting the role of the aggressor. It was clear, however, that he intended to transition to the offence as soon as possible. To facilitate this transition and to protect his ally Bavaria, he therefore wanted to establish his defence as close to the Austrian border as prudence would permit. Napoleon's thinking had been evident in several letters, but now he distilled his thoughts and dictated a lengthy epistle entitled 'Instructions for the Major General' on 30 March to equip his faithful chief of staff with his vision for the coming conflict: 'I will let him know my plans, so that he can execute them without waiting for my orders if circumstances are pressing.'[159]

Napoleon founded his planning on two key assumptions. First, he estimated that he had at least two more weeks before war erupted, and that Austrian activities would provide some advance warning. He thus began this remarkable document by reiterating his conviction that 'the Austrians are not at the point of declaring war' and that they were unlikely to initiate a campaign before 15 April. Second, all of the intelligence he had received up to 30 March clearly and correctly placed the bulk of the Austrian army in Bohemia. As a result, his strategic concept, though flexible, was designed primarily to counter an Austrian thrust from that region. Both of these assumptions, of course, were wrong. Napoleon did not yet have the new reports indicating the Austrian shift to the Danube, and he did not judge that Charles would attack on 10 April before the Austrian army was truly ready. The former mistake was a result of the communications means available in Napoleon's day, the latter, however, was an error in his assessment of the enemy. It is hardly surprising, therefore, that the 30 March 'Instructions', based on erroneous assumptions, contributed to the disarray and near disaster the French experienced in the first days of the war. Fortunately for the French, the plan was fundamentally sound, sufficiently adaptable and robust to be a major factor in absorbing the Austrian invasion and turning a grim situation to Napoleon's advantage.

In essence, Napoleon envisaged forming a huge battalion square on the Danube as he had for the invasion of Prussia in 1806, albeit this time for defensive purposes initially. Davout, concentrated around Nuremberg and Bayreuth with his three original divisions, a new reserve division, the 2nd Heavy Cavalry Division, and his light cavalry brigade was the left point of the square. He would also have a division of troops from the small German states under his command, but this was still to the rear at Würzburg in the early stages of formation. The Bavarian corps along the Isar comprised the right, and Massena was in the Augsburg area as the rear-most component of the square. The forward point of this grouping was to be the Cavalry Reserve and a new corps under Marshal Jean Lannes. Lannes's command would include Oudinot's infantry and light cavalry, St Hilaire's division, and the 3rd Heavy Cavalry Division. The Cavalry Reserve, destined for Marshal Jean-Baptiste Bessières, was to be composed of two light and two heavy cavalry divisions as well as the division of provisional dragoons forming at Strasbourg. The Imperial Guard, which Napoleon hoped would reach Strasbourg by 15 April, and the Württemberg corps would constitute a general reserve. When finally in place by mid- to late April, the various elements of the Army of Germany would all be within four to five marches of one another and thus capable of uniting rapidly in any direction. With this general template of dispositions in mind, Napoleon considered how to deploy his formations on the ground. Two factors determined the answer to this question: the readiness of his own forces and the timing of the expected Austrian offensive. Assuming that the Austrians were attacking out of Bohemia, the emperor's clear desire was to assemble on Regensburg: 'My goal is to take my headquarters to Regensburg and to make that the central point of my entire army'.[160] With Regensburg as a pivot, he could command the bridges over the Danube and operate north or south of the river as the situation demanded. Given that he did not expect an enemy advance before 15 April and that he believed his own units could be in place by the 10th, he felt confident of his ability to occupy Regensburg with 30,000 infantry and seven regiments of horse before the Habsburg legions crossed the border.

However, he also planned for an earlier Austrian move: 'Headquarters at Donauwörth and the line of the Lech is a position to occupy in a case where the enemy anticipates me.'[161] Though not developed in as much detail as the Regensburg option, the notion that the army would not be able to reach Regensburg and would thus have to defend along the Lech River was clear in his mind and clearly communicated to others. In discussing logistics for the campaign, for example, he took 'the incertitude that we can arrive at Regensburg ahead of the enemy' into account in deciding to store hardtack biscuit at Donauwörth, 'a point which we are in a position to defend today', rather than at more vulnerable Regensburg.[162]

As indicated by the decisions on collecting hard rations, Napoleon carefully integrated logistics into his operational planning. The 30 March 'Instructions' summarised the extensive correspondence that had flowed between the emperor and Daru.[163] Ulm, Augsburg, and Donauwörth were to be the key forward magazines for food and the sites of numerous bakeries; at the latter alone the bakers were to prepare two million bread rations. Daru was to lease boats and crews at Ulm to provide transportation on the Danube and was to organise a relay of wagons between Ulm and Strasbourg to move 'all that the army needs, among other things, three to four million cartridges, 6,000 muskets . . . 12,000 tools which the engineers should have, as well as the hospital supplies and shoes which can be found at Strasbourg'. Hospitals, engineer parks, transport battalions, spare artillery equipment, and a host of other administrative and logistic concerns all attracted the emperor's attention.[164] The problem, of course, was that many of these measures would still be in their infancy when the war began. As a consequence, the French administrative services, just like the combat troops, would have to establish, organise, and equip themselves while supplying the army's requirements, all under the pressure of an active war of movement.

Napoleon's logistic preparations illustrate the importance of fortresses in his administrative planning, but the key fortified cities along the Danube were also central to his operational intentions. Augsburg and Donauwörth were important as magazines, but also as bridgeheads across key rivers. The same was true of Ingolstadt, of the bridgeheads on the Lech and, to a lesser degree, of Straubing. These crossing points gave Napoleon the freedom to operate on both banks of these two rivers and he expended no little effort to see that they were properly prepared for defence.[165] He paid particular attention to Passau, directing that it be capable of withstanding a siege of two to three months as he envisaged using it as a major supply base for the eventual counter-offensive into Austrian territory.[166]

With the 30 March 'Instructions', Napoleon thus established the conceptual framework for an initial defensive deployment, a 'strategic ambush', which would allow him to absorb the first Austrian blow and then transition rapidly to an offensive of his own.[167] Centred around Regensburg, the French army could oppose any Austrian advance out of Bohemia. If the Habsburg troops marched towards the Danube through Waldmünchen or Cham, for example, Napoleon would gather his corps along the Regen; he would be in a position to cut off an Austrian thrust toward Nuremberg or Bamberg; and he could counter a move on Dresden by an advance of his own into Bohemia. In the unlikely event of an enemy offensive on both flanks, he planned to 'accept the centre', assembling on the Lech with Augsburg as a garrison. He also considered the possibility of an Austrian advance towards Innsbruck, but dismissed this relatively small force of 'ten or twelve regiments' as irrelevant to the outcome of the principal struggle: 'they will learn of the defeat of their troops in Bohemia by our arrival in Salzburg'.[168] Although he expected Vienna to foment an insurgency in the Tyrol, he told Berthier: 'Let the Austrians do what they will in the Tyrol, as I do not want to engage in a war in the mountains under any circumstances.'[169] The clear-sighted focus on the enemy's main army and determination to avoid unnecessary entanglements in secondary operations would inform his thinking throughout the coming campaign.[170]

With all of this information, Berthier, who may have reviewed the 'Instructions' with Napoleon in person, should have been well equipped with his master's guidance for the initial defensive phase of the war when he departed for Strasbourg on 31 March.[171] Over the following week, Napoleon issued several directives that refined the 30 March 'Instructions', adding greater detail and introducing a few new orders. The principal new element was that Bernadotte in Dresden was to prepare to march for the Danube.[172] Among the refinements, Napoleon directed Davout to move one or two of his infantry divisions as well as his cuirassier division to the area between Nuremberg and Regensburg so that they could reach the latter city in one day's march.[173] These orders were consistent with the general tenor of the 30 March 'Instructions', but Napoleon's repeated references to Regensburg and his edging of some of Davout's troops closer to the city suggest that he was anxious to concentrate a large force there as early as possible. He may also have been experiencing second thoughts about the suitability of Oudinot's relatively weak command for the demanding mission at the closest point of approach for the Austrians.[174] The stress he placed on Regensburg, however, influenced Berthier's thinking, leading the harried chief of staff to lend even greater importance to the city in the days immediately following the Austrian invasion.[175]

THIS SKILFUL DISPOSITION OF THE ARMY

According to what the admiring Jean-Jacques Pelet, then an officer on Massena's staff, later called 'this skilful disposition of the army', by early April, Napoleon had the beginnings of an imposing force stretched across southern Germany from Dresden to Munich. The new army, soon to be named the 'Army of Germany', would consist of three predominantly French corps (2nd, 3rd, 4th), four German corps (7th, 8th, 9th, 10th), the Guard, and the Cavalry Reserve.[176] In the event, this organisation was not achieved until several months into the war, but it is important as it represented the general structure that Napoleon had in mind as he strove to cobble together his ad hoc army.

The heart of the Army of Germany was Davout's 3rd Corps. Though appellatives such as 'Napoleon's X Legion' smack more than a little of hyperbole, it is no exaggeration to say that 3rd Corps was the largest, best trained, best organised, and best equipped corps in the army with the highest proportion of veterans and the greatest degree of unit cohesion. They made a considerable impression. Encountering a column of men from the corps in mid-March, for example, an officer from the 4th Rheinbund Regiment recorded that 'the appearance of these march- and combat-experienced soldiers was a good example for our young troops, and our soldiers stared wide-eyed at the heavy packs that the French carried with ease'.[177] The men were full of confidence. Proud to be serving under Davout—'one of the leading warriors of that time'—Chef de Bataillon Jean-Pierre Bial, the new commander of I/72nd Ligne, felt that the marshal could be pleased 'to have under his hands the best troops of the empire'.[178] Similarly, Capitaine Alexander Coudreux of the 15th Léger wrote to his brother that 'the army has never been more magnificent, never better supported'.[179]

The high quality of the corps also reflected the many years its officers and men had spent on campaign as a unit with a distinctive identity. In the first place, Davout had commanded 3rd Corps since its creation on the Channel coast in the summer of 1805. Second, there had been few changes in either its order of battle or its senior leadership since its establishment. Of the fifteen infantry regiments in the three original divisions of the corps (that is, not counting St Hilaire's), twelve had served together in the same divisions for nearly four years, including extensive combat and campaigning through the wars of 1805, 1806, and 1807. Each of the other three 'newer' regiments (7th Léger, 15th Léger, and 65th Ligne) had been with its division for two years. Moreover, the three division commanders were not only soldiers of long experience and superior talent, they had all held their commands at least through the campaigns of 1806 and 1807; two had led their divisions through the 1805 war as well. The significance of these long associations for unit efficiency, cohesion, and battlefield performance cannot be overestimated.

Beyond their extended tenures in command within 3rd Corps, Davout and his divisional generals represented a remarkable collection of military ability. Charles Antoine Louis Alexis Morand, who had a fine education to match his sharp intellect, was 38 and had led the 1st Division since 1806. He had given up a legal career to volunteer in 1792 and was considered 'one of those men who made war best and with total commitment'.[180] GD Louis Friant, 51 years old and a former corporal in the Royal Army, was tall, brave, tough, and honest. He had assumed command of the 2nd Division in August 1805. Coming from the opposite end of the social spectrum was the 3rd Division commander, GD Charles Etienne Gudin de la Sablonnière, 'one of the six best infantry officers in the army'.[181] The son of a noble officer, he was 41 and had repeatedly distinguished himself since joining the Royal Guard in 1782. All three had amassed combat records of extraordinary achievement, particularly in senior commands during the great imperial campaigns of 1805, 1806, and 1807.

'The brave General St Hilaire, one of the glories of the army' was another officer from the old Royal Army, having enrolled as a cavalry cadet in 1777 at the age of 11. In 1805, it was his division that captured the Pratzen Heights at Austerlitz; in 1806, he ably manoeuvred his command on the French right at Jena; and in 1807, he fought with great credit at Eylau and 'saved the army' at Heilsberg.[182]

The cavalry brigadiers, Claude Pierre Pajol, Charles Claude Jacquinot, and Hippolyte Rosnyvien, Comte de Piré were all talented and experienced light horsemen. They were soon to be joined by GD Louis Pierre Montbrun, one of the finest cavalrymen to ever serve Napoleon. Also attached to 3rd Corps was the 2nd Heavy Cavalry Division under GD Raymond Gaspard de Bonardi, Comte de St Sulpice. As with Davout's infantry, these four cuirassier regiments had served together in the same brigades since the division's formation in the summer of 1805; St Sulpice had been with the division for the entire period, first as a brigadier and since 1807 as the commander.

As for Davout, 'the Iron Marshal' was a 'tough nut' in the eyes of his men, but they were proud to serve under his stern gaze.[183] Possibly the most capable marshal, he had led the corps on its gruelling march from Vienna to hold the French right wing at Austerlitz in 1805, had coolly brought victory against overwhelming odds at Auerstädt the following year, and had nearly succeeded in crushing the Russian left at Eylau in the cruel February of 1807. Possessed of a fine intellect, he was studious, serious and hard on the enemy, his men and, most of all, himself. Though he lacked the flamboyant charisma that characterised some of his fellow marshals, he could inspire his troops and his tactical ability certainly earned their trust and respect.[184] Beyond tactical competence and strategic vision, 39-year-old Davout was a thorough and efficient administrator, and, as we have seen, he managed extremely effective intelligence operations.[185] If his generals sometimes found him harsh or brusque, relations with his division commanders were good in 1809 and together they made a formidable team.[186]

Reflecting Napoleon's confidence in Davout, 3rd Corps was extraordinarily large. It was founded on the three large, five-regiment infantry divisions, the light cavalry brigade, and artillery of Davout's corps in 1807. In addition to this powerful force, 3rd Corps now included a fourth five-regiment division, a heavy cavalry division, and an additional five light cavalry regiments. Furthermore, a fifth infantry division was organised under GD Joseph Laurent Demont as a holding command for the recruits of the new fourth battalions of the 1st, 2nd, and 3rd divisions. Including the 3,215 men of Demont's reserve division, 3rd Corps numbered 55,500 officers and men in its infantry and cavalry units. The artillery complement was sixty-six guns: fifteen per infantry division and six more with the heavy cavalry.[187]

By 9 April, on the very eve of war, Davout's corps was the principal French force north of the Danube. Its cavalry outposts covered the routes of egress from Bohemia with Pajol's horsemen on both sides of Waldmünchen and Jacquinot's brigade stretching from Braunetsried away to the Eger road in the north. The 2nd Infantry Division was posted at Bayreuth, and Gudin's 3rd Division was at Nuremberg with Davout's headquarters. The 12th Ligne and a squadron of the 5th Hussars were stationed at Amberg to cover the gap between Friant and Pajol. Morand's division extended from Neumarkt to the south-west along the road to Regensburg, while St Hilaire's men were tightly concentrated around the city itself. St Sulpice's cuirassiers were cantoned around Windsbach. Not far away at Ansbach, Demont was assembling his thin division of recruits. Still en route were the 105th Ligne of St Hilaire's division and three more light cavalry regiments.[188] Finally, Davout was also responsible for the division of four Rheinbund regiments slowly coming into existence at Würzburg under GD Marie François Rouyer. Not included in the totals above, Rouyer's division was supposed to number nine battalions with some 6,000 men, but was only in the earliest stages of formation when the war opened.[189]

Also in Davout's immediate operational area was the large 1st Heavy Cavalry Division. The division's commander, GD Etienne Marie Antoine Champion, Comte de Nansouty was known as a tough and competent professional with a haughty demeanour and a powdered queue, reflecting his aristocratic heritage. One of his fellow generals described him as possessing 'an accurate and rapid *coup d'oeil*, a character of rare firmness, an imposing authority', but even his admirers disliked the tendency towards sarcasm and mockery that blighted his interactions with peers and subordinates alike.[190] Nor was he regarded as a general who would seize the initiative instinctively or seek innovative solutions to tactical and administrative predicaments as a matter of course. He had commanded the division since its creation in 1805 and all six regiments had served continuously in the same brigades for the past four years. Nansouty had departed in 1808 to replace Caulaincourt as the Master of Horse in Napoleon's household. He had thus gone to Spain with the emperor and was still on his way back to Germany when the war with Austria began. Leadership of this fine division thus temporarily devolved to GB Antoine Louis Decrest, Comte de St Germain. Two of Nansouty's six regiments (2nd and 12th Cuirassiers) were with St Hilaire around Regensburg. The remaining four were further west near Denkendorf. In total, the division counted at least 4,880 troopers, supported by twelve guns.[191]

Two French corps were quartered in the towns and villages south of the Danube. In the triangle formed by the Danube and the Lech was Marshal

Massena's 4th Corps. Though perhaps leavened with more conscripts than Davout's battalions, Massena's infantry regiments were solid, well-established units with excellent reputations and superb leadership at all levels. The regiments of the 1st and 2nd Divisions had served together in their respective divisions for almost four years as elements of Soult's old 4th Corps. The regiments of the 3rd and 4th Divisions had been together for less time and had not been embroiled in the crucial battles of 1805 to 1807, but they had been with their divisions for at least two years. Reviewing the men in early April, Massena found them in 'the best appearance' and 'already accustomed to marching'; he further noted that 'the beardless faces of the conscripts contrasted with those of their older comrades', but he left convinced that the new troops had 'already adopted their easy manner, their high spirits and their cheerfulness'.[192] A Westphalian officer who saw one of 4th Corps's regiments near Strasbourg was also impressed: 'The troops were in the finest condition and excited general admiration among us.'[193] Unlike 3rd Corps, however, the regiments and divisions of Massena's command had never served together as a corps, so the officers and men, the staffs and commanders did not know one another or enjoy the easy familiarity that helps lubricate the machine of war.

Massena's 4th Corps was also smaller than Davout's. Where the four infantry divisions of 3rd Corps (not including Demont) totalled sixty French battalions, Massena's four divisions could only field thirty-two. Four additional battalions were under orders to join their regiments from depots in Italy by marching through the Tyrol. As we shall see, however, the vagaries of war would preclude this union. To help fill the ranks, therefore, Napoleon turned to his German allies, allotting the contingent from Baden to the 1st Division under GD Claude Juste Alexander Legrand and that of Hesse-Darmstadt to GD Jean François Carra Saint-Cyr's 2nd Division. The inclusion of these two brigades also brought the corps two additional light cavalry regiments and two and one-half artillery batteries. Massena was fortunate that the Hessians and Badeners were some of the best Rheinbund troops. They 'rivalled the French in zeal and devotion', and their French comrades would soon discover they were a valuable asset for the corps.[194] French officers, however, 'were not a little horrified' to learn that the Baden and Hessian infantry muskets were incompatible with French cartridges. Moreover, the Baden Jäger carried a rifled musket that required yet another type of ammunition. There being no time to exchange all of these weapons for French muskets before the war began, the German troops had to cope with this complexity throughout the campaign.[195]

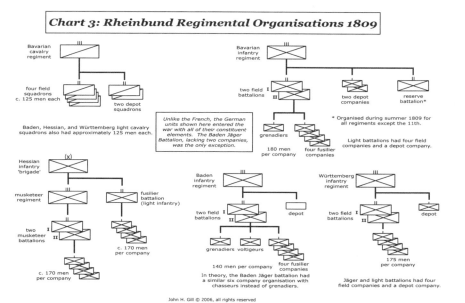

Chart 3: Rheinbund Regimental Organisations 1809

The other crucial asset in 4th Corps was its leaders. The division commanders were all first rate: solid, reliable, experienced. Legrand stood out from the rest as one of the few in whom Napoleon descried the 'sacred fire' (*feu sacré*) that distinguished officers of especial dedication, determination, and inspirational ability.[196] Above all, however, 4th Corps benefited from having Massena as its commander. Though completely different from Davout in background, education, personality, and outlook, Massena at 51 was an extraordinarily gifted leader, one of the two or three marshals capable of commanding armies on independent operations. His abilities were the result of natural talent rather than study, but he had honed his skills across a lengthy career of victorious service. He had begun as a common soldier in the old Royal Army and had repeatedly displayed his competence during the wars of the Revolution, most notably during his exemplary campaign in Switzerland in 1799. His passions for women and riches have tarnished the sheen of his reputation, but Napoleon remarked that the marshal was 'eminently noble and brilliant under fire and in the disorder of battle; the sound of cannon clarified his thoughts, gave him spirit, penetrating insight, and cheerfulness.'[197] Accompanying him on the campaign was his son, Sous-

Lieutenant Prosper Massena, decked out in a glowing white hussar uniform as an officer on his father's staff. Several days behind followed his mistress, Madame Henriette Le Berton.[198]

With the addition of the two German contingents, Massena would command a total of 36,060 infantry and cavalry of whom 4,570 were Hessian and 6,170 from Baden.[199] There was, however, considerable disparity in strength among the infantry divisions. With the addition of the Rheinbund troops, the 1st and 2nd Divisions mustered 10,000 and 11,050 officers and men respectively, while GD Gabriel Molitor had 6,830 in his 3rd Division and GD Jean Boudet only 5,260 in the 4th Division. The unusually large light cavalry component of the corps included four French and two German regiments under the talented GD Jacob François Marulaz. Unfortunately for Massena, all six of these regiments were significantly under strength, totalling only some 2,830 troopers. Each infantry division included twelve French guns, while the Baden and Hessian contingents contributed a further twelve and six pieces to their respective divisions.

Assembling between the Lech and Ilm Rivers was the third major French formation, 2nd Corps, temporarily under GD Oudinot pending the arrival of Marshal Lannes. The corps was neither as large nor as rich in veterans as its sister formations. Though founded on Oudinot's famous combined grenadier division of 1806 and 1807, it had lost this elite character by 1809 and now contained a high percentage of conscripts. Furthermore, it lacked the cohesion and history of the other formations, having been rudely hammered together in the weeks immediately prior to the opening campaign. Leadership was also a problem. The division and brigade commanders were good to excellent, but there was noticeable dissatisfaction with some of the junior officers in 2nd Corps, and Oudinot's qualities were hardly stellar. The future marshal was a solid, tactically adroit officer with enormous courage and a knack for inspiring his troops, but his intelligence was limited and his capability for independent command very small. He was ideal for leading an infantry charge or fighting a tough defensive action, as long as he had a superior to guide him. Although he had a violent temper, he could be surprisingly gentle at times. He had earned a good reputation during the wars of the Revolution, including service under Massena in Switzerland, and had served with distinction under the empire. Always at the centre of danger in combat, by 1809 he had already accrued more than one dozen wounds.

Oudinot's 2nd Corps was an ad hoc formation, composed for the most part of fourth battalions that were being created for regiments in Spain.[200] It was still awaiting some 8,000 men when the war began and most of its battalions had only two fusilier companies instead of the required four. Being thrown together from loose battalions with no regimental structure, Napoleon reached into the past and used the Revolutionary term 'demi-brigades' for groupings of three battalions; two demi-brigades made a brigade and each division included three brigades. The 1st Division under GD Jean-Victor Tharreau was slightly smaller with 6,940 officers and men compared to the 8,700 in GD Michel Claparède's 2nd Division. Claparède's division was also distinguished by the inclusion of two large independent battalions of superb light infantry: the Tirailleurs du Po and the Tirailleurs Corses. For cavalry, 2nd Corps disposed of GB Edouard Colbert's 'Brigade Infernale' (2,180 men)—as fine a body of light horse as one was likely to find—and the attached four cuirassier regiments in GD Espagne's 3rd Heavy Cavalry Division (2,900 men). As with its sister divisions, the 3rd Heavy Cavalry had not changed its composition since its constitution in 1805, so the regiments all knew one another. They also knew their general, renowned for his attention to discipline and order, as he had taken command in November 1806. A Portuguese contingent of some 1,700 men was slated to join the corps, but it was still well inside France on 10 April. Each of Oudinot's infantry divisions had eighteen guns and Espagne's six pieces brought the corps total to forty-two.

Bavaria supplied the largest German contingent and these men, 25,110 strong with an exceptionally powerful artillery complement of seventy-eight guns, were gathered in 7th Corps under Marshal François Lefebvre. An additional 4,560 men were on garrison duty in the Tyrol.[201] Unlike the French formations, the Bavarians integrated their cavalry into their three infantry divisions, giving each a brigade of two mounted regiments. The corps was also unusual in that Lefebvre had a substantial artillery reserve of four batteries at his disposal. The men were reliable, well trained, and generally well led. They also understood war against their old foe Austria.[202]

The Bavarian division commanders made an interesting gallery. Crown Prince Ludwig, a passionately intense young man of 22 who detested Napoleon, had hoped to command the contingent and thus acquired another reason to resent the French emperor when Napoleon insisted on Lefebvre, telling King Maximilian Joseph: 'If the crown prince had been through six or seven campaigns at all levels, then he could command them.'[203] The youthful Ludwig instead became commander of the 1st Division with an able veteran, GM Clemens von Raglovich as his chief of staff. General-Leutnant (GL) Carl Philipp Freiherr von Wrede, aged 42, led 2nd Division. A competent soldier and an often inspiring leader who could get the most from his men, he was also highly ambitious and could be a most difficult subordinate. During the tense days immediately preceding the Austrian invasion, he also displayed 'a certain nervousness', responding to every rumour and report from across the border.[204] At the head of 3rd Division was the veteran GL Bernhard Erasmus Graf von Deroy, dependable, calm, and capable, a true 'old war horse' of 66 who elicited much affection from his men. Napoleon's choice of Lefebvre to lead the corps seemed a good one. Lefebvre may not have been the most imaginative of France's marshals, but he had a solid military record and easily surpassed most of his Austrian contemporaries. He was another officer in whom Napoleon detected the *feu sacré*.[205] A key consideration was that he spoke German, albeit with a heavy Alsatian accent, and relations between him and his new command began on a professional, if not especially cordial, note. At 54, he was the oldest of the French corps commanders. Napoleon reinforced the corps' leadership by assigning the talented and experienced GD Jean-Baptiste Drouet, Comte d'Erlon as Lefebvre's chief of staff.

In early April, the three Bavarian divisions were deployed to cover the army's right flank against Austrian forces in the Danube valley. Marching to their assigned positions, the men encountered the same vile weather that was plaguing the Austrians across the frontier. A soldier in Wrede's 2nd Division wrote that his battalion 'departed its quarters before midnight and marched the entire night through … a very fine rain fell steadily and an icy cold wind came up at dawn out of the north, so that the left side of my helmet (called a casquet in those days) and my musket were completely covered over with ice'.[206] Weather notwithstanding, Wrede established his men generally between Straubing and Weichshofen, but with the 13th Infantry, 6th Light Battalion, and 3rd Chevaulegers north of the river to tie in with Pajol's horsemen near Cham and to monitor the Bohemian border. The bulk of the 3rd Division was gathered around Freising and the crown prince's men were located due east of Munich. Cavalry outposts observed the line of the Inn, Vils, and Traun Rivers. The Tyrol garrison, under the elderly and infirm GL Georg Kinkel, was scattered in major towns from Innsbruck to Brixen. Though not technically part of 7th Corps, six of the twelve 'reserve battalions' requested by Napoleon were in the initial stages of organisation, Bavaria's financial resources and its pool of qualified officers and NCOs being inadequate to support the larger number at this early date.[207]

As with the Bavarians, diplomatic friction also accompanied the assignment of GD Dominique Joseph René Vandamme to another large German contingent, the Württembergers of 8th Corps. Though he was an excellent tactician with great drive and energy, Vandamme was also crude, proud, and difficult to the point of insubordination. He had commanded the

Württemberg contingent during the 1806–7 campaign, but his coarseness, arrogance, and penchant for illicit profit had disgusted most of the senior Württemberg officers and had come to the attention of their formidable sovereign. Most offensive in the eyes of King Friedrich was Vandamme's constant interference in the internal affairs of the contingent, matters that the king jealously guarded as his own personal prerogatives. Friedrich complained bitterly to Napoleon that Vandamme's 'callousness and rudeness' during 1806–7 were 'beyond sufferance', but his petitions were in vain.[208] The emperor, recalling Vandamme's earlier successes with the Württembergers and convinced that French officers had to be set over all allied contingents, refused to reconsider his decision.[209] Vandamme would stay.

The Württembergers were originally assigned an independent role in Napoleon's thinking, but by early April he had decided to allocate them to 8th Corps. This formation was to include Dupas's small French division and Rouyer's division of miscellaneous Rheinbund troops, all under the command of Marshal Charles Augereau.[210] As events unfolded, however, this organisation was not fully implemented: Augereau never came to Germany and Dupas's infantry (with Rouyer's men attached) remained semi-independent. Though technically assigned to Vandamme for about three weeks from mid-April to mid-May, these two divisions (Dupas in overall command of both) were never physically close to the Württembergers and operated more or less on their own under missions assigned by army headquarters. The Württemberg contingent under its 39-year-old commander thus became the *de facto* 8th Corps. One of the best Rheinbund armies, the 11,830 men of the contingent were divided into an infantry division of three brigades and a two-brigade cavalry division; twenty-two guns provided artillery support.[211]

By the end of March, the infantry regiments were in quarters from Ellwangen down to the Danube while their cavalry compatriots were lodged further west near Kirchheim. The soldiers were tough, well-trained and well-led, satisfying even the hard-eyed Vandamme. The cavalry and horse artillery were especially good, and the light infantry brigade would prove itself a truly crack unit during the coming campaign.[212] The large foot battery, on the other hand, proved cumbersome despite the best efforts of its personnel. As with the other elements of the Army of Germany, a sense of pressing excitement pervaded the atmosphere. 'It was a time of joy for the young officers', recalled brand new Leutnant Leo Ignaz von Stadlinger, 'All of one's senses were engaged and concentrated themselves at that point in the brain where the drive to combat resides'. Private Johann Georg Schäffer of the Light Brigade left a slightly different impression in one of his letters home: 'We Jägers would have had it good in our quarters if it weren't for all the drilling, but not a day goes by when we don't drill, marching out with all of our gear.'[213]

These were the principal components of the Army of Germany immediately available to meet the Austrian invasion on 10 April. All in all, they amounted to some 160,000 infantry and cavalry with at least 286 guns. Other troops, however, were also en route to the theatre of war. Most prominent among these was the Imperial Guard, making its way from Spain with the infantry loaded in wagons. Urgency was in the air, as Grenadier Corporal Jean-Roche Coignet recorded of the journey: 'There was not a moment lost; each man felt the need of doing his duty. We travelled 25 leagues a day. It was as though a streak of lightning passed from south to north.'[214] This mode of travel, however, was 'neither easy nor commodious', in the words of a soldier in the Fusilier-Grenadiers: 'On the seventh day after our departure from Bordeaux, we arrived in Paris, our limbs feeling dislocated and quite happy to be delivered from this new means of transporting men to butchery.'[215]

Two other major bodies of French troops destined for the Army of Germany were Dupas's division (some 4,850 infantry and cavalry), marching down from Hanover, and the six provisional dragoon regiments (2,070 men) just beginning to assemble as a division in Strasbourg under GD Marc Antoine de la Bonière, Comte de Beaumont.[216] At Dresden, Marshal Bernadotte was overseeing the embodiment of most of the Saxon army (some 13,890 men) into the Army of Germany as 9th Corps.[217] Although a small number of troops would be left behind in the kingdom, 9th Corps too would soon find itself on the road for the Danube. As a contingency reserve, Napoleon ordered Marshal Mortier's 5th Corps of the Army of Spain from Saragossa to Burgos where it would meet local operational requirements, but where it would also be easier to call for a 'return to France, if the apparently imminent war with Austria should make this necessary'.[218]

While most of the Army of Germany would be employed against the Austrian Main Army, Napoleon designated 10th Corps under his brother Jerome to maintain order between the Rhine and the Elbe, to hold Magdeburg, and to watch the Bohemian border. Jerome's men would also be available to operate against landings on the North Sea coast if required. The corps, however, was a patchwork creation. Based on Jerome's Westphalian army, the mobile elements of the 10th Corps also included a Dutch division, a small contingent from Berg, some of the Saxons left behind once Bernadotte departed for the Danube, and a few French troops. In addition to this field force, 10th Corps had responsibility for the garrisons of Stettin, Küstrin, and French-occupied Swedish Pomerania. Napoleon thus hoped to have a

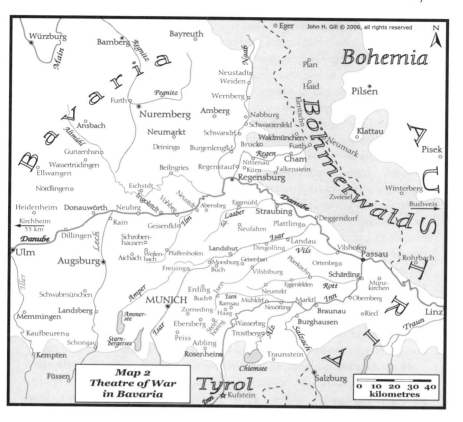

**Map 2
Theatre of War
in Bavaria**

mobile force of at least 14,000 men to operate in central Germany as well as garrisons for the key fortresses in his rear. This number was nearly achieved by early April (12,910 infantry and cavalry), but troop quality was questionable as many of the units were newly created or composed of untrained depot detachments.[219] Leadership, particularly in the Westphalian army, was also problematic. Moreover, the various units were scattered over large areas and unable to act in concert on short notice.

Napoleon was keenly aware of the weaknesses of his reserves and sought to establish conditions under which they could enforce tranquillity in his rear areas without resorting to the chancy business of combat. He thus relied on pervasive deception to intimidate potential adversaries by creating the image of an unassailably powerful force capable of responding quickly and decisively across the face of Germany. 'It would not be a bad idea', he told

Jerome, 'to spread the rumour that you command an army of 40,000 men formed from your troops, the Dutch troops, and a supplement of French.'[220] Furthermore, by granting Jerome's force its imposing title as 10th Corps, he linked it directly to the main French army and hoped to contribute to the impression that it was a fully-formed, combat-ready organisation.

From the Westphalians of 10th Corps deep in the army's rear to the troopers of the 1st French Chasseurs watching their Austrian counterparts on the Bohemian border, Napoleon's astonishing energy and vision, combined with the enormous power of his centralised state apparatus, had managed to assemble a tremendous army on the frontiers of the Habsburg Empire. On 10 April, however, it was still very much in the process of formation. Another seven to ten days were required at a minimum to gather additional reinforcements, assimilate march battalions into their regiments, and move to the locations Napoleon had envisaged in his 30 March 'Instructions'. This situation gave the Army of Germany an ad hoc, 'under-construction' character that had important implications for its structure. Moreover, with much of the old Grande Armée committed to Spain, the new Army of Germany's appearance would be noticeably different from its famous predecessors of 1805, 1806, and 1807. The army would change during the course of the campaign, coming closer to these earlier paradigms, but several points concerning its organisation and composition in the first few days and weeks deserve mention.

In the first place, Napoleon himself was absent, still waiting in Paris when the Austrians crossed the border. As a result, Berthier would have to serve—most uncomfortably—as the interim commander until the emperor could arrive on the scene.[221] Berthier was perhaps not a happy choice for this role, but Napoleon could hardly place a marshal of Massena's pride and prestige under Davout.[222] Nor could he subordinate Davout to Massena. Instead, to clarify the command situation until he could appear, he authorised Berthier to leave Davout in charge his Army of the Rhine units (minus Oudinot) and to give Massena temporary command south of the river if operational exigencies warranted.[223] This logical measure would create two 'wings' of the army in effect, but it did not address Vandamme and could lead to confusion in the various chains of command as units shifted across boundaries. Second, some of the regular features of the Grande Armée were missing initially. There were no Guard units yet available and thus neither an artillery reserve at the army level nor escorts for Napoleon when he reached Germany; in their place he accepted Rheinbund cavalry as his escort, an honour that did much to bind the German soldiers to him personally. Nor was there a true cavalry reserve in the first weeks. Although specified in Napoleon's conception of the army's organisation, the opening of the war found the constituent elements of the future reserve scattered about assigned to individual corps. This dispersal of the cherished heavy cavalry and its attachment to *corps d'armée* was in itself a unique feature of the Army of Germany. Not only was there no cavalry reserve, but its designated commander, Marshal Bessières had not yet reached the theatre of war. Other key imperial luminaries still en route included the 2nd Corps commander Marshal Lannes and Nansouty of the 1st Heavy Cavalry Division, as well as GD Antoine Charles Louis Lasalle and Montbrun, both of whom were to command light divisions of the cavalry reserve.[224]

Finally, the Army of Germany is noteworthy for the large number of Germans within its ranks. Some 80,000 Rheinbund troops were already 'present under arms' when the conflict opened, and many thousands more would find themselves in combat before the year was out. Napoleon's German allies thus played a greater part in 1809 than they had in any previous conflict, especially in the opening battles.[225]

As the chill night fell on 9 April 1809 and thousands of French and Allied soldiers went about the quotidian business of finding food and shelter, Napoleon could be satisfied that his vast energy had brought together the beginnings of a great army in a remarkably short period of time. If the Duchy of Warsaw had only assembled a field force of 15,520 men in distant Poland and the mobile component of Marmont's Army of Dalmatia numbered no more than 11,780, Viceroy Eugene had more than 72,000 immediately at hand in northern Italy and Napoleon could count on at least 160,000 in southern Germany, not including fortress garrisons or the Bavarian troops in the Tyrol.[226] More were on the way: Dupas and Bernadotte in Germany, GD Pierre Durutte in Italy. In addition, there were thousands of replacements collecting in depots or trudging across the miles in march battalions. Thousands more, French and Allied alike, were gathering to join the 12,910 men of 10th Corps in securing the army's strategic rear. It would be many weeks more before all of the rear area security units were in place, but the formed front-line units and most of the new replacements would reach their allotted positions in no more than seven to ten days. This brief window thus represented the period of maximum French vulnerability. It was a time, moreover, during which Napoleon and several other key senior commanders would not be present. The initiative lay with Austria. Having missed the opportunity of striking in March, the question now was whether Archduke Charles and his army could move fast enough and hit hard enough to exploit this French vulnerability and open the campaign with a major victory.

CHAPTER 4

It Is War

Napoleon's achievement in nailing together a large ad hoc army in southern Germany by early April was remarkable and well beyond the capability of any other contemporary state or monarch. His troops were gathering, his intelligence apparatus was busy collecting data from across the continent, and he had promulgated a flexible, reasonable plan as a basis for future operations. Austria, however, held the initiative. As a result, when Charles opened the war on 10 April, he enjoyed two important advantages: he had a slight numerical edge over Napoleon's Army of Germany and his Hauptarmee was much better concentrated than the available French forces.[1]

AUSTRIAN DISPOSITIONS

The Austrian decision to shift the principal line of advance from Bohemia to the Danube valley placed the bulk of the Main Army along the Inn River on 9 April. Though wearied and bedraggled by the long, rain-soaked march from their assembly areas in Bohemia, the six corps with their 127,000 men were well concentrated and poised to invade Bavaria. On the right, collected near Schärding was FML Franz Fürst von Rosenberg with IV Corps, and I Reserve Corps under GdK Johannes Fürst Liechtenstein. Rosenberg's command was the weakest of the line corps: ten battalions and two infantry companies were still en route, while Infantry Regiment No. 40 (former *Josef Mittrowsky*), a squadron of *Stipsicz* Hussars No. 10, and an artillery battery had been detached to blockade the little Bavarian fortress of Oberhaus at Passau.[2] Fourth Corps was thus left with only 15,000 infantry and cavalry on hand in addition to its sixty-two guns. To remedy these deficiencies in part, army headquarters had attached the brigade of GM Peter Freiherr von

Vécsey (6,190 infantry and cavalry) to Rosenberg from II Corps. Vécsey's mission, however, was to form the link with I and II Corps north of the Danube. He was therefore expected to operate semi-independently, brushing the Danube with his right flank as the advance progressed, so Rosenberg could not rely on having this brigade available in his order of battle.

Rosenberg himself was 48, a veteran cavalryman of demonstrated bravery. He had fought against the Turks early in his career, then participated in the campaigns against Revolutionary France in Germany and Switzerland under Charles. Though reputedly a man of few words, he had openly criticised some of the senior leaders in 1800. This, apparently, was not a unique occurrence and he was sent into temporary forced retirement. He was back in service under Charles for the Italian campaign of 1805 at the head of a mixed division of infantry and cavalry, but this experience provided

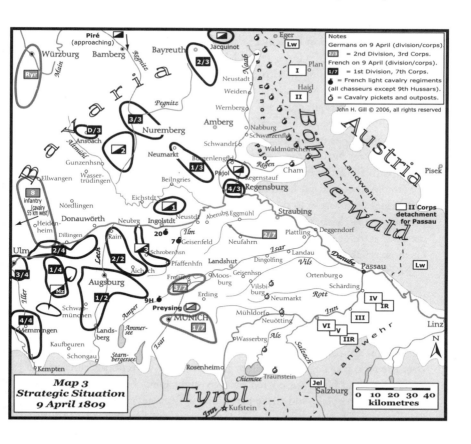

Map 3
Strategic Situation
9 April 1809

Notes
Germans on 9 April (division/corps).
2/3 = 2nd Division, 3rd Corps.
French on 9 April (division/corps).
1/7 = 1st Division, 7th Corps.
● = French light cavalry regiments (all chasseurs except 9th Hussars).
○ = Cavalry pickets and outposts.

John H. Gill © 2006, all rights reserved

only limited background in senior command before his assignment to IV Corps in February 1809.

Fürst Liechtenstein, commanding I Reserve Corps, was another cavalryman who had taken part in the Turkish wars. He had repeatedly distinguished himself in campaigns against France in the Netherlands, Italy, and Germany, culminating in leading the reserve corps that helped to save the army after the disaster at Hohenlinden in December 1800. Five years later, in another calamitous winter campaign, he had been the nominal commander of the Austrian forces at Austerlitz and then served as the principal Austrian negotiator in the diplomacy leading to the Treaty of Pressburg. Competent and courageous if not especially brilliant or imaginative, he was in the curious position of being the prince of a state that belonged to the Rheinbund. His corps, assembling near Schärding, numbered 14,370 grenadiers and cuirassiers backed by thirty-four guns. Missing from the corps order of battle was GM Heinrich Graf Rottermund's dragoon brigade of two regiments; it had been left behind in Bohemia to serve under II Corps.

To the left of IV Corps was FML Friedrich Franz Xavier Fürst von Hohenzollern-Hechingen with the 23,730 men and ninety-six guns of his III Corps. As with Rosenberg, Hohenzollern's command was incomplete, lacking a hussar regiment, two line battalions, a volunteer battalion, and twelve line infantry companies who were still marching to join the army. Hohenzollern was 52 in 1809 and had seen thirty-three years of service under the Habsburgs against the Turks and the French after starting his military career with Holland. He had won acclaim for his performance in Italy from 1797 to 1800, often at the head of small semi-independent commands. He too had a close connection to the Confederation of the Rhine: his elder brother, Hermann Friedrich Otto, was the ruler of Hohenzollern-Hechingen, a member state of the Rheinbund. Charles considered Hohenzollern one of his most reliable subordinates.[3]

Next in line along the Inn was V Corps under one of Charles's younger brothers, FML Archduke Ludwig. Ludwig, 25 years old, had been raised under tutelage arranged by his eldest brother, Kaiser Franz, from the time of their father's death when Ludwig was a boy of 8. Although much of his education focused on military matters, he seems to have evinced neither interest nor aptitude for an army career and turned over his command shortly after the 1809 war began. His corps, gathering near Obernberg, consisted of 23,840 foot and horse supported by sixty-eight guns, but was missing two battalions of regulars and three battalions of Vienna Volunteers when the conflict opened. Noteworthy in V Corps was the presence of the future

Field Marshal Josef Radetzky, then a talented major general and commander of the corps' advance guard. Weak leadership at the top, however, would hamper the corps in the April battles and make its morale vulnerable to the shock of setbacks.

FML von Hiller commanded the 31,790 men and ninety-six guns of VI Corps. Unlike many of the other corps, Hiller's command had all of its assigned regular troops and was only missing its allotted three battalions of Vienna Volunteers. Hiller, aged 61, had first donned a uniform in 1763 and had extensive experience in the Turkish wars (1788–91), in fighting against France, and along the Military Border in Croatia. Though little better than an adequate commander, he was superior to most of his compatriots in many respects and could display occasional flashes of determination and competence. The son of a self-made army officer, he was the only corps commander who had not been born into the old aristocracy, a fact that speaks well for his abilities as compared with his peers. He was also one of the few with considerable experience as an independent commander. At the same time, he was an ambitious, outspoken, and sometimes unruly subordinate whose stubbornness and refractory behaviour led to a clash with Charles in 1808 over issues associated with the administration of the Grenzer in Croatia. He also seems to have exhibited a tendency towards mulish sullenness when he felt thwarted or slighted. This trait and his strained relationship with Charles boded ill for smooth and prompt functioning of the army's chain of command.[4]

While most of Hiller's large corps was assembling at Braunau, FML Franz Freiherr Jellacic de Buzim was detached to Salzburg with his division of 9,340 men and fourteen guns. From that city, he was to advance on Munich and protect the left flank of the Main Army as it launched itself across the Inn. His division was also to send a small detachment into the Tyrol to support the planned uprising against the Bavarians. Unfortunately for Austria, Jellacic proved a poor choice for this independent command. 'It is difficult to comprehend', writes a noted Austrian military historian, 'why the Austrian military leadership again entrusted such an influential and independent command to a man who had, to the great detriment of the state, repeatedly displayed his haplessness and utter incapacity in difficult situations.'[5] Moreover, the detachment left Hiller with only 22,450 troops and eighty-two guns, thus giving that prickly general another cause for complaint against Charles.[6]

The final regular formation in the Danube valley was FML Michael Freiherr Kienmayer's small II Reserve Corps. Assigned to Braunau to cross

the Inn behind Hiller, Kienmayer had only 6,690 men and twenty guns at
his disposal in five grenadier battalions and two regiments each of dragoons
and cuirassiers. The bulk of Kienmayer's thirty-five-year military career
had been in the cavalry, and he had shown himself to be a bold and resolute
soldier capable of commanding small independent forces. These qualities
would prove useful in the latter part of the 1809 war, but were wasted in his
role at the head of II Reserve Corps.[7]

Table 5: Austrian Main Army—Units Detached or Not Arrived on 10 April

Infantry and cavalry only. Units in parentheses not included in strength
calculations

	Detached	En Route	approx. strength
I Corps	III/*A. Mittrowsky* III/*Erbach* 2 Sqdns/*Schwarz.* Uhlans	1st, 2nd Moravian Volunteers	4,980
II Corps	III/*J. Colloredo* (Oberhaus*) (one brigade detached to IV Corps)	–	1,340
III Corps	–	III/*Würzburg* III/*Württemberg* 3rd *EH Karl* Legion Two companies each from III Battalions of: 1, 7, 12, 20, 29, 56 Inf *Hessen-Homburg* Hussars	7,480
IV Corps	(Oberhaus*)	*Deutsch-Banat* Grenz *Wallach-Illyria* Grenz* 5th, 6th *EH Karl* Legion III Bns of: 9th, 44th, 46th, 55th Inf Two companies each from III Bns of: 22, 40* Inf	12,630
V Corps	–	III/*Stain* III/*Beaulieu* 1st, 2nd, 3rd Vienna Vols.	5,680

VI Corps	–	4th, 5th, 6th Vienna Vols.	3,000
I Reserve Corps	(one cavalry brigade detached to II Corps)	–	0
II Reserve Corps	–	–	0
Total	3 x battalions	23 x battalions	35,110
	2 x squadrons	16 x companies	
		8 x squadrons	

*Additionally, the following were detached for the blockade of Oberhaus (Passau):

II Corps	IV Corps
III/18th Inf. (former *Stuart*)	40th Inf. (former *J. Mittrowsky*) (minus two comps)
Plt/*Merveldt* Uhlans	Sqdn/*Stipsicz* Hussars
	6-pdr battery

Note: The *Wallach-Illyria* Grenz Regiment No. 13 later replaced Inf. Regt. No. 40 at Oberhaus.
Source: Krieg, vol. I, Annex XIII.

A string of Landwehr battalions covered the frontier behind the regular forces. GM Ignaz Freiherr von Legisfeld had the four Salzburg battalions, the 3rd Innviertel and two battalions from Oberst Thomas MacDermott's brigade (1st and 2nd Hausrück) on the left at Salzburg. Legisfeld's command was to support Jellacic's advance and the small incursion into the Tyrol. MacDermott, on the other hand, was posted at Braunau with his three Traunviertel battalions, while the 2nd Innviertel was detached from his brigade and placed at Hochburg under the commandant of Braunau. Oberst Hermann Nesslinger von Schelgengraben commanded a brigade of four battalions at Münzkirchen near Schärding, but Nesslinger himself and six companies were to participate in the blockade of Passau.[8] Just north of the Danube, GM Rudolf Graf Sinzendorf and his brigade of four Mühlviertel battalions were south of Rohrbach. They were to seal the ring around Passau from the Bohemian side.[9] The next section of the border in Bohemia was held by the ten Landwehr battalions of GM Johann von Richter's brigade. Richter, with a small regular detachment of regular troops from II Corps and his headquarters at Winterberg, was also slated to support the investment of Passau, but his ten battalions were spread along the frontier as far as Klattau.

GM Friedrich von Oberdorf covered the frontier on both sides of Eger with eight Landwehr battalions and a squadron of *Schwarzenberg* Uhlans on or near the border and an additional four Landwehr battalions assembled in the Beraun Forest to the rear.[10] Finally, to guard against an incursion from Saxony, GM Karl Freiherr Am Ende commanded a brigade six Landwehr battalions in and around Theresienstadt, supplemented by two line battalions and another *Schwarzenberg* squadron.[11]

Between Oberdorf's and Richter's Landwehr brigades were the two regular corps that constituted the northern wing of the Austrian offensive. On the left was II Corps, just south-west of Haid with 23,420 men and sixty-five guns under Feldzeugmeister (FZM) Johann Karl Graf Kolowrat-Krakowsky. Most of the units allotted to II Corps were on hand on 9 April, but the corps' prescribed order of battle had been altered in several ways. As we have seen, Vécsey's brigade had been detached to IV Corps and Kolowrat had received Rottermund's two dragoon regiments as partial compensation. One infantry battalion (III/*Josef Colloredo*) was absent quelling a mutiny among Bohemian Landwehr and another battalion (III/*Stuart*) along with a platoon of *Merveldt* Uhlans and a half-battery were sent south to assist in the blockade of Passau under Richter's command. Furthermore, within his own resources, Kolowrat decided to form a strong advance guard of six battalions and most of his cavalry under FML Johann Graf Klenau. Even this advance guard lacked some of its elements: a company of the 8th Jägers and some *Merveldt* Uhlans were detached to advance up the Waldmünchen road on the left flank of the corps. The remaining troops came under two rather unbalanced infantry divisions, each with three squadrons of *Erzherzog Johann* Dragoons.

A scion of one of the oldest noble families in Bohemia, Kolowrat, at 61, was in his forty-third year of military service to the House of Habsburg. He had begun his career in 1766 in the cavalry, but switched to an infantry regiment when he purchased his captaincy in 1768. Having demonstrated great courage against the Turks, he changed branches again when he moved to the artillery in 1792. He had a reputation for chivalry and fairness that was apparently rewarded by the loyalty of his subordinates, but he had never commanded a major field formation in a campaign of manoeuvre, let alone an organisation such as the corps that now stood under his orders.

On Kolowrat's right was GdK Bellegarde's I Corps. The 53-year-old Bellegarde had been born in Dresden and began his military life in the electoral Saxon army. He transferred to Austrian service in 1772 and came to know Charles well while serving on the archduke's staff in 1796. He had been entrusted with the Austrian army in Italy during the retreat from Marengo in 1800 and had remained in Italy during the peaceful years thereafter as army commander until he led the centre at Caldiero in 1805, again under Charles. As with Hohenzollern, Charles considered Bellegarde a reliable officer who exhibited conspicuous courage on the battlefield. The Habsburg authorities saw him as a possible army commander (after Liechtenstein) should Charles be incapacitated.

Bellegarde's corps consisted of 25,700 cavalry and infantry with sixty-two guns that he organised into an advance guard, two divisions, and a composite reserve. As with the other corps, several units were missing from his order of battle as the initial campaign opened: two battalions of Moravian volunteers (4th *Erzherzog Karl* Legion had been assigned in their stead), as well as two line battalions and two squadrons of *Schwarzenberg* Uhlans that had been detached to support the Landwehr on the Bohemian border. In overall command of the advance of I and II Corps, Bellegarde was also to exercise control over the Landwehr, depot troops and fortresses in Bohemia.

As the Austrian battalions were closing on their assembly areas, the Habsburg leadership was concluding its final preparations for war. On 6 April, Charles left Vienna for the Inn, the Bavarian border was closed to all traffic, and Austrian troops assumed outposts along the frontier.[12] The 6th also saw Charles issue a stirring order of the day announcing to the soldiery that 'the defence of the fatherland calls us to new deeds' and appealing to the men to 'loose the chains' of their 'German brothers' who would soon be joining in the fight against 'the common foe'. Meanwhile, a host of printing presses was busily engaged in finishing two other proclamations, one addressed 'To the German Nation' and the other to the 'Brave Warriors of Bavaria'. Designed to make the hope of German defection from Napoleon a reality, thousands of copies were to be distributed by the army as it advanced into Bavaria.

In Vienna that evening, Stadion expressed this hope when he told Charles Stuart, the unauthorised British representative, that many in Germany were 'ready to rise against the Enemy on the appearance of the first Austrian Soldier'. Stadion, however, also provided further evidence of the complete breakdown of Austrian political–military co-ordination. Although he was the chief promoter of the coming war and despite the influence that close associates of his had exerted to shift the Hauptarmee from Bohemia to the Danube, it seems that Stadion had only the vaguest notion of the army's plans. Talking to Stuart, who had arrived in the Habsburg capital that very day, he stated that Austria had three of its corps in Bohemia; of these, Bellegarde would strike north towards Dresden and Kolowrat would advance on Bayreuth, while Rosenberg marched through Waldmünchen to defeat Wrede at Straubing before joining Charles 'in the vicinity of Munich'.[13] He even suggested that any French reinforcements withdrawn from Spain would be sent to Italy 'where Bonaparte means to command in person'. What is one to make of this exposition, so at odds with reality? These are not items of military trivia, but important aspects of strategy with direct relevance to diplomacy (Prussia's stance, the attitudes of the key Rheinbund princes, etc.). The foreign minister can reasonably be expected to have mastered such operational information, especially given the life-or-death character he personally ascribed to this war. Either Stadion had no idea of the army's actual intentions or he was deliberately misleading the presumed agent of a much-sought ally for no apparent reason. In either case, Stuart instantly perceived the weakness of the strategy as explained to him and, at the risk of appearing 'invidious', he 'hazarded' his own 'reflection upon what is here the object of enthusiasm and admiration': 'I cannot but consider that these corps, like so many rays diverging from the same centre, though at first successful, will progressively grow weaker as they advance towards the enemy's frontier'. Still, he chided himself for unfairly entertaining 'such views' and concluded that 'something decisive may be looked for hourly'.[14]

While Stuart pondered Stadion's remarks, Austrian preparations along the frontier continued apace. On 8 April, Charles sent one of his adjutants to convey a conciliatory letter to Bavaria's King Max Joseph, declaring his intention to enter Bavaria but promising not to treat the kingdom as a hostile land until Max Joseph had determined his government's policy. Also on the 8th, Kaiser Franz left Vienna and released a proclamation of his own announcing his departure for the front to be with the 'brave defenders of the fatherland' on the empire's frontiers and calling on all of his subjects to make sacrifices for the monarchy.[15] Supplementing all of these noble sentiments, troop morale was also to be raised by the provision of a free ration of brandy and meat as well as the distribution of a cash 'gratuity' equivalent to three days' pay.

On an equally practical note, the generalissimus arrived at his headquarters in Ried on 7 April. He called his corps commanders and FML Jellacic to a meeting there on the morning of the 8th to have the final orders for the invasion read aloud and handed out in written form. In typical Austrian fashion, this disposition occupied seven densely written pages and required a two-page supplement.[16] The army staff also prepared a host of other directives specifying roads to be taken, the order of march within each column, logistical arrangements, and the allocation of artillery batteries. Charles was confident that the army would encounter no serious resistance for the first few days of the war and used these initial instructions to detail the army's movements through to 12 April. At that point, he hoped to have concentrated the bulk of the Hauptarmee tightly along the line of Eggenfelden-Pfarrkirchen (III, IV, V, and I Reserve Corps), with VI Corps just behind at Wurmannsquick and II Reserve Corps further back at Obertürken. The specifics of this initial concept did not survive the first day of the invasion, and Charles would make adjustments to accommodate his growing concern for reports of French forces on the Lech, but the general idea of an advance to the Isar remained consistent during the opening phase of the campaign.[17]

Hiller used the meeting to argue, apparently with some vigour, that the detachment of Jellacic to the far left flank was a wasteful diversion. He proposed instead that he be allowed to march his entire corps down the Inn to Füssen, where he believed he would be in a position to force Massena out of Augsburg and make himself master of Donauwörth and the upper Danube. None of the other corps commanders supported him, and Charles curtly dismissed this wildly unrealistic proposal, so that Hiller departed feeling resentful and self-righteous.[18]

Hiller's willingness to take the initiative was evident again on 9 April. That afternoon, he mustered his advance guard in the main square of Braunau having noted that the only reaction on the Bavarian side to the recent Austrian activity was that the customs official on the Inn River bridge had closed the tollgate and that two Bavarian chevaulegers had ridden off at full gallop to report the Austrian movements. While Hiller was busy with his troops, two generals and two colonels from the army staff had approached the customs man and endeavoured to persuade him to open the gate. This worthy official rebuffed their entreaties and refused again when Hiller himself repeated the request. Hiller thereupon ordered sappers to force the gate before the Bavarians could take steps to destroy the bridge. When FML Grünne, one of the staff officers on the bridge, asked if Hiller had reported his actions to Charles, the haughty commander stiffly replied that Grünne could accept the report on the spot as a representative of army headquarters and proceeded to send a detachment across the river.[19] There was a tiny flurry of activity at Schärding in the IV Corps zone as well, when two men of *Czartoryski* Infantry No. 9 seized a Bavarian vedette around midnight, but the corps did not actually begin to cross until the predawn hours of 10 April.[20]

OVER THE RUBICON AND INTO BAVARIA:
THE AUSTRIAN OFFENSIVE OPENS

'My Dearest Uncle,' wrote Charles to Herzog Albert of Sachsen-Teschen on 8 April from Ried, 'I arrived here yesterday and not without suffering considerably from the cold ... everything here is covered with snow. I will depart after dinner for Altheim, I will be at Braunau tomorrow evening, and the day after tomorrow I will cross my Rubicon before the break of day ...'[21]

The Rubicon metaphor also occurred to other Austrians in April 1809. One of these was Carl Friedrich Freiherr Kübeck von Kübau, a war ministry official travelling with the army, who wrote in his diary that 'Thus was the Rubicon crossed, by a Caesar against an emperor.'[22] There was a general sense of embarking on something grand and momentous, but emotions were mixed: enthusiastic cheers for Charles as he rode across the bridge at Braunau mingling with foreboding and uncertainty as unexpected problems arose during the early stages of the army's advance.

The crossing of the Inn on 10 April, however, proceeded without a hitch. Vécsey's brigade led the way at Schärding, passing over the intact bridge at 4 a.m. and turning to the north-west to assume his role as the right flank guard of IV Corps. He was followed by GM Josef Reinwald von Waldegg with a detachment destined for Passau to seal the southern segment of the ring around the Bavarian fortress at Oberhaus. Next came GM von Stutterheim at the head of the IV Corps advance guard, then the main body of IV Corps, and finally Liechtenstein's I Reserve Corps. The III Corps advance guard crossed in boats at Obernberg to provide security for a pontoon bridge to be constructed near Mühlheim. This work having been accomplished between 4 a.m. and 10 a.m., the bulk of the corps marched across and headed for Rotthalmünster. Charles placed these three northern corps temporarily under Liechtenstein while he himself crossed at Braunau with VI Corps, followed by V Corps. Kienmayer's II Reserve Corps remained on the Austrian side of the Inn. FML Jellacic and his division remained around Salzburg, but he sent a small detachment of regulars and Landwehr into the Tyrol under Oberstleutnant Paul Freiherr von Taxis to show support for the uprising there and to establish communications with Chasteler's detachment as it advanced up the Pusterthal.[23]

By the evening of the 10th, Vécsey was at Ortenburg, IV Corps on the post road south of Griesbach, and III Corps at Rotthalmünster, all with advance detachments posted further to the north and west. First Reserve Corps bivouacked just across the Inn from Schärding. Of the southern group,

VI Corps had its advance guard at Marktl, where the bridge had fallen into its hands intact. Patrols reported, however, that Bavarian light cavalry had burned the span at Neuötting. The main body of the corps camped around Stammham with V Corps behind it on the road to Braunau. Second Reserve Corps settled into billets in Braunau where Charles had established the army's headquarters. Nowhere during the day had the Austrians encountered active resistance.

Despite the generally favourable outcome of the first day's operations, the Austrian army was already experiencing severe problems. First, the weather was execrable. 'The regiment arrived late at the riverbank,' recorded Oberleutnant Pierre-Martin Pirquet of the *Beaulieu* Infantry No. 58 in V Corps, 'the weather was abominable and it snowed continually.'[24] The incessant precipitation turned roads into muddy sloughs, retarding the

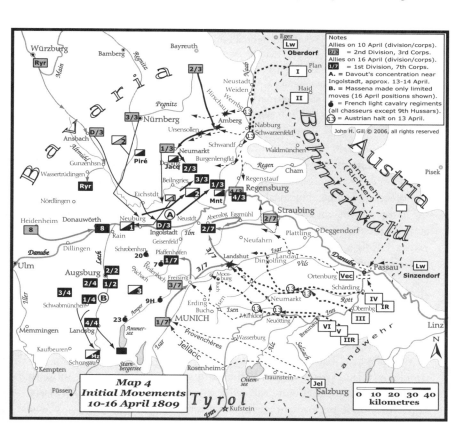

army's movements and ruining equipment. Poor march discipline made the situation worse. As a consequence, the frequent delays along the route were lengthy and enervating, accentuating the misery of the common soldiers.[25] Furthermore, in an effort to limit the depredations caused by the invasion and thus win Bavaria to the Habsburg cause, Charles had directed that the army would bivouac in Bavaria rather than quarter itself on the population. Cold, hungry, exhausted, and thoroughly soaked after hours of slogging through the cloying mud, the soldiers could only look forward to a night in cramped and cheerless camps on rain-drenched fields. Health and morale suffered. Another Oberleutnant, Karl Johann Ritter von Grueber of the *Herzog Albert* Cuirassiers No. 3, noted the effect on his men when they were caught in a sudden storm:

> The gale drove the gouts of rain so heavily against the heads of our horses, that all of them, throughout the entire column, even as we marched one behind the other four abreast, turned right about as if on command and reversed the heading of the column. We had to exert all our strength to turn the horses back and continue our march. For a time, our men regarded this accidental and easily explained phenomenon as an evil omen, and we officers had considerable trouble removing this disheartening image from their minds. We marched in the heaviest rain under lightning and thunder through the day and into the sinking night without a pause . . .[26]

Compounding the negative impact of the rain, snow, and cold was the failure of the logistics train to meet the soldiers' most basic needs. Several factors combined to hamper logistical and administrative support of the army. In the first place, the underlying assumption was that the invading troops would support themselves from the new 'mobile magazines', but these organisations proved hardly mobile at all. Ponderous and slow, they were too far to the rear and arrangements to send wagons back for replenishment from the heads of the columns only served to exacerbate the excruciating traffic situation on the muddy and over-crowded roads. Second, the Austrians had hoped that requisitioning would supplement supplies from the mobile magazines, but this practice was inhibited by the desire to limit the invasion's impact on the Bavarian population. Moreover, the Austrian army was neither accustomed to nor adept at requisitioning and in many places the local citizenry was decidedly unco-operative. Third, the army's logistical personnel seem to have done little to ameliorate 'the awkwardness of the entire administrative apparatus', their performance was characterised rather by indolence and incapacity.[27] As early as 11 April, Charles complained to Karl Graf Zichy, the army minister:

> During the advance of our army yesterday, the arrangements for subsistence were extraordinarily poor, or, better stated, no arrangements were made at all. The soldier, uncared for, was left to his own devices ... the consequence of these poor arrangements was that the civilian inhabitants fled into the hills and left us an empty landscape ...[28]

Strict new orders were issued to regulate march columns and the administrative personnel were chastised, but little real improvement resulted. The army was simply unprepared for rapid, mobile warfare. What did result was an operational pause. On the evening of 12 April, only three days into the campaign, Charles declared the 13th as a rest day. The archduke hoped that this break would give the troops a chance to repair shoes, harness, and other equipment while allowing the mobile magazines to catch up. The pause was certainly beneficial, but the supply system remained problematic when the advance resumed on the 14th. In III Corps, for instance, the logistical apparatus proved incapable of delivering a free issue of wine that Charles had granted to the men to boost morale.

The 'diabolical weather', poor march organisation, and a general lack of urgency had also resulted in limited advances.[29] On 11 April, for example, Vécsey's men only made sixteen to seventeen kilometres. Third Corps recorded similar progress and none of the other columns achieved much more. By the 12th, the Main Army had only reached the line from Eichendorf on the right (Vécsey) through Pfarrkirchen and Eggenfelden to Mühldorf on the left wing (Hiller). This was more or less as Charles had specified in his 8 April conference, but it hardly represented a major accomplishment. No significant movements occurred on the 13th, but the renewal of the march on 14 April saw a reprise of the previous difficulties with III Corps spending thirteen painful hours on the road to advance a mere eighteen kilometres.

The want of enterprise and organisation was also reflected in the collection and reporting of intelligence. Although Radetzky, leading the V Corps advance guard, performed very well and Stutterheim at the head of IV Corps reported what he could uncover, few of their fellows matched their efforts.[30] Charles, who had lamented that he 'knew little of the strength, organisation, and movements of the French troops' before he crossed the Inn, found himself equally ignorant as he pushed into Bavaria and desperately needed good intelligence.[31] The limited information that did make its way to headquarters was vague, contradictory, and often days out of date. As one staff officer saw things, Austrian intelligence capabilities were 'at such a level of infancy' that the army was left nearly blind and could only 'tap its way forward in a foreign land as if in a fog'.[32] Furthermore, reporting was often inexplicably lethargic. In one especially egregious example, an important 10 April report from Vécsey only reached Charles on the 13th.[33] By that time it was virtually useless.

The renewed Austrian advance on 14 April reflected Charles's evolving perception of the operational situation. As early as the 11th, he seems to have concluded that the Allied forces south of the Danube were concentrating on the Lech (as indeed Napoleon intended) and that only the Bavarians stood between him and the Danube.[34] Moreover, he apparently believed that he could gather the Hauptarmee in the space south of Regensburg and unite with Bellegarde's two corps without fighting a major engagement.[35] Looking forward from the 13th, the next major obstacle was the Isar. Charles saw Landshut as the most advantageous crossing point over this river and told Kaiser Franz that he hoped to force a passage there on the 17th or 18th. He also wrote to Bellegarde, instructing him to arrive at Regensburg at the same time that the Main Army passed the Isar.[36] The dispositions for 14 April therefore directed the V, III, I Reserve, and II Reserve Corps towards Landshut with IV Corps on the right towards Frontenhausen and VI Corps south-west of Neumarkt on the left.

'Tapping their way' northward on the 14th in accordance with this operational concept, the Main Army's advance units had their first encounters with the foe. In the VI Corps zone, a half-squadron of the *Liechtenstein* Hussars from GM Armand von Nordmann's avant-garde skirmished with the Bavarian 4th Chevaulegers at Erding.[37] Further south, two squadrons of *Liechtenstein* attacked and scattered forty or fifty troopers of the Bavarian 1st Chevaulegers at Ramsau. The Bavarians lost eighteen men and Chef d'Escadron Gabriel Montélégier, one of Lefebvre's staff officers, was almost captured in the melee.[38] Bavarian dragoons also fired on parts of Jellacic's division near Wasserburg during the day. In all of these cases, the Bavarians retired, but the active resistance indicated that Max Joseph's army would oppose the Austrian invasion. Efforts to subvert or disarm Bavarian forces bore no fruit.[39]

Other than these fleeting cavalry squabbles, 14 April was much like the preceding days: a long, slow slog over miserable roads. By the end of the day, Vécsey was astride the Isar at Landau and Stutterheim's advance patrols were ensconced in Dingolfing where they trapped and captured a handful of Bavarian troopers. There were no serious enemy forces in sight. As noted above, V Corps had patrols in Landshut, while Hiller's forward troops were near Aich, Erding, and Haag. Although these patrols had reached the Isar, the vast bulk of the army was still tightly packed in and around Neumarkt. Other than small outposts, even the advance guards had still not reached the river in most cases. The rain had let up but the weather remained cold and raw.

The rain returned on the 15th and the army dragged itself toward the Isar under the seemingly ceaseless downpour. There were several encounters with Bavarians, but almost no actual fighting. Instead, curious palavers ensued, during which Bavarian officers at Landshut and Dingolfing notified their Habsburg counterparts that they were under orders to treat the Austrians as enemies. Austrian efforts to negotiate safe passage failed.[40]

These minor incidents had no influence on the ponderous Austrian advance. By nightfall on the 15th, Vécsey had his brigade across the river at Hienhart and had ordered the local Bavarian authorities to repair the bridge at Straubing (destroyed on Wrede's orders on the 9th). Advance guard elements from the other corps had closed on the Isar at Dingolfing, Wörth, Landshut, and Moosburg. The bridge at Dingolfing had already been secured by IV Corps, and a VI Corps advance guard detachment under Major Karl von Scheibler rapidly repaired the span at Moosburg after the Bavarian company guarding it withdrew. All of the detachments in these forward locations were small: Scheibler, for instance, had only one battalion, two squadrons, and two companies of Grenzer.[41] The main power of the Austrian Hauptarmee was still many muddy miles to the rear: IV Corps around Frontenhausen, VI Corps at Velden, and V Corps on the Landshut road between Geisenhausen and Zeiling, with III Corps and the two reserve corps stacked up behind it all the way to Neumarkt. Further to the rear, the six battalions of Vienna Volunteers, finally across the Inn, were slowly making their way to the army.[42] Jellacic had his main body at Peiss and GM Karl Dollmayer von Provenchères's division at Zorneding, but forward patrols reached the gates of Munich near evening to learn that the city was undefended and that the court had fled.

Meanwhile, Charles had changed his mind about the little fortress of Oberhaus above Passau. He had initially envisaged a simple blockade operation that could be entrusted to the Landwehr, but he now decided that the fortress had to be reduced rapidly. The Landwehr having shown themselves flighty, ill-equipped, and discontented with serving outside Austria, on 14 April Charles issued orders diverting the *Wallach-Illyria* Grenz

Regiment No. 13 from IV Corps to FML Josef von Dedovich's blockading force. Furthermore, he authorised Dedovich to retain the services of his other regular troops pending the arrival of the Grenzer. For several days in mid-April therefore, the 900 Bavarians and French in Oberhaus absorbed the attentions of almost ten times their number in Austrians. The vigilant and well-provisioned defenders evinced no inclination to surrender.[43]

RAIN, UNCERTAINTY, AND CAUTION:
BELLEGARDE ENTERS BAVARIA

As Charles and the Main Army invaded Bavaria across the Inn, Bellegarde was advancing from Bohemia with I and II Corps. Like Charles, Bellegarde delivered a curt letter of intent to the French outposts on 9 April: 'Sir, according to a declaration from His Majesty the Emperor of Austria to the Emperor Napoleon, I have the honour to inform the officer commanding the French outposts that I have orders to advance with the troops under my command and to treat as enemies all those who offer me resistance.'[44] Many of the men had bivouacked in the snow on the night of 9/10 April, but early the following morning, the two corps crossed the border with the soldiers cheering the advance and acclaiming their monarch despite the foul weather.[45] The distribution of the three-days' pay as a gratuity also helped to boost spirits among the troops.[46]

Bellegarde's strategic situation replicated that of the Main Army in miniature. Just as Charles had a chance, albeit limited, to catch elements of Napoleon's Army of Germany and defeat them in detail, Bellegarde stood before a fleeting opportunity to smash Friant's division of Davout's corps if he could move rapidly. Friant, stretched between Bayreuth and Haag, was considerably closer to his Austrian enemies than he was to his own corps. His infantry regiments would require at least a day to assemble, and the available light cavalry was even more dispersed. A quick strike by Bellegarde's two corps could conceivably snare and break Friant's command before Davout could come to its assistance.

Unfortunately for Austria, the northern arm of the invasion was hampered by cautious, indecisive leadership and by the same dreadful weather that soaked the whitecoats crossing the Inn. Success depended on speed, but Colonel André Méda, commanding the 1st Chasseurs-à-Cheval, reported on 10 April that the Austrians 'are marching very slowly, I do not think they will pass the Naab today.'[47] Indeed not: Bellegarde had planned completely ordinary marches and did not intend to unite his two corps

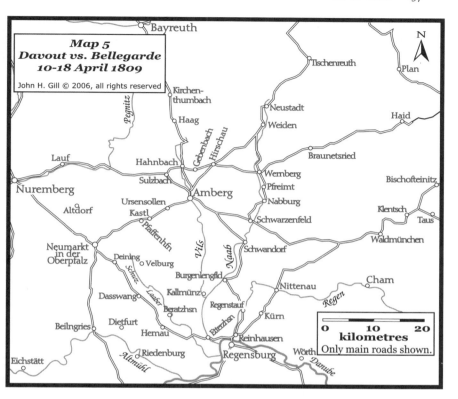

Map 5
Davout vs. Bellegarde
10-18 April 1809

N

around Wernberg on the Naab until 12 April. From Wernberg, he would be able to operate toward Nuremberg, Neumarkt, or Regensburg as the situation demanded. However, with only vague instructions at hand and with no reliable communications to Charles, Bellegarde's initiative and intuition would determine the army's actions once it reached Wernberg.

Friant moved to a different clock. Without waiting for directions from Davout, he issued orders to begin assembling his division towards Amberg. The weather was no better for the French, of course—'much snow fell during those two days' as trooper Charles Henri Lejeune of the 11th Chasseurs noted[48]—but by dint of hard marching, Friant had gathered his regiments around Amberg by the evening of the 11th. The following day, undisturbed by the enemy, he crossed the Vils and took up a position at Neumarkt.[49] Davout could report with satisfaction that 'General Friant did not lose a single wagon during his march.'[50]

Morale in 3rd Corps was good despite the ugly weather. Hippolyte d'Espinchal, capitaine adjutant-major in the 5th Hussars, recalled that news of the Austrian invasion 'was greeted by the regiment with repeated cries of "Vive l'Empereur!"' and the 15th Léger's Capitaine Coudreux wrote confidently to his brother that the corps was 'quite well disposed to open the ball whenever they want; too bad for those who lose the measure'.[51]

SKIRMISHING WITH DAVOUT: HIRSCHAU, AMBERG, URSENSOLLEN, REINHAUSEN (11–15 APRIL)

On the Austrian side, I and II Corps reached their concentration areas along the Naab near Wernberg on 12 April as planned, after three days of slogging through the freezing rain along narrow mountain roads. Resistance had been light. In most cases, French scouts and pickets had withdrawn without opposing the Austrian advance. The only skirmish took place on 11 April at Hirschau as an advance detachment from II Corps under Oberst Josef Steffanini probed west from Wernberg. Learning that the French held Hirschau in some strength and therefore posed a potential threat to II Corps around Wernberg, Steffanini decided to attack. With 800 men of his own 7th Jägers and 260 troopers in two squadrons of *Merveldt* Uhlans, he pushed elements of Colonel Méda's 1st Chasseurs (approximately 300 troopers) back through the town and managed to occupy a ridge line just to the west, deploying his Jägers as skirmishers on both sides of the road and holding the uhlans in reserve. Méda's chasseurs rallied on a battalion of the 33rd Ligne near Gebenbach and were reinforced by a battalion of the 111th Ligne and two 4-pounders from Hahnbach, but the French showed no inclination to press matters and the little action ended at nightfall with Steffanini still in possession of Hirschau. The French, their mission of covering their own division's movements accomplished, withdrew early the following morning.[52] The French lost some twenty-two men in this engagement, the Austrians fifty-two, most of them from the 7th Jägers.[53] In his report, Steffanini praised his detachment and explained 'the high casualties among the Jäger of my battalion' by claiming that 'the excessive zeal and good will of the men, among whom are many brand new recruits', made it difficult to hold them back in combat.[54] One may assume that inadequate training was also an important contributing factor.

Reconnaissance and security detachments such as Steffanini's continued to explore the countryside west and south of the Naab as the main bodies of the two corps settled their cantonments on the 12th. Second Corps lay stretched between Pfreimt and Schwarzenfeld with GM Ludwig Karl Graf

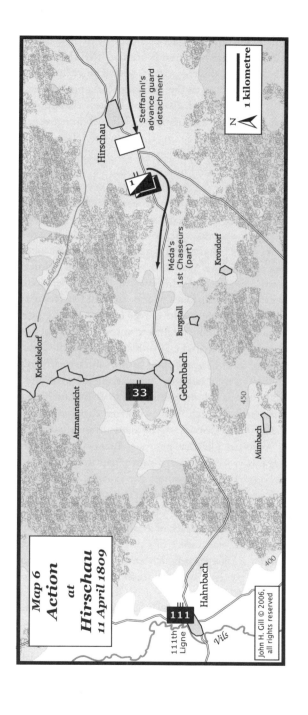

Map 6
Action
at
Hirschau
11 April 1809

Steffanini's
advance guard
detachment

Hirschau

1

Méda's
1st Chasseurs
(part)

Krondorf

Burgstall

Krickelsdorf

Gebenbach

33

Atzmannsricht

450

Mimbach

N

1 kilometre

T. Schweinbach

Hahnbach

111

111th
Ligne

Vils

400

John H. Gill © 2006,
all rights reserved

Folliot de Crenneville's advance guard brigade at Schwandorf to the south, scouting towards Burgenlengfeld and Nittenau. FML Klenau and the rest of the II Corps advance guard were posted west of the Naab; its detachments entered Amberg and reported French outposts near Ursensollen on the Neumarkt road. Bellegarde's I Corps took over the previous II Corps encampments at Wernberg with its advance guard on the road to Hirschau and other security elements screening the army's northern flank.

Having accomplished the first stage of his plan by uniting his two corps at Wernberg, Bellegarde lapsed into inaction. His situation was unenviable: he had no information on the Main Army, he was uncertain about enemy activity and, just as the Main Army, his force was suffering from the miserable weather and serious logistical problems. Assessing these circumstances, Bellegarde reached the same conclusion as Charles and ordered his two corps to rest on 13 April. That evening he compounded his error by deciding to hold in place on the 14th as well. He based this decision on erroneous intelligence that the French had reinforced their troops in Neumarkt and on his concern over the continuing lack of contact with Charles. Fearing that the French might threaten his right if he moved on Regensburg as Kolowrat was suggesting, and anxious that he might err in some way, Bellegarde elected to wait. He did not move the main body of his force until the 15th, and this was only a minor change as II Corps shifted from Nabburg to Schwandorf and I Corps took its place in the Nabburg–Schwarzenfeld area. The fundamental result remained a pointless operational pause on the northern front from 13 to 15 April. Any chance to catch Friant's isolated division was lost.

While the main bodies of I and II Corps lingered on the Naab, Friant had kept the Austrian advance guard elements busy. From Neumarkt, where his division covered 3rd Corps' movement to the Danube, he ordered Méda to reconnoitre towards Amberg on 13 April with two squadrons of his 1st Chasseurs and two voltigeur companies from the 111th Ligne. Easily driving in the uhlan picket at Ursensollen, Méda came upon their supports approximately four kilometres west of Amberg at 6 a.m. and a lively skirmish ensued. The Austrians, two squadrons of *Merveldt* Uhlans and a company of 8th Jägers under Major Emanuel Mensdorff, were determined and well posted. The combat swayed back and forth for some time until Mensdorff, wounded and feeling outnumbered, withdrew through Amberg, hoping for reinforcements.[55] Méda, on the other hand, feared a trap and restrained his troopers from entering the town. Luckily for the Austrians, Oberst Steffanini and his 7th Jägers appeared on the scene by accident shortly after 9 a.m. Steffanini immediately sent his men forward and Méda, his command tired and outnumbered, fell back slowly on his supports in the long, forested defile between Ursensollen and Kastl.[56] The morning's encounter cost each side some forty men killed and wounded, but the bold French advance may have contributed to convincing Bellegarde that the enemy was at Neumarkt in strength and that his two corps could not risk a march south to Regensburg.[57]

On the French side, Friant was convinced that 'the enemy will attempt to take his revenge and will move against me in force' following Méda's success at Amberg.[58] He therefore moved the 15th Léger and two 4-pounders to Kastl to reinforce the 1st Chasseurs.[59] Meanwhile, the commander of the I Corps advance guard, FML Johann Karl Graf Fresnel von Hennequin, had received orders to push his outposts west to Kastl so that Klenau and the II Corps troops could shift south. A lively but pointless fusillade thus developed when GM Ferdinand Freiherr von Winzingerode-Ohmfeld brought the 3rd Jägers and two squadrons of *Blankenstein* Hussars against the French position on the morning of 14 April. Coming upon this scene Fresnel was annoyed by the waste of ammunition. Content to observe the French, he ordered the cavalry to dismount and the Jägers to cease firing.[60] Friant, on the other hand, wanted to know more about the enemy forces to his front. The French had noticed that all of their encounters to this point had been with light troops and Friant needed intelligence on the number and location of the line troops to ascertain Bellegarde's position and possible intentions.[61] He also believed that an aggressive advance on Amberg would intimidate the Austrians and 'make them fear that they would be taken in the flank'. He therefore ordered his men forward at noon. Fresnel withdrew in the face of the French attack, but halted his command at Ursensollen where II/*Erzherzog Johann* was drawn up in support. The appearance of this battalion and the speedy arrival of three cavalry guns allowed the Austrians to hold the French advance and a see-saw fight raged until nightfall.[62] Friant, 'assured that the number of troops opposing me was much larger than I had previously assessed', felt that he had accomplished his mission and retired to Kastl.[63] Fresnel, satisfied with having contained the French thrust, returned to Amberg, leaving Wintzingerode to maintain the outpost line at Ursensollen.[64]

This little engagement cost each side between 100 and 200 casualties, but does not seem to have achieved the desired effect on Bellegarde's thinking.[65] Instead, the Austrian commander concluded that the French force at Neumarkt was indeed no more than a rear guard. He thus edged closer to Regensburg when he finally moved on 15 April.[66] Still, as previously noted, the move was very limited—a mere twenty kilometres for I Corps from

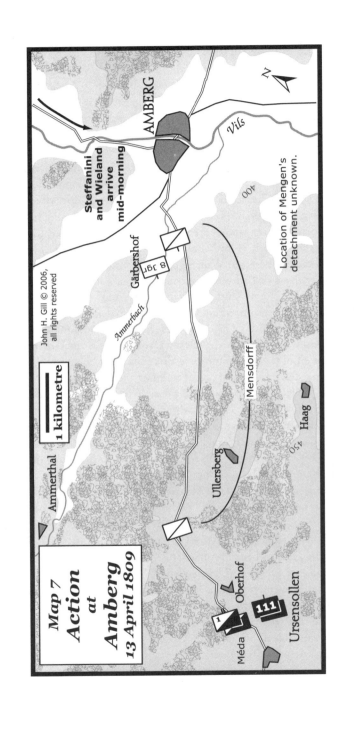

Map 7
Action
at
Amberg
13 April 1809

Ammerthal

1 kilometre

N

AMBERG

Vils

**Steffanini
and Wieland
arrive
mid-morning**

Gärbershof

Ammerbach

8 Jgr

400

Mensdorff

Location of Mengen's
detachment unknown.

Ullersberg

450

Haag

Oberhof

Méda

1

111

Ursensollen

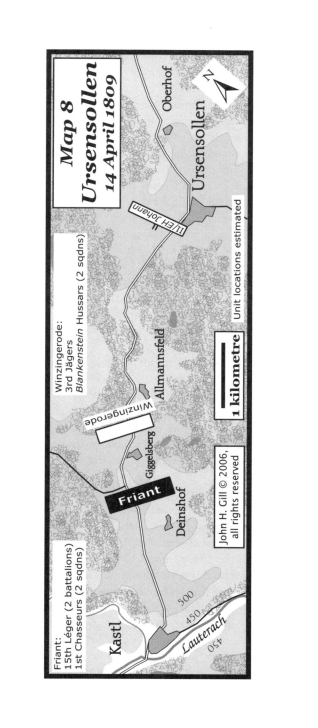

Map 8
Ursensollen
14 April 1809

Winzingerode:
3rd Jägers
Blankenstein Hussars (2 sqdns)

Friant:
15th Léger (2 battalions)
1st Chasseurs (2 sqdns)

Winzingerode

Friant

IV/EH Johann

Ursensollen

Oberhof

Allmannsfeld

Giggelsberg

Deinshof

Kastl

Lauterach

500

450

450

N

1 kilometre

Unit locations estimated

Wernberg to Schwarzenfeld and even less for II Corps from Nabburg to Schwandorf—and Bellegarde remained preoccupied with the possibility of French forces debouching from the Neumarkt area for several more days.

While some Austrian advance guard elements were contending with Friant's forays, small reconnaissance detachments from Crenneville's brigade had been probing towards Regensburg. Crenneville had most of his men at Schwandorf by the evening of the 12th with patrols as far as Burgenlengfeld and Nittenau. At the latter place, Rittmeister Ludwig Freiherr von Mallowetz with his squadron of *Merveldt* Uhlans was joined by the company of the 8th Jägers and the platoon of uhlans that had marched over the Bohemian mountains from Klentsch.[67] The following day, Crenneville established himself at Burgenlengfeld and Mallowetz reached Reinhausen, causing some alarm among the French in Regensburg when he drove off pickets from the 11th Chasseurs. Mallowetz and Crenneville remained in place from 13 to 15 April, but Bellegarde's hesitant shift south brought Klenau with the remainder of the II Corps advance guard to Nittenau on the 15th. The 15th also saw the restoration of communications with the Hauptarmee when Mallowetz's troopers made contact with one of Vécsey's patrols on the north bank of the river late that night.

The long delay in establishing direct liaison between the two wings of the Austrian Main Army illustrates the challenges of conducting co-ordinated operations over long distances during the early nineteenth century. The absence of direct communications during the first six days of the war, however, also highlights serious weaknesses in Austrian planning and preparation. The problems of communications were not unknown to Charles and his staff, yet they and their subordinates did nothing to ameliorate the situation. The Austrian official history especially laments the lack of a chain of dispatch riders or estafettes, and contends that a regular courier service would have allowed messages to pass between Charles and Bellegarde within twenty-four to thirty hours.[68] Such a service could have been established easily before the war. Instead, four to five days were consumed in passing information: Bellegarde's first note to Charles, for example, was dispatched on 9 April but did not reach the archduke until the 13th.[69]

As previously noted, the severe difficulties inherent in co-ordinated operations were compounded by Bellegarde's qualities as a commander. In the words of a contemporary Austrian staff officer, Bellegarde was 'of the noblest character as a man, uncommonly brave as a soldier, but always irresolute as a commander', particularly 'in an uncertain undertaking' where he knew little of the enemy. Rather than press the French, 'he sought only to protect everything and did nothing decisive'.[70] In explication of Charles's choice of Bellegarde for this difficult role, it must be remarked that the poverty of the senior Habsburg leadership was such that no other Austrian commander of the appropriate rank is likely to have done any better, but the end result after six days of hostilities was that the northern wing of the Austrian invasion had contributed almost nothing toward a victorious outcome for the campaign or a successful conclusion of the war.

IN THE MASTER'S ABSENCE:
ALLIED OPERATIONS 10 TO 15 APRIL

Word of the Austrian invasion reached Berthier in Strasbourg on 11 April. At 5.30 a.m. that morning, he received a 9 April message from Oudinot forwarding a letter from Lefebvre: 'the enemy is in Bavarian territory; they crossed the Inn yesterday (8 April) near Braunau'.[71] This missive and numerous similar notes launched a legion of couriers out into the cold and wet across southern Germany, alerting commanders and setting thousands of troops in motion.[72] But it was false. Lefebvre's report to Oudinot was based on messages he had received from Crown Prince Ludwig and Wrede stating that the Austrians had crossed the Inn on 8 April. Ludwig was passing on information from his outposts, while Wrede claimed that the fortress commandant of Oberhaus had given the pre-arranged signal for the Austrian invasion (three cannon shots). Wrede added that he also had information from the 14th Infantry at Landshut that the Austrians had crossed on the 8th. These reports, of course, were erroneous, rumour transformed into fact by the pervasive tension of those early April days.[73] In fact, as we have seen, the Austrians did not actually cross the Inn in force until the morning of 10 April. As evening fell on 9 April, it was clear to the French and Bavarian leadership of 7th Corps that 'the Imperial Austrian troops have not crossed at all' and that 'a completely unfounded report' had generated the initial excitement.[74] Lefebvre, vastly annoyed at the alarmist reporting, reprimanded his officers for accepting at face value what they were told by local peasantry and instructed them to make direct personal observations.[75] He also tried to recall what was doubtless for him an embarrassing series of dispatches alerting his superiors and fellow commanders. By then, however, the word was already spreading up the French chain of command. Ironically, this erroneous alarm did more good than harm to the French cause.

At the local level, these false reports afforded Allied commanders in Bavaria twelve to twenty-four hours' advance notice of the invasion. Oudinot, for example, had Lefebvre's report in his hands by 5 p.m. on the evening of 9 April, just as Hiller's men were seizing the customs barricade at Braunau. Inherent delays in travel and transmission meant that the advantage in time diminished to some twelve hours for Berthier and Napoleon, but this still proved significant. When Berthier accepted Oudinot's report as fact on the morning of the 11th, therefore, he was only twenty-four hours behind the actual Austrian crossing of the Inn; and the arrival of a copy of Archduke Charles's letter to the Bavarian king at 3 p.m. on the 11th merely served to confirm something Berthier thought he already knew.[76] As a result of this error, generals in Bavaria were able to issue key orders to their troops almost as the Habsburg battalions were beginning their advance. More important, the prompt delivery of this mistaken information meant that Napoleon in Paris knew of the invasion by 8 p.m. on 12 April. 'They have crossed the Inn, it is war,' he told a small group of advisers.[77] A little more than eight hours later he would be on the road for the Danube.

Advance notice aside, French reporting at this point is noteworthy for its remarkable speed. Lefebvre's 9 April letter announcing the (erroneous) Austrian invasion, for instance, travelled the 400 kilometres to Strasbourg in only thirty-three hours, despite passing through Oudinot's headquarters en route.[78] The Austrian record hardly bears comparison with this impressive achievement. The advantages of the French and their allies in message transmission and other military administration would not always be so dramatic, but the general level of competence and energy was considerably higher than that evident among their foes. At the same time, Allied commanders and staffs at all levels exercised great professional care in disseminating information to neighbouring headquarters, exchanging information and orders as the situation evolved. Furthermore, a high level of tactical readiness allowed the Army of Germany to concentrate almost immediately.[79] As we shall see, however, for all of the French and German proficiency in staff work, readiness, and communications, their reporting fell far short of meeting the high command's needs for intelligence on Austrian activity.

While Berthier's letter made its way to Napoleon in Paris, French and German troops were already on the move in response to news of the invasion. The initial operational requirements and existing instructions were clear enough that the corps commanders felt confident to act on their own without awaiting new orders. For Massena, this meant pulling his scattered companies and battalions into more tightly concentrated brigades and divisions, issuing rations, flints, shoes, and ammunition, and ensuring that a hundred other small actions were completed so that the corps could march on short notice.[80] 'A Rubicon has been crossed', GB François Roch, Baron Ledru des Essarts wrote to his sister, unconsciously echoing the enemy's metaphor as he described preparations in 4th Corps.[81] This was not a period of clockwork precision for Massena's command, rather a flurry of confusion, frustration, haste, and error as staff officers and commanders attempted to do everything at once. Leaders continued to press training with vigour while cavalry patrols pushed east to the Amper and south towards the Tyrol. Lodgings were often poor and everyone suffered from the foul weather. For Philippe René Girault, a musician of the 93rd Ligne, the persistence of winter 'was an evil beginning, but we would see much harder times'.[82]

Confusion, delay, snow, and inefficiency aside, the battalions and squadrons got where they needed to go. As night fell on 11 April, Massena's light cavalry was on the Lech south of Augsburg; by the evening of the 12th, his infantry divisions were within a day's march of the river. Simultaneously, Oudinot, operating under Massena's orders, collected his corps between Augsburg (1st Division) and Aichach (2nd Division), with Colbert's light horsemen and most of Espagne's cuirassiers posted well to the east.

On Massena's left, just north of the Danube, Vandamme moved with his customary energy to concentrate his somewhat separated Württemberg troops between Dillingen and Heidenheim. 'Press this movement so as not to lose a minute', he urged General Leutnant Franz von Neubronn, the senior Württemberg officer. He reminded his subordinates that they must be 'perfectly ready to fight at any moment' and issued orders for the Württemberg staff officers to inspect all of the cantonments and 'assure themselves that everyone is occupied actively with training the troops and that all are constantly prepared to move wherever circumstances require'.[83]

As command arrangements were vague, Lefebvre acted according to his own understanding of Napoleon's extant directives. In the 1st and 3rd Divisions this meant assembling and concentrating their regiments in preparation for action—a somewhat easier process as compared to 4th Corps because the Bavarians had not been as dispersed as Massena's troops. The Bavarians, moreover, had been on a high state of alert for several days as Lefebvre, prudently responding to the numerous alarms, readied 7th Corps for 'the sort of rapid march we might be called upon to conduct' at a moment's notice.[84]

Wrede, however, immediately caused a minor stir by abandoning Straubing on his own initiative as soon as he received the erroneous signal that the Austrians were across the Inn.[85] Departing the area on the evening of the 9th, his division marched through the night to reach Abensberg, weary and bedraggled, at midmorning on 10 April. Although constantly in motion, it spent the next several days in this general vicinity 'marching first left and then right ... without ever seeing the enemy', in the words of one bemused soldier.[86] Wrede's action irritated Lefebvre, but the reproach he fired off to his nominal subordinate only provoked the testy Wrede to reply with an indignant and lengthy epistle—accompanied by six attachments— defending his move and demanding satisfaction.[87] The press of events soon overwhelmed this miniature tempest, but it contributed to the sour relations between Lefebvre and Wrede that would plague 7th Corps throughout the war. The 1st and 3rd Bavarian Divisions were neither as peripatetic nor as dyspeptic as the commander of the 2nd; 12 April found them at Munich and Freising respectively, well concentrated, but more or less where they had been when hostilities began.

Unfortunately for the Allies, in the course of their movements, the Bavarians largely lost contact with the invading Austrians. The intelligence that made its way to Berthier and eventually to Napoleon was therefore scanty and speculative, especially as it related to the Austrian forces in the Danube valley. This weak reporting left a gap in the Allied appreciation of the enemy situation, a shadowed area that would influence Berthier's decisions during his brief stint as the de facto commander of the Army of Germany.

North of the Danube, Davout had a better, if still far from perfect, picture of Austrian strength and location, telling Berthier on the morning of the 13th that 'Bellegarde commands the army that is debouching at Waidhaus; it numbers between 30,000 and 40,000 men.'[88] As soon as he learned of the Austrian invasion, Davout had ordered his scattered command to assemble in the area just north of Ingolstadt in accordance with his existing instructions and, by the evening of the 13th, as the marshal established his headquarters at this important crossing point, his corps was collecting as directed.[89] The 1st and 3rd Infantry Divisions as well as the 2nd Heavy Cavalry Division and Demont's Reserve Division were already in place; the 1st Heavy Cavalry Division was en route; and the bulk of St Hilaire's division had reached Hemau from Regensburg. This concentration took place behind a shield of other 3rd Corps units: Piré at Nuremberg, Jacquinot with the 2nd Chasseurs at Altdorf, Friant with Colonel Méda's 1st Chasseurs between Kastl and Neumarkt, the newly arrived GD Montbrun at Velburg at the head of an ad hoc cavalry-infantry command, and GB Pajol at Regensburg with a mixed detachment of light infantry and cavalry.[90] With these dispositions, Davout believed, 'the orders given to me to unite my corps with the French troops on the Lech are fulfilled'.[91]

Shortly after noon on the 14th, however, Davout received a disturbing letter from Berthier directing him to move his headquarters to Regensburg while sending St Hilaire, Montbrun, and the 1st Heavy Cavalry to the Isar (either Freising or Landshut) as soon as 3rd Corps was established in the vicinity of Regensburg. From these instructions and a copy of an order for Wrede, Davout also learned that the Bavarians were to withdraw to the Lech 'if the enemy makes a move'.[92] The marshal thus suddenly faced the unexpected and decidedly uncomfortable prospect of placing his corps in an exposed position at Regensburg, with his left more or less in the air, the Austrians approaching on both flanks, and his nearest supports several days' march to the west. In the process, he would lose several key components of his command as one of his infantry divisions and half of his cavalry were to march off to the banks of the Isar.[93] What had happened to occasion this dramatic shift?

To answer this, we must return to Berthier. The chief of staff, having departed Strasbourg around midnight on the night of 11/12 April, had arrived in Donauwörth on the evening of the 13th and had immediately busied himself with dispatching a hail of letters and orders. Events were to determine that these orders came in two distinct batches. The first group, hurried off into the rainy darkness around 8 p.m., sent Wrede back to Straubing and Deroy to Landshut, while pushing Oudinot to Regensburg where he was to join St Hilaire and the Cavalry Reserve; Massena and Vandamme were to stay on the Lech and Davout was to remain near Ingolstadt north of the Danube; army headquarters itself would move to Ingolstadt.[94] This was essentially what Napoleon envisaged.

The second batch of messages, however, written between 11 p.m. and 11.30 p.m., halted Oudinot on the Lech, directed the Bavarians to prepare for withdrawal, and shoved Davout forwards to his precarious position at Regensburg. The difference was a 10 April letter from Napoleon.[95] This missive, intended as a supplement to a brief telegraphic message, arrived at Berthier's headquarters in Donauwörth at 11 p.m. on the 13th. It apprised Berthier of Napoleon's belief 'that Austria will commence hostilities, if it has not already done so'. The emperor, following the pattern he had used in the 30 March 'Instructions for the Major General', then outlined two general sets of dispositions for the army: one to be followed if the Austrians attacked before the 15th, and one in the event that 'as the Austrians are very slow, it is possible that they will not have attacked before the 15th'. In the former case (an early attack), Davout's entire command (including St Hilaire and the Cavalry Reserve) and the Bavarians, 'all will retire to the Lech' to join

Massena. If the Austrians had still not invaded by the 15th, however, Berthier was to direct Davout to Regensburg, the Bavarians would stay in place, and St Hilaire et al. would move to the Isar (Freising or Landshut 'according to circumstances'), where they could support 7th Corps.

Berthier did not understand. Napoleon's letter left too much to his harried chief of staff's limited powers of imagination and interpretation. Perhaps Berthier would have penetrated the sense of the letter if he had had in hand the message Napoleon had dispatched via the French optical telegraph system shortly before the courier had ridden off with the actual letter. The letter may have lacked precision, but the telegram was unmistakable: 'if the enemy has attacked before the 15th, you must concentrate the troops at Augsburg and Donauwörth and have everyone ready to march'.[96] The telegram, however, was absent, a victim of the accidents of war. Bad weather had evidently delayed its transmission (Berthier did not receive it until 6 a.m. on the 16th in Augsburg) and the copy that was supposed to accompany the letter was missing from the packet Berthier read in Donauwörth late on that night of 13 April. That left the tired and stressed marshal to deal with the letter alone. Unfortunately for Davout in particular and the French cause in general, Berthier misinterpreted a key clause in his emperor's instructions. In the paragraph describing how the army should array itself if the Austrians had *not* attacked before 15 April, Napoleon stated that Davout 'will have his headquarters in Regensburg; his army arrayed within one day's march of that town, and this under all circumstances'. Berthier, mindful of the 30 March 'Instructions'—which he considered as 'formal'—and burdened by the importance Napoleon seemed to attach to Regensburg, ignored the premise in Napoleon's letter ('If the enemy has not made any movement' before the 15th) and focused on the phrase 'under all circumstances'. He thus ordered Davout to Regensburg while drawing most of the army back toward the Lech.

Nor was the passage about Davout the only one that Berthier misread. He also misinterpreted Napoleon's intentions for the Bavarians as outlined in the same paragraph. Again, Berthier ignored Napoleon's underlying premise that this portion of the orders was based on Austria delaying the invasion until after 15 April. Where the emperor wrote that 'The Bavarians will not make any movement if the enemy has made none' (clearly meaning 'if the Austrians have not crossed the border'), Berthier mistakenly applied this guidance to the situation prevailing on the 13th, even though the war had already begun. As a result, the orders to Wrede and Lefebvre were equivocal, couched in Napoleon's phrases, but misapplying Napoleon's purpose: 'If the enemy makes any movement', Berthier wrote, the Bavarians were to retire on the Lech, but if not, he directed them to remain where they were—far forward, vulnerable, and unsupported—presumably until such time as the Austrians advanced even deeper into their country.[97]

Berthier's false reading of the operational situation, his often-difficult relations with his fellow marshals, his general incapacity for command, and what Binder von Kriegelstein calls 'the looming pressure to do something' in Napoleon's absence, compounded his serious misunderstanding of his master's intentions.[98] Each of these points warrants a small comment. As far as Berthier's understanding of the operational situation is concerned, this was conditioned by the limited information at his disposal on 13 and 14 April. Much of the reporting he had received stressed Austrian interest in and forces near Salzburg and the Tyrol. Furthermore, he was well aware that the region was in open revolt. He also knew from Davout's reporting that Bellegarde and some 40,000 men had entered Bavaria from Bohemia and were operating on the Allied strategic left. What he did not have was a reliable picture of the Austrian forces that had crossed the Inn. He thus concluded that 'It seems that they are manoeuvring on the flanks, in the Upper Palatinate [Oberpfalz] and in the Tyrol.' He seems to have accepted the intelligence on the Tyrol uncritically, even relating to Napoleon that as many as 40,000 Austrians might have marched into the area 'to turn your flank'.[99] Charles would have been delighted to read this. As a consequence of his faulty analysis, Berthier gave undue attention to the long but unmenaced Alpine flank and failed to appreciate the real threat slowly approaching the Isar in the Allied centre. Furthermore, in gluing himself to a literal reading of Napoleon's evolving instructions, Berthier seemed to give no heed to Bellegarde's command: Davout was to go to Regensburg even though Berthier was well aware that a major enemy force was present around Amberg.

Berthier's incapacity for the weighty responsibility he now bore grew more manifest with each passing day. Having never held a major command of any sort and accustomed to working under Napoleon's close supervision, he was unsure of himself and painfully aware of his awkward position as a temporary commander whose orders might be questioned, especially in coping with fellow marshals.[100] He therefore repeatedly invoked Napoleon's name in his orders even in cases where he was not truly relaying the emperor's words. A 13 April note to Davout will suffice as an example: 'His Majesty wants to centralise his troops at Regensburg and plans to establish his quarters there.'[101] This was partly true, but quite misleading and certainly stretched the authority of the emperor's communications.

Furthermore, though difficult to prove definitively, Binder seems correct in his instinct that Berthier felt compelled to *do something* when it might have been better to wait and allow the situation to ripen.[102] Circumstances demanded at least some action, a modicum of independent decision making, as Napoleon had recognised in preparing the 30 March 'Instructions', and Berthier was understandably anxious to satisfy his domineering sovereign. Unfortunately, in his efforts to do so, he overreached his own capabilities, as he himself soon began to realise. By midnight on the 14th, with the situation increasingly murky, complex, and slipping out of his tenuous grasp, he was penning an infamously plaintive note to the emperor: 'In the current state of affairs, I greatly desire the arrival of Your Majesty to avoid the orders and counter-orders which circumstances, as well as the instructions and orders of Your Majesty, necessarily entail.'[103] One of his staff officers, Colonel Louis François Lejeune, watched with anguish as 'the anxiety of Prince Berthier now [15 April] became greater than ever, and it grieved me very much to see a man who was always so calm and courageous under fire, and whom no personal danger could intimidate, trembling and sinking beneath the weight of responsibility thrown upon him now'.[104]

Berthier's discomfort was as obvious to many of the Army of Germany's officers as it was to the chivalrous Lejeune, but many of these were far less charitable. 'It seemed that Major General Berthier only preceded him [Napoleon] to the army in order to place in evidence his complete incompetence', wrote Colonel Pierre Berthezène, commanding the 10th Léger.[105] The perspective on matters was similar from the lower ranks as recounted by a sub-lieutenant of the 33rd Ligne: 'In hesitant comings and goings we endured the hours under an avalanche of counter-orders ... we commenced to march more "for the Capuchins" [i.e., without rhyme or reason] and to be manipulated by the enemy.'[106]

Davout clearly grasped the potential calamity inherent in Berthier's orders and sent a professional protest on 14 April.[107] His objections were in vain. Berthier remained focused on having 3rd Corps in Regensburg as he believed his emperor desired. During the course of 14 April, he sent Davout four letters reminding him of the importance of this placement. In one brief missive, Berthier stressed Regensburg three times: 'The essential, as I have told you, is that you concentrate your corps at Regensburg ... in all cases, your corps must concentrate at Regensburg ... I tell you again, Duke, your headquarters at Regensburg and your entire army corps within one march of that town.'[108] He repeatedly used Napoleon's authority to lend weight to his instructions.[109] Left with little choice, Davout dutifully but reluctantly set his corps on the road to Regensburg.[110] His orders register for the day included the note that 'the marshal resisted the execution of an order that events could render extremely dangerous, and it was only after repeated orders sent in duplicate copies that he decided to make the ordered movement'.[111]

Davout's men thus spent 15 April on the 'detestable' roads leading east and south to Regensburg.[112] This meant that most of 3rd Corps had to turn about and retrace its steps after a series of tough marches in the vile weather. Officers and men were understandably confused, annoyed, and apprehensive: this was not the sort of manoeuvring they had come to expect as soldiers of the Grande Armée. As the sodden evening of 15 April closed in, St Hilaire's division was concentrated at Regensburg with Pajol's command, Morand was on the east bank of the Altmühl around Dietfurt, Gudin and St Sulpice were just west of Riedenburg, while Friant remained at Neumarkt, and Demont at Ingolstadt. Also at Ingolstadt were the carabinier and cuirassier regiments of the 1st Heavy Cavalry Division, following their orders to head for the Isar. In the rear, Rouyer's Germans had reached Gunzenhausen, having departed Würzburg on the 13th.

As for the Bavarians, 7th Corps remained scattered on 15 April. Wrede, after his hasty withdrawal from Straubing on the night of 9/10 April, had spent the next five days marching back and forth between Biburg and Eggmühl in response to Berthier's fluctuating instructions and his own conceits. The 15th found him with his infantry assembled between Abensberg and Langquaid; he had posted his two chevaulegers regiments at Rottenburg (3rd Regiment) and Pfeffenhausen (2nd Regiment) where they could warn of an Austrian approach and support Deroy at Landshut. Additionally, at Berthier's direction, he had placed a battalion (II/3rd Infantry) at Vohburg to guard the bridge. Deroy's 3rd Division had arrived at Landshut early on the 15th after a long night's march, leaving a company of the 10th Infantry and a gun at Moosburg.[113] As noted earlier, however, the infantry company withdrew towards Pfeffenhausen when Scheibler's detachment appeared, and the Austrians soon repaired the bridge. Further west, the 1st Bavarian Division was assembled at Au after 'a foul march . . . it snowed dreadfully for two hours so that one was completely soaked through'.[114] Ludwig had detachments at Allershausen and Attenkirchen, but was hardly positioned to support either of the other two Bavarian divisions.[115] Lefebvre and the corps headquarters were at Mainburg, planning to move to Geisenfeld on the 16th, a proposition that earned Berthier's praise.[116] In that location he would be more than twenty kilometres away from his closest division (the 1st) and utterly unable to influence the 3rd Division's upcoming action at

Landshut. As a result of these deployments, all executed in accordance with Berthier's directives, the area towards Straubing was completely denuded of Allied units. The only troops on St Hilaire's right (south), therefore, were Austrians, while Deroy was on his own at Landshut with both flanks completely in the air.

The forces along the Lech were more solidly situated. Vandamme had a light battalion and four squadrons forward at Neuburg, but the rest of the Württemberg contingent was well established between Rain and Donauwörth. Oudinot and Massena had made only minor moves. The former had his 1st Division at Augsburg and his 2nd between Aichach and Rain; his light cavalry was further east, with the 9th Hussars watching the crossings over the Amper. Espagne's four cuirassier regiments were dispersed between Augsburg and the Amper. Most of Massena's infantry was still quartered west of the Lech, but Boudet had one brigade at Landsberg and another forward at the southern end of the Ammersee. Some of the 4th Corps divisions, however, would require a day to collect themselves before they could march. Marulaz's chasseurs screened the southern end of Massena's line and scouted toward the Alps, alert to reports of the Tyrolian insurrection and the danger of incursions from that direction.

In addition to the operational mistakes that left the army divided and unarticulated, Berthier also committed a number of 'technical' errors that suggest that his unfamiliar responsibilities as commander were detracting from the meticulous care he usually applied to his chief of staff functions. These mistakes fall into two broad categories. First, he repeatedly disrupted the chain of command, sending orders to subordinate leaders without informing their superiors, as occurred with Lefebvre, St Hilaire, and Wrede.[117] The potential for misunderstanding, even disaster, made this more than a minor detail. Second, Berthier's correspondence during this period is replete with imprecision and contradiction, lax staff work indicating a mind unequipped to cope with the numerous tasks it faced. Planning for St Hilaire's move to the Isar on the 14th illustrates this point.[118] Stolidly trying to cleave to the letter of Napoleon's instructions, Berthier would have had St Hilaire marching south to Landshut or Freising, crossing paths with Wrede and Deroy, who were retiring north to Ingolstadt (why take this route to Augsburg in the first place?). He did nothing to ensure communications between Lefebvre and St Hilaire, and did not make clear to 7th Corps that St Hilaire's move was contingent on developments at Regensburg.[119] When he decided to send St Hilaire on a more logical route through Schrobenhausen,[120] the chief of staff neglected to inform Lefebvre and Deroy of the change, leaving them to think the French division would be marching into Landshut on 16 April.[121] In reality, Deroy stood alone.

This was only one of the many instances of shoddy staff work during the opening days of the campaign. Taken together, they leave the reader 'swimming in incoherence', in the words of a modern observer.[122] They were not necessarily debilitating errors, but they were numerous and fraught with danger. Fortunately for Napoleon, the level of dedication and professionalism among the Allied commanders and staffs was very high. Furthermore, the Austrians were poorly served by their intelligence apparatus and were slow to exploit French mistakes. These factors and a good dose of luck reduced the negative impact of Berthier's decision making, but his 'technical' faults in staff processes exacerbated his operational mistakes and contributed to the pervasive sense of unease that spread through the army during those dismal April days.

Historical commentary tends to divide sharply in apportioning responsibility for this potentially catastrophic state of affairs. Many observers castigate Berthier for his 'terrible blunders', especially his failure to understand the 'clear and precise' instructions from the emperor that left 'nothing to desire, nothing to interpret'.[123] Berthier's partisans, on the other hand, argue that the emperor's 30 March 'Instructions' were 'detailed but imprecise' and that the crucial 10 April dispatch was 'very ambiguous'.[124] They thereby attempt to shift the blame to Napoleon and exculpate the chief of staff. Certainly, Napoleon's communications to Berthier between 28 March and 10 April were not without flaws, and the emperor often failed to discipline the inspired passion and velocity of his concepts to match his recipient's intellect.[125] The phrase 'under all circumstances' was especially unfortunate. However, Berthier's defenders misread Napoleon's orders as egregiously as did Berthier.[126] Even accounting for the benefits of hindsight, Berthier's misinterpretations are 'difficult to comprehend', especially if campaign historian Charles Saski is correct in asserting that Napoleon dictated the 30 March 'Instructions' to his chief of staff personally.[127] GD Drouet, who met with Napoleon on 11 March en route to his posting as 7th Corps chief of staff, had no doubts about the emperor's desire to concentrate the army on the Lech. He and Lefebvre were thus surprised when Berthier 'changed all of the dispositions originally determined by the emperor'.[128] Despite thirteen years of close association with Napoleon, Berthier utterly failed to grasp the essentials of his master's thinking for the upcoming campaign, most importantly the clear distinction Napoleon drew between the different actions to take if the Austrians invaded before or after 15 April. Instead, Berthier 'adopted as absolutes' measures that were supposed to be contingent and thus 'made a salad of all the dispositions contained in the orders and instructions of the emperor'.[129] Mental stress and physical exhaustion help explain but do not excuse his errors.[130] Berthier was an excellent chief of staff to Napoleon, more than a mere 'tool' or 'nullity' as some of his detractors state, but his thinking was often slow and 'the fear of responsibility dominated all his actions'.[131] The result was the series of increasingly incomprehensible and conflicting instructions to the Army of Germany that were 'contrary to the orders of the emperor and in direct opposition to the exigencies of the situation'.[132]

The other criticism frequently levelled against Napoleon in the spring of 1809 is that he erred badly in appointing Berthier as interim commander in the first place. Here, too, the analysis is often shallow. In fact, Napoleon had no other realistic options, given that he did not want to precipitate a war by moving to Germany himself before Austria attacked. As noted earlier, the emperor could hardly appoint Davout over Massena, or place Massena over Davout. Of the imperial relatives with any military capability whatsoever, Murat was unavailable, Jerome too feckless and inexperienced. Berthier was the only viable alternative and even he was not to go beyond Strasbourg unless Austria actually crossed the border. Napoleon thus took a risk, but one that he considered acceptable under the circumstances: (1) an Austrian invasion was unlikely before 15 April in his estimation, by which time the Army of Germany would be in its designated defensive positions; (2) counting on Austrian torpor, he expected to join the army before any major action occurred, so Berthier would not be in command for more than a few days; and (3) Berthier had detailed instructions outlining the emperor's intentions for a wide variety of contingencies while Napoleon travelled from Paris to Germany. Although the march of events brought the army to the edge of disaster, the original decision to give temporary command to Berthier was therefore both reasonable and unavoidable as a compromise between competing political and military requirements.

Thus stood the Army of Germany on the eve of its first major engagement. Thanks to Berthier's misunderstandings, it was divided into two groups separated by at least four 'marches de guerre' or five more normal days on the road: the 68,700 men of 2nd, 4th, and 8th Corps generally along the Lech between Landsberg and Donauwörth, and Davout, approaching Regensburg with the 52,300 infantry and cavalry of his own corps (minus Demont), St Hilaire's division, St Sulpice's cuirassiers, and the light cavalry allotted to Montbrun.[133] Lefebvre's corps of 25,100 Bavarians occupied the yawning gap between these two groups, but its three constituent divisions were poorly positioned as far as mutual support was concerned. The Austrians, tightly concentrated and slowly moving on Landshut, had therefore a real chance to overwhelm the disjointed 7th Corps, reach the Danube at Kehlheim, and split the Army of Germany before the Allies could react effectively.

In addition to leaving the army in this dangerously vulnerable position, Berthier's period of command had a negative influence on Allied morale. Days of marching and counter-marching through wretched weather for no apparent purpose demonstrated quite clearly that the reins of command rested in unsteady hands. In the words of GB Guillaume de Latrille, Baron de Lorencez, a brigade commander in St Hilaire's division, 'Our anxiety was great, as the enemy's advantage over us increased each day, our position became more and more critical.' Owing to Berthier's 'hesitations' and the 'uncertainty of his schemes', recalled Lorencez, 'The simple soldiers themselves were astonished at all of the counter-marches and began to grow uneasy.'[134] From top to bottom, the Army of Germany grumbled and questioned. Officers and men, French and German alike, looked over their shoulders and wondered when 'he' would arrive.

CHAPTER 5

Eight Days in April, I: The War Opens and the Tide Turns

'He' was already on the road for the Danube. Learning of the Austrian invasion on the evening of 12 April, Napoleon immediately made preparations to depart.[1] He met with Arch-Chancellor Cambacérès at 8 p.m., dined at 9 p.m., then took coffee in his office while dictating a series of notes and letters around 10 p.m., met with Fouché at 11 p.m. to give the minister of police final instructions on keeping Paris secure, and lay down at about midnight. GD Marie François Auguste Caffarelli woke him at 2.30 a.m. on the 13th, and by 4.20 he was seated in his travelling office coach with Josephine, heading east for war. The travelling party was small and moved rapidly despite the heaviness of the emperor's special coach. Other than notifying the post relays to have fresh horses ready, there had been no time to make advance arrangements, and towns along the route were surprised when their sovereign passed through on the way to the Rhine. The Oudinot family was taken aback, for example, when Napoleon suddenly appeared at their door in Bar-le-Duc for a brief call on the morning of the 14th before pushing on to Strasbourg, where the party pulled up at dawn the following day. Josephine, exhausted after two straight days in the carriage, sought out a bed in the Rohan Palace, but Napoleon only stayed long enough to receive reports from GD Beaumont and consume lunch. Bidding farewell to the empress, he was in his coach and rattling his way east once again by early afternoon. In retrospect, it was potentially a poignant moment, as Napoleon would return from the Austrian war intent upon divorcing Josephine and entering into a marital alliance with the defeated House of Habsburg. But all of that lay in the future. On 15 April, his immediate concern was repulsing the Austrian invasion of Bavaria.

Napoleon crossed the Rhine at Kehl that afternoon, making two stops as he traversed the Grand Duchy of Baden: first to see his niece, Stephanie de Beauharnais (he urged her to join Josephine in Strasbourg), and later to discuss France's interests and the tangled intrigues of the grand ducal court with his ambassador, Louis Pierre Bignon. The next two major halts also concerned his Rheinbund allies. The first was Ludwigsburg, residence of the corpulent but forceful King Friedrich of Württemberg. Driving through the night, the emperor's party entered Friedrich's courtyard at 4 a.m. on 16 April where 'everything was at the peak of excitement owing to the arrival of the imperial guest'.[2] The two monarchs discussed the Austrian invasion and Friedrich asked Napoleon about his plans. 'We will go to Vienna', was the reply. Napoleon also used the opportunity to send dispatches in all directions, even employing Württemberg officers as couriers. By 10.30 a.m., however, the emperor was once more in his carriage, under escort by Württemberg cavalry in the absence of his own guard. His passage created a sensation. 'The town and the villages were in motion, the entire population took itself to the highway', noted a French commissary official who happened upon the emperor's route of travel, 'Taken for members of his suite, we received the salutes addressed to his carriages.'[3]

Napoleon now headed for Dillingen to reassure Max Joseph of Bavaria, temporarily evicted from his capital by Jellacic's advance.[4] En route, he and his companions experienced some of the dreadful weather that had made the men of both armies miserable for the past week: when the party's third night on the road fell, it was utterly black and a violent storm drenched the struggling staff officers and escorts. The interview with Bavaria's king took place in the earliest hours of 17 April, the emperor telling the anxious Max Joseph that he would be able to re-enter Munich in a few days. But the halt was brief. After only an hour's conversation, the cavalcade was pressing on for army headquarters at Donauwörth, passing through the gates of the astonished little town at 5 a.m.[5] Annoyed not to find Berthier at headquarters, Napoleon immediately set to work reading through the army's recent correspondence. As he had told Ambassador Otto in March, he had indeed come to the theatre of war 'like a lightning bolt', but there was much to do and he was not a moment too soon if he was to retrieve the situation.[6]

16 APRIL: ACROSS THE ISAR

Meanwhile, the Austrians were slowly advancing. Charles's plan for 16 April called for the Main Army to force the Isar at three points along its existing lines of march. The principal crossing would be at Landshut, where Radetzky would lead the way, followed by the remainder of V Corps, then III Corps, and finally the two reserve corps. On the army's right, Rosenberg would cross at Dingolfing, defeat Wrede if necessary, and then turn left to outflank Deroy's position at Landshut. Vécsey would seek contact with Bellegarde along the Danube. On the left, Hiller was to protect the army's western flank by continuing his move on Moosburg, bringing up the main body of his corps to reinforce the small detachment that had seized this bridge on the 15th.

Information on the enemy, however, was scanty. Charles, assuming that Davout was entirely north of the Danube occupied with Bellegarde, was most concerned with the Allied forces south of the river. He believed that these, with the exception of the Bavarians, were concentrated on the Lech, posing a potential threat to his left. To his immediate front, he knew that Deroy stood at Landshut with one Bavarian division, but intelligence on the whereabouts of the other two was contradictory, leading the Austrian staff to conclude that the entire Bavarian army might be arrayed behind the Isar with Wrede north of Dingolfing and the crown prince somewhere near Freising or Moosburg. The Hauptarmee would have to be prepared for serious resistance at any of these sites.

Landshut, the principal crossing site, had received its first visit from Habsburg troops—a patrol of uhlans—on 13 April, but the Austrians did not establish a presence in the city until the 15th, when Radetzky sent General Staff Hauptmann Joseph von Simbschen there with a platoon of *Erzherzog Karl* Uhlans. Simbschen endeavoured to persuade the Bavarians to permit an unopposed Austrian crossing, but his entreaties were politely rebuffed.[7] There was, however, no fighting. Instead, a curious atmosphere of tense peace prevailed while anxiety mounted among the local citizenry. Radetzky reinforced Simbschen with two companies of *Gradiska* Grenzer in the evening and sent another two Grenzer companies and a squadron of *Karl* Uhlans to outpost the river on both sides of Landshut. In addition, the pioneer divisions from III and V Corps arrived during the night. Otherwise all was quiet.

Radetzky and the remainder of the V Corps advance guard (the other eight companies of *Gradiskaner*, two squadrons of *Kienmayer* Hussars, one platoon of *Karl* Uhlans and a cavalry battery) joined the forward elements of his command at Landshut as day was breaking, bright and clear.[8] It was 16 April, the first day of good weather since the campaign had opened and doubtless a most welcome change for the men on both sides. Radetzky straight away set his pioneers to work repairing the two bridges and sent an officer across the river to persuade the Bavarians not to interfere. GL Deroy, however, informed the Austrian emissary that he would order his men to fire on the Habsburg pioneers if they did not cease work at once. Radetzky quickly called off his men and the next several hours passed peacefully, while the Austrians assembled in the city and the Bavarians waited tensely on the northern bank.

The terrain at Landshut favoured an attacker coming from the south. Although the river, swollen and swift from the recent rain, was a major obstacle, the southern (right) bank was substantially higher than the northern, allowing Austrian artillery to dominate the broad meadows on the far side, while the hills and buildings on the Austrian side afforded Habsburg commanders a superb view of almost anything Deroy might care to undertake. The city offered two bridges. One of these, the 'Spitalbrücke', connected the city's central square to an island in the middle of the Isar and thence with the northern bank. The suburbs here offered good protection to the Bavarian defenders. The other bridge, known as the 'Lendbrücke', led to open ground that could be swept by Austrian guns and gave Radetzky a chance to outflank the defence of the Spitalbrücke. The low water meadows north of the river, absolutely flat and nearly devoid of cover, extended for three kilometres to a fringe of hills. This high ground made a fine defensive position, but was so far from the bridges that Bavarian guns posted on the heights would be unable to place effective fire on Austrian troops at the crossing sites. The wide meadows were sodden and soft, unsuitable for the manoeuvre of formed troops. They could only be traversed via the two main roads and a few paths, a circumstance that could hinder the withdrawal of the Bavarians on the river's margin, but would also hamper pursuit.

The terrain complicated Deroy's already difficult task of defending the river against a greatly superior force with both flanks open and no support in sight. The old general saw clearly that he could neither commit his entire division (7,600 infantry, 1,070 cavalry, eighteen guns) to a fight at the riverbank nor leave the Austrians to cross unmolested. He thus placed about half of his force along the river to contest the repair and passage of the bridges, while retaining the other half and most of his artillery on the heights to the north to cover the inevitable retreat. The five battalions of 1st Brigade stood at the river with a foot battery and three cavalry squadrons: 5th Light Battalion in the houses on the northern end of the Spitalbrücke, II/9th Infantry and two guns near the paper mill at the exit from the Lendbrücke, two other guns slightly closer to the bridge near a large farmstead, I/9 north of Seligenthal, I/10th Infantry in the Am Rennweg suburb, and II/10 with the three squadrons north of the St Nikolaus suburb to serve as the rear guard when the brigade withdrew.[9] Of his remaining resources, Deroy placed I/5th Infantry in Altdorf to hold that critical defile, while sending a squadron of *Bubenhofen* Chevaulegers and two companies of the 7th Light to Bruckberg to guard his right; he also sent a detachment of Schützen from II/5 to Gündlkofen to maintain contact with the men at Bruckberg. The rest he positioned on the hills north-east of Altdorf: three line battalions, the other two companies of the 7th Light, four squadrons, and two batteries.[10] Thus situated, Deroy awaited the Austrian advance.

Rather than attack, the Austrians made two more abortive attempts to negotiate a free passage of the river. With further palaver clearly futile, Charles, who had now arrived in Landshut and established his headquarters in the Trausnitz castle, ordered Radetzky to 'drive the Bavarian posts from the far bank and immediately restore the bridges'.[11] At 11 a.m., the Austrians opened fire, the cavalry battery of Radetzky's command reinforced by two V Corps batteries positioned opposite the Lendbrücke.[12] The Bavarians replied with alacrity and a lively exchange was soon in progress.

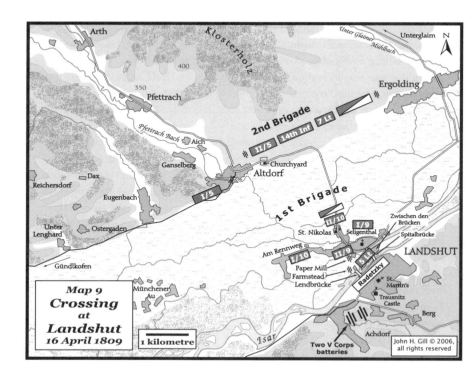

Map 9
Crossing
at
Landshut
16 April 1809

1 kilometre

Bombardment notwithstanding, the men of the 5th Light held to their posts near the Spitalbrücke and inflicted notable losses on the Austrians. Upstream, on the other hand, the situation rapidly turned against the Bavarians. Heavy fire from the Austrian batteries on the southern shore quickly forced the two guns near the farmstead to withdraw and drove off the skirmishers who had been sniping at the Austrian pioneers on the Lendbrücke. The two guns at the paper mill also had to pull back. Although Radetzky's small force only numbered some 2,880 infantry and cavalry, the positioning and strength of the Austrian artillery made the defence of the Lendbrücke untenable.[13] Restoring the bridge proved difficult, but by 1.30 p.m., it was passable and Radetzky was pushing a small mixed force of Grenzer, pioneers, and cavalry across the river.[14]

At about this time, Deroy learned that Austrians had crossed the Isar at Moosburg, compromising his right flank.[15] With the Habsburg troops beginning to collect on the northern bank in front of him and no word on when, or if, St Hilaire was to arrive, he gave orders for the 1st Brigade to fall back from the river and asked Wrede for support.[16] Wrede, for his part, had already set his 1st Brigade on the road to Pfeffenhausen after his cavalry commander, GM Maximillian von Preysing, reported sounds of combat from the direction of Landshut. Likewise, Preysing on his own initiative had sent an officer to Deroy at 12.30 p.m. to report on 3rd Division's situation. Indeed, it was this officer, Leutnant Madroux of the *König* Chevaulegers, who copied Deroy's request to Wrede into his notebook and carried the message back to his division commander.[17] Thanks to the professionalism of his compatriots, therefore, a modicum of help was on the way to Deroy, but first he had to extricate his division from its uncomfortable position. This he accomplished with great skill and aplomb.

The 1st Brigade's withdrawal from the banks of the Isar posed no great challenge as the Austrians did not yet have enough troops on the northern shore to interfere. Although the small Austrian detachment moved into the Seligenthal suburb and secured the northern end of the bridge from Zwischen den Brücken, the Bavarians conducted a model withdrawal. With two companies of the 10th Infantry as its rear guard to face down the Austrian cavalry, the brigade retired behind Altdorf in an orderly fashion and marched north for Pfettrach. Curiously, the Schützen from II/5 at Gündlkofen were told to return to the main road at Altdorf, a decision that forced the divisional rear guard to hold in place until the detachment was recovered. With the 1st Brigade safely on its way north, Deroy started to pull out the rest of his infantry, leaving I/5 west of Altdorf and GM Kurt von

Seydewitz with the cavalry brigade and two batteries on the slopes north of the churchyard.

It was now approximately 4 p.m., and elements of the V Corps main body were crossing the Isar, so Radetzky could act more boldly. He sent ten of his twelve Grenzer companies off towards Ergolding in an effort to outflank Deroy while pushing his cavalry, his battery, and the remaining two Grenzer companies forward against the Bavarian rear guard. A fierce cavalry clash erupted as Radetzky's four available squadrons (two each of *Karl* Uhlans and *Kienmayer* Hussars) attempted to crash through Seydewitz's rear guard.[18] Seydewitz, numerically superior, held his ground until the Bavarian infantry had made good its withdrawal, whereupon he broke off the fight and retired towards Pfettrach. Radetzky, conscious of his command's weakness, reined in his troopers to await reinforcements.

While the cavalry fight had been swirling on the hillside, the two Grenzer companies, supported by sixty volunteers from the *Sztaray* Infantry No. 33 from the Am Rennweg suburb, had occupied the eastern portion of Altdorf and seized the bridge over the Pfettrach. The men of I/5th Infantry who had shielded the withdrawal of the detachments from Gündlkofen and Bruckberg thus narrowly escaped being cut off by crossing the unfordable stream on a small footbridge.[19]

Deroy had cunningly selected the narrow defile at Pfettrach for his next rear guard position and, concerned about the possible threat to his right from the Austrians reported at Moosburg, he simultaneously sent two companies of the 7th Light to Gammelsdorf and the battalion's other two companies with a squadron of 2nd Dragoons and a gun to Furth.[20] Despite their fine position at Pfettrach, the Bavarians were not allowed to tarry long. With the Schützen of II/5 and the 14th Infantry in the hamlet, the cavalry on its southern edge, and the light battery unlimbered to the north, Deroy covered the withdrawal of the rest of his force. The Austrian commander, now reinforced by the other six squadrons of the *Karl* Uhlans and a battalion of *Erzherzog Karl* Infantry No. 3, attempted an advance, but was dissuaded by the strength of the Bavarian position. Instead, Radetzky turned to his cavalry battery, which soon set the little village aflame and forced Deroy's men to decamp shortly after 5 p.m.[21]

Deroy's retrograde movement continued for two more hours with brief exchanges of fire at Arth and Weihmichl. Radetzky, now more than seven kilometres from the main body of V Corps back at Altdorf, out of touch with most of his Grenzer, and very aware that he was outnumbered by an enemy who was clearly full of fight, decided that he had done enough for the day

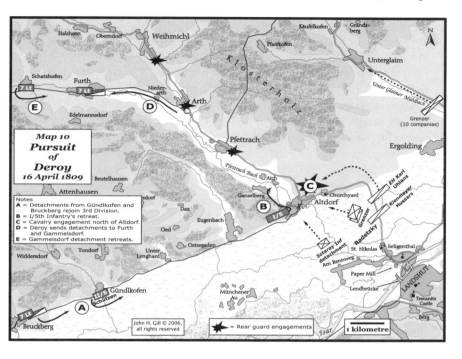

and returned to Pfettrach. The ten companies of Grenzer rejoined him there during the evening after their fruitless march to Unterglaim and over the hills covered by the Klosterholz. Deroy, once he was satisfied that the pursuit had been called off, put his troops back on the road. Marching through the night, they passed through Wrede's supporting position at Pfeffenhausen and went into bivouac on the western side of the Abens opposite Siegenburg at 5 a.m. on the 17th for a well-deserved respite after nine hours of combat and a march of some thirty-eight kilometres.[22]

Losses in killed, wounded, and missing were relatively minor for both sides: ninety-six Austrians and 168 Bavarians. This was less, indeed, than the casualties suffered at Ursensollen two days earlier. Moreover, some forty of the Bavarians were deserters from the 7th Light Battalion. Recruited in the Tyrol, few of these men had any interest in serving King Max Joseph and many took the opportunity to slip off into the hills and forests. Other than this blemish on the 7th Light's record, both sides had performed very well during the day. Radetzky conducted an active pursuit even though the force he had immediately at hand was outnumbered, and his men displayed courage, skill, and energy. For his part, Deroy made the best of a bad situation: delaying the inevitable Austrian crossing by most of a day, breaking off the defence at the right moment, and conducting a textbook withdrawal. His troops responded to his calm professionalism and excellent leadership at all levels by showing steadiness under pressure and recovering quickly from setbacks. Charles was not exaggerating when he later told a group of Bavarian officers that 'the masterful conduct of the retreat' had gained his 'respect and admiration'.[23]

Charles, on the other hand, missed a chance to attain a more significant victory. Making no real effort to damage or destroy Deroy's division, he concerned himself with simply getting his army onto the northern shore. Some additional energy and direction might have made Deroy's task far more challenging and dangerous.[24] Still, the Austrians *were* now across the Isar, the price of passage had been minimal, and little stood between the Hauptarmee and the Danube.[25] It remained to be seen whether the archduke and his army could exploit the day's success.

With the northern bank of the Isar cleared of troublesome Bavarians, III and V Corps crossed the river to camp on the hills and meadows around Ergolding and Altdorf respectively. The two reserve corps remained south of the river for the night, stretched along the road leading from the Isar to the Vils. All suffered from short rations owing to the poor logistical arrangements and the foul weather of the previous week. This led to hardship for the local population, and the citizens of Landshut—with 'most of their property stolen or ruined'—did not recall the hungry Austrian occupation with any great kindness.[26]

To the right of the central Austrian column, Rosenberg had also brought his corps north of the river, but his excessive caution, bad roads, and the long distance his men had to cover meant that his forward elements did not arrive east of Ergolding until 5 p.m. Stutterheim's troopers skirmished with a squadron of Wrede's 3rd Chevaulegers around Postau for four hours before the Bavarians retired on their supports at Neufahrn, but IV Corps had no other encounters with the enemy during the day.[27] The corps spent the night with its advance guard around Essenbach and the main body at Wörth. Vécsey continued his lone march up the Danube, halting at Leiblfing with a small detachment in Straubing and outposts as far as the Kleine Laaber. He was, however, able to notify Rosenberg that his patrols finally had contact with II Corps.

On the army's left flank, VI Corps had closed up on the Isar after a long and painful march over execrable side roads. Only at 11 p.m. was Hiller able to report that 'all troops of the army corps as well as guns have arrived in the area of Aich and Moosburg'.[28] Even so, the rearmost combat elements were several kilometres to the rear at Buch am Erlbach.[29] Of Hiller's other detachments, GM Nordmann was at Berglern after a wearing march up from Erding, and Oberst Albert de Best of *Klebek* Infantry No. 14 occupied Moosburg with two battalions of his regiment and two squadrons of *Rosenberg* Chevaulegers.[30] While the rest of the corps was struggling towards the Isar, Major Scheibler had energetically scouted the region north of the river. In addition to sending an infantry/cavalry detachment to Freising, he personally led a reconnaissance patrol of *Rosenberg* Chevaulegers towards Pfeffenhausen, capturing five men from a patrol of the 2nd Bavarian Chevaulegers at Gammelsdorf before being turned back by a squadron of the regiment south of Pfeffenhausen.

On the army's farther flanks, Jellacic's advance guard entered Munich and Bellegarde did nothing. Lending credence to false reports of a French division in Nuremberg and a possible French advance against Amberg from Sulzbach, the I Corps commander, 'true to his previous passivity', decided to hold in place and await further developments. Austrian activity north of the Danube was thus limited to local reconnaissances and minor movements by the advance guard elements of the two corps.[31] 'Another day was thereby lost in inactivity' commented the Austrian official history.[32]

On the Allied side, the various components of the Army of Germany continued their efforts to comply with Berthier's confused instructions. Sandwiched between Charles and Bellegarde, Marshal Davout arrived in Regensburg on 16 April. St Hilaire and Pajol's detachment were already in and around the city, but the 2nd Heavy Cavalry and the bulk of 3rd Corps were still north of the Danube along the road to Dasswang, with Friant's rear guard at Deining under Jacquinot. Two of the Bavarian divisions, as we have seen, were in the process of retiring on the Abens during the night, although Wrede still had his cavalry forward at Rottenburg and Pfeffenhausen. The 1st Division, on the other hand, had moved from Au to Pfaffenhofen, and Lefebvre himself had his headquarters at Geisenfeld.[33] Demont remained at Ingolstadt and most of the Württemberg contingent was still around Donauwörth and Rain. The two Württemberg light infantry battalions, the *Herzog Louis* Jäger-zu-Pferd, and three guns, however, were posted further east at Neuburg, where the 1st Heavy Cavalry was also gathered. Rouyer had his Germans at Oettingen. These movements occurred in an atmosphere of tumult, worry, and uncertainty, leading an observant Bavarian to note that 'after eight days everything closely resembled a retreat'.[34]

The atmosphere in Berthier's headquarters was equally frenetic and anxious, but the marshal seemed pleased with the dispositions he had ordered, essentially a dangerously thin cordon stretching some 140 kilometres from Regensburg through Augsburg to Landsberg on the Lech. His satisfaction dissipated when he finally received Napoleon's 10 April telegram along with a 12 April letter. The telegram having directed Berthier to 'concentrate the troops at Augsburg and have everyone ready to march', Napoleon had assumed in the 12 April note that 'you are in Augsburg and have assembled my entire army on the Lech'. Berthier must have been appalled. He wrote a plaintive postscript at the end of a message he had been about to dispatch to his emperor: 'I would have been saved a great embarrassment if your telegraphic message of 10 April, arriving at Strasbourg on the 13th and handed to me here on the 16th, had reached me earlier.'[35]

The authors of the Austrian official history point out that all was not yet lost: there was still time to call 3rd Corps back to Ingolstadt and order the Bavarians to retire to the Lech.[36] Such bold strokes were beyond poor Berthier. He restricted himself to sending minor messages to Lefebvre and Oudinot before climbing in his carriage at 10 a.m. to hurry off to Donauwörth. Clattering into town at 4 p.m., he was doubtless dismayed to discover that Napoleon was not there. After six hours of restless waiting, he concluded that the emperor must have gone to Augsburg, so at 10 p.m. he clambered aboard his coach once more and set off for his starting point.[37] Had he waited and managed to get some decent sleep, he could have greeted Napoleon when he stepped down from his travelling office at dawn on 17 April.

17 APRIL:
NAPOLEON ARRIVES AND CHARLES DELIBERATES

For the Austrians, the 17th was another day of hesitancy. Charles, left in a murk of uncertainty by poor reconnaissance and intelligence, knew very little about the enemy situation on the night of 16/17 April. Deroy's route of retreat was clear enough and it seemed likely that all or part of the Bavarian corps would assemble, at least temporarily, behind the Abens, but he held almost no specific information about Davout and had only a vague picture of French strength and activity on the Lech. Preparing his 'disposition' for the following day, therefore, he 'came to no definitive conclusion'.[38] The result was almost no forward movement by the main bodies of the Hauptarmee. Instead, Charles allowed the day to pass in arranging his corps north of the Isar on their likely avenues of future advance: V Corps around Arth, III

Corps (with the *Levenehr* Dragoons No. 3 attached) at Türkenfeld, and IV Corps near Essenbach.[39] The two reserve corps were simply brought north of the Isar, while Hiller's command collected itself around Moosburg and Jellacic halted the main body of his division on the Isar east of Munich. In the army's rear, the Vienna Volunteers were finally approaching the area of operations. Hiller's contingent (4th, 5th, and 6th Battalions) was just south of Landshut by the nightfall of the 17th, and those allotted to V Corps (1st, 2nd, and 3rd Battalions) were back at Ganghofen between the Rott and the Vils. Additionally, the *Wallach-Illyria* Grenz Regiment No. 13 had arrived at Passau/Oberhaus on 16 April, allowing GM Josef Reinwald von Waldegg to depart for the Hauptarmee on the 17th with half of the regular troops previously assigned to that mission.[40]

There was a similar lack of enterprise north of the Danube. Some movement occurred as Bellegarde directed Kolowrat to have II Corps outside Stadtamhof by 18 April. Kolowrat marched the bulk of his command to Nittenau in response to these orders and sent FML Klenau forward towards Regensburg with the advance guard. The other half of Bellegarde's force, however, did little. Bellegarde was paralysed by false intelligence reports indicating that fifteen French infantry regiments and Davout himself might be located between Kastl and Neumarkt. As a result, he held his own I Corps at Schwarzenfeld for the 17th, although he did extend his cantonments south to Schwandorf as Kolowrat's men pulled out.

If the major elements of the eight Austrian corps made only limited moves on 17 April, their advance guards were quite active, leading to several small scuffles with Allied screening forces.[41] Advancing to Pfeffenhausen with the V Corps advance guard, Radetzky sent a battalion and a squadron to scout towards Rottenburg and pushed two squadrons of *Karl* Uhlans and two companies of Grenzer north on the road to Siegenburg in the wake of the retreating Bavarians. The latter encountered Preysing's cavalry brigade around Schweinbach and were forced to retire to Oberhornbach after a smart cavalry engagement.[42] On Radetzky's right, a patrol from the III Corps advance guard reached the Danube opposite Kehlheim to report that the French held the northern bank and that the bridge had been destroyed.[43] Fourth Corps scouts found French outposts at Köfering, and elements of the *Klenau* Chevaulegers from Vécsey's brigade clashed with the 11th Chasseurs at Geisling.[44] These patrols and skirmishes collected exactly the information Charles needed to plan the Hauptarmee's next move: that Davout was in Regensburg with 30,000 infantry and substantial cavalry. Scheibler's patrols west from Nandlstadt, on the other hand, produced nothing, and Jellacic's troopers exchanged fire with the French 9th Hussars near Moosach, but undertook nothing to learn more about Allied activity on the Lech.[45] In general, the Austrian advance guards, far ahead of their respective corps, were too weak to force their way through the screens of Allied cavalry. If some patrols were lucky, most discovered 'those places where some enemy forces might be found, without having the capability of procuring complete and satisfactory intelligence'.[46]

Unfortunately for Charles, the crucial intelligence gathered by IV Corps and Vécsey did not reach his headquarters until the morning of 18 April.[47] As he dictated his dispositions for the 18th, therefore, he was relying on an increasingly inaccurate picture of Allied deployments. The general view in the headquarters of the Hauptarmee on the evening of the 17th was that the French and their German allies were stretched out in an immense cordon with Davout north of the river from Regensburg to Neumarkt opposing Bellegarde, the Bavarians in the process of crossing the Danube to the north, the Württembergers in the general vicinity of Rain, and the remaining French forces on the Lech towards Augsburg. Charles thus perceived an opportunity to smash through this imagined cordon: 'I will pass the Danube at some point between Regensburg and Ingolstadt, and make for Eichstätt,'[48] he wrote to Bellegarde. With the Austrian Hauptarmee ensconced on the Altmühl, any French forces at Regensburg would have to retreat, indeed Davout would have to evacuate all of eastern Bavaria. Moreover, the French would be manoeuvred out of their position on the Lech in classical eighteenth-century style without the necessity of a major battle. With these exciting thoughts in mind, his staff drafted instructions that would send the central elements of the Main Army forward in the general direction of Kehlheim and Neustadt on 18 April.

Two observations are useful here. First, Charles was correct in perceiving an opportunity 'because', as he told Bellegarde, 'the French army is still so divided'.[49] He was wrong in assessing the precise nature of this opportunity, principally because he mistakenly assumed Davout to be preoccupied with Bellegarde, but the opportunity certainly existed. Second, however, is the surprising lack of urgency in his orders and the completely ordinary marches the corps were called upon to conduct on the 18th. Having largely wasted the 17th by making only minimal forward movements, and facing an enemy acknowledged to be enterprising and impetuous, one might have reasonably expected a high degree of energetic haste. But this was not in evidence. Instead, V Corps was to proceed to Ludmannsdorf on the right, III Corps to Unter-Eulenbach, and IV Corps to Rottenburg. The reserve corps were to move to Pfeffenhausen, while Hiller was instructed 'to march

slowly through Au towards Pfaffenhofen' as a flank guard.[50] Charles expected no combat on the 18th and brought the army's trains across the Isar
at Landshut, a decision that would have significant negative consequences
during the coming days.

In the absence of significant Austrian activity, the Bavarians were able
to move with considerable freedom. Although Wrede's cavalry skirmished
with Radetzky's troopers, his infantry remained in combat formation behind
the Abens for most of the day, awaiting an enemy who never appeared.
Protected by Wrede, Deroy's men rested after their exertions of the 16th and
their long night march. New orders arrived as evening fell. The two divisions
were to withdraw north of the Danube during the night, Deroy to Ingolstadt
and Wrede opposite Vohburg. Meanwhile, the crown prince's division
established itself at Reichertshofen on the south side of the river. Berthier
hopefully envisaged this attenuated Bavarian position as the link between
the troops on the Lech and Davout at Regensburg. One need not think long
to imagine how Davout perceived this situation. As far as Deroy and Wrede
were concerned, however, orders were orders. While Wrede's men burned
the bridge over the Abens at Siegenburg and ordered all potential bridging
material near Vohburg transported to the north bank, Deroy's division
marched off into the darkness towards Neustadt and its new position north
of the great river. Wrede soon followed.[51]

Davout spent a tense day in Regensburg as Austrian forces slowly closed
in on him from north, east, and south. Increasingly concerned about the
column approaching from the Isar, albeit slowly, and assessing it to be the
principal Habsburg host, he brought Gudin's division and Montbrun's light
cavalry south-west of the city to protect his right flank. At the same time, he
wanted to keep his communications on the north bank of the Danube open
as long as possible; he therefore maintained Friant, St Sulpice, and Jacquinot
along the Nuremberg road as far as Dasswang and Piré at Dietfurt on the
Altmühl.

Other elements of Davout's corps engaged in a long firefight with
the II Corps advance guard when Klenau tried to probe French defences
on the Regen just north of Stadtamhof. Klenau approached Sallern from
the north-east on the morning of the 17th and established his troops in a
concealed position near the town.[52] At 1 p.m., he ordered patrols to push
towards Reinhausen and deployed III/*Zedtwitz*, the 7th Jägers, the *Riesch*
Dragoons, and a cavalry battery in the low ground near Weichs. At the same
time, a battery unlimbered on the hills east of Sallern and opened fire on
the town.[53] The French only had light forces on the east bank of the Regen:

the three voltigeur companies of the 17th Ligne in Reinhausen and a weak outpost in Weichs. The principal French position was on the heights to the west where St Hilaire had established himself to protect the road leading north. Outnumbered, the French quickly abandoned Weichs, but had no intention of giving up Reinhausen and its bridge without a serious fight. This the Austrians were not prepared to offer. Klenau limited himself to sending skirmishers from Steffanini's Jäger battalion against the village and setting some of its buildings alight with his howitzers. The cavalry battery in the low ground also availed itself of the opportunity to lob shot and shell at the French troops crossing the stone bridge.[54] Beyond inflicting misery on the terrified inhabitants, the results of the bombardment were minimal, and Klenau failed to learn that Davout already had some 35,000 men and forty-five guns tightly collected around Regensburg. The Austrians lost fifty-seven men during the exchange, while Davout reported 'twenty or so' casualties.[55]

As Davout's and Lefebvre's men were skirmishing with Austrian probes on the fringes of the army, their emperor was applying his intense energy to piercing the fog surrounding the situation. He had only vague information about his own troops and knew even less about the enemy. What he did know—that the army was not assembled on the Lech—surprised and angered him. Moreover, to his vast irritation, no one in Donauwörth could depict recent developments and current status in any useful detail. Vandamme, who rode in during the morning, could only report on his own contingent and supply the alarming but incorrect news that the Austrians held Regensburg! Fortunately, one of Massena's staff officers could at least describe the positions of 2nd and 4th Corps. Napoleon thus sent a courier to recall Berthier to Donauwörth post-haste and began to read through the dispatches of the past several days. Guided more by his intuition and experience than by the information in these vague and contradictory messages or Berthier's sketchy reports, he rapidly developed a general picture of the situation.[56] He dismissed Bellegarde at once; he probably felt confident that the force from Bohemia was no larger than the 40,000 reported by Davout and it was moving with such extreme deliberation as to pose no immediate danger. Similarly, he gave no heed to Berthier's anxieties about the Tyrol. Instead, he focused on the column that had crossed the Isar. He remained alert to the possibility that a major Austrian force, perhaps the bulk of the enemy army, might be moving toward the Amper from Munich and Freising, but he concentrated his attention on the Habsburg troops north of Landshut as both an imminent threat and a tremendous opportunity. When GB Monthion, Berthier's chief of staff, told him that

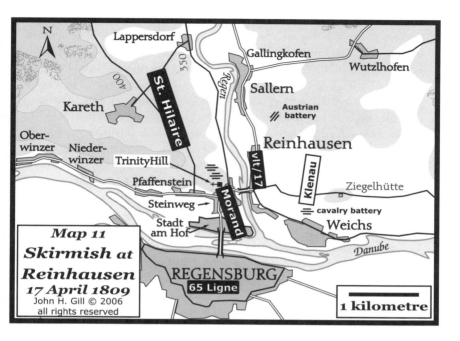

Map 11
Skirmish at Reinhausen
17 April 1809
John H. Gill © 2006
all rights reserved

1 kilometre

the Austrians had crossed the Isar and were marching on Regensburg, the emperor was incredulous: 'that is impossible!' On being assured that this was indeed the case, disbelief gave way to excitement and he delightedly exclaimed 'that army is lost!'[57] He still needed detailed confirmation, but with this general image in mind, he acted immediately to stave off this closest Austrian danger, to concentrate the army in a central position, and, above all, to gather information on friend and foe alike. By midmorning on the 17th, couriers were speeding away with urgent messages for the corps commanders.

The emperor attached the highest priority to recalling Davout from Regensburg, but the distance from Donauwörth was daunting (130 kilometres) and the security of the roads uncertain. Napoleon, after dictating instructions for Davout at 10 a.m., thus sent four copies of his orders during the late morning, dispatched two similar letters in the afternoon, and directed both Lefebvre and Wrede to pass his instructions to Regensburg as well.[58] The thrust of this pressing correspondence was that 3rd Corps was to withdraw to Ingolstadt via Neustadt south of the Danube with the stipulation that Friant should fall back on the northern side of the river, leaving outposts on the Altmühl.[59] Lefebvre would protect Davout's movement by holding in check 'the corps from Landshut'.[60] Napoleon, however, did not want to confine himself to simple withdrawal. He correctly surmised that 3rd Corps's march would surprise the Austrians and thus gave both marshals specific instructions to 'fall upon the column from Landshut' if Davout's unexpected move generated 'a superb occasion' to 'do some harm' to the enemy without diverting too far or long from his route of march. While evincing considerable confidence and his irrepressible offensive impetus, he remained acutely conscious of his lack of reliable information, and pressed Davout and Lefebvre for data: 'I await with impatience news of the enemy'.[61]

Davout and Lefebvre represented one aspect of Napoleon's nascent concept of operations for the coming several days. The other major theme in his planning centred around Massena. Treating Massena as commander of Oudinot's men and Espagne's cuirassiers as well as the marshal's own 4th Corps, the emperor's messages implied an exciting possibility: if the Austrian troops near Munich were simply a flank guard and if major enemy forces were located between the Isar and the Danube, he would hold them in front with 3rd and 7th Corps while Massena took them in the flank by surprise.[62] He arrived at this assessment as early as midmorning on the 17th and his impression was reinforced during that day as further information reached Donauwörth.[63]

The first step in making this concept a reality was an immediate move by Massena from Augsburg and Aichach to Pfaffenhofen. 'The purpose of your march is to combine with that of the army to catch the enemy *en flagrant délit* and destroy his columns', he explained to Massena. The marshal was also to 'push strong patrols towards Dachau to make certain when you move that enemy infantry has not arrived in that position', but Napoleon clearly did not expect these patrols to find anything of consequence. He was already anticipating a major engagement north of the Isar where the power of Massena's flank attack would be amplified by surprise. He therefore abjured Massena to prepare his command with the greatest possible speed, but to preserve the strictest secrecy concerning his destination and to circulate rumours that he was planning an advance on Munich or towards the Tyrol. He also issued detailed guidance for the fortification of Augsburg.[64] Always prudent, Napoleon needed Augsburg to be secure against any surprise and wanted to ensure that all Allied detachments, baggage, and other impedimenta were safely stowed within its walls. Nothing was to slow Massena or distract the Army of Germany from its principal aim: the defeat of the Austrian field army.

Psychological and political factors were also integral to Napoleon's operational planning. He had carved precious hours out of his compressed schedule to reassure the monarchs of both Württemberg and Bavaria on his way to the Danube and now took care to issue a stirring proclamation. Published in German as well as French and rapidly distributed to the army and the public at large, his compact declaration explained the cause of the war, inspired Allied co-operation, announced his arrival in the theatre of war, and promised victory in simple but powerful statements.[65] At the same time, his words subtly wove a bond between the common soldiers and their imperial commander, emphasising common experiences of past triumph in a familiar, confiding tone.

> Soldiers! The territory of the Confederation has been violated! The Austrian general hopes that we will flee at the aspect of his arms and that we will abandon the territory of our allies. I have arrived among you with the speed of an eagle.
>
> Soldiers! You were with me when the Austrian sovereign came to my bivouac in Moravia. You heard him implore my clemency and promise me eternal friendship. Defeated in three wars, Austria owes everything to our generosity: three times it has been faithless! Our past successes are a certain guarantee of the victory that awaits us. March now, and let the enemy know their conquerors![66]

With this initial proclamation on its way to printing presses across Germany, Napoleon returned to the operational situation, outlining his vision for the coming several days in a comprehensive letter to Davout on the evening of the 17th: 'Tomorrow will be a preparatory day for us to concentrate, and I expect that we will be able to manoeuvre against the columns that have debouched from Landshut and elsewhere on Wednesday [19 April] to rout those that are between the Danube, the Isar, and perhaps even the Inn.'[67] Napoleon's predictive assessment was accurate, but his timing proved optimistic. Whether as a leadership technique to spur his subordinates or from an excess of confidence, he was asking the impossible of his officers and troops. Massena, who was ordered to have his combat elements clear of Friedberg by 4 a.m. on the 18th, did not have his final instructions in hand until 2 a.m. that morning. His first three divisions, quartered in small villages west of the Lech, would require many hours just to assemble; Boudet at Landsberg and Marulaz still further south at Schongau could not possibly even receive their instructions until midmorning on 18 April. As for Oudinot, his infantry was fairly well concentrated, but much of his light cavalry would take time to gather. The men of 2nd and 4th Corps exerted themselves to the uttermost to comply with their sovereign's intent, but there were not enough hours in the day. Even if we accept Bonnal's complaint that Massena was 'no longer the man of Zürich, Rivoli, and Genoa', the marshal could hardly have done more at this stage.[68]

Likewise, Napoleon wanted to see Davout's corps in Neustadt by the evening of 18 April, but Davout only received the first of the emperor's urgent messages at 8 a.m. that very morning. At that point, Friant, St Sulpice, and some of his light cavalry were still well north of the Danube. Friant, the corps rear guard, could not pass through Regensburg until

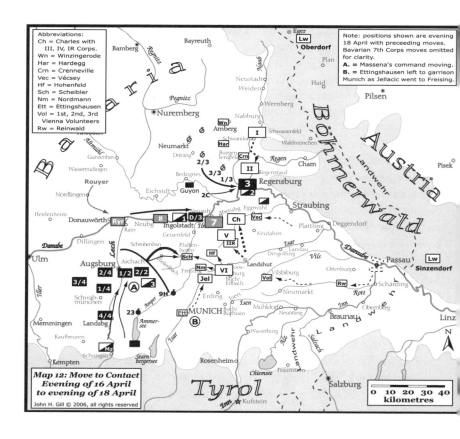

Map 12: Move to Contact
Evening of 16 April
to evening of 18 April

John H. Gill © 2006, all rights reserved

evening, and Davout, concerned for his command's integrity and security, decided to await his subordinate's arrival south of the river before beginning the march west.

As a result of these considerations, carefully explicated by both marshals in letters to the emperor on the morning of the 18th, neither Davout nor Massena would be available until 19 April at the earliest.[69] Napoleon's desired timetable would be set back by a full day.

18 APRIL: PREPARATIONS AND TENTATIVE CONTACT

Like 3rd and 4th Corps, the Bavarian 7th Corps was unable to comply with the Emperor's operational desires for 18 April. While Davout and Massena were assembling on the night of 17/18 April, the Bavarians, still operating according to Berthier's earlier instructions, had begun to retire north of the Danube. Deroy's 3rd Division left its bivouacs west of Siegenburg at 6.30 p.m. on the 17th. Crossing the Danube at Vohburg, the division halted in its new assembly area at Grossmehring around 3.00 a.m. on 18 April after an exhausting 28-kilometre night march. The last units finally pulled in as the sun rose. They enjoyed only the briefest respite. Deroy had expected to continue on to Neuburg and hoped to rest his men there, but new orders reached him shortly after dawn and, by 8 a.m., the lead elements of his division were once more on the road, retracing their steps east towards Neustadt under the urgency of Napoleon's energy.[70]

Wrede, for his part, had burned the little span at Siegenburg and marched for the Neustadt bridge at 9 p.m. on the night of the 17th. Some of his men were already on the north bank of the Danube 'when, near Neustadt, a courier of His Majesty the Emperor brought the lieutenant general commanding an order to reoccupy the position behind the Abens'.[71] It was 2 a.m. Wrede turned his wet and weary column about and headed back to the east.

An hour earlier, Crown Prince Ludwig had received similar instructions at his headquarters in Reichertshofen. 'His Imperial and Royal Majesty, who has arrived in Donauwörth, has changed the dispositions ordained for you for tomorrow', began Drouet's note. Marching 'with the greatest possible celerity' via Ingolstadt and Vohburg on the north bank of the Danube, Ludwig was to join the corps on the Abens, 'knowing that it is important that the division arrive on line with the other two in the position at Siegenburg'.[72] By the early hours of 18 April, therefore, the entire 7th Corps was on the move in accordance with the emperor's will.

Napoleon's intention was that Lefebvre should have his corps in position at Neustadt between 9 and 11 a.m. in order to 'make a diversion that will occupy a number of men equal to your own' in support of Davout.[73] This proved impossible. The 2nd Division reassembled itself at Neustadt during the day but could not return to the heights west of Siegenburg until 5 p.m. The 1st and 3rd Divisions, exhausted after wearing marches in the wretched weather (the crown prince had covered forty-nine kilometres from Reichertshofen), only took over Wrede's bivouacs outside Neustadt during the late afternoon.[74] Even though 7th Corps had not been able to assemble and move against the Austrians during the morning of the 18th as Napoleon had hoped, it was now, for the first time in the campaign, united and functioning under unambiguous orders from army headquarters: 'tell the Bavarians what I expect of them in the coming days,' Napoleon wrote to Lefebvre, 'you understand the urgency of the circumstances; I do not have to instruct you to act accordingly.'[75]

Wrede's advance guard approached the Abens opposite Siegenburg as afternoon was melting into evening. Radetzky's troops had exchanged fire with Wrede's rear guard east of the Abens earlier in the day and restored the Siegenburg bridge as the Bavarian 2nd Division withdrew. During the afternoon, a half-squadron of uhlans ventured across the little river. When Wrede returned in response to Napoleon's new orders, therefore, his lead elements (13th Infantry, 2nd Chevaulegers, and one battery) came upon this reconnaissance party in the Dürnbucher Forst and sent it flying. Left in possession of the west bank, Wrede established outposts along the Abens, placed a regiment each in Abensberg and opposite Siegenburg, and settled the rest of his troops into a bivouac around Altdürnbuch.[76]

Vandamme's Württemberg troops were also headed for Neustadt and the Abens. Relieved at Donauwörth and Rain by Rouyer's men, 8th Corps moved east on 18 April under 'a terrible rain'.[77] The muddy roads along the north bank of the Danube were clogged with heavy cavalry and vehicles, imposing additional burdens on the slogging infantry and artillery. Napoleon was on the same road, accompanied by Marshal Lannes, just arrived from Spain. Departing Donauwörth at 1 p.m. escorted by Württemberg light horse, he stopped in Rain to inspect the bridgehead and lavish personal attention on its garrison, the Light Battalion of the 4th Rheinbund Regiment from the so-called 'Saxon Duchies' in Thuringia.[78] He then pressed on for Ingolstadt, missing no opportunity to connect with his army en route.[79] He halted his carriage to compliment GL von Neubronn on the appearance and discipline of the Württemberg troops and stopped again later to offer similar plaudits to the commander of the Light Brigade, GM Friedrich August von Hügel. The Württemberg contingent ended its day in camps and quarters stretched between Neuburg and Ingolstadt, with one battalion (II/*Camrer*) assigned to garrison the latter city.

The 1st Heavy Cavalry camped near Grossmehring. Its commander, the mordantly patrician GD Nansouty, had now arrived from Spain and was horrified to see that his colonels had authorized their men to shear off their queues and adopt a more fashionably modern short hairstyle in his absence. Catapulted into a state of high dudgeon, he placed his colonels under arrest for this affront. The colonels soon reappeared at the heads of the regiments, but the queues were gone forever.[80]

East of the discomfited heavy cavalry and its indignant commander was GD Demont with his slender division of conscripts. They held Vohburg along with II/1st Bavarian Infantry. The Bavarians also left two battalions, forty cavalry, and two guns from Deroy's division to guard the intersection of the Vohburg and Geisenfeld roads south of Münchmünster.[81]

Napoleon's arrival on the Danube was now making itself felt across the army. The effect was electric. In addition to the Württembergers and Rheinbund men vouchsafed a glimpse of the famous hat and greatcoat, a new spirit surged through the ad hoc Army of Germany as the imperial proclamation was read and, perhaps even more important, as order, purpose, and decision replaced the uncertainty and incoherence of the preceding week. 'Finally!' remembered GB Lorencez, 'an order of the day filled all with confidence; it announced the presence of the emperor.'[82] 'This news produced its customary effect; everyone was animated by a new confidence and certain of victory,' wrote Colonel Berthezène of the 10th Léger.[83] 'Let the Kaiserliks [Austrians] come!' summarised the views from the lower ranks.[84] The French were not alone in their relief and excitement. 'A proclamation issued from Donauwörth on 17 April announced his [Napoleon's] arrival and the coming defeat of the enemy,' noted a soldier of the Bavarian 6th Light Battalion.[85] 'From then on,' recalled another Bavarian, 'no more retrograde movements took place; everything went forward relentlessly.'[86] There would be no more retreats.

Davout spent the 18th in his positions around Regensburg awaiting the arrival of his remaining forces from north of the Danube and meticulously planning his march to Neustadt. While a staff engineer conducted a thorough reconnaissance of the planned routes of march, he sent an officer and twenty-five troopers of the 5th Hussar Regiment to make certain the bridge at Siegenburg was intact. He also moved I/30th Ligne to secure the defile at Abbach.

There were only minor engagements during the day for 3rd Corps. Montbrun and Pajol, probing south, had brushes with elements of Vécsey's brigade along the Grosse Laaber, and Morand's men clashed again with Klenau's detachment on the Regen. In the latter case, Morand sent the 1st and 2nd Battalions of the 17th Ligne across the Regen to reinforce the three voltigeur companies in Reinhausen at 8 a.m. when the Austrians seemed to be preparing a new attack. The fighting quickly subsided only to flare anew in the afternoon as a battalion of the 65th Ligne relieved the 17th in its defensive positions. By 4 p.m., however, the musketry had died down and the 17th Ligne retired south across the Danube, with the rest of Morand's division, leaving the 65th under Colonel Louis François Coutard to garrison Regensburg. The lone battalion did not remain long in Reinhausen. Burning the bridge over the Regen, it withdrew to Stadtamhof and the Trinity (Dreifaltigkeits) Hill during the evening. The tentative Austrian action at Reinhausen did nothing to slow the passage of Davout's remaining troops over the Danube.[87] By 8 or 9 p.m., St Sulpice, Friant, and the last of the light cavalry had passed through Regensburg to occupy bivouacs south of the city.

Other than parts of Colonel Coutard's regiment, the only French troops now north of the Danube were Colonel Claude Raymond Guyon with his 12th Chasseurs, I/111th Ligne, and two companies of III/15th Léger. Deployed at Hemau and on the Altmühl, Guyon's tiny detachment of 1,700 infantry and cavalry would monitor the movements of Bellegarde's 25,000 men during the coming crucial days.

To the south, Montbrun advanced along the road towards Eggmühl with two hussar regiments (5th and 7th) and two battalions of the 7th Léger. His advance guard exchanged blows with two squadrons of *Klenau* Chevaulegers from Vécsey's brigade during the morning near Höhenberg, but the two sides pulled back after inflicting a few wounds on each other. Similarly, the advance guard of Pajol's 11th Chasseurs encountered elements of the *Klenau* Chevaulegers near Pfatter. The Austrians overthrew the leading French forces, but Pajol brought up the rest of the 11th to restore the situation, forcing the Habsburg troopers to retire behind the Grosse Laaber after two hours of skirmishing. With no infantry support, Pajol left one squadron of the 11th Chasseurs at Pfatter and fell back to Geissling with the other two.[88] Thus ended the day for the flanking forces along the Grosse Laaber.

While Davout was readying his corps for its next move, Massena's men were on the road, embarked on the first stages of what was to become an epic march. Napoleon, conveying the confidence and intimacy he felt towards

Massena, had sent a letter on the morning of the 18th exhorting the marshal to make every possible exertion:

> With one word you will understand what is happening. Prince Charles, with his entire army, debouched from Landshut towards Regensburg yesterday; he has three army corps estimated at 80,000 men . . . Everything leads to the conclusion that all of the affairs of Germany will be decided between the 18th, 19th, and 20th . . . We will not have much action here before the 19th, and you will recognise instantly, at a glance, that circumstances demand activity and speed as never before . . . I regard the enemy as lost if Oudinot and your three divisions have debouched before dawn and if, in this critical situation, you tell my troops what it is that they must do.[89]

In his own hand, Napoleon added the famous lines 'Activity, activity, speed! I rely upon you.' in the margins of the letter. Although the emperor had read and understood Massena's message explaining his inability to comply with the initial instructions (those of 17 April), he still hoped that the bulk of Massena's two corps could reach Pfaffenhofen early on 19 April 'to fall on the rear of Prince Charles's army'.[90] Massena, receiving this note at 2 p.m., when his corps was already moving, forwarded it to Oudinot with a note promising to 'do the impossible to march through the night and share the glory that awaits you'.[91] He also sent copies to his division commanders to imbue the lower echelons of his command with the driving urgency of the emperor's will.

Massena's initial orders for the march east reached his subordinate divisions during the night of 17/18 April and into the morning of the 18th. Oudinot was able to comply promptly. His corps, led by Colbert's light cavalry and followed by Espagne's heavies, arrived east of Pfaffenhofen with the dawn to engage Major Scheibler's detachment (see below). The three closest divisions of 4th Corps, on the other hand, had their troops dispersed in quarters as far as thirty-nine kilometres from Augsburg. Massena's first regiments (Legrand's division), therefore, had already completed a respectable day's march when they reached the city late in the morning. But their trials had only begun. Leaving behind all baggage and almost all vehicles, they were told 'to carry as much bread as possible' and hurried out of Augsburg after a brief rest.[92] Normal march routine called for brigades to move as units, but now individual regiments were pushed east as soon as they were ready. The next station was Aichach, where Legrand's men arrived weary and wet at 10 p.m. They had come fifty kilometres since early that morning, but only enjoyed some two hours of rest before the drums called them to their feet once more and they headed out into the night. The weather was execrable, a vile combination of cold and rain that sapped the men's strength as they pressed on numbly through the darkness. Most units marched by the paved post road through Schrobenhausen, but, in an effort to save an hour or two, some of the infantry found themselves assigned to the direct 'traverse': a muddy secondary road via Weilenbach that only increased the misery of man and horse. For some units, paucity of food compounded the grinding fatigue of the march: 'We arrived in Aichach without any food at all, and here as well no distribution could take place owing to scarcity of supplies.'[93]

Trailing stragglers, Legrand's lead elements reached Pfaffenhofen at 10 a.m. on the 19th, well after Oudinot's fight with Scheibler had concluded.[94] Several more hours passed before the division was fully assembled. Carra Saint-Cyr's men arrived during the late afternoon and evening, Molitor at 6 p.m. Boudet and the French light cavalry came in during the night. The condition of the men may be imagined. The journal of the Baden brigade recorded that the 2nd Infantry Regiment, marching on the Weilenbach traverse, 'arrived in the hamlet of Singenbach [fourteen kilometres west of Pfaffenhofen] at 9 a.m. in such a state of exhaustion that our men fainted to the ground'.[95] Enduring this punishing pace, some of Massena's regiments slogged 100 kilometres in the space of those two days and Marulaz's troopers rode 110. Even Oudinot's men, many of them inexperienced conscripts, covered between fifty and sixty kilometres and fought a small engagement in a period of slightly more than twenty-four hours. In a march that rivals better-known exploits of the era, the German troops and the young Frenchmen were beginning to learn how Napoleon made war.[96] More such instruction was to come.

As the Army of Germany was turning itself about in accordance with Napoleon's intentions, Charles was changing his own plans.[97] The disposition issued on the 17th oriented the Hauptarmee generally towards a crossing of the Danube 'at some point between Regensburg and Ingolstadt'. As new intelligence reached him during the morning hours of 18 April, however, Charles came to recognise that he had a unique opportunity to strike Davout's isolated corps. The key message came from Vécsey relating a prisoner's comments that Marshal Davout was south of Regensburg 'with 30,000 men and four light cavalry regiments'.[98] Forwarding Vécsey's report and other intelligence at 6 a.m. on the 18th, Rosenberg expressed exaggerated anxieties about his own right flank but added that 'the movement Your Imperial Highness is making today will cost him [Davout] dearly if stays in this position until tomorrow.'[99] In Stutterheim's words: 'We found it hard to believe, because this position [Davout's] could be extremely embarrassing for the French; but eventually reliable information arrived from every direction and removed all doubts.'[100]

Having thus suddenly awakened to Davout's vulnerability, Charles issued new orders at 10 a.m. re-organising the Hauptarmee to accomplish two tasks: to fall on the isolated Davout while protecting the Austrian left flank against the possible arrival of French reinforcements from the Lech. Based on the road network and the existing positions of the various corps, he chose Rohr as the central assembly point for the strike force he intended to employ against Davout on the 19th, and orders were hurried off directing III Corps, IV Corps, and I Reserve Corps to concentrate around this town. Charles supplemented this force with FML Karl Freiherr von Lindenau's division from V Corps and GM Andreas von Schneller's cuirassier brigade from II Reserve Corps, placing them under Liechtenstein along with Vécsey's brigade. According to the tentative plan for the 19th, Liechtenstein would command Lindenau, Vécsey, and his own cuirassier brigades as well as Schneller's troopers, while losing his twelve battalions of grenadiers; nominally designated to join IV Corps, the grenadiers actually functioned as an army reserve under Charles's hand. By these measures, Charles was able to mass some 66,700 infantry and cavalry around Rohr, not including Vécsey's 6,100 men near Eggmühl.[101]

On the Austrian left, the remaining units of V Corps and II Reserve Corps, some 18,650 in all, would form the flank shield along the Abens. Continuing their march in accordance with these directions, V Corps spent the night at Ludmannsdorf with Radetzky's outposts on the eastern side of the Abens, a detachment under GM Josef Freiherr Mesko de Felso-Kubinyi at Attenhofen, and another detachment at Mainburg to await Hiller's arrival.[102] Kienmayer, now reduced to five grenadier battalions and four squadrons of *Knesevich* Dragoons, halted around Pfeffenhausen for the night. Back at Landshut, the local citizens were amazed by the mass of Austrian supply vehicles and other baggage rumbling through their city: 'wagons without number ... It seemed as if these gentlemen had it in mind to pack all of Bavaria into wagons and ship it back to Vienna.'[103] This great agglomeration of vehicles, horses, conscripted civilian drivers, sutlers, government officials, women, children, and other rear area impedimenta would soon pose a dangerous embarrassment to the army. Charles, acutely conscious of Landshut's importance to his logistical support, ordered Hiller to Au 'as rapidly as possible' to guard that segment of the Abens as 'protection for the line of communications'.[104] Concern for his supply lines also moved Charles to leave Jellacic in Munich 'so that Landshut and the whole area of the upper Isar do not remain open'.[105]

Hiller, however, made no move to comply with his orders, contenting himself with reporting to Charles that VI Corps would march to Au on the 19th and to Mainburg on the following day. Nightfall on 18 April thus found the corps still around Moosburg with its advance guard at Zolling and GM Otto Graf Hohenfeld's brigade at Nandlstadt.[106] Scheibler pushed all the way to Pfaffenhofen. Additionally, Hiller had called Jellacic forward from Munich. That general, leaving GM Konstantin Ettinghausen with two battalions and two squadrons in the Bavarian capital, had dutifully marched up to Freising on the 18th. Now, to Hiller's vast irritation, he had to issue orders sending Jellacic back to Munich: 'I leave to the judgement of every informed person ... if it would have been more sensible to follow my suggestion and post FML Jellacic at Moosburg'. [107] For once, he was right.

For his forces north of the Danube, Charles used unusually active and aggressive language in ordering Kolowrat to 'do every possible to eradicate this enemy corps [Davout] completely'.[108] He gave no indication that either I or II Corps should come south once Regensburg was in Austrian hands; Kolowrat was merely to co-operate from the northern bank of the river. Kolowrat, however, did not receive this order until the morning of 19 April, so he spent the day preparing to attack Stadtamhof on the 19th as previously instructed. Although Klenau grappled with Davout's troops at Reinhausen off and on during the day as we have seen, it was clear that the defences would not be overcome easily. Kolowrat thus decided to attack via the west bank of the Regen on the 19th and marched the bulk of II Corps direct from Kürn to Regenstauf to effect a crossing of the river. Klenau, leaving Rottermund with a detachment at Reinhausen, joined Kolowrat at Regenstauf and the corps crossed the Regen there during the night. Bellegarde had patrols as far west as Neumarkt and Velburg, but otherwise undertook no significant moves. He was satisfied with remaining around Schwarzenfeld and Schwandorf to prepare himself for his upcoming march to Amberg (19th) and Neumarkt (20th).[109]

By nightfall on 18 April, therefore, Charles had positioned his army—apart from I Corps—for a decisive stroke against Davout on the following morning. Moreover, he and his staff had acted with uncharacteristic promptness and energy to exploit the opportunity they had detected. As darkness settled over Rohr and the white-coated battalions established their bivouacs, however, the planning for the next day was still preliminary; the details of his movements for the 19th would be decided during the night and issued in the early morning hours of the day they were to be executed.

19 APRIL: MEETING ENGAGEMENT

The first major combat of the war and the turn of the tide against Austria came on 19 April. The fighting, however, is best viewed as a meeting engagement on a grand scale rather than a single, coherent 'battle' in the style of Austerlitz. Under lowering grey skies, the two armies, each ill-informed about the location of its foe, fought a series of interrelated actions as they groped towards one another over a hilly, forested landscape that precluded the various commanders from achieving a comprehensive view of the battlefield and put a premium on tactical agility and independent leadership at all levels of command. The nature of fighting under these conditions afforded the French significant advantages. Where the Austrians were slow, rigid, and tightly confined in outdated tactical norms, their opponents were adaptable, flexible, accustomed to taking the initiative, and expected to assume responsibility with minimal guidance. These qualities, combined with a tremendous confidence in themselves and their leaders made the French and their German allies much more comfortable dealing with the uncertainty that characterised the coming five days.

Hausen–Teugn: Charles vs. Davout

The initial Austrian plan for the 19th was dictated to the corps commanders and their chiefs of staff in the Rohr post-house (the 'Gaststätte zur Post') shortly after midnight on the night of 18/19 April. It was based on the assumption that Davout was planning a move west to Neustadt and that he may have already reached Abbach. Charles thus decided to interpose his army, or part of it, between Lefebvre and Davout by occupying a position between Grossmuss and Oberschambach, more or less athwart Davout's presumed line of march.[110] This plan would have placed the Hauptarmee between Lefebvre and Davout, but it is not clear whether Charles intended to attack or simply wanted to await Davout in an advantageous 'position'.[111] The defensive tone implied here was certainly incongruous when contrasted with the aggressive verbiage used on the 18th. This initial disposition was soon abandoned, but it sheds light on the prevailing sense of caution—hardly an item in short supply in the Austrian army—that would persist in the next set of orders and in the army's actions during 19 April as well.

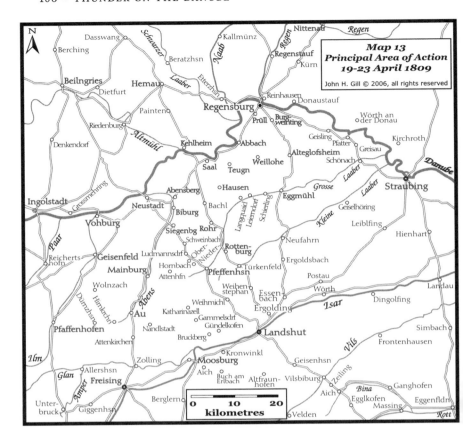

The corps commanders and staff officers had barely left army headquarters when Charles cancelled the orders just issued and began preparing a new set of instructions. At 3.30 a.m., as the generalissimus was finishing a message to Ludwig apprising him of the day's disposition, Hohenzollern's advance-guard commander, FML Philipp Freiherr von Vukassovich, forwarded a prize piece of intelligence to the post-house in Rohr. An outpost of *Ferdinand* Hussars near Reissing had halted and questioned a Bavarian civilian whose behaviour had aroused suspicion and discovered that he was bearing an important message from Lefebvre to Davout, dated 4 p.m. on the 18th:

> You know, my dear marshal, that I am here to support you and to draw upon myself part of the enemy's forces if you are attacked.

For this purpose, I have sent a division to Siegenburg and Biburg. Two others are ready to follow and march against the enemy's left flank if you are attacked.[112]

Many in Charles's headquarters at first thought this find too good to be true, a French ruse intended to discourage an Austrian advance on Regensburg. Subsequent reports confirmed the letter's authenticity, but produced a mistaken interpretation of its contents. As read in Rohr that chill night, Lefebvre's note and some of the other intelligence awakened two thoughts: first, that Davout might remain in place on 19 April as he had, inexplicably, on the previous day; and second that, if at all possible, the Hauptarmee should endeavour to engage Davout beyond range of Lefebvre's immediate support. The second point should have been obvious regardless of Davout's status, but the first represented a definite, if erroneous, change from the previous Austrian understanding of the operational situation. Countervailing information seems to have been ignored.[113] The result of this revised view was a second disposition issued between 6 and 7 a.m. on 19 April. Stutterheim summarised the deliberations: 'news arrived announcing that the Marshal Duke of Auerstädt would not move from Regensburg and that his troops occupied a camp between Prüll and Burgweinting; it was believed that he would be found there on the 19th again, and it was decided to move to the attack.'[114]

Where the first concept envisaged a limited move north from Rohr, the new instructions pushed the bulk of the Hauptarmee to the north-east more directly towards Regensburg. As in the first disposition, Hohenzollern would be on the left and would leave a brigade opposite Biburg and Abensberg. The new orders, however, called for the remainder of III Corps (18,550) to advance from its bivouacs near Rohr north-east through Hausen to Teugn. Here the column would split: one portion bearing left to Abbach, the other swinging to the right to reach Peising. Rosenberg with his corps and the twelve grenadier battalions of I Reserve Corps (26,900) would march through Langquaid, Paring, and Dünzling to Weillohe in the centre.[115] On the right, Liechtenstein, now commanding Lindenau, Schneller, and the cuirassiers of his own corps (12,900), was to move via Langquaid, Schierling, Obersanding, and Gebelkofen to approach Regensburg from the south.[116] Vécsey's brigade (6,100), also under Liechtenstein's authority, was to advance from Eggmühl to Alteglofsheim on the post road. The mission assigned to V Corps and II Reserve Corps (18,650) was largely unchanged: 'occupy the enemy near Siegenburg.'[117] Additionally, Charles placed the III Corps brigade near Biburg under Ludwig's orders. Hiller (25,100) was to accelerate his march to join V Corps and, as the most senior officer, was to command the three corps upon his arrival.[118] Should retreat be necessary, the left wing, including Hiller, was to withdraw through Pfeffenhausen to Landshut.

On the French side, Davout was planning to move through some of the same villages that Charles had used to delineate the Austrian lines of advance. Like the Austrians, the French would move in several columns. While the cumbersome trains rolled along the paved main road from Abbach towards Abensberg escorted by the 2nd Chasseurs and an infantry battalion (I/30), the bulk of the 3rd Corps' combat power would move in two large columns over poor secondary roads further south. In the French centre, Morand's 1st Division, followed by St Hilaire's 4th, was to march from Isling through Seedorf, Peising, and Teugn to Buchhofen and Abensberg. Gudin would lead the column on the left from Burgweinting through Hinkofen and Weillohe towards Saalhaupt, trailed by Friant. Each of these two main columns included light cavalry and a brigade of St Sulpice's cuirassiers. Montbrun, assigned a route from Alteglofsheim through Luckenpaint and Dünzling, would guard the southern flank with three light horse regiments and two battalions of the 7th Léger. Davout selected the routes of march with great care and, as far as the close terrain allowed, he picked roads and trails that permitted mutual visibility between his columns 'so that it will be possible to place the four divisions in line of battle at any point the enemy chooses to attack'.[119] Left behind in Regensburg was Colonel Coutard and the 2,080 men of his 65th Ligne. Also absent was Colonel Guyon's miniature command, spread along the Altmühl to observe the hesitant Bellegarde. Other than these small detachments, the entire 3rd Corps would be on the move. With 40,800 infantry and nearly 8,000 cavalry, Davout's force was considerably larger than anyone in the Habsburg high command expected.[120] It was chill and damp at 5 a.m. as dawn seeped into the sky, but the lead French elements were already moving along the muddy roads west, light infantry and cavalry scouring the wooded hills to front and flanks.[121]

The Habsburg troops did not break camp until 6 a.m., in accordance with the initial disposition for the day and then, in at least some cases, had to change direction when the revised orders reached them some time after 7 a.m. As a result, the lead French divisions and the baggage train slipped past the Austrian attempt at interception. Morand and Gudin were already passing through Teugn and Saalhaupt respectively at 8.30 a.m., when cavalry scouts reported encountering Austrian patrols not far to the south. Interrogation of local peasants and Austrian marauders confirmed the enemy's approach

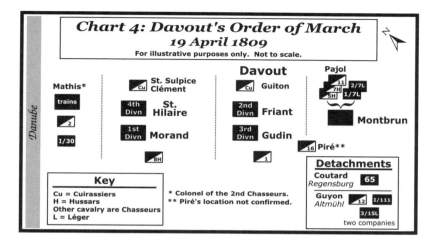

Chart 4: Davout's Order of March
19 April 1809
For illustrative purposes only. Not to scale.

Davout   **Pajol**

Mathis*   St. Sulpice   **Cu** Guiton   **11** **7H** **5H** **2/7L** **1/7L**
                Clément

trains   **4th** **Divn** St. Hilaire   **2nd** **Divn** Friant   **Montbrun**

2   **1st** **Divn** Morand   **3rd** **Divn** Gudin

I/30   **8H**   **1**   **16** Piré**

Detachments

Coutard
Regensburg   **65**

Key

Cu = Cuirassiers   * Colonel of the 2nd Chasseurs.   Guyon   **12** **I/111**
H = Hussars   ** Piré's location not confirmed.   Altmühl
Other cavalry are Chasseurs   **3/15L**
L = Léger   two companies

in strength. Davout, concerned for the safety of his trains and his link to Lefebvre, immediately ordered Morand (at Teugn) and Gudin (heading up the valley from Saalhaupt) to march for Obersaal on the high road along the Danube with all possible speed. Skirmish fire began to snap in the distance to the south and west as the two divisions accelerated their pace towards the Danube. It was approximately 9 a.m.

These initial shots came from encounters near Schneidhart between French vedettes and scouting parties from Stutterheim's IV Corps advance guard. Stutterheim had been waiting at Langquaid for the rest of IV Corps to march up from Rohr, when a patrol of the *Vincent* Chevaulegers returned from Abbach at 6 a.m. From the patrol's prisoners he heard that Davout had 80,000 men in Regensburg and other exaggerated nonsense, but he also learned that the French planned to evacuate the city. Stutterheim immediately forwarded this information to Rohr, but seems to have done nothing to scout the proposed IV Corps route of march. Instead, some three hours passed before Rosenberg's columns appeared at Langquaid and Stutterheim took his detachment north-east past Hellring, sending a patrol of *Vincent* Chevaulegers off through Schneidhart towards Saalhaupt. A rider from the chevaulegers soon came pelting back with the news that there were French in Schneidhart and the woods to the north, so Stutterheim deployed his troops near Hellring and almost instantly found himself in a firefight with French skirmishers in the woods beyond the hamlet.

The time was now edging towards 10 a.m., and Charles, arriving on the heights north of Langquaid near Grub, ordered IV Corps to halt and deploy facing north until Hohenzollern could come up on the left. Rosenberg put his men into two lines between Leierndorf and Grub, while Stutterheim took the French under fire with his cavalry battery and pushed a battalion of *Deutsch-Banat* Grenz Regiment No. 12 into the woods. The Grenzers' foes among the trees were from III/7th Léger under GB Claude Petit.[122] This battalion had been the 3rd Division's advance guard on the march to Saalhaupt and Gudin had sent them into clear the wooded hills south of the village to protect his left flank as he continued on to Obersaal.[123] Their struggle with Stutterheim's men, however, quickly settled into sporadic musketry. Charles, observing the appearance of Hohenzollern's columns on his left and the inconsequential skirmishing to his front, ordered Rosenberg to proceed with his march to Dünzling.[124] Petit headed up the valley to catch up with Gudin's division.

As IV Corps reassembled in march columns and turned east, Stutterheim was left with four squadrons, one battalion of *Deutsch-Banat*, a cavalry battery, and instructions 'to advance from Schneidhart on Abbach'—a clear indication that the Austrian leadership had no idea of Davout's dispositions. The rest of his advance guard went off with the main body of the corps. Stutterheim duly occupied Schneidhart but found the woods full of French and the terrain impossible for the cavalry and guns of his diminished detachment. Reporting these conditions, he received new orders simply 'to hold near Schneidhart and cover this post'.[125] His Grenzer, however, remained in the woods where, as we will see, they soon found themselves in combat with advance elements of Friant's 2nd Division.

Charles and his staff, from his command post on the heights near Grub, could see Stutterheim's small action but little else.[126] It was clear, however, that Hohenzollern was involved in an increasingly noisy fight, so the archduke kept the twelve grenadier battalions at Grub when Rosenberg resumed his march to Dünzling. On his own initiative, Rosenberg deposited Oberst Karl von Steyrer with two squadrons of *Vincent* Chevaulegers and I/*Chasteler* No. 46 at Paring to secure communications with the grenadiers.[127]

It was at this time (late morning), that Charles, questioning Stutterheim's prisoners, learned of Napoleon's arrival in the theatre of war.

The focus of action now shifted from the prolonged sparring in the woods between Schneidhart and Saalhaupt to the major engagement that was rapidly developing north of Hausen.[128] Hohenzollern's men had left their bivouacs near Rohr some time between 7 and 8 a.m. to slog up the road to Bachl. In accordance with the new disposition, GM Ludwig Chevalier Thierry de Vaux headed off to Kirchdorf with his brigade and the *Levenehr* Dragoons

(5,900) to a defensive position opposite Biburg and Abensberg under Archduke Ludwig. Hohenzollern also elected to leave a small detachment at Bachl as a connection to Thierry.[129] GM Josef von Pfanzelter thus remained behind in this tiny hamlet with I/*Peterwardein* Grenz Regiment No. 9 and two squadrons of *Erzherzog Ferdinand* Hussars No. 3 (1,350) while the corps continued its march east.[130]

Hohenzollern had intended to divide his corps once it reached Teugn, sending Vukassovich and FML Franz Marquis Lusignan's division towards Abbach while FML Josef Franz Graf St Julien headed for Peising. His outriders, however, soon discovered French skirmishers in Hausen. At about the same time, he and his staff could hear the crackle of musketry and the occasional deep growl of cannon from the direction of Schneidhart. Other than the vague information that Davout was somewhere south of Regensburg with something over 30,000 men, Hohenzollern knew nothing about the enemy ahead and the wooded rise beyond Hausen blocked his view of everything to the north.[131] He thus decided to assault Hausen in full force, sending Vukassovich around to the left while Lusignan prepared to attack the town directly. These measures proved unnecessary as the French light troops hastily decamped and 'vanished into the woods'.[132] Concluding that the French presence in Hausen had been insignificant, Hohenzollern continued north. Accompanied by Lusignan, GM Nikolaus von Kayser's brigade led the advance, marching up the road to Teugn with a squadron of hussars while Vukassovich poked through the woods on Kayser's left with II/*Peterwardein* followed by 1st *Erzherzog Karl* Legion. As Kayser's battalions slowly emerged from the defile through the woods between Hausen and Teugn and his skirmishers began to descend the slopes towards the latter village, however, they came under unexpectedly heavy fire. Vukassovich's Grenzer were likewise surprised as they attempted to move north from the woods around Roith. Lusignan, recognising that he had encountered serious resistance, hastened to get Kayser's men and his battery through the narrow gap in the forest and deployed on the low hills south of Teugn.

The Engagement of Hausen–Teugn was concentrated in a confined space between the two villages. The initial fighting roared back and forth across two small ridges and a thin isthmus of forest in an area of approximately four square kilometres. The northern ridge, known as the Buchberg, rises up from the southern side of Teugn and is separated from the southern ridge, or Hausener Berg, by a shallow swale. The road north from Hausen twists through the narrow neck of trees just beyond Saladorf before crossing the two

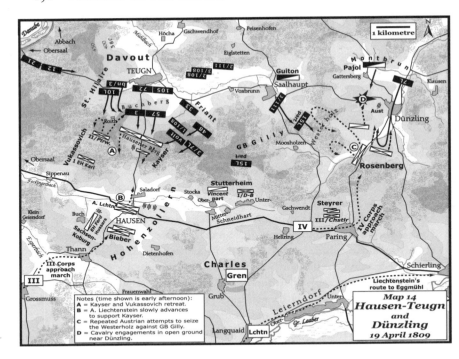

Notes (time shown is early afternoon):
A = Kayser and Vukassovich retreat.
B = A. Liechtenstein slowly advances
      to support Kayser.
C = Repeated Austrian attempts to seize
      the Westerholz against GB Gilly.
D = Cavalry engagements in open ground
      near Dünzling.

Map 14
Hausen-Teugn
and
Dünzling
19 April 1809

ridges to drop into Teugn. On either side of the road are low but broad ridges thick with conifers; they completely obscure observation from one town to the other. Neither the Austrian commanders on the heights above Hausen, nor their French counterparts in the valley formed by the little Mühlbach could see much beyond the slopes and dark forests to their immediate fronts.

It was approximately 11 a.m. when Lusignan, hearing the exchange between his skirmishers and the French in Teugn, rushed the nearest formed units forward to the Buchberg while hurrying the two available regiments into position on the Hausener Berg: *Wenzel Colloredo* No. 56 on the left and *Schröder* No. 7 on the right. The Habsburg skirmishers initially encountered the tail elements of Gudin's division, but these continued on their way to Saal and soon departed the battlefield.

Behind Gudin came St Hilaire's five regiments, including some of the best in the army. The lead regiment, the 10th Léger, had just passed through Teugn on its way towards the Danube, but the next regiment in the column of march, the 3rd Ligne, was immediately available. Davout, not wanting the Austrians to establish a foothold north of the forest, grabbed this regiment and threw it at the white-coated skirmishers on the Buchberg while a messenger pounded off to recall the 10th. Every moment counted, so the marshal gave the 3rd no time to form, but sent the entire regiment forward in skirmish order. Reaching the crest breathless and disorganised, the regiment was repulsed with relative ease by 'a cloud of light troops' and tumbled back down the slopes, disordered but not disheartened.[133] Though unsuccessful in seizing the rise for Davout, the 3rd Ligne's attack gained precious minutes for more of St Hilaire's troops to arrive. The 57th Ligne was now on hand and had time to organise itself for a proper assault. Proud to have been christened 'the Terrible' by Napoleon for its performance during the 1797 campaign in Italy, the 57th coolly advanced up the Buchberg and pushed the Austrians off its summit. The 57th 'certainly justified its name that day, promptly gaining ground', wrote the brigade commander, GB Lorencez.[134] The regiment's trials had only just begun, however, for the men were now exposed to punishing infantry and artillery fire from the main body of Kayser's brigade on the Hausener Berg and the left flank had to form square for a time to repel an attack by the hussar squadron. They held firmly despite this pressure and Davout felt that the situation was sufficiently stable for him to leave Teugn in St Hilaire's hands and ride off to assess the possibility of an attack against the Austrian flank by Morand and Gudin.

By this time, St Hilaire had posted his 72nd and 105th regiments on the heights north of Teugn and was organising the 3rd Ligne in the valley west of the town. The 10th Léger was also west of Teugn in reserve, but St Hilaire only had three guns at hand; the remainder of his artillery, having been left behind 'by an inconceivable mistake', would not arrive on the battlefield until early afternoon.[135]

On the other side of the Buchberg, however, Lusignan was not idle. Before long, he began to lead *Wenzel Colloredo* and *Schröder* forward against the sorely pressed 57th Ligne, while Vukassovich's battalion of Grenzer, supported by the 1st *Erzherzog Karl* Legion, advanced from the woodline to threaten the French right. The Austrian attacks seem to have been conducted in sequence by battalion rather than simultaneously, lessening their impact, but the 57th's situation was looking grim when Davout returned from Obersaal.[136] Peering up from Teugn, the 10th Léger's Colonel Berthezène watched as 'the 57th maintained itself energetically; but the artillery and musket fire was ravaging its ranks considerably, we could see them thin before our eyes and it became urgent to go to their assistance'.[137]

The French acted with decision to answer the Austrian advance. With the 72nd and 105th Ligne in support, the 10th Léger pushed forward against the little tongue of woods by Roith and the 3rd Ligne moved up on the right of the 57th. These moves simultaneously halted the Grenzer near Roith and endangered the left of Kayser's line. Austrian casualties mounted and the advance came to a standstill. Lusignan's situation was now critical. In addition to the heavy losses sustained in the failed frontal attacks against the 57th and the threat to his left from the 3rd Ligne and 10th Léger, he was taking fire on his right flank as the lead elements of Friant's division and GB Petit with III/7th Léger began to appear from Saalhaupt. His requests to Hohenzollern did not bring the immediate assistance he needed. Unsupported and exposed, Lusignan ordered Kayser's battered brigade to retire but fell badly wounded as he organised the retreat. The French did not hesitate to press their advantage, pursuing Kayser into the band of trees with the 3rd and 57th Regiments. A terrible struggle surged to and fro in the woods for a time before the French forced Kayser's men out. The two French regiments, however, had suffered heavily and were running short of ammunition, so St Hilaire brought forward the 72nd and 105th Ligne to replace them. The Austrian battalions now slowly forming themselves to counter-attack would thus encounter two fresh French regiments as they drove towards the woods.[138]

Lusignan was unsupported because Hohenzollern had kept the rest of his infantry behind Hausen while Kayser's brigade and Vukassovich advanced on Teugn. GM Fürst Alois Liechtenstein's brigade was eventually chosen to help Lusignan, but it first had to go through the cumbersome process of organising itself to advance and then had to cover some two kilometres before it came into action. By that time, Kayser's brigade had already been defeated and his men were reeling back out of the woods towards Hausen, not panicked, but weakened by casualties and in considerable disorder.

Though he did not know it yet, Hohenzollern's situation was equally grave on his left, where a battalion of the 3rd Ligne that Davout had held in reserve managed to cut off and capture a large number of *Peterwardein* Grenzer in the protruding tongue of woods near Roith. The remaining Grenzer fell back into the forest under the cover of the 1st *Erzherzog Karl* Legion.

We must return to the action between Saalhaupt and Schneidhart for a moment to bring Friant and his 2nd Division into the picture. When Friant's column emerged from the trees into the open ground around Saalhaupt, the general noted Austrian skirmishers in the forested hills to the south. Petit having marched off towards Teugn to rejoin his division, these Grenzer had taken advantage of his departure to probe through the forest.[139] Friant was not going to tolerate this threat to his flank. He quickly dispatched

GB Jacques Laurent Gilly with the 15th Léger to clear the woods and screen his route of march. Four companies under Chef de Bataillon Jean François Auguste Sarraire soon pushed the Grenzer back towards the south, but his light infantrymen and I/*Deutsch-Banat* became entangled in an inconclusive fight over the hills north of Schneidhart during the afternoon. As the day progressed, the enervating combat began to tell on Sarraire's soldiers, and Friant sent four companies of the 108th Ligne to back up the tiring foot chasseurs.[140] The French did not press their attacks, but their mission only required them to secure Friant's flank and they were satisfied keeping Stutterheim's infantry away from the main column. Gilly, responsible for the flank as far as Dünzling, would soon have to contend with a much more serious threat from that direction.

Friant, having shielded his left, kept marching. Leaving a battalion of the 111th Ligne at Saalhaupt to protect his trains, he pushed on for Teugn with the rest of the division just in time to contribute to Lusignan's discomfiture. As he approached the battle, Friant sent Chef de Bataillon Nicholas Schmitz with I/108th Ligne and the combined voltigeur companies of the 33rd, 48th, 108th, and 111th Regiments into the forest on Lusignan's right. GB Petit and III/7th Léger, making their way from Saalhaupt, joined Schmitz and his men in the woods. Before long, therefore, a swarm of 2,000 French light infantry was nattering away at the beleaguered Austrians on the Hausener Berg and nimbly chasing them through the trees as they sought to retire towards Hausen. Friant soon added the 48th Ligne to his advance. Of the 2nd Division's other regiments, he deployed the 33rd Ligne south-east of Teugn with a battery, and held II/111th and the remaining two battalions of the 108th in reserve east and north-east of the village.[141]

As Alois Liechtenstein advanced north along the Teugn road towards the glowering forest ahead, therefore, Kayser's shaken battalions were retreating south towards him in confusion and large numbers of French infantry were appearing along the woodline to his front. Liechtenstein sent his lead regiment, *Manfredini* No. 12, towards the woods against increasingly heavy French fire. The regiment charged forwards with great determination and apparently pressed some distance into the trees, where it became entangled in a brutal and bloody firefight. Liechtenstein, hoping to restore momentum to the attack, personally led the three battalions of *Würzburg* No. 23 along the road in support. Astride his horse, he made a conspicuous and inspiring figure, the more so as he grabbed one of the regiment's standards and held it high as he rode forward. A number of men from Kayser's brigade, apparently reinvigorated by his courage, joined the advance, but they and the men of

Würzburg marched into a murderous crossfire as they pressed into the notch formed by the trees where the road enters the woods. The woodline on their right was full of Frenchmen whose enfilading fire brought down dozens of Austrians.[142] Liechtenstein was soon wounded and the attack collapsed.[143]

Hohenzollern desperately sought some way to retrieve the battle. He had already deployed several batteries in front of Hausen and, concerned by reports of French forces at Obersaal, had posted Oberst Ferdinand Prinz von Sachsen-Koburg on the heights near Buch with five squadrons of his *Ferdinand* Hussars and a cavalry battery. He had only two intact infantry regiments left. One of these, *Kaunitz* No. 20, had been pushed forward to support the failed attacks on the woodline, but had not yet become engaged. As he watched the Grenzer and Legion troops streaming out of the woods on his left, however, Hohenzollern saw no choice but to commit this regiment. Led by FML St. Julien and GM Moritz Fürst Liechtenstein, Alois's brother, the regiment charged up the gentle slope toward the treeline and succeeded in arresting both the flight of the *Peterwardeiner* and the advance of the 10th Léger. But the men of *Kaunitz* could not hold long. Under galling fire, the regiment lost 486 men in a matter of minutes.[144] Moritz Liechtenstein was among the badly wounded and *Kaunitz* fell back towards Hausen to reform.

In the meantime, GM Josef von Bieber had brought III Corps' last untouched infantry unit into action, leading parts of *Württemberg* No. 38 forward east of the road in an attempt to restore the deteriorating situation on the Austrian right flank.[145] Here too, however, a gallant attack broke in bloody ruin along the forest's edge, where the French, through a combination of ingenuity and energy, had managed to reinforce their hard-fighting infantry with a number of guns.[146] Bieber received a wound and the regiment fell back towards Hausen.

It was now approximately 3 p.m. and Hohenzollern, having exhausted his last remaining infantry, recognised that all hope for victory had vanished. He pencilled a note to Charles—'the forest is now lost, I will establish myself behind Hausen'—and ordered his much-diminished regiments to withdraw under the protection of the artillery. The French, equally exhausted by the furious fight, were unable to advance out of the trees in the face of the Austrian guns and the depleted but unbroken infantry.

Combat also flashed briefly on the northern edge of the battlefield. Early in the fight, Davout had ridden to Obersaal and instructed Morand to secure the defile at Oberfeking while Gudin marched west towards the Bavarians.[147] The marshal then galloped back to Teugn, but these orders resulted in the 17th Ligne making a brief appearance around 5 p.m. as Morand cautiously advanced towards Rohr. On the division's left flank, the 17th was marching along the Feckingerbach when it encountered Prinz Sachsen-Koburg's hussars west of Buch. Attacked by the hussars and effectively shelled by the cavalry battery, the 17th lost thirteen men killed and twenty-nine wounded before darkness and a thunderstorm brought the brief skirmish to an end. This was the last French attempt at offensive action. But one more violent act had yet to play itself out before the combat ceased between Hausen and Teugn.

Charles had remained near Grub with the grenadiers all day. Although much of the detail of Hohenzollern's fight was obscured by the terrain and later by battle smoke, there could be no doubt in his headquarters that III Corps was heavily engaged. Yet he had made no move to intervene. Now, between 5 and 6 p.m., whether in response to Hohenzollern's pencilled message or some other impulse, he sent reinforcements towards Hausen. These took the form of four grenadier battalions under GM Viktor Prinz Rohan-Guemenée and Stutterheim with four squadrons of *Vincent* Chevaulegers and his cavalry battery.[148] Charles accompanied the grenadiers personally. This small effort accomplished nothing. Just as at Schneidhart, the terrain precluded any useful employment of Stutterheim's cavalry, and the four grenadier battalions were far too weak to reverse Habsburg fortunes at Hausen.[149] A lone battalion, *Leiningen*, advanced towards the treeline to the right of Hausen while the other three deployed in front of the village, but this only served to allow subsequent French regimental historians an opportunity to claim that their units had repelled an attack led by the generalissimus in person. *Leiningen* lost eighteen men in a short, sharp firefight before withdrawing. As the grenadiers turned back towards Hausen, a violent storm broke over the battlefield to bring fighting to a definitive conclusion. The sky had begun to cloud over during the late afternoon and now hurled down a pounding deluge that sent men of both sides scurrying under whatever shelter they could find. Some of the French benefited from the protection of the forest and a few of the Austrians were able to take refuge in Hausen and other villages, but many of the men, thoroughly exhausted after the long day's struggle, would find themselves utterly drenched as the cold evening came on.

Dünzling: Montbrun Detains Rosenberg

While Hohenzollern's corps was wasting itself in fruitless attacks north of Hausen, Rosenberg and his men continued on their way to Dünzling. Subtracting the troops deposited with Stutterheim and Steyrer, IV Corps was left with fourteen battalions, nine or ten squadrons (approximately 13,000 infantry and 1,400 cavalry), and fifty guns as it made its way through the woods north of Paring between 11 a.m. and noon.[150] Here scouts from the *Vincent* Chevaulegers rode up to report that they had encountered French troops on the heights north of Dünzling.

The French were troops of Montbrun's small detachment: three light cavalry regiments and two battalions of the 7th Léger for a total of some 1,920 infantry and 1,830 cavalry (Montbrun had no artillery). The men had left their encampments around Alteglofsheim and Langenerling late in the morning and bumped into the Austrian chevaulegers as they rode through Luckenpaint to assume their position on Davout's left flank. As the chevaulegers sent messengers galloping back to find Rosenberg, Montbrun moved his detachment into the bowl around Dünzling, placing most of his cavalry on the right near Gattersberg where the terrain would allow it to manoeuvre and ordering the 7th Léger to attack the town itself. The light infantrymen conducted their advance with speed, skill, and élan. Chasing Austrian skirmishers from Dünzling, they seized a cannon that had unlimbered adjacent to the town and then drove up the slopes to the south against Rosenberg's main body where it was deploying from the woods. Montbrun, however, soon recognised that he was facing overwhelming numbers and pulled the 7th back to the woodline east of Gattersberg.

The sudden and violent onset of the 7th Léger seems to have shocked Rosenberg. The impetuous charge suggested the presence of a powerful French force, reinforcing the Austrian commander's natural caution. He could probably see all or most of Montbrun's command, but he worried that there might be other French lurking in the trees, a concern that seemed validated when his men discovered French skirmishers ensconced in the woods (Westerholz) on his left. From Rosenberg's perspective, he was facing an energetic enemy of unknown size in difficult terrain that suited French tactics and temperament. He sent a battalion of *Koburg* Infantry No. 22 to secure the Westerholz and prepared for a careful advance on Dünzling.[151]

Skirmishers from *Koburg* soon poked through the treeline onto the high ground above Saalhaupt, but the French, part of Gilly's 15th Léger, gave them a hot reception.[152] Outflanking the Austrian left, Gilly's troops threw them back into the Westerholz and its northern extensions, where the confused fight among the trees soon turned against the whitecoats. Habsburg casualties were heavy: ejected from the forest, *Koburg* lost twenty killed, fifty wounded, and 110 prisoners, including its colonel, Oberst Wenzel Vetter von Lilienberg. By this time, all three battalions of *Koburg* were in action in the forest and

Rosenberg felt himself compelled to send the three battalions of *Erzherzog Ludwig* No. 8 there as well. He later added II/*Chasteler* and a battalion from *Reuss-Greitz* No. 55, but was unable to dislodge the tenacious French. Facing eight Austrian battalions committed in and around the Westerholz, Gilly, with at most eight companies after detaching Sarraire, 'employed all means of resistance' and searched desperately for reinforcements.[153] The only available unit was III/111th Ligne guarding the division trains at Saalhaupt. Gilly did not hesitate. Calling the battalion forward on his own authority, he threw it into the fight for the Westerholz. It arrived just in time to help fend off some of the heaviest Austrian assaults. As one Habsburg attack column neared the woodline, Gilly broke out of the trees with the 15th Léger's two carabinier companies to charge against one flank of the advancing enemy while the grenadier company of III/111th stormed in from the opposite side. A brief flurry of brutal hand-to-hand fighting ensued before the surprised Austrians recoiled back down the slope.[154] Threatened by I/*Czartoryski* and parts of *Reuss-Greitz* from near Dünzling, Gilly retired to the safety of the woods.

While Gilly was struggling for possession of the Westerholz with Rosenberg's left, the remainder of IV Corps was contending with Montbrun. The Austrians, following the 7th Léger as it retired from its audacious advance, regained their lost gun, but the French commander, intent on keeping Rosenberg's clearly superior force distracted, launched his cavalry in a series of attacks that absorbed Rosenberg's attention throughout the afternoon. Before sounding the charge, however, he brazenly 'had our regiments pass in review as if on the exercise field despite the grape shot and musket balls'.[155] Review complete, Montbrun sent the 5th Hussars against the *Stipsicz* Hussars in the open ground west of Dünzling. The two hussar regiments, both clad in variations of sky blue, clashed in a whirling melee over the fields until parts of the *Vincent* Chevaulegers intervened to turn the tide. The 5th Hussars retreated, but musketry from the 7th Léger dissuaded the Austrians from serious pursuit. Rosenberg had pushed the other two battalions of *Czartoryski* and the remaining battalion of *Reuss-Greitz* forward to Dünzling in the meantime, but with more than half of his infantry embroiled in the battle on his left flank and only two battalions (*Bellegarde* No. 44) left uncommitted, he forbore to press Montbrun any further.[156] Vigorous cavalry engagements roiled back and forth during the afternoon as the three French light horse regiments charged in sequence to keep their counterparts occupied, using their offensive activity to hide the weakness of their force. Rosenberg, however, did not stir. Content with having accomplished the letter of his mission by reaching Dünzling, the Austrian commander ordered his men to camp where they were, as night and the terrific thunderstorm brought combat to a close.[157]

Montbrun retired to Peising and Abbach.[158] It had been a challenging day for his command: the colonels of the 5th Hussars and 7th Léger were wounded, Pajol had taken a cut on the arm from a *Stipsicz* hussar, Montbrun's horse had been shot out from under him, and his men had expended all of their ammunition.[159] He and Gilly, however, had occupied a far superior enemy force for the better part of a day, preventing it from achieving anything of consequence and allowing Davout a free hand to deal with Hohenzollern.

As Rosenberg's troops were arranging their bivouacs south of Dünzling, the men of Liechtenstein's column were doing the same at Höhenberg five kilometres to the east. Assigned the same road as IV Corps, Liechtenstein had been forced to wait at Laaber while Rosenberg's battalions marched ahead. When he was able to continue his move, his route through Langquaid to Schierling took him directly south of the battle at Hausen–Teugn, Charles's command post near Grub, and Rosenberg's engagement around Dünzling, but there is no evidence that he made any effort to enquire about the fighting or that anyone in army headquarters thought to alter his direction of march to support the other corps. He thus proceeded to Schierling as instructed. Leaving two battalions and a cuirassier regiment at Eggmühl under GM Ignaz Freiherr von Lederer, he marched the rest to Höhenberg on the Landshut–Regensburg highway and camped for the night. Oberst Josef Mayer with a small detachment of four companies and two squadrons continued on to Obersanding.[160]

Vécsey, supposed to serve as Liechtenstein's advance guard, was equally unenterprising. Starting the day at Eggmühl, his activity for 19 April consisted of advancing up the main road to Alteglofsheim, a distance of ten or twelve kilometres, and placing some outposts along the Pfatter stream another kilometre or so further north.[161] He did not arrive in the town until 8 p.m., where 'the large stock of beer . . . was consumed by the troops in the village'.[162] Nor did he perform any useful reconnaissance. Indeed, the reports he did submit were wildly inaccurate, claiming 'the arrival of a powerful enemy column in Langenerling, a strong enemy army corps around Geisling and Pfatter, and Regensburg full of troops'.[163] Liechtenstein likewise reported spectres, worrying that his right flank was in danger from French near Langenerling and Triftlfing. There were, of course, no French forces at all in these locales, leading to a scathing condemnation of intelligence gathering by Liechtenstein's command in the Austrian official history.[164] Neither Liechtenstein nor Vécsey had any contact with the enemy during the day.

Losses during the engagements at Hausen–Teugn, Schneidhart, and Dünzling fell most heavily on Hohenzollern on the Austrian side and on St Hilaire and Friant among the major French formations. Hohenzollern, entering the fray with approximately 17,200 infantry and cavalry (minus Thierry and Pfanzelter), lost 3,862 dead, wounded, captured, and missing, or some 22 per cent of his initial strength.[165] Rosenberg's corps contributed another 1,084 men to the casualty rolls, more than half of these from *Koburg*. The short-lived appearance of the grenadiers at Hausen led to an additional twenty-four casualties giving a grand total of 4,970 men lost during the day. French casualties are more difficult to assess. It seems clear that St Hilaire lost approximately 1,800 and Montbrun 215, but Friant's toll varies from 377 to 2,016 according to the source consulted. Moreover, some accounts tally more than 300 casualties in Gudin's division as well. The results thus range from a low of 2,400 to a high of almost 4,400 with the most likely figure hovering around 3,600. Whatever the precise numbers, the Austrians certainly lost several hundred men more than the French. Additionally, most of the Austrian wounded from Hohenzollern's corps (some 2,400 men) would be captured over the coming two days in Rohr and Landshut.[166] Just as clear is that both sides, in the words of one contemporary French account, 'deployed an equal valour'.[167] This was a very hard-fought engagement and neither army stinted when it came to praising the bravery and determination of its enemy.

Casualties and courage notwithstanding, the outcome did not favour the Habsburg cause. As downpour and darkness closed 19 April, Hohenzollern had been handed a decided repulse, Rosenberg had allowed his corps to fritter its strength away against inferior forces, and Liechtenstein had succumbed to imaginary enemies. Davout, on the other hand, had handled the enemy severely and accomplished his mission: 'the fruit of that day was the reunion of 3rd Corps with the rest of the Army of Germany'.[168] This was a crucially important operational result: Davout was no longer in danger of being defeated in isolation.[169] The psychological consequences were equally significant. The French had no doubt that they had won the day; their self-confidence was confirmed. Davout reported that two of his divisions had sufficed to defeat a numerically superior enemy in an advantageous position.[170] As we shall see, the day's events left a vastly different impression on the Austrian Hauptarmee, one close to the attitude expressed by a soldier in the 7th Léger: 'This contact reminded the Austrians that the soldiers of Austerlitz, Jena, and Friedland were at their heels.'[171]

Although it was the largest combat of the day, the fighting among the trees and hills from Hausen to Dünzling represented only one of the engagements on 19 April, and it is now time to turn our attention to the action along the Abens.

ACTIONS AT ARNHOFEN AND ALONG THE ABENS

Charles's dispositions for the 19th specified that III Corps detach a brigade to cover its left and rear. After some discussion, the choice fell on GM Thierry.[172] Thierry, a Luxembourger by birth, was 56 years old in 1809, had served the Habsburg crown for more than three decades, and had especially distinguished himself by his courage at the siege of Valenciennes in 1793. His capacity for independent command in dicey tactical circumstances however, was questionable. He had little understanding of the enemy situation that April morning or of the operational context in which his brigade was to perform a crucial role and, in the words of an Austrian historian 'it is nearly impossible to grasp the degree of naiveté and the unmilitary appreciation of the situation' that he would display over the next two days.[173] He had no map. His command consisted of three infantry battalions from *Kaiser* No. 1 (2,670 men), three from *Lindenau* No. 29 (2,470 men), the *Levenehr* Dragoons No. 4 under Oberst Anton Graf Hardegg (725 sabres), and eight guns. Each of the infantry regiments, however, was short two companies from its 3rd Battalion and *Kaiser* included some 450 recruits with almost no training.

Thierry's initial orders came from Hohenzollern and directed him to Kirchdorf to 'observe' the Bavarian troops at Biburg. Departing the encampment near Rohr shortly after 6 a.m., he and his brigade were negotiating the muddy roads towards the Abens when they were joined by Oberst Xaver Richter von Binnenthal of the General Staff. Shortly thereafter, an artillery officer brought four guns from a position battery to support Thierry. Finally, around 8 a.m., another officer rode up with new orders, this time from Charles himself, requiring Thierry to 'cover the area on the right bank of the Abens between the crossing at Biburg and that by Abensberg'.[174] The orders specified in great detail the locations he was to occupy with sub-detachments and placed him under Ludwig's command while instructing him to send reports directly to Charles as well.

The brigade reached the heights west of Kirchdorf after a dreary trudge through the bottomless trails from Rohr. Thierry, at the insistence of Oberst von Richter (who did have a map), dutifully placed his detachments as directed: III/*Kaiser* and a half-squadron of dragoons at Hörlbach and *Lindenau* in the low ground near Bruckhof with three and a half squadrons and four guns. He and Richter, however, believed that Bavarian troops might be moving north-east out of Abensberg, so they decided to take Thierry's remaining force (reduced to two battalions of *Kaiser*, two dragoon squadrons, and four guns) through the woods (Seeholz) towards Arnhofen to intercept.[175] In what was surely one of the examples that caused Charles to lament generals who 'appealed' to staff officers 'in every case' and 'unconditionally paid homage to all of their remarks', Thierry had largely abdicated operational responsibility for the brigade to Richter.[176] Regardless of who held the reins of command, the two men saw only a few Bavarian cavalry vedettes atop a set of low hills as the diminished command emerged from the Seeholz just before 11 a.m.[177] These hills blocked the Austrian view of the Abensberg–Regensburg road, so Thierry had no idea of the enemy's strength and dispositions when he ordered his men to continue their advance.

The force on the other side of the hill was GM Friedrich von Zandt's cavalry brigade, serving as advance guard for Crown Prince Ludwig's 1st Bavarian Division. Lefebvre, hearing cannon fire in the distance around 10 a.m., had ordered the division to advance towards Regensburg to support Davout as specified in Napoleon's instructions.[178] Zandt's troopers had just passed through Abensberg and were jangling up the road to Arnhofen with the division's main body close behind. As their outriders reported Austrians on the edge of the Seeholz, however, Lefebvre ordered the 1st Chevaulegers forward at the trot. Wheeling right, the regiment crested the low rise and presented Thierry with an unpleasant surprise.

The unexpected appearance of the Bavarian cavalry did not deter Thierry. Seeing no infantry, he accepted battle in what he later conceded was a spirit of 'rather inappropriate zeal', sending the *Levenehr* Dragoons forward and opening up with his four guns.[179] Unfortunately for Thierry, a second Bavarian surprise now appeared as Hauptmann Ferdinand Regnier's light battery dashed up and unlimbered on a small knoll to the left of the chevaulegers with professional skill and celerity. Accurate fire from Regnier's six pieces dismounted two of the Habsburg guns after only fifteen minutes of firing. The Austrian dragoons at first advanced on this dangerous battery, but a hail of canister caused Hardegg to swing his squadrons left towards the chevaulegers. The Bavarian horsemen had the apparent advantage of being uphill from their opponents, but their colonel ordered his troopers to receive the Austrian attack in a stationary posture. The Bavarians fired their carbines and pistols at the onrushing dragoons, but this only served to disorder their own ranks and they found themselves tumbling back the way they had come after a brief hand-to-hand fight. Regnier, observing this turn of events, hastened to limber and retire his battery before the Habsburg horse could overrun him.

Luckily for the Bavarian artillery, a timely intervention by the 1st Dragoons gave the 1st Chevaulegers time to rejoin the battle and the combined pressure of the two Bavarian regiments forced Hardegg back to the edge of the Seeholz. The Bavarian squadrons did not press their advantage, but their success allowed Regnier to return to the fray. His men resumed a lively fire against the Austrian cavalry and guns north of the Seeholz as well as the

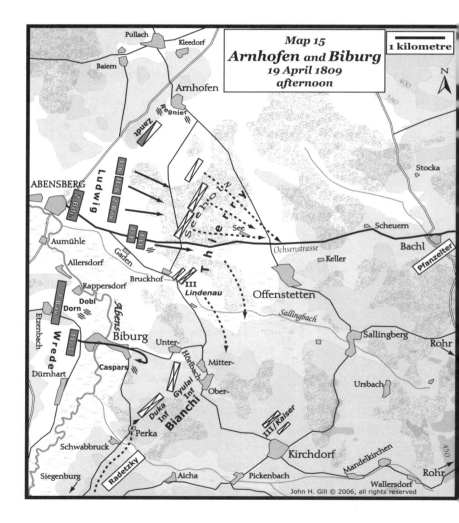

Map 15
Arnhofen and Biburg
19 April 1809
afternoon

1 kilometre

infantry battalions deployed on the western fringe of the woods. He would later receive the cross of the Legion of Honour for his actions on the 19th.

Bavarian artist Albrecht Adam had an opportunity to observe the results of the cavalry battle and the dreadful work of Regnier's battery:

> ... I came upon the traces of a bloody combat. Among the many badly wounded, I encountered here a group that looked artistically beautiful and hideous at the same time. Two men and two horses lay in a knot next to one another; they had been standing one behind the other and had been smashed down by a ball fired into their ranks by a Bavarian battery. This had torn away the first man's hip and the left leg of the second, mortally wounding the one horse in the throat, the other on the breast and shoulder. The entire group literally swam in blood.

The dragoon with the mangled leg had himself cut away his dangling foot after failing to persuade a Bavarian civilian to perform this grisly task on his behalf. 'With incredible presence of mind' he related his story to Adam and asked for a drink of brandy. Adam rode off, secured the desired libation, and was pleased when sympathetic local farmers carried both wounded men off to the field hospital in Abensberg.[180]

While this spirited and sanguinary cavalry engagement was in progress, Thierry, concerned for his left flank, had placed his two battalions of *Kaiser* in the woodline opposite Abensberg. Skirmishers probing towards the town, however, provoked a Bavarian response and an infantry fight erupted west of the Seeholz as the Bavarian 6th Infantry *Herzog Wilhelm* deployed into line between the town and the woods. Although this regiment was part of Wrede's 2nd Division, it was the only infantry immediately at hand, so Lefebvre personally led it forward towards the Seeholz. The two battalions unfolded from their march columns and advanced, but their first three attacks failed. Finally, a fourth attack, this time made in column behind a thick screen of Schützen, successfully penetrated into the woods. Thierry, however, had called forward part of his reserve while the cavalry engagement was in progress at Arnhofen, and two battalions of *Lindenau* arrived just in time to throw the 6th Infantry out of the Seeholz.

The Bavarians were also rushing up reinforcements. As 1st Brigade, 1st Division arrived on the scene, the men could hear the action developing up ahead: 'skirmish fire spiced with cannon shots' in the words of an artillery drummer.[181] The 2nd Infantry *Kronprinz*, attacking to the right of the 6th, pushed into the woods, the Schützen capturing an Austrian gun in the process. To the right of the 2nd Infantry, the 1st Light, I/1st Infantry, and a battery advanced cautiously east along the road to Offenstetten, threatening Thierry's left and eventually achieving a position near See from which the battery could fire on the Austrian flank and rear.[182] On the Bavarian left, the energetic Regnier also manoeuvred his battery aggressively. He noted that he could approach the Austrian right unseen by moving through Arnhofen and took three guns through the village streets to appear unexpectedly on Thierry's flank 'as if by magic'. His cannon raked the shocked Austrians with enfilading fire and pursued the Habsburg troops with whistling shot as they fled to seek the protection of the Seeholz.[183]

Thierry had now committed most of his scattered reserves but the Bavarians were pressing him steadily back. Feeling outnumbered and unsupported, he ordered a withdrawal between 3 and 4 p.m. Falling rapidly into disorder, most of the dragoon regiment and about half of his infantry component dropped back towards Offenstetten, but other elements fled south towards V Corps. Fortunately for Thierry, the Bavarian pursuit was uninspired and he was able to restore some cohesion to the troops who collected around Offenstetten in the late afternoon. Here, as elsewhere, the weather erased all thought of further combat as the day came to an end: 'Towards evening a storm unloaded itself so that the lightnings of nature competed with those of the guns, and the thunder rolled its bass above to accompany the cacophony below and the victory songs of the soldiers.'[184]

Though the Bavarian advance had been rather tentative, there was no denying that Lefebvre's men had gained a victory or that the Austrians had suffered a repulse. Thierry's brigade was badly shaken, much reduced by losses, and in only tenuous contact with its neighbouring units as the men sought shelter from the storm. Its condition did not augur well for its ability to fight effectively on the following day. Thierry himself was demoralised: 'I was so upset that I was incapable of making any decisions and needed, but did not receive, help from Oberst Richter, who alone knew the disposition and orders.'[185] Concerned that his right flank was 'completely unconnected', he considered retreating to Rohr but changed his mind after one of Archduke Ludwig's staff officers arrived at 9 p.m. to inform him that Bianchi would provide support on his left and that FML Emanuel Freiherr von Schustekh was at Rohr with a small detachment.[186] He also took solace from the presence of Pfanzelter's tiny force at Bachl. Thus reassured, Thierry settled in for the night at the manor house in Offenstetten.

If the Bavarian advances on 19 April were cautious, those of the Austrian V Corps were confused and lethargic. During his five-hour battle with the

1st Bavarian Division, Thierry received no meaningful assistance from his comrades to the south. In part, Thierry and Richter had themselves to blame for their isolation. Incredibly, they had seen no reason to co-ordinate their actions with Ludwig or even to send him a routine report during the morning. One of the brigade's patrols had made contact with Radetzky's troops and that, for Thierry and Richter, was sufficient. But neither did Ludwig or Charles exert themselves on Thierry's behalf. A staff officer, dispatched by Thierry or Richter, did reach Ludwig during the early afternoon, but the V Corps response was limited. Likewise, a message sent to Charles at 1.15 p.m. prompted no action from the generalissimo.

Meanwhile, V Corps made no attempt to communicate with Thierry until some time after midday. Indeed, everything V Corps did that day seemed painfully slow. Archduke Ludwig had received his initial orders from Charles at 6 a.m., but the corps delayed three hours before decamping from Ludmannsdorf and did not establish itself around Siegenburg until noon. It had required six hours to organise itself and march seven kilometres. Ludwig and his staff were with Radetzky's advance guard on the heights south of Perka when the officer from Thierry's brigade found them, probably at around 1 p.m.[187] The danger was clear and FML Heinrich XV Fürst Reuss-Plauen's division was detailed to move north from its position just east of Siegenburg. GM Friedrich Baron Bianchi's brigade duly marched off, but more to cover V Corps' right flank than to help the hard-pressed Thierry in any active sense.[188] The two battalions of *Beaulieu* No. 58 followed Bianchi's march later in the afternoon. Reuss was serving as an adviser to Archduke Ludwig, so Bianchi assumed interim command of the division.[189]

As he rode up the heights near Hörlbach between 2 and 3 p.m., Bianchi saw Bavarian infantry crossing the Abens at Biburg and immediately deployed his brigade along the high ground to oppose them. The Bavarians were elements of the 3rd Infantry *Prinz Karl* and an artillery battery led forward by Wrede in support of the 1st Division's advance.[190] Wrede intended to distract Thierry, but heavy fire from Bianchi's infantry and artillery persuaded him to recall his own infantry almost at once. He left one battery east of the Abens for nearly two hours, however, occupying the Austrians with the support of a 12-pounder reserve battery and half of another 6-pounder battery from the west bank. The 6-pounders eventually ran out of ammunition and had to withdraw, leaving their heavier cousins to continue the cannonade until the thunderstorm concluded the day's combat.[191] Wrede's brief advance across the stream with at most a lone regiment sufficed to prevent Bianchi from entertaining any thought, however remote, of marching to Thierry's assistance. Writing to Ludwig at 9.30 p.m., Bianchi lamely stated that he was 'not in a position to give Your Imperial Highness a definitive report concerning the situation of General Thierry'.[192] This despite the fact that a substantial portion of Thierry's brigade had found refuge at Hörlbach under the protection of Bianchi's battalions.

Further south along the Abens, Ludwig endeavoured to divert the Bavarians by conducting a limited demonstration and by bombarding elements of Wrede's division that were visible on the edge of the Dürnbucher Forst. Second Reserve Corps had arrived at Umelsdorf at approximately 3 p.m., so the archduke was able to add its cavalry battery to two from V Corps. The effect was hardly worth the effort. Opened at 4 p.m., the artillery barrage achieved nothing beyond the killing or wounding of some Bavarian infantrymen and came to a halt with the onset of the rainstorm not long after it had begun.

As far as the Austrians were concerned, the fighting on the Abens thus ended in a situation similar to the outcome at Hausen–Teugn and Dünzling: a definite setback on one flank (Hohenzollern and Thierry) and ineffectual efforts along the other parts of the front (Rosenberg and Ludwig). Although Pastor Franz Xaver Stoll of Abensberg noted that 'the fields and woods were sown with corpses', the cost of the fighting at Arnhofen had been relatively small.[193] The record does not allow us to disentangle Thierry's losses on the 19th from those suffered on the 20th, but it is safe to assume that his casualties at Arnhofen, while significant, were hardly crippling. The Bavarians at Arnhofen paid for their victory with 227 casualties. Wrede lost at least thirty men from 3rd Infantry at Biburg and forty-two among the units that Ludwig bombarded in the Dürnbucher Forst.[194] Archduke Ludwig's casualties in killed and wounded at Biburg and Siegenburg were roughly the same as Wrede's: thirty-six. Curiously, Ludwig's losses also included an astonishing thirty-two captured and 113 missing from Bianchi's brigade in an engagement where the Austrians should have dominated the field.[195] Most of these men were almost certainly deserters who took advantage of the brigade's first combat to flee the ranks.[196] It was an ominous sign.

Fighting on the Fringes: Pfaffenhofen and Stadtamhof

There was also combat on both flanks on 19th of April. At Pfaffenhofen on the extreme left of the Austrian advance, Major Scheibler's little detachment clashed with the lead elements of Oudinot's corps early in the morning. Scheibler had reached Pfaffenhofen on the evening of the 18th and had pushed his two *Warasdin-St Georg* Grenzer companies across the Ilm west of town while holding most of his men on the hills to the east. When Oudinot's column appeared on the road from Schrobenhausen at approximately 4 a.m., Scheibler rode forward with a half-squadron each of *Rosenberg* Chevaulegers and *Liechtenstein* Hussars to support the Grenzer and assess the enemy. He left the rest of his command (II/*Klebek*, one and one-half squadrons of *Rosenberg* and a half-squadron of *Liechtenstein*) on the heights east of Pfaffenhofen.

Colbert led Oudinot's column with the 7th and 20th Chasseurs, followed closely by GD Claparède's infantry division. Scheibler, who had neglected to scout west of Pfaffenhofen, was unpleasantly surprised by the size of the French force. He was further discomfited when the French foot soldiers, despite the high percentage of young conscripts, deployed rapidly to attack. Scheibler wisely decided to retire and ordered Major Heinrich von Jamez, commanding II/*Klebek*, to post a company on the western edge of Pfaffenhofen to cover the withdrawal. Jamez, however, thought a lone company was insufficient and decided to advance his entire battalion. Scheibler thus received another unwelcome surprise as he observed the bulk of his command marching down the slopes contrary to his orders and deploying north and south of Pfaffenhofen on the east side of the Ilm.

The outcome of the combat was never in doubt. Advancing with the 7th Chasseurs and GB Louis Jacques Coëhorn's 1st Brigade at 6.30 a.m., Oudinot had more than 4,000 infantry and 750 cavalry in his first line. These included two excellent veteran battalions, the Tirailleurs du Po and Tirailleurs Corses, which probably accounts for the speed and skill with which the French deployed. The 20th Chasseurs and GB Joseph Lesuire's 2nd Brigade followed in support. Oudinot held the 3rd Brigade (GB Florentin Ficatier) in reserve. Under fire from a battery of three guns to which he could not reply and outflanked by French infantry that crossed the Ilm at the Sägmühle, Scheibler, with only some 1,300 infantry and at most 400 cavalry, had no choice but retreat. This he conducted with considerable skill, bringing off his overcommitted command in good order despite courageous charges by the 7th Chasseurs. The fighting faded away by midmorning. Having lost 187 men, the Austrians withdrew through Dürnzhausen to Hirnkirchen, where the cavalry and part of the Grenzer arrived around midday.[197] From Hirnkirchen, Hiller ordered Scheibler to Au and Mainburg, while Jamez and his battalion, who had become separated from Scheibler, made their own way back to their regiment. French losses

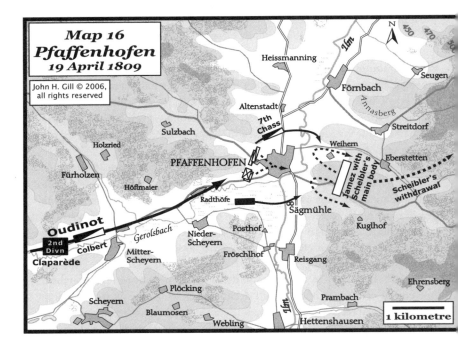

in the brief engagement were perhaps 170, and Oudinot called off the pursuit after his weary men had reached the heights between Kuglhof and Eberstetten.[198] The curtailment of operations earned Oudinot a rebuke from Massena: 'You should have exploited your initial success; you cannot excuse, under any pretext, neglecting to order General Colbert to harass the enemy with his light cavalry ... You know the intentions of the emperor, that should suffice for you.'[199]

Massena's and Oudinot's reports of the engagement grossly exaggerated the foe, claiming that 'General' Scheibler had had as many as 4,000 men in six battalions and two or three cavalry regiments. Napoleon had a clearer picture of the overall situation. While acknowledging the report, he replied to Massena that 'there is not much at Au and Freising' and directed the marshal to prepare for a march on Landshut.[200] However, this report bolstered the emperor's disparaging mental image of incompetent Austrian troops fleeing before energetic French assaults, and he told Massena that '12,000 to 15,000 of that rabble that you defeated this morning may be attacked headlong by 6,000 of our men.'[201]

As Scheibler was retreating towards Au, FZM Kolowrat was attempting to storm Stadtamhof at the other end of the operational battlefield. Davout had left Coutard and the 65th with instructions to hold the heights north of the Danube until the enemy approached, then to withdraw into the town and defend it until night. Coutard was then to rejoin his division at Abensberg. These orders made no mention of destroying the stone bridge over the Danube, which Coutard lacked the means to contemplate in any case.[202]

Kolowrat thus found the Trinity Hill, the suburbs north of the Danube and the islands in the river held against him when his corps arrived near Kareth at 1 p.m. Standing on the heights above the river that afternoon, Kolowrat could hear the artillery at Hausen–Teugn rolling out its lugubrious song to the south-west and could see with no little astonishment that the area around Regensburg was devoid of French troops. He had, however, no idea of the garrison's strength. Having sent a detachment under GM Crenneville towards Etterzhausen (5,050 men, four guns) and posted FML Franz Freiherr Weber von Treuenfels at Regenstauf with a reserve of two battalions (2,640) and twelve guns, Kolowrat approached his task with 9,700 infantry and 1,260 cavalry supported by twenty-six guns. An additional 4,800 men and eighteen guns had been left just across the Regen under GM Rottermund.[203] Coutard's regiment numbered just over 2,080 men and had no artillery, but it was a tough, veteran outfit firmly ensconced in a formidable position.

The Austrians advanced at 2 p.m., III/*Froon* No. 54, two companies of *Zedtwitz*, and the 8th Jägers (four companies) attacking the Trinity Hill from Kareth while the 7th Jägers crossed a hastily constructed bridge at Reinhausen to charge in from the French right. The defending battalion, I/65, finding itself under assault from several directions at once, retired towards the fortified walls of Stadtamhof. The Austrian attack, however, had developed such momentum that the French were hard pressed to repel an attempt against the gates of Stadtamhof itself. Most of Rottermund's detachment had now crossed over the Regen, and Kolowrat ordered his numerous artillery to bombard the French position. Austrian shot soon demolished the Stadtamhof gate and III/*Froon* charged up the main street towards the Danube bridge in a thick column, while Jägers and elements of *Zedtwitz* attempted to penetrate via side streets and alleys. The assault failed. The *Froon* battalion thrust headlong into the middle of Stadtamhof but found its path blocked by a ditch just short of the entrance to the stone bridge. The French had raised the small wooden drawbridge over the ditch and the

Austrians thus found themselves in an impossible situation. Packed together in a surging mass on a street dominated on both sides by French infantry firing from fortified houses, they began to take casualties and lose cohesion. Advance was out of the question. With the bonds of control loosening, the battalion began to retreat. Coutard chose this moment to launch a vigorous counter-attack with the bayonet and a wild melee ensued as the Austrians were driven out of the suburb in disorder.[204] In an intense hand-to-hand struggle, III/*Froon* lost its colours and a number of prisoners.[205] The French also succeeded in evicting the other Habsburg groups, and at 6 p.m., Kolowrat called off the assault. He had, as the Austrian official history notes, 'made no use of his numerous available reserves'.[206] Lieutenant Georges Geoffroy Eissen of the 65th described the battle in a letter to his father several days later: 'we fought in the streets at ten paces' distance, later hand to hand with the bayonet; bullets, shells, and balls rained on us, but we did not cede an inch of terrain . . . the streets were covered with the dead and dying'.[207] Those dead and dying numbered between 450 and 500 (including 150 captured) on the Austrian side.[208] French losses were probably 100 to 150 dead, captured, and missing with an unknown number of wounded.[209]

Although Coutard had reason to be proud of his regiment in its successful defence of the bridgehead, he was now in desperate straits. His men had exhausted their ammunition and he could hardly have been cheered when Chef d'Escadron Trobriand, arrived at 8 p.m. bearing firm orders from Davout to defend the city at all costs and to destroy the stone bridge. The destruction of the bridge was beyond the 65th's capacity and Coutard feared for the defence of the city. He sent Trobriand back to Davout with an account of the day's battle and a plea for ammunition: 'I will hold, Your Lordship, but send me cartridges'. Davout attempted to comply. He directed Trobriand to take three ammunition wagons to Regensburg, escorted by I/7th Léger. Unfortunately, the battalion was late. Trobriand waited at Abbach with his caissons until 4 a.m. on the 20th before deciding that he could delay no longer. Setting off with only a few cavalrymen as escort, his little column was attacked and captured by some of Vécsey's cavalry two kilometres south of Regensburg.[210]

The 7th Léger's 1st Battalion eventually appeared, reaching Abbach shortly after daybreak, but by then it was too late. Having fired most of its ammunition on the 19th at Dünzling, the battalion skirmished briefly with Vécsey's horsemen and retired.[211] Coutard was left to his own limited resources. The Austrians, therefore, despite the poorly organised attack on the 19th, were on the verge of seizing the vital bridge over the Danube. With this span in his hands, Charles would be able to unite the two segments of his army. Moreover, although his thoughts were not yet turned in this direction, possession of the Regensburg bridge would offer him a crucial escape route should the Habsburg invasion of Bavaria falter.[212]

Into the Cold, Wet Night: Austria Abandons the Initiative

'Soaked to the skin', shivering, and exhausted, the men of the two armies sought whatever repose and sustenance they could find against the cold April night.[213] The Austrians seemed stunned after the day's combat. The Hauptarmee lay spattered across the landscape in loosely connected bits and pieces, not quite disarticulated, but ill positioned to face the coming dawn. It was divided into three groups. First, on the north bank of the Danube, Bellegarde had the main body of I Corps in Amberg with Fresnel's advance guard towards Kastl and outposts between Neumarkt and Hersbruck. Kolowrat had clustered his men north of Stadtamhof between Kareth and Reinhausen, but had posted Crenneville at Etterzhausen and a sub-detachment at Kallmünz to guard against fictional foes beyond the Naab.[214] Second, Charles and the Main Army's right wing remained where combat and marching had left them south of the Danube: Liechtenstein concentrated between Alteglofsheim and Eggmühl on the Regensburg highway, Rosenberg around Dünzling, and Hohenzollern's corps licking its wounds at Hausen.[215] Pfanzelter's small 'brigade', occupied the heights south-west of Bachl. Army headquarters and the grenadiers moved to Paring for the night.[216] The third group was the army's left wing, to be commanded by FML Hiller when he arrived on the 20th. Thierry was recovering east of Offenstetten, but nearly half of his brigade ended the day at Hörlbach under Oberst Anton Hammer of *Lindenau*. Most of V Corps (ten and two-thirds battalions, ten and three-quarters squadrons) was on Hammer's left along the Abens and behind Siegenburg with II Reserve Corps, but Schustekh was in Rohr with four squadrons of *Kienmayer* Hussars and Mesko was marching up from Attenhofen with his detachment of Grenzer and hussars.[217] Hiller himself was in Mainburg with the bulk of VI Corps, but a significant portion of his corps was scattered about south along the Abens or en route to rejoin the main body.[218]

The archduke's plans for 20 April reveal the demoralisation that had already taken hold of the Hauptarmee. Unnerved by the first day of real combat, Charles intended to recoil from his contact with Davout: III Corps, whose defeat he had witnessed in its final phases, was to pull back to Leierndorf, while Rosenberg held his post at Dünzling and Liechtenstein probed towards Regensburg. The psychological impact was evident, however, even before the fighting at Hausen had concluded. Writing to his brother Ludwig at 3.30 p.m., Charles outlined his intention to withdraw and assume a defensive posture the following day.

> I stand with the grenadier corps on the heights behind Schneidhart and cannot yet tell if my columns will reach their assigned objectives.
>
> In this uncertain situation, and given the high probability that the enemy will renew the battle in force tomorrow, and that it will have to be continued by us in any event, I find it necessary that Your Grace march to my support at nightfall via Rohr and Langquaid, and aim to arrive here by tomorrow morning.
>
> Your Grace will direct FML Hiller to assume your previous position and will for this purpose call him forward at once if he has not yet arrived. It goes without saying that Your Grace's march with the troops under your command can only take place if you have no concerns about your current position.[219]

This curious order speaks volumes about Charles's thinking as 19 April drew to a close. In the first place, he had decided to abandon his offensive strategy and switch over to the defensive. The very tone of the letter reflects the hesitancy, anxiety, and caution that had flooded into army headquarters by late afternoon and deepened as evening came on. The language contrasts starkly with French directives (e.g. Napoleon to Massena: 'I assume that you will push the 4,000 men you have in front of you so that they will not escape'), yet the situation was not all that grim.[220] The engagement at Hausen–Teugn had clearly gone against the Austrians, but it was hardly a major battle, the Allies were still only tenuously linked, and the Hauptarmee was neither crippled nor outnumbered. Indeed, a rough parity prevailed between the forces immediately available to each side: approximately 93,000 Austrians to 89,000 Allies.[221] Nonetheless, the setback at Hausen–Teugn and the news of Napoleon's arrival led to a complete revision in the Austrian plans. Charles abandoned the initiative to Napoleon.

These instructions are also questionable on a more practical level. Charles knew full well that Ludwig faced a numerically superior foe along the Abens. He knew from the captured letter that Lefebvre had orders to assist Davout by offensive action. He should have known that Hiller's corps was unlikely to reach the Abens until some time on the 20th. How then could Ludwig fail to have 'concerns' about his current position? How could Charles realistically expect his brother to execute these orders? Furthermore, consummation of these instructions would have left Hiller dangerously isolated on the Abens with an enormous gap between him and the bulk of the army north-east of Langquaid.[222] It is not clear what Charles had in mind when he issued this bizarre order; perhaps it is only explicable as the result of too much haste and his personal experience of witnessing the defeat of III Corps. Whatever the motivation, the afternoon instructions to Ludwig carry the taint of unreality, suggesting that the army high command lacked a clear strategic concept, misperceived the tactical situation, and could only respond to local setbacks and changed circumstances by precipitous retreat.[223] Combined with the evening's orders for Hohenzollern to fall back to the Laaber, they helped set the stage for the coming defeat.

For Napoleon, 19 April was a day of preparation and planning. He had already issued his orders and now had to wait for their implementation. By 6 a.m., he had Davout's message outlining the 3rd Corps march from Regensburg, but did not know the status of the other critical branch of his offensive: Massena's forced march to Pfaffenhofen. He was no longer worried about Austrian forces advancing through the Dürnbucher Forst and did not feel that his presence was necessary with 7th Corps, so rather than taking himself to the Abens, he remained in Ingolstadt through the morning, awaiting word from Massena.[224] Once he had the marshal's report in hand, he rode forward to Neustadt and reconnoitred the area around Abensberg.[225]

As evening came on, he returned to Vohburg. The news from all quarters was encouraging. In addition to Massena's exaggerated account of the skirmish at Pfaffenhofen, a staff officer brought Davout's report of success against daunting odds at Hausen-Teugn, and Lefebvre wrote to announce that the enemy had been 'routed' with the loss of 400 prisoners.[226] Perhaps most important was a second letter from Lefebvre, stating that he had seen Gudin's and St Sulpice's divisions encamped on the Regensburg road to his left.[227] Napoleon could thus be satisfied with the day's encounters. Moreover, he now knew that a large enemy force was located between Abensberg and Teugn, that this force had failed to intercept Davout, and that Davout and Lefebvre had inflicted a fairly serious defeat on parts of it. He did not know, however, that a significant portion of the Habsburg host was located east of Paring and Dünzling.[228] Additionally, the inflated reports from the three marshals reinforced Napoleon's pre-existing contempt for Austrian fighting capabilities and led him to overestimate the amount of damage suffered by the Hauptarmee. At the moment in the campaign when the Austrians had fallen under a pall of doubt and anxiety, therefore, the day's action had reaffirmed

Napoleon's confidence in the ability of his men to defeat superior numbers of Habsburg troops. These factors help explain his decision making over the coming two days. For the moment, however, he was justifiably pleased with his subordinates and confident of exploiting their successes to complete the destruction of the Austrian army.

By evening, the left wing of the Army of Germany was arrayed along a line running generally from the Dürnbucher Forst to Abbach on the Danube. Davout held the left with Friant and St Hilaire encamped in the dank woods around the battlefields of Teugn and Saalhaupt while Montbrun covered the extreme northern flank towards Regensburg. The three Bavarian divisions on the Abens constituted the right flank with Vandamme and Nansouty close behind. Further to the rear, Demont was at Vohburg, and Rouyer's division, leaving detachments at Donauwörth and Rain, arrived in Neuburg late in the afternoon 'under thunder, lightning, snow, and hail'.[229] Concentrated around Reissing and Teuerting, Morand's and Gudin' infantry divisions, St Sulpice's cuirassiers, and Jacquinot's chasseurs comprised the centre of the forward line. Napoleon assigned Marshal Jean Lannes to command this powerful force.

Lannes, the son of a farmer, exemplified the 'baton in the knapsack' aphorism. Though lacking a formal education, his skill, determination, loyalty, and conspicuous courage had carried him through the officer ranks to become a marshal of the empire and Duke of Montebello. Superb performances in Italy and Egypt led to key command assignments in 1800, 1805, 1806, and 1807 where he consistently distinguished himself, especially the tense early hours of the Battle of Friedland. By 1808, however, the 40-year-old marshal was in need of an extended period of recuperation. Continual campaigning, physical exhaustion, and multiple wounds weighed heavily. Instead, Napoleon sent him to Spain, where he demonstrated unexpected skill at siege warfare in the capture of Saragossa in February 1809. Even though volatile, stubborn, and 'prone to depression', he had grown under Napoleon's tutelage to become a first-rate commander, inspiring to his own men and deadly to the enemy.[230] He was also one of Napoleon's few true friends and one of the very few who could converse with the emperor in candour.

Lannes carried a black cloud of gloom with him when he arrived in Vohburg at 11 p.m. that night. The brutal siege in Spain on top of long years of war and absence from his family had left him grim, bitter, and discouraged. He reproached Napoleon for involvement in yet another war after an almost unbroken string of conflicts. The emperor, deploying all of his personal charm, countered that the current war had been brought on by

Austrian aggression and that he would aim for a peace that would ensure tranquillity for years to come. Appealing to Lannes's vanity and sense of loyalty, Napoleon stressed the importance of his friend's task in the coming battle and described the superb troops he would command. 'Who knows the road to Vienna better than you?' he asked. His depression diminished but not dispelled, Lannes merely replied 'Sire, I will do as you command,' and Napoleon, taking him by the arm, escorted him to the door of the chateau as he departed for his own lodgings. 'My arrival has brought the emperor the greatest pleasure,' Lannes wrote his wife the next day, 'He said the most agreeable things to me.'[231] The morose mood would continue to cling to him, but it had no influence on his battlefield abilities. In less than twelve hours, he would be leading the troops who smashed through the centre of the Austrian army. In one man, Napoleon had gained an invaluable reinforcement.

On his far right flank, Napoleon was expecting reinforcement of a more substantial sort from another of his most famous and capable marshals. Massena had some 53,400 men around Pfaffenhofen and Napoleon wanted them available for two roles: 'to send reinforcements to Abensberg by one of the two routes and to march on Landshut'.[232] Massena had thus posted one of Oudinot's divisions on the road to Geisenfeld and another in the direction of Zolling; each was accompanied by two light cavalry regiments. His remaining four infantry divisions, Espagne's cuirassiers, and Marulaz with five regiments of light horse were concentrated at Pfaffenhofen, mostly west of the Ilm.

In his commentary on the Bavarian phase of the 1809 war, General Bonnal sharply criticises Napoleon for these orders to Massena. Bonnal argues that they reveal the emperor's predisposition to march on Vienna, thereby intentionally avoiding a grand battle and returning to a form of eighteenth-century manoeuvre warfare aimed at *geographic objectives* rather than the Napoleonic goal of destroying the *enemy army*. Extrapolating, he contends that Napoleon should have brought Massena's entire force directly against the Austrian left via Au to crush the Hauptarmee and end the war in April.[233] Bonnal, however, perhaps captive of his own thesis (that Napoleon was focused on capturing Vienna from the beginning of the war), ignores the context created by Napoleon's earlier instructions. The specific directions in the imperial messages and, above all, their tone, clearly communicate Napoleon's desire to 'fall on the column from Landshut' (to Davout), 'to crush the enemy debouching from Landshut' (to Wrede), and, to Massena 'to take the enemy *en flagrant délit* and destroy his columns'.[234]

This is hardly the language of someone seeking to avoid battle or simply trying to manoeuvre the Austrians out of Bavaria. Sending Massena to Au may have been just as effective in defeating the Hauptarmee. Indeed, it may have been the better course of action given the actual outcome of events. But Napoleon was aiming at a greater object, an annihilating blow, cutting Charles off from his base of support to demoralise, surround, and destroy him. Napoleon may be faulted for expecting too much of his men, but this was a brilliant piece of operational thinking, a strike in depth that would place Massena across the enemy's line of communication. The Austrians, of course, might evade the planned envelopment and attempt to flee over the Danube, but Napoleon knew that Regensburg was still in French hands and that the bridge at Straubing was burned. An Austrian retreat across the Danube would thus involve a difficult passage of a major river across a pontoon bridge or a repaired span—in either case, a dangerous and potentially crippling withdrawal *away* from the Hauptarmee's principal line of communications. Napoleon may have believed that the capture of Vienna would be a necessary feature of the war whatever the result in Bavaria, and he may have erred in not pursuing Charles after the victory at Regensburg on the 23rd, but there is no doubt that he purposed nothing less than the destruction of the Austrian army between the Danube and the Isar during that cold and rainy April. He came within a hair of achieving it.

The emperor's intentions notwithstanding, the Army of Germany's positions that night of 19/20 April were by no means ideal and might have been problematic in the face of a more aggressive foe. Under Napoleon, however, and facing an almost intimidated Austrian high command, the Allies now posed two distinct threats to Charles. The most immediate danger was from the provisional corps Lannes would command, poised as it was at the seam between the left and right wings of the Hauptarmee (although neither side knew this). Equally menacing, but more distant, was Massena's command, preparing to drive deep behind the Austrian left against the line of communications through Landshut. Massena would not come into play until the 21st at the earliest, but Lannes, in co-ordination with Lefebvre, could strike on the 20th. Moreover, the Army of Germany was now infused with the emperor's confidence and will to action.[235] 'This day of victory concluded with the reassuring news that Napoleon would arrive tomorrow morning and would personally command the principal forces,' noted Pastor Stoll of Abensberg, 'Now no one had any doubt about the happy success of the coming day.'[236] The dawn creeping into the dull eastern sky thus promised a severe challenge for Charles and his army.

Actions on 19 April: Courage and Contrasts

Some commentary on the battles of 19 April is useful before proceeding. Although officers and men of both sides displayed great valour and tenacity during these engagements, in almost every instance, the Allies, French and German alike, came out on top. In the case of Pfaffenhofen, the weight of numbers made any other outcome impossible, but in the battles at Hausen, Arnhofen, and Biburg, the Allied troops had little if any numerical advantage.[237] Tactical and operational superiority, not numbers, explain the results of these battles.

In the first place, the archduke's planning for the day was muddled and indecisive, 'utterly incomprehensible'.[238] Poor planning was followed by flawed and half-hearted execution. At the operational and grand tactical levels, for instance, Charles and his subordinates weakened the attempted thrust against Davout by dispersing their strength. Advancing across a front of sixteen kilometres in close terrain, the three Austrian columns were compartmented, unable to support one another and acting as unconnected individuals rather than an articulated army. The result was a series of more or less isolated combats for III and IV Corps, while Liechtenstein marched off to the far right flank, where he was untroubled by contact with the enemy.

This dispersal also had a negative effect on Charles's ability to command his army on the 19th. The wooded and hilly terrain precluded Charles and his subordinates from gaining a comprehensive view of the battlefield and concealed the enemy's strengths and weaknesses. The effect was nearly debilitating. With no clear picture of the enemy or friendly situation and challenged to communicate with Rosenberg or Liechtenstein in a timely manner, Charles fell into indecision. Weak leadership at the corps and division level compounded the lack of a firm hand at the top. The corps commanders were uncomfortable with the new organisational structure and the demands it placed on their initiative and ability to act at least semi-independently. Additionally, Charles regularly disregarded the corps organisation that he had emphasised in the approach to war.[239] Liechtenstein's conglomerate command is a prime example of this. Thus even the generalissimus fell back into the old pattern of cobbling together 'columns' and ad hoc formations rather than utilising the corps organisations in which he had placed so many hopes.

A passion for detachments also weakened the Austrian advance. The most important of these was Thierry. The presence of an additional 6,000 men at Hausen might have made a difference in the result, even if only to limit the sense of demoralisation and defeat that set in among the Austrians after the battle. The other detachments were not militarily significant, but they highlight the army's operational culture and norms. The habit of detaching forces in dribs and drabs about the battlefield provides additional testimony to the prevalence of a deadening sense of caution in Austrian thinking and a predilection for guarding everything at the risk of being too weak at the principal point of contact. This tendency was amplified by the sense of inferiority vis-à-vis the French, so that Austrian leaders often attributed unrealistic operational options to their opponents.[240]

Serious problems also emerged at the tactical level. Rosenberg's disappointment with his infantry was evident in his report:

> Although the enemy losses in dead and wounded was greater than ours [he erred in this judgement], the number of prisoners was out of all proportion, and so it will remain in every forest engagement, because our infantry has too little capability and too much awkwardness when compared to the French, ours is so accustomed to closed ranks and the word of command that one cannot count on independent decision making.[241]

In addition, the Austrian commanders displayed a tendency to throw their battalions, regiments, and brigades forward in courageous but unsupported, unco-ordinated attacks. Hohenzollern was unable to exploit the advantages of surprise and quantitative superiority he had over St Hilaire at the beginning of the engagement because he did not have any supporting units at close hand, and Rosenberg pushed isolated units against the outnumbered Gilly, allowing the hard-pressed French to repel piecemeal attacks.

There was also a failure to co-ordinate at the army command level. Charles contented himself with simply observing what little he could of the action from a distance and may have allowed himself to become captivated by Stutterheim's minor skirmishing to his immediate front. There is no evidence that he sent staff officers to report on Hohenzollern's and Rosenberg's actions, and his two corps commanders seem to have done little to keep him informed or even ask for assistance prior to Hohenzollern's plaintive 'the forest is now lost' note at 3 p.m.[242] Charles allowed Rosenberg to march off to Paring and failed to alter Liechtenstein's outdated instructions. As a result of Charles's action and inaction, Hohenzollern was left unsupported, Rosenberg spent the day occupied with far inferior forces, and Liechtenstein never saw the enemy.

In contrast, the French leaders had employed their men with skill and intelligence, consistently concentrating numbers and firepower to gain local advantage. Just like the Austrian brigade and division commanders, the French generals demonstrated exemplary courage and determination, but they brought superior tactical abilities and greater agility to the contests. It was a winning combination.

Davout had added another fine performance to his record. From the meticulous planning and careful implementation of the morning's march to his rapid response to the Austrian attack, he had been cool, sure, and deft. He and his chief of staff were constantly in evidence where the combat burned hottest.[243] The comparison with Charles is illuminating. Although Charles was the army commander and had to concern himself with more than a lone corps, his failure to ride the few kilometres from Grub to Hausen and assess the situation for himself is inexplicable, especially as he did little else to orchestrate the manoeuvres of his three attack 'columns'. At the same time, Davout can be criticised for not pressing Morand and Gudin to attack earlier and with greater energy. The impact of one or both of these veteran divisions rolling into Hohenzollern's thinly held left flank could have been disastrous for III Corps. Perhaps the overriding importance of establishing a firm link with the rest of the army at Abensberg led him to be prudent.[244] Even in the absence of an energetic flank attack, however, Davout had accomplished his primary mission and inflicted a severe rebuff on the Hauptarmee under Charles's personal (if somewhat detached) leadership. He thus made a substantial contribution to the theme of French tactical superiority and psychological domination that would colour the remainder of the campaign.

The story along the Abens was similar. Where Lefebvre made his presence felt and personally led the first available regiment forward to counter Thierry, neither Archduke Ludwig nor any of his senior staff officers took the time to trot a few kilometres north to investigate the action east of Abensberg. Thierry was left largely to his own devices and V Corps headquarters was left largely ignorant of the dangerous situation on their vulnerable right flank.

The French and German soldiers not only responded to this personal style of leadership, they exhibited impressive tactical abilities. The Bavarian infantry retained their cohesion despite setbacks, and the Bavarian artillery was especially well handled. In 2nd and 3rd Corps, French commanders heaped accolades on their troops. Oudinot reported that his 'old grenadiers and voltigeurs gave new proof of their bravery in the successive charges that they made' and 'the young conscripts, encouraged by this truly admirable example, behaved well', while Davout honoured the men of St Hilaire's and Friant's divisions, especially the 57th and 72nd 'who covered themselves with glory'.[245]

Friant's tactical analysis of the fighting on the 19th emphasised 'the constant superiority that our skirmishers obtained over the Austrians'. Describing the 'rolling and murderous fire' maintained by the combined voltigeurs of his division, he concluded that their ability to 'repulse during the evening a charge directed by the Generalissimus Charles is a new proof of the superiority of our musketry' and that 'the officers of the voltigeurs justify more and more the excellence of their institution'.[246] Friant's confidence and his proud satisfaction with the performance of his division make an interesting contrast to Rosenberg's sour frustration.

The 19th of April was a pivotal day in the war of 1809. It would, in Stutterheim's words, 'have a great influence on the outcome of the war'.[247] As rain, thunder, and night closed around the two armies, the tide in the opening campaign, the Austrian invasion of Bavaria, was already turning. There had been as yet no grand battle, but the French and their Bavarian allies had demonstrated indubitable dominance of the battlefields at Hausen–Teugn, Dünzling, and Arnhofen. They had won several small physical victories, but far more important was the psychological triumph they had achieved: 'all moral power of resistance had been undermined' among the Austrians.[248] Moreover, Napoleon was now on the scene, bringing with him, as a Bavarian commentator observed, 'confidence and victory'.[249] He and his men had gained the initiative and started the process of establishing an unassailable psychological ascendancy over their opponents that would cripple Austrian planning and leadership, leaving the Hauptarmee stunned and disarticulated; still courageous, but incapable of reacting effectively to the blows it was about to receive.

CHAPTER 6

Eight Days in April, II: Four More Victories

The day dawned 'dreary, raw, and rainy', the skies leaden and overcast.[1] Bright campfires flickered into life across the monochrome hills and forests, accentuating the prevailing greyness, as the troops of both armies, waking from whatever sleep they had been able to catch during the cold night, sought relief from the damp chill that soaked into their uniforms, into their bones. Low fog clung to the dewy grass and the smoke from the campfires 'crept along the ground and rose only painfully into the air'.[2] Huddled over the flames in the hopes of hot food or at least some bodily warmth, the men expected a renewal of the previous day's struggle, but the early hours of 20 April passed quietly as Napoleon ordered his forces for an offensive strike that would capitalise on the Allied success of the previous day and introduce four days of muddle and ill-fortune for the Austrians.

20 APRIL: THE BATTLE OF ABENSBERG

Napoleon's headquarters was active well before dawn. Couriers rode out into the darkness at 3 a.m. with initial orders for Lefebvre and Massena, followed three hours later by instructions for Vandamme and updates for Massena. Curiously, there is no record of a message to Davout. Having thus set the army in motion, the emperor left Vohburg at 6.30 a.m. for Abensberg, accompanied by Marshals Lannes and Bessières.

Waiting under arms or preparing their breakfasts that chill, grey morning, the Bavarians of 7th Corps were wondering what the day would bring when 'a universal cheer of joy announced the arrival of His Majesty the Emperor of the French', recalled Christian Schaller, an artillery corporal in the 1st Division. 'As if touched by an electrical charge,' he continued, 'the entire army was suddenly filled with joy and hope.' The corporal recognised Napoleon 'not from the similarity to the busts of him that I have seen, but from the simplicity of his clothing'. This 'simplicity of clothing', a conscious affectation that set Napoleon apart from his brightly bedizened staff in a striking fashion, was an effective bit of leadership, widely remarked and remembered in this and other campaigns. As described by Schaller: 'He wore a light grey great coat buttoned to his neck, white breeches, and a completely undecorated hat of something less than middle size.'[3] Similarly, Albrecht Adam was sketching when 'a noisy shouting in the distance became audible and came ever closer: "the Emperor!"' Edging up to the imperial entourage, Adam, with his artist's eye, got his first glimpse of Napoleon:

> There he sat on his little white Arabian in a somewhat slack posture with that little hat on his head and dressed in the renowned dust-coloured great coat, in white breeches and big boots, so unprepossessing that no one would have suspected in this person the great emperor, the victor of Austerlitz and Jena, before whom monarchs had to humble themselves, had one not already seen him in manifold illustrations. With his pale face, the cold features, the earnest, sharp gaze, he made an almost eerie impression on me; the brilliance of the many uniforms about him heightened the contrast of this unprepossessing apparition.[4]

Riding to the top of a small knoll just east of Abensberg, the emperor gathered the Bavarian officers and addressed them, his speech translated by Crown Prince Ludwig and transmitted to the men by their commanders:

> Bavarian soldiers! I stand before you not as the Emperor of France but as the protector of your country and of the Confederation of the Rhine. Bavarians! Today you fight alone against the Austrians. Not a single Frenchman is in the first line, they are in reserve and the enemy is unaware of their presence. I have complete faith in your bravery. I have already expanded the borders of your land; I see now that I have not yet gone far enough. I will make you so great that you will not need my protection in any future war with Austria. For 200 years, the Bavarian flag, supported by France, has fought heroically against Austria. We march to Vienna, where we will punish it for all the evil it has caused your Fatherland. They want to divide your nation and enrol you in Austrian regiments! Bavarians! This war shall be the last you fight against your enemies. Attack them with the bayonet and destroy them![5]

'A loud cheer rang out as he ended' and the officers dispersed to convey Napoleon's finely crafted message to their men. If some parts were lost in the process, the central themes were crystal clear: Austrian turpitude, Franco-Bavarian solidarity, certain triumph, and, most especially, the emperor's personal faith in the loyalty and competence of the Bavarian army. 'I only know this much,' wrote artillery drummer Reichold, 'that this great man assured us that he placed the same trust in us as in his Frenchmen and that we alone would therefore reap the honours of the day.'[6]

The Allied commanders, meanwhile, were receiving their final instructions from the emperor in person. Dismounting, 'Napoleon gathered his generals about him, had a large map spread out on the ground, sat down and made his dispositions. It was said he indicated the points where he wanted to strike the Austrians.'[7]

On the opposite bank of the tiny Abens, some Austrian officers sensed the looming danger and were decidedly uneasy about their position. One key Habsburg leader, however, was oblivious to the impending attack. At about the same time that Napoleon was explaining his intentions to his subordinates, FML von Hiller was examining the enemy's movements from the heights just north of Siegenburg. Hiller, in accordance with Charles's instructions to support Ludwig and assume command of the army's left wing, had departed Mainburg at daybreak with four squadrons of *Rosenberg* Chevaulegers under FML Vincent and two infantry brigades (GM Nikolaus Ungnad Graf Weissenwolff's and GM Josef Hoffmeister von Hoffeneck's). The column reached Niederhornbach around 8 a.m. and Hiller rode off to reconnoitre while the troops enjoyed a prolonged rest. Arriving at Ludwig's headquarters in Pürkwang at approximately 9 a.m., Hiller, apparently haughty and stiff, had a rather brusque discussion with the young archduke and then went to Radetzky's position to see what he could ascertain of the terrain and the enemy.[8] His conclusion, as the Austrian official history notes, was rather 'strange': the Allies were withdrawing to seek safety north of the Danube! Observing the obvious Bavarian advance from Abensberg, he decided that this was merely a diversionary move 'that could only be intended to cover a crossing at Kehlheim'.[9]

On returning to Ludwig, he read a dispatch that Charles had sent at 7.30 that morning. In it, the generalissimus warned of the possible danger to Ludwig's right flank and suggested, in an imprecise, conditional fashion, that Ludwig should probably withdraw to Rottenburg and that Hiller should take up a defensive position at Pfeffenhausen. Hiller, however, dismissed this vague order as no longer appropriate and replied that the key was to repel the supposed Allied covering attack and push the enemy back towards Kehlheim. He thus decided to leave V Corps and II Reserve Corps along the Abens and to move the lead elements of his own corps to Rohr. It is difficult to reconcile Hiller's decision with the current situation as the delay involved in sending instructions to the two VI Corps brigades, still resting west of Pfeffenhausen, and getting the troops up to Rohr certainly precluded any timely support to Thierry and Pfanzelter.[10] Hiller nonetheless seemed satisfied with his actions and rode to rejoin his men at Niederhornbach.[11] Unfortunately for him, his entire conception of the situation on the Abens was about to collapse.

Offenstetten to Rottenburg

The Allied attack on 20 April can be viewed as developing, through many small engagements and often unco-ordinated actions, along two general axes: the eastern one (Allied left flank) from Abensberg and Reissing through Bachl to Rohr and Rottenburg, the other just to the west (Allied right flank) from Biburg to Schweinbach and eventually to Pfeffenhausen. In accordance with Napoleon's plans, fighting on 20 April opened on the first of these, the eastern, or left flank axis.[12]

Crown Prince Ludwig's division, inspired by Napoleon's speech, threw out skirmishers and advanced east from Abensberg, emerging from the woods near See at approximately 10 a.m.[13] On the right along the Ochsenstrasse, the 1st Brigade soon cleared a small Austrian detachment from Offenstetten but encountered some difficulty in evicting a rear guard company from the 'Sommerkeller' (Keller on the maps), a small, walled farmstead on the rise just east of the village. South of Ludwig, GM von Hügel was advancing up the valley of the Sallingbach into the gap between Thierry and Bianchi, apparently unopposed.

East of Offenstetten, Thierry's men in the Sommerkeller resisted stoutly at first. With the Bavarian 1st Light marching up the road, I/1 pressing up the gentle slope from Offenstetten, and II/1 threatening them from their right, however, they finally fled to the temporary shelter of the woods to their rear. Hoping to relieve the pressure on their countrymen, two squadrons of *Levenehr* Dragoons launched a sudden charge at I/1st Infantry, but the Bavarians coolly formed square and repelled the Austrian horsemen with loss. Bavarian Schützen killed and captured a number of the dragoons as the cavalrymen attempted to retreat through the woods towards Sallingberg. Meanwhile, the 2nd Brigade had passed through the forest on the Bavarian

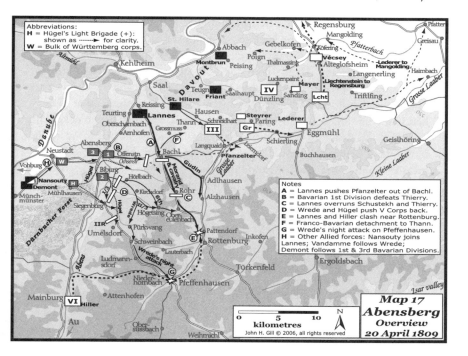

Abbreviations:
H = Hügel's Light Brigade (+):
shown as ----▶ for clarity.
W = Bulk of Württemberg corps.

Notes
A = Lannes pushes Pfanzelter out of Bachl.
B = Bavarian 1st Division defeats Thierry.
C = Lannes overruns Schustekh and Thierry.
D = Wrede and Hügel push V Corps back.
E = Lannes and Hiller clash near Rottenburg.
F = Franco-Bavarian detachment to Thann.
G = Wrede's night attack on Pfeffenhausen.
H = Other Allied forces: Nansouty joins
Lannes; Vandamme follows Wrede;
Demont follows 1st & 3rd Bavarian Divisions.

Map 17
Abensberg
Overview
20 April 1809

kilometres
John H. Gill © 2006, all rights reserved

left and entered the dewy meadow north of the Ochsenstrasse. Leading the attack, the brigade's Schützen had overcome Habsburg resistance and were pressing through the band of trees west of Scheuern as 1st Brigade surged past the Sommerkeller some time between 11 a.m. and noon.

Early that morning, the luckless Thierry, completely ignorant of what the Main Army was doing and barely in touch with Archduke Ludwig, had believed that Bavarian movements betokened an imminent retreat. He learned to his alarm that the opposite was true when Richter and Hardegg returned from a personal reconnaissance just before 10 a.m. Based on their information, Thierry decided to withdraw, but by then it was too late to leave without a fight: Bavarian uniforms were already visible along the treeline west of Offenstetten and skirmish fire was beginning to pepper the grey morning. Though under pressure, his brigade held up fairly well at first, maintaining its posts at the Sommerkeller and in the woods west of Scheuern. However, the successful Bavarian attack on the Sommerkeller, the repulse of the dragoons, and the appearance of Württemberg skirmishers from Hügel's brigade near Sallingberg confirmed Thierry in his decision to retreat. He returned two

3-pounders borrowed earlier that morning from Pfanzelter and hurried to get the rest of his command back to the supposed safety of Rohr.

The end, however, was near. Coming out of the woods and looking down into the bowl around Bachl, Thierry and his men were dismayed to find not Pfanzelter, but French light cavalry. These men, the 1st and 2nd Chasseurs of Jacquinot's brigade, had already swept up the two 3-pounders that Thierry had sent trundling back to Pfanzelter unescorted, and they now blocked the road to Rohr. Reacting quickly, the chasseurs struck the surprised Austrians in the flank before they could form square to defend themselves. Thierry's brigade rapidly unravelled. Abandoning their guns, the Austrians streamed into the woods between Bachl and Rohr, seeking safety in flight and losing their cohesion in the process.

Probing ahead of Lannes's ad hoc corps, Jacquinot's men had driven in Pfanzelter's outposts by 7.30 a.m., but a lull then ensued until late morning when Morand's division, the 13th Léger in the lead, began to appear near Stocka north of Bachl. Close behind Morand were GB François Clément de la Roncière's cuirassier brigade (GB Adrien François Guiton's brigade had been left behind to guard the defile at Saal) and Gudin's infantry. Pfanzelter, who already had orders to retire to the new III Corps position on the Laaber at Langquaid and Leierndorf, was in no mood to oppose the powerful force deploying to his front and hastened to withdraw as directed. He was not quick enough to escape unscathed. The French light cavalry and infantry fell on his little command in a fury, capturing his two 3-pounders (the pair he had retained after sending two to Thierry) as well as two companies of his *Peterwardein* Grenzer. The remainder of his chastened brigade hurried off to Langquaid, grateful that Morand did not choose to molest them further. Although he notified Schustekh of his withdrawal, Pfanzelter neglected to tell Thierry, hence that hapless brigadier's astonishment when he discovered Jacquinot's chasseurs at Bachl. If Pfanzelter got away with relatively minor losses, Thierry and Schustekh were not so lucky: Lannes, with Jacquinot's light horse, Morand's infantry, and Clément's two cuirassier regiments, was headed down the highway to Rohr.

The fight at Rohr was brief. By midday, Schustekh knew that Thierry was under attack by superior forces and that Pfanzelter was withdrawing towards Langquaid; shortly thereafter, Thierry's men, badly disorganised, began to flow into town from the woods along the western edge of the Bachl–Rohr road. Schustekh had only four squadrons of hussars and eight companies of Grenzer and could not expect reinforcement from VI Corps until at least 6 p.m., but he decided to cover Thierry's flight as well as possible. Rohr, nestled in a small, deep valley, was clogged with vehicles of every description as supply troops and civilian drivers endeavoured to escape Thierry's catastrophe, so Schustekh collected his men on a ridge south of town.[14] Thierry soon arrived with three infantry companies and a pair of dragoon platoons that had kept some sense of cohesion during their retreat, but the French were immediately behind the fleeing Austrians. Jacquinot's two regiments led the French advance, followed closely by a horse battery, Clément's heavy troopers, and Morand's foot soldiers. Complicating the Austrian situation, Zandt's two Bavarian regiments appeared from Sallingberg. Schustekh, hoping at least to delay the enemy, launched his hussars and the available dragoons against a regiment of French chasseurs that was moving towards the Austrian right. The Habsburg cavalry gained a momentary initial success, but they were, in their turn, completely overthrown when the cuirassiers hit them from the flank. The Austrians retreated in irreparable confusion, carrying Schustekh away in their desperate flight. The French cavalry, now joined by Zandt's troopers, allowed their foes no respite. One of Napoleon's staff officers, a Polish captain named Dezydery Chlapowski, observed the ensuing attack with a combination of enthusiasm and professional detachment: 'the cuirassiers fell upon the enemy infantry with more vigour than the latter had expected; instead of forming up . . . they [the Austrian infantry] broke apart'.[15]

Intermingled with the routing hussars and dragoons, many of the French and Bavarian riders bypassed the bewildered enemy infantry in the open fields and broke into the disorderly mob of troops, wagons, servants, and other detritus that was trying to escape down the main road to Rottenburg. Other Allied troopers charged in among the Habsburg foot soldiers. Chef d'Escadron Jean Dieudonné Lion of the 2nd Chasseurs seized two Austrian standards—the first trophies of the campaign—with his regiment's elite company as they rounded up a huge mass of prisoners.

Meanwhile, the French infantry was deploying, 13th Léger and 17th Ligne swinging to the right, 30th Ligne advancing on the left and in the centre. Schustekh's detachment and the remains of Thierry's brigade dissolved in panic. Thierry himself was taken captive as he bravely dismounted in an effort to rally his demoralised troops. In the fighting and rout, the *Kaiser* Infantry ceased to exist as an effective combat unit, the *Levenehr* Dragoons were almost wiped out, the eight companies of *Brod* Grenzer nearly annihilated, and a wealth of supply and ammunition wagons fell into French hands.[16] The tangled moil of fleeing Austrians and jubilant French tumbled down the highway towards Rottenburg.

Where was Hiller? At about the time that Schustekh was reporting the arrival of Thierry's first refugees and Jacquinot's chasseurs were trotting out of the woods north of Rohr, Hiller departed Niederhornbach. He had ridden back to the town to set his men in motion and at approximately noon, after an extended rest, VI Corps was on the move for Rottenburg.[17] The corps marched on the road through Pfeffenhausen and then south of the Laaber, but Hiller and his staff rode off north of the little river on their own.[18] They did not get far. According to Hiller's account: 'Hardly had I arrived in the vicinity of Pattendorf when I encountered a substantial number of disorganised, retreating soldiers, who said in answer to my enquiries that they belonged to the troops of FML Schusteck [sic], who had been at Rohr, but that they had been defeated, General Thierry taken prisoner, and the entire detachment wiped out.'[19] Still, Hiller remained confident, telling Ludwig that within three hours he would have two infantry brigades and some cavalry at Rohr to support Schustekh. It was approximately 3 p.m.[20] He soon discovered that the soldiers' statements were accurate. He did not have three hours.

By the time he made his way to Rottenburg, his two infantry brigades were up, having experienced great difficulty fighting their way through roads jammed with vehicles and hundreds of fugitive soldiers. Vincent and the *Rosenberg* Chevaulegers chased away some French scouts, but numerous French of all arms were now evident everywhere across the Laaber. Although evening was closing in, Hiller ordered Vincent and Weissenwolff to attack the French while Hoffmeister established his men east of the river. Vincent's troopers succeeded in repulsing the lead French cavalry units, but a subsequent infantry assault met a very different fate. Led by the corps' chief of staff, Oberst Markus von Csollich, *Deutschmeister* attacked the wooded high ground opposite Rottenburg. At great cost, the soldiers of *Deutschmeister* pushed their way into the woods in the gathering gloom. They could not hold. The 13th Léger and 17th Ligne struck the Austrians in the left flank, forcing *Deutschmeister* to retire to Rottenburg with a loss of more than 1,200 men.[21] As if this bloody rebuff were not enough, Hiller now had another worry: the leading French troops were throwing their hats in the air and cheering, while the few French prisoners assured him that 'Napoleon himself had reached the army yesterday'. Under such circumstances, Hiller believed, 'there remained nothing else for me to do' but to hold his position as best he could until nightfall brought some level of surcease.[22] Later that night he withdrew his corps to Türkenfeld, five kilometres south of the Laaber on the highway to Landshut.

While Morand and most of the cavalry from Lannes's temporary corps were encompassing the destruction of Thierry and Schustekh, Gudin slanted off to the south-east to Adlhausen on the Laaber, ending the day on the west bank of the little river between that village and Alzhausen. His route thus took him away from Pfanzelter, who was able to slip off to Langquaid with no further loss.

As for other Allied forces, Deroy and Demont halted around Bachl, while Nansouty and St Sulpice (Guiton rejoined that evening) bivouacked between that village and Rohr. Crown Prince Ludwig's division camped north of Rohr. Napoleon kept them in this central position out of concern for Davout's safety, going so far as to send part of the heavy cavalry, Seydewitz's light cavalry brigade, Deroy's two light battalions, and three guns to Grossmuss and Thann at 4 p.m. when a report came in that Austrian troops were still in that area.[23] This force collected an appreciable number of stragglers, but had no significant interaction with the enemy. Similarly, a detachment consisting of I/5 Bavarian Infantry, some light cavalry, and one cannon under Chef de Bataillon Jean Maingranaud, one of Lefebvre's staff officers, probed down the road towards Langquaid in the evening and took two prisoners, but returned quickly on encountering greatly superior numbers of enemy along the Laaber.

Biburg to Pfeffenhausen

Fighting along the other axis (Biburg to Pfeffenhausen) opened around midday just as Lannes's men were pressing forward against Schustekh and Thierry. Wrede, supported by his foot artillery on the hills west of the Abens, took his infantry across the little bridge at Biburg and deployed to attack Bianchi's positions on the heights. The soldiers were aware that Napoleon, 'whom we all saw', was watching their manoeuvres from the knoll to their left rear.[24] The 7th Infantry and 6th Light carried the brunt of the assault against the Austrian centre, while the 6th Infantry advanced toward the Hörlbachs on the left and the 13th climbed the bluffs to seize the woods on the right. Slightly further right, II/3rd Infantry had the task of securing the wooded high ground near Perka, but its sister battalion continued down the valley of the Abens directly on Siegenburg. The Austrians, well posted and equal to the Bavarians in strength, offered firm resistance and the Bavarians did not initially push their attacks with any great vigour. Similarly, the attack of II/3 Infantry stalled after seizing Perka and the surrounding woods. As the afternoon wore on, however, the pace and pressure of the attack increased,

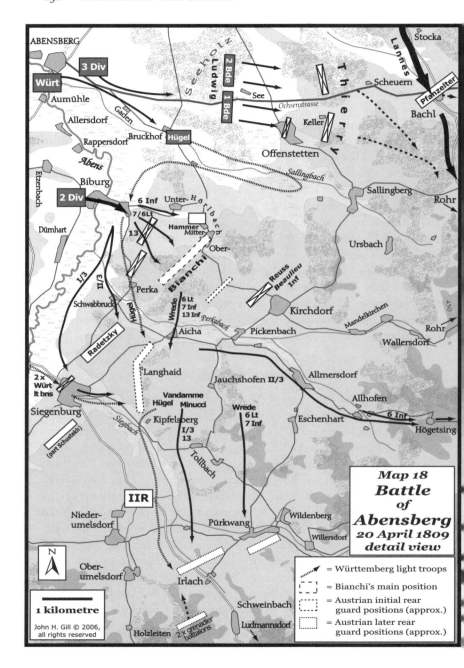

ABENSBERG

3 Div

Würt

Aumühle

Allersdorf

Rappersdorf

Gaden

Bruckhof   Hügel

Abens

Biburg

Etzenbach

2 Div

Dürnhart

6 Inf   Unter-

7/6Lt

13

Hammer

Mitter-

Ober-

Schwabbruck

Perka

I/3

II/3

Radetzky

2 x
Würt
lt bns

Siegenburg

(part Schustekh)

Bianchi

Hügel

Wrede

6 Lt
7 Inf
13 Inf

Aicha

Perkabach

Langhaid

Vandamme
Hügel   Minucci

Kipfelsberg
I/3
13

Stegbach

Tollbach

IIR

Nieder-
umelsdorf

N

1 kilometre

John H. Gill © 2006,
all rights reserved

Ober-
umelsdorf

Horlbach

See

2 Bde

1 Bde

Seeholz
Ludwig

Ochsenstrasse

Keller

Offenstetten

Sallingbach

Thierry

Stocka

Scheuern

Pfanzelter

Bachl

Sallingberg

Rohr

Ursbach

Reuss
Beaulieu
Inf

Kirchdorf

Mandelkirchen

Pickenbach

Rohr

Wallersdorf

450

Jauchshofen II/3

Allmersdorf

Allhofen

Wrede
6 Lt
7 Inf

Eschenhart

6 Inf

Högetsing

Wildenberg

Pürkwang

Willersdorf

Irlach

Schweinbach

Holzleiten   2 x grenadier
battalions

Ludmannsdorf

Map 18
Battle
of
Abensberg
20 April 1809
detail view

= Württemberg light troops

= Bianchi's main position

= Austrian initial rear
guard positions (approx.)

= Austrian later rear
guard positions (approx.)

probably because Napoleon, once he learned of the success at Rohr, decided that the time had come to push forward with his right wing.[25]

It was now between 1 and 2 p.m., and Napoleon had Vandamme's Würt temberg contingent at hand to intensify the attack. The Württembergers were split in three groups. GM von Hügel's Light Brigade had started the day west of Siegenburg behind Wrede, but the general himself and two of his battalions (Jäger Battalion *König* and 1st Light Infantry Battalion *von Wolff*) had been called forward to cover the Bavarian 1st Division's advance towards Offenstetten. These men (approximately 1,300) thus found themselves between Bruckhof and Sallingberg, while the other two battalions of the brigade, a light artillery battery, and the Leib-Eskadron of the *Herzog Louis* Jäger-zu-Pferd waited west of the Abens opposite Siegenburg. The remainder of 8th Corps had been diverted from Siegenburg owing to the clogged roads, and found itself east of Abensberg when the emperor 'approached our two battalion columns, riding into the interval between the battalions.'[26] The Württembergers were then treated to a Napoleonic peroration similar to that delivered to the Bavarians several hours earlier. As in his address to the Bavarians, Napoleon selected themes that would resonate with the Württemberg soldiers and spoke in short, dramatic sentences that conveyed direct, comprehensible messages and were easy for the German officers to translate. He concluded with:'I have never turned my back on the enemy and I certainly will not do so today! In one month we will be in Vienna!'[27]'At this point "Vive l'Empereur!" sounded from the entire regiment,' remembered Dr H. von Gross of the *Kronprinz* Infantry.[28]

Although Napoleon headed for the growing sound of combat east of the Abens, most of the Württemberg corps did not. The Light Brigade, however, took the first steps on what was to become a three-day odyssey of rapid marching and heavy fighting. Having decided to push his right flank forward, Napoleon called Hügel's two battalions back from Sallingberg, placed the *Herzog Heinrich* Chevauleger Regiment and a light battery under the general's command and sent the group along the Abens to reinforce Wrede. The Württembergers joined II/3 Bavarian Infantry near Perka and immediately attacked the hills to the south, crashing into Radetzky's right flank as they drove for Langhaid. At the same time, I/3 and the other two battalions of Hügel's brigade were advancing out of Siegenburg pressing Radetzky's left. The Bavarian battalion, coming down the east bank of the Abens, chased the Austrian defenders out of Siegenburg, thereby clearing the way for the Württemberg detachment. On his own initiative, Oberst Karl von Neuffer led his battalion of Jägers, the 2nd Light Infantry *von Brüsselle*, the *Louis* Jäger Leib-Eskadron, and the light battery across the bridge to join the attack on Radetzky.

Radetzky had been reinforced by four companies of *Brod* Grenzer and two squadrons of *Kienmayer* Hussars, but his position was becoming untenable and he was doubtless relieved when he received orders to withdraw to the south.[29] Archduke Ludwig and his staff, convinced that their corps was now in the sort of danger Charles had outlined in his 7.30 a.m. message and knowing that Hiller was marching for Rottenburg, had issued orders for V Corps to retire to Pfeffenhausen. Radetzky fell back accordingly, halting briefly to skirmish at Langhaid. He reached the heights near Irlach and Pürkwang at approximately 5 p.m. Bianchi was also withdrawing in conformity with Ludwig's instructions. His rear guard, using the 'battalion mass' formation for the first time, first took up a position just west of Kirchdorf,[30] before continuing to Pürkwang, where they were also able to help cover Radetzky's withdrawal. Under this protection, the main bodies of both forces took the crowded road south through Ludmannsdorf to the Laaber.

Wrede followed Bianchi across the Perkabach, but inflicted few losses on the retreating Austrians, and the latter were able to secure a good rear guard position near Pürkwang. Though casualties were not heavy, the momentum of the day was against the Habsburg troops and they soon found themselves under pressure again as Wrede approached from the north with 6th Light, 7th Infantry, his cavalry, and his light battery.[31] At the same time, the Württemberg Light Brigade and other Bavarians were advancing from the north-west, generally parallel to the highway. After evicting Radetzky from the area around Langhaid, Hügel consolidated his brigade on the plateau and crossed the Siegbach to move on Irlach from the southern side of the valley. On his left, north of the stream, three of GM Minucci's Bavarian battalions (I/3 and 13th Infantry) and two foot batteries were also marching for Irlach. General Vandamme, much to Wrede's irritation, had commandeered these men and guns after the fight at Langhaid and had ordered Minucci to attack in conjunction with Hügel. The Austrians, however, held off their pursuers. Leading forward two grenadier battalions, GM Konstantin Freiherr d'Aspre repulsed Hügel's lead unit, the *König* Jägers, allowing Radetzky time to reorder his uhlans and deploy his cavalry battery. Covered by these troops, the rest of the rear guard withdrew down the highway and Radetzky eventually retired to Ludmannsdorf. The Allied commanders renewed their advance through Irlach, but with their troops tired, ammunition low, and night falling, they were content to let the Austrians go and did not press much beyond the village.

Minucci remained at Irlach for the night and Hügel's brigade bivouacked around Umelsdorf. The rest of the 8th Corps, which had spent most of the day near Bruckhof in reserve, came up during the evening and established a camp east of Siegenburg. The other pieces of Wrede's division, however, had wandered off during the battle. The 6th Infantry and II/3, trailing Austrian units, had both arrived in Högetsing some time in the late afternoon after 'an adventurous march through forest and fen'; apparently without orders, they marched off on their own to Obereulenbach, where they camped for the night.[32] Three battalions, one-third of Wrede's infantry, were thus out of his immediate control and unable to contribute to the day's concluding actions.

Indeed, V Corps was fortunate to escape as lightly as it did. In part this was the result of the timeliness of the pullout and tactical skill of the local Austrian commanders, but the ineffective co-ordination of the Allied pursuit was also a major factor. Although the tactical performance of the Bavarian and Württemberg units was generally excellent, lack of unified leadership hampered the overall effort so that combat power was applied in a diffuse manner. Napoleon, focused on the Rohr axis, left the conduct of the battle along the Abens to Vandamme and Wrede, and these two testy and independent generals failed to co-operate with one another. Marshall Bessières's presence on the battlefield did nothing to ameliorate this problem. With no orders or authority, Bessières's only contribution was to oversee the actions of the Württemberg Leib Chevaulegers and a horse battery for part of the afternoon. On the other hand, it should also be noted that the Rheinbund troops achieved success even though they did not enjoy any numerical advantage over V Corps. In round numbers, the forces were roughly equal: against 18,000 Austrians, the Allies had some 19,000 men, of whom approximately 11,300 Bavarians and Württembergers were actually engaged while 7,700 Württemberg troops followed in general reserve.[33]

For Wrede, however, the day was not yet over. At about 10 p.m., he received new orders from Napoleon instructing him to seize Pfeffenhausen that night. Although he and his men were exhausted, Wrede led the 6th Light, a squadron of the 2nd Chevaulegers, and II/7th Infantry down the highway towards the Laaber. Near Oberhornbach they discovered deserted campfires (a failed Austrian ruse) and just beyond Niederhornbach they had a brief skirmish with the trail elements of the V Corps rear guard (five companies of Grenzer and two squadrons of uhlans). The Austrians withdrew and the Bavarians pressed ahead with little loss of time.[34] As they reached the heights north of Pfeffenhausen, Wrede could see that the enemy in and around the town outnumbered his small force, but he also observed that the streets were crammed with men, horses, and vehicles of every description.

Down in the town, news of Wrede's approach merely confirmed a decision that Ludwig and his staff were already inclined to make.[35] Although they had found considerable reinforcements awaiting them in Pfeffenhausen when they had arrived late that evening (at least 12,000 men), the V Corps leadership was inclined to flight.[36] The first reports of Wrede's skirmish with his rear guard led the anxious Ludwig to write to Hiller: 'General Radetzky, whom I left on the heights above Ludmannsdorf, is being heavily attacked and must withdraw quickly; I will therefore depart here as soon as possible and I advise you to do the same'. Then, shortly before Wrede and his detachment appeared north of Pfeffenhausen, Ludwig sent a second dispatch to Hiller stating that 'today's events force me to march to Landshut tonight' and requesting that the VI Corps commander 'likewise leave Rottenburg by the main road so that we can unite our forces there'.[37] As a result, most of the units around Pfeffenhausen were already slogging south through the mud and darkness when Wrede arrived.

The Bavarian general, looking down from the hills north of town, could discern the widespread confusion among the Austrians. He sensed an opportunity and decided to attack. Forming the 6th Light in long thin lines above the town, he ordered the drummers and hornists to sound the charge on his signal and sent a detachment forward to seize the bridge. His timing was upset when the officer leading the detachment stopped to skirmish with some Austrians, thereby alerting the enemy and giving them time to set fire to the bridge. Wrede immediately called for a different company to capture the bridge. The bold move succeeded. Accompanied by drums, horns, and shouting, the Bavarian company fell upon the bridge's defenders, overthrew them, and stormed over the burning span into the village. It was midnight and the chaos in Pfeffenhausen was absolute. As panicked Austrians struggled to escape the apparently overwhelming enemy attack, the Bavarians captured horses and wagons by the score, along with ammunition, stores, and other booty of war. Ludwig and several of his generals were lucky to escape.[38] In the first hours of 21 April, the 6th Light and the chevaulegers established pickets south of town while other men extinguished the fire on the bridge. Wrede brought the 7th and 13th Regiments along with I/3 and his artillery to Pfeffenhausen, granting them a few precious hours of rest in the knowledge that the chase would resume at daybreak.[39]

As Wrede was encouraging Ludwig's departure for Landshut, Hiller was also headed for that city and the safety of the Isar. The general was already in Türkenfeld when he received Ludwig's anxious messages and he soon had VI Corps on the march, joining his troops and trains to the stream of men and vehicles clogging every road south. He was deeply discouraged, writing to Charles that 'with my exhausted troops and poor vehicles, I will be most satisfied if the enemy does not seriously pursue me'.[40]

The congeries of small engagements known as the Battle of Abensberg thus came to a close. For the Habsburg Main Army, it was an even more serious reverse than that at Hausen–Teugn. Napoleon had now driven a deep wedge, albeit unintentionally, between the two halves of the Hauptarmee, leaving it in shock and confusion, incapable of acting as a unified force. The Allies were exuberant. Oberst Honorius von Theobald of Württemberg, for instance, reported proudly on 'how brilliantly the Royal Army Corps has debuted'.[41] Once again, the commanders and soldiers of the Army of Germany, imbued with emperor's will and now inspired by his physical presence, inflicted a severe setback on the Austrians despite difficult terrain and an extended battlefield that prevented Napoleon from exerting direct control on the entire action. Although V Corps managed to extricate itself from its position along the Abens with minimal casualties, Thierry's brigade was destroyed, Schustekh's shattered, and the Austrian left wing, at first thrown back to the Laaber, twelve to fourteen kilometres from its starting positions, was now retreating to Landshut in considerable disorder. Losses for the Austrian left wing on 19 and 20 April totalled twelve guns and more than 7,200 officers and men, by far the majority of those on the 20th.[42] Many of these were captured and missing; while this could be expected in Thierry's and Schustekh's circumstances, it was also the case for the infantry regiments under Reuss and Radetzky, where 73 per cent of the 955 total casualties were either missing or prisoners of war. In contrast, French and German casualties during the two days were approximately 1,000, some 730 of whom were lost on the 20th.[43]

Equally important was the psychological impact on the Habsburg soldiers and commanders. The Austrians were still capable of determined resistance and most of them still held to their colours, but, having suffered two unmistakable defeats in the two days since Napoleon's appearance on the battlefield, they were shaken and apprehensive. Many of them were already mentally beaten. In Landshut with the war minister's staff, Freiherr Kübeck visited the badly wounded Oberst von Lilienberg of the *Koburg* Infantry, who 'had little good to say about the leadership of the Austrian army, opining that everyone had lost his head at the unexpected news of Napoleon's arrival and that the affair should be considered as good as lost'.[44] Leutnant Pirquet agreed: 'Our generals have lost their heads', he noted in his diary.[45]

The Fall of Regensburg

While the Austrian left wing was retiring to the Isar in confusion, the right wing was cautiously advancing on Regensburg. In essence the Hauptarmee pivoted about the IV Corps's position at Dünzling during the day: the battered III Corps falling back from Hausen across the Laaber near Leierndorf, the grenadiers shifting to a position between Schierling and Eggmühl, and Liechtenstein scouring the countryside south of Regensburg with his ad hoc command.[46] Anxiety prevailed and there was no suggestion of attacking or pursuing the enemy, indeed no 'guiding concept' at all.[47] Liechtenstein's hesitant march north, for instance, was accompanied by extensive probes east (Lederer with two battalions and a cuirassier regiment) to Haimbach and Pfatter, chasing phantoms in areas where there had never been any significant French forces. The attitude in the archduke's headquarters was summed up in a report Charles sent to the Kaiser that morning: 'I am placing the troops in battle order and *awaiting the further movements of the enemy*' (emphasis added).[48]

Opposite Charles, Davout's corps maintained a watchful vigilance on the 20th. It is not clear what orders, if any, the marshal received, but at the end of the day, he clearly had no information on the army's situation or the whereabouts of Morand, Gudin, and St Sulpice.[49] The apparent neglect of Davout indicates a serious lapse in the Army of Germany's command and staff functions, but also illustrates Napoleon's faith in Davout's skills.[50] The marshal who had defeated an overwhelming Prussian force at Auerstädt three years earlier could be trusted to act on his own now that he was no longer in danger of being entrapped in Regensburg. In any case, most of Davout's corps, in the absence of other instructions, remained in the positions it had occupied the previous evening, Friant around Teugn and Montbrun at Peising.[51] The only offensive action was a careful advance by Piré's brigade and the 10th Léger against Hohenzollern's troops around Hausen. French pressure built only slowly, but Charles, who was still in Hausen when skirmishing began around 10 a.m., was worried about the condition and safety of III Corps and gave Hohenzollern detailed instructions on withdrawing over the Laaber and setting up a protected position south of the little river.[52] Vukassovich remained around Hausen until midafternoon when, apparently feeling isolated and jumpy, he retired to the Laaber.[53] St Hilaire bivouacked between Hausen and Dietenhofen.

Despite uncertainties and anxieties about the enemy and near-total ignorance of his own left wing's predicament, Charles was able to conclude the day with an accomplishment of far-reaching consequences: the capture of Regensburg and its vital bridge. Liechtenstein, entrusted with the mission of seizing the city, marched slowly, cautiously covering his advance with detachments to right and left. Oberst Josef Mayer, advancing on Poign with his four infantry companies and two chevauleger squadrons, skirmished with Montbrun's outposts, while Vécsey marched off west of the city. As noted in the previous chapter, these detachments intercepted Davout's attempt to resupply the city's garrison with ammunition. On the other hand, Lederer, of course, found nothing in his expedition to Pfatter and was recalled to Mangolding in the evening, while FML Lindenau with two battalions and a cuirassier regiment held a pointless support position at Gebelkofen. The corps, now reduced to six and one-third battalions and four cuirassier regiments, arrived under Regensburg's walls late in the afternoon, having taken most of the day to cover the twenty kilometres from Eggmühl.

In the city, Colonel Coutard of the 65th Ligne had been in contact with Kolowrat since late morning and had managed to delay his regiment's fate until first 4 and later 5 p.m. by claiming that a relief column was en route. Liechtenstein's arrival, however, destroyed any hopes of holding the city. According to the capitulation signed that evening, the regiment would march out with the honours of war, and Coutard's officers, retaining their baggage and personal weapons, could return to France after giving their pledge not to take up arms against Austria for the remainder of the war. Having delayed as long as he could, Coutard wrapped the 65th's eagle in the captured Austrian battle flags, hid the lot, and surrendered at 6 p.m., some 2,000 French going into captivity as Liechtenstein's men took possession of the city.[54]

With the capture of Regensburg, Charles had an alternative route of escape should things go ill south of the great river. Napoleon could not now pin his army against the Danube. Charles also acquired a solid link to the two corps north of the river, some 48,000 men who had as yet contributed little to the campaign. Instead of bringing Kolowrat to the south bank, however, he had II Corps continue towards Hemau, its previous destination. Likewise, I Corps remained well north at Neumarkt. Charles's reasoning here is unclear. The authors of the official history offer a possible explanation by speculating that he expected Napoleon to attack towards Regensburg in the next day or two. If the French emperor intended such an attack, according to Austrian thinking, it would have to be made along both banks of the Danube. Charles, therefore, may have decided to keep I and II Corps on the northern bank to oppose this presumed French advance, while protecting his line of communications with Bohemia and perhaps encouraging the

French to make more substantial detachments to the north. For these early twentieth-century Austrian historians, this mode of reasoning exemplified the archduke's faith in 'the apparently overwhelming power of manoeuvre', but they noted sardonically that Napoleon, planning according to a different strategic style, 'sought and found protection for his communications in a powerful offensive in the direction where he expected to find his enemy's main force'.[55]

Kolowrat met with Charles that evening at army headquarters in Alteglofsheim before returning north to join his men as they marched off through the night towards Hemau.[56] Bellegarde, meanwhile, bivouacked his corps around Neumarkt with security detachments to the west and south. One of these forward detachments, Oberst Ignaz Graf Hardegg with three platoons of *Schwarzenberg* Uhlans and four companies of the 2nd Jäger Battalion, encountered I/111th Ligne and elements of the 12th Chasseurs at Berching.[57] The brief but violent engagement that followed cost the Austrians ten casualties and the French approximately three times as many. The French retired behind the Altmühl and withdrew to Ingolstadt that evening.[58]

At the other end of the operational theatre, Massena's men had again stretched themselves to the limit to meet their emperor's expectations. As the history of the 56th Ligne dryly comments: 'in such circumstances, war is in the legs'.[59] The corps marched in two great columns, one over poor secondary roads through Allershausen, the other south down the Munich highway to Unterbruck, then east on an unpaved road via Giggenhausen. The initial destination for both was Freising. The lead elements of the first column (Claparède and Marulaz), however, continued through the town to halt for the night with Marulaz's advance guard just short of Moosburg and its bridge over the Isar.[60] These men had covered more than forty kilometres during the day. The other component of the first column, Carra Saint-Cyr's infantrymen, bivouacked around Freising when they reached the town at 1.30 a.m. on the 21st (twenty-seven kilometres). The way was often miserable: 'We marched on the worst possible road, full of large holes and resembling a ditch full of water for long stretches,' according to a Hessian account.[61] Again, the condition of these exhausted units is not known with precision, but each Hessian battalion apparently left seventy to eighty men behind. The march of the second column (Legrand, Molitor, and Espagne, with much of the artillery and trains) was just as gruelling. Legrand's men did not reach Freising until 6 a.m. the following morning.[62] Molitor had a brief rest at Unterbruck, but his division was on the march again at 2 a.m., with Espagne close behind and the guns and trains bringing up the rear.[63] This column had

(clockwise from top left)

1. **Franz I** (1768–1835) assumed the throne in 1792, became the first Emperor of Austria (1804), before laying aside the crown of the Holy Roman Empire in 1806.
2. **Maria Ludovica** (1787–1816), from the Este branch of the Habsburg family, was Franz's cousin and third wife (1808). Influential, she advocated war.
3. **Johann Philipp Graf Stadion** (1763–1824) resigned in July 1809, but played a key diplomatic role in 1813 and served as finance minister from 1815.
4. **Clemens von Metternich** (1773–1859) took Stadion's place as foreign minister in 1809; he was one of Europe's foremost diplomats for half a century.

5. **Tsar Alexander I** (1777–1825), Napoleon's inconsistent ally in 1809, he provided much of the motive force behind the Coalition campaigns against the French emperor from 1812–15.

6. **Friedrich Wilhelm III** (1770–1840) was finally permitted to return to Berlin at Christmas 1809. Remained closely tied to the tsar, but also a French ally/client until circumstances forced him to change sides in March 1813.

7. **Friedrich Wilhelm von Goetzen** (1767–1820), Governor General of Silesia from 1807 to 1812, his duties brought him into contact with Stadion and other anti-Napoleon luminaries in Austria during 1808–9.

(clockwise from top)
8. Archduke Charles (1771–1847), relieved of command after Znaim, was briefly
  fortress commandant in Mainz in 1815, but never held an active post again.
9. Anton Mayer von Heldensfeld (1765–1842) was promoted to FML and recalled from
  internal exile in Brod in September 1809 to advise the desperate court.
10. Philipp Graf Grünne (1762–1854), one of Charles's closest confidants through
  1809, served as head of his household until the archduke's death in 1847.

(clockwise from top left)

15. EH Ludwig (1784–1864) turned over command of V Corps in May owing to illness and left military life until 1822 when he became director general of artillery.

16. Johann von Hiller (1748–1819) departed the army just before Wagram, supposedly for health reasons, but commanded the Military Border later that year.

17. Johannes Fürst Liechtenstein (1760–1836) commanded the army after Charles's departure in July, but never again held a military position.

18. Michael Freiherr von Kienmayer (1755–1828) was Commandant in Galicia, Transylvania, and Moravia until 1826, but 1809 was his last active command.

19. **Napoleon** (1769–1821) regarded the 'manoeuvre of Eggmühl' and the Danube crossing prior to Wagram as two of his greatest military achievements. The war brought him a new wife: the young Habsburg Archduchess Marie Louise (1791–1847).

20. **Marshal Alexander Berthier, Prince of Neuchâtel** (1753–1815) became Prince of Wagram in 1809; he remained Napoleon's loyal chief of staff through 1814.

21. **Antoine François Andréossy** (1761–1828) was a veteran artillery officer who also served in many diplomatic functions (including governor of Vienna after its capture in May).

(clockwise from top left)

22. Marshal Jean Lannes, Duke of Montebello (1769–1809) died of his wounds in May, depriving Napoleon of a superb commander and a candid friend.

23. Marshal Louis Nicholas Davout, Duke of Auerstädt (1770–1823), named Prince of Eckmühl in 1809, he held key corps commands in 1812 and 1813–14.

24. Marshal André Massena, Duke of Rivoli (1758–1817) received the title Prince of Essling for his performance in 1809, but suffered defeat in Iberia in 1810–11.

25. Louis Pierre Montbrun (1770–1812) performed brilliantly in April 1809 and later in Spain and Portugal; he was killed at Borodino leading 2nd Cavalry Corps.

(clockwise from top left)

26. **Marshal François Lefebvre, Duke of Danzig** (1755–1820) commanded the Old Guard in 1812 and again in 1814.

27. **Marshal Jean-Baptiste Bessières, Duke of Istria** (1768–1813), a thorough patrician, commanded in northern Spain in 1811.

28. **Dominique René Vandamme** (1770–1830) led the Westphalian 8th Corps into Russia but was relieved and sent back to France; recalled in 1813.

29. **Nicolas Charles Oudinot** (1767–1847) was made a marshal and Duke of Reggio after Wagram, he occupied Holland in 1810.

(clockwise from top left)

30. French Light Infantry: the stamina and experience of hard-marching men like these gave Napoleon an enormous advantage in speed and flexibility. The gentleman with the bearskin is a carabinier, light infantry equivalent of grenadiers.

31. French Line Infantry: these were the core of the Army of Germany. Shown here in full dress uniforms are representatives of the two elite companies in each battalion: a grenadier (left) and a voltigeur (right).

32. French Cuirassier: these elite troops impressed all observers. The 1st (shown) and 5th Regiments of Clément's brigade broke the Austrian defences at Eggmühl.

33. French Carabinier: these were in the forefront at Regensburg on 23 April. Their uniform, with the distinctive bearskin cap, led many Austrians to think they were Horse Grenadiers of the Imperial Guard.

34. Württemberg Jäger zu Fuss: the crack Light Brigade wore a handsome dark green uniform jacket with black facings for Jäger (König Jäger shown here) and light blue for the light battalions. (Alfred Umhey)

35. Bavarian Infantry: Bavarian infantry uniform was a unique 'cornflower blue' colour with the 'Raupenhelm' also worn by Baden troops. Note the kettle that was key to preparing rations; the dents indicate that this essential item of equipment has seen tough service.

36. Bavarian Cavalry: Dragoons (as shown here) wore white, chevaulegers green; both had the 'Raupenhelm'. One regiment of each participated in the charges at Eggmühl.

(clockwise from top left)

37. **Austrian Infantry**: an NCO, officer, and private (from left) of three 'German' regiments. Hungarian regiments already had shakos, but the helmets would not be replaced in all German regiments until after the war. (Alfred Umhey).

38. **Austrian Hussar**: hussars and their distinctive uniforms originated in Hungary; many troopers in 1809 were still of Magyar origin. The Stipsicz Hussars and Vincent Chevaulegers helped stave off disaster for IV Corps at Eggmühl.

39. **Austrian Grenadiers**: regiments recruited from Hungary wore tight, sky-blue trousers (as here), while 'German' regiments and their grenadiers (such as Nissel's ill-fated battalion) had conventional white breeches with black gaiters.

40. **Austrian Cuirassiers**: uniformed in white, Austrian cuirassiers wore a black half-cuirass that covered the trooper's chest but left him vulnerable to thrusts from behind in the wild press of a mounted melee, such as those at Alteglofsheim and Regensburg.

41. Battle of Abensberg (20 April): Napoleon issues orders in the centre foreground; Crown Prince Ludwig's 1st Bavarian Division advances against Thierry's brigade in the Seeholz (centre). Behind the trees is the church steeple of Offenstetten. A Bavarian light artillery battery is exiting the gates of Abensberg (left) and two Württemberg Jäger are visible in the lower right. (Anne S. K. Browne Collection)

42. Battle of Landshut (21 April): as French infantry and Allied cavalry storm across the burning bridge, Bavarian GM von Zandt receives his mortal wound (centre). Bavarian light infantry in the foreground provide supporting fire to the assault. In the distance, Claparède's infantry advances against Austrians south of the river. (Anne S. K. Browne Collection)

43. Battle of Eggmühl (22 April): St Hilaire's men (left) have captured Unterlaichling in the centre, assisted by Deroy's Bavarians (the old general is the central figure). Allied infantry presses into the little copse beyond the village and Allied cavalry charges the smoke-wreathed Austrian battery (right background). 'How to describe such a scene that impressed all who beheld it!' exclaimed Chef de Bataillon Bial of I/72nd Ligne. (Anne S.K. Browne Collection)

44. **Storming of Regensburg** (23 April): 'Fire broke out in two locations simultaneously,' wrote Albrecht Adam, 'and in the windless conditions the smoke rose straight up into the sky in red-grey columns, horrible and majestic.' The city burns in the distance as French troops collect scaling ladders and Napoleon's wound is dressed. The French entering through the breach (centre) have opened the gate (left) for their comrades. (Anne S. K. Browne Collection)

45. Scaling the Walls of Regensburg: the leading two officers up the ladders help each other to the honour of being first of the wall. These may have been Marbot and La Bédoyère as Marbot tells it (and as shown here), but other officers were also on hand.

covered thirty-nine kilometres during the day. The emperor could hardly have asked for more from his men.

Napoleon, in his two early morning dispatches, had also ordered Massena to detach Oudinot's corps to Neustadt in support of the army's right wing. Tharreau, posted north-east of Pfaffenhofen that morning, was hurried towards the Danube at once with his infantry and Colbert's two chasseur regiments. Claparède, however, was already on his way to the Isar, so Massena sent Boudet from Pfaffenhofen rather than call back Claparède. This fine example of the marshal's common-sense leadership met Napoleon's intentions fully and saved the army hours of pointless counter-marching. Tharreau and Colbert were in Geisenfeld by 4 p.m. and both divisions closed in on Neustadt late that night.[64] Oudinot himself was nearing Freising when a messenger handed him the recall order, so he did not arrive in Neustadt until the morning of the 21st.

As to the respective army commanders, Napoleon's activities are fairly clear: after addressing the Bavarians and Württembergers, he remained near Abensberg through the morning, but rode to Bachl in the midafternoon, and spent the night at Rohr in the 'Gaststätte zur Post' where Charles and his commanders had held their conclave on the night of 18/19 April.[65] Of Charles, on the other hand, we know little. He visited Rosenberg in Dünzling at 6 a.m., and then made his way to Hausen, where he was still to be found at 11 a.m. Thereafter, he and his staff vanish from the records until 6.30 p.m. when they reappear in Alteglofsheim, the new army headquarters. This extended absence at a critical point in the opening campaign of the war is baffling and has left many to conclude that the archduke was afflicted by an epileptic seizure on 20 April. Charles suffered from several health problems, including periodic seizures, so this is a plausible hypothesis, but nothing concrete has yet been unearthed to allow subsequent historians to make a definitive assessment.[66] Whatever the cause, Charles's odd invisibility that afternoon contributed to the indecision and lethargy that characterised Austrian operations. We may reasonably conclude, for instance, that this exacerbated the army's command and control problems and that it may have delayed or precluded recognition of the catastrophe that had befallen the left wing. Otherwise it is difficult to explain the army leadership's apparent indifference to the tentative reports Hohenzollern sent relating disturbing news from the left flank. Nor did anyone from the high command enquire about the left wing or so much as send an officer to assess the situation personally.[67] Furthermore, the lack of firm leadership at the top was almost certainly a factor in the precipitous decline in the army's morale, fuelling the growing sense of foreboding expressed by Oberst von Lilienberg and felt by many other men at all ranks. 'Oh, no!' lamented a simple Austrian wagon driver in Landshut that evening, 'we've already been beaten again!'[68]

21 APRIL: PURSUIT TO LANDSHUT

Two great columns of retreating Habsburg troops converged on Landshut during the grey and drizzly morning of 21 April. Coming from Pfeffenhausen, the lead elements of Archduke Ludwig's long, weary column emerged from the defile at Altdorf around 5 a.m. Totalling some 29,000 men, Ludwig's force included most of his V Corps, II Reserve Corps, Oberst Hammer's III Corps troops, and substantial parts of VI Corps. Hiller with the bulk of VI Corps, perhaps 13,000 men, marched on the highway from Rottenburg at a similarly early hour.[69] The other VI Corps detachments north of the Isar were also called to join the main body at Landshut, but the only substantial reinforcement Hiller found in the city was six squadrons of *Hessen-Homburg* Hussar Regiment No. 4 that had just reached the army from Austria.[70] The sight that greeted these generals and their men as the Isar valley came into view was hardly cheering: hundreds of wagons, carts, and miscellaneous vehicles, sometimes three or four abreast, jammed the roads leading to the bridges over the Isar 'in the greatest disorder'.[71] 'The dreadful confusion of everything we encountered is not to be described,' Ludwig told Franz, 'the disorder was so great and the vehicles so jammed up, that one could hardly get them to move.'[72] Pandemonium reigned as each commander sought to force *his* men or *his* guns or *his* supply wagons through the tangled traffic to the safety of the south bank. Although Hiller commanded the wing, he preferred to blame Ludwig and the V Corps chief of staff for 'taking no useful measures to undo the confusion and to bring the thousands of vehicles . . . through the defile'.[73]

The author Clemens Brentano watched the chaos during the night as 'an endless, anxious, wild, exhausted, hurrying stream' of vehicles tried to get through the city so that 'all of the streets were jammed with wagons'.[74] Bavarians observed that 'the soldiers were frequently without muskets or cartridge boxes, without hats or helmets, wounded, etc.'[75] The situation only grew worse as daylight brought Hiller's and Ludwig's men, guns, and horses to the same inadequate bridges. There were only two crossing points: the Spital-brücke and Lendbrücke, both hastily repaired and the former only accessible after crossing onto the Zwischen den Brücken island. A temporary bridge above the Lendbrücke had actually been dismantled and no one thought to use the fifty-six available pontoons to construct another crossing.

Hiller did manage to get II Reserve Corps and Ludwig's three Vienna Volunteer battalions on the heights south of the river and he posted a few guns and some infantry at each of the bridges, but most of his command was still north of the Isar when the Allies began to push against his rear guards shortly after daybreak. Ludwig's corps was north-east of Altdorf and Hiller's was on the outskirts of the Seligenthal and St Nikolas suburbs. Radetzky, with the *Karl* Uhlans and *Gradiska* Grenzer, covered the Pfeffenhausen highway at Arth, his forward post somewhat further north. Four squadrons each of *Kienmayer* and *Hessen-Homburg* Hussars under Vincent were posted at Ergolding to watch the road from Rottenburg, supported by I/ *Benjovszky*.[76]

While Hiller was back-pedalling toward the Isar as quickly as possible, Napoleon was trying to determine the location of Charles and the principal Austrian forces. Although he held an inflated image of the success achieved on the 20th—'another Jena' as he told Davout—he was not sure that the enemy's main body was in front of him on the roads to Landshut.[77] 'Some maintain that he [Charles] was marching for Regensburg at 3 p.m. today, others that he has turned towards Eggmühl in order to retire on Landshut from there,' Berthier wrote to Davout on the evening of 20 April, 'And now your report of 5 p.m. leads to the conclusion that he still stands in front of you.'[78]

During the night, Napoleon decided that the bulk of the Austrian army was indeed retreating on Landshut and he made that city his focus for 21 April. Several factors apparently contributed to this assessment. In the first place, he had several reports that the main Austrian force was withdrawing to the south. The fact that the army had captured prisoners from a multitude of regiments doubtless reinforced this impression. Many of those captured, as it happened, were men of Hohenzollern's corps who had been wounded at Hausen on the 19th, and their presence clouded the picture of which units were actually retreating in front of Wrede and Lannes. Second, the archduke's lassitude during the 20th led Napoleon to believe that the forces opposing Davout must be a mere screen. Third, as far as Napoleon knew (in the early hours of 21 April) Regensburg was still in French hands. The most likely course of action for Charles, therefore, would be a retreat to the Isar or Straubing, not a concentration around Regensburg.[79] Indeed, had this scenario been correct, there would have been every reason to expect to find Austrian baggage trains, parks, and other rear area elements strung out along the south bank of the Danube in an attempt to escape towards

Straubing. Finally, he was analysing the situation under the false assumption that he had already dealt the Hauptarmee a telling blow on the 20th. Had Abensberg truly been 'a second Jena', it was logical to deduce that Charles would be thinking only of retreat.

The emperor's orders for the 21st thus set most of the army in motion towards Landshut. Davout, supported by Boudet and Lefebvre, would evict the remaining Austrians from the area around Regensburg (north and south of the Danube), but Lannes, Wrede, Vandamme, Tharreau, Nansouty, and the Bavarian crown prince would press on for Landshut, where Napoleon optimistically hoped Massena had already arrived.[80]

Vandamme was already marching on his own initiative. Parts of 8th Corps were on the move by 1 a.m. on 21 April and the Württemberg cavalry somehow passed through Wrede's division to lead the initial advance to the Isar.[81] A Württemberg gunner noted the signs of the Austrian retreat as he rode south: 'cannons, ammunition, and provisions lay about in the ditches right and left of the highway'.[82] The Württemberg horsemen slowly forced Radetzky's rear guard troops back through Arth to the position at Altdorf, where Austrian resistance temporarily halted the advance. It was now approximately 9 a.m. Preysing's Bavarian cavalry brigade and, apparently, some French cuirassiers had joined the Württemberg light horse, and Wrede was assembling most of his division around Altdorf. Ludwig had already marched the main body of V Corps back through Landshut to take up positions south of the city; Radetzky soon followed with the rear guard. Though V Corps moved before it came under direct attack, its withdrawal only proceeded with difficulty as 'the entire army found itself trying to cross these bridges all at once . . . the regiments could not be rallied . . . the wagon drivers cut the traces and abandoned their vehicles'.[83]

At the same time that V Corps was struggling across the Isar (c.9 a.m.), French cavalry began to appear near Ergolding opposite the hussars of Vincent's rear guard. Before long, a major cavalry engagement was in progress across the flat, boggy meadows north of the Isar: twenty Austrian squadrons against as many as forty-eight French and Bavarian.[84] The Austrian horse, badly outnumbered, sacrificed itself to gain time for its countrymen to escape. Those Austrians still trying to reach the bridges included the detachments under Nordmann and Scheibler: coming from Katharinazell, Nordmann had to fight his way across the meadows and lost two companies of Grenzer captured in the process; Scheibler, with two squadrons, came riding down the river after finding it impossible to cross at Moosburg.[85] Both of these detachments and most of the V and VI Corps infantry made it to the southern bank, but the Allied mounted regiments soon succeeded in sweeping the Habsburg troopers from the field and came roaring up against the remaining rear guard infantry: two of Bianchi's battalions drawn up in masses on either side of the highway north of St Nikolas and I/*Kerpen* in Seligenthal.[86] Austrian musketry emptied a few saddles, but the Habsburg infantrymen quickly retreated to the relative safety of Zwischen den Brücken and greeted the charging French troopers with a 'lively fusillade'.[87] A brief pause ensued as the French waited for their own infantry to appear. In the meantime, French artillery under GD Jacques Law, Comte de Lauriston, another recent arrival from Spain, occupied the heights between Altdorf and Ergolding and began to bombard the retreating Austrians, increasing the panic and confusion in the city.

Morand's division was leading Lannes's column from Ergolding. Two of his regiments, 13th Léger and 17th Ligne, came up at about 11 a.m. and were soon embroiled in a firefight with the Austrians in Zwischen den Brücken. The French, joined by two Württemberg light companies and the Bavarian 7th Infantry, were about to storm across the bridge when the Austrians withdrew.[88] Hiller had seen that there was no hope of saving any more of the impossibly tangled train and had ordered the rear guard to pull out. The Allies immediately attacked. Two companies of I/*Benjovszky* fell into French hands when their retreat route was cut off, but most of the men succeeded in reaching the south bank. The 6th Pioneer Division, however, charged with igniting the piles of incendiary material on the Spitalbrücke, waited a few moments too long. Delaying their departure to allow a hurrying battalion of Grenzer to cross, eighty of the pioneers were captured by the French infantry that appeared on the heels of the Grenzer. Nonetheless, the surviving men managed to set the bridge alight as they withdrew.[89]

Unfortunately for the Austrians, the light rain that had been falling most of the morning had left everything damp, so both the flammable material and the bridge timbers were slow to burn. The French thus had time to assemble an attack force and Napoleon sent GD Georges Mouton, one of his staff generals, to energise the assault. Mouton placed himself at the head of III/17th Ligne's grenadiers, told them not to fire, and led them across the smoking bridge, despite heavy Austrian fire, at approximately 12.30 p.m. He became thereby the subject of a famous commemorative painting commissioned by the grateful emperor.[90] Once on the other side, the battalion's sappers broke through the city's wooden gates with axes while men of the 13th Léger clambered over the span.[91] As the gates flew open, two squadrons of the Bavarian 3rd Chevaulegers, three Bavarian battalions, and the two Württemberg companies joined their French allies, breaking into the city and fanning out through the streets, collecting booty and pushing the Austrians back as they went.[92] The fighting was often intense, but the issue was not in doubt. By 1 p.m., Landshut was in Allied hands.[93]

By this time, Hiller was also coming under pressure from the lead elements of Massena's corps. Fortunately for the Austrians, the marshal was not riding with his advance guard when they arrived near Achdorf south of the Isar around 10 a.m. These initial troops were outriders of Marulaz's light cavalry division, soon followed by Claparède's hustling infantrymen. Marulaz had had his troopers up and moving early in the morning, riding towards the bridge at Moosburg. The lead regiment, the 23rd Chasseurs, galloped through Moosburg to find Austrians occupying the south bank and the bridge in flames. The defenders, two companies of *St Georg* Grenzer and a half-squadron of *Liechtenstein* Hussars, soon withdrew, however, so the chasseurs leaped from their horses, extinguished the fire with the help of local citizens, and continued their advance south of the Isar.

North of the river, a detachment of the 23rd scouting beyond the Amper ran into Major Scheibler's two squadrons. The enterprising Scheibler, hoping to cross the Isar at Moosburg, attacked the French patrol and chased it back to the town, but found his further progress blocked by the arrival of the Baden Light Dragoons. The Badeners charged at once, driving off the Austrians, freeing some of the captured French chasseurs, and inflicting a few casualties at no loss to themselves.[94] Scheibler, thus repulsed, turned about and headed for Landshut, followed for a distance by the Baden regiment. Before long, Claparède also appeared at Moosburg. He detached Ficatier's brigade to guard the Amper crossing with the Baden horse, and took the rest of his division south of the Isar towards Landshut. Many kilometres behind came Carra Saint-Cyr, Legrand, Molitor, and Espagne, all weary from the extended marching of the past four days.

Approaching Achdorf and the noisy battle in progress north of Landshut, therefore, Claparède had only two of his brigades, perhaps 5,800 fatigued infantrymen, at hand. Marulaz had some 3,100 light cavalry in six regiments, but neither general knew how strong the large enemy force was, nor how long they might have to wait for reinforcements. Marulaz, in the lead, called for infantry support and Coëhorn hurried forward to assist with his brigade. Claparède, however, hesitated. Despite the urgings of Massena's principal aide-de-camp, Claparède was unwilling to attack without orders from the marshal. He therefore called back Coëhorn and waited.[95] At last, around midday, he sent one battalion towards the Achdorf heights in skirmish order to harass the Habsburg defenders. His decision, while understandable, helped save the Austrian left wing.

Even this limited effort caused considerable anxiety for the Austrian commanders.[96] Kienmayer, who was guarding the southern approaches to Landshut with three of his grenadier battalions and the *Knesevich* Dragoons, immediately worried about the safety of Geisenhausen on the line of retreat and sent the *Brzezinski* Grenadiers and two dragoon squadrons to secure the town.[97] Hiller, moreover, recognised that he could not hold along the Isar as he had hoped and would have to withdraw further south. Worse, word that they were 'outflanked' or 'surrounded' spread quickly among the troops in Landshut, heightening their sense of panic, desperation, and abandonment.

Arriving on the scene shortly after 1 p.m., Massena immediately sent Claparède's infantry forward against the Austrian left flank, but it was too late to trap Hiller in Landshut. The Austrian rear guard, arranged in a loose hook with the left facing west on the heights above the city and the centre and right astride the road to Geisenhausen on the hills south of Landshut, courageously resisted Allied efforts to break through their defences. The pressure, however, intensified as Massena advanced and as more and more French and Bavarians pushed out from the city. Posted on a hilltop near Achdorf at the angle of the hook, for example, I/*Kerpen* No. 49 was almost caught in a vice as Allied forces gained ground on both of its flanks. Apparently forgotten in the confusion, the battalion commander, Major Johann Freiherr O'Brien, coolly held his men together and fell back fighting until GM Hoffmeister could rush up to his rescue with *Jordis*.

The Austrian retreat continued south in a confused series of rear guard actions entrusted, once again, to Radetzky with his Grenzers, uhlans, and parts of the *Liechtenstein* and *Kienmayer* Hussar Regiments. By now, all of Morand's division, three of Wrede's infantry battalions (7th Infantry and I/3), two squadrons of the Bavarian 3rd Chevaulegers, Marulaz's light horse, and at least part of Claparède's division were involved in the pursuit. This increasing French pressure forced Hiller to commit GM d'Aspre with the *Scovaud* and *Scharlach* Grenadier Battalions and three guns to hold off his pursuers.

Active pursuit faded away as the Austrians struggled south from Geisenhausen. The situation among the retreating Austrian units, however, worsened. Hiller had wanted to halt at Vilsbiburg, but V Corps, leading the march, arrived there 'in complete disorder'.[98] Many men had by now 'scattered into the woods' according to Ludwig's report, and the VI Corps chief of staff recorded that 'a panicky fright filled these dispersed men'.[99] Kienmayer's troops and most of the VI Corps units seem to have retained a reasonable degree of military order, but V Corps had had enough. Much of the column dissolved into a crowd of terrified fugitives wildly fleeing before rumours and apparitions. The roads and fields were strewn with abandoned vehicles and equipment of every description. Judging the situation in Vilsbiburg irreparable, Ludwig recommended that the retreat continue and Hiller reluctantly agreed.[100] The lead units, thoroughly exhausted and disheartened, reached Neumarkt an der Rott between 1 and 2 a.m. on the 22nd. Radetzky and Vincent, left at Vilsbiburg and Zeiling with rear guard detachments, withdrew behind the Bina when French scouts appeared at Vilsbiburg shortly after midnight.[101]

In the confusion, the three V Corps Vienna Volunteer battalions became separated from the rest of the army and wandered off to the east. Led by Oberstleutnant August Freiherr von Steigentesch, commander of the 2nd Battalion, the Viennese tried to rejoin their corps at Vilsbiburg during the night, but found the town occupied by French cavalry and hastily withdrew to Frontenhausen. For the next three days, the bulk of the little force stumbled about the Bavarian countryside, constantly harassed by French cavalry, until they finally reached Schärding on 24 April. During the night of 21/22 April, two detachments serving as rear guard lost contact with the main body and had to make their separate ways back to the fold. The first group found Hiller after several days and retreated across the Inn with the rest of the left wing. The other group, including Steigentesch himself, arrived in Passau on the 24th after a perilous trek through Landau and Vilshofen.

Some time during the 21st, Hiller also gained a small reinforcement in the form of GM Reinwald with 2,800 men and four guns. Reinwald's men had departed the blockade of Passau on 17 April to join Rosenberg, but for the next several weeks they would find their fates tied to Hiller's command.[102]

On the French side, the bulk of the force under Napoleon's direct command was concentrated around Landshut as evening settled over the Isar valley. Legrand, Espagne, and Molitor, however, were stretched along to road south of the river as far as Moosburg. GM von Preysing from Wrede's division was also at Moosburg with six of his squadrons. In the rear, Oudinot was around Abensberg and Boudet at Neustadt. Crown Prince Ludwig had halted his division (minus its cavalry brigade) at Rottenburg as directed. During their march on the 21st the men of the 1st Division 'were visually persuaded as to the loss of the *Kaiserlichen* on the previous day; as one saw a great number of muskets—although most were broken—sabres, bayonets, helmets, hats, dead men, and horses lying about, as well as ammunition wagons that they had turned over . . . this scene lasted from Rohr to Rottenburg.'[103]

As graphically depicted in this Bavarian soldier's observations, the Austrian left wing was, at least temporarily, neutralised. Many commentators have noted that Hiller and his men managed to cover a lot of ground very rapidly on their retreats during 20 and 21 April despite rainy weather (approximately thirty-five to forty kilometres on the 21st from Ergolding to Neumarkt for example), a skill that seemed to elude them during the advance into Bavaria the previous week. The three corps of the left wing had lost 8,000 men in the fight at Landshut and the succeeding retreat, almost 80 per cent of those from VI Corps. Allied losses for the 21st were small in comparison: seventy-six Germans and several hundred French, probably less than 1,000 overall.[104] Reflecting the nature of the action, 74 per cent of the Austrians lost were listed as prisoners or missing.[105] Major O'Brien of I/*Kerpen* explained this high percentage by noting that 'Among this number were many foreigners who grabbed the opportunity to go over to the enemy; also many young men who were overcome by the unaccustomed burdens of the continuous marches of the 19th to the 22nd, day and night, with no time to prepare meals, in the vilest weather.'[106] Also gone were eleven guns, fifty-six pontoons, hundreds of other vehicles, all manner of field gear, and much of the army's baggage. Adding the casualties from 20 April, the Hauptarmee's left wing had lost at least 15,000 men and nineteen guns in less than three days.[107]

On the other hand, the bulk of Hiller's troops and guns escaped. In part, this was a result of his ability to extricate key combat elements from their dire situation at Landshut after having failed utterly to prepare the army's logistical apparatus for withdrawal. In part, it was his good fortune that Massena was not with Claparède on the morning of the 21st and that the French 4th Corps could not bring more troops to bear that day. Additionally, he could thank the younger generals, such as Radetzky, Nordmann, and d'Aspre as well as numerous junior officers who kept their men with the colours and continued to offer dogged resistance in the face of chaos and defeat. He was being nothing less than honest when he praised 'the bravery of the grenadiers and hussars' for fending off the French pursuit.[108] Though badly injured and momentarily stunned, the Austrian left wing had lived to fight another day.

Davout and Charles

While Napoleon chased Hiller and the Austrian left wing, Davout had to contend with Charles and the bulk of the Hauptarmee. Napoleon, fairly

confident that most of the Austrian forces were before him on the roads
leading to Landshut, had left the marshal only the vaguest orders: 'If you do
not receive instructions, the standing order in a case such as this is to take
yourself where the enemy is and destroy him.'¹⁰⁹ The following morning, the
emperor elaborated, outlining his assessment that 3rd Corps only faced a
'screen of three infantry regiments' and ordering Davout to support Lefebvre
as the latter swept up this supposed Austrian rear guard. The two marshals
were then to cross the Danube and attack the Austrian forces north of the
river so as to 'purge' the left bank and drive the 'debris' into Bohemia.¹¹⁰ By the
time these expansive orders reached his headquarters, however, Davout was
already on the move.

The morning of 21 April found the remaining elements of 3rd Corps
camped in the damp woods around Hausen, Teugn, and Abbach. Davout had
Friant's and St Hilaire's infantry divisions and Montbrun's cavalry division
of approximately 22,700 officers and men. In accordance with his orders to
locate and destroy the enemy, he roused his corps early and the two infantry
divisions were already moving south-east towards the Laaber by 5 a.m.

Davout's advance guard, the 10th Léger and Piré's light cavalry, came into
contact with Hohenzollern's outposts just north of Langquaid around 6 a.m.
The Austrian commander at once rode out with the *Erzherzog Ferdinand*
Hussars and a cavalry battery to assess the situation. It was immediately
evident to Hohenzollern that the enemy was advancing in full force: heavy
French columns were approaching from Hausen, the woods near Grub were
already in French hands, and the rolling sound of French drums could be
heard off to the Habsburg right. Indeed, the Austrians could clearly see a
large group of officers (Davout and his staff) along the woodline. Before
Hohenzollern could take any definitive counter-measures, however, he was
surprised by the sudden appearance of GB Piré. With true light cavalry
panache, the French general had ridden ahead of his own men to seek out
the enemy commander. Intercepted by Major Franz Freiherr von Hundt, one
of Hohenzollern's staff officers, Piré brazenly stated that the Austrians were
outflanked and demanded their surrender. The Austrians reacted to this
suggestion with indignation, sent Piré packing, and scattered Davout and
his staff with a few well-placed cannon balls, but not before the 'imprudent'
Hundt had revealed that Regensburg had fallen and that the bulk of the
Austrian army was between that city and the Laaber.¹¹¹ Davout scribbled a
hasty report to Napoleon ('The army from Bohemia has debouched through
Regensburg ... They have effected their junction with Prince Charles, who is
bringing all of his troops to this bank') and continued his advance: St Hilaire

moving on Schierling parallel to the Laaber, and Friant pushing for Paring on his left.[112] Hohenzollern, who had as yet received no orders for the day, pulled his advance guard south of the Laaber and withdrew to the east, establishing his corps in a new position between Schierling and Mannsdorf.[113]

North of III Corps, Rosenberg was also falling back. Oberst Steyrer, whose little detachment (one battalion and two squadrons) had spent the night just east of Schneidhart, found himself facing Friant's division as dawn's grey light began to colour the day. Fortunately, he was reinforced by Stutterheim (one battalion, four squadrons, one battery) before the French got too close and was able to retire with his battalion as Stutterheim assumed the mission of protecting the IV Corps withdrawal.[114] Rosenberg had decided to retreat. Although he was under no pressure at Dünzling, he was nervous, bewildered by uncertainty, believing himself under threat from vastly superior enemy forces that were advancing very rapidly against his left flank.[115] These French troops were the 33rd, 108th and 111th Ligne, followed by Friant's other two regiments. Even if Rosenberg exaggerated their numbers, they certainly had the advantage of Stutterheim. Placing his lone battalion in Paring, Stutterheim conducted a fine fighting withdrawal, but the 108th Ligne eventually ejected his infantry from the village and forced him to fall back towards Laichling.

As Davout drove in the Austrian advance guard detachments, Lefebvre came up on his right. The marshal had only one Bavarian division, Deroy's 3rd, under his command on the morning of 21 April. The rest of his temporary command was composed of Demont's conscripts and St Germain's cuirassiers. The instructions issued to Lefebvre early on the 21st reflected Napoleon's belief that Lefebvre and Davout stood before an opportunity to sweep aside a small rear guard and capture much of the Hauptarmee's logistics train: 'Pursue the enemy with your sword in his back and announce to the emperor by evening that you have taken from the enemy his parks, his baggage, his wounded . . . with great activity, it is impossible that the enemy's parks will not fall into your hands.'[116]

Approaching Langquaid and Leierndorf shortly after 7 a.m., Lefebvre could see Hohenzollern's III Corps still in the woodline south of the Laaber and resolved to remove this threat to his flank despite the difficulties presented by the marshy terrain. His lead element, Demont's weak and inexperienced division, pressed into Leierndorf, but found that the Austrians had destroyed the bridges. With no way to cross the Laaber and its swampy surroundings and under a heavy artillery bombardment that soon set the village on fire, Demont pulled his men out of the town and out of range.

Before long, however, III Corps fell back towards the Allersdorferbach, and Lefebvre was able to resume his advance. By 11 a.m., therefore, with no intervention from Charles, the Austrian IV (13,800) and III (14,500) Corps had withdrawn three to five kilometres to take up positions along the line from the Laichlings through Schierling and extending some two kilometres south along the Allersdorterbach; Davout (19,200) and Lefebvre (13,400) were approaching this line in the relatively narrow open space between the Laaber and the woods north of Paring.[117]

While these small actions were in progress, Austrian headquarters in Alteglofsheim was issuing a new, painfully detailed 'disposition' that illustrated how little the archduke and his staff knew of the situation on the ground. Evidently with an eye towards some sort of offensive movement on the 22nd through Abbach to Bachl, Charles wanted to assemble the bulk of his army between Regensburg and Eggmühl behind a screen of light troops stretching in an extended cordon from Weillohe through Dünzling and Paring to a point opposite Adlhausen south of the Grosse Laaber. Kolowrat's corps would turn about and march through Regensburg behind the right flank of this position, while Ludwig with V Corps, II Reserve Corps, Thierry's brigade, and Pfanzelter would shift to Eggmühl. On the farther flanks, Hiller should hold Pfeffenhausen and Rottenburg to guard the routes to Landshut, and Bellegarde would bring most of his corps to Hemau.[118] Out of date before they were issued, these instructions suggest a high degree of detachment and unreality in army headquarters. In particular, this disposition did not cater for the potential actions of an active enemy, even though Charles knew that Napoleon himself was on the field; the high command assumed that the Hauptarmee would be able to carry out its repositioning undisturbed.

In the event, the Austrians were forced to react to a rapidly changing situation. This initial disposition had not even reached its recipients when reports from III and IV Corps necessitated a new set of instructions, but the revised set of orders was also overtaken by events and could not be implemented.[119]

The fighting that interfered with Charles's new orders began around midday as Davout and Lefebvre, pushing east, came up against Rosenberg's new defensive positions. On withdrawing from Dünzling and Paring, the Austrian general had established his corps on the heights above Unterlaichling:

- ✦ five companies of *Deutsch-Banat* Grenzer and a squadron of *Stipsicz* Hussars in the open ground toward Kolbing;

+ the remaining seven Grenzer companies in the woods on the right, supported by I/*Bellegarde;*
+ infantry regiments *Ludwig, Koburg,* and *Chasteler* on the heights north-east of Oberlaichling with several batteries;
+ Neustädter's brigade in Oberlaichling and on the hill to the south supported by two squadrons of *Vincent* Chevaulegers;
+ II/*Bellegarde* in Unterlaichling and the small copse behind it; and
+ Stutterheim in the Laaber valley with the remaining twelve cavalry squadrons (six each of *Vincent* and *Stipsicz*) and his cavalry battery on the hill between Schierling and Unterlaichling (Hill 402).[120]

This was a fine position, but the large woods on the right were vulnerable to penetration and the isolated spur of high ground on the left (Hill 402) had to be held to prevent an unobserved enemy approach from the area around Schierling. Moreover, Rosenberg was deeply concerned about his flanks. The grenadiers had moved from Eggmühl towards Alteglofsheim, providing some support to his right rear, but Rosenberg became alarmed when, looking south, he saw Hohenzollern's troops withdrawing from their position along the Allersdorferbach. Soon only Vukassovich and some of Bieber's men were on the south bank.

Hohenzollern's orders to withdraw came from Charles himself. The archduke had ridden to Rosenberg's corps late in the morning and concluded that a major attack was imminent. Still expecting V Corps to appear south of the Laaber, Charles sent instructions for Hohenzollern to leave a detachment at Lindach to await Ludwig, while the rest of his corps occupied the grenadiers' former position north of Eggmühl. As Hohenzollern's infantry crossed the little bridge 'at double time', their commander received orders to move to the heights above Unterlaichling. Third Corps was only beginning to debouch from Eggmühl when one of the archduke's staff officers galloped up with instructions to post a brigade at Haus. St Julien's two regiments and their attached battery dutifully followed this imperial adjutant, but, shortly thereafter, FML Archduke Maximilian d'Este appeared and likewise demanded a brigade. In no position to refuse a member of the Habsburg family, Hohenzollern handed over his last infantry, Kayser's brigade and the *EH Karl* Legion battalion, which Maximilian led off to a support position behind Rosenberg's left flank. Hohenzollern, left with just four squadrons of *Ferdinand* Hussars, moved to the Bettelberg above Kraxenhöfen.[121] 'Totally chopped up, I remained on the ridge,' complained the frustrated prince in his corps's operations journal.[122] In the space of a few minutes, therefore, an entire corps had been broken up and strewn across the battlefield, destroying command arrangements and disrupting unit cohesion. Fortunately for the Austrians, this thoughtless scattering of III Corps had no adverse impact on 21 April, but the incident was emblematic of the confusion, careless haste, and outmoded thinking that prevailed in Austrian headquarters.[123]

On the other side of the field, Davout was unaware of Hohenzollern's vexation. Convinced by Montbrun's detailed reports and other intelligence that he faced the bulk of the Austrian army, however, he knew that he had to play for time against superior forces. He thus undertook an energetic offensive first to gain a strong defensive position and second to persuade the Austrians that his corps was more powerful than in fact it was. While Lefebvre's men attacked Schierling, therefore, he sent Friant and St Hilaire into the wooded hills opposite the Laichlings to seize this excellent position and create the impression of an aggressive and numerically strong force. St Hilaire's men cleared out the Grenzer and hussars near Kolbing, while the 15th Léger, supported by the 3rd Ligne, advanced deep into the wood. The light infantrymen quickly evicted the Grenzer and only stayed their progress when Rosenberg threw a battalion each of *Bellegarde* and *Ludwig* into the fray.

St Hilaire launched brief forays towards Oberlaichling and Unterlaichling to occupy the Austrians, but Davout clearly had no intention of entangling his corps in a full-scale attack.[124] Combat between Kolbing and the Laichlings thus devolved into back-and-forth skirmishing and a heavy cannonade. Similarly, Lefebvre's command was nearly quiescent after the capture of Schierling. The northern edge of the town had been captured by the 7th Light Battalion, but an ill-advised attempt to push this frangible battalion towards Hill 402 broke in the face of Austrian grape shot and a charge by the *Vincent* Chevaulegers. The battalion lost 150 men in short order and had to be withdrawn from the fight. Lefebvre then sent Oberstleutnant Butler with the 5th Light and one of Demont's battalions against Schierling. Attacking from the north, the Bavarians and French secured the town after a tough fight, but efforts to advance into the water meadows beyond were thwarted by Austrian artillery and Stutterheim's vigilant troopers. South of the Laaber, one of Demont's brigades advanced to the Allersdorferbach, but otherwise made no effort to press forward.[125]

The heavy fighting on Rosenberg's right, however, grew in intensity and came to dominate the day. Friant sent the 33rd Ligne to support the 15th Léger in the forest; and Rosenberg, feeding battalion after battalion into the struggle, managed to maintain himself in the eastern edges of the woods,

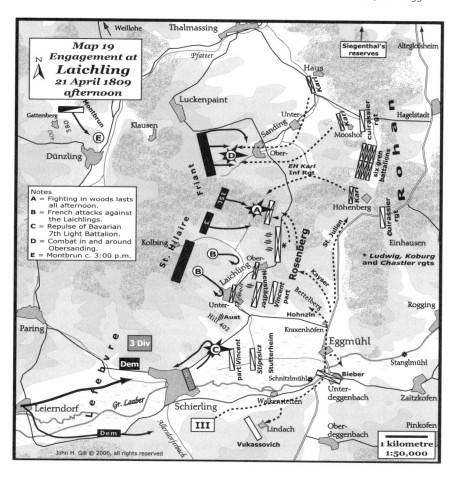

Map 19
Engagement at
Laichling
21 April 1809
afternoon

Notes
A = Fighting in woods lasts all afternoon.
B = French attacks against the Laichlings.
C = Repulse of Bavarian 7th Light Battalion.
D = Combat in and around Obersanding.
E = Montbrun c. 3:00 p.m.

* Ludwig, Koburg and Chastler rgts

1 kilometre
1:50,000

but could not expel the French. Other elements of Friant's division began appearing in the open ground north of the wood in the late afternoon, threatening to outflank Rosenberg on the right. The capture of Obersanding by a battalion of the 48th Ligne made the danger acute.[126] At this critical moment, Archduke Charles arrived at the head of his own regiment. Bringing up this reserve in response to Rosenberg's repeated calls for help, Charles sent one battalion into the woods, while the other two cleared Obersanding and advanced towards the high ground to the west. As darkness fell, however, Chef de Bataillon Schmitz of I/108th Ligne led his two elite companies in a flank attack that broke the Austrian advance and effectively brought an end to the day's 'very hot' fighting.[127] These actions cost the Allies some 1,930, the greatest number from Friant's division. Austrian losses totalled approximately 3,400, all but 150 to 200 coming from IV Corps.[128]

Charles endeavoured to push some of Liechtenstein's men towards Wolkering to threaten Davout's left flank, but this effort came to naught, as the Austrian reserves were incapable of reacting quickly. Although no great distance was involved, it took the reserve formations all afternoon to get into position. By that time, the archduke was satisfied that his front would hold. He therefore elected to keep the remaining troops out of the fight so as to preserve them for an offensive he was planning for the 22nd. Torpor and confusion thus made 21 April a 'lost day' for the Austrians, who 'with a little vigour', in the opinion of a French observer, 'could have overthrown all before them'.[129]

Night found the armies in the northern portion of the theatre aligned generally along a north–south axis running from Abbach to Schierling. On the French side, Montbrun had part of his command at Dünzling, where he had appeared around 3 p.m.; the rest remained on the left wing near Abbach and Peising. Friant and St Hilaire rested opposite Obersanding and Unterlaichling respectively, and Lefebvre held Schierling with the bulk of his command while keeping one brigade south of the Laaber. Davout had achieved his objective of intimidating the Austrian command with his aggressive posture and calculated offensive moves.[130] In the rugged, wooded terrain, the Austrians could not tell that there was very little behind the units actually in contact.[131] The French marshal, on the other hand, was painfully conscious of his vulnerable position and, during the evening, he directed Boudet to move the bulk of his division from Abensberg to Abbach to support Montbrun; at the same time, Boudet was to detach 1,000 to 1,200 men to reinforce Colonel Guyon along the Altmühl. Davout bombarded his emperor with situation reports stressing that he was facing the principal Austrian force immediately south of Regensburg, but he could take some comfort in the news that Napoleon had placed Oudinot, with Tharreau's division and Colbert's two chasseur regiments, at his disposal. He ordered Oudinot to move from Schweinbach to Langquaid, and learned later (probably in the early hours of 22 April), that he could also call on the 1st Bavarian Division at Rottenburg.[132]

On the Austrian side of the field, Charles presided over tangled dispositions and woolly intentions to undertake an offensive some time during 22 April, while the troops bivouacked according to a disposition issued at 7 p.m. that evening:

+ Liechtenstein, with four cuirassier regiments in Köfering, had half of Vécsey's brigade opposite Montbrun on the Abbach road and the other half near Weillohe, Lindenau's division (minus *Erzherzog Karl*) around Gebelkofen, one battalion of Lindenau's in Regensburg, and two cuirassier regiments at Obertraubing.
+ The bulk of III Corps assembled near Alteglofsheim. It was once more under Hohenzollern's direct command, but, given the detachments to Rosenberg, it consisted of only two infantry brigades, four hussar squadrons, and the corps artillery. Additionally, two squadrons of cuirassiers under Major Anton Klehe (one each from *Kaiser* and *Gottesheim*) were on outpost duty near Thalmassing.[133]
+ The grenadiers and *Erzherzog Karl* were at Haus and Mooshof under Rohan.
+ Rosenberg remained in the positions he had defended during the afternoon with command over Vukassovich and Bieber, both of whom were south of the Laaber.
+ Vukassovich sent an officer and forty men of the *Erzherzog Ferdinand* Hussars south to Ergoldsbach in an effort to locate Archduke Ludwig and V Corps.
+ Kolowrat, leaving GM Crenneville behind at Hemau with the 7th and 8th Jäger Battalions and two uhlan squadrons, was under urgent orders to move south of the Danube.
+ Bellegarde was to march to Hemau.

Plans in the Night

Charles and his staff spent the night in the manor house (Schloss) in Alteglofsheim. Here they drafted a plan to assume the offensive on the 22nd. According to the village chronicle, however, 'one observed among the senior officers a conspicuous and silent dejection' as they arrived at the chateau.[134] Charles himself was deeply weary and annoyingly inconvenienced because he had already sent much of his own baggage, servants, and other amenities to the rear with some of the army's administrative material. He was also burdened by the gravity of the situation, writing to his adoptive uncle that night that 'Success hangs in the balance.'[135]

The orders issued between 7 and 8 a.m. on the 22nd envisaged a general offensive by the Austrian right formed into three 'columns'. The first column, composed of Kolowrat's II Corps with half of Vécsey's command (three battalions, four squadrons, six guns) as its advance guard, was to push west towards Abbach along the high road and 'seize this position by frontal attack'. Liechtenstein would command the second column, an ad hoc force comprised of Lindenau's division and the other half of Vécsey's brigade (two battalions, four squadrons). This column was directed to 'march through Weillohe against the enemy right flank in the area around Peising'. The third column, under Hohenzollern, had the two brigades and four squadrons of III Corps with the *Erzherzog Karl* Infantry as its advance guard. This column, too, was to advance on the supposed enemy 'right flank' near Peising (via Luckenpaint). The first and third columns were to initiate their advances at noon, followed by the second column at 1 p.m. Rosenberg's corps (11,000 infantry, 1,950 cavalry, fifty-six guns), on the other hand, would remain in the positions it had occupied on the 21st as an anchor upon which the three columns would pivot in their advance. Additionally, Vukassovich's and Bieber's brigades (5,300 infantry, 500 cavalry, fourteen guns) were placed under Rosenberg's orders and given the task of guarding the army's extreme left flank south of the Laaber.[136] Indicative of Charles's ignorance of the calamity that had befallen his left wing, he assigned Rosenberg a contingency mission to advance in support of the third column if the situation permitted.[137] The grenadiers and cuirassiers were held back as an army reserve, the former apparently near Alteglofsheim and the latter with two regiments at Thalmassing and four at Köfering. It is interesting to note the disregard for the army's order of battle, especially in Liechtenstein's case where none of the troops under his orders belonged to his I Reserve Corps.

Two key factors dominated this plan and ensured its failure. First, as illustrated by the wording of the disposition, Charles founded his thinking on the erroneous assumption that he was facing the bulk of the Army of Germany and that this force, under Napoleon's personal command, was to be found immediately south of the Danube near Abbach with its fictional right flank around Peising. In reality, the only French troops covering the six or seven kilometres between Dünzling and Abbach were the three light cavalry regiments and two light infantry battalions of Montbrun's tiny 'division' (some 3,500 men total).[138] Charles had received one or two vague reports from his left wing by 10 p.m. that night and knew that Hiller and Ludwig had experienced some setbacks, but he did not know that they had been roundly beaten and that Napoleon was in Landshut with a large force, free to move against the Austrian left flank on the Grosse Laaber.[139] Where nearly 50,000 Austrian troops with 156 guns in their three 'columns' were assigned to move against Montbrun near Peising, therefore, Charles allocated less than 5,000 to his extreme left south of the Laaber. Even including Rosenberg's 13,000, the Austrian left, the flank upon which Napoleon's assault would fall, was dangerously weak and ill-disposed to meet the approaching threat.

The second determining factor was the time delay imposed by Charles's decision to make II Corps a major component of the planned offensive. Believing that he would be fighting the main French army and the emperor himself, Charles called Kolowrat south of the Danube on the afternoon of the 21st. That general marched at once, but his men only dragged into their bivouacs south of Regensburg between 6 and 8 a.m. on 22 April. They were exhausted by their long night march on the muddy roads and Charles agreed to postpone the start of his attack until noon so that II Corps would have time to rest and eat. By then it would be too late.

Away to the south, across many kilometres of wet, grey Bavarian country-side, Napoleon was also planning an offensive for 22 April. The challenge for the French emperor was deciding which direction to carry the massive force he had concentrated around Landshut. Although he had trumpeted the Battle of Abensberg as a 'second Jena' that morning and was thoroughly pleased with the rapid fall of Landshut early in the afternoon, by evening he was concerned that he did not know enough about the enemy's locations. He 'did nothing but interrogate everyone around', vexed that his rapid departure from Paris had left him without his normal staff of secretaries and equipage.[140] In addition to the forces pursuing Hiller south of the Isar, he thus attached the Württemberg Light Brigade and *Herzog Louis* Jäger-zu-Pferd to GD St Sulpice and ordered that general to push reconnaissance patrols from Essenbach out along the roads to Regensburg, Straubing, and Landau and to 'send me, this evening, the reports of all his outposts, scouts and spies'.[141] Similarly, he sent a strong patrol composed of Bavarian light horse towards Regensburg during the evening under the command of a relatively young imperial staff officer, Chef d'Escadron Charles Eugène Montesquiou-Fezensac.[142] Perhaps the ease of the victories on the 20th and 21st was beginning to trouble him despite his low estimation of Austrian fighting qualities.

The emperor's subordinates provided invaluable reporting as he pondered his next moves during the night. If some of the information supplied by commanders along the Abensberg–Landshut axis exaggerated the scale of the French achievement on the 20th, Davout, Montbrun, Lefebvre, and the scouts north-east of Landshut were precise, persistent, and timely. Davout's contributions were crucial to changing Napoleon's view of Austrian deploy-ments. Forwarding Montbrun's detailed reports and his own assessments,

Davout sent four letters to Napoleon between 7 a.m. and 5 p.m. on 21 April, informing his master that Regensburg had fallen, that what he termed the Austrian 'Army of Bohemia' (Bellegarde's force) had joined Charles, and that he was engaged in heavy fighting against Charles in person commanding a force three times larger than his own.[143] 'The entire enemy army is before me,' he scribbled on the back of one of Montbrun's messages.[144] Lefebvre added to the accumulating evidence, writing at 9 a.m. that the enemy was present 'in great force' and that his prisoners claimed 'this is the army of Archduke Charles'.[145]

Chef d'Escadron Joseph Szymanowski, an officer on Davout's staff, carried one of the marshal's messages that afternoon. He arrived in Landshut, however, just as a member of Lannes's staff was reporting to Napoleon that *his* commander's ad hoc corps was facing the main Austrian army. Szymanowski dutifully made his own report, but the emperor was not convinced. 'Return to your marshal and tell him that he is mistaken,' said Napoleon, 'The principal Austrian forces are down here, not in front of him.' Szymanowski faced a storm of anger when he presented himself to Davout. The marshal demanded to know why Szymanowski had not told Napoleon what he had seen with his own eyes and, impatient with Szymanowski's reply, exclaimed: 'This is what always happens to me! The emperor has confidence in those who make false reports to gain credit for themselves and he never believes me.'[146]

Davout's choler, however, was misplaced. By the time the unfortunate Szymanowski had returned to 3rd Corps headquarters, the scales had already fallen from the emperor's eyes.[147] The turning point in Napoleon's thinking came with the arrival of GB Piré at approximately 2 a.m. on 22 April. Davout, frustrated at what he saw as the lack of response from Napoleon and concerned that his command would be overwhelmed, had taken the unusual step of sending a general to make a personal report to the emperor. Armed only with a two-sentence note from Davout, Piré must have been persuasive. Immediately after his arrival in imperial headquarters, orders were on the way to Lannes, Vandamme, and St Sulpice instructing those commanders to put their troops on the road to Regensburg between 4 and 6 a.m. Vandamme with the Württemberg Light Brigade and three of the Württemberg cavalry regiments was to serve as the advance guard, followed by Gudin, St Sulpice, and Morand for a total of some 20,000 infantry and 5,500 cavalry. He sent a second letter to Lannes at 3 a.m. enjoining all possible speed and simultaneously directed Massena to march north with Espagne's cuirassiers and three of his four infantry divisions. The marshal was to leave one of his divisions (he selected the most distant and exhausted, Molitor's) in Landshut to support Bessières, who would continue the pursuit of Hiller's forces with his light cavalry and Wrede's Bavarians.[148] While the Württemberg light troops led the advance and the *Neubronn* Fusiliers garrisoned Landshut, the remaining four line regiments and the foot artillery of 8th Corps would bring up the end of the long column. Napoleon also considered rear area security, directing GD Jean François Moulin in Augsburg to send a force to Dachau to protect the army's line of communications against threats from the south and placing all forces along the Danube under GD Rouyer in Ingolstadt with instructions to fall back on that fortress or on Augsburg in case of emergency.[149]

The speed and decision with which Napoleon completely changed direction reflect his titanic energy and flexibility of mind, but also suggest that he had already been harbouring doubts about the extent of the victory on the 21st. That is, his resolute orders in the early morning hours of the 22nd connote a pre-existing readiness to accept and act upon a dramatically different view of the operational situation. In the space of an hour that cold, grey morning, he had put at least 50,000 infantry, 14,000 cavalry and 114 guns on the road to Eggmühl.[150] Additionally, as we have seen, Oudinot and Crown Prince Ludwig were already under orders to join Davout, and Boudet was nearby. Many of these troops (notably Massena's trail division, Legrand) could not possibly arrive in time to participate in a major battle on the 22nd, but they would all be on hand if needed the following day.

This near-instantaneous turnabout from Landshut to Regensburg also provides another illustration of Napoleon's dynamic leadership and his rare ability to infuse the entire hierarchy of his army with his own resolution and driving spirit. In his 3 a.m. order to Lannes, for instance, he wrote 'you will march to Eggmühl and attack the enemy from all sides'.[151] Similarly, just before leaving Landshut, he sent final instructions to Davout and Lefebvre, telling them that he planned to be in a position to attack 'vigorously' by 3 p.m. and concluding with characteristic vivacity: 'I am determined to exterminate Prince Charles's army today or tomorrow at the latest.'[152]

Ponderously preparing his own offensive, Charles had only the vaguest hints of trouble along the Isar and was unaware of Napoleon's approach. The latter's staff officer, Chef d'Escadron Montesquiou, reported during the morning that he had taken prisoner a large number of wounded Austrians who were being evacuated to Landshut. 'They are all surprised to learn that Your Majesty has arrived ahead of them,' he wrote.[153] The Austrian left wing thus had no warning of the juggernaut driving steadily north up the Landshut road.

22 APRIL: THE BATTLE OF EGGMÜHL

While Napoleon was interviewing Piré and issuing his revised orders, St Sulpice was sending a strong force from Essenbach towards Ergoldsbach in accordance with his earlier instructions. The hard-marching Württemberg Light Brigade had barely reached Essenbach at 1.30 a.m. on the 22nd when St Sulpice pushed them north with a squadron of cuirassiers and Montesquiou's squadron of Bavarian chevaulegers. He placed them under the tough GB Clément, a tall horseman 'with a martial bearing, imposing and severe.'[154] Clément's little command reached Ergoldsbach at 4 a.m. and discovered it occupied by Austrian cavalry, the detachment of *Ferdinand* Hussars that Vukassovich had sent down the road towards Landshut late in the afternoon of the 21st. The Habsburg troopers had paid little heed to their own security, and the Württembergers were able to capture nearly all forty in a swift, sudden attack. 'We arrived in the first light of dawn and found the houses full of sleeping Hungarian hussars', recorded Surgeon Heinrich von Roos, 'There was firing into and out of the windows; a dreadful tumult ensued; one saw frightful countenances of terror among the ambushed and the inhabitants; there were dead and wounded, but mostly prisoners.'[155] This handy little feat of arms accomplished, the exhausted men of the Light Brigade were finally granted a short rest, having marched more than sixty kilometres and fought in two major engagements during the preceding forty-eight hours.

Their respite was to be all too brief. Vandamme arrived with three of the Württemberg cavalry regiments (the Leib Chevaulegers were left behind in Essenbach to scout along the Isar) and the two horse batteries at 7 a.m., shook Hügel's weary men out of their sleep, and pushed them ahead towards Eggmühl.[156] Reaching Buchhausen some time around 1 p.m., the Württembergers encountered Vukassovich's troops: the much reduced *Peterwardein* Grenzer, four squadrons of *Ferdinand* Hussars, and a cavalry battery. After a short exchange of fire, the *König* Jäger charged into the village and chased away a few Grenzer. The Württemberg light infantrymen then proceeded to clear the woods and slopes on either side of the main road, creating space for the cavalry and artillery to deploy. Trotting through Buchhausen to unlimber west of the road, the two Württemberg batteries opened a lively duel with Vukassovich's guns.

Napoleon soon arrived at the head of the column, where he 'dismounted, withdrew a telescope from his grey greatcoat and laid it on the shoulder of one of his adjutants to observe the enemy'.[157] He also personally directed some of the Württemberg pieces as he waited for the long, muddy columns slogging up from Landshut. Vukassovich, observing the steadily accumulating mass of Allied power, quickly concluded that any further resistance would be both otiose and dangerous. He withdrew his little command to Eggmühl. By approximately 2 p.m., therefore, Vandamme and his Württembergers had gained control of the bluffs that dominate the south bank of the Grosse Laaber and had opened the way for the deployment of the main army. 'Napoleon's arrival, and everything that one saw', observed Surgeon Roos, 'pointed to the approach of battle.'[158]

It is important to note that Napoleon would not enjoy a numerical superiority in the engagement that Roos could feel approaching like a great storm. Indeed, adding up the troops engaged and immediately available (perhaps loosely defined as those that could see the battlefield), the Allies were at a slight quantitative disadvantage. In gross numbers, Charles had some 75,000 men at hand in the area south of Regensburg as compared to the 70,000 Napoleon would bring to the battle.[159] The emperor, however, was about to array some 66,000 of these against Rosenberg's 18,700.[160] Even if more than 18,000 of these Allied troops hardly fired a shot all day, this would be an irresistible concentration of power.[161] The surprise factor would multiply the impact of this force. Furthermore, slow decision making, laborious command procedures, and general awkwardness meant that much of the Hauptarmee would not encounter the enemy at all during the day, and those elements that did come against the advancing Allies would do so in a piecemeal, disjointed fashion.

Eggmühl: This Imposing Spectacle

North of the Grosse Laaber, the morning had passed quietly. The night had been bitingly cold and Deroy reported that daybreak found 'everything frozen over and covered with white rime'.[162] The chill night also left behind an impenetrable fog that cloaked the surroundings in mystery during the first hours after dawn, but even when the sun broke through the mist around 8 a.m., there was little activity on either side. The Austrians slowly regrouped themselves into the three 'columns' described in Charles's attack orders and Kolowrat's tired troops rested in their bivouac south-west of Regensburg. Kolowrat rode forward to take a personal look at Abbach, a cuirassier

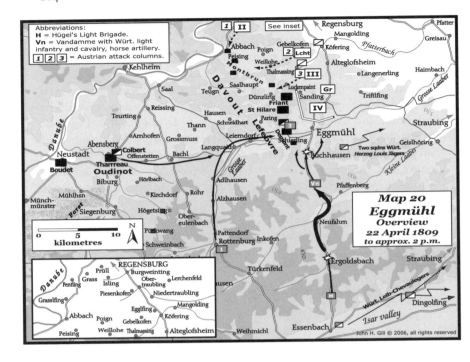

patrol from Liechtenstein's column probed tentatively in the direction of Dünzling, and the *EH Karl* Infantry moved north of Obersanding to await the arrival of the third column, but none of the Habsburg commanders pressed his reconnaissance with much vigour and the Austrians remained largely ignorant of the enemy forces to their front, specifically the weakness of Davout's left flank.[163] On the southern end of the Austrian line, the officers of IV Corps, peering west through the dissipating fog, noticed some French troops shifting north opposite the Laichlings, but saw little else of immediate concern: the Allied cavalry in the low ground near Schierling remained dismounted, the French troops were preparing meals, and 'the greatest tranquillity reigned' on Rosenberg's front.[164]

This placid tableau began to change in the early afternoon. Just at midday, Vukassovich, probably alerted by survivors of the Württemberg attack on Ergoldsbach, apprised Rosenberg that enemy cavalry was advancing up the road from Landshut. He followed this with two increasingly anxious reports: that his force was dangerously weak, and that Bieber's brigade had pulled back north of Eggmühl.[165] Rosenberg, already uneasy in his exposed position, did not yet know the strength of the Allied force or that Napoleon himself was present on this wing. Before long, however, he could see enemy troops on a small segment of the highway near Buchhausen visible from his position; the rising pillars of smoke from the village combined with the growing sound of gunfire to remove all doubt that a major enemy force had arrived on his left.[166] By 2 p.m., he could also see Lefebvre's French and Bavarian cavalry in the valley mounting up. These and other movements among the Allied troops indicated an attack was imminent. His messages to army headquarters, however, elicited no response.

Rosenberg did not know that Charles had already reached a decision. The archduke was near Thalmassing when Rosenberg's urgent messages and the dull rumble of the guns reached him between 1 and 2 p.m. Without riding to IV Corps to make a personal assessment, he immediately decided to call off the nascent Austrian offensive and issued new orders. The first set of instructions went to IV Corps at 2 p.m., directing Rosenberg to 'withdraw from the engagement as best he could', pulling back through Alteglofsheim to a position behind the Pfatter if necessary.[167] He then told the three attack columns to retire 'temporarily' to a line generally running from Grass on the right through Gebelkofen and Thalmassing to Sanding, while the grenadiers assumed a post between the latter villages and Höhenberg. Curiously, the orders for Kolowrat, issued at 4 p.m., show that Charles continued to believe that Napoleon had a powerful force near Abbach/Peising. In these instructions to II Corps, he thus expressed his concern that the Kolowrat's column might be subjected to 'serious attacks' and he enjoined his subordinate to 'defend the heights near Grass with the utmost tenacity' so that the rest of the army would have time to concentrate near Regensburg. Equally curious is the fact that no one was directed to support Rosenberg. Charles did not believe that there was time to shift his clumsy army ninety degrees from a westward to a southern orientation, so he restricted himself to establishing positions in the rear from which his reserves could cover Rosenberg's withdrawal. Not only was IV Corps left more or less to its own devices, but by the time this new disposition reached Rosenberg, his corps was inextricably engaged in a desperate fight for its life. On the other hand, Charles finally issued instructions for Bellegarde to march for Regensburg.

While Charles and his staff were drafting these lengthy missives, the united Allied army was advancing on Rosenberg's corps under Napoleon's personal direction. From his position near Lindach, the emperor enjoyed a splendid view of the coming battlefield and could clearly see Rosenberg's formations wedged between the gathering Allied forces.[168] The dramatic vista spreading out before them left a deep impression on the French and German officers standing on that hillside. Capitaine Pelet, who had accompanied Massena, left a vivid description:

> On top of the Lindach heights, we saw the broad field of battle sloping gently up like an amphitheatre. The summits were crowned with beautiful forests, the valleys opened before us, rather bare, but cultivated and separated by slight promontories. We noted above all, the Eggmühl valley, through the middle of which snaked the highway to Regensburg, and the Laichling valley, where the two villages were separated by a bouquet of trees ... At our feet we saw the Laaber, flowing from the large village of Schierling on our left and running through green and wet pastures. We followed the sinuousities of its bed, edged with willows and poplars, through the bottom of a valley [three kilometres] wide, decorated with pretty villages, divided by channels and tree-shaded roads, and yet the heights were gently sloped. Towards our right, we saw the wooded bluffs of Rogging rising up, strongly dominating the environs and likely destined to play an important role in the battle. These aspects offered us a countryside of remarkable freshness. But this valley, though delightful, was at the same time difficult and perilous to cross. In the middle of this smiling tableau, across the different bouquets of trees, we could perceive the movement of troops, the establishment of enemy batteries, all the apparel and apparatus of battle ... One could nonetheless discern with ease the white line of Rosenberg's corps, which took shape on the left slope of the Laichling valley and then successively unrolled itself, like a ribbon, along the Laaber to occupy Eggmühl and to gain the support of the wooded bluffs above Rogging.[169]

Observing the scene from the heights opposite the Laichlings, Chef de Bataillon Bial of the 72nd Ligne similarly tried to absorb the details of a 'truly marvellous' sight, 'a spectacle admirable and terrible of which I have retained a profound memory'.[170]

It was now about 2 p.m. Only twelve hours had passed since Piré's arrival in Landshut, but the Army of Germany, despite a 180-degree change in orientation, had covered the thirty-five kilometres from the Isar and was prepared to attack. On the right, Lannes's two divisions, Gudin in the lead, swung east from the highway and made for Rogging while Davout, supported by Lefebvre, advanced towards Unterlaichling on the left. Crown Prince Ludwig's 1st Division (infantry and artillery) had marched from Rottenburg that morning to join Lefebvre and was now formed up in battalion columns outside Schierling.[171] South of the Laaber, a mass of heavy and light cavalry was assembling near Napoleon in the centre of the French line just south of Eggmühl, including ten regiments of cuirassiers 'in glittering steel equipment creating a dreadful and warlike din'.[172] Yet further south, Massena's weary men were hastening forward. 'A heavy cannonade, arising around midday at a distance of several hours' march ahead of us, accelerated our march,' wrote one of Massena's Hessians, 'In such circumstances, the French marching pace, lively as it is under normal conditions, resembles a full-out run.'[173]

On the Austrian side, Rosenberg had hastily arrayed his corps to meet the coming attack. Dismayed that the *EH Karl* Infantry had been pulled out to serve as the advance guard for the third column in Charles's offensive, he had shifted the *Koburg* Infantry towards Obersanding and left his Grenzer and *EH Ludwig* defending the large wood on his right. Next in line was *Chasteler*, posted on the ridge north-east of Oberlaichling, while *Reuss-Greitz* held the village itself. Seeing little purpose in trying to hang on to Unterlaichling, Rosenberg placed the two battalions of *Bellegarde* Infantry behind the village, their position centred on a little copse that covered the steep slope ascending to the east. Two companies, however, were detailed to defend the walled churchyard in the little town. As Pelet and his colleagues could observe, the Austrian line made a near ninety-degree turn at this point to swing east and south-east towards Rogging. Rosenberg had withdrawn the forces sent to Hill 402 in the morning, placing the two position batteries on the low hill south-east of Unterlaichling (the Vorberg) with the corps's two light cavalry regiments in support under Stutterheim's command. The *Czartoryski* Infantry, on the other hand, was stationed on the Bettelberg above Kraxenhöfen with Vukassovich's cavalry battery. The hard-used *Peterwardein* Grenzer held Eggmühl: the 1st Battalion protecting the bridge and the 2nd nestled into the hamlet and its wall-encircled Schloss. Bieber's brigade (four and two-thirds battalions), lining the slopes above the Stanglmühle, constituted Rosenberg's extreme left, but beyond Rogging this flank was entirely in the air. This was a strong position, but not as strong as the Austrians thought. The general staff officers who had surveyed the Laaber had reported that the bridge at Eggmühl was the only practicable crossing site.[174] The French were about to prove them wrong.

French deployments from the march had allowed Rosenberg time to make these adjustments to his defence, but Napoleon wasted no time in advancing. French staff officers behind the emperor were still discussing 'the nature of the divers dispositions and the formation of the two armies' when they noticed that imperial adjutants, 'departing in all directions, were

already on the way with orders'.[175] Before long, the crowd of observers on
the hillside were treated to one of military history's most majestic scenes,
'the most remarkable manoeuvre of all my campaigns' as Roos described it.[176]
Pelet was one of those with a ringside seat:

> Soon the firing commenced. Both sides engaged, and the fire extended along
> the entire line, perfectly sketching the positions of the two armies by two
> bands of light haze, marked now and again by the whitish smoke and flashes
> of the batteries. Suddenly the armies appeared in the middle of this beautiful
> landscape as if by magic. All discussion ceased in front of this imposing
> spectacle that excited the greatest interest, this magnificent field of battle on
> which would be decided the fates of the two armies and of Germany.[177]

All attention now came to focus on the centre of the field, the little bridge
at Eggmühl. Contrary to Austrian expectations, there were other crossing
sites, especially at the mills that dotted the river, and the small stream was
fordable at some points. Nonetheless, the Eggmühl bridge carried the highway
from Landshut to Regensburg and represented the best means for artillery
and formed units to cross. To accomplish its capture, Napoleon once again
called on the Württemberg Light Brigade, and personally directed Major
Ludwig von Stockmayer of the *König* Jäger to attack.[178] The four battalions,
'still inspired by the successes of the morning', were twice repulsed, but a
third charge, launched with 'a terrifying shout' and well supported by the
Württemberg light batteries, overwhelmed the defending Grenzer.[179] Without
pausing, the Württembergers drove ahead into the village and assaulted the
Schloss. Three Jägers broke in the doors and a fierce hand-to-hand struggle
ensued in corridors and courtyards, but the Grenzer, losing a standard and
seeing themselves surrounded by the approach of one of Gudin's battalions
(III/12th Ligne) from the Stanglmühle, soon surrendered. 'There then arose
a cry of joy such as I have never heard before or after', wrote Roos.[180]

The Jägers and light infantrymen, though thoroughly jubilant at their
achievement, were exhausted, disorganised, and out of ammunition. Some
led away their prisoners—300 taken in the Schloss alone—and the soldier
who presented the captured battle flag to Napoleon earned the cross of the
Legion of Honour and twenty gold napoleons, but what the men welcomed
most was the chance to rest after their exertions of the previous three days.[181]
The battle, of course, continued around them.

As the Württemberg Light Brigade was gaining its measure of the day's
glories, French and Bavarian battalions were advancing on Unterlaichling.

Around 10 a.m., Davout, having received Napoleon's instructions from Landshut, had ridden to the 10th Léger and discussed the Austrian dispositions and the upcoming attack with the regiment's commander, Colonel Berthezène. 'You see that high tower on our right?' asked the marshal, pointing to the south-east, 'That's Eggmühl! The emperor will be there at about one o'clock; as soon as you see his advance guard engaged with the enemy, without waiting for any further orders, you are to seize that village (indicating Unterlaichling) and thereafter the woods.' Berthezène, who had accurately estimated that the two Austrian regiments in the Laichlings outnumbered his own, had his doubts, but launched his attack as directed at about the same time that the Württembergers were storming Eggmühl. The 10th Léger swept into Unterlaichling in their first rush without firing a shot and captured the two companies in the churchyard just as the Bavarian 14th Line from Deroy's division entered from the south-west.

Deroy had placed two batteries on Hill 402 and pushed his cavalry brigade forward as well. The rest of the division followed with the 14th Line in the lead, and, while the Bavarian guns duelled with the heavy Austrian batteries on the Vorberg, the old general sent this regiment forward as Berthezène's men made their move for Unterlaichling. Side by side, the French and Bavarian infantry now advanced up the steep slope above the village, clearing it of Austrians despite the hindrance of some hastily erected abatis. 'The occupation cost us dearly', wrote Berthezène, but *Bellegarde* and *Reuss-Greitz* fell back and the two Allied regiments deployed swarms of skirmishers onto the open plateau east of the little copse. Fortunately for Rosenberg, Stutterheim spotted the danger. He quickly brought up four squadrons of *Vincent* Chevaulegers, reanimated the withdrawing infantry, and led them all forward in a combined counter-attack that scattered the Allied skirmishers and regained part of the wood for the Austrians, albeit at heavy cost.

Despite Stutterheim's local success, the situation for IV Corps was clearly dire. Some of Davout's officers thought he would never give the order to advance, but at the right moment, he snapped shut his telescope and shouted 'Gentlemen, to your posts! And advance!'[182] As a result, more of St Hilaire's regiments were now moving on Oberlaichling in support of the 10th Léger, and Friant was exerting heavy pressure on the Austrian right wing. On Rosenberg's left, Gudin's battalions were across the Laaber shoving Bieber's men back into the woods above Rogging, and Morand's division would have been visible following behind Gudin. Even more alarming for the Austrians was the mass of cavalry gathering in the low ground just north of the

Laaber as squadron after squadron coolly trotted over the Eggmühl bridge or crossed over the shallow stream at Walkenstetten and the Schnitzlmühl. Leaving the protection of the corps' retreat principally in the hands of the cavalry and artillery, Rosenberg ordered *Czartoryski* to withdraw up the main road.

The men of *Czartoryski* had not yet begun to displace when the first of a series of cavalry charges broke over the Austrian batteries on the heights. GM von Seydewitz, commanding Deroy's light cavalry brigade, was waiting with some impatience on the southern slope of Hill 402 when he received an order to capture the Habsburg guns on the hills to his front. At approximately

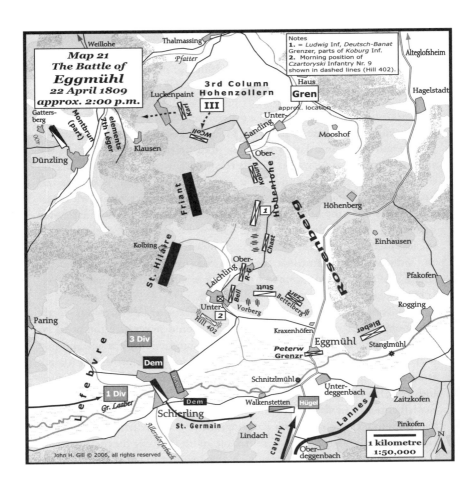

Map 21
The Battle of
Eggmühl
22 April 1809
approx. 2:00 p.m.

Notes
1. = *Ludwig* Inf, *Deutsch-Banat* Grenzer, parts of *Koburg* Inf.
2. Morning position of *Czartoryski* Infantry Nr. 9 shown in dashed lines (Hill 402).

1 kilometre
1:50,000

2.30 p.m., Seydewitz, skilfully using the terrain, led his six and one-half squadrons across the little brook south of Unterlaichling and into some low ground where they could not be seen by the Austrian gunners.[183] Swiftly wheeling left into line, the Bavarian horsemen charged up the slope, braved a blast of canister from the surprised Habsburg artillerymen, and charged in among the guns. Their success, however, was transitory. Stutterheim, leading four squadrons each of *Vincent* Chevaulegers and *Stipsicz* Hussars, crashed into the disordered Bavarians and sent them flying. But Stutterheim's victory was equally evanescent. Well-directed fire from the Bavarian guns on Hill 402 and nearby squares of Deroy's infantry repelled the Austrians, giving Seydewitz time to rally his troopers.

The pressure on the Austrian centre, however, was unrelenting. The Allied cavalry that had been suffering under Austrian artillery fire on the Lindach heights had now crossed the Laaber and deployed in the water meadows west of Eggmühl. With ten Württemberg squadrons and the 14th Chasseurs on the left, and St Sulpice's cuirassiers on the right followed by Nansouty's division, Napoleon had amassed fifty-eight and one-half squadrons for a total of at least 8,000 horsemen.[184] Splendidly accoutred and 'manoeuvring as if on the exercise field', they made a breath-taking sight in the afternoon sunlight, even though they were tired and muddy from the marches and combats of the previous several days.[185] 'I have never seen a more beautiful display,' wrote Markgraf Wilhelm of Baden, 'The sun sparkled on the brightly polished cuirasses and the visages of the old warriors showed much courage and confidence in victory.'[186] The Austrian gunners soon had the range of the French heavy squadrons, so the cuirassiers 'crossed the meadow at a gallop, the horses often sinking in the mud up to the chest, and falling into deep ruts which hundreds of balls were tearing out beneath our feet, covering us with splashes of black peat and mud'.[187]

The Württemberg squadrons had assisted in the repulse of Stutterheim's counter-attack, but were thrown back by musket fire from *Czartoryski* and canister from the batteries when they attempted to charge up the slope. They launched a second charge to hold off Austrian pursuit and were again overthrown, but the stage was set for the final assault on Rosenberg's centre. It was now approximately 3.30 p.m. and Seydewitz threw his regiments forward a second time. His starting position (Württemberg squadrons on his left, French on his right) did not allow any clever manoeuvres on this occasion, so his men drove straight for the guns, once again rode in amongst the desperate gunners and were once again stymied by Stutterheim. The Austrian general plunged down the gentle slope with four squadrons of

Vincent and three of *Stipsicz*, but the Bavarians were only ejected when he threw in four more squadrons of *Vincent*—those that had just contributed to checking a renewed French effort to advance out of the woods above Unterlaichling. 'The sun glinted a thousandfold on the bare swords of the combatants,' recalled a Bavarian soldier, 'Neither side wanted to yield.'[188]

Time, however, had now run out for the Austrians. Although observers could see 'iron helmets flying into the air and many men and horses falling' from the fire of the heavy Austrian guns, the ten cuirassier and carabinier regiments of St Sulpice's and Nansouty's divisions were trotting forward in a stately mass to the acclamations of Lannes's infantry, who halted in their advance along the heights east of Eggmühl to admire the fantastic spectacle.[189] Supported on their left by the Württembergers and Seydewitz's Bavarians, the French heavies rolled forward on a two-regiment front.[190] Clément's brigade was in the lead and suffered accordingly in the brutal combat, first from the Austrian artillery fire and then in the hand-to-hand melee. The 5th Cuirassiers lost at least forty men, and Clément himself, at the head of his brigade, 'should have been killed a thousand times'.[191] He survived, but received multiple wounds, one of which resulted in the amputation of his left arm. Despite great courage and tenacity on the part of the Austrian troopers, however, the cuirassiers were unstoppable. Compounding the Austrian predicament, Oberstleutnant Nikolaus von Jobbagyi, contrary to orders and to Stutterheim's frustration, 'bravely but also imprudently' hurled the last of the Austrian mounted reserve (the remaining four squadrons of *Stipsicz*) at the cuirassiers. The results were predictable: the hussars were defeated and the guns were finally well and truly lost, as 'the two Austrian regiments were thrown into disorder and the confusion became general'.[192] Fortunately for the Austrians, the *Czartoryski* Infantry had retired in accordance with its orders by the time the last Allied charge rolled in, or it too would have been engulfed in the collapse of the front. As it was, efforts by Rosenberg and his staff officers to remedy the confusion were in vain; 'they did not have the means to oppose such forces or to stop an army that was attacking them from all sides'.[193]

While this drama was playing itself out in the amphitheatre provided by the Laaber valley, the French were also driving in Rosenberg's flanks. Friant's 33rd and 108th Regiments soon pushed the Grenzer out of the forest on the Austrian right, while *Koburg* No. 22 struggled to hold back the 48th and 111th Regiments near Obersanding. A counter-attack by *EH Ludwig* delayed the French in the woods and allowed time for the artillery batteries above Oberlaichling to limber up and depart, but time was clearly running out for the Austrians on this part of the field as well. The order to withdraw was given, apparently by FML Ludwig Fürst Hohenlohe-Waldenburg-Bartenstein, who could see that the copse above Unterlaichling had been lost and that French infantry had made its way onto the plateau above the wood on his left. With both flanks in danger and facing a numerically and tactically superior enemy, he evidently decided to retreat while his troops were still intact. The three regiments therefore withdrew through the Sandings towards Thalmassing in relatively good order.[194]

Meanwhile, Bieber's brigade on the Austrian left was also in trouble as the French unexpectedly leaped the barrier of the Laaber. Skirmishers from Gudin's division, led by the intrepid Capitaine Pelet, crossed the little river near the Stanglmühle and advanced up the heights above Rogging.[195] The rest of Gudin's division was right behind them, contributing to the isolation of the *Peterwardein* Grenzer in Eggmühl and driving back Bieber's troops as the cavalry struggle by Kraxenhöfen began. Exploiting his numerical advantage, Gudin kept slipping troops to the east towards Bieber's left, forcing the Austrians to cede ground. Bieber's men defended themselves as best they could in the woods atop the heights, but finally had no choice but to retreat towards Altegglofsheim with heavy losses.[196] On the French side, casualties were relatively light and fell almost entirely on Gudin's troops; Morand followed Gudin across the Laaber but took little part in the fighting.[197]

Not long after 4 p.m., Austrian IV Corps was in full retreat. Rosenberg himself, with the battered remains of Neustädter, Stutterheim, Vukassovich, and Bieber, fell back along the post road toward Altegglofsheim and Köfering. Hohenlohe retired towards Thalmassing with his three regiments.[198] All were in considerable confusion, some in panicked flight. The sacrifices of the artillery and light cavalry had granted the bulk of Rosenberg's troops time to escape, but IV Corps had been badly damaged and was in no condition to offer coherent resistance. The French were close on its heels.

As Rosenberg's defence was collapsing, the other elements of the Hauptarmee were beginning to respond to the orders Charles had issued between 2 and 4 p.m. Having concluded that his attack columns could not turn about in time to support IV Corps, the archduke directed the army to occupy defensive positions south of Regensburg to cover Rosenberg's withdrawal. As noted, Charles continued to labour under the delusion that Napoleon had a powerful force near Abbach, so Kolowrat was detailed to defend against this illusory threat on the army's right, while Hohenzollern, Liechtenstein, and the grenadiers dealt with the attack from the south. Hohenzollern would take up a position between Sanding and Thalmassing,

Liechtenstein would occupy the area from the latter village to Gebelkofen, and the grenadiers would move from Haus to Höhenberg. Charles apparently entertained a relatively benign and badly mistaken view of the situation. At the very least, a message he sent to Kaiser Franz late that afternoon generated an optimistic glow among the members of the imperial court in Schärding when his courier reached that lovely little town at 9 p.m. on the 23rd. The army's 'Ninth Daily Report' published in Vienna on the 25th happily announced that 'Fortune favoured the Austrians' on 22 April and that both Abbach and Luckenpaint as well as 'a great number of prisoners' had been captured!'[199] 'The Kaiser at once hastened to proclaim the battle as won via a courier expedited to Vienna,' recalled Herzog Albert.[200]

The rapid pace of events, however, soon disabused Charles of his illusions and overwhelmed his instructions. Indeed, the archduke found himself entangled the maelstrom of defeat, retreat, and rear guard actions as darkness enveloped the field. As a result, in the closing phases of the battle unified command and control evaporated, army headquarters had little influence on the fighting, and individual units were left to struggle or succumb as best they could with their own luck and their own resources.

Eggmühl: Pursuit

'The fighting now expanded along the entire line from Gailsbach to Luckenpaint' as Davout's two divisions, hinged on the latter village, swung to the north, Lefebvre accompanied them on their right flank, and Napoleon drove up from the Laaber towards Regensburg with the cavalry and Lannes.[201] By the time Davout and Lefebvre had reformed their commands, however, they were too late to catch Hohenlohe's half of IV Corps. Probing north, the Allies initially found little resistance, but they encountered Hohenzollern's III Corps as they approached the Pfatterbach.

It will be remembered that FML Hohenzollern had been charged with leading the third 'column' of the abortive Austrian offensive. With *EH Karl* Infantry in the lead, the corps had moved off on schedule, but almost immediately ran into elements of Montbrun's command. Caution seems to have been the order of the day. The white-coated infantrymen engaged in a lively skirmish with several companies of the 7th Léger west of Luckenpaint and reported French cavalry and infantry between Dünzling and Gattersberg but did not press the badly outnumbered French. All enterprise disappeared when Hohenzollern, trying in vain to find a vantage point near Luckenpaint, noticed the increasing volume of fire from the direction of Rosenberg's corps and began to worry about the security of his left flank. Much to Hohenzollern's relief, the revised orders from Charles soon arrived calling the column back to the east. Hohenzollern lost no time in reorienting his command. Leaving the *Karl* Infantry near Luckenpaint with II/*Wenzel Colloredo*, he placed Kayser's brigade (*Schröder* and the other two battalions of *W. Colloredo*) on the right flank with two battalions forward atop the low ridge south of Thalmassing. Two of Kayser's companies were also sent to hold Schloss Haus, a large manor on the southern fringe of the Alteglofsheim forest. Hohenzollern set his remaining infantry, regiments *Würzburg* and *Manfredini*, on the high ground north of Thalmassing with most of the artillery. As for his cavalry, he found a place on the left of the line for Prinz Sachsen-Koburg's four squadrons of *Ferdinand* Hussars and held Major Klehe's two cuirassier squadrons near Thalmassing.

Davout, thrusting north, had not yet encountered Hohenzollern, when, some time near 5 p.m., a new order arrived from Charles. The prince was now to occupy the large wood between Haus and Alteglofsheim, but was to move the bulk of his command to the area south of Köfering. Why Charles decided to pull Hohenzollern east toward the Regensburg highway is unclear. He was doubtless anxious for the safety of the road, but this change potentially left the field free for Davout. It thus seems likely that Charles, still misreading the situation, did not perceive the French near the Laichlings as a real threat or did not believe that they would pursue Hohenlohe. The generalissimus seemed increasingly out of touch with the battle. Hohenzollern, not yet in contact with Davout, gave the mission of holding the forest to FML St Julien, and began to ponder how to shift the rest of his men to fulfil his instructions.

St Julien, with Kayser's brigade (minus II/*W. Colloredo*) and accompanied on his right flank by Sachsen-Koburg's hussars, was beginning his shift to the east, when thick swarms of skirmishers from St Hilaire's division suddenly appeared on the ridge north of Untersanding. Sachsen-Koburg moved quickly to counter this threat, launching his hussars in a charge that scattered the French skirmishers. His men likewise overthrew the French 8th Hussars when that green-clad regiment pounded forward to succour its countrymen. St Hilaire, however, swiftly brought forward his infantry in tight columns accompanied by artillery, seized the ridge, and drove off the Austrian hussars. Little daunted, Sachsen-Koburg reformed his men and charged another relatively vulnerable target: skirmishers of the 33rd Ligne. This regiment, the right flank of Friant's division, had come into view as it crested the ridge in its advance from Obersanding, a dense cloud of skirmishers leading the way. Although the skirmishers were soon dispersed, the veteran 33rd formed squares and chased off the Austrian hussars with well-delivered musketry. A charge against Friant's left flank regiment, the 111th Ligne, was similarly fruitless and Sachsen-Koburg 'disappeared into the darkness' with his hussars.[202] Friant pressed forward with little delay: the 15th Léger brought up from the reserve, and the 48th Ligne advancing between the 33rd and 111th (the 108th now following in reserve). The 15th succeeded in clearing determined Austrian infantry from two small clumps of trees near Luckenpaint, but nightfall finally brought an end to the fighting on Davout's front. The last flash of serious combat occurred just south of Thalmassing as advancing French and Württemberg cavalry repulsed an attack by two squadrons of *Ferdinand* Hussars, only to be attacked and overthrown by Major Klehe's cuirassiers.[203]

As the firing diminished and darkness spread across the hills, Davout established his headquarters in Obersanding and his two divisions bivouacked in the fields north of the twin villages. For Hohenzollern, on the other hand, the day was not yet finished. Before concluding his command's tribulations, however, we have to catch up with the other pieces of the battle.

On Davout's right, Deroy and Demont covered the area up to the Regensburg post road. The old Bavarian general initially kept the 14th Line in the lead, but the broken nature of the terrain and the regiment's losses soon led him to replace the 14th with the combined Schützen of the entire division supported by some of the division's grenadiers and, as the ground allowed, by his artillery.[204] The division encountered only scattered resistance and eventually emerged from the woods south of Alteglofsheim to exchange some final shots with the Austrians in the darkness to the north. As the firing died away, the 3rd Division established its bivouac close to Alteglofsheim. Demont encamped nearby. Although Crown Prince Ludwig alarmed his entourage by remaining calmly under fire in various exposed positions for much of the afternoon, his 1st Division saw no action. Following behind Deroy during the pursuit, the division also bivouacked near Alteglofsheim while Ludwig's staff located quarters for the prince in the village.

The rest of the Allied army, having broken Rosenberg's resistance, paused only briefly to reorganise before pursuing the retreating elements of IV Corps. Gudin, followed by Morand, inclined to the right and advanced generally through Langenerling. Other than prisoners, Lannes's men saw little more of the enemy. The cavalry, on the other hand, followed the Regensburg highway accompanied by Napoleon. Nansouty led the pursuit

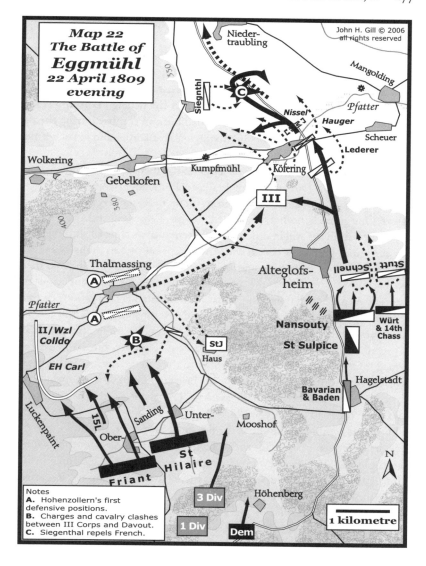

Map 22
The Battle of
Eggmühl
22 April 1809
evening

Niedertraubling

Mangolding

Siegnthl

Pfatter

Nissel

Hauger

Scheuer

Lederer

Wolkering

Kumpfmühl

Köfering

Gebelkofen

III

Thalmassing

Alteglofs-heim

Schnell

Stutt

Pfatter

II / Wzl
Colldo

Nansouty

St Sulpice

Würt & 14th Chass

EH Carl

StJ

Haus

Bavarian & Baden

Hagelstadt

Luckenpaint

15L

Sanding

Unter-

Mooshof

Ober-

St Hilaire

Friant

N

Notes
A. Hohenzollern's first defensive positions.
B. Charges and cavalry clashes between III Corps and Davout.
C. Siegenthal repels French.

Höhenberg

3 Div

1 Div

Dem

1 kilometre

up the post road, but the exhaustion of the cuirassiers (they had already covered at least forty kilometres and participated in a major action), the closed nature of the terrain, and periodic Austrian resistance retarded the

French advance. Some two to three hours thus passed before the next major action of the day.[205]

Charles was fortunate that some IV Corps units retained their cohesion and held off the French, because many of the retreating elements were completely incapable of organised resistance. The inhabitants of Alteglofsheim observed the 'panicked terror' of the fleeing Habsburg troops and noted that 'the Austrian forces that had been in combat during the day came back between 5 and 6 p.m. in unimaginable disorder and in such a mob that the reserves were unable to advance'.[206]

This mass of confused troops apparently included the bulk of the grenadier division. Directed from Haus to Höhenberg some time after 2 p.m., the grenadiers seem to have been swept up in Rosenberg's undisciplined retreat. One grenadier officer described *Hauger*, *Leiningen*, and *Georgy* as 'the only three battalions still in order', and Hohenzollern's chief of staff reported that 'the entire grenadier corps, with the exception of battalions *Nissel* and *Hauger*, ran off in fragments and in the greatest disorder'.[207] Indeed, these two battalions are almost the only ones that receive any notice in the historical record for that evening. Most of the grenadiers, in various degrees of dissolution, evidently fled north towards Regensburg with the jostling crowd of broken and bewildered units. Charles, in Alteglofsheim, faced an urgent requirement to protect this horde of fugitives, but had no fresh, formed infantry at hand. He thus turned to the reserve cavalry and ordered GM Andreas von Schneller to bring his brigade of cuirassiers south of the Pfatterbach to hold off the dark mass of French horse that was trotting steadily up the road from Eggmühl.

Dusk was coming on rapidly as the pursuing French cavalry broke into the open area between Hagelstadt and Alteglofsheim. To their front Nansouty's men could see Schneller's two regiments, their white coats gleaming in the fading light. These were the *Kaiser* Cuirassiers No. 1 and Cuirassier Regiment No. 6 (formerly *Gottesheim*) and they were posted east of the highway on a low rise with *Gottesheim* on the left and *Kaiser* on the right next to the road. To Schneller's left, the indefatigable Stutterheim had assembled the much-reduced *Vincent* Chevaulegers and *Stipsicz* Hussars along with four weak squadrons of *Ferdinand* Hussars from Vukassovich's brigade. Taken together, the Austrians had a nominal twenty-nine squadrons, but the two fresh cuirassier regiments only had five squadrons each and the exhausted light regiments were badly depleted.[208] Finally, to Schneller's right, west of the highway, was a lone cavalry battery that immediately opened fire on the approaching French.

The Austrian gunners certainly had plenty of targets. As the twenty-four squadrons of Nansouty's 1st Heavy Cavalry Division unfolded across the barren, rolling hills, sixteen more heavy squadrons from St Sulpice's division were clattering up behind, followed by Württemberg, French, Bavarian, and Baden light cavalry for a grand total of sixty-two and one-half squadrons, or close to 10,000 horsemen.[209] Galloping up in support were three horse batteries; these rapidly unlimbered and laid a heavy and accurate fire on Schneller's cuirassiers. The imbalance in numbers was obvious despite the growing twilight, and the Austrian battery soon decamped to avoid being captured in what was clearly an increasingly perilous situation.

It was one of the great cavalry engagements of the era, played out in dusk and moonlight. Nansouty deployed his six regiments in a line three regiments wide and two deep, the two carabinier regiments in the centre flanked on each side by two cuirassier regiments. Officers called repeatedly 'Close up, cuirassiers, close up!' in firm, steady voices, with sergeants echoing the admonition as the sun sank and the moon shone. Behind Nansouty, St Sulpice arrayed his two brigades in columns side by side, while the two Württemberg regiments and the French 14th Chasseurs swung off to the right to engage Stutterheim's men. The Bavarian and Baden regiments remained in reserve behind the centre and right rear of this enormous mass of horsemen. Although there was no overall commander for this Allied mounted host, the regiments, brigades, and divisions co-operated with admirable harmony.

Unitary senior leadership was also missing on the Austrian side. Although Charles was in Alteglofsheim and Liechtenstein not far away to the north, neither intervened in the combat. GM von Lederer's cuirassier brigade (*Kronprinz* and *Hohenzollern* Cuirassiers) was called forward to Köfering, apparently on Charles's orders, but GM Heinrich Bersina von Siegenthal's twelve squadrons were left north of the Pfatter and no effort was made to co-ordinate Lederer's actions with Schneller and Stutterheim.[210] With the top commanders absent, leadership fell to Schneller and Stutterheim. The latter saw Austria's salvation in putting up a bold front long enough for night to fall so the Habsburg regiments could escape into the darkness with impunity, but Schneller, the senior of the two, had other ideas and 'the order was given for *Gottesheim* to attack'.[211]

It was 7 p.m. when the former *Gottesheim* Cuirassiers, led by Oberst Nicholas François Chevalier Roussel d'Hurbal, a Frenchman by birth, advanced on Nansouty.[212] With twilight ebbing, the light of the waxing moon was visible 'reflected from the sabres, helmets, and breastplates of the imposing arrays of the thousands of horsemen who were about to cross swords.'[213] Commanding 'Squadrons! Forward march!' the French general sent his men forward so as not to be caught at the halt by the Austrian charge. One hundred paces from the enemy, however, the carabiniers in the centre of the line indeed stopped while the command rang out to the flanking cuirassier regiments: 'Squadrons! At the trot! March!' As the cuirassiers advanced to either side, the carabiniers raised their carbines and, when Roussel's troopers were within thirty or forty paces, let loose a volley at the onrushing Austrians. They then reached for their sabres. Charged in the flanks and front simultaneously by superior numbers of French, *Gottesheim* recoiled, fell back, and rallied on *Kaiser*, which was jogging up in support. The opposing lines now crashed into each other with great violence, riders penetrating into their adversary's ranks, sabres rising, falling, stabbing, and swinging in the dense mass of horsemen.[214]

The Austrian artillery had already fled and the French guns now fell silent to avoid hitting their own men. The battlefield was given over to the barbarous cacophony of mounted hand-to-hand combat: 'All that could be heard was the horrible rattling of combat with cold steel, sabres ringing on helmets and cuirasses like hammers on anvils, the sharp sound of trumpets, the frightful cries of the combatants.'[215]

In addition to being badly outnumbered, the Austrian troopers were at a distinct tactical disadvantage in this close melee because their half-cuirass covered their chests but left their backs exposed.[216] The unequal contest could not long continue. The Austrians cuirassiers soon crumbled, broke, and fled towards Köfering. The *Stipsicz* Hussars made a bold charge to halt the pursuit and allow Schneller's men to recover, but the French heavy cavalry overran the hussars and pressed ahead. Similarly, the Allied light cavalry intercepted Stutterheim's attempt to intervene with the *Vincent* Chevaulegers, the 14th Chasseurs conducting itself 'in a manner most distinguished' but losing its colonel in the process.[217] Falling on the Austrian flank, the Allies dispersed the chevaulegers and almost captured the mettlesome Stutterheim. An effort by the *Ferdinand* Hussars was no more successful. The Austrians were now in full flight, mingled with and followed by jubilant Frenchmen who drove their pursuit relentlessly north into the darkness.[218] Schneller was wounded and Charles, suddenly finding himself entangled in the press and confusion of the panicked horsemen, was lucky to escape capture. 'The fleeing cavalry and the disorder that they spread everywhere in their flight carried him [Charles] to Regensburg,' he recounted ruefully in later years, 'He was thus lost to the army at the decisive moment.'[219]

The 'terrible and majestic' fight at Alteglofsheim had been brief, and the swirling mass of fugitives and combatants now surged towards Köfering.[220] For the local villagers, the short, ferocious struggle resembled a momentary dream of vivid intensity: 'Like the most violent thunderstorm, where all the elements are in the greatest turmoil, the battle flew over our village and away.'[221] For the Allied and Austrian soldiers, however, there remained a final act to the day's drama.

Hohenzollern had appeared south of Köfering just as the cavalry battle was about to commence. His corps was marching up behind him along the south bank of the Pfatter, but the post road and adjacent fields were crowded with retreating troops. Hohenzollern, unable to either deploy as directed or withdraw, halted his command to see if the ground would clear. As he waited, however, he could easily discern the rapidly unfurling lines of French heavy cavalry beyond Alteglofsheim. Recognising immediately that the situation was dangerous and probably hopeless, he hastened to get his artillery to the north side of the Pfatter. This small stream, like many others in the area, was bordered by broad, marshy meadows, so Hohenzollern's batteries were restricted to the main highway and a narrow dam. With no desire to see his guns caught on the wrong bank when the French unleashed their attack, he sent his gunners bouncing off pell-mell for these two sites. Bieber's brigade peeled away from Rosenberg's jumbled column and rejoined III Corps at this point, its battalions and others forming masses, while Hohenzollern himself rode to Köfering. Here he found Lederer's two cuirassier regiments and warned them of the impending attack.

The French mounted storm now broke over the Austrian cavalry. Schneller's and Stutterheim's men were soon streaming to the rear in rout, intermingled with French cuirassiers in a great mass of slashing, hacking, shouting horsemen. Lederer desperately tried to use the *Kronprinz* Cuirassiers No. 4 to stem the Allied tide, but it was no use. The regiment advanced but was almost immediately carried away by the irresistible press of fleeing Austrian troopers and the wildly pursuing French. 'All at once, the enemy heavy cavalry fell upon both wings with superior numbers,' in the words of Leutnant Maximilian Ritter von Thielen, 'the regiment was rolled up towards the middle and forced to retreat'.[222] Its sister regiment, *Hohenzollern* Cuirassiers No. 8, vanished in the chaos without even having a chance to charge. Fearing catastrophe, FML Hohenzollern, still in Köfering, ordered his infantry to withdraw across the Pfatter and directed the *Hauger* Grenadier Battalion to hold the bridge as long as possible.

He then made his way through the increasing darkness and disorder to meet his shaken command on the far side of the little stream. The French cavalry, however, was already flooding exultantly across the twilight fields north of Alteglofsheim, attacking the III Corps foot soldiers and pressing their retreat. Most of Hohenzollern's infantry maintained its coherence and withdrew relatively intact, but several companies at the tail of the column were broken and destroyed.[223] Additionally, one of the batteries that Hohenzollern had been so keen to preserve lost its way in the mayhem around the village and literally galloped into French hands.[224]

In Köfering, Major Franz Hauger's grenadiers defended the bridge with skill and courage for a time, finally managing to retreat in fair order even though the battalion had been split in two pieces by the French advance. The *Nissel* Grenadiers were not so fortunate. The battalion apparently held off several probes, but somewhere north of Köfering it was ridden over by Austrian cavalry, lost all cohesion, and fell victim to charging French cuirassiers. Major Johann Nissel was taken prisoner and the battalion destroyed.[225]

Crossing the Pfatter, the French horsemen seemed to discover new vigour, for they launched themselves at Hohenzollern's retreating men with redoubled fury. The French heavy troopers shattered III/*Schröder* and captured some 250 hapless infantrymen before St Julien was able to restore the situation with *Kaunitz, Wenzel Colloredo*, and a few platoons of cuirassiers. Here too, however, disordered Austrian cavalry crashed into its own infantry and artillery, ruining all efforts to conduct an organised withdrawal.[226] The men of Hohenzollern's and Rosenberg's corps tumbled north through the darkness in a confused, disheartened tangle. Behind them roared the 'terrible shouts' of the exhausted but exhilarated French cavalry.[227]

Three factors combined to save Charles and the Hauptarmee in this critical situation. In the first place, except for the moonlight, it was now completely dark.[228] This certainly magnified the fear of the retreating Austrians and hindered the efforts of their officers to re-establish a semblance of order, but it also hampered the French commanders in conducting their pursuit.

Second, there was still one fresh brigade of Austrian cuirassiers on the field. These were the two regiments (*Erzherzog Franz* and *Herzog Albert* Cuirassiers) under GM von Siegenthal's command and they now, some time between 8 and 9 p.m., arrived west of the highway near Egglfing.[229] Siegenthal and the men of his brigade were watching in horror as 'the Austrian troops streamed back in a rout up the road towards Regensburg' when Liechtenstein rode up.[230] Charles, supposedly dragged up the highway by the terrified press of troops, was out of the picture, but Liechtenstein and Siegenthal saw a desperate opportunity. The prince ordered the brigade to charge. Led by the *Albert* Cuirassiers, the formed Austrian squadrons smashed into the exhausted and disordered French and sent them flying to the south after a brief, savage struggle.[231]

Now it was the turn of the French to retire in confusion and the third saving grace for the Hauptarmee came into play: the utter physical exhaustion of the French. As the jumble of heavy cavalry fell back south of the Pfatter, Napoleon and his marshals were near Alteglofsheim discussing their next moves. Lannes urged continued pursuit to exploit the successes of the day and complete the destruction of the Austrian army. Massena, on the other hand, spoke of the army's exhaustion and reminded the emperor that the success achieved in night battles was rarely proportional to the casualties suffered. Napoleon agreed and orders went out directing the enervated divisions to bivouac where they were and prepare for renewed combat in the morning.[232]

The weariness of his soldiers, however, did not deter Napoleon from giving a final assignment to the Württemberg light cavalry. Reviewing Wöllwarth's meagre six squadrons under the moonlight near Alteglofsheim at 9 p.m., he sent them east towards the Danube in the hopes of intercepting the Austrian baggage trains he expected them to find along the Regensburg–Straubing highway. The Württemberg regiments did not have quite the success that the emperor had hoped, but the *Herzog Louis* Jäger surprised and captured an entire squadron of *Riesch* Dragoons caught sleeping in Geisling.[233] Similarly, the *König* Jägers seized a large number of wagons and their 160-man infantry escort at Pfatter.[234]

While the Württemberg mounted Jägers were scouring the countryside towards the Danube, the rest of Napoleon's bone-weary men began to seek shelter and sustenance to see them through to the next dawn. The bulk of the army bivouacked in and around Alteglofsheim so that the area was crowded with troops: Lannes, the heavy cavalry, the 1st and 3rd Bavarian Divisions, Demont, the Württemberg Light Brigade, and Wöllwarth's six squadrons.

On the Allied left, Davout's two divisions were between the Sandings and Thalmassing with Piré and the Württemberg *Herzog Heinrich* Chevaulegers. Montbrun's little command, in an example of superb cavalry–infantry co-operation, had spent the day skirmishing energetically with various Austrian advance guards, reacting to every enemy probe with musketry from covered positions and vigorous cavalry charges. The Austrians, however, never pressed very hard and the French encamped where they had spent the preceding several days: between Abbach and Dünzling.[235] Elements of Boudet's division came up in the rear as a support for Montbrun, but were not engaged.[236]

As for Massena, the marshal himself had accompanied Napoleon during the day, but his 4th Corps did not reach Eggmühl until well after dark. Indeed it was midnight before Legrand's men encamped. Claparède and Saint-Cyr stopped just short of Alteglofsheim, while Legrand bivouacked at Eggmühl and Espagne at Schierling. They found the battlefield 'covered with corpses' and the pitiable wounded: 'It was hideous when the severely wounded awoke during the night as it began to get cold and started a penetrating howling for help; many people were sent out to retrieve these unfortunates and provide them some help, but many could not be moved and breathed their last.'[237] Unteroffizier Benedikt Peter of the *König* Jägers was less sensitive to such sentiments: 'They [the Austrians] annoyed us with cannon balls for a time, but disregarding this we celebrated our victory on the battlefield among the dead and dying.'[238]

Of the more distant Allied forces, Tharreau was at Langquaid, part of Boudet near Neustadt, the Württemberg line infantry and foot artillery in detachments along the post road from the Kleine Laaber to Landshut.[239] Molitor, having received instructions to support Bessières south of the Isar, departed the area around Ergolding at 11 p.m. and marched through the night to reach Vilsbiburg at 9 a.m. on 23 April. His subsequent actions and the rest of the pursuit south of Landshut will be covered in the next volume. Along the Danube, Rouyer guarded the crossings from Donauwörth to Ingolstadt, while Guyon continued to observe Bellegarde along the Altmühl.[240]

Napoleon, his marshals, his staff, and most of the senior officers found lodgings for the night in Alteglofsheim Schloss, the same building where Charles had made his headquarters only hours earlier: 'all of the rooms were jammed full of officers, and one saw generals and staff officers who were sleeping on the bare stone without straw; only one work room remained free from lodgers'. The scene in the little town was no different: 'all the houses, stables, gardens, and alleys were crammed with troops'.[241] A Bavarian soldier from Ludwig's division looked on with disgust and cynicism as he observed the French, 'our friends', pillaging Alteglofsheim with frightful thoroughness.[242] Some of these men, through negligence or malice, ignited the thatched roof of a house and started a fire that soon raged out of control, destroying part of the town and increasing the misery of its unfortunate citizens.[243]

Charles was in Regensburg. How he ended up in the city is unclear. He had been temporarily swept away by the tide of fugitives at Alteglofsheim, but it is difficult to envisage a press of soldiers so dense and so urgent that he could not have disentangled himself at some point during the ten- or twelve-kilometre ride from Köfering. Perhaps he had given the battle up as lost and decided to take steps to save the army knowing that darkness was likely to bring the French pursuit to a halt before much further damage was done. Whatever the explanation, the experience left a mark on his personal morale and he arrived in Regensburg around 11 p.m. 'sad and alone'.[244]

The disjointed components of the Hauptarmee collected south of Regensburg: IV Corps on the heights north of Obertraubling, Liechtenstein's cavalry astride the highway near Obertraubling, his infantry at Burgweinting, Hohenzollern (with Bieber) at Isling, and Kolowrat, untouched by the day's fighting, from Isling to Grass. Second Corps also had four battalions in Regensburg and Stadtamhof. Stutterheim and his weary hussars were concentrated at Obertraubling with outposts from Piesenkofen through Niedertraubling to Lerchenfeld. Vécsey screened the area from Stutterheim's right to the Danube near Grasslfing. North of the Danube, Crenneville's small force was marching to Regensburg and Bellegarde had reached Hemau with his advance guard probing towards the Altmühl.[245] Fortunately for Charles, the bridge train arrived north of Regensburg.[246]

The Battle of Eggmühl was a disaster for Charles and his army. Despite the bravery and tenacity of IV Corps and its attached III Corps units, especially the artillery and cavalry, the Hauptarmee had been driven back more than twelve kilometres at heavy cost in men, material, and morale. Total Austrian casualties came to more than 10,700 with IV Corps and its attached elements suffering by far the greatest proportion of these: almost 8,000 men, or some 43 per cent of Rosenberg's strength when the day began. Hohenzollern's 'column' lost approximately 1,200, the grenadiers 1,300, and Schneller's cuirassiers 173. The *Peterwardein* Grenzer had been effectively wiped out, as had the 1st *Erzherzog Karl* Legion and the *Nissel* Grenadiers. On top of this, thirty-nine guns had fallen into Allied hands.[247] Allied losses, on the other hand, were comparatively low, perhaps something over 3,000 officers and men. St Hilaire's division paid the heaviest toll on the French side (1,000 to 1,500) with the 10th Léger suffering the most.[248]

The archduke's complete misreading of the situation on the morning of 22 April and the late hour he set for the start of the Austrian offensive (however understandable) set the stage for the day's defeat. Tactical errors compounded these fundamental operational mistakes. Efforts to respond to Napoleon's sudden appearance along the Laaber were clumsy and spasmodic. Charles seemed unaware of the situation in Hohenzollern's sector, for example, when he ordered that general to march his corps to Köfering, and he was thus lucky that dogged resistance by a few elements of III Corps and the onset of night prevented Davout from exploiting Habsburg weakness near Thalmassing. Likewise, he could thank Rosenberg's determined defence and rear guard actions for delaying the collapse of the southern flank. This was crucial because the available reserves, though substantial, were badly managed. With the exception of two or three battalions, the grenadiers seemed to vanish from the battlefield, Lindenau's division never came into action, and the sequential commitment of the cuirassiers is certainly debateable. Writing after the war, Charles complained about the cavalry's performance, but he did nothing at the time to influence the action. Although he was very close by in Alteglofsheim, he implied that he had to be 'informed' of Schneller's charges and only then rode forth to find himself engulfed in the tide of retreat and swept away to the north. The surprise, speed, and violence of Napoleon's unexpected flank attack granted the Allies a significant advantage, but this combination of cumbersome operational reaction, confused command relationships, dubious tactical decisions, and misapprehension of the situation on the Austrian side magnified the material and psychological scope of the Hauptarmee's defeat. Reeling back towards Regensburg in the darkness, Charles could only hope that he would be able to get his wounded army across the Danube without further significant loss.

23 APRIL: THE BATTLE OF REGENSBURG

Arriving in Regensburg late on the night of 22 April, Charles was grim and dispirited. He had witnessed, indeed participated in, the 'panicky flight' following the cavalry melee at Alteglofsheim and was now resigned to withdrawal across the Danube and into Bohemia.[249] His personal involvement in the desperate rout that evening probably left him with an exaggerated sense of the day's defeat, but there was no question that rapid retreat was his only realistic option. At some point during the night, he somehow heard the depressing news that Hiller had been thrown across the Isar with heavy losses.[250] A mood of despondency and desperation thus pervaded army headquarters as it reconstituted itself in Regensburg.[251] The Hauptarmee was by no means crushed, but neither was it in any condition to fight another major battle against a numerically and psychologically superior enemy, especially with a major river at its back.

Earlier in the day, Charles had initially thought that he might rest the army for a day or two and then undertake a new advance against the enemy. How he imagined that a French army under Napoleon's personal leadership was going to allow him any respite whatsoever is difficult to comprehend, but the letter sent to Kaiser Franz some time in the late afternoon of the 22nd announced this intention.[252] The letter, written before the battle turned irremediably against the Hauptarmee, strongly suggests that the archduke, despite his intelligence and experience, still did not understand either his foe or the new nature of warfare. This optimistic thought vanished in the chaos of the rout up the Regensburg highway and Charles now turned his efforts to putting the Danube between his army and Napoleon's as quickly as possible.

Personally demoralised, Charles wrote to his imperial brother in the early morning hours of the 23rd. This dejected missive described half the army as 'dissolved' and announced the archduke's intention to 'march for Bohemia' if he could first 'bring the army over the Danube with honour'. Having outlined a grim situation, Charles then appealed to his brother to seek peace while 'a reasonable arrangement might still be achieved. Once the enemy is in our country, where he is certainly coming, Your Majesty's lands, like the Prussians, will be ruined and occupied for years to come.' 'I can no longer guarantee anything,' he concluded ominously.[253]

The army's baggage trains and artillery parks rumbled and jumbled across the stone bridge at Regensburg all through the pre-dawn hours of 23 April while the combat troops sorted themselves into some kind of order for the coming day. The sky was clear and moonlight illuminated the city and surrounding countryside, reducing somewhat the considerable confusion inherent in the retreat. GM Karl von Fölseis of II Corps was given the unenviable task of holding Regensburg long enough to allow the army to escape. With two battalions of *Zach* Infantry No. 15, three battalions of (former *Zedtwitz*) No. 25, and a brigade battery, he was to defend the city until nightfall and then withdraw the bulk of his brigade, leaving only 300 men to surrender the fortress on the morning of the 24th. Curiously, the Austrians again disregarded their order of battle by pulling Fölseis away from his own brigade and giving him two battalions originally assigned to two other brigades.[254] Nonetheless, as vehicles of every description were slowly making their way through Regensburg's twisting streets and the snarl of traffic leading to the stone bridge, at least some of Fölseis's men were busy barricading two of the city's three gates: the East Gate on the Straubing highway and Peter's Gate on the road to Eggmühl. Only Jacob's Gate, through which the road from Abbach passed, remained open to allow ingress for the retreating troops.[255] Simultaneously with all this activity, Austrian engineers hastened to throw a pontoon bridge over the Danube. The officers selected a site just downstream from the mouth of the Regen and pontooneers began work at 5 a.m. Three hours of feverish labour later, Charles had a crucial second crossing site.

Another Great Cavalry Battle

Daybreak came at 5.30 a.m., but the French did not. This was most fortunate for the Hauptarmee because confusion reigned in arrangements for the withdrawal. Hohenzollern, for instance, marched to the site of the pontoon bridge with much of his command and parts of IV Corps, only to find that the span was still under construction and the approaches already jammed with traffic.[256] He had no choice but to turn about and march all the way around Regensburg's walls to Jacob's Gate. Nonetheless, his men, followed by Rosenberg's, made the journey safely and passed over onto the northern bank, albeit in no little disorder, to reassemble east of the Regen.[257] As IV Corps and the greater part of III Corps were making their way through the city streets, St Julien brought other pieces of III Corps across on the pontoon bridge, mingled with a host of baggage wagons. The grenadiers, most of Lindenau's men, and, apparently, Schneller's cuirassiers were preparing to follow.[258] So far, things had proceeded more easily than the Austrian commanders had any right to expect, but between 8 and 9 a.m. the sounds of combat finally began to roll up towards Regensburg's walls from the south.

The French, exhausted after five days of combat and long, gruelling marches, were up and stirring between 5 and 6 a.m. that morning, but several hours passed before they engaged the Austrian rear guard. As they prepared for another day of battle and movement, the rising sun 'announced a beautiful day', but also revealed a gruesome tableau of war's wrack populated by furtive looters and other ghouls plying their grisly trades.[259]

> We rode over the battlefield and saw here the consequences of war in their worst aspect . . . The entire region for a distance of up to four hours' march was full of dead and wounded. The moans of the latter filled the air . . . What most outraged me, however, was the behaviour of the marauders, the female sutlers, and a mass of vile riff-raff who plundered the wounded and, if these would not give up their possessions willingly, often abused them dreadfully or even murdered them. This impression, drawn from my first battlefield, has always remained with me.[260]

Young Markgraf Wilhelm of Baden, the memoirist who recorded this unsettling scene, was not, however, en route to Regensburg. Napoleon recognised that the huge force he had at hand—more than 110,000 men— greatly exceeded that required to clear the south bank of the Danube.[261] He therefore sent one-third of the available troops south and east on other missions. He was also, of course, already thinking about the next move in the campaign and thus posturing the army for a rapid pursuit down the Danube valley. Massena was dispatched to Straubing to seize the temporary bridge the Austrians had constructed there and 'to push patrols in all directions to intercept the enemy's baggage and columns on both banks of the Danube'.[262] Wilhelm, serving on Massena's staff, thus found himself riding south through Eggmühl absorbing grim visions of war from all sides. At the same time, the 1st Bavarian Division (minus 1st Chevaulegers) headed down the road towards Landshut to reinforce Bessières in pursuit of Hiller.[263] The Württemberg line infantry and foot artillery, on the other hand, were brought north so that the kingdom's contingent, with the exception of the *Neubronn* Fusiliers garrisoning Landshut, was consolidated around Alteglofsheim by the evening of 23 April. These detachments left the emperor with 74,000 infantry and cavalry, including some 7,000 cuirassiers and carabiniers.[264] These latter led the advance up the Eggmühl–Regensburg road when it finally started rolling, and they were the first to encounter the Austrian rear guard near Obertraubling between 8 and 9 a.m.

Charles still had most of his troops south of the Danube as the French approached. Prinz Rohan had responsibility for protecting the pontoon bridge with *Stain*, two battalions of *Rohan*, and two squadrons of *Albert* Cuirassiers on the south bank, while Charles posted a line of 12-pounders north of the Danube protected by five grenadier battalions.[265] On the Austrian right Vécsey's brigade, minus the two battalions of *Rohan*, watched the Abbach road.[266] Behind Vécsey, II Corps was marshalling itself just outside Regensburg's walls in preparation for entering the city to pass over the Danube. Siegenthal's and Lederer's cuirassier brigades sat astride the Landshut highway south of Burgweinting, while Stutterheim and his three battered regiments manned the outpost line near Obertraubling. Additionally, III/*EH Karl* under Major Johann Graf Paar occupied Burgweinting, because the post road passed through a defile near the village and an unnamed General Staff officer thought this would be a good position to delay any French cavalry advance.[267] Jogging down the road to relieve Stutterheim's weary troopers were six squadrons of *Merveldt* Uhlans with FML Klenau at their head.

Coming up the road were Nansouty's heavies, 1st Carabiniers in the lead. The stage was set for another epic cavalry battle: perhaps some 5,000 Habsburg horsemen contesting the advance of nearly 8,000 French under Napoleon's leadership.[268] Chasseurs scouted the way for the French heavy regiments, but the small streams and broken terrain north of Köfering meant that the carabiniers and cuirassiers arrived, initially at least, as individual regiments and squadrons rather than as a single coherent body.[269] Nonetheless, Nansouty's leading squadrons, pressed by emphatic orders from the emperor, smashed into Klenau's uhlans and overthrew them before the Austrians were properly organised. The uhlans fled north, intermingled with pursuing carabiniers and cuirassiers. Stutterheim had placed his light cavalry in two lines between Obertraubling and Burgweinting, as a support for the uhlans. Seeing the enemy arrive pell-mell with Klenau's men, he advanced his tired troopers and succeeded in halting the French momentarily. Major Mensdorff imposed a further delay on the cuirassiers by rallying two uhlan squadrons and hurling them at the French left flank. The French, however, 'constantly reinforced' as the Austrians saw things, re-ordered their ranks and resumed their advance.

The swirling cavalry battle assumed a see-saw aspect as individual Austrian regiments threw themselves at the steadily encroaching French. West of the highway, GM Lederer deployed the *Hohenzollern* Cuirassiers into line and attacked. As with Stutterheim and Mensdorff, Lederer repulsed the first French line, but retreated under the implacable pressure of supporting squadrons. The story was the same with the *Kronprinz* Cuirassiers when they charged in their turn. Siegenthal's two regiments were also committed, and defeated, piecemeal. The Austrian generals, including Liechtenstein, displayed great valour but little sense as they repeatedly placed themselves at the heads of their regiments and charged into the enemy ranks. Trading sabre blows with French troopers may have been personally satisfying for the Habsburg leaders, but they lost their perspective and thus their ability to influence the outcome of the ferocious fighting. Despite enormous bravery, therefore, the Austrians found themselves inexorably driven back by the superior numbers and more intelligent generalship of the French. The French horse artillery, skilfully handled, also made a valuable contribution, while almost all of the Austrian guns had already escaped across the river. As the combat roiled north, Major Paar and his hapless battalion of *EH Karl* were surrounded, cut up, and forced to surrender. The decision to leave them behind had been a pointless waste. Fortunately for the honour of the regiment, Gefreiter Thomas Kosibek tore the battalion's standard from its pole, stuffed it inside his tunic, and carried it to safety by swimming the Danube.[270] The French seem to have gathered up other infantry remnants as well.

In an effort to outflank their tiring foes and perhaps cut them off from Regensburg, the French steadily edged to the west as they pressed the Austrians towards the Danube. This persistent slippage to the French left had two effects. First, it brought the French carabiniers and cuirassiers into contact with the last untouched Austrian cavalry: the *Klenau* Chevaulegers of Vécsey's brigade. Second, the action pulled the French away from the pontoon bridge.

The fighting had by now drifted to the vicinity of Prüll and the left flank of Vécsey's command. Vécsey, reinforced by the 7th Jägers, had been focused on Montbrun, and had slowly pulled his infantry back towards Regensburg during the morning, but the approach of the French heavy cavalry forced him to look to his other flank.[271] To ward off the danger, he and Klenau placed themselves at the head of the *Klenau* Chevaulegers and stormed into Nansouty's advancing troopers. Stutterheim rode along in support with his hearty band, and a lone squadron of *Erzherzog Johann* Dragoons No. 1 (left behind when II Corps withdrew) participated with distinction. The Austrian onslaught threw back the leading French squadrons, but victory was again transitory. Not only did the French heavy cavalry return to the attack, they were joined by the 5th Hussars and 11th Chasseurs of Montbrun's division and a squadron of 8th Hussars from Piré's brigade.[272] Despite some initial moments of indecision in trying to distinguish between friend and foe in the confusing tableau before them, Montbrun and his men soon made an impact.[273] The French light horse took the Austrians in the flank and, combined with their heavy brethren, finally succeeded in driving the Habsburg squadrons from the field. 'We overthrew all who offered resistance,' remembered Capitaine Espinchal. 'Pursuing that disordered cavalry relentlessly', the French troopers pressed their advantage and a wild cavalcade of intermixed regiments tumbled back towards Jacob's Gate.[274] The Austrian infantry at the gate, alarmed by the confused snarl of friendly and enemy mounted combatants rolling towards them, pushed the gate closed before all of their countrymen could escape. A number of French saddles were emptied by musketry from the ramparts as the wave of cavalry lapped up against the city's walls, and a sizeable group of *Stipsicz* Hussars were stranded outside when the gates slammed shut. Some of the trapped troopers sought safety by swimming their mounts across the Danube to the north bank, but at least fifty drowned, man and horse, in the attempt.

The bulk of II Corps, followed by Vécsey's infantry and artillery, retreated hurriedly through Jacob's Gate while the cavalry fight was in progress. As the trail unit in Kolowrat's command, however, FML Weber's 'division' (*Frelich* and *Froon* Infantry) had to march in combat formation and suffered 500 casualties, mostly prisoners and missing, before reaching the protection of Regensburg's walls.[275] The experience of Vécsey's foot units was similar. Though he had no artillery and was outnumbered 2:1 by Vécsey in infantry, Montbrun pressed his opponent with energy and skill.[276] Pushed from the west by Montbrun and threatened from the south-east by the advancing French cavalry, Vécsey got most of his foot soldiers back through Jacob's Gate before it closed, but lost more than 1,000 men in the process.[277] As with Weber's losses, most of these were listed as prisoners and missing.

The closing of Jacob's Gate and the direction of the fighting also caused problems for the Austrian cuirassiers. Having fought valiantly all morning, they now found themselves hemmed in with Regensburg's walls to the west, the French to the south, and the Danube at their backs. The city's defenders refused to open the East Gate, so the cuirassiers, profiting from the distraction caused by the attacks of the *Klenau* Chevaulegers, launched a final series of charges that cleared enough space for them to retreat towards the pontoon bridge. Like the *Stipsicz* Hussars, some sought safety in swimming the Danube, and some may have made their way into Regensburg, but the majority apparently reached safety via the pontoon bridge.[278]

The pontoon bridge itself was now under threat. Unaware of its existence, the French cavalry had pushed towards Regensburg in its struggles with the Austrian horse. By midday, however, the Austrian retreat had exposed the span. Lannes immediately moved to attack, but with his infantry still some distance to the rear, the best he could do was to have his guns open fire on the bridge and the mass of vehicles, horses, and men struggling to get across. Rohan, entrusted the defence of the bridge, was soon wounded and command fell to GM Josef von Mayer and Oberst Maximilian Chevalier von Paumgartten, Liechtenstein's chief of staff. Led by Mayer, the two battalions of *Stain*, joined by two batteries, succeeded in holding off the French cavalry and provided a firm foundation for the two squadrons of *Albert* Cuirassiers to chasten the French horse with a bold charge. The Austrian guns on the north bank also contributed to holding the French in check. French shot and shell continued to pound the crossing area and some men fell to their deaths from the bridge's crowded deck, but Austrian disorder did not give way to panic. Other than the harrowing bombardment, even the rear guard troops (*Rohan* Infantry, *Albert* Cuirassiers, and a company of *Stain*) were able to pass over the now-damaged span with little interference from the enemy. Remarkably, the bulk of the *Stain* Infantry, finally given the order to retreat, slipped along the riverbank and somehow made its escape over the stone bridge in Regensburg.

Although the Austrian commanders got their troops across the pontoon bridge, they could not save the span itself. Punishing French fire made recovery of the bridge elements impossible, so the engineers finally cut the anchor ropes only to watch helplessly as the bridge floated to the south and fell into enemy hands.

The Storming of Regensburg

The time was now shortly after noon. Although the French had taken only three guns and a number of munitions wagons as trophies from the morning's combat, the Hauptarmee had been driven from the right bank of the Danube, and dense columns of French infantry were closing on the last Austrian redoubt south of the river, Regensburg itself.

Founded during the reign of Marcus Aurelius and the seat of the imperial diet from 1663 to 1806 under the Holy Roman Empire, Regensburg in 1809 belonged to Carl Theodor von Dalberg, the Prince Primate of the Confederation of the Rhine. A fortified city, it was surrounded by a wide dry moat some six metres deep and shielded on the land side by a high, irregular wall that offered numerous opportunities for enfilading fire against an attacking force. Though ill suited to withstand a formal siege, it was well protected against a hasty assault or *coup de main*.[279]

As we have seen, GM von Fölseis, charged with the defence of the city, had reinforced its fortifications by barricading the three main gates and emplacing the guns of his brigade battery on platforms and bastions along the walls. Fölseis allotted the two battalions of *Zach* to the eastern side of the city and the three battalions of *Zedtwitz* to the west; he put I/*Zach* in the rear at Stadtamhof, and left himself a reserve of two companies in Regensburg proper. With only six battalions and one battery of field guns, Fölseis did not have the strength to conduct an extended defence, nor was that his mission. By retaining such a minuscule reserve, however, he deprived himself of the ability to react to penetrations and thus left himself vulnerable to a breakthrough.

Napoleon was intent on taking Regensburg as quickly as possible. By 1 p.m., the French had encircled the city. Gudin's 3rd Division, marching up the Landshut road, was the first infantry to come within striking distance. He wasted no time in sending III/7th Léger and the 12th Ligne forward on the left and the 85th Ligne on the right in an attempt to rush the walls. Finding the fortifications formidable and the defenders alert, however, 'the attack could not have any advantageous result', so the French infantry fell back without making a serious effort.[280] There being no option but to organise a more formal assault, Napoleon established a breaching battery of eight 12-pounders and 8-pounders near the Landshut post road opposite Peter's Gate and 500 to 600 paces from the wall. Other cannon and howitzers unlimbered next to the battery and directed their fire against the flanks of the intended breach. Gudin's division was arrayed in this sector with Morand in close support and Lefebvre behind with Deroy and Demont. Davout sealed the ring on the left with his two infantry divisions and Montbrun, while Lannes set Gudin's men to constructing ladders, collecting material for fascines, and otherwise readying themselves for the assault.

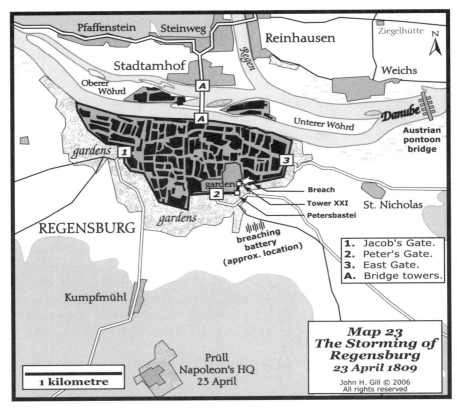

1. Jacob's Gate.
2. Peter's Gate.
3. East Gate.
A. Bridge towers.

Map 23
The Storming of
Regensburg
23 April 1809

1 kilometre

The battle now settled into an extended, noisy lull, a thunderous, anticipatory pause as both sides awaited the results of the breaching battery's efforts and the other preparations for the coming escalade. The dull, rolling roar of the French artillery punctuated the incessant sharp crackle of musketry as thick lines of French skirmishers nestled in the gardens and buildings outside the city and traded shots with the Austrian defenders.

Inside the city, the citizens were in a state of frantic apprehension. Fear had been the dominant emotion all day and the disturbances occasioned by the hurrying, disorderly crowds of retreating Austrian troops led to the cancellation or curtailment of early morning religious services (23 April was a Sunday): 'As early as 7.30 a.m., the sermon in the Neupfarrkirche among others could not be held, so the assembled congregation was released after the reading of a few psalms and prayers.' As the morning wore on and the battle began, 'everyone fled to the cellars or other hiding places.'[281] Now they cowered under the terrifying bombardment or sought to save their possessions from the hungry flames.

During this enforced pause, as French iron thudded into the old stone of Regensburg's walls and accompanying shells burst among Austrian soldiers and hapless civilians alike, Napoleon suffered a slight wound. Observing the bombardment from the low heights south of the city, he was struck on the foot by a spent bullet. The ball did not break the skin, but did cause a painful contusion that required medical attention. Calmly calling for Dr Alexander Urbain Yvan, one of his personal surgeons, Napoleon seated himself on a drum and allowed the injury to be dressed. He then quickly, if painfully, remounted and went about the business of command. News of his wound had spread through the army like wildfire, sparking a momentary flash of anxiety, so his first priority was to reassure the army. Conspicuously mounted on his white horse, he rode to the nearest units and 'galloped through their ranks in the midst of enthusiastic cheering and touching expressions of devotion.'[282]

He also reviewed some of the troops who were not involved in preparations for the assault. He gave special attention to St Hilaire's division, which he credited with much of the success on the 22nd. With each brigade assembled, he distributed rewards and decorations with his usual flair: calling for the bravest officers and men, exchanging a few personal words with each, and announcing their individual boons to the lively acclamations of their fellow soldiers. 'He complimented me on the vigour of our combat the preceding day,' wrote GB Lorencez, 'Everything that I requested for the officers, non-commissioned officers, and soldiers ... was granted on the spot.' Lorencez himself received the Order of the Iron Crown he had long desired.[283] Common soldiers were promoted, junior officers were elevated to the imperial nobility (a distinction previously reserved for senior officers and generals), and, culminating his review of St Hilaire's men, he clapped the general on the shoulder and declared, 'Very well, you have earned a marshal's baton and you shall have it!'[284] Little wonder that officers and men responded with devotion and the desire to do their utmost in Napoleon's service.

Meanwhile, the French breaching battery continued to thud away. The Austrians on the walls 'could observe each and every little movement of the enemy troops', but 'all of that just seemed preparation for an assault that might take place during the night or at dawn'.[285] The French, however, had no intention of waiting so long. Fortunately for Lannes, his guns, though light for their work, eventually had the desired effect: at approximately 3 p.m., part of Tower XXI and the outer wall of a house near the Petersbastei (Peter's Bastion) collapsed into the dry ditch, partially filling it with debris. According to the standards of the day, the breach was still inadequate, but the French decided that the moment had come to place scaling ladders on the rubble so the storming parties could climb out of the ditch and assault the city. Lannes immediately called for volunteers. A courageous band charged forward in answer to his appeal, but it was soon driven back, 'streaming with blood', by heavy fire from the Austrian defenders.[286] A second attempt met a similar fate. Once more, Lannes shouted for volunteers, but the troops' enthusiasm had dimmed in the face of two failures and the grim sight of corpses strewn before the city walls. The fiery marshal, beside himself with fury and impatience, harangued his men in vain and, when this had no perceptible impact, himself grabbed a scaling ladder and declared 'Well, I will show you that I was a grenadier before I was a marshal, and still am one!' Aghast, his staff officers rushed to restrain their commander, and a brief comedy of tugging and pulling ensued before the young officers persuaded Lannes to relinquish the ladder. The sight of the marshal thus quarrelling with his staff officers over the honour of leading the assault re-inspired the division and, after a short pause to organise the attack, the men surged forward once again, Lannes's gallant staff and an engineer officer in the lead. In short order, the ladders were in place and two of Lannes's officers, Jean Baptiste Marbot and Charles François Huchet de la Bédoyère, were over the wall. The other two staff officers, the engineer, and dozens of men of the 25th and 85th Ligne were right behind them, and the assault force quickly spread along the walls and into the nearby houses. The Austrians put up a stubborn fight from Tower XXI and the buildings surrounding the breach, but the 85th found a poorly guarded postern that allowed GB Jean Duppelin to push more men inside the walls.[287] Exploiting their momentum, the French now drove for Peter's Gate from the rear. The Austrian battalion charged with defending it (III/Zach), taken completely by surprise and facing assailants within and without the walls, had no choice but surrender.[288] Clearing the barricades from the gate and throwing a hasty bridge over the ditch took only a few minutes, and soon the rest of Gudin's division was swarming into Regensburg's tangle of streets and alleyways. It was 4 p.m.[289]

The French swiftly overran the burning city. By the time Fölseis learned that the wall had been breached, Gudin's troops were already approaching the stone bridge, cutting off the garrison's retreat. Disjointed resistance continued for several hours but sputtered out as night came on. Fighting house to house and street to street, the combatants were often brutal, and the confused welter of intense fighting and pitiless looting by both sides left cruel images of bitter struggles at close quarters, charred corpses, and buildings reduced to ashes. The Frenchmen, eager to press their advantage and establish a foothold on the north bank, plunged ahead in the gathering gloom of smoke and dusk.[290] It took time, however, to force a passage of the river. Although two hastily summoned guns knocked down the gate on the south end of the stone bridge, several efforts to cross the arched span withered in the face of determined defence by I/Zach. French artillery fire finally broke the gate at the bridge's northern terminus around 9 p.m., but with II Corps ensconced on the heights above the river, Gudin's weary men could not progress beyond Stadtamhof. That night, as the Austrians withdrew from the suburb, Kolowrat's guns set it afire, completing the horror of its unfortunate citizens.[291]

Austrian artillery fire finally tapered off around midnight as Kolowrat, covered by a rear guard under Crenneville, pulled his corps out to head east towards Bohemia.[292] It had been another costly day for Charles. The army had lost some 8,900 men, most from II Corps and Vécsey's brigade. The losses of the Regensburg garrison alone included Fölseis, eight guns, and more than 3,700 men killed, wounded, or captured. Regiments Zach and Zedtwitz as well as the 7th Jägers lost more than 50 per cent and an entire battalion of EH Karl was destroyed. That the great majority of these losses were prisoners, many from units that were not much engaged, suggests the degree of disorder and despair that afflicted portions of the Hauptarmee. Charles also lost his second pontoon train of the campaign, but was fortunate that only three guns fell into French hands beyond those captured in Regensburg (for a total of eleven). Indeed, the archduke was lucky to have brought away most of his shaken army relatively intact. The French suffered an estimated 1,000 casualties, about half of these coming from Gudin's division.[293]

The prizes the French recovered in Regensburg included Colonel Coutard and most of the officers of the 65th Ligne. While the regiment's men had been shipped off down the Danube shortly after their surrender on 20 April, Coutard and his officers, having given their paroles, were still in the city when it fell. Reporting to Napoleon several days later, Coutard expected to be received as a hero for his stout resistance, but found instead an irate emperor. 'Where is your regiment?' demanded Napoleon, 'What have you done with my soldiers?' Coutard's explications did little to mollify his stern monarch, who then asked pointedly 'And my eagle? What have you done with my eagle?' Coutard hurriedly sent for the eagle, removed the two Austrians flags in which it had been lovingly wrapped, and presented it to Napoleon. 'That is different, that is different,' said the emperor.[294] Coutard was allowed to keep his regiment, which he reformed and commanded until 1811, when he was promoted to général de brigade while serving in Spain.

Such illuminating army anecdotes aside, in reviewing the cost of the day's battle, one should not forget the countless sufferings of Regensburg's inhabitants, subjected to abuse, assault, pillage, and artillery fire from both sides as their ancient city burned around them.

Positions on the Night of 23/24 April

As Lannes's troops moved to occupy ruined Stadtamhof late that night and the injured Napoleon retired to his new headquarters in the charterhouse at Prüll, the bulk of the Army of Germany was concentrated between Regensburg and the Pfatterbach: Davout, Lefebvre (Deroy and Demont), Oudinot (Tharreau and Colbert), Nansouty's and St Sulpice's heavy cavalry divisions, the 1st Bavarian Chevaulegers, and two Württemberg light horse regiments.[295] Boudet was nearby at Abbach and Vandamme had assembled his weary Württembergers around Alteglofsheim (*Neubronn* Fusiliers in Landshut). Massena occupied Straubing—where he was in a good position to block any Austrian adventurism across the Danube—to restore the bridge and operate on the north bank itself if necessary, or to lead the march into Austria proper once Napoleon was satisfied that Charles was genuinely retreating. The 1st Bavarian Division reached Ergoldsbach. Further afield, Guyon continued to screen along the Altmühl, Rouyer's division was spread from Vohburg west to Neuburg, and Moulin held Augsburg with the Baden 3rd Infantry forward at Odelzhausen.

As to the Austrians, Charles and the Hauptarmee staff somehow decided that it was important to issue detailed instructions for the next five days' march at approximately 1 p.m. that afternoon while the army was still trying to get itself safely over the Danube. The army's operations journal dolefully recorded, however, that 'the dispersion and disorder of the troops made the fulfilment of this disposition impossible'.[296] The army retired in the general direction of Waldmünchen and Cham after destroying the bridge at Reinhausen. Third Corps and I Reserve Corps halted at Nittenau, and IV Corps, along with Charles, spent the night at Kürn. Charles dispatched St Julien towards Cham to cover the army's left, but his small ad hoc force did not get much beyond Falkenstein that night.[297] Five squadrons of *Hessen-Homburg* Hussars were already in Cham and a sixth guarded the north bank at Deggendorf.[298] Kolowrat took his corps over the Regen at Regenstauf at 1 a.m. on the 24th, followed some hours later by Crenneville's detachment. Bellegarde, who still had small detachments in Nuremberg, Neumarkt, and Amberg, marched to Burgenlengfeld according to orders he had received at Etterzhausen that afternoon while en route to Regensburg from Neumarkt.[299] He left a rear guard at Hemau under GM Johann Nepomuk Graf Nostitz-Reineck to cover the withdrawal of his trains and artillery.[300] On the distant left flank, FML Jellacic marched out of Munich at 10 p.m. on the night of 23 April to head for Ebersberg. He left one flanking detachment at Hohenlinden and another towards the Tyrol, and prepared to collect two Landwehr battalions occupying Bavarian towns in his rear.[301] Dedovich maintained his blockade of the Oberhaus fortress at Passau.

South of the Isar, Bessières had reached the Rott River at Neumarkt and Hiller was attempting to revive his command on the Inn around Altötting. It is to their confrontation and the race to Vienna that we will turn our attention in the next volume.

The Regensburg Campaign: Observations

The fall of Regensburg brought the first campaign of the 1809 war to a close. Despite a poor beginning characterised by Berthier's bungling, confused communications, operational surprise, and incomplete deployment, Napoleon had seized the initiative and led his French and German troops in a series of bold manoeuvres at lightning pace. Only two weeks after the opening of the Austrian invasion, one week after his arrival in the theatre of operations, and five days after the start of serious combat operations, he had inflicted a string of punishing defeats on the lumbering Austrians and completely reversed the strategic situation. Austrian casualties for this period came to at least 44,700 men, seventy-three guns, nearly 100 pontoons, and a multitude of other vehicles as compared to Allied losses of approximately 16,300 soldiers.[302] Operationally, Napoleon had concentrated his forces and repelled the Austrian invasion of Bavaria; his army now stood closer to Vienna than the archduke's and was poised to carry the war into the 'heart of the Austrian monarchy'.[303] Beyond the staggering physical and operational blows inflicted on the enemy, he had gained a significant psychological advantage, reaffirming his army's moral edge while vividly demonstrating his own personal dominance of Charles and the lesser Austrian commanders. Furthermore, as will be seen, the victory in Bavaria nullified the advance Archduke Johann had made into Italy and dealt a severe blow to the hopes of Austrian sympathisers elsewhere in Europe.[304] And all of this was achieved, as Moltke noted, 'without a major battle being fought'.[305] Looking back, Napoleon repeatedly commented that 'the Battle of Abensberg, the manoeuvres of Landshut, and the Battle of Eggmühl were the most brilliant and most skilful manoeuvres' of his career.[306]

This breathtaking series of Allied victories requires some explanation, at the centre of which are two key factors: the character of the Allied army and Napoleon's leadership. Napoleon's 1809 Army of Germany was not the superb force that had bested the Austro-Russians at Austerlitz in 1805 and the Prussians at Jena–Auerstädt the following year. It retained, however, some of the qualities of organisation, tactics, experience, and, above all, morale and leadership that had made its predecessors so formidable. Although the Army of Germany as an operational entity and several of its key components (notably 2nd and 4th Corps) were ad hoc constructions, other formations were long established with the corresponding benefits to unit cohesion. Davout's 3rd was the most striking example of this, but the heavy cavalry divisions and, to a lesser extent, the Bavarians and Württembergers, were also comfortable in their organisational structures. Tactically, the French and their quick-learning German confederates repeatedly demonstrated a decided superiority in the free-wheeling combat that raged as a giant meeting engagement in the hills and forests south of Regensburg. In a situation where the two armies were moving to contact and where the opposing senior commanders seldom enjoyed an overview of their scattered forces, the Allied advantage in dispersed tactics, skirmishing, and independent lower-level leadership was decisive. Despite the confused circumstances, French and

German leaders, from generals to junior officers, showed themselves adept at exercising their own initiative within the general context provided by Napoleon's guidance. A tradition of victory and an unrelenting confidence in its officers and emperor infused these other characteristics, giving the army an aggressive, impetuous spirit perfectly suited to the urgent forced marches and fluid, close-quarters fighting of the opening campaign.

The remarkable marching capacity of the French and German units, despite the youth and inexperience of the many new recruits, deserves special mention. Massena's forced marches from his cantonments in the Augsburg area to Landshut and Eggmühl have been discussed in some detail, but just as astonishing were the marches and battles of Morand, Gudin, the French heavy cavalry, and the Württemberg Light Brigade. From 19 to 23 April, the two French infantry divisions, accompanied by Nansouty's and St Sulpice's troopers, covered some 150 kilometres under dreadful weather and often on indescribably bad roads.[307] On top of this, of course, elements of all four divisions participated in intense engagements each day. Hügel's Württemberg light troops amassed a similar record of long marches and tough fights over four consecutive days, culminating in one of the pivotal attacks at Eggmühl. Nor should the Bavarians be neglected. All three Bavarian divisions put in impressive performances from the 18th to the 20th; Wrede's improvised drive to Rottenburg and Landshut was especially noteworthy. The troops were understandably exhausted by the 23rd, but their vigour and endurance had made a major contribution to the successful conclusion of the campaign.

The army, of course, both reflected its supreme commander and enabled his bold operations. Napoleon not only soared above his adversaries in the scope of his strategic vision and his terrifyingly intuitive grasp of warfare, he was also far beyond them in seemingly ceaseless activity and ruthless resolution.[308] With something approaching awe, Charles remarked on 'the speed of his decisions and their implementation'. 'Thus', he concluded, 'were those enemies overpowered who were not possessed of similar decisiveness.'[309]

Moreover, Napoleon used the remarkable relationship he cultivated with his soldiers to imbue the army with this determination and drive, energising men at all levels. Espinchal, describing Napoleon's arrival on the field outside Regensburg, echoed the sentiments of French and Germans alike when he wrote that 'the sudden appearance of the emperor produced an electric effect throughout the army'.[310] It is crucial to note, however, that the confidence was mutual. As they trusted him, so he relied upon them. This dynamic between leader and led allowed him to undertake operations of unparalleled audacity and speed, bordering on the rash, and gave him the means to exploit the opportunities he either recognised or created. If at times he asked more of his men than was humanly possible, the astonishing pace of his operations left the Austrians in a constant state of surprise and anxiety. The admiring Pelet wrote that 'Napoleon's activity doubled the time available, devouring space and obstacles, multiplying thereby the means of victory.'[311] Repeatedly stunned by the unexpected appearance of large Allied forces on their flanks, the Austrians could only back-pedal in haste and hope for respite. In addition to compounding his advantages, of course, the agility, initiative, and spirit that Napoleon nurtured in his officers and men also granted him considerable margin for error. With troops who could march like Massena's corps and fight like Davout's, he could redeem Berthier's mistakes and recover from his own miscalculations (underestimating when the Austrians would launch their invasion, for example, or exaggerating the victory at Abensberg). Napoleon, eager to capitalise on every Austrian vulnerability, found in the Army of Germany an instrument, albeit flawed, that was still capable of implementing most of his designs.

The Austrian army and its commander, on the other hand, were ill suited for the task they had been handed. There was no lack of physical, combat courage in the Austrian ranks at any level, but the army was slow and awkward, its leaders often indolent, trammelled by cumbersome command processes and hesitant execution.[312] Where Napoleon *acted*, they hesitated, deliberated, reconsidered, and finally produced pedantic dispositions of dubious value. Caught in fast-moving battles that required an unfamiliar degree of individual initiative, generals who were brave enough in the face of musketry and cannon fire could not find the moral courage and self-confidence to deviate from the comfort of written instructions. Leaders and soldiers alike were unaccustomed to rapid marches and consecutive engagements, expecting a pause after every encounter to regroup and reassess. Napoleon offered no such respite. The Austrians, repeatedly surprised and battered, soon became bewildered and lost the hopeful spirit with which they had entered the campaign. Writing during the armistice, Grünne expressed the army's shock and bafflement as he reflected on the calamities Napoleon had inflicted on the Hauptarmee between 19 and 22 April: 'we were outflanked and attacked almost before we knew of Archduke Ludwig's misfortunes.'[313]

'In war, the power of opinion shows itself in its full extent,' Charles had once observed, 'In identical circumstances, one often gains victory through the simple conviction of the soldiers that they are physically or psychologically superior to the enemy.'[314] Unfortunately for the Austrian cause, this conviction lay with the French and Germans in April 1809.

Nor was Charles the man to overcome his army's imperfections. Entering the war with considerable reluctance, he lacked Napoleon's killer instinct and could not instil in his subordinates the drive needed to exploit Austria's initial advantages. Where the French and Germans marched twenty to forty kilometres in twenty-four hours despite poor roads and horrendous weather, the Austrians made twelve or thirteen and then clamoured for rest. There was often a marked lethargy about army headquarters and the archduke himself. His physical infirmity may account for his mysterious absence on the 20th, but what explains his failure to ride to the centre of action on the 19th and 22nd? Or the failure to send a responsible senior officer to report on the left wing on the 20th and 21st? Curiously, Charles several times referred to Napoleon and the French as an 'active' or an 'enterprising' enemy as if this was a new, unforeseen characteristic of the French troops and their soldier-emperor.[315] Had not Austria been engaged off and on with the armies of France since 1792? Had not the Habsburg Empire suffered at Napoleon Bonaparte's hand in various campaigns since 1796? Whatever the explanation for these odd adjectives, the Austrian command apparatus, faced with this 'very active enemy', seemed seized with paralysis at several critical points during the campaign.

Charles indulged in no little self-criticism after the war, blaming himself for vacillating and for founding his actions on the enemy's moves, disadvantages that were compounded because he dispersed his forces in an attempt to imitate Napoleon's swift advances. He also censured himself for not recognising his army's weaknesses, and lamented especially the incapacity of the corps commanders who lacked the 'determined will and skilfulness' to fulfil their orders despite obstacles.[316] Charles did not discuss, however, his own morale. It is evident in letters he wrote at the time as well as his subsequent analyses, that he, like his subordinates and soldiers, became frustrated and gloomy as the initial gleam of the campaign faded. These sentiments eroded morale to leave the army and its commander vulnerable to the dual shocks of the setback at Hausen-Teugn and Napoleon's arrival in the theatre of war. By 23 April, he was psychologically beaten and saw no alternative but a rapid retreat to put the Bohemian mountains between his shaken army and Napoleon's victorious battalions.

Intermezzo

THE FIRST CAMPAIGN

The 23rd of April is one of the most important in the history of our times; it brought the war into the heart of the Austrian monarchy; dashed or changed the moral and political dispositions that could have turned in its favour, deranged the general plan of that war and decided it, despite the opportunities that later offered themselves to the Austrians.[1]

So wrote Stuttheim in 1811, summing up the campaign in Bavaria. The campaign's outcome is all the more remarkable considering that the Austrians began the war with an impressive list of advantages: the numerically superior Hauptarmee was well concentrated, Napoleon was in Paris, and, having achieved operational surprise, the Austrians held the initiative. The nature of the Austrian army, however, particularly the quality of its leadership, made the offensive into Bavaria a dubious proposition regardless of these advantages. Charles did have a real chance to inflict a serious blow on the Allies before they concentrated and before Napoleon arrived on the scene, but it was a narrow chance and fleeting. Stadion and the war party in Vienna, ignorant of military realities, had gambled the monarchy's fate on a risky venture where the odds were stacked against Habsburg success. The evanescent Austrian advantages were soon squandered and Napoleon's arrival gave the Allies a decisive superiority in leadership, a psychological dominance that complemented the Allied tactical and organisational edge for an almost unbeatable combination in this sort of rapid, mobile warfare. In the words of a soldier of the 7th Léger: 'Napoleon was constantly among us, victory could not quit our side, and nothing slowed the rapid flight of our eagles.'[2]

'And yet, Napoleon's hopes were far from being entirely realised', Charles and his army had escaped.[3] The war would continue. Moreover, in the glow of yet another victory over the 'Kaiserliks', the French do not seem to have noticed that the Austrians offered tenacious resistance when their mission was clear and the field of battle open. Charles bemoaned his army's inability to conduct offensive operations in broken terrain, but he recognised its capabilities and would look to make the next fight a set-piece battle on open ground. For Napoleon, on the other hand, the April battles validated his negative, almost dismissive, impressions of Austrian military prowess. These perceptions would inform the decisions of both commanders as the war now moved into the Austrian heartland.

TABLE OF COMPARATIVE MILITARY RANKS

Austrian and German Ranks (Abbr.)	French Ranks (Abbr.)	Modern British or U.S. Equivalents
Feldmarschall (FM)	(no equivalent rank)	Field Marshal or General
Feldzeugmeister (FZM) or General der Kavallerie (GdK)	(no equivalent rank)	Lieutenant General
Feldmarschall-Leutnant (FML) or General-Leutnant (GL)	Général de Division (GD)	Major General
General-Major (GM)	Général de Brigade (GB)	Brigadier General
[staff] Oberst	Adjutant-Commandant	[staff] Colonel
Oberst	Colonel	Colonel
Oberstleutnant (OTL)	Major	Lieutenant Colonel
Major (MAJ)	Chef de Bataillon or Chef d'Escadron	Major
Stabs-Hauptmann	Adjoint	[staff] Captain
Hauptmann, Rittmeister (cavalry), or Kapitän	Capitaine	Captain
Oberleutnant (OLT) or Premierleutnant (PLT)	Lieutenant	Lieutenant, First Lieutenant
Leutnant	Sous-Lieutenant	Subaltern, Second Lieutenant

Notes:
1) All comparisons are approximate, protocol and functions could vary widely.
2) Contemporary Austrian and German sources frequently use 'Lieutenant' vice 'Leutnant' in all of the above (e.g., Oberstlieutenant). Additionally, 'Obrist' was often used in place of 'Oberst' (e.g., Obristlieutenant).
3) Although the rank of Feldmarschall-Leutnant was unique to the Austrian military (the Germans used General-Leutnant), the ranks of Feldzeugmeister, General der Kavallerie (or Infanterie) and even Feldmarschall were occasionally used by Napoleon's German allies.
4) In the French Army, the title 'Major Général' indicated a function rather than a rank and was unique to Berthier. Similarly, the title 'Generalissimo' was unique to Archduke Charles. Technically, the French title of 'Marshal' was also an appointment rather than a rank.

Appendices

INTRODUCTORY NOTE:
UNIT STRENGTHS AND ORDERS OF BATTLE

> I have my unit strength reports presented to me every day. I do not have the
> memory to retain a verse of poetry, but I do not forget a syllable of my strength
> reports. This evening I will find them in my chamber; I will not go to bed
> without having read them.
>
> Napoleon in conversation with Senator Pierre Louis Roederer,
> 11 February 1810[1]

Unit strengths. Few historical details are more interesting, more important,
and yet more difficult to calculate or uncover than unit strengths. I have
attempted to be as accurate as possible using the available source material.
Wherever feasible I have tried to use archival records (with the recognition
that these have their own problems: such as officers who might submit false
reports, simple transcription errors, delayed entries, etc.). In many cases,
however, I have had no recourse but to turn to secondary sources. In using
these tables, therefore, readers should recognize that they are only estimates.
Even the officers preparing these reports doubtless knew that the best they
could do was to come close to the actual figures and that minor discrepancies
did not really matter in the larger scheme of things anyway. I have used the
following guidelines in calculating and depicting unit strengths throughout
the book:

- In almost all cases, strength figures in the main text give numbers of
  infantry and cavalry only. If the figure includes other troops (artillery,
  train, etc.), I have tried to indicate this in the text or in an endnote.
  The idea is to give the number of muskets and sabres available by
  listing officers and men of infantry and cavalry units; I let the artillery's

guns speak for that branch. For those who wish to do so, one may add approximately 100 men per battery as a rule of thumb.

+ All strength figures are based on the number of 'effectives' or 'present under arms' (*présens sous les armes, Summa der Dienstbaren, bleibt zum Dienst*, etc.), and thus do not include detached troops (often substantial), those in hospital, or prisoners—all of whom remained on the formal rolls of units in many countries until they returned to duty or were mustered out of service. My aim has been to portray the number of soldiers actually available on the battlefield.

+ All figures agglomerate officers and men (including drummers, light infantry hornists, and cavalry trumpeters). Some of these persons were considered 'non-combatants' in some armies. This can lead to minor discrepancies, but seldom any of a major order.

+ I did not calculate losses to march attrition or illness. Unless I had a source that gave a specific piece of data (such as several consecutive tables for a single unit—very rare), I therefore carried the old numbers forward and continued to use those until I had new information. This means that units may sometimes appear stronger than they actually were, but I felt it was better to give the available figures and allow the reader to calculate march attrition, sickness rates, desertion, etc. according to his or her own formulae. Moreover, in most cases, I suspect that the *ratio* of forces on the battlefield (as opposed to actual raw numbers) would not be much affected by trying to guess attrition rates.

+ I did adjust figures for battle losses as well as the available information allowed. Where a unit has had losses deducted (or where data is otherwise uncertain), I have used 'c.' (*circa*) to indicate the adjustment.

Orders of battle. This can be more challenging than one would imagine, especially determining unit subordination at any particular moment during the war. Officers were promoted, transferred, dismissed, or fell ill throughout the year, but the exact dates of these events are frequently difficult to pinpoint 200 years later. Likewise, commanders often changed the formal order of battle to suit their own preferences without recording the specific subordination scheme. As with unit strengths, therefore, the structures outlined here should be considered guides or best estimates based on the available information.

APPENDIX I

The Austrian Army, April 1809

The following lists combat formations as they were allocated at the onset of hostilities. Note, however, that not all of the following had reached their assigned corps when the war began.

Line Infantry Regiments	Assignment (10 April)
Kaiser No. 1	III Corps
Hiller No. 2*	V Corps
Erzherzog Karl No. 3	V Corps
Deutschmeister No. 4	VI Corps
the numbers 5 and 6 were vacant in the sequence of line infantry regiments.	
vacant (formerly *Schröder*) No. 7	II Corps
Erzherzog Ludwig No. 8	IV Corps
Czartoryski No. 9	IV Corps
Anton Mittrowsky No. 10	I Corps
Erzherzog Rainer No. 11	I Corps
Manfredini No. 12	III Corps
Reisky No. 13	IX Corps
Klebek No. 14	VI Corps
Zach No. 15	II Corps
Lusignan No. 16	VIII Corps
Reuss-Plauen No. 17	I Corps
vacant (formerly *Stuart*) No. 18	II Corps
Allvintzi No. 19*	IX Corps
Kaunitz No. 20	III Corps
Rohan No. 21	II Corps [to IV Corps]
Koburg No. 22	IV Corps
Würzburg No. 23	III Corps
Strauch No. 24	VII Corps
vacant (formerly *Zedtwitz*) No. 25	II Corps
Hohenlohe-Bartenstein No. 26	VIII Corps

Strassaldo No. 27	VIII Corps
Frelich No. 28	II Corps
Lindenau No. 29	III Corps
de Ligne No. 30	VII Corps
Benjovszky No. 31*	VI Corps
Esterhazy No. 32*	VI Corps
Sztaray No. 33*	V Corps
Davidovitch No. 34*	VII Corps
Erzherzog Johann No. 35	I Corps
Kolowrat-Krakowksy No. 36	I Corps
Weidenfeld No. 37*	VII Corps
Württemberg No. 38	III Corps
Duka No. 39*	V Corps
vacant (formerly *Josef Mittrowsky*) No. 40	IV Corps
Kottulinsky No. 41	VII Corps
Erbach No. 42	I Corps
Simbschen No. 43	IX Corps
Bellegarde No. 44	IV Corps
de Vaux No. 45	VI Corps
Chasteler No. 46	IV Corps
Vogelsang No. 47	I Corps
Vukassovich No. 48*	VII Corps
Kerpen No. 49	VI Corps
Stain No. 50	V Corps
Splenyi No. 51*	VI Corps
Erzherzog Franz No. 52*	IX Corps
Johann Jellacic No. 53*	VIII Corps
Froon No. 54	II Corps
Reuss-Greitz No. 55	IV Corps
Wenzel Colloredo No. 56	III Corps
Josef Colloredo No. 57	II Corps
Beaulieu No. 58	V Corps
Jordis No. 59	VI Corps
Gyulai No. 60*	V Corps
St Julien No. 61*	VIII Corps
Franz Jellacic No. 62*	VIII Corps
Baillet No. 63	VII Corps

* Indicates a Hungarian regiment, that is, one raised in what was broadly considered Hungary; these had distinctive uniforms and were organised with a slightly higher establishment in each infantry company (238 men per company). All others were raised in Habsburg hereditary lands (Erbländer) and were considered 'German' regardless of actual ethnic composition; infantry companies in these regiments ideally numbered 218 men.

Line infantry regiments that changed Inhaber during 1809:

No.	Initial Name	Later Name (as of)	Later Name (as of)
7	vacant (Schröder)	Würzburg (18 November)	
10	Anton Mittrowsky	Reisky (1 December)	
12	Manfredini	Alois Liechtenstein (after 17 May)	
18	vacant (Stuart)	d'Aspre (24 May)	Reuss-Greitz (18 November)
25	vacant (Zedtwitz)	de Vaux (after July)	
27	Strassaldo	Chasteler (18 November)	
33	Sztaray	H. Colloredo-Mansfeld (8 December)	
35	Erzherzog Johann	Argenteau (1 May)	
40	vacant (J. Mittrowsky)	Württemberg (6 December)	
48	Vukassovich	Simbschen (November)	

Grenz Infantry Regiments	Assignment (10 April)
Licca No. 1	Dalmatia
Ottocac No. 2	IX Corps
Ogulin No. 3	IX Corps
Szulin No. 4	IX Corps
Warasdin-Kreuz No. 5	VI Corps
Warasdin-St Georg No. 6	VI Corps
Brod No. 7	V Corps
Gradiska No. 8	V Corps
Peterwardein No. 9	III Corps
1st Banal No. 10	VIII Corps
2nd Banal No. 11	VIII Corps
Deutsch-Banat No. 12	IV Corps
Wallach-Illyria No. 13	IV Corps
1st Szekel No. 14	VII Corps
2nd Szekel No. 15	VII Corps
1st Wallach No. 16	VII Corps
2nd Wallach No. 17	VII Corps

Jäger Battalions	Assignment (10 April)
1st	I Corps
2nd	I Corps
3rd	I Corps
4th	I Corps
5th	II Corps [to IV Corps]
6th	II Corps [to IV Corps]
7th	II Corps
8th	II Corps
9th	VIII Corps

Volunteer Battalions	Assignment (10 April)
1st *Erzherzog Karl* Legion ('Prager Jäger')	III Corps
2nd *Erzherzog Karl* Legion	II Corps
3rd *Erzherzog Karl* Legion	III Corps
4th *Erzherzog Karl* Legion	II Corps [detached to I Corps]
5th *Erzherzog Karl* Legion	IV Corps
6th *Erzherzog Karl* Legion	IV Corps
1st Vienna Volunteers (Major Bigot St Quentin)	V Corps
2nd Vienna Volunteers (Oberstlt. von Steigentesch)	V Corps
3rd Vienna Volunteers (Major Waldstein)	V Corps
4th Vienna Volunteers (Oberstlt. Küffel von Küffelstein)	VI Corps
5th Vienna Volunteers (Major Salis)	VI Corps
6th Vienna Volunteers (Major Managetta)	VI Corps
1st Moravian-Silesian Volunteers	I Corps
2nd Moravian-Silesian Volunteers	I Corps

Cuirassier Regiments	Assignment (10 April)
Kaiser No. 1	II Reserve Corps
Erzherzog Franz No. 2	I Reserve Corps
Herzog Albert No. 3	I Reserve Corps
Kronprinz Erzherzog Ferdinand No. 4	I Reserve Corps
Sommariva No. 5	VII Corps
vacant (formerly *Gottesheim*) No. 6	II Reserve Corps
Lothringen No. 7	VII Corps
Hohenzollern No. 8	I Reserve Corps

Dragoon Regiments	Assignment (10 April)
Erzherzog Johann No. 1	I Reserve Corps [to II Corps]
Hohenlohe No. 2	IX Corps
Knesevich No. 3	II Reserve Corps
Levenehr No. 4	II Reserve Corps
Savoy No. 5	IX Corps
Riesch No. 6	I Reserve Corps [to II Corps]

Hussar Regiments	Assignment (10 April)
Kaiser No. 1	VII Corps
Erzherzog Josef No. 2	IX Corps
Erzherzog Ferdinand No. 3	III Corps
Hessen-Homburg No. 4	III Corps
Ott No. 5	VIII Corps
Blankenstein No. 6	I Corps
Liechtenstein No. 7	VI Corps
Kienmayer No. 8	V Corps

Frimont No. 9	IX Corps
Stipsicz No. 10	IV Corps
Szekler No. 11	VII Corps
Palatinal No. 12	VII Corps

Chevauleger Regiments	**Assignment (10 April)**
Kaiser No. 1	VII Corps
Hohenzollern No. 2	VIII Corps
O'Reilly No. 3	VI Corps
Vincent No. 4	IV Corps
Klenau No. 5	II Corps [to IV Corps]
Rosenberg No. 6	VI Corps

Uhlan Regiments	**Assignment (10 April)**
Merveldt No. 1	II Corps
Schwarzenberg No. 2	I Corps
Erzherzog Karl No. 3	V Corps

Cavalry regiments that changed Inhaber during 1809:

No.	Initial Name	Later Name (as of)
Cuirassiers No. 6	vacant (*Gottesheim*)	*Moritz Liechtenstein* (approx. 22 April)
Dragoons No. 3	*Württemberg*	*Knesevich* (4 April)

Orders of Battle for the April Campaign in Bavaria

AUSTRIAN MAIN ARMY, 10 APRIL 1809

The Archduke Charles of Austria

Staff Dragoons (one squadron)
Staff Infantry (two companies)

	baons/ sqdns	present under arms
I Corps: GdK Bellegarde[2]		
Staff Dragoons (one wing)		
Staff Infantry (one company)		
1st Pioneer Division (two companies)		
Advance Guard: FML Graf Fresnel		
Brigade: GM Hardegg		
1st Jäger Battalion	1	
2nd Jäger Battalion	1	
4th Jäger Battalion	1	
Schwarzenberg Uhlans No. 2	4	
1 x 6-pounder battery (nonstandard: 6 x 6-pounders, one howitzer)		
Brigade: GM Wintzingerode		
3rd Jäger Battalion	1	
Erzherzog Johann Infantry Regiment No. 35	3	
Blankenstein Hussars No. 6	2	
1 x 6-pounder battery (nonstandard: 6 x 6-pounders, one howitzer		
Division: FML von Ulm		

Brigade: GM von Wacquant
    Erzherzog Rainer Infantry Regiment No. 11   3
    Vogelsang Infantry Regiment No. 47   3
    1 x 6-pounder battery
Division: FML von Vogelsang
  Brigade: GM von Henneberg
    Reuss-Plauen Infantry Regiment No. 17   3
    Kolowrat Infantry Regiment No. 36   3
    1 x 6-pounder battery
  Brigade: GM Wartensleben
    Blankenstein Hussars No. 6   6
Reserve: GM Nostitz
    Anton Mittrowsky Infantry Regiment No. 10   2
    Erbach Infantry Regiment No. 42   2
    4th *Erzherzog Karl* Legion   1
    Schwarzenberg Uhlans No. 2   2
    1 x 3-pounder brigade battery
Artillery Reserve:
    2 x 12-pounder position batteries
    1 x 6-pounder position battery
    1 x cavalry battery
Infantry: 23,600
Cavalry: 2,100
Guns: 62

Notes:
a. Bellegarde made fairly drastic changes to the 'standard' Austrian corps order of battle.
b. Two squadrons of the *Schwarzenberg* Uhlans were detached in Bohemia as were the third battalions of *Erbach* and *Anton Mittrowsky*.
c. Although two battalions of Moravian Volunteers were supposed to be allotted to Bellegarde, they were not ready when the war began and did not march with the corps. In partial recompense, the corps received the 4th Battalion of the *Erzherzog Karl* Legion (originally slated for II Corps). The 1st Moravian Volunteers reached the Inn at Braunau on approximately 25 April.

II Corps: FZM Kolowrat-Krakowsky[3]

Staff Dragoons (one wing)
Staff Infantry (one company)
2nd Pioneer Division   –   99
Advance Guard: FML Klenau
    7th Jäger Battalion   1   501[4]
    Infantry Regiment No. 25 (formerly *Zedtwitz*)   3   3,649
    Merveldt Uhlans No. 1   3   (see below)
    Riesch Dragoons No. 6   6   785
    1 x cavalry battery
    ½ pioneers

Brigade: GM Crenneville		
8th Jäger Battalion	1	829
2nd *Erzherzog Karl* Legion	1	895
Merveldt Uhlans No. 1	5	(total) 1,061
1 x cavalry battery		
Division: FML von Brady		
½ pioneer company		
Brigade: GM Buresch von Greiffenbach		
Zach Infantry Regiment No. 15	3	3,517
Josef Colloredo Infantry Regiment No. 57	2	1,670
1 x 6-pounder brigade battery		
Brigade: GM von Wied-Runkel		
Infantry Regiment No. 18 (formerly *Stuart*)	2	2,465
Cavalry Brigade: GM Rottermund (attached)		
Erzherzog Johann Dragoons No. 1	3	(see below)
Division: FML Weber von Treuenfels		
Brigade: GM Fölseis		
Frelich Infantry Regiment No. 28	3	3,659
Froon Infantry Regiment No. 54	3	3,626
Erzherzog Johann Dragoons No. 1	3	764 (total)
1 x 6-pounder brigade battery		

Artillery Reserve: 65 guns
    2 x 12-pounder Position Batteries
    1½ x 6-pounder position batteries
    1 x 6-pounder brigade battery
    1 x 3-pounder brigade battery
Infantry: 20,811 (as of 6 April)
Cavalry: 2,610 (as of 6 April)
Guns: 65

Notes:
a. As with Bellegarde, Kolowrat made substantial changes to the prescribed corps order of battle.
b. Rottermund's brigade (1,549) was attached from I Reserve Corps. This was to compensate for the detachment of GM Vécsey's brigade to IV Corps.
c. III/*Josef Colloredo* was engaged in repressing a mutiny among Landwehr in Bohemia.
d. 4th *Erzherzog Karl* Legion was detached to I Corps.
e. A small force was detached to assist in the blockade of the Bavarian fortress of Oberhaus: III/*Stuart* (1,235 men), a platoon (thirty-one troopers) of *Merveldt* Uhlans, and one-half of a 6-pounder position battery.
f. Available records do not give a break down for the various components of the *Merveldt* Uhlans or the *EH Johann* Dragoons. The figures here (1,061 and 764 respectively) are the totals for each regiment.

III Corps: FML Hohenzollern-Hechingen[5]

Staff Dragoons (one wing)
Staff Infantry (one company)
3rd Pioneer Division
Advance Guard: FML von Vukassovich
    Brigade: GM Moritz Liechtenstein

1st *Erzherzog Karl* Legion	½	498
Erzherzog Ferdinand Hussars No. 3	4	(see below)
1 x cavalry battery		
Brigade: GM Pfanzelter		
Peterwardein Grenz Infantry Regiment No. 9	2	2,334
Division: FML Lusignan		
Brigade: GM von Kayser		
Schröder Infantry Regiment No. 7	3*	2,861
Wenzel Colloredo Infantry Regiment No. 56	3*	2,944
Brigade: GM Thierry		
Kaiser Infantry Regiment No. 1	3*	2,673
Lindenau Infantry Regiment No. 29	3*	2,479
Division: FML St Julien		
Brigade: GM Alois Liechtenstein		
Manfredini Infantry Regiment No. 12	3*	2,678
Würzburg Infantry Regiment No. 23	2	1,631
Brigade: GM von Bieber		
Kaunitz Infantry Regiment No. 20	3*	2,728
Württemberg Infantry Regiment No. 38	2	1,953
Erzherzog Ferdinand Hussars No. 3	4	1,048 (total)

Artillery:
    3 x 12-pounder position batteries
    3 x 6-pounder position batteries
    4 x 6-pounder brigade batteries
    2 x 3-pounder brigade batteries
    1 x cavalry battery
Infantry: 22,679 (as of 16 April)
Cavalry: 1,048 (as of 16 April)
Guns: 96

Notes:

a. In those regiments marked with an asterisk (*), the third battalions only had four companies (not the required six) at the start of the war. One company of *Wenzel Colloredo*, however, did arrive before 19 April.[6]

b. The third battalions of *Würzburg* and *Württemberg* were still en route to the army. These reached the Inn at Braunau (III/*Würzburg*) and Schärding (III/*Württemberg*) on approximately 25 April.

c. Intended for M. Liechtenstein's brigade, the 3rd *Erzherzog Karl* Legion did not reach the Inn until late April.

d. Pfanzelter was to receive the *Hessen-Homburg* Hussars, No. 4 (998 men); six squadrons (approximately 780) arrived at Landshut on 21 April; the remaining two squadrons did not join the regiment until early May.

e. Only part of the 1st *Erzherzog Karl* Legion was present (498 men) on 10 April; the rest were still en route to the army and did not reach the Inn at Braunau until 25 April.

f. Available records do not give a break down for the various components of the *Ferdinand* Hussars. The figure here (1,048) is the total for the regiment.

g. Strength for artillery, train and *Handlanger* combined was 2,142.

IV Corps: FML von Rosenberg[7]

Staff Dragoons (one wing)
Staff Infantry (one company)
4th Pioneer Division
Advance Guard: GM von Stutterheim

Erzherzog Ludwig Infantry Regiment No. 8	3	
Stipsicz Hussars No. 10	4	

1 x cavalry battery
Division: FML Somariva
   Brigade: GM Neustädter

Czartoryski Infantry Regiment No. 9	2	
Reuss-Greitz Infantry Regiment No. 55	2	
Stipsicz Hussars, No. 10	3	
Vincent Chevaulegers, No. 4	8	

Division: FML Hohenlohe-Waldenburg-Bartenstein
   Brigade: GM von Riese

Koburg Infantry Regiment No. 22	3*	
Bellegarde Infantry Regiment No. 44	2	
Chasteler Infantry Regiment No. 46	2	

Brigade: GM Vécsey

5th Jäger Battalion	1	
6th Jäger Battalion	1	
Rohan Infantry Regiment No. 21	3	
Klenau Chevaulegers No. 5	8	962

Artillery:
   2 x 12-pounder position batteries
   1 x 6-pounder position battery
   3 x 6-pounder brigade batteries
   1 x 3-pounder brigade battery
   1 x cavalry battery
Infantry: 18,029
Cavalry: 3,162
Guns: 62

Notes:

a. In the *Koburg* infantry (*), the third battalion only had four (not the required six) at the start of the war. It is not clear when the missing two companies rejoined their regiment.

b. The third battalions of *Czartoryski*, *Reuss-Greitz*, *Chasteler*, and *Bellegarde* were still en route to the army.

c. Vécsey's brigade was attached from II Corps (5,229 infantry and 962 cavalry).

d. The corps was supposed to include two Grenz regiments. One of these, *Deutsch-Banat*, No. 12, arrived on 15 April 1809. The other, *Wallach-Illyria* No. 13, 2,157 strong, reached the theatre of war at the same time, but was diverted to the blockade of Oberhaus.

f. The 5th and 6th Battalions of the *Erzherzog Karl* Legion were en route to the corps.

g. Detached for the blockade of Oberhaus: FML Dedovich and GM Reinwald with Infantry Regiment No. 40 (formerly *J. Mittrowsky*), one squadron of *Stipsicz* Hussars, a pioneer detachment and a 6-pounder position battery.

V Corps: FML Archduke Ludwig[8]

Staff Infantry (one company)		
5th Pioneer Division	–	96
Advance guard: GM Radetzky		
Gradiska Grenz Infantry Regiment No. 8	2	2,352
Erzherzog Karl Uhlans No. 3	2	282
Kienmayer Hussars No. 8	2	283
Pioneers	–	48
1 x cavalry battery		
Division: FML von Lindenau		
Brigade: GM von Mayer		
Erzherzog Karl Infantry Regiment No. 3	3	2,864
Stain Infantry Regiment No. 50	2	2,156
Brigade: Oberst Hessen-Homburg		
Hiller Infantry Regiment No. 2	3	3,144
Sztaray Infantry Regiment No. 33	3	2,576
Division: FML Reuss-Plauen		
Brigade: GM von Bianchi		
Duka Infantry Regiment No. 39	3	1,982
Gyulai Infantry Regiment No. 60	3	2,370
Brigade: Oberst Fröhauff		
Beaulieu Infantry Regiment No. 58	2	1,686
Division: FML von Schustekh		
Brigade: GM Mesko de Felsö-Kubinyi		
Brod Grenz Infantry Regiment No. 7	2	2,462
Erzherzog Karl Uhlans No. 3	6	837
Kienmayer Hussars No. 8	6	849
Artillery:		
2 x 12-pounder position batteries		
2 x 6-pounder position batteries		

3 x 6-pounder brigade batteries
1 x 3-pounder brigade batteries
1 x cavalry battery
Infantry: 21,592 (as of 12 April)
Cavalry: 2,251 (as of 12 April)
Guns: 68

Notes:
a. The third battalion of *Stain* (consisting entirely of recruits 'who have not fired a shot even in training') and the Stabsdragoner (one wing) were absent on 10 April, but joined the corps on the 14th.
b. The third battalion of *Beaulieu* was still en route to the army.
c. Three battalions of Vienna Volunteers (1st, 2nd, 3rd) joined the corps on 20 April.
d. Two of the brigadiers were absent (reassignment and sickness respectively) and were replaced by the senior regimental commander in their brigades.

VI Corps: FML von Hiller[9]
  Staff Dragoons (one wing)
  Staff Infantry (one company)
  6th Pioneer Division
  Advance Guard: GM von Nordmann

Warasdin-St Georg Grenz Infantry Regiment No. 6	2	
Liechtenstein Hussars No. 7	4	
1 x cavalry battery		

  Division: FML von Kottulinsky
    Brigade: GM Hohenfeld

Klebek Infantry Regiment No. 14	3	
Jordis Infantry Regiment No. 59	3	

  Division: FML von Vincent
    Brigade: GM Weissenwolf

Deutschmeister Infantry Regiment No. 4	3	
Kerpen Infantry Regiment No. 49	3	

    Brigade: GM Hoffmeister von Hoffeneck

Benjovszky Infantry Regiment No. 31	3	
Splényi Infantry Regiment No. 51	3	
Rosenberg Chevaulegers No. 6	8	
Liechtenstein Hussars No. 7	4	

  Artillery:
    3 x 12-pounder position batteries
    3 x 6-pounder position batteries
    3 x 6-pounder brigade batteries
    1 x 3-pounder brigade battery
    1 x cavalry battery
  Detached Division: FML Jellacic
    Advance Guard: GM von Provenchères

Warasdin-Kreuz Grenz Infantry Regiment No. 5	2	2,534

O'Reilly Chevaulegers No. 3	8	1,057
Brigade: GM von Ettingshausen		
Esterhazy Infantry Regiment No. 32	3	2,511
de Vaux Infantry Regiment No. 45	3	3,083

1 x 6-pounder brigade battery
1 x 3-pounder brigade battery
Infantry (including Jellacic): 28,543
Cavalry (including Jellacic): 3,249
Guns (including Jellacic): 96

Notes:

a. FML Jellacic was detached to move towards Munich.

b. Three battalions of Vienna Volunteers (4th, 5th, 6th) joined the corps on 18 April and were assigned to Weissenwolf's brigade.

I Reserve Corps: GdK Liechtenstein[10]

    Division: FML Hessen-Homburg

        Grenadier Brigade: GM Rohan

Mayblümel Grenadier Battalion (8, 22, 60)	1
Leiningen Grenadier Battalion (25, 35, 54)	1
Hohenlohe Grenadier Battalion (1, 29, 38)	1
Hauger Grenadier Battalion (40, 44, 46)	1
Cappy Grenadier Battalion (12, 20, 23)	1
Peccaduc Grenadier Battalion (9, 55, 56)	1
Weiniawsky Grenadier Battalion (10, 11, 47)	1
Nissel Grenadier Battalion (15, 28, 57)	1
Stark Grenadier Battalion (7, 18, 21)	1
Georgy Grenadier Battalion (17, 36, 42)	1
Bissingen Grenadier Battalion (3, 50, 58)	1
Hahn Grenadier Battalion (2, 33, 39)	1

        Brigade: GM von Siegenthal

Erzherzog Franz Cuirassiers, No. 2	6
Herzog Albert Cuirassiers, No. 3	6

        Brigade: GM von Lederer

Kronprinz Erzherzog Ferdinand Cuirassiers, No. 4	6
Hohenzollern Cuirassiers, No. 8	6

    2 x 6-pounder brigade batteries
    3 x cavalry batteries
Infantry: 11,619
Cavalry: 2,750
Guns: 34

Notes:

a. The numbers in parentheses indicate the regiments from which the grenadiers were drawn (two grenadier companies per regiment).

b. GM Rottermund's dragoon brigade was detached to II Corps

II Reserve Corps: FML Kienmayer[11]

  Grenadier Brigade: GM d'Aspre

Puteany Grenadier Battalion (14, 45, 59)	1	(787)
Brzezinski Grenadier Battalion (24, 30, 41)	1	(275)
Scovaud Grenadier Battalion (4, 49, 63)	1	(804)
Kirchenbetter Grenadier Battalion (34, 37, 48)	1	(520)
Scharlach Grenadier Battalion (31, 32, 51)	1	(753)

  Brigade: GM von Schneller

Kaiser Cuirassiers, No. 1	6	(640)
Cuirassier Regiment No. 6 (formerly *Gottesheim*)	6	(?)

  Brigade: GM von Clary

Knesevich Dragoons No. 3	6	(680)
Levenehr Dragoons No. 4	6	(739)

  1 x 6-pounder brigade battery
  2 x cavalry batteries
Infantry: 3,870 (as of 10 April)
Cavalry: 2,820 (as of 10 April)
Guns: 20

Notes:

a. The numbers in parentheses following the grenadier battalion names indicate the regiments from which the grenadiers were drawn (two grenadier companies per regiment).

b. The individual regimental/battalion strength figures are as of 30 March. At that point, Brzezinski had only two companies and Kirchenbetter only four; the arrival of the missing six companies (all had arrived by 8 April) brought the corps infantry strength to the total shown for 10 April. The table for 30 March from which these numbers are drawn did not show a figure for the *Gottesheim* Cuirassiers, but they evidently numbered some 761.

Oberhaus Blockade: FML von Dedovich[12]

  GM Reinwald von Waldegg (IV Corps)

Infantry Regiment No. 40 (formerly *Josef Mittrowsky*)	2	*c.*2,700
Stipsicz Hussars No. 10	1 wing	*c.*130
part of a 6-pounder position battery (2 x 6-pounders, one howitzer)	–	

  Oberst Nesslinger

III/*Josef Mittrowsky* Infantry Regiment No. 40 (IV Corps)	2 companies	(incl. above)
1st Innviertel Landwehr	2 companies	*c.*400
4th Traunviertel Landwehr	1	809

  GM Sinzendorf

III/*Josef Mittrowsky* Infantry Regiment No. 40 (IV Corps)	2 companies	(incl. above)
Stipsicz Hussars, No. 10 (IV Corps)	1 wing	(incl. above)
two 6-pounders (IV Corps)	–	

1st Mühlviertel Landwehr	1	
2nd Mühlviertel Landwehr	1	
3rd Mühlviertel Landwehr	1	
	(1st through 3rd)	2,431
4th Mühlviertel Landwehr	1	810
GM Richter		
III/*Stuart* Infantry Regiment No. 18 (II Corps)	1	1,235
Merveldt Uhlans No. 1 (one platoon) (II Corps)	–	31
1st Klattau Landwehr	1	772
2nd Klattau Landwehr	1	695
3rd Klattau Landwehr	1	769
1st Prachin Landwehr	1	1,017
2nd Prachin Landwehr	1	858
3rd Prachin Landwehr	1	1,003
4th Prachin Landwehr	1	813
1st Budweis Landwehr	1	849
2nd Budweis Landwehr	1	978
3rd Budweis Landwehr	1	826

Notes:

a. The strength for J. *Mittrowsky* includes all elements present at Passau; two companies of III/*Josef Mittrowsky* were still en route.

b. The *Wallach-Illyria* Grenz Regiment No. 13 (IV Corps) joined the blockade force on 16 April with 2,157 men.

c. Although technically part of the blockade, all but three of Richter's battalions remained on the frontier. These three (2nd, 3rd, and 4th Prachin) and the II Corps troops (III/*Stuart* and the uhlans) arrived at the scene on 15 April.

d. Strength for the 1st, 2nd and 3rd Mühlviertel Battalions combined totaled 2,431; the 4th Battalion is listed separately. These figures and the strengths for Richter's Bohemia Landwehr battalions are from reports in March.

TROOPS EN ROUTE TO THE ARMY

Note: This list shows troops en route to the army and their *intended* destinations; some of them did not actually join the corps to which they were nominally assigned.

For I Corps

1st Moravian Volunteers	1
2nd Moravian Volunteers	1

For III Corps

III/*Würzburg* No. 23	1
III/*Württemberg* No. 38	1
Two companies of III/*Kaiser* No. 1	1/3

Two companies of III/*Schröder* No. 7	1/3	
Two companies of III/*Manfredini* No. 12	1/3	
Two companies of III/*Kaunitz* No. 20	1/3	
Two companies of III/*Lindenau* No. 29	1/3	
Two companies of III/*Wenzel Colloredo* No. 56	1/3	
3rd *Erzherzog Karl* Legion	1	
Hessen-Homburg Hussars No. 4	8	998

For IV Corps

III/*Czartoryski* No. 9	1
III/*Chasteler* No. 44	1
III/*Bellegarde* No. 46	1
III/*Reuss-Greitz* No. 55	1
Two companies of III/*Koburg* No. 22	1/3
Two companies of III/*Josef Mittrowsky* No. 40	1/3
Deutsch-Banat Grenz Infantry Regiment No. 12	2
Wallach-Illyria Grenz Infantry Regiment No. 13	2

 Note: Destination was initially IV Corps, but it was detached to the Oberhaus blockade force.

5th *Erzherzog Karl* Legion	1
6th *Erzherzog Karl* Legion	1

For V Corps

III/*Stain* No. 50	1
III/*Beaulieu* No. 58	1
1st Vienna Volunteers	1
2nd Vienna Volunteers	1
3rd Vienna Volunteers	1

For VI Corps

4th Vienna Volunteers	1
5th Vienna Volunteers	1
6th Vienna Volunteers	1

FRENCH ARMY OF GERMANY, 10 APRIL 1809

The Emperor Napoleon I
Commanding through Marshal Alexander Berthier

	baons/ sqdns	present under arms
2nd Corps: [Marshal Lannes en route][13]		
Under GD Oudinot:		
1st Division: GD Tharreau		

1st Brigade: GB Conroux		
1st Light Demi-Brigade		2
IV/6th Léger	1	504
IV/24th Léger	1	540
IV/25th Léger	1	430
3rd Light Demi-Brigade		9
IV/9th Léger	1	417
IV/16th Léger	1	458
IV/27th Léger	1	399
2nd Brigade: GB Albert		
1st Line Demi-Brigade		2
IV/8th Ligne	1	441
IV/24th Ligne	1	287
IV/45th Ligne	1	435
2nd Line Demi-Brigade		9
IV/94th Ligne	1	415
IV/95th Ligne	1	431
IV/96th Ligne	1	315
3rd Brigade: GB Jarry		
3rd Line Demi-Brigade		2
IV/28th Ligne [not yet arrived]	–	–
IV/54th Ligne	1	353
IV/63rd Ligne	1	523
4th Line Demi-Brigade	1	
IV/4th Ligne	1	491
IV/18th Ligne	1	505
IV/46th Ligne [not yet arrived]	–	–
Artillery and Train	–	176
2nd Division: GD Claparède		
1st Brigade: GB Coëhorn		
2nd Light Demi-Brigade		3
IV/17th Léger	1	519
IV/21st Léger	1	471
IV/28th Léger	1	506
4th Light Demi-Brigade		2
IV/26th Léger	1	519
Tirailleurs Corses	1	899
Tirailleurs du Po	1	1,118
2nd Brigade: GB Lesuire		
5th Line Demi-Brigade		4
IV/27th Ligne	1	456
IV/39th Ligne	1	515
IV/50th Ligne [not yet arrived]	–	–
6th Line Demi-Brigade		3
IV/59th Ligne	1	476

IV/69th Ligne	1	482
IV/76th Ligne	1	443
3rd Brigade: GB Ficatier		
7th Line Demi-Brigade		2
IV/40th Ligne	1	498
IV/75th Ligne [not yet arrived]	–	–
IV/88th Ligne	1	498
8th Line Demi-Brigade		2
IV/64th Ligne	1	520
IV/100th Ligne	1	383
IV/103rd Ligne	1	395
Artillery and Train	–	158
Light Cavalry Brigade: GB Colbert		7
9th Hussars	3	793
7th Chasseurs-à-Cheval	3	761
20th Chasseurs-à-Cheval	3	615
3rd Cuirassier Division (attached): GD d'Espagne		
1st Brigade: GB Reynaud		
4th Cuirassiers	4	665
6th Cuirassiers	4	693
2nd Brigade: GB Fouler		
7th Cuirassiers	4	701
8th Cuirassiers	4	838
Artillery and Train	–	212

Infantry: 15,642
Light cavalry: 2,169
Heavy cavalry: 2,897
Guns: 42 = 4 x 12-pounders, 14 x 8-pounders, 14 x 4-pounders, 10 x howitzers.
These were distributed 18 per infantry division, and 6 for d'Espagne's cavalry.

Note: The four battalions listed as 'not yet arrived' never did join Oudinot's command. All four ended up assigned to various reserve formations in Germany.

3rd Corps: Marshal Davout[14]

1st Division: GD Morand		
1st Brigade: GB Guiot de Lacour		
13th Léger	3	1,862
17th Ligne	3	2,325
30th Ligne	3	2,239
2nd Brigade: GB L'Huillier		
61st Ligne	3	2,124
65th Ligne	3	2,086
Artillery and Train	–	429
2nd Division: GD Friant		
Brigade: GB Gilly		

15th Léger	3	2,251
Brigade: GB Grandeau		
33rd Ligne	3	2,138
48th Ligne	3	2,228
Brigade: GB Gautier		
108th Ligne	3	2,189
111th Ligne	3	2,226
Artillery and Train	—	408
3rd Division: GD Gudin		
1st Brigade: GB Petit		
7th Léger	3	2,894
12th Ligne	3	2,085
21st Ligne	3	2,182
2nd Brigade: GB Duppelin		
25th Ligne	3	1,708
85th Ligne	3	2,202
Artillery and Train	—	472
4th Division: GD St Hilaire		
1st Brigade: GB Lorencez		
10th Léger	3*	2,505
3rd Ligne	3*	2,033
57th Ligne	3*	1,934
3rd Brigade: GB Destabenrath		
72nd Ligne	3*	2,224
105th Ligne	3*	2,161
Artillery and Train	—	473
5th (Reserve) Division: GD Demont		
IV/7th Léger	1	316
IV/12th Ligne	1	219
IV/17th Ligne	1	660
IV/21st Ligne	1	747
IV/30th Ligne	1	183
IV/33rd Ligne	1	223
IV/61st Ligne	1	188
IV/65th Ligne	1	214
IV/85th Ligne	1	219
IV/111th Ligne	1	246
Light Cavalry Brigade: GB Jacquinot		
1st Chasseurs-à-Cheval	3	553
2nd Chasseurs-à-Cheval	3	749
12th Chasseurs-à-Cheval	3	773
Light Cavalry Division (attached): [GD Montbrun en route]		
Brigade: GB Pajol		
5th Hussars	3	585
7th Hussars	3	557

11th Chasseurs-à-Cheval	3	693
Brigade: GB Piré		
8th Hussars	3	884
16th Chasseurs-à-Cheval	3	655
2nd Cuirassier Division (attached): GD St Sulpice		
1st Brigade: GB Clément		
1st Cuirassiers	4	793
5th Cuirassiers	4	792
2nd Brigade: GB Guiton		
10th Cuirassiers	4	846
11th Cuirassiers	4	812
Artillery and Train	–	168
Corps Artillery Park	–	1,817
Sappers and Miners	–	921
Equipment Train	–	585

Infantry: 46,811
Light cavalry: 5,449
Heavy cavalry: 3,243
Guns with the infantry divisions: 60 = 8 x 12-pounders, 24 x 8-pounders, 8 x 6-pounders, 12 x 4-pounders, 8 x howitzers. These were distributed 15 per division, with 15 additional guns en route for Demont's division.
Guns with St Sulpice's division: 6 = 4 x 8-pounders, 2 x howitzers

Note: The fourth battalions in St Hilaire's division were still under construction. The grenadier and voltigeur companies of these fourth battalions were included in the third battalion of each regiment (as noted with an asterisk*). The fusilier companies of the fourth battalions did not begin to depart Strasbourg until late April and early May.

4th Corps: Marshal Massena[15]

1st Division: GD Legrand		20
1st Brigade: GB Ledru		
26th Léger	3	1,993
18th Ligne	3	2,312
2nd (Baden) Brigade: GB Kister (French) and		
GM von Harrant (Baden)		
1st Baden Infantry Regiment *Grossherzog*	2	1,696
2nd Baden Infantry Regiment *Erbgrossherzog*	2	1,713
3rd Baden Infantry Regiment *Graf Hochberg*	2	1,718
Baden Jäger Battalion *Lingg*	1	572
French Artillery and Train	–	340
Baden Artillery and Train	–	369
2nd Division: GD Carra Saint-Cyr		25
1st Brigade: GB Cosson		
24th Léger	3	2,262

2nd Brigade: GB Dalesme		
4th Ligne	3	2,217
46th Ligne	3	2,331
3rd (Hessian) Brigade: GB Schiner (French) and		
GM von Nagel (Hesse-Darmstadt)		
Leib-Garde Brigade	3	2,141
Leib Brigade	3	2,095
French Artillery and Train	–	349
Hessian Artillery and Train	–	140
3rd Division: GD Molitor		16
1st Brigade: GB Leguay		
2nd Ligne	2	1,537
16th Ligne	3	2,110
2nd Brigade: GB Viviès		
37th Ligne	3	1,699
67th Ligne	2	1,485
Artillery and Train	–	308
4th Division: GD Boudet		13
1st Brigade: GB Fririon		
3rd Léger	2	1,545
2nd Brigade: GB Valory		
56th Ligne	3	2,306
93rd Ligne	2	1,417
Artillery and Train	–	347
Light Cavalry Division: GD Marulaz		3
Brigade:		
3rd Chasseurs-à-Cheval	2	438
14th Chasseurs-à-Cheval	2	391
Brigade:		
19th Chasseurs-à-Cheval	3	599
23rd Chasseurs-à-Cheval	3	594
Brigade:		
Baden Light Dragoons	4	475
Hessian Chevaulegers	3	340

Infantry: 33,223
Light cavalry: 2,837
Guns: 8 x 12-pounders, 32 x 6-pounders, 8 x howitzers evenly distributed among the four divisions. The Baden contingent provided the 1st Division with an additional eight 6-pounders and four howitzers, while the 2nd Division artillery was increased by five 6-pounders and one howitzer of the Hessian artillery; the total number of pieces thus stood at 66.

Notes:
a. Fourth battalions for 3rd Léger, 2nd Ligne, 67th Ligne, and 93rd Ligne were to join Massena's corps from Italy via the Tyrol.

b. The Baden Jäger Battalion had only five of its six companies; its 3rd Company had been left behind until it could be brought up to authorised strength. In a letter to his sister on 17 April, GB Ledru stated that the Baden Jäger were assigned to his brigade. This may have been a concept, but if so, it was never implemented as it finds no mention in the records of the battalion or of the contingent.

c. The Hessian 'brigades' were the functional equivalent of regiments. Each consisted of a two-battalion musketeer regiment (line infantry) and a battalion of fusiliers (light infantry).

d. One squadron of the 3rd Chasseurs was with Marmont's Army of Dalmatia.

7th Corps: Marshal Lefebvre[16]

1st Division: GL Crown Prince Ludwig		
staff company from 2nd Infantry depot	–	189
staff cavalry from V/1st Chevaulegers	1	137
1st Brigade: GM von Rechberg		
1st *Leib* Infantry Regiment	2	1,602
2nd Infantry Regiment *Kronprinz*	2	1,615
1st Light Infantry Battalion *Habermann*	1	813
2nd Brigade: GM Stengel		
4th Infantry Regiment	2	1,645
8th Infantry Regiment *Herzog Pius*	2	1,619
Cavalry Brigade: GM von Zandt		
1st Dragoon Regiment	2	265
1st Chevaulegers *Kronprinz*	4	529
Artillery and Train	–	418
Line (Foot) Batteries: Wagner, Hofstetten		
Light (Mounted) Battery: Regnier		
2nd Division: GL von Wrede		
staff company from 3rd Infantry depot	–	184
staff cavalry from V/2nd Chevaulegers	–	66
1st Brigade: GM von Minucci		
3rd Infantry Regiment *Prinz Karl*	2	1,594
13th Infantry Regiment	2	1,592
6th Light Infantry Battalion *La Roche*	1	794
2nd Brigade: GM von Beckers		
6th Infantry Regiment *Herzog Wilhelm*	2	1,542
7th Infantry Regiment *Löwenstein*	2	1,597
Cavalry Brigade: GM von Preysing		
2nd Chevaulegers *König*	4	512
3rd Chevaulegers *Leiningen*	4	500
Artillery and Train	–	406
Line (Foot) Batteries: Dorn, Berchem		
Light (Mounted) Battery: Caspers		
3rd Division: GL von Deroy		
staff company from 13th Infantry depot	–	179

staff cavalry from V/4th Chevaulegers	–	64
1st Brigade: GM von Vincenti		
9th Infantry Regiment *Ysenburg*	2	1,594
10th Infantry Regiment *Junker*	2	1,549
5th Light Infantry Battalion *Butler*	1	810
2nd Brigade: GM von Siebein		
5th Infantry Regiment *Preysing*	2	1,540
14th Infantry Regiment	2	1,610
7th Light Infantry Battalion *Günther*	1	718
Cavalry Brigade: GM von Seydewitz		
2nd Dragoons *Thurn und Taxis*	4	543
4th Chevaulegers *Bubenhofen*	4	527
Artillery and Train	–	430
Line (Foot) Batteries: Peters, Roys		
Light (Mounted) Battery: Gotthardt		
Corps Reserve Artillery: Major Göschl		
Reserve (12-pounder) Batteries: von Dietrich, Dobl, Leiningen		
Light (Mounted) Battery: van Douwe		

Infantry: 22,234 (not including staff companies)
Light cavalry: 2,876 (not including staff cavalry)
Guns: 78

Notes:
a. See below for Bavarian forces in the Tyrol.
b. 'Mounted artillery' is used to translate the German '*reitende Artillerie*' for the Bavarian light artillery batteries whose crewmembers rode on the limber of their piece (the so-called 'Wurst' wagons).
c. Each line and light battery included four 6-pounders and two howitzers; the reserve batteries contained four 12-pounders and two howitzers each.

8th Corps: GD Vandamme[17]

Infantry Division: GL von Neubronn		
1st Line Brigade: GM von Franquemont		
Kronprinz Infantry Regiment	2	1,331
Herzog Wilhelm Infantry Regiment	2	1,383
I/*Neubronn* Fusilier Regiment	1	702
2nd Line Brigade: GM von Scharffenstein		
Camrer Infantry Regiment	2	1,359
Phull Infantry Regiment	2	1,387
II/*Neubronn* Fusilier Regiment	1	691
3rd Light Brigade: GM von Hügel		
Jäger Battalion *König*	1	704
Jäger Battalion *von Neuffer*	1	695
1st Light Infantry Battalion *von Wolff*	1	674
2nd Light Infantry Battalion *von Brüsselle*	1	689

Cavalry Division: GL von Wöllwarth
1st Brigade: GM von Röder

Leib Chevaulegers	4	565
Herzog Heinrich Chevaulegers	4	545

2nd Brigade: GM von Stettner

König Jäger-zu-Pferd	4	555
Herzog Louis Jäger-zu-Pferd	4	549
Artillery and Train	–	413

    Line (Foot) Battery: 8 x 6-pounders and 2 x howitzers
    1st Light Battery: 4 x 6-pounders and 2 x howitzers
    2nd Light Battery: 4 x 6-pounders and 2 x howitzers
Infantry: 9,615
Light cavalry: 2,214
Guns: 22

Notes:
a. Although termed a 'fusilier regiment', *von Neubronn* differed in no way from the other infantry regiments.
b. The 'Situation' in Charles Saski, *Campagne de 1809*, Paris: Berger-Levrault, 1899–1902, shows the two royal cavalry regiments under GM von Röder and the other two under Stettner, but other reports make it clear that the chevaulegers regiments and the Jäger-zu-Pferd regiments were brigaded together from the start of the war (VIII Corps, 'Situations', dated 1, 15, and 19 April 1809, AG, *Armée d'Allemagne*, C2/508; General von Camrer, 1 April 1809 report, HStAS, *Kabinet, Geheimer Rat, Ministerien 1806-1945*, E271aNr.50).

9th Corps: Marshal Bernadotte[18]
1st Division: GL von Zezschwitz
    1st Infantry Brigade: GM von Hartitzsch

combined Leib Grenadier Guard Battalion	1	559
2nd Grenadier Battalion (Major von Bose)	1	570
3rd Grenadier Battalion (Major von Hake)	1	551
König Infantry Regiment	2	962
I/*Dyherrn* Infantry Regiment	1	471

    2nd Infantry Brigade: GM von Boxberg

Prinz Maximilian Infantry Regiment	2	1,092
Prinz Friedrich August Infantry Regiment	2	1,080
Prinz Anton Infantry Regiment	2	1,033

    Cavalry Brigade: GM von Gutschmid

Garde du Corps Regiment	2	240
Karabinier Regiment	2	150
Hussar Regiment	3	214
Prinz Clemens Chevaulegers	4	300
Herzog Albrecht Chevaulegers	1	74

2nd Division: GL von Polenz
    1st Infantry Brigade: GM von Lecoq

Prinz Clemens Infantry Regiment	2	1,077
von Low Infantry Regiment	2	1,023
von Cerrini Infantry Regiment	2	1,030
2nd Infantry Brigade: GM von Zeschau		
1st Grenadier Battalion (Major von Radeloff)	1	540
4th Grenadier Battalion (Major von Winkelmann)	1	483
von Niesemeuschel Infantry Regiment	2	977
II/*von Oebschelwitz* Infantry Regiment	1	421
Cavalry Brigade: GM von Feilitzsch		
Leib-Garde Cuirassiers	4	499
Prinz Johann Chevaulegers	4	497
Artillery and Train	–	520
1st Heavy Battery (Hoyer): 4 x 8-pounders and 2 x howitzers		
2nd Heavy Battery (Coudray): 4 x 8-pounders and 2 x howitzers		
1st Light Battery (Bonniot): 4 x 8-pounders and 2 x howitzers		
2nd Light Battery (Huthsteiner): 4 x 8-pounders and 2 x howitzers		
Two spare guns were with the artillery park		
Pontoon Detachment	–	73
Garrisons of Glogau and Danzig (see below).		

Infantry: 11,869
Cavalry: 1,974
Guns: 24 (+2 spare)

Notes:

a. Moritz Exner (*Die Antheilnahme der Königlich Sächsischen Armee am Feldzug gegen Oesterreich und die kriegerischen Ereignisse in Sachsen im Jahre 1809*, Dresden: Baensch, 1894, pp. 16–21) gives substantially higher numbers for each unit to arrive at a total of 19,096 for the Saxons. This figure seems much too high, even taking into account that Exner includes a War Commissariat of 1,157 men under a Sous-Lieutenant. Exner apparently miscalculated in at least one instance and may have counted detached troops, those in hospital and others (rather than just those 'present under arms'). Other lower numbers come from an April 'Etat Sommaire' that credits the Saxon troops with only 14,030 personnel, an 'Etat Sommaire' of 20 May that provides a similar figure (13,440), and a Saxon history written several years after the war (13,365). I have therefore opted for the strength figures above.

b. Grenadier battalion composition:
   von Radeloff: Prinz Anton & von Niesemeuschel
   von Bose: Prinz Friedrich August & von Burgsdorff
   von Hake: Prinz Clemens & von Oebschelwitz
   von Winkelmann: von Low & von Cerrini

c. Bernadotte also had nominal command of the Polish troops in the Grand Duchy of Warsaw.

10th Corps: King Jerome of Westphalia[19]

Westphalian 1st Division:
   1st Brigade: GB Bernterode

Guard Grenadier Battalion	1	950
Guard Jäger Battalion	1	570
5th Infantry Regiment	2	1,277
2nd Brigade: GB d'Uslar		
1st Infantry Regiment	2	1,965
6th Infantry Regiment	2	846
Jäger Carabiniers [en route from France]	1	362
Cavalry Brigade: GB d'Albignac		
Guard Chevauxlegers	3	440
1st Cuirassiers	4	650
Artillery and Train	–	193
Guns: 12 (evenly divided between one foot battery, one horse battery)		
Dutch 2nd Division: GD Gratien		
1st Brigade: GB Anthing		
6th Infantry Regiment	2	1,056
7th Infantry Regiment	2	1,129
2nd Brigade: GB van Hasselt		
8th Infantry Regiment	2	1,044
9th Infantry Regiment	2	1,318
2nd Cuirassiers	3	513
Artillery and Train	–	442
Guns: 12 (evenly divided among one foot battery, two horse batteries)		
French battalion: Col. Chabert [en route from Mainz]		
27th Ligne	–	100
30th Ligne	–	140
33rd Ligne	–	140
28th Léger	–	300
5th Sappers	–	50

Total: 790
Garrisons of Magdeburg, Stettin, Küstrin, Swedish Pomerania (see below).
Infantry: 11,307 (including Chabert's detachment and the Jäger Carabiniers)
Cavalry: 1,603
Guns: 24

Notes:
a. Chabert's battalion also included sixty men from the 33rd Ligne who were designated to join their regiment.
b. The Jäger Carabiniers had initially marched for Spain with the Westphalian 2nd Division; they were recalled, however, shortly after the division crossed the Rhine.

1st Cuirassier Division: GD Nansouty[20]
1st Brigade: GB Defrance		
1st Carabiniers	4	825
2nd Carabiniers	4	811
2nd Brigade: GB Doumerc		

2nd Cuirassiers	4	781
9th Cuirassiers	4	854
3rd Brigade: GB St Germain		
3rd Cuirassiers	4	767
12th Cuirassiers	4	795
Artillery and Train	-	252

Guns: 12 = 8 x 8-pounders, 4 x howitzers
Total: 4,833
Guns: 12

German Division: GD Rouyer[21]

2nd Rheinbund (Nassau)	2	1,550
4th Rheinbund (Saxon Duchies)	3	2,370
5th Rheinbund (Anhalt & Lippe)	2	840
6th Rheinbund (Schwarzburg, Reuss, Waldeck)	2	970

Total: 5,730

Note: Only the excellent 4th Rheinbund was complete when the war began, the other three regiments did not begin to approach full strength until later in the campaign. The 2nd Regiment received a missing contingent of 181 men from the Hohenzollern principalities on 5 June. The 5th Rheinbund had only three Anhalt and three Lippe companies at this point: the other three Anhalt companies and the regimental commander were in Metz and would not join the regiment until 25 April (see below); the remaining Lippe troops arrived in early June. All of the companies of the 6th Rheinbund were on hand, but they totaled only eight and all were somewhat under strength.

OTHER TROOPS EN ROUTE TO THE ARMY

	baons/ sqdns	present under arms
Infantry Division: GD Dupas[22]		
Brigade: GB Gency		
5th Léger	2	1,350
Brigade: GB Veaux		
19th Ligne	3	2,120
Artillery and Train	—	692
Guns: 12		
Cavalry Brigade: GB Bruyère[23]		
13th Chasseurs-à-Cheval	3	767
24th Chasseurs-à-Cheval	3	611

Imperial Guard[24]
Division: GD Curial

Brigade: GB Roguet

Tirailleurs Chasseurs	2	1,334
Tirailleurs Grenadiers	2	1,116

Brigade: GB Gros

Fusiliers Chasseurs	2	1,272
Fusiliers Grenadiers	2	1,269

Brigade: GB Dorsenne

Chasseurs	2	1,519
Grenadiers	2	1,324

Cavalry: GD Arrighi

Chevaulegers		414
Chasseurs-à-Cheval		363
Dragoons		254
Grenadiers-à-Cheval		219
Gendarmes d'élite	–	55
Artillery and Train	–	163

Dragoon Division: GB Beaumont[25]

1st Provisional Dragoon Regt (1st, 2nd, 3rd, 4th Dragoons)	4	335
2nd Provisional Dragoon Regt (5th, 6th, 8th, 9th Dragoons)	4	214
3rd Provisional Dragoon Regt (10th, 11th, 12th, 13th Dragoons)	4	291
4th Provisional Dragoon Regt (14th, 15th, 16th, 17th Dragoons)	4	342
5th Provisional Dragoon Regt (18th, 19th, 20th, 21st Dragoons)	4	387
6th Provisional Dragoon Regt (22nd, 25th, 26th, 27th Dragoons)	4	501

Note: Original regiments contributing personnel and horses to each of these provisional regiments are indicated in parentheses.

Three companies of the Anhalt Battalion (I/5th Rheinbund)[26]	–	c.420
1st Provisional Chasseur-à-Cheval Regiment[27]	4	693
Neufchatel Battalion[28]	1	703
1st and 2nd Staff Hussar Companies[29]	–	202

French Naval Units[30]

44th Naval Battalion	1	1,178
Battalion of Naval Artificers	1	533

Portuguese contingent[31]

13th Elite Demi-Brigade	3	1,471
Provisional Chasseurs-à-Cheval Regiment	2	293

French reserve demi-brigades were not yet formed.

APPENDIX 3

Orders of Battle for the Battle of Abensberg and the Pursuit to Landshut[32]

AUSTRIAN MAIN ARMY, EVENING 19 APRIL 1809

The Archduke Charles of Austria

	baons/ sqdns	present under arms
Staff Dragoons (one squadron)		
Staff Infantry (two companies)		

Grenadier Reserve
Division: FML Hessen-Homburg
Grenadier Brigade: GM Rohan

	baons/ sqdns	present under arms
Mayblümel Grenadier Battalion (8, 22, 60)	I	
Leiningen Grenadier Battalion (25, 35, 54)	I	
Hohenlohe Grenadier Battalion (1, 29, 38)	I	
Hauger Grenadier Battalion (40, 44, 46)	I	
Cappy Grenadier Battalion (12, 20, 23)	I	
Peccaduc Grenadier Battalion (9, 55, 56)	I	
Weiniawsky Grenadier Battalion (10, 11, 47)	I	
Nissel Grenadier Battalion (15, 28, 57)	I	
Stark Grenadier Battalion (7, 18, 21)	I	
Georgy Grenadier Battalion (17, 36, 42)	I	
Bissingen Grenadier Battalion (3, 50, 58)	I	
Hahn Grenadier Battalion (2, 33, 39)	I	

Infantry: 11,610

I Corps: GdK Bellegarde (as in Appendix 2)
Infantry: 23,400
Cavalry: 2,100
Guns: 62

II Corps: FZM Kolowrat-Krakowsky[33]
Staff Dragoons (one wing)
Staff Infantry (one company)
2nd Pioneer Division (two companies)

2 x pontooneer divisions	–	99
Detachment: GM Crenneville (Etterzhausen and Kallmünz)		
Frelich Infantry Regiment, No. 28	3	3,650
8th Jäger Battalion	1 company	c.130
2nd Erzherzog Karl Legion	1	890
Merveldt Uhlans No. 1	3	c.380
½ cavalry battery		
Main Body		
Advance Guard: FML Klenau		
7th Jäger Battalion	1	c.710
8th Jäger Battalion	4 companies	c.520
Infantry Regiment No. 25 (formerly Zedtwitz)	3	3,640
Merveldt Uhlans No. 1	5	c.640
1 x cavalry battery		
Division: FML von Brady		
Brigade: GM Buresch von Greiffenbach		
Zach Infantry Regiment No. 15	3	3,510
Josef Colloredo Infantry Regiment No. 57	2	c.1,670
Riesch Dragoons No. 6	6	780
1 x 6-pounder brigade battery		
Brigade: GM von Wied-Runkel		
Infantry Regiment No. 18 (formerly Stuart)	2	2,460
Cavalry Brigade: GM Rottermund (attached)		
Erzherzog Johann Dragoons No. 1	6	760
Division: FML Weber von Treuenfels		
Brigade: GM Fölseis		
Froon Infantry Regiment No. 54	3	3,620
1 x 6-pounder brigade battery		

Artillery Reserve:
2 x 12-pounder Position Batteries
1 and 1/2 6-pounder position batteries
1 x 6-pounder brigade battery
1 x 3-pounder brigade battery
Infantry: c.20,800
Cavalry: c.2,560
Guns: 65

Notes:

a. The organisation given here for the corps main body is speculative. The available data do not provide a breakdown of command responsibilities within the main body at this point.

b. One company of the 8th Jägers is absent from the existing sources.

III Corps: FML Hohenzollern-Hechingen
Staff Dragoons (one wing)
Staff Infantry (one company)
3rd Pioneer Division
Advance Guard: FML von Vukassovich

II/*Peterwardein* Grenz Infantry Regiment No. 9	1	c.1,000
1st *Erzherzog Karl* Legion	1/2	c.350
Erzherzog Ferdinand Hussars No. 3	6	c.780
1 x cavalry battery		

Brigade: GM von Kayser

Schröder Infantry Regiment No. 7	3*	c.2,200
Wenzel Colloredo Infantry Regiment No. 56	3*	c.2,300

Division: FML St Julien
Brigade:

Manfredini Infantry Regiment No. 12	3*	c.1,200
Würzburg Infantry Regiment No. 23	2	c.1,100

Brigade: GM von Bieber

Kaunitz Infantry Regiment No. 20	3*	c.2,100
Württemberg Infantry Regiment No. 38	2	c.1,500

Brigade: GM Pfanzelter

I/*Peterwardein* Grenz Infantry Regiment No. 9	1	c.1,160
Erzherzog Ferdinand Hussars No. 3	2	c.260
½ x 3-pounder brigade battery		

Artillery:
3 x 12-pounder position batteries
3 x 6-pounder position batteries
(the ½ battery sent to Thierry had rejoined the corps)
3½ x 6-pounder brigade batteries
1½ x 3-pounder brigade batteries
½ cavalry battery

Infantry: c.12,910
Cavalry: c.1,040
Guns: 89

Note: See below for changes on 21 April. Regiments marked * are missing two companies.

IV Corps: FML von Rosenberg
Staff Dragoons (one wing)
Staff Infantry (one company)
4th Pioneer Division (two companies)

Advance Guard: GM von Stutterheim
  Deutsch-Banat Grenz Infantry Regiment No. 12   2
  Vincent Chevaulegers No. 4   4
  1 x cavalry battery
Main Body
  Erzherzog Ludwig Infantry Regiment No. 8   3
  Stipsicz Hussars No. 10   7
  Vincent Chevaulegers No. 4   2
  Division: FML Somariva
    Brigade: GM Neustädter
      Czartoryski Infantry Regiment No. 9   2
      Reuss-Greitz Infantry Regiment No. 55   2
  Division: FML Hohenlohe-Waldenburg-Bartenstein
    Brigade: GM von Riese
      Koburg Infantry Regiment No. 22   3*
      Bellegarde Infantry Regiment No. 44   2
      II/*Chasteler* Infantry Regiment No. 46   1
  Detachment: Oberst von Steyrer
    I/*Chasteler* Infantry Regiment No. 46   1
    Vincent Chevaulegers No. 4   2
Artillery:
  2 x 12-pounder position batteries
  1 x 6-pounder position battery
  3 x 6-pounder brigade batteries
  1 x 3-pounder brigade battery
Infantry: *c.*13,900
Cavalry: *c.*2,030
Guns: 56
Detached (en route to Hauptarmee from Oberhaus/Passau):
  GM Reinwald von Waldegg
    Infantry Regiment No. 40 (formerly *Josef Mittrowsky*)   3*   *c.*2,700
    Stipsicz Hussars No. 10   1   *c.*130
    2/3 x 6-pounder position battery (2 x 6-pdrs, 2 x howitzers) —

Note: Grenz Regiment *Deutsch-Banat* No. 12 had arrived on 15 April. Regiments marked
* are missing two companies.

V Corps: FML Archduke Ludwig[34]
Staff Infantry (one company)
5th Pioneer Division   —   96
III/*Stain* Infantry Regiment, No. 50   1   *c.*1,000
Advance guard: GM Radetzky
  Gradiska Grenz Infantry Regiment No. 8   2   *c.*2,190
  Erzherzog Karl Uhlans No. 3   8   *c.*1,060
  1 x cavalry battery
Division: FML Reuss-Plauen

Brigade: GM von Bianchi		
Duka Infantry Regiment No. 39	3	*c.*1,980
Gyulai Infantry Regiment No. 60	3	*c.*2,370
Brigade: Oberst Fröhauff		
Beaulieu Infantry Regiment No. 58	2	1,680
Detachment: FML von Schustekh		
Kienmayer Hussars No. 8	4	*c.*560
Brigade: GM Mesko de Felsö-Kubinyi		
Brod Grenz Infantry Regiment No. 7	2	*c.*2,460
Kienmayer Hussars No. 8	4	*c.*560

Artillery:
2 x 12-pounder position batteries
2 x 6-pounder position batteries
1 x 6-pounder brigade battery
1 x 3-pounder brigade batteries
1 x cavalry battery
Infantry: *c.*11,840
Cavalry: *c.*2,190
Guns: 68
Attached:

Brigade: GM Thierry at Offenstetten		
Kaiser Infantry Regiment No. 1	10 companies	–
Lindenau Infantry Regiment No. 29	6 companies	–
Levenehr Dragoons No. 4	4¾	–
½ battery		
Oberst Hammer at Hörlbach (from Thierry's brigade)		
Kaiser Infantry Regiment No. 1	6 companies	–
Lindenau Infantry Regiment No. 29	10 companies	–
Levenehr Dragoons No. 4	1¼	–
½ battery		

Notes:
a. Three battalions of Vienna Volunteers (1st, 2nd, 3rd) destined for V Corps reached Pfeffenhausen by evening on 20 April.
b. This is the early morning situation. Eight companies of *Brod* Grenzer were detached to Schustekh at Rohr and arrived at approximately 10.30 a.m.

VI Corps: FML von Hiller[35]
Staff Dragoons (one wing)
Staff Infantry (one company)
6th Pioneer Division
Detachment: Major von Scheibler (Abens)

Warasdin-St Georg Grenz Infantry Regiment No. 6	2 companies
Rosenberg Chevaulegers No. 6	1
Liechtenstein Hussars No. 7	1

Detachment: Rittm Spannagel (Attenhofen)
Benjovszky Infantry Regiment No. 31   2 companies
Liechtenstein Hussars No. 7   1
Advance Guard: GM von Nordmann (Au)
Warasdin-St Georg Grenz Infantry Regiment No. 6   1
Liechtenstein Hussars No. 7   3
Detached Brigade: GM Hohenfeld (Au and Abens)
Klebek Infantry Regiment No. 14   3
Jordis Infantry Regiment No. 59   3
Liechtenstein Hussars No. 7   3
½ cavalry battery
Corps Main Body (Mainburg)
Detachment: FML von Vincent
Rosenberg Chevaulegers No. 6   4
Brigade: GM Weissenwolf
Deutschmeister Infantry Regiment No. 4   3
Kerpen Infantry Regiment No. 49   3
4th, 5th, 6th Vienna Volunteers   3
Brigade: GM Hoffmeister von Hoffeneck
Benjovszky Infantry Regiment No. 31 $2\,^1/_3$
Splényi Infantry Regiment No. 51   3
Rosenberg Chevaulegers No. 6   1
En route to Pfeffenhausen to join main body from Scheibler:
Rosenberg Chevaulegers No. 6   1
En route to Pfeffenhausen to join main body from Nordmann
Warasdin-St Georg Grenz Infantry Regiment No. 6   4 companies
Benjovszky Infantry Regiment No. 31   2 companies
Rosenberg Chevaulegers No. 6   1
1/2 cavalry battery
Artillery:
3 x 12-pounder position batteries
3 x 6-pounder position batteries
3 x 6-pounder brigade batteries
1 x 3-pounder brigade battery
1 x cavalry battery
Infantry: c.22,810
Cavalry: c.2,140
Guns: 82

Notes:
a. Jellacic's division, detached to Munich, is not included in these figures.
b. Added 2,700 (est.) to the 10 April figures for the three Vienna Volunteers battalions.
   Subtracted losses for Scheibler's command.

Provisional Corps (I Reserve Corps): GdK Liechtenstein

	infantry	5,229
Brigade: GM Vécsey		
5th Jäger Battalion	1	
6th Jäger Battalion	1	
Rohan Infantry Regiment, No. 21	3	
Klenau Chevaulegers, No. 5	8	*c.*900
1 x cavalry battery		
Division: FML von Lindenau		
Brigade: GM von Mayer		
Erzherzog Karl Infantry Regiment No. 3	3	2,864
Stain Infantry Regiment No. 50	2	2,156
1 x 6-pounder brigade battery		
Brigade: GM Reinhard		
Hiller Infantry Regiment No. 2	3	3,144
Sztaray Infantry Regiment No. 33	3	2,576
1 x 6-pounder brigade battery		
Brigade: GM von Siegenthal		
Erzherzog Franz Cuirassiers No. 2	6	
Herzog Albert Cuirassiers, No. 3	6	
Brigade: GM von Lederer		
Kronprinz Erzherzog Ferdinand Cuirassiers No. 4	6	
Hohenzollern Cuirassiers No. 8	6	
Brigade: GM von Schneller		
Kaiser Cuirassiers No. 1	6	640
Cuirassier Regiment No. 6 (formerly *Gottesheim*)	6	670
1 x cavalry battery		
2 x 6-pounder brigade batteries		
3 x cavalry batteries		

Infantry: 15,969
Light Cavalry: *c.*900
Heavy Cavalry: 4,060
Guns: 64

Note: Newly promoted GM Reinhard arrived on 19 or 20 April to take command of his brigade.

II Reserve Corps: FML Kienmayer

Grenadier Brigade: GM d'Aspre		
Puteany Grenadier Battalion (14, 45, 59)	1	
Brzezinski Grenadier Battalion (24, 30, 41)	1	
Scovaud Grenadier Battalion (4, 49, 63)	1	
Kirchenbetter Grenadier Battalion (34, 37, 48)	1	
Scharlach Grenadier Battalion (31, 32, 51)	1	
Brigade: GM von Clary		
Knesevich Dragoons No. 3	6	680

1 x 6-pounder brigade battery
1 x cavalry battery
Infantry: 3,870
Cavalry: 680
Guns: 14

Note: One cavalry battery apparently went with Schneller's brigade to Liechtenstein's ad hoc command.

FRENCH ARMY OF GERMANY, EVENING 19 APRIL 1809

The Emperor Napoleon I

	baons/ sqdns	present under arms
3rd Corps: Marshal Davout		
2nd Division: GD Friant[36]		c.9,000
Brigade: GB Gilly		
15th Léger	3	–
Brigade: GB Grandeau		
33rd Ligne	3	–
48th Ligne	3	–
Brigade: GB Gautier		
108th Ligne	3	–
111th Ligne (II and III)	2	–
Artillery and Train	–	408
4th Division: GD St Hilaire[37]		c.9,150
Brigade: GB Lorencez		
10th Léger	3	–
3rd Ligne	3	–
57th Ligne	3	–
Brigade: GB Destabenrath		
72nd Ligne	3	–
105th Ligne	3	–
Artillery and Train	–	473
5th (Reserve) Division: GD Demont – detached with Napoleon (see below)	–	–
Light Cavalry Division: GD Montbrun		
Brigade: GB Pajol		c.1,700
5th Hussars	3	–
7th Hussars	3	–
11th Chasseurs-à-Cheval	3	–
7th Léger (I and II)	2	c.1,800
Light Cavalry Brigade: GB Piré		
8th Hussars	1?	c.290

16th Chasseurs-à-Cheval	3	655
Detachment: Col. Guyon (12th Chasseurs)		
12th Chasseurs-à-Cheval	3	773
I/111th Ligne	1	c.750
two companies from 15th Léger	–	c.200
Regensburg garrison: Col. Coutard (65th Ligne)		
65th Ligne (losses on 19th not reflected here)	3	2,086
Corps Artillery Park	–	1,817
Sappers and Miners	–	921
Equipment Train	–	585

Infantry: 20,230 (not including the 65th Ligne or Guyon's detachment)
Light cavalry: 2,800 (not including the 12th Chasseurs)
Guns with the infantry divisions: probably 30 (15 per division).

Notes:

a. The two detached companies from the 15th Léger were probably from its Third Battalion.

b. Part of the 8th Hussars, perhaps as much as two of its large squadrons (as reflected here), somehow ended up in the pursuit to Landshut and participated in the Battle of Neumarkt on 24 April.

Provisional Corps: Marshal Lannes
 1st Division: GD Morand
  1st Brigade: GB Guiot de Lacour

13th Léger	3	1,862
17th Ligne[38]	3	c.2,240
30th Ligne	3	2,239

  2nd Brigade: GB L'Huillier

61st Ligne	3	2,124
Artillery and Train	–	429

 3rd Division: GD Gudin
  1st Brigade: GB Petit

III/7th Léger[39]	1	c.900
12th Ligne	3	2,085
21st Ligne	3	2,182

  2nd Brigade: GB Duppelin

25th Ligne	3	1,708
85th Ligne	3	2,202
Artillery and Train	–	472

 2nd Cuirassier Division (attached): GD St Sulpice
  1st Brigade: GB Clément

1st Cuirassiers	4	793
5th Cuirassiers	4	792

  2nd Brigade: GB Guiton

10th Cuirassiers	4	846

11th Cuirassiers	4	812
Artillery and Train	–	168
Light Cavalry Brigade: GB Jacquinot		
1st Chasseurs-à-Cheval[40]	3	c.470
2nd Chasseurs-à-Cheval	3	749
8th Hussars	2?	c.580

Infantry: c.17,530
Light cavalry: c.1,800
Heavy cavalry: 3,243
Guns with the infantry divisions: probably 30 (15 per division)
Guns with St Sulpice's division: 6 = 4 x 8-pounders, 2 x howitzers

Note: One or two squadrons of the 8th Hussars apparently joined Jacquinot in the pursuit to Landshut.

Under Marshal Massena

4th Corps: Marshal Massena		
1st Division: GD Legrand		20
1st Brigade: GB Ledru		
26th Léger	3	1,993
18th Ligne	3	2,312
2nd (Baden) Brigade: GB Kister (French) and GM von Harrant (Baden)		
1st Baden Infantry Regiment *Grossherzog*	2	1,696
2nd Baden Infantry Regiment *Erbgrossherzog*	2	1,713
Baden Jäger Battalion *Lingg*	1	572
French Artillery and Train	–	340
Baden Artillery and Train	–	369
2nd Division: GD Carra St-Cyr		25
1st Brigade: GB Cosson		
24th Léger	3	2,262
2nd Brigade: GB Dalesme		
4th Ligne	3	2,217
46th Ligne	3	2,331
3rd (Hessian) Brigade: GB Schiner (French) and GM von Nagel (Hesse-Darmstadt)		
Leib-Garde Brigade	3	2,141
1st Leib Fusilier Battalion	1	c.680
French Artillery and Train	–	349
Hessian Artillery and Train	–	140
3rd Division: GD Molitor		16
1st Brigade: GB Leguay		
2nd Ligne	2	1,537
16th Ligne	3	2,110
2nd Brigade: GB Viviès		
37th Ligne	3	1,699

67th Ligne	2	1,485
Artillery and Train	–	308
4th Division: GD Boudet		13
1st Brigade: GB Fririon		
3rd Léger	2	1,545
2nd Brigade: GB Valory		
56th Ligne	3	2,306
93rd Ligne	2	1,417
Artillery and Train	–	347
Light Cavalry Division: GD Marulaz		3
3rd Chasseurs-à-Cheval	2	438
14th Chasseurs-à-Cheval	2	391
19th Chasseurs-à-Cheval	3	599
23rd Chasseurs-à-Cheval	3	594
Hessian Chevaulegers	3	340
3rd Cuirassier Division (attached): GD d'Espagne		
1st Brigade: GB Reynaud		
4th Cuirassiers	4	665
6th Cuirassiers	4	693
2nd Brigade: GB Fouler		
7th Cuirassiers	4	701
8th Cuirassiers	4	838
Artillery and Train	–	212

Infantry: c.30,000
Light cavalry: 2,362
Heavy cavalry: 2,987

Guns: 8 x 12-pounders, 32 x 6-pounders, 8 x howitzers. The Baden contingent provided the 1st Division with an additional eight 6-pounders and four howitzers, while the 2nd Division artillery was increased by five 6-pounders and one howitzer of the Hessian artillery; the total number of pieces for 4th Corps thus stood at 66. D'Espagne's division had an additional 6 guns.

2nd Corps: GD Oudinot

1st Division: GD Tharreau		
1st Brigade: GB Conroux		
1st Light Demi-Brigade		2
IV/6th Léger	1	504
IV/24th Léger	1	540
IV/25th Léger	1	430
3rd Light Demi-Brigade		9
IV/9th Léger	1	417
IV/16th Léger	1	458
IV/27th Léger	1	399
2nd Brigade: GB Albert		
1st Line Demi-Brigade		2

IV/8th Ligne	I	441
IV/24th Ligne	I	287
IV/45th Ligne	I	435
2nd Line Demi-Brigade		9
IV/94th Ligne	I	415
IV/95th Ligne	I	431
IV/96th Ligne	I	315
3rd Brigade: GB Jarry		
3rd Line Demi-Brigade		2
IV/54th Ligne	I	353
IV/63rd Ligne	I	523
4th Line Demi-Brigade		I
IV/4th Ligne	I	491
IV/18th Ligne	I	505
Artillery and Train	–	176
2nd Division: GD Claparède		
1st Brigade: GB Coehorn		c.3,400
2nd Light Demi-Brigade	3	
IV/17th Léger, IV/21st Léger, IV/28th Léger		
4th Light Demi-Brigade	3	
IV/26th Léger, Tirailleurs Corses, Tirailleurs du Po		
2nd Brigade: GB Lesuire		c.2,470
5th Line Demi-Brigade	2	
IV/27th Ligne, IV/39th Ligne		
6th Line Demi-Brigade	3	
IV/59th Ligne, IV/69th Ligne, IV/76th Ligne		
3rd Brigade: GB Ficatier		
7th Line Demi-Brigade		2
IV/40th Ligne	I	498
IV/88th Ligne	I	498
8th Line Demi-Brigade		2
IV/64th Ligne	I	520
IV/100th Ligne	I	383
IV/103rd Ligne	I	395
Artillery and Train	–	158
9th Hussars	3	793
Baden Light Dragoons	4	475
Light Cavalry Brigade: GB Colbert		7
7th Chasseurs-à-Cheval	3	700
20th Chasseurs-à-Cheval	3	615

Infantry: c.15,500
Light cavalry: 2,584
Guns: 36 (distributed 18 per infantry division)

7th Corps: Marshal Lefebvre
1st Division: GL Crown Prince Ludwig
staff company from 2nd Infantry depot —
staff cavalry from V/1st Chevaulegers 1
1st Brigade: GM von Rechberg
I/1st *Leib* Infantry Regiment 1 *c*.800
2nd Infantry Regiment *Kronprinz* 2 *c*.1,540
1st Light Infantry Battalion *Habermann* 1 813
2nd Brigade: GM Stengel
4th Infantry Regiment 2 1,645
8th Infantry Regiment *Herzog Pius* 2 1,619
Cavalry Brigade: GM von Zandt
1st Dragoon Regiment 2 *c*.260
1st Chevaulegers *Kronprinz* 4 *c*.470
Artillery and Train — 418
Line (Foot) Batteries: Wagner, Hofstetten
Light (Mounted) Battery: Regnier
2nd Division: GL von Wrede
staff company from 3rd Infantry depot —
staff cavalry from V/2nd Chevaulegers —
1st Brigade: GM von Minucci
3rd Infantry Regiment *Prinz Karl* 2 *c*.1,560
13th Infantry Regiment 2 *c*.1,585
6th Light Infantry Battalion *La Roche* 1 *c*.790
2nd Brigade: GM von Beckers
6th Infantry Regiment *Herzog Wilhelm* 2 *c*.1,450
7th Infantry Regiment *Löwenstein* 2 1,597
Cavalry Brigade: GM von Preysing
2nd Chevaulegers *König* 4 *c*.450
3rd Chevaulegers *Leiningen* 4 500
Artillery and Train — 406
Line (Foot) Batteries: Dorn, Berchem
Light (Mounted) Battery: Caspers
3rd Division: GL von Deroy
staff company from 13th Infantry depot —
staff cavalry from V/4th Chevaulegers —
1st Brigade: GM von Vincenti
9th Infantry Regiment *Ysenburg* 2 1,594
10th Infantry Regiment *Junker* 2 *c*.1,540
5th Light Infantry Battalion *Butler* 1 *c*.730
2nd Brigade: GM von Siebein
5th Infantry Regiment *Preysing* 2 *c*.1,530
14th Infantry Regiment 2 1,610
7th Light Infantry Battalion *Günther* 1 *c*.650

Cavalry Brigade: GM von Seydewitz

2nd Dragoons *Thurn und Taxis*	4	c.520
4th Chevaulegers *Bubenhofen*	4	527
Artillery and Train	–	430

Line (Foot) Batteries: Peters, Roys
Light (Mounted) Battery: Gotthardt
Corps Reserve Artillery: Major Göschl
Reserve (12-pounder) Batteries: von Dietrich, Dobl, Leiningen
Light (Mounted) Battery: van Douwe
Vohburg garrison

II/1st *Leib* Infantry Regiment	1	c.800

Infantry: c.21,850 (including II/1 at Vohburg, not including staff companies)
Light cavalry: c.2,730 (not including staff cavalry)
Guns: 78

Note: The four batteries of the corps reserve were distributed to the divisions on 19 April: von Leiningen (1st Division), Dobl (2nd Division), von Dietrich and van Douwe (3rd Division).

8th Corps: GD Vandamme
Infantry Division: GL von Neubronn
1st Line Brigade: GM von Franquemont

Kronprinz Infantry Regiment	2	1,331
Herzog Wilhelm Infantry Regiment	2	1,383
I/*Neubronn* Fusilier Regiment	1	702

2nd Line Brigade: GM von Scharffenstein

I/*Camrer* Infantry Regiment	1	c.650
Phull Infantry Regiment	2	1,387
II/*Neubronn* Fusilier Regiment	1	691

3rd Light Brigade: GM von Hügel

Jäger Battalion *König*	1	704
Jäger Battalion *von Neuffer*	1	695
1st Light Infantry Battalion *von Wolff*	1	674
2nd Light Infantry Battalion *von Brüsselle*	1	689

Cavalry Division: GL von Wöllwarth
1st Brigade: GM von Röder

Leib Chevaulegers	4	565
Herzog Heinrich Chevaulegers	4	545

2nd Brigade: GM von Stettner

König Jäger-zu-Pferd	4	555
Herzog Louis Jäger-zu-Pferd	4	549

Ingolstadt garrison

II/*Camrer* Infantry Regiment	1	c.650
Artillery and Train	–	413

Line (Foot) Battery: 8 x 6-pounders and 2 x howitzers

1st Light Battery: 4 x 6-pounders and 2 x howitzers
2nd Light Battery: 4 x 6-pounders and 2 x howitzers
Infantry: 9,615 (including Ingolstadt garrison)
Light cavalry: 2,214
Guns: 22

Augsburg Garrison: GD Moulin		
3rd Baden Infantry Regiment *Graf Hochberg*	2	1,718
Hessian Leib Regiment	2	1,408

5th (Reserve) Division, 3rd Corps: GD Demont[41]

Brigade		
IV/30th Ligne	1	183
IV/61st Ligne	1	188
IV/65th Ligne	1	214
Brigade		
IV/33rd Ligne	1	223
IV/111th Ligne	1	246
Brigade		
IV/7th Léger	1	316
IV/12th Ligne	1	219
IV/21st Ligne	1	747
IV/85th Ligne	1	219

Infantry: 2,555
Possibly 15 guns

Detached at Vohburg: IV/17th Ligne	1	660

1st Cuirassier Division: GD Nansouty[42]

1st Brigade: GB Defrance		
1st Carabiniers	4	825
2nd Carabiniers	4	811
2nd Brigade: GB Doumerc		
2nd Cuirassiers	4	781
9th Cuirassiers	4	854
3rd Brigade: GB St Germain		
3rd Cuirassiers	4	767
12th Cuirassiers	4	795
Artillery and Train	–	252

Guns: 12 = 8 x 8-pounders, 4 x howitzers
Total: 4,833
Guns: 12

German Division: GD Rouyer[43]

2nd Rheinbund (Nassau)	2	1,550
4th Rheinbund (Saxon Duchies)	3	2,370
5th Rheinbund (Anhalt and Lippe)	2	840
6th Rheinbund (Schwarzburg, Reuss, Waldeck)	2	970

Total: 5,730

Notes:
a. The division was concentrated at Donauwörth and Rain.
b. The 5th Rheinbund had only three Anhalt and three Lippe companies at this point in the war.

MAJOR ORDER OF BATTLE CHANGES FROM 20 TO 21 APRIL

Note: The following changes are useful for understanding the actions on 21 April. Otherwise, the orders of battle for both sides remained more-or-less as outlined above.

Austrian

Austrian III Corps elements on the afternoon of 21 April
Near Lindach (south of the Laaber)
Advance Guard: FML von Vukassovich

Peterwardein Grenz Infantry Regiment No. 9	2	c.1,700
Erzherzog Ferdinand Hussars No. 3	4	c.500
1 x cavalry battery		

Brigade: GM von Bieber

Kaunitz Infantry Regiment No. 20	3*	c.2,100
Württemberg Infantry Regiment No. 38	2	c.1,500

In reserve near Haus
FML St Julien:

Manfredini Infantry Regiment No. 12	3*	c.1,200
Würzburg Infantry Regiment No. 23	2	c.1,100

Behind left wing of IV Corps
Brigade: GM von Kayser

Schröder Infantry Regiment No. 7	3*	c.2,200
Wenzel Colloredo Infantry Regiment No. 56	3*	c.2,300
1st *Erzherzog Karl* Legion	1/2	c.350

Under FML Fürst Hohenzollern on the Bettelberg

Erzherzog Ferdinand Hussars No. 3	4	c.500

Note: The *Hessen-Homburg* Hussars No. 4 were destined for III Corps, but only joined the corps on the Bohemian border after the retreat from Regensburg. Six squadrons did reach Landshut on 21 April and some participated in the fighting there on 21 April (see Chapter 6). The other two squadrons did not join the regiment until early May.

Allied

7th Corps: Marshal Lefebvre's Command on 21 April
  3rd Division: GL von Deroy
    1st Brigade: GM von Vincenti

9th Infantry Regiment *Ysenburg*	2	1,594
10th Infantry Regiment *Junker*	2	c.1,540
5th Light Infantry Battalion *Butler*	1	c.730

    2nd Brigade: GM von Siebein

5th Infantry Regiment *Preysing*	2	c.1,530
14th Infantry Regiment	2	1,610
7th Light Infantry Battalion *Günther*	1	c.650

    Cavalry Brigade: GM von Seydewitz

2nd Dragoons *Thurn und Taxis*	4	c.520
4th Chevaulegers *Bubenhofen*	4	527
Artillery and Train	—	430

    Line (Foot) Batteries: Peters, Roys
    Light (Mounted) Battery: Gotthardt
    Reserve (12-pounder) Battery: von Dietrich
  5th (Reserve) Division, 3rd Corps: GD Demont

IV/7th Léger	1	316
IV/12th Ligne	1	219
IV/17th Ligne	1	660
IV/21st Ligne	1	747
IV/30th Ligne	1	183
IV/33rd Ligne	1	223
IV/61st Ligne	1	188
IV/65th Ligne	1	214
IV/85th Ligne	1	219
IV/111th Ligne	1	246

    Possibly 15 guns
  3rd Brigade, 1st Heavy Cavalry Division: GB St Germain

3rd Cuirassiers	4	767
12th Cuirassiers	4	795

APPENDIX 4

Orders of Battle for the Battle of Eggmühl[44]

AUSTRIAN MAIN ARMY, 22 APRIL 1809

The Archduke Charles of Austria

	baons/ sqdns	present under arms
Staff Dragoons (one squadron)		
Staff Infantry (two companies)		

North of the Danube
I Corps: GdK Bellegarde (as in Appendix 2)
Infantry: 23,400
Cavalry: 2,100
Guns: 62

Detached from II Corps		
GM Crenneville (Hemau)		
7th Jäger Battalion[45]	I	*c.*710
8th Jäger Battalion	I	*c.*780
Merveldt Uhlans, No. 1	2	*c.*250

South of the Danube
1st 'Column' (II Corps): FZM Kolowrat-Krakowsky[46]

Staff Dragoons (one wing)		
Staff Infantry (one company)		
2nd Pioneer Division (two companies)		
2 x pontooneer divisions	–	99

Main Body
  Advance Guard: FML Klenau

2nd *Erzherzog Karl* Legion	1	890
Merveldt Uhlans No. 1	6	*c.*750
1 x cavalry battery		
Division: FML von Brady		
Brigade: GM Buresch von Greiffenbach		
Zach Infantry Regiment No. 15 (II and III)	2	*c.*2,340
Josef Colloredo Infantry Regiment No. 57	2	*c.*1,670
1 x 6-pounder brigade battery		
Brigade: GM von Wied-Runkel		
Infantry Regiment No. 18 (formerly *Stuart*)	2	2,460
1 x 6-pounder brigade battery		
Cavalry Brigade: GM Rottermund (attached)		
Erzherzog Johann Dragoons No. 1	6	760
Riesch Dragoons No. 6	5	650
Division: FML Weber von Treuenfels		
Brigade: GM Fölseis		
Frelich Infantry Regiment No. 28	3	3,650
Froon Infantry Regiment No. 54	3	3,620
1 x 6-pounder brigade battery		
Artillery Reserve:		
2 x 12-pounder Position Batteries		
1 and 1/2 6-pounder position batteries		
1 x 3-pounder brigade battery		
Attached: GM Vécsey		
5th Jäger Battalion	1	*c.*800
6th Jäger Battalion	1	*c.*800
I/*Rohan* Infantry Regiment No. 21	1	*c.*800
Klenau Chevaulegers No. 5[47]	4	*c.*450
1 x cavalry battery		

Infantry: *c.*17,000
Cavalry: *c.*2,630
Guns: 71

Notes:
a. The organisation given for the column is speculative. The available data do not provide a breakdown of command responsibilities within the main body at this point.
b. It is not clear how Vécsey's battalions were distributed; the representation here is speculative.
c. One squadron of *Riesch* Dragoons detached to reconnoitre towards Straubing.

Regensburg Garrison (detached from II Corps)[48]

Infantry Regiment No. 25 (formerly *Zedtwitz*)	3	3,640
I/*Zach* Infantry Regiment, No. 15	1	*c.*1,170

2nd 'Column': GdK Liechtenstein[49]

Attached from Vécsey's Brigade:

Rohan Infantry Regiment No. 21 (II and III)	2	*c*.1,700
Klenau Chevaulegers No. 5	4	*c*.650

Division: FML von Lindenau

Brigade: GM von Mayer

Stain Infantry Regiment No. 50	3	*c*.3,150

1 x 6-pounder brigade battery

Brigade: GM Reinhard

Hiller Infantry Regiment No. 2	3	3,144
Sztaray Infantry Regiment No. 33	3	2,576

1 x 6-pounder brigade battery

Infantry: *c*.10,500

Cavalry: *c*.650

Guns: 16

Note: It is not clear how Vécsey's battalions were distributed; the representation here is speculative.

3rd 'Column' (III Corps): FML Hohenzollern-Hechingen[50]

Staff Dragoons (one wing)

Staff Infantry (one company)

3rd Pioneer Division

Advance Guard

Erzherzog Karl Infantry Regiment No. 3	3	2,850

Brigade: GM von Kayser

Schröder Infantry Regiment No. 7	3*	*c*.2,200
Wenzel Colloredo Infantry Regiment No. 56	3**	*c*.2,300
1st *Erzherzog Karl* Legion	½	*c*.350

Division: FML St Julien

Brigade:

Manfredini Infantry Regiment No. 12	3*	*c*.1,200
Würzburg Infantry Regiment No. 23	2	*c*.1,100

Cavalry:

Erzherzog Ferdinand Hussars No. 3	4	*c*.500

Attached cavalry: Major Klehe

Kaiser Cuirassiers No. 1	1	*c*.100
Cuirassier Regiment No. 6 (formerly *Gottesheim*)	1	*c*.110

Artillery:

3 x 12-pounder position batteries

3 x 6-pounder position batteries

3½ x 6-pounder brigade batteries

1½ x 3-pounder brigade batteries

Infantry: *c*.10,000

Cavalry: *c*.710

Guns: 69

Note: It is not clear that Klehe's two squadrons were formally attached to Hohenzollern, but they were operating in his area. Infantry Regiment No. 56 was missing one company (**); the others missing two companies as before (*).

IV Corps: FML von Rosenberg
  Staff Dragoons (one wing)
  Staff Infantry (one company)
  4th Pioneer Division (two companies)

Deutsch-Banat Grenz Infantry Regiment No. 12	2	
Cavalry: GM von Stutterheim		
Stipsicz Hussars No. 10	7	
Vincent Chevaulegers No. 4	8	
1 x cavalry battery		
Right Wing: FML Hohenlohe-Waldenburg-Bartenstein		
Erzherzog Ludwig Infantry Regiment No. 8	3	
Koburg Infantry Regiment No. 22	3*	
Chasteler Infantry Regiment No. 46	2	
Left Wing: FML Somariva		
Brigade: GM Neustädter		
Czartoryski Infantry Regiment No. 9	2	
Reuss-Greitz Infantry Regiment No. 55	2	
Brigade: GM von Riese		
Bellegarde Infantry Regiment No. 44	2	
Attached:		
FML von Vukassovich		
Peterwardein Grenz Infantry Regiment No. 9	2	*c.*1,700
Erzherzog Ferdinand Hussars No. 3	4	*c.*500
1 x cavalry battery		
Brigade: GM von Bieber		
Kaunitz Infantry Regiment No. 20	3*	*c.*2,100
Württemberg Infantry Regiment No. 38	2	*c.*1,500

  Artillery:
    2 x 12-pounder position batteries
    1 x 6-pounder position battery
    3 x 6-pounder brigade batteries
    1 x 3-pounder brigade battery
Infantry: *c.*16,300
Cavalry: *c.*2,450
Guns: 70

Detached (en route to Hauptarmee from Oberhaus/Passau):
  GM Reinwald von Waldegg

Infantry Regiment No. 40 (formerly *Josef Mittrowsky*)	3*	*c.*2,700

Stipsicz Hussars, No. 10	I	*c.*130
2/3 x 6-pounder position battery (2 x 6-pounders, 2 x howitzers)	–	

Note: GM von Riese's role on 22 April is unclear. Regiments marked * are missing two companies.

Grenadier Reserve
Grenadier Brigade: GM Rohan

Mayblümel Grenadier Battalion (8, 22, 60)	I
Leiningen Grenadier Battalion (25, 35, 54)	I
Hohenlohe Grenadier Battalion (1, 29, 38)	I
Hauger Grenadier Battalion (40, 44, 46)	I
Cappy Grenadier Battalion (12, 20, 23)	I
Peccaduc Grenadier Battalion (9, 55, 56)	I
Weiniawsky Grenadier Battalion (10, 11, 47)	I
Nissel Grenadier Battalion (15, 28, 57)	I
Stark Grenadier Battalion (7, 18, 21)	I
Georgy Grenadier Battalion (17, 36, 42)	I
Bissingen Grenadier Battalion (3, 50, 58)	I
Hahn Grenadier Battalion (2, 33, 39)	I

2 x 6-pounder brigade batteries
Infantry: 11,610 (this figure may be high, actual 'present under arms' strength may have been as low as 9,000)

Cuirassier Reserve
Brigade: GM von Siegenthal

Erzherzog Franz Cuirassiers No. 2	6
Herzog Albert Cuirassiers No. 3	6
1 x cavalry battery	

Brigade: GM von Lederer

Kronprinz Erzherzog Ferdinand Cuirassiers, No. 4	6
Hohenzollern Cuirassiers No. 8	6
1 x cavalry battery	

Brigade: GM von Schneller

Kaiser Cuirassiers No. 1	5	*c.*530
Cuirassier Regiment No. 6 (formerly *Gottesheim*)	5	*c.*550
1 x cavalry battery		

Heavy Cavalry: 4,060

Other
Six squadrons of *Hessen-Homburg* Hussars No. 4 (intended for III Corps, estimated at some 780 troopers) were also in the general area of the Hauptarmee on 22–3 April. Two squadrons escorted the army headquarters' baggage (one split off at Straubing to destroy the bridge at Deggendorf); the other four crossed the Danube (probably at Straubing or Deggendorf) and joined the Main Army at Cham (details unknown). The regiment's remaining two squadrons arrived in the army's camps in Bohemia in the first days of May.

FRENCH ARMY OF GERMANY, 22 APRIL 1809

The Emperor Napoleon I

Northern sector (near the Laaber River):
3rd Corps: Marshal Davout

2nd Division: GD Friant		c.7,900
Brigade: GB Gilly		
15th Léger	3	–
Brigade: GB Grandeau		
33rd Ligne	3	–
48th Ligne	3	–
Brigade: GB Gautier		
108th Ligne	3	–
111th Ligne (II and III)	2	–
Artillery and Train	–	408
4th Division: GD St Hilaire		c.8,700
1st Brigade: GB Lorencez		
10th Léger	3	–
3rd Ligne	3	–
57th Ligne	3	–
3rd Brigade: GB Destabenrath		
72nd Ligne	3	–
105th Ligne	3	–
Artillery and Train	–	473
Light Cavalry Division: GD Montbrun		
Brigade: GB Pajol		c.1,700
5th Hussars	3	–
7th Hussars	3	–
11th Chasseurs-à-Cheval	3	–
7th Léger (I and II)	2	c.1,800
Light Cavalry Brigade: GB Piré		
8th Hussars	1?	c.290
16th Chasseurs-à-Cheval	3	655
Detachment: Col. Guyon (12th Chasseurs)		
12th Chasseurs-à-Cheval	3	773
I/111th Ligne	1	c.750
two companies from 15th Léger	–	c.200
Corps Artillery Park	–	1,817
Sappers and Miners	–	921
Equipment Train	–	585

Infantry: 18,400 (not including Guyon's detachment)
Light cavalry: 2,800 (not including the 12th Chasseurs)
Guns with the infantry divisions: probably 30 (15 per division).

Notes:
a. The two detached companies from the 15th Léger were probably from its Third Battalion.
b. The 8th Hussars were split between Piré and Bessières. The figures above represent a best estimate that one squadron (*c.*290) remained with Piré while two (*c.*580) rode with Bessières; the reverse may have been true.

7th Corps: Marshal Lefebvre
3rd Division: GL von Deroy
  staff company from 13th Infantry depot —
  staff cavalry from V/4th Chevaulegers —
  1st Brigade: GM von Vincenti
    9th Infantry Regiment *Ysenburg* — 2 — 1,594
    10th Infantry Regiment *Junker* — 2 — *c.*1,540
    5th Light Infantry Battalion *Butler* — 1 — *c.*730
  2nd Brigade: GM von Siebein
    5th Infantry Regiment *Preysing* — 2 — *c.*1,530
    14th Infantry Regiment — 2 — 1,610
    7th Light Infantry Battalion *Günther* — 1 — *c.*650
  Cavalry Brigade: GM von Seydewitz
    2nd Dragoons *Thurn und Taxis* — 4 — *c.*520
    4th Chevaulegers *Bubenhofen* — 4 — 527
  Artillery and Train — — — *c.*650
    Line (Foot) Batteries: Peters, Roys
    Light (Mounted) Batteries: Gotthardt, van Douwe
    Reserve (12-pounder) Battery: von Dietrich
5th (Reserve) Division, 3rd Corps: GD Demont
  IV/7th Léger — 1 — 316
  IV/12th Ligne — 1 — 219
  IV/21st Ligne — 1 — 747
  IV/30th Ligne — 1 — 183
  IV/33rd Ligne — 1 — 223
  IV/61st Ligne — 1 — 188
  IV/65th Ligne — 1 — 214
  IV/85th Ligne — 1 — 219
  IV/111th Ligne — 1 — 246
  Possibly 15 guns
3rd Brigade, 1st Heavy Cavalry Division: GB St Germain
  3rd Cuirassiers — 4 — 767
  12th Cuirassiers — 4 — 795
Infantry: *c.*10,190 (not including staff companies)
Heavy cavalry: 1,562
Light cavalry: *c.*1,047 (not including staff cavalry)
Guns: 24 Bavarian and possibly 15 French (with Demont)

Detached: IV/17th Ligne (guarding bridge at Vohburg till 26 April)   1   660[51]

4th Division, 4th Corps: GD Boudet
Division staff   13
  1st Brigade: GB Fririon
    3rd Léger   2   1,545
  2nd Brigade: GB Valory
    56th Ligne   3   2,306
    93rd Ligne   2   1,417
  Artillery and Train   –   347
Infantry: 5,268 (perhaps 1,000 to 1,200 detached to Guyon north of the Danube)
Guns: 12

2nd Corps: GD Oudinot
  1st Division: GD Tharreau
    1st Brigade: GB Conroux
      1st Light Demi-Brigade   2
      IV/6th Léger   1   504
      IV/24th Léger   1   540
      IV/25th Léger   1   430
      3rd Light Demi-Brigade   9
      IV/9th Léger   1   417
      IV/16th Léger   1   458
      IV/27th Léger   1   399
    2nd Brigade: GB Albert
      1st Line Demi-Brigade   2
      IV/8th Ligne   1   441
      IV/24th Ligne   1   287
      IV/45th Ligne   1   435
      2nd Line Demi-Brigade   9
      IV/94th Ligne   1   415
      IV/95th Ligne   1   431
      IV/96th Ligne   1   315
    3rd Brigade: GB Jarry
      3rd Line Demi-Brigade   2
      IV/54th Ligne   1   353
      IV/63rd Ligne   1   523
      4th Line Demi-Brigade   1
      IV/4th Ligne   1   491
      IV/18th Ligne   1   505
    Artillery and Train   –   176
  Light Cavalry Brigade: GB Colbert   7
    7th Chasseurs-à-Cheval   3   700
    20th Chasseurs-à-Cheval   3   615
Infantry: 6,944

Light cavalry: 1,315
Guns: 18

1st Bavarian Division: GL Crown Prince Ludwig

staff company from 2nd Infantry depot	–	
staff cavalry from V/1st Chevaulegers	1	
1st Brigade: GM von Rechberg		
1st *Leib* Infantry Regiment	1	*c.*800
2nd Infantry Regiment *Kronprinz*	2	*c.*1,540
1st Light Infantry Battalion *Habermann*	1	813
2nd Brigade: GM Stengel		
4th Infantry Regiment	2	1,645
8th Infantry Regiment *Herzog Pius*	2	1,619
Artillery and Train	–	*c.*550
Line (Foot) Batteries: Wagner, Hofstetten		
Light (Mounted) Battery: Regnier		
Reserve (12-pounder) Battery: von Leiningen		

Infantry: *c.*6,410

Note: Regnier's light battery may have gone to Landshut with Zandt's cavalry brigade.

Southern sector (Landshut and vicinity): under Napoleon's direct command

Provisional Corps: Marshal Lannes

1st Division: GD Morand[52]		
1st Brigade: GB Guiot de Lacour		
13th Léger	3	*c.*1,650
17th Ligne	3	*c.*2,170
30th Ligne	3	*c.*2,170
2nd Brigade: GB L'Huillier		
61st Ligne	3	*c.*1,770
Artillery and Train	–	429
3rd Division: GD Gudin		
1st Brigade: GB Petit		
III/7th Léger	1	*c.*900
12th Ligne	3	2,085
21st Ligne	3	2,182
2nd Brigade: GB Duppelin		
25th Ligne	3	1,708
85th Ligne	3	2,202
Artillery and Train	–	472

Infantry: *c.*16,840
Guns with the infantry divisions: probably 30 (15 per division)

4th Corps: Marshal Massena

1st Division: GD Legrand	20

Unit		
1st Brigade: GB Ledru		
26th Léger	3	1,993
18th Ligne	3	2,312
2nd (Baden) Brigade: GB Kister (French) and GM von Harrant (Baden)		
1st Baden Infantry Regiment *Grossherzog*	2	1,696
2nd Baden Infantry Regiment *Erbgrossherzog*	2	1,713
Baden Jäger Battalion *Lingg*	1	572
French Artillery and Train	–	340
Baden Artillery and Train	–	369
2nd Division: GD Carra Saint-Cyr		25
1st Brigade: GB Cosson		
24th Léger	3	2,262
2nd Brigade: GB Dalesme		
4th Ligne	3	2,217
46th Ligne	3	2,331
3rd (Hessian) Brigade: GB Schiner (French) and GM von Nagel (Hesse-Darmstadt)		
Leib-Garde Brigade	3	2,141
1st Leib Fusilier Battalion	1	c.680
French Artillery and Train	–	349
Hessian Artillery and Train	–	140
2nd Division, 2nd Corps: GD Claparède[53]		
1st Brigade: GB Coehorn		c.3,400
2nd Light Demi-Brigade	3	
IV/17th Léger, IV/21st Léger, IV/28th Léger		
4th Light Demi-Brigade	3	
IV/26th Léger, Tirailleurs Corses, Tirailleurs du Po		
2nd Brigade: GB Lesuire		c.2,470
5th Line Demi-Brigade	2	
IV/27th Ligne, IV/39th Ligne		
6th Line Demi-Brigade	3	
IV/59th Ligne, IV/69th Ligne, IV/76th Ligne		
3rd Brigade: GB Ficatier		
7th Line Demi-Brigade		2
IV/40th Ligne	1	498
IV/88th Ligne	1	498
8th Line Demi-Brigade		2
IV/64th Ligne	1	520
IV/100th Ligne	1	383
IV/103rd Ligne	1	395
Artillery and Train	–	158
Light cavalry:		
14th Chasseurs-à-Cheval	2	391
9th Hussars	3	793
Baden Light Dragoons	4	475

3rd Cuirassier Division (attached): GD d'Espagne
  1st Brigade: GB Reynaud

4th Cuirassiers	4	665
6th Cuirassiers	4	693

  2nd Brigade: GB Fouler

7th Cuirassiers	4	701
8th Cuirassiers	4	838
Artillery and Train	–	212

Infantry: c.30,000
Light cavalry: 1,659
Heavy cavalry: 2,987
Guns: 60 with the infantry and 6 for d'Espagne's cavalry.

1st Cuirassier Division: GD Nansouty[54]
  1st Brigade: GB Defrance

1st Carabiniers	4	825
2nd Carabiniers	4	811

  2nd Brigade: GB Doumerc

2nd Cuirassiers	4	781
9th Cuirassiers	4	854
Artillery and Train	–	252

  Guns: 12 = 8 x 8-pounders, 4 x howitzers
Total: 3,271
Guns: 12

2nd Cuirassier Division: GD St Sulpice
  1st Brigade: GB Clément

1st Cuirassiers	4	793
5th Cuirassiers	4	792

  2nd Brigade: GB Guiton

10th Cuirassiers	4	846
11th Cuirassiers	4	812
Artillery and Train	–	168

Total: 3,243
Guns: 6 = 4 x 8-pounders, 2 x howitzers

Cavalry Brigade, 1st Bavarian Division: Oberst von Vieregg

1st Dragoon Regiment	2	c.260
1st Chevaulegers *Kronprinz*	4	c.470

Total: c.730

Note: Regnier's light battery may have gone to Landshut with this brigade.

8th Corps: GD Vandamme
  Infantry Division: GL von Neubronn

1st Line Brigade: GM von Franquemont

Kronprinz Infantry Regiment	2	1,331
Herzog Wilhelm Infantry Regiment	2	1,383
I/*Neubronn* Fusilier Regiment	1	702

2nd Line Brigade: GM von Scharffenstein

I/*Camrer* Infantry Regiment	1	c.650
Phull Infantry Regiment	2	1,386
II/*Neubronn* Fusilier Regiment	1	691

3rd Light Brigade: GM von Hügel

Jäger Battalion *König*	1	c.653
Jäger Battalion *von Neuffer*	1	c.683
1st Light Infantry Battalion *von Wolff*	1	c.638
2nd Light Infantry Battalion *von Brüsselle*	1	c.684

Cavalry Division: GL von Wöllwarth

1st Brigade: GM von Röder

Leib Chevaulegers	4	565
Herzog Heinrich Chevaulegers	4	c.527

2nd Brigade: GM von Stettner

König Jäger-zu-Pferd	4	c.538
Herzog Louis Jäger-zu-Pferd	4	547

En route to battlefield

II/*Camrer* Infantry Regiment	1	c.650

Artillery and Train	–	413

Line (Foot) Battery: 8 x 6-pounders and 2 x howitzers
1st Light Battery: 4 x 6-pounders and 2 x howitzers
2nd Light Battery: 4 x 6-pounders and 2 x howitzers
Infantry: 9,450 (including II/*Camrer*)
Light cavalry: 2,170
Guns: 22

Line of communications
Augsburg Garrison: GD Moulin

3rd Baden Infantry Regiment *Graf Hochberg*	2	1,718
Hessian Leib Regiment	2	c.1,400

German Division: GD Rouyer[55]

2nd Rheinbund (Nassau)	2	1,550
4th Rheinbund (Saxon Duchies)	3	2,370
5th Rheinbund (Anhalt and Lippe)	2	840
6th Rheinbund (Schwarzburg, Reuss, Waldeck)	2	970

Total: 5,730

The division was concentrated at Donauwörth and Rain.

Abbreviations

AE	Archives du Ministère des Affaires Étrangères,
AG	Archives de la guerre, Service historique de la armée de terre
AN	Archives Nationales, *Secrétairerie d'État Impériale: Guerre*
BKA	Bayerisches Hauptstaatsarchiv, Abt. IV, Kriegsarchiv
du Casse, *Eugène*	Eugene de Beauharnais, *Mémoires et Correspondance*, ed. Albert du Casse, Paris: Lévy, 1858–60
Collingwood	*Selection from the Public and Private Correspondence of Vice-Admiral Lord Collingwood*, New York: Carvill, 1829.
Correspondance	Napoleon I, *Correspondance de Napoléon Ier publiée par ordre de l'Empereur Napoléon III*, Paris: Imprimerie Impériale, 1858–70.
GLA	Generallandesarchiv Karlsruhe
HHStA	Haus-, Hof- und Staatsarchiv (Vienna)
HStAS	Hauptstaatsarchiv Stuttgart
Hiller	Manfried Rauchensteiner (ed.), 'Das sechste österr. Armeekorps im Krieg 1809. Nach den Aufzeichnungen des FZM Johann Freiherr v. Hiller (1748–1819)', in *Mitteilungen des österr. Staatsarchivs.*
KAFA	Kriegsarchiv, Alte Feldakten
MOL	Magyar Orszagos Leveltar
Nachl.	Nachlässe
NA	US National Archives

Napoleon, War Archives	*Unpublished Correspondence of Napoleon I Preserved in the War Archives*, ed. Ernest Picard and Louis Tuetey, New York: Duffield, 1913.
ÖMZ	*österreichische militärische Zeitschrift* or *Streffleurs österreichische militärische Zeitschrift*
PRO	Public Records Office (now UK National Archives)
PRO/FO	Public Records Office/Foreign Office
SächsHStA	Sächsisches Hauptstaatsarchiv Dresden
Stadion	Hellmuth Rössler, *Graf Johann Philipp Stadion: Napoleons deutscher Gegenspieler*, Vienna: Herold, 1966.
VPR	*Vneshniaia Politika Rossii*, Moscow, 1965.

Notes

PREFACE

1 Letter from the French Foreign Minister, Jean-Baptiste de Nompère de Champagny, to Napoleon's ambassador in Vienna, Général de Division Antoine-François Andréossy, printed in extract in Napoleon I, *Correspondance de Napoléon Ier publiée par ordre de l'Empereur Napoléon III*, Paris: Imprimerie Impériale, 1858–70 [hereafter *Correspondance*], no. 14254, 16 August 1808.

2 Jean-Jacques Pelet, *Mémoires sur la guerre de 1809 en Allemagne*, Paris: Roret, 1824–6, vol. IV, pp. 166.

3 Edmond Buat, *1809 De Ratisbonne à Znaïm*, Paris: Chapelot, 1909, vol. I, p. II.

4 Wilhelm Meier, *Erinnerungen aus den Feldzügen 1806 bis 1815*, Karlsruhe: Müller, 1854, pp. 50–2.

5 As John Elting was wont to point out, however, it is well to remember that Napoleon fought numerous successful *battles* after 1809.

6 Contemporary Germans frequently referred to Napoleon as the 'Schlachtenkaiser' or 'Emperor of Battles'.

7 Louis Madelin, *Histoire du Consulat et de l'Empire*, Paris: Hachette, 1944, vol. VIII, p. 238.

8 'Feu sacré' was Napoleon's term for the combination of devotion and determination that inspires some commanders; at various times, Napoleon cited Lefebvre and Legrand as officers possessing this quality. See also Colonel Vachée, *Napoleon at Work*, trans. G. Frederic Lees, London: Charles Black, 1914, p. 21.

9 In 1815, Charles briefly returned to military life as commandant of Mainz, hardly a position for the man who had once served as generalissimo of the entire Habsburg host and contested the field with Napoleon.

CHAPTER I: WAR IS UNAVOIDABLE

1 As the Austrian ambassador (Graf Metternich) in Paris wrote: 'There can be no peace with a revolutionary system' and 'a state of calm and quiet' is impossible 'so long as Napoleon lives'; see Clemens Lothar Wenzel von Metternich-Winneburg, *Memoirs of Prince Metternich*, New York: Fertig, 1970, vol. II, p. 205.

2   See Paul W. Schroeder, *The Transformation of European Politics 1763–1848*, Oxford: Oxford University Press, 1994; and Frederick W. Kagan, *The End of the Old Order: Napoleon and Europe 1801–1805*, Cambridge: Da Capo Press, 2006, pp. 4–7.

3   He was the second Holy Roman Emperor to bear the name 'Franz' (Maria Theresa's husband, Franz Stefan of Lorraine/Lothringen, had been the first), and was consequently known as Franz II until 1804. On 11 April of that year, he was declared 'Franz I, Emperor of Austria' and thus managed to retain his imperial title when he abdicated as Holy Roman Emperor in 1806.

4   Armand Lefebvre (completed by Eduard Lefebvre de Béhaine), *Histoire des Cabinets de l'Europe pendant le Consulat et l'Empire*, Paris: Amyot, 1868, vol. III, p. 44.

5   *Krieg 1809*, prepared by the staff of the k. und k. Kriegsarchiv, Vienna: Seidel & Sohn, 1907–10, vol. I, pp. 37–8. Franz's cabinet minister, Fürst Franz von Colloredo-Mansfeld, came to the same conclusion: 'We see well that all which has occurred at Tilsit has been done in hatred of England and Austria, and that our demise is decided; but, if we must perish, at least we will fall with honour and with our swords in our hands' (quoted in Edouard Driault, *Tilsit*, Paris: Alcan, 1917, p. 221).

6   This isolation was partially self-inflicted: suspicion of everything foreign pervaded the court, particularly the Kaiser's close advisers and sycophants (Adolf Beer, *Zehn Jahre österreichischer Politik 1801–1810*, Leipzig: Brockhaus, 1877, p. 213).

7   A further Napoleonic inconvenience for the Stadion family came when the Holy Roman Empire disappeared and their ancestral lands in Schwaben fell under the suzerainty of corpulent King Friedrich of Württemberg. That dread monarch promptly sequestered the Stadion land revenues. The French chargé in Vienna, Claude Dodun, described Stadion's ire in a 23 March 1809 report (no. 8), Archives du Ministère des Affaires Étrangères, *Correspondence politique: Autriche* [hereafter AE], vol. 382.

8   Conversation between Stadion and Graf Hardenberg in October 1808 (Lefebvre, vol. IV, pp. 60–1).

9   See Archduke Charles, 'Denkschrift über die millitärisch-politischen Verhältnisse Oesterreichs von 1801–1809', *Ausgewählte Schriften*, Vienna: Braumüller, 1893, vol. VI, p. 328: 'From the time he assumed the ministry, Stadion set his eye on a break with France.'

10   Stadion wanted to return 'everything to its state before and after the Peace of Pressburg, up to the introduction of the Rheinbund Act' (undated memorandum entitled 'Bemerkungen über den Marsch der Kays. Königl. Armee nach Deutschland', in Hellmuth Rössler, *Oesterreichs Kampf um Deutschlands Befreiung*, Hamburg: Hanseatische Verlagsanstalt, 1940, vol. I, p. 505). See also Enno E. Kraehe, *Metternich's German Policy*, Princeton: Princeton University Press, 1963, vol. I, p. 80; and James Allen Vann's fine essay 'Habsburg Policy and the Austrian War of 1809', *Central European History*, vol. VII, no. 4 (December 1974), pp. 291–2, 299. Although Charles believed that Metternich shared the foreign minister's aim ('Denkschrift', *Ausgewählte Schriften*, vol. VI, pp. 326–7), Manfred Botzenhart cogently destroys this perception in *Metternichs Pariser Botschafterzeit*, Münster: Aschendorff, 1967.

11   Stadion, quoted in Oskar Criste, *Erzherzog Carl von Oesterreich*, Vienna: Braumüller, 1912, vol. II, p. 418. Furthermore, Stadion had initially counselled

defiance of Napoleon in the autumn of 1806—albeit without seriously addressing the military requirements of such a policy (Helmut Hertenberger and Franz Wiltschek, *Erzherzog Karl*, Graz: Styria, 1983, p. 193).

12 Stadion, quoted in Beer, pp. 292–3.

13 This analysis draws on Vann and Botzenhart. Napoleon saw the danger of the expatriates' bellicose influence (to Jerome, 15 February 1809, *Supplément a la Correspondance de Napoléon Ier*, Paris: Dentu, 1887, p. 113).

14 '. . . your princes travel through your provinces, your proclamations call your people to the defence of the fatherland . . .' from a conversation with Metternich on 15 August 1808 (in Champagny to Andréossy, 16 August 1808, *Correspondance*, no. 14254. Napoleon had used almost exactly these words one year earlier in a letter to Champagny (12 August 1807, *Correspondance*, no. 13023).

15 With thanks to Mr. Mark van Hattem.

16 Vann, pp. 300–4.

17 In contrast to Charles's military credentials, the performances of Ferdinand and Johann as senior commanders in 1805 hardly inspired confidence. Among the loudest proponents of war were such courtiers as 'the baleful' Baron Anton von Baldacci (Johann averred that Baldacci would have made a good adjutant for Tamerlane, see Gustav Just, *Der Friede von Schönbrunn*, vol. IX of *Das Kriegsjahr 1809 in Einzeldarstellungen*, Vienna: Stern, 1909, p. 37). The comment on Baldacci is from 'Tagebuch eines Ungenannten', entry for 29 September 1809, quoted in Eduard Wertheimer, *Geschichte Oesterreichs und Ungarns im ersten Jahrzehnt des 19. Jahrhunderts*, Leipzig: Duncker & Humblot, 1890, vol. II, p. 421; see also Viktor Bibl, *Der Zerfall Oesterreichs: Kaiser Franz und seine Erbe*, Vienna: Rikola, 1922, p. 153.

18 Unfortunately, there is no good, scholarly biography of Franz. The best is Bibl's *Zerfall*, but it suffers from a number of weaknesses. C. Wolfsgruber, *Franz I.*, Vienna, 1899, and W. C. Langsam, *Francis the Good*, New York: Macmillan, 1949, only take his life to 1792 when he began his reign. Hermann Meynert, *Kaiser Franz I.*, Vienna, 1872, uncritical and curiously organised, offers little insight. Heinrich Drimmel, *Kaiser Franz*, Vienna: Amalthea, 1981, is eccentric, poorly documented, occasionally tendentious, and puffed up with florid (if often evocative) prose. Andrew Wheatcroft provides interesting insights in *The Habsburgs*, London: Viking, 1995.

19 Napoleon to Champagny, 21 September 1809, *Correspondance*, no. 15832; Bibl, *Zerfall*, pp. 152–5. Archduke Johann described his brother in similar terms (Hans Magenschab, *Erzherzog Johann*, Graz: Styria, 1981, p. 183). For other comments on Franz, see Beer, pp. 211, 313, 314. The French ambassador observed 'This regime lacks a certain decisiveness . . . At the top there is no skill for leadership and underneath no talent for administration' (Andréossy in Hellmuth Rössler, *Graf Johann Philipp Stadion: Napoleons deutscher Gegenspieler*, Vienna: Herold, 1966 [hereafter *Stadion*], p. 307. Herta Steiner provides a good summary of Napoleon's views in 'Das Urteil Napoleons I. über Oesterreich', dissertation, University of Vienna, 1946, pp. 103–8.

20 Napoleon's larger ambitions against Britain played the key role in determining his actions in Spain as well as his sense of tidiness, his disgust with the Spanish court, and his overestimation of Spain's value as a strategic possession. As Michael

Broers points out 'Napoleon moved out of exasperation rather than as a result of a premeditated plan' (*Europe Under Napoleon 1799–1815*, London: Arnold, 1996, p. 149). For Napoleon's sense of Spain's treachery in 1806–7, see R. B. Mowat, *The Diplomacy of Napoleon*, London: Arnold, 1924, pp. 208–9.

21 For Spain, see David Gates, *The Spanish Ulcer*, New York: Norton, 1986; Charles Esdaile, *The Peninsular War*, London: Penguin, 2002.

22 The complex details of these events are beyond the scope of this study, but a general understanding of the sequence of events is important for comprehension of the Austrian decision to go to war.

23 Stadion drew this parallel between the Spanish Bourbons and the Austrian Habsburgs vividly and specifically in a 13 April 1808 memorandum for the Kaiser (in Rössler, *Oesterreichs Kampf*, vol. I, p. 304). Archduke Johann wrote: 'Spain's experience stood clearly before our eyes' (Johann, Archduke of Austria, *Erzherzog Johanns 'Feldzugserzählung' 1809*, ed. Alois Veltzé, Vienna: Seidel & Sohn, 1909, p. 16).

24 Broers, p. 165.

25 Metternich's 30 March 1808 report is printed in Wilhelm Oncken, *Oesterreich und Preussen im Befreiungskriege*, Berlin, 1879, vol. II, pp. 588–92. In any event, Napoleon's intervention in Spain was, in fact, more a case of opportunism than long-term planning. See David G. Chandler, *The Campaigns of Napoleon*, New York: Macmillan, 1966, pp. 594–601; and Gates, pp. 5–7.

26 Both memoranda quoted extensively in Rössler, *Oesterreichs Kampf*, vol. I, pp. 304–5. The quote is from 15 April.

27 Stadion's 15 April memorandum quoted in Criste, *Carl*, vol. II, pp. 433. A slightly different version of this statement ('among his *familial* creatures and generals …') is in Rössler, *Oesterreichs Kampf*, vol. I, p. 305, and Botzenhart, p. 217. Watching the growing inertia towards war, the sceptical in Vienna were disgusted and worried. The 73-year-old Feldmarschall Prince Charles Joseph de Ligne, for example, lamented 'this miserable salon diplomacy of *I think* and *I hope* and this miserable politics based on the hypothesis of *perhaps*! Because this is the grand word: *perhaps* Napoleon will attack us. Why not just let him exhaust himself in the Pyrenees?' (*Fragments de l'Histoire de Ma Vie*, Paris: Plon, 1928, vol. II, p. 170).

28 Charles to Franz, 14 April 1808, in *Ausgewählte Schriften*, vol. VI, p. 292. Noting the sudden shift, Johann recorded 'we leaped from one extreme to the other' (Johann, *Feldzugserzählung*, p. 7).

29 Plans for the establishment of reserve battalions and the Landwehr had been prepared in 1807, materially easing their implementation a year later (see Rainer Wohlfeil, 'Der Volkskrieg im Zeitalter Napoleons', in Wolfgang v. Groote and Klaus-Jürgen Müller (eds), *Napoleon I. und das Militärwesen seiner Zeit*, Freiburg: Rombach, 1968).

30 As Stadion wrote at the time: 'I sought to promote in the Kaiser a confidence in my advice which would earn me an influence over him that I could exert on the most important issues.' No issue was more important to the foreign minister than the coming war with Napoleon. Quoted in Vann, p. 300.

31 Gunther E. Rothenberg, *Napoleon's Great Adversaries: The Archduke Charles and the Austrian Army 1792–1814*, Bloomington: Indian University Press, 1982, p. 121.

In contrast to the vast outpouring of German-language propaganda, only a few pamphlets were translated into Czech; Hungarians and other nationalities were almost completely ignored.

32   From a 27 September 1808 memorandum quoted in Rössler, *Oesterreichs Kampf*, vol. I, p. 380; also his 13 April 1808 note to the Kaiser (Rössler, *Oesterreichs Kampf*, vol. I, p. 305). There is an extensive literature on the question of German nationalism in Austria in the Napoleonic period. As a starting place, see Walter C. Langsam, *The Napoleonic Wars and German Nationalism in Austria*, New York: Columbia University Press, 1930.

33   Stadion's 13 April 1808 memorandum (Rössler, *Oesterreichs Kampf*, vol. I, p. 304).

34   One of the most celebrated pamphlets was an account by the Spanish foreign minister, Don Pedro Cevallos, of the humiliating negotiations in Bayonne (see Peter Rassow, 'Die Wirkung der Erhebung Spaniens auf die deutsche Erhebung gegen Napoleon I', *Historische Zeitschrift*, vol. 167 (1943)). A former French officer returning from Austria in March 1809 specifically mentioned it (letter to Marshal Massena quoted in Edouard Gachot, *1809 Napoléon en Allemagne*, Paris: Plon, 1913, p. 17). Spanish representatives also approached Kaiser Franz with pleas for weapons and political recognition; these requests generated little material or diplomatic support, but the exposure to the Spanish war certainly helped lay the groundwork for Austria's resistance to Napoleon. See, for example, Hannsjoachim W. Koch, *Die Befreiungskriege*, Starnberger See: Türmer, 1987, chapters 6 and 7; Otto W. Johnston, 'The Spanish Guerrillas in German Literature During the Peninsular War', in Alice D. Berkeley (ed.), *New Lights on the Peninsular War*, Almada: The British Historical Society of Portugal, 1991; and Criste, *Carl*, Vol II, pp. 435–6.

35   The German patriot, Ferdinand von Schill, for instance, hoped to turn Stralsund into a 'second Saragossa' when he entered that Baltic port in May 1809 at the head of his small band of insurgents.

36   The French ambassador in Vienna noted 'The affairs of Spain have made a vivid impression on the government' (Andréossy to Champagny, no. 21, 10 June 1808, AE, vol. 381).

37   Stadion to Metternich, 30 June 1808, in Rössler, *Oesterreichs Kampf*, vol. I, p. 331. Stadion was referring to domestic projects ('System'), but the comment shows the tenor of his thinking. One month later, he told the Kaiser: 'the present external circumstances offer us many hopes' (26 July 1808 memorandum in Beer, p. 313).

38   Stadion to Metternich, 8 August 1808, Rössler, *Oesterreichs Kampf*, vol. I, p. 373.

39   Hardenberg to Münster, 8 October 1808, relating a conversation with Stadion (in Paul Hassel, *Geschichte der Preussischen Politik 1807 bis 1815*, Leipzig: Hirzel, 1881, pp. 537–8). See also his 11 October 1808 letter, where he wrote that Austria was approaching Britain for assistance 'in the firm persuasion ... that war is inevitable, and perhaps with the premeditated intention of profiting from the favourable circumstances of the moment by seizing the first pretext to begin it [the war]' (Hassel, pp. 538–9).

40   First quote: Stadion to Feldmarschall-Leutnant Philipp Grünne, 27 September 1808, Rössler, *Oesterreichs Kampf*, vol. I, p. 383. Grünne was Charles's adjutant general. Second quote: Stadion memorandum of 12 October 1808, Rössler, *Oesterreichs Kampf*, vol. I, p. 393. See also *Krieg*, vol. I, p. 57.

41 Andréossy to Champagny, no. 40, 14 August 1808, AE, vol. 381. Andréossy noticed a distinctly offensive theme in Austrian thinking as early as October: reports of 8, 13, and 16 October 1808, nos. 49–51, AE, vol. 381.

42 Rössler avers that Stadion 'decided on war' in September 1808 (Rössler, *Oesterreichs Kampf*, vol. I, p. 377).

43 Metternich might also be considered an 'obstacle' to Stadion's war plans. See below.

44 As Manfried Rauchensteiner observes, Archduke Charles 'represented a political power which could not be bypassed' (*Kaiser Franz und Erzherzog Karl*, Vienna: Verlag für Geschichte und Politik, 1972, p. 83).

45 Stadion to Metternich, 8 and 31 August 1808, Rössler, *Oesterreichs Kampf*, vol. I, pp. 373, 376.

46 Charles to Franz, 14 April 1808, *Ausgewählte Schriften*, vol. VI, p. 292ff.

47 From a letter to Herzog Albert II of Sachsen-Teschen, 20 July 1808, in Hertenberger/Wiltschek, pp. 205–6.

48 Hardenberg, for example, noted Charles's opposition to an offensive war in his 10 September 1808 letter to Münster (Hassel, p. 535). Archduke Johann noted 'the War Department was inclined towards peace up to the end of October and even later' (Johann, *Feldzugserzählung*, p. 13).

49 Briefing to the Kaiser, *Ausgewählte Schriften*, vol. VI, p. 300ff. Rössler argues persuasively that this memorandum, annotated 'January 1809?' in the *Ausgewählte Schriften*, was actually composed in September 1808 (Rössler, *Oesterreichs Kampf*, vol. II, p. 305, note 178). See also a 16 July 1808 letter to Johann: '. . . the attitude of our cousin Ferdinand, who seems to have taken as his credo that the war is on the point of breaking out, does not sit well with me. Let us not imitate the young officers (gens d'armes) and mob of Berlin, or things will end for us as they did there. If the war begins before everything is organised, all that will harm rather than serve us. I beg you not to lose sight of these observations and not to believe that the uprisings in Spain have robbed Napoleon of all his power for the indefinite future' (*Krieg*, vol. I, pp. 55–6). Charles's reliance on a defensive strategy is also evident in a 25 June 1808 memorandum (*Ausgewählte Schriften*, vol. VI, p. 295ff.); this pessimistic document contains no mention whatsoever of offensive action on Austria's part. For other comparisons with 1806 Berlin, see Andréossy, no. 54, 3 December 1808 and Dodun, no. 4, 11 March 1809 (AE, vols 381, 382).

50 Stadion to Grünne, 29 September 1808, Rössler, *Oesterreichs Kampf*, vol. I, p. 383. See Criste, *Carl*, vol. II, p. 450ff. for additional extracts from Grünne's letters (written on Charles's behalf). Grünne also refers to Stadion's frustration with Charles in a letter to Prince de Ligne written the following year during the armistice and published in a Hamburg journal: Grünne to de Ligne, 23 September 1809, copy in the Archives Nationales, *Secrétairerie d'État Impériale: Guerre* [hereafter AN], AF/IV/1639: Campagne d'Autriche.

51 The opinion of Prussia's ambassador, Karl Reichsgraf Finck von Finckenstein, from a letter to Friedrich Wilhelm, 17 September 1808; see also his 27 August 1808 report (both in Hassel, pp. 524, 525).

52 Charles, 'Ein Beitrag zur Geschichte des Krieges zwischen Oesterreich und Frankreich im Jahre 1809', *Ausgewählte Schriften*, vol. VI, p. 357.

53 Criste, *Carl*, vol. II, p. 470; Hertenberger/Wiltschek, p. 207. Recalling the pre-war events in Vienna, the French ambassador wrote that 'Archduke Charles could not resist the tears of the empress and, against his better judgement, agreed to a war whose evil outcome he had foreseen' (in Criste, *Carl*). Maria Ludovica's biographer sheds no light on this issue: Eugen Guglia, *Kaiserin Maria Ludovica*, Vienna: Graeser, 1894. See also Wertheimer, *Geschichte*, vol. II, p. 256. It is worth noting that Charles was not entirely consistent in his attitude towards war in the twelve months between April 1808 and April 1809 (Hertenberger/Wiltschek, p. 210).

54 Grünne to Stadion, 28 September 1808, Rössler, *Oesterreichs Kampf*, vol. I, p. 383. After the war, Grünne wrote that 'the preponderance of generally held opinion turned the war into an affair of honour' and implied that Franz had 'already declared for war' (to Prince de Ligne, 23 September 1809 in AN, AF/IV/1639).

55 'Denkschrift', *Ausgewählte Schriften*, vol. VI, p. 329. Herzog Albert of Sachsen-Teschen recorded similar sentiments in his 'Mémoire sur la Guerre éclatée en 1809 entre l'Autriche et la France et sur les Evénements qui l'ont précédé et amené', Magyar Orszagos Leveltar [hereafter MOL] P300/1/100. Brief quotes are printed in Wertheimer, *Geschichte*, vol. II, p. 259, where Wertheimer paraphrases Albert: Charles came to believe that 'all efforts to stave off war were in vain'. See also a memoir by Carl Friedrich von Lindenau, 'Ausweis über den Stand, die Eintheilung und Stellung der beiderseitigen Armeen im Jahr 1809', MOL, P300/1/98: 'the decision for war was seen as already made, so his objections had become utterly superfluous'.

56 Rauchensteiner, *Franz*, p. 89; Vann, p. 299; also Drimmel, vol. I, p. 265. Much of the following drawn from Vann, pp. 308–10. Dodun also makes this argument in report no. 4, 11 March 1809 (AE, vol. 382).

57 First quote from Johann, *Feldzugserzählung*, pp. 13 and 14; second quote from Vann, p. 306.

58 Franz's notes from 17, 20 and 21 August 1808, cited in Beer, p. 327. See also Finckenstein to Friedrich Wilhelm, 14 May 1808 (Hassel, pp. 517–18).

59 Stadion to Metternich, 11 April 1808 (Botzenhart, p. 218). In autumn 1807, Stadion wrote Metternich: '... you will do the fatherland a great service if you highlight in your reports the danger that threatens us from this direction [France] if we do not act with intelligence and energy' (Rössler, *Stadion*, vol. I, p. 289). The French believed Franz was routinely manipulated by his court and ministers (Andréossy report no. 10, 18 February 1809, AE, vol. 382).

60 Metternich worked to restrain his foreign minister during the spring and summer of 1808; indeed, he believed that Napoleon's empire, at odds with the European system and riven with internal contradictions, would eventually collapse owing to its own inherent weaknesses. War was thus indeed inevitable in his opinion, but the danger was by no means as immediate as Stadion portrayed it and the counter-strategy was completely different. His goal was to preserve and rebuild Austria until such time as the Napoleonic edifice began to crack; with this in mind, he endeavoured to guide Stadion towards a policy of accommodation with France. See Botzenhart's excellent study wherein he effectively destroys the long-standing belief that Metternich was a member of the war party throughout 1808. Metternich finally came round to Stadion's viewpoint in November–December 1808 when he

learned of the extent of Austrian preparations for war (previously kept from him) and saw which way the domestic political-bureaucratic winds were blowing. See also Metternich, *Memoirs*, vol. I, pp. 82–4, 389–91.

61 Johann, *Feldzugserzählung*, p. 8.

62 'Mémoire sur la Guerre éclatée en 1809', MOL, P300/1/100.

63 Metternich to Stadion, 23 June 1808; 1 July 1808, (complete version in Oncken, vol. II, 595); and 2 August 1808, in Metternich, *Memoirs*, vol. II, pp. 215, 221, 231.

64 The Diet also voted 20,000 recruits to fill the Hungarian infantry regiments of the regular army and promised to approve further assistance on short notice in case of war. See Wertheimer, *Geschichte*, vol. II, pp. 286–97.

65 Quote from Prince de Ligne, vol. II, p. 185.

66 See Metternich, *Memoirs*, vol. I, pp. 81–3 and note 29 on p. 390 (this latter is the source for the quotation); as well as Botzenhart, pp. 270–1, 284.

67 Botzenhart, p. 262, 270–1. Andréossy repeatedly used the term 'exasperation' to describe the atmospherics in Vienna (to Champagny no. 52, 14 November; no. 54, 3 December; no. 56, 13 December 1808, AE, vol. 381).

68 'Mémoire sur la Guerre éclatée en 1809', MOL, P300/1/100.

69 Chargé Ivan O. Anstett to Count Alexander Saltykoff, 23 November 1808, in Fedor Martens, *Recueil des Traités et Conventions conclus par la Russie avec les Puissances Etrangères*, St Petersburg, 1876–1908, vol. III, p. 32.

70 The exact sequence of meetings and decisions is poorly recorded. Rössler concludes that the key session was held on either 15 or 17 December; the 23 December conference at Stadion's sickbed appears to have been limited to the subject of Metternich's instructions (Rössler, *Oesterreichs Kampf*, vol. I, pp. 398–9, and vol. II, p. 306). These decisions, however, were not final; Franz continued to vacillate on into the initial weeks of 1809.

71 Stadion's memorandum of 4 December 1808 (Haus-, Hof- und Staatsarchiv [hereafter HHStA], *Vorträge 1808/XII*, Kart. 180).

72 Stadion's memorandum of 4 December 1808 (HHStA, *Vorträge 1808/XII*, Kart. 180), portions quoted in Rössler, *Oesterreichs Kampf*, vol. I, p. 397 and Wertheimer, *Geschichte*, vol. II, p. 262.

73 The memoranda are in Beer, pp. 516–35. Botzenhart provides an excellent summary (pp. 272–81). Note Charles's conviction that Metternich's assessments were coloured by the company he kept in Paris: 'persons of the dissatisfied groups, who viewed everything associated with the government in the most negative light and consequently regarded the regime as weak and easily overthrown' ('Denkschrift', *Ausgewählte Schriften*, vol. VI, p. 328).

74 Botzenhart's trenchant analysis dismantles the arguments of many other historians who have seen these memoranda as crucial to the Austrian decision for war. As he rightly points out: (1) the monarchy was already on a nearly irreversible course toward conflict by November/December 1808, and (2) even in these notes, Metternich continued to discuss the advantages of peace. None the less, many in Vienna would have found in these papers and their optimistic tone important evidence in support of an early venture into war. In presenting the notes to the Kaiser, for example, Stadion gave them a decidedly pro-war cant (see his memorandum of 4 December 1808, HHStA).

75 The Austrian allegation that this proclamation signalled Napoleon's intention to place Joseph on the Habsburg throne was made directly to Napoleon's ambassador in St Petersburg, General Armand Caulaincourt, by the Austrian chargé d'affaires (see Caulaincourt's 15 January 1809 letter to Napoleon in Grand Duke Nicholas Mikhaïlowitch (ed.), *Les Relations Diplomatiques de la Russie et de la France d'aprés les Rapports des Ambassadeurs d'Alexandre et de Napoléon*, St Petersburg, 1905, vol. III, p. 25). The Prussian ambassador, Finckenstein, believed that this proclamation finally pushed Charles into the war faction (Finckenstein's reports of 4 and 21 January 1809, cited in Udo Gaede, *Preussens Stellung zur Kriegsfrage im Jahre 1809*, Hanover: Hahn, 1897, pp. 25–6). See also, Metternich, *Memoirs*, vol. II, p. 311.

76 Rössler, *Oesterreichs Kampf*, vol. I, pp. 385, 397 (Charles to Stadion, 26 November 1808); and the 4 December memo.

77 Metternich to Stadion 26 August (Metternich, *Memoirs*, vol. II, p. 259) and 24 September 1808 (Constantin de Grunwald, 'La Fin d'une Ambassade: Metternich à Paris en 1808–1809', *Revue de Paris*, 1 and 15 October 1937, p. 838); Botzenhart, p. 261; Stadion's 4 December 1808 memo (HHStA).

78 Botzenhart, pp. 250–1; Stadion's 4 December 1808 memo (HHStA).

79 Stadion memorandum of 10 December 1808 (Beer, p. 338).

80 The 'three-decisions' construct from Rössler, *Oesterreichs Kampf*, vol. I, p. 399. See also Botzenhart, p. 271.

81 Botzenhart, p. 272. Andréossy to Champagny, no. 52, 14 November and no. 54, 3 December 1808, AE, vol. 381.

82 Stadion's 13 April 1808 briefing in Rössler, *Oesterreichs Kampf*, vol. I, 307–8.

83 Berlin, being surrounded by French garrisons, was considered too dangerous for King Friedrich Wilhelm III, and he held court in distant Königsberg through most of 1808. It is interesting to note that Stein directed Goetzen to contact Archduke Ferdinand because Charles 'drags everything out' (Stein to Goetzen, 4 or 5 September 1808, in Wladyslaw de Fedorowicz, *1809: Campagne de Pologne*, Paris: Plon, 1911, vol. I, p. 16).

84 For initial Austro-Prussian contacts and the anxiety about the Silesian fortresses, see Rössler, *Oesterreichs Kampf*, vol. I, pp. 372, 378; Beer, p. 353 (Stadion note to Hruby, 29 August 1808); Finckenstein to Friedrich Wilhelm, 18 June 1808 (Hassel, p. 520); and 23 July 1808 instructions for Graf Goetzen (Hassel, pp. 542–3). It is interesting that Hassel (p. 201) describes the instructions prepared for Austria's envoy (Hruby) as 'utterly devoid of substance'.

85 Stein memorandum to King Friedrich Wilhelm III, 11 August 1808 (in Georg Heinrich Pertz, *Das Leben des Ministers Freiherrn vom Stein*, Berlin: Reimer, 1851, vol. II, p. 199ff.). See also note from the foreign minister, Graf August Friedrich von der Goltz, to the king, 24 December 1808 (in Gaede, p. 11–12).

86 Friedrich Wilhelm III, undated memorandum, in Rössler, *Oesterreichs Kampf*, vol. I, 391. As one sample of the dire results the Prussian activists expected: 'If Napoleon is fortunate in Spain and against Austria, he will never let us remain' (Gneisenau, 5 February 1809, in Georg Heinrich Pertz, *Das Leben des Feldmarschalls Grafen Neithardt von Gneisenau*, Berlin: Reimer, 1864, vol. I, p. 464). See also Gaede, pp. 37, 48; Scharnhorst, 8 August 1808, in Pertz, *Stein*, vol. II, p. 197; and Gneisenau's

memoranda in Friedrich Thimme, 'Zu den Erhebungspläne der preussischen Patrioten im Sommer 1808', *Historische Zeitschrift*, vol. 86 (1901).

87 First quote: Friedrich Wilhelm to Baron Schladen (Prussian ambassador to Russia), 30 July 1808, in Hassel, p. 205. Second quote: Scharnhorst to Stein, 23 August 1808, in Pertz, *Stein*, vol. II, pp. 210–11.

88 Friedrich Wilhelm to tsar, 28 August; tsar's reply, 12 September 1808; in Paul Bailleu, *Briefwechsel König Friedrich Wilhelm's III und der Königin Luise mit Kaiser Alexander I.*, Leipzig: Hirzel, 1900, pp. 174–9.

89 The king had no faith in Austria and set impossible preconditions for Prussian action (Max Lehmann, *Scharnhorst*, Leipzig, 1887, vol. II, pp. 188, 253–4, 261; Pertz, *Gneisenau*, vol. I, p. 427; Gaede, p. 58).

90 Prussia's communications with Austria originated from varying sources (the king, Goltz, Stein, Goetzen) and ran through several channels, both routine (Ambassador Finckenstein) and covert (Goetzen et al.). Friedrich Wilhelm's role in all this is uncertain. For example, it is not clear how much of this correspondence had royal authorisation and how much might have been undertaken by Stein and others without the monarch's specific approval. Hardenberg believed these secret contacts were conducted with the king's knowledge, see his letter to Münster, 26 November 1808, in Hassel, pp. 540–2. From Gneisenau's correspondence, however, one develops the distinct impression that the monarch was being kept in the dark about some of the links to Austria (see Chapter III of Karl Griewank, *Gneisenau: Ein Leben in Briefen*, Leipzig: Koehler & Amelang, 1939). Similarly, Lehmann and Gaede point out that Stein often acted 'on his own hook' (Lehmann, vol. II, pp. 193–4; Gaede, pp. 5, 46, 53–4).

91 The Prussian foreign minister as reported by Hruby in a 31 July 1808 letter to Stadion (Beer, pp. 352–3).

92 Goetzen's promises to Bubna from an October meeting on the Silesian border (Bubna's 11 October 1808 report of the meeting in *Mittheilungen des K. K. Kriegs-Archivs*, 1882; also Beer, p. 355; and Hassel, pp. 268–70, 555–6). Goetzen was also involved in cloaking unofficial, covert support for German patriots in Bohemia (Anton Ernstberger, *Die deutschen Freikorps 1809 in Böhmen*, Prague: Volk und Reich, 1942, pp. 44–62).

93 The two Prussian officers, Major Graf Lucey and Hauptmann Karl von Tiedemann, rode off for Vienna in July and October respectively; Lucey was still there in late December. Lucey's initial contacts included Archduke Maximilian d'Este and two of Charles's senior staff officers (Hassel, pp. 268–73, 287–9, 296–7, and Lucey's reports pp. 554–8). Their vague—and unrealistic—planning led even the passionately nationalistic Austrian historian Hellmuth Rössler to comment wryly: 'After these gentlemen had thus completely won the war on paper, Lucey continued with his visits.' Although both Lucey and Tiedemann later met with Charles, Stadion was at first suspicious of Lucey and refused to see him (Rössler, *Oesterreichs Kampf*, vol. I, p. 378). Goetzen referred to their sojourn as unofficial (19 October 1808 to Stein in Pertz, *Gneisenau*, vol. I, p. 435), and Lucey claimed not to have given any indication of Prussian intentions, but his mere appearance in Vienna would have been taken by many as an important signal (see his 30 August 1808 report in Hassel, p. 544ff.). Pertz (p. 431) avers that

Lucey, Tiedemann, and others were to develop specifics for joint operations, but cites no evidence.

94 The key report is 5 December 1808 in which Hruby quoted the Prussian foreign minister as saying: 'His Majesty proposes to do everything possible to elude that engagement [his treaty obligation to France], but if he cannot back out of it at the commencement of the war, he will not fail to join Austria at the first favourable occasion, and it is with this in view, that His Majesty desires timely information as to the plans of your court [Austria] so he may take measures in conformity' (Beer, p. 356). Gaede, however, avers that Hruby erred badly, indeed egregiously, in reporting this conversation with Goltz. The internal Prussian view of the Goltz–Hruby conversation presents a much more reserved position: 'my sentiments of friendship, of confidence, of good neighbourliness, are constantly the same and at every occasion, the side that I will embrace, if circumstances allow me to chose, will be that which corresponds with our mutual interests' (Instructions for Major Graf Heinrich von der Goltz, December 1808, in Gaede, p. 8). Gaede allows that the Prussian foreign minister may have overstepped his brief in talking with Hruby, but thinks this unlikely given Goltz's behaviour in other situations (pp. 8–10). The key here is not so much what Goltz actually relayed in his king's name, but rather the impression Hruby's report left in the minds of his superiors in Vienna (see, for example, Stadion's instructions for Schwarzenberg, 29 January 1809, no. 1, HHStA, *Russland III/36*; Gaede, p. 46).

95 In his 28 August 1808 letter to the tsar, Friedrich Wilhelm wrote 'I do not know Your Imperial Majesty's opinion of the current state of affairs, but in the critical situation in which I find myself, it is important for my tranquillity to understand completely the nature of the current relationship between Your Imperial Majesty and France—and above all to know which side Your Majesty will take in the inevitable case of a war between France and Austria' (Bailleu, *Briefwechsel*, p. 176). See also Goltz to Major Reinhold Otto von Schöler (Friedrich Wilhelm's personal emissary to the tsar), 29 August 1808 (in Hassel, p. 414). One of the Prussian king's most important foreign policy goals was the amelioration of the harsh punitive measures Napoleon had imposed upon his realm in 1807. He counted on the tsar's help in this endeavour, and throughout 1808 Alexander pressed Napoleon to reduce the contributions Prussia was obligated to pay into French coffers; see, for example, Count Peter Tolstoi to Champagny, 22 April 1808 (Bittard des Portes, 'Les Préliminaires de l'Entrevue d'Erfurt', *Revue d'Histoire Diplomatique*, 1890, pp. 106–7), and Caulaincourt to Napoleon, 20 December 1808 (Mikhaïlowitch, vol. III, p. 9).

96 See 15 January and 5 February 1809 letters from Caulaincourt in Mikhaïlowitch, vol. III, pp. 20–32. Also Albert Vandal, *Napoléon et Alexandre Ier*, Paris: Plon, 1918, vol. II, p. 37.

97 Schwarzenberg to Stadion, 15 February 1809, no. 1A, HHStA, *Russland III/9* (parts in Max Duncker, 'Friedrich Wilhelm III. im Jahre 1809', *Preussischer Jahrbücher*, vol. 41 (1878), p. 139). This report, however, also contained some distinctly hopeful phrases; Prussia's ambassador reported that Schwarzenberg was not convinced by the tsar's warnings and was telling Vienna that Russia might alter its course if Austria won a success or two (Schladen's 17 February 1809 report in Gaede, p. 38).

98 Vienna's attitude from Finckenstein's 3 January 1809 report citing discussions with Franz and Stadion (Gaede, p. 17). Schwarzenberg's sudden departure (his Order of the Golden Fleece had to be sent after him) is from Hugo Kerchenawe and Alois Veltzé, *Feldmarschall Karl Fürst zu Schwarzenberg*, Vienna: Gerlach & Wiedling, 1913, p. 86. Stein and others attempted to dissuade the king from undertaking the journey to Petersburg (Hassel, p. 301). It is interesting to note that rumours of Schwarzenberg's appointment came to Andréossy's ears as early as August 1808 (Andréossy to Champagny, no. 37, 2 August 1808, AE, vol. 381).

99 Instructions for Major Goltz, 7 January 1809 (Duncker, p. 139). Similar directions had been issued prior to his departure and he was adjured again on 6 February 1809 (instructions in Gaede, p. 26).

100 Stadion's realisation from a 31 January 1809 letter to Hruby (Wertheimer, *Geschichte*, vol. II, p. 269). Beer (p. 357) states that Goltz presented a draft convention in Vienna, which Kaiser Franz approved. Both Rössler (*Oesterreichs Kampf*, vol. I, p. 408) and Duncker (pp. 138–9) strongly disagree. Duncker argues that there is no indication ('not a single syllable') of a convention in any of Goltz's reports. Nor is there mention of any such convention in Stadion's 29 January 1809 instructions for Schwarzenberg (HHStA, *Russland III/36*, no. 1).

101 From Stadion's 17 January 1809 briefing to the Kaiser in Rössler, *Oesterreichs Kampf*, vol. I, p. 408.

102 Franz to Friedrich Wilhelm III, 31 January 1809 in Beer, p. 478.

103 From 20 February 1809 instructions for Johann Freiherr von Wessenberg, the new Habsburg ambassador to Prussia (in Rössler, *Oesterreichs Kampf*, vol. I, p. 408). See also Stadion's 8 March 1809 letter to Wessenberg in Fedorowicz, p. 40; and 29 January 1809 (no. 1) instructions for Schwarzenberg (HHStA). Goetzen also contributed to Austrian misperceptions by claiming that his king supported the anti-French *Tugendbund* (Anton Ernstberger, 'Oesterreich und der preussische Tugendbund 1809', *Zeitschrift fuer sudetendeutsche Geschichte* (1939)).

104 Wessenberg's 7 March 1809 report from Alfred Ritter von Arneth, *Johann Freiherr von Wessenberg*, Vienna: Braumüller, 1898, vol. I, p. 105. Report by Capitaine Flolard, 31 March 1809, in Herman Granier (ed.), *Berichte aus der Berliner Franzosenzeit 1807–1809*, Leipzig: Hirzel, 1913, pp. 384–7. See also the French ambassador's reports in Alfred Stern, *Abhandlungen und Aktenstücke*, Leipzig: Duncker, 1885, p. 278ff.

105 For a broader reinterpretation of the king's behaviour, see Otto W. Johnston, 'Was the Prussian Monarchy under Friedrich Wilhelm III Vacillating?', paper presented at the Consortium on the Revolutionary Era, March 2006.

106 Gaede, pp. 8–11, 27. Austria was already looking at an advance into Poland as a means of *forcing* Prussia into an alliance (Friedrich Gentz to Stein in Rössler, *Oesterreichs Kampf*, vol. I, p. 410). Bernd von Münchow-Pohl offers a fine analysis of Prussia's situation in *Zwischen Reform und Krieg*, Göttingen: Vandenhoeck & Ruprecht, 1987.

107 Friedrich Wilhelm was aware of the threat to his policies as represented by some of his officers. On 12 March 1809, for example, he sent a firm missive to the firebrand Goetzen warning of the 'disadvantageous and unpredictable consequences' that could result 'if such outbursts are not guided by intelligence and occur at an

inopportune moment'. The king abjured Goetzen to avoid creating an 'explosion from inopportune enthusiasm' and cautioned that he would view those who did not follow his orders as 'irresponsible and punishable'. Friedrich Wilhelm hand-written note to Goetzen, 12 March 1809, quoted in Thomas Stamm-Kuhlmann, *König in Preussens grosser Zeit: Friedrich Wilhelm III., der Melancholiker auf dem Thron*, Berlin: Siedler, 1992, p. 305.

108   Gaede, p. 34. Stuck in Berlin far from the court to which he was accredited, Wessenberg was in an unenviable position for an ambassador, a situation made worse by Hruby's habit of sending reports directly to Vienna without informing Wessenberg. See his complaint to Stadion, 8 March 1809, in Fedorowicz, p. 139.

109   Stadion letters to Wessenberg, 8 March 1809, and Stadion to Archduke Ferdinand, same date (Fedorowicz, p. 140–6). Stadion told the archduke that the news from Königsberg did 'not respond entirely to our expectations'. See also Lehmann, vol. II, p. 245. Gaede summarises the 13 March 1809 note (p. 47).

110   This section compiled from Arneth, pp. 106–11; Duncker, pp. 140–4; Gaede, pp. 30–5, 53–4; Rössler, *Oesterreichs Kampf*, vol. I, pp. 409–12; Wertheimer, *Geschichte*, vol. II, p. 270. See also Münchow-Pohl, pp. 133–42.

111   Wessenberg to Stadion, 7 April 1809 (Fedorowicz, p. 251).

112   From the 13 April 1808 memorandum, Rössler, *Oesterreichs Kampf*, vol. I, pp. 309–10.

113   Stadion's opening to Russia in July 1808 suggested Austria would recognise Russia's possession of the Danubian Principalities (Moldavia and Wallachia, with the exception of Little Wallachia). See letter from Prince Alexander Kurakin (Russian ambassador in Vienna) to Alexander, 14 July 1808, in *Vneshniaia Politika Rossii*, Moscow, 1965, vol. IV, pp. 291–5 [hereafter *VPR*]; Alexander's reply to Kurakin, 26 August 1808, *VPR*, vol. IV, p. 315. In a separate note the same day, the tsar admonished Kurakin not to make any commitments to Austria: 'I desire that you apply yourself with extreme care not to engage me in anything' (*VPR*, vol. IV, p. 316).

114   By September, Stadion even began to profess that Austria alone could withstand the *combined* efforts of France and Russia, given that both of those powers were constrained by their military commitments elsewhere (Rössler, *Oesterreichs Kampf*, vol. I, p. 380). Several months later, Tsar Alexander asked the Austrian ambassador: 'if France alone is already a formidable enemy for Austria, to what dangers shall she not be exposed if she forces me to draw my sword against her in consequence of the engagements I have established with the Emperor Napoleon and which I have not hidden from the Emperor of Austria?' (Alexander's account of his initial discussion with Schwarzenberg in Alexander to Rumiantsev, 14 February 1809, *VPR*, vol. IV, p. 493).

115   Among numerous statements of this policy, see Alexander to Kurakin, 2 October 1808, and Alexander to Rumiantsev, 14 February 1809 (*VPR*, vol. IV, pp. 351, 493).

116   Alexander to Kurakin, 8 September 1808 (*VPR*, vol. IV, p. 331). Hardenberg reported that Kurakin had made 'strong representations against all measures that could lead to a rupture with France' on 10 September 1808 after receiving a courier from St Petersburg (Hardenberg to Münster, 17 September 1808, Hassel, p. 535ff.). See also Schladen to Friedrich Wilhelm, 3 September 1808, and Schöler to

Friedrich Wilhelm, 7 September 1808: 'haste would therefore be a great, indeed the greatest mistake, as Emperor Napoleon, with his customary speed, would give up Spain and fall upon Austria'. Furthermore, the Prussian envoys used these letters to report the Tsar's disapproval of Goetzen's activities (Hassel, pp. 415–16).

117 Alexander to Kurakin, 26 October 1808 (*VPR*, vol. IV, p. 386). See also *Krieg*, vol. I, p. 61; and Wertheimer, *Geschichte*, vol. II, pp. 263–4.

118 Alexander to Maria Feodorovna, 5 September 1808 in Alan Palmer, *Alexander I*, New York: Harper & Row, 1974, p. 157. He later told Schwarzenberg the same thing: 'a propitious day for vengeance will come' (Schwarzenberg to Stadion, 15 February 1809, no. 1C, HHStA). General Ludwig von Wolzogen, a German who had taken service with the tsar, was in St Petersburg and noted 'relations between the court of the dowager and the court of the tsar were not always characterised by perfect harmony as the former enjoyed involving herself in things that the latter wanted to keep to himself', in *Memoiren des königlich preussischen Generals der Infanterie Ludwig von Wolzogen*, Leipzig: Wigand, 1851, p. 49.

119 Quotes from Schwarzenberg to Stadion, 15 February 1809, no. 1C, HHStA. Alexander had no faith in the Austrian army and feared a repeat of the 1805 debacle; specifically telling Schwarzenberg that the Austrians would collapse before Russian succour could reach the theatre of war (Schwarzenberg to Stadion, 28 February 1809, no. 2A, HHStA). Correspondingly, the tsar regarded Napoleon's military talents with awe (in addition to the two reports cited above, see those of 3 March, 21 March, and 15 April). On 15 April 1809, Schwarzenberg also wrote to his wife that the Russians were terrified of Napoleon: 'the idea of opposing his designs seems gigantic to them' (Carl Fürst zu Schwarzenberg, *Briefe des Feldmarschalls Fürst zu Schwarzenberg an seine Frau*, Vienna: Gerlach & Wiedling, 1913, p. 167).

120 Schwarzenberg to Stadion, 15 February, no. 1C, and 3 March, no. 3A, HHStA. See also Lefebvre, vol. IV, pp. 36–7, 47; Palmer, p. 155. At Erfurt (September 1808), Napoleon attempted to enlist the tsar in a joint démarche to Vienna; Russia and France should threaten to break off diplomatic relations if Franz failed to disarm and recognise the new kings of Spain and Naples (Joseph Bonaparte and Joachim Murat respectively); Alexander demurred (Vandal, vol. I, pp. 431–5, 485–7).

121 Alexander to his foreign minister, Count Nikolai Rumiantsev, 10 February 1809 (Vandal, vol. II, p. 39). Two months earlier, he had written: 'The great goal, that is preventing Austria from attacking France and provoking a general conflagration, has been attained' (Alexander to Rumiantsev, 18 December 1808, Vandal, vol. I, p. 486). The tsar repeatedly adjured his ministers to avoid committing him to Austria or nourishing Austrian hopes of Russian neutrality (Alexander to Kurakin, 26 August 1808 and Rumiantsev to Kurakin, 14 February 1809, *VPR*, vol. IV, pp. 316, 497).

122 It is worth noting that Stadion was wholly Machiavellian in his approach to Russia. He was quite prepared to incite Sweden and the Ottoman Empire to greater efforts against the tsar should Alexander demonstrate any intention to menace Austria (see Rössler, *Oesterreichs Kampf*, vol. I, p. 414; Rössler, *Stadion*, vol. I, pp. 318–19; and Stadion to Wessenberg, 20 February 1809, in Fedorowicz, p. 95). As part of this plan, London would also be requested to urge Russia's foes to increased activity

(Instructions for Wallmoden, 29 January 1809, HHStA, *Russland III/36*; parts in Wertheimer, *Geschichte*, vol. II, p. 273; see also Wagner's instructions in Fedorowicz, p. 67ff). Additionally, Schwarzenberg carried authorisation to threaten the tsar if Russia proved recalcitrant; if necessary, he was to ascribe to Archduke Ferdinand's force in Galicia a strength of 120,000 men, to promise Austrian support for Turkey, and to hint at the restoration of Poland (Stadion to Schwarzenberg, 4 April 1809, HHStA, *Russland III/36*; Beer, p. 351).

123 For Stadion's view, see letters to Wessenberg (20 February, 8 March, and 21 April 1809) in Fedorowicz, pp. 95, 140–1, 322; and Rössler, *Oesterreichs Kampf*, vol. I, p. 395. Pertz, *Stein* (vol. II, pp. 227–9), discusses Stein's briefing in detail. it is also mentioned in Lefebvre, vol. IV, pp. 44–5 and Palmer, pp. 157–8. General von Wolzogen (p. 50) comments that 'the Russians also wanted Austria to be victorious, and one can say that ... a veritable fermentation in favour of Austria dominated among the public'—by which term he meant, of course, the social elites among whom he travelled.

124 Kurakin's reports from Vienna during July to October 1808 in *VPR*, vol. IV, pp. 291–394. Quote from Kurakin to Rumiantsev, 28 August 1808, *VPR*, vol. IV, p. 320; Stadion replied 'then we can await developments tranquilly'.

125 Anstett to Saltykoff, 23 November 1808 in Martens, *Recueil*, vol. III, p. 32.

126 Rössler, *Oesterreichs Kampf*, vol. I, p. 310 (citing Stadion to Metternich, 11 April and 29 May 1808).

127 Wolzogen, p. 50.

128 From a 3 March 1809 letter to Stadion appended to no. 3B, HHStA. See also Schwarzenberg's letters to his wife in Schwarzenberg, pp. 163–72. Roger de Damas, one of the more prominent French émigrés in Vienna, recorded on 4 April 1809 that one of Schwarzenberg's couriers had arrived the preceding day: 'The news appears satisfying, but I do not share this view; I am inquiet. Russia continues to counsel the court in Vienna not to make war ... it shows, it is true, a desire to preserve its neutrality ... [but] it makes no promises. I find nothing reassuring in this manner of expression' (*Mémoires*, Paris: Plon, 1912–14, vol. II, p. 92). Similarly, on 6 April, Archduke Joseph wrote: 'that it [Russia] will take an active part in the conflict to our benefit is hardly to be hoped' (Joseph to Franz, 6 April 1809, in *Jozsef nador irasi (Palatin Josefs Schriften)*, ed. Sandor Domanovszky, Budapest: n.p., 1935, p. 436).

129 Schwarzenberg to Stadion, 3 March 1809, no. 3A, HHStA.

130 Stadion memo of 27 February 1809, in *Krieg*, vol. I, p. 64. He also sought support from the strongly anti-French Russian community in Vienna (Andréossy to Champagny, 15 January 1809, AE, vol. 382).

131 Schwarzenberg to Franz, 21 April 1809, with a cover letter from the tsar (Gustav Just, *Politik oder Strategie?*, Vienna: Seidel & Sohn, 1909, pp. 69–70).

132 Friedrich Heller von Hellwald, *Der Feldzug des Jahres 1809 in Süddeutschland*, Vienna: Carl Gerold's Sohn, 1864, p. 231.

133 Report from British agent Charles Stuart to George Canning, 12 April 1809, no. 3 (Public Records Office/Foreign Office [hereafter PRO/FO] 342/2). The French embassy also reported continuing faith in Russian loyalty (Dodun, reports: 1, 2, 5, 6, 11; AE, vol. 382).

134 First quote from Canning's 15 June 1808 speech to Parliament, second from a 10 June 1808 letter to the British agent in Stockholm (both cited in John M. Sherwig, *Guineas and Gunpowder*, Cambridge, MA: Harvard University Press, 1969, p. 197).

135 Much of the communication between Vienna and London passed through an odd channel: the residual ministers of Hanover. Left in place when Napoleon erased their state, Graf August von Hardenberg in Vienna and Graf Ernst von Münster-Ledenburg in London conducted a lively correspondence that apparently excited little French interest. See Charles S. B. Buckland, *Metternich and the British Government from 1809 to 1813*, London: Macmillan, 1932, pp. 31–4; and Wertheimer, *Geschichte*, vol. II, p. 271.

136 See Canning's famous lines to John H. Frere, 10 December 1808 (in William F. P. Napier, *History of the War in the Peninsula*, London: Constable, 1992, vol. II, p. 616) and 19 April 1809 (in Rory Muir, *Britain and the Defeat of Napoleon 1807–1815*, New Haven, CT: Yale, 1996, p. 94).

137 Rössler, *Oesterreichs Kampf*, vol. I, p. 414. An early English overture, vague and tentative, was a 3 August 1808 letter from Lord Granville Leveson Gower to Stadion cited in Rössler, *Oesterreichs Kampf*, vol. I, pp. 311–12; see also Münster's 5 August 1808 letter to Hardenberg, wherein he discusses this missive and Canning's intentions (Hassel, pp. 533–5). The letter was delivered in great secrecy by Britain's confidential agent to Austria, J. M. Johnston (see Finckenstein's report of 17 September 1808 in Hassel, p. 526). Another avenue was through Robert Adair, the British envoy to the Ottomans. Formerly ambassador in Vienna, the energetic and imaginative Adair corresponded with Stadion (and later Hardenberg as well) through the summer and autumn of 1808 and was authorised to negotiate with Austria in his new post as soon as a general treaty was signed. In his initial letter, Adair told the Austrian minister that 'our dispositions towards you remain the same' and that he was 'authorised to furnish the most satisfactory proofs' (Adair to Stadion, 26 June 1808, in Robert Adair, *The Negotiations for the Peace in the Dardanelles in 1808–9*, London: Longman, Brown, Green, and Longman, 1845, vol. I, p. 8–9). Canning sent a message through Sicilian diplomatic channels on 1 November 1808 offering general support to Austria in the case of a new struggle with France, but remained sceptical of Vienna's intentions (Muir, p. 82)—see below.

138 'Substance of a Communication', Vienna, 11 October 1808, PRO/FO 7/89. Key elements published in Hassel, pp. 538–9. Sherwig calls it 'breathtaking' (p. 208); see also Muir, p. 82.

139 Canning to Adair, 2 December 1808, PRO/FO 78/60.

140 'Answer to the Austrian Government', 24 December 1808, PRO/FO 7/89. Canning expressed similar sentiments in a 20 April 1809 letter to Wallmoden (PRO/FO 7/90); see also Münster to Hardenberg, 23 December 1808 (Wertheimer, *Geschichte*, vol. II, p. 274). Note that Stadion tried to prompt British military intervention by invoking the effect such a move would have on *Denmark*, suggesting that a landing in northern Germany or a naval demonstration off the Danish coast would prevent Danish troops from intervening on the Danube (Stadion to Starhemberg, 15 April 1809, Fedorowicz, pp. 286–7).

141 Canning to Adair, 20 December 1808, PRO/FO 78/60.

142 The other actor in this little drama was Commander Alvaro Ruffo, the Sicilian envoy in Vienna. Tracking the relevant correspondence is rather torturous. The original letter from London to Vienna is Castelcicala to Ruffo, 1 November 1808 (PRO/FO 70/35). Ruffo received this on 5 January 1809 and met with Stadion twice during the following several days. Ruffo reported these meetings in letters to Castelcicala dated 7 and 8 January 1809, but these did not reach London until 30 March(!) as relayed in Castelcicala to Canning, 31 March 1809 (PRO/FO 70/37). Ruffo also wrote to his own foreign minister, Tommaso di Somma, Marquis of Circello, in Palermo on 10 January, and Circello dutifully shared this report with the British crown's representative, Joseph C. Mellish, recounting in the process Ruffo's rather unproductive interviews with Stadion: Mellish to Canning, no. 22, 27 February 1809 (PRO/FO 70/33). This interaction is outlined in Piers Mackesy, *The War in the Mediterranean 1803–1810*, Westport, CT: Greenwood, 1981, pp. 306, 308.

143 Stadion's 28 January 1809 instructions for Wagner are printed in Fedorowicz, p. 67ff. Wagner's 12 March 1809 note to the British government (PRO/FO 7/90) speaks much of subsidies and outlines the general results Austria hoped to achieve, but had only a few vague remarks to make on military operations (continued British effort in Spain, requests for assistance in Italy, request for diversion at the mouths of the Weser in Germany).

144 Sherwig, pp. 208–11; Wertheimer, *Geschichte*, vol. II, pp. 271–8. Wagner and Wallmoden arrived in London on 12 and 28 March respectively. Wallmoden travelled via Malta and from thence aboard HMS *Success* (Gentz to Stein, 17 April 1809 in Pertz, *Stein*, vol. II, p. 362). Wagner was unaccountably delayed on the north German coast: although he reached Hamburg on 8 February, he did not depart for Britain until 2 or 3 March (Wagner to Bankhaus Arnstein & Eskeles, 10 February, 13 February, and 2 March 1809, HHStA, *England: Varia*, K. 13, Konv. 1809).

145 'Observations sur une Coopération Austro-Britannique', 15 April 1809, in Fedorowicz, p. 282. This was part of the instructions for Austria's new ambassador to the Court of St James, Fürst Ludwig von Starhemberg. Stadion made similar points in a March 1809 letter to Wallmoden in London (PRO/FO 7/90); my thanks to the graciousness of the late Mrs Jane Hoyle for locating this item on my behalf.

146 Stuart wrote that because Stadion was 'aware of the eclat and bad consequences which might arise from the communication of this Letter to those Members of the Cabinet who are not so staunch as himself, he determined to suppress the whole & merely to make known the general substance to the Emperor and his Council', in Stuart to Canning, 12 April 1809, no. 2 (PRO/FO 342/2); and reports from Hardenberg (8 and 11 March 1809) in Wertheimer, *Geschichte*, vol. II, p. 274. See also Rössler, *Oesterreichs Kampf* I, p. 379ff., where he quotes Stadion on 27 September 1808 arguing the necessity of delaying the opening of the war until spring 1809. The 11 October 1808 communications to Münster and the British government also mention Stadion's desire to wait until spring (Hassel, p. 539 and PRO).

147 Adair's 26 June 1808 missive, Gower's of 3 August and Canning's 1 November letter through the Sicilians seem to have been the only British encouragements and they were imprecise and indirect at best (see note above); indeed, Stadion complained

to Adair that he would have preferred 'a more precise explanation ... respecting the dispositions of the British Government towards Austria', and also regarding the 'proofs' which Adair had mentioned in the 26 June letter (Adair to Canning, 18 November 1808, in Adair, vol. II, p. 120; and Adair to Canning, 10 November 1808, PRO/FO 78/63).

148 As of 15 April, when he was preparing the instructions for Starhemberg, Stadion was clearly unsure of British support in Germany (see instructions for Starhemberg in Fedorowicz, pp. 279–86 and letter to Starhemberg, pp. 286–7). Rössler states that Wagner brought home a promise of British military support, specifically, that an expeditionary force would be landed at the mouth of the river Weser in late May; he offers no evidence, however, to support this assertion (*Oesterreichs Kampf*, vol. I, p. 421, vol. II, p. 11). As late as 20 April 1809, however, Canning was still telling Wallmoden that any plans for military co-operation would have to be referred to 'a more particular discussion' in the future (Canning to Wallmoden, 20 April 1809, PRO/FO 7/90). In the absence of confirmatory documentation, it seems highly unlikely that Canning, or any other British official, would have given Wagner a firm commitment on British military action in Germany at this early stage. No extant report from Wagner has been located, despite diligent searching by the courteous staffs of the HHStA and Kriegsarchiv.

149 Canning to Bathurst, no. 1, 16 February 1809, PRO/FO 7/88.

150 Canning told Stuart that his appearance in Austria had caused 'great inconvenience'. Having made his journey to Austria 'without the authority or knowledge' of his government, Canning ordered him to return at once (Canning to Stuart, 13 May 1809, PRO/FO 342/2). Stuart was indiscreet in discussing funding options as demonstrated by Stadion's 15 April 1809 instructions for Starhemberg (in Fedorowicz, p. 280). Stuart reached Vienna on 6 April from Cadiz; Bathurst landed at Trieste on the 19th and reached the Austrian capital a week later. J. M. Johnston, another British representative, was already in Vienna and had reported pessimistically and inaccurately in January 1809 that the Austrians were unlikely to undertake anything serious. Yet another Englishman, Alexander Horn, had established himself in Prague and a further agent (Janson) made his way to the Tyrol to help foment unrest there. See Buckland, especially pp. 42–3; Koch, p. 255; Mackesy, p. 309.

151 Hardenberg to Münster, 3 December 1808, in Wertheimer, *Geschichte*, vol. II, p. 271. Still, many Germans expected English intervention as soon as Austria moved (Friedrich Thimme, 'Die hannoverschen Aufstandspläne im Jahre 1809 und England', *Zeitschrift des Historischen Vereins für Niedersachsen* (1897), p. 286).

152 Specifically, General Stuart sent a letter to the Sicilian court on 4 December 1808 suggesting 'the advantage which could result if, during the negotiations then in train in Vienna, that court were informed of my dispositions to act in conformity with the authority I was going to receive' (Stuart to de La Tour, 16 April 1809, in Giuseppe Gallavresi and Victor Sallier de La Tour de Cordon, *Le Maréchal Sallier de La Tour*, Turin: Bocca, 1917, p. 89). Also Mellish to Canning, no. 13, 31 December 1808 in PRO/FO 70/33; and Collingwood to Mulgrave, 17 March 1809, in *Selection from the Public and Private Correspondence of Vice-Admiral Lord Collingwood*, New York: Carvill, 1829, [hereafter *Collingwood*] p. 370. In the event, the British

commanders in the Mediterranean received no specific instructions to assist Austria until July. Although many in Britain were attracted to the idea of action in Italy, from the British cabinet's perspective, problems of distance and the reluctance to commit the army made major activity in this theatre distinctly unappealing. See Mackesy, pp. 301, 313.

153 Stadion's quote from 'Observations sur une Coopération Austro-Britannique', 15 April 1809, in Fedorowicz, p. 283. Stuart to Castlereagh, 27 April 1809, in Gallavresi/de La Tour, pp. 91–2. Note that Adair apparently wrote to Vienna in mid-November urging Austria to 'concert immediately with Sir John Stuart the plan of campaign for Italy'; he simultaneously informed Canning and Stuart of his actions (Adair to Stuart and Adair to Canning, both 18 November 1808, in Adair, vol. II, pp. 119–21).

154 See Collingwood, pp. 365–72; and Joseph Freiherr von Helfert, Königin Karolina von Neapel und Sicilien, Vienna: Braumüller, 1878, p. 373. The first Austrian communication to Collingwood was a 20 April 1809 letter from Johann; an example of both the tyranny of distance and Austrian dilatoriness, the letter did not reach the admiral until mid-June! (Collingwood to Johann, 22 June 1809, Collingwood, p. 391). At Stadion's request, Adair also transmitted Vienna's desire for naval support in the Adriatic to Collingwood, but his letter was not dispatched until 27 April, only days before Johann's forces were ordered to withdraw from Italy entirely (Adair, vol. II, 159).

155 The Austrian representative to Sardinia, Oberstlieutenant Chevalier de St Ambroise, reached Caligari around the same time, but became discouraged and soon departed—before the first letter from de La Tour had even reached him! De La Tour, however, was the principal envoy to both courts and corresponded directly with Sardinia's King Victor Emmanuel from Palermo, leaving his courier, a Hauptmann Bertina, in Caligari as Vienna's representative. See Gallavresi/de La Tour. Note that St Ambroise had apparently travelled to Sardinia in November 1808 (Johann, Feldzugserzählung, p. 14; and Joseph Hormayr, Das Heer von Innerösterreich, Leipzig: Brockhaus, 1817, p. 13), but if so, he could hardly have conducted any substantive planning as Austria's own intentions were still being debated in Vienna. Austrian agents were also sent to Liguria, Dalmatia, and Albania (Johann, Feldzugserzählung, p. 19), and Vienna attempted to enlist British assistance in these areas as well (Adair to Captain William Leake, 29 April 1809, Adair, vol. II, p. 161).

156 Stuart to the Sicilian Court, 22 April 1809, and Stuart to Castlereagh, 27 April 1809 (Gallavresi/de La Tour, pp. 91–2, 98). Also Mackesy, pp. 317, 324–6; Desmond Gregory, Sicily: The Insecure Base, Rutherford: Fairleigh Dickinson University Press, 1988, p. 75. On de La Tour's ignorance of the 4 December offer, de La Tour to Stadion, 8 May 1809 (Gallavresi/de La Tour, p. 104).

157 Quote from de La Tour's letter to the Sicilian court, undated, in Gallavresi/de La Tour, pp. 80–2; parts quoted in Sir Henry Bunbury, A Narrative of Military Transactions in the Mediterranean 1805–1810, London: Boone, 1851, p. 162. Stuart learned of the Austrian's arrival on 29 March 1809, de La Tour met with one of Stuart's subordinates on 3 April, went to see Stuart in Messina on the 11th, and sent his first direct letter to the British general on the 13th (Stuart to Castlereagh, 14 April 1809, de La Tour to Stuart, 13 April 1809, de La Tour to Stadion, 8

May 1809, all in Gallavresi/de La Tour, pp. 83–104). For the Austrian desire for simultaneous offensive operations in the north and south of Italy, see Stadion's 3 March instructions to de La Tour; Laval Nugent to de La Tour, 6 March; and Archduke Johann to de La Tour, 4 April 1809, all in Gallavresi/de La Tour, pp. 68–83.

158 See instructions for Leutnant Wagner in Fedorowicz, pp. 67–73. The extraordinary difficulties of communicating between London and the Mediterranean have already been mentioned. Rössler's contention that in early 1809 'the English government ... promised to support the Austrian army in Italy by an expedition to Naples in combination with the Bourbon King of Sicily and the King of Sardinia' is wildly misleading (Rössler, *Oesterreichs Kampf*, vol. I, p. 415); as Bunbury, de La Tour, Gregory, and Mackesy clearly demonstrate, the English leaders in the Mediterranean and their Sicilian allies debated courses of action until June of 1809.

159 Stadion did not send new instructions to his representative in Spain until 1 April 1809 and even then saw no purpose in requesting negotiations for a formal alliance. Stadion did not trust the junta's envoy in Vienna, Don Diego de la Quadra (who in the space of one year had managed to transform himself from the Bourbon ambassador to Joseph Napoleon's representative to the central junta's agent), and rejected a December 1808 offer to negotiate an alliance; the new Spanish emissary, Don Eusebio de Bardaxi y Azara, did not reach Trieste until 19 April. For Vienna's approaches to Spain, see Rössler, *Stadion*, vol. I, p. 318.

160 Rössler, *Stadion*, vol. I, p. 318. As related in his memoirs, Crossard had a rather grandiose appreciation of his mission: to reorganise the entire Spanish war effort! (*Mémoires Militaires et Historiques*, Paris: Migneret, 1829, vol. III). The instructions for Wagner and Wallmoden included requests for additional British pressure in Spain (see also Wagner's 12 March 1809 note to the British government; PRO/FO 7/90).

161 From a 10 January 1807 letter to Grünne quoted in Criste, *Carl*, vol. II, pp. 434–5.

162 Quotations taken from Stadion's correspondence as follows: 13 April 1808 memo, undated (February 1809) memo, 3 October 1808 letter to Grünne, 25 August 1808 memorandum, 4 December 1808 memorandum, 27 September 1808 memorandum. The memoranda are from HHStA and Rössler, *Oesterreichs Kampf*, vol. I, pp. 314, 380, 499. The letter to Grünne is quoted in Criste, *Carl*, vol. II, p. 451. In his 27 September 1808 briefing to the Kaiser, Stadion wrote 'the developments in Spain, as well as the recent excesses of the French troops in Germany, have inflamed many minds, especially in northern Germany, and generally raised the idea of an insurrection against the French yoke' (in *Krieg*, vol. I, p. 59).

163 Goetzen to Stadion, 22 December 1808 in Rudolf Vaupel (ed), *Das Preussische Heer von Tilsiter Frieden bis zur Befreiung*, Leipzig: Hirzel, 1938, vol. I, pp. 825–6. On the Tugendbund and Austria, see Ernstberger, 'Tugendbund'. For Friedrich Stadion's reports on conditions in Bavaria, see Eduard Wertheimer, 'Berichte des Grafen Friedrich Lothar Stadion ueber die Beziehungen zwischen Oesterreich und Baiern (1807–1809)', *Archiv für österreichische Geschichte*, vol. 63 (1882). Quotes here are taken from letters of 7 August and 12 October 1808. For the behaviour of Bavaria's callow Crown Prince Ludwig, see especially the letters of 20 September and 18 December 1808 along with those of 15 January and 22 February 1809. Some

fiery extracts from Friedrich Stadion's correspondence are in Rössler, *Oesterreichs Kampf*, vol. I, pp. 417–18.

164 Dörnberg's plan on going to Vienna is from Rössler, *Oesterreichs Kampf*, vol. I, pp. 419–20. Metternich's report on this discussion with Talleyrand (who certainly maintained his own private agenda!) is in Metternich to Stadion, 11 January 1809, no. 1/I (HHStA, *Frankreich: Berichte 1809*, Kart. 205).

165 In the 27 September 1808 memorandum, Stadion wrote 'The time may be very near when we will be in a position to make use of such [anti-French] sentiment and to stoke the fire glowing under the ashes; and I am already busying myself with how, given such conditions, I can locate apt people for such an undertaking' (in Wertheimer, *Geschichte*, vol. II, p. 267, and *Krieg*, vol. I, p. 59). Austrian Hauptmann Paulsen met with Prussian patriots in late February (Wertheimer, *Geschichte*, vol. II, p. 404); Wessenberg established similar contacts and, according to Rössler, supplied Major Schill with substantial funds (Rössler, *Stadion*, vol. II, p. 35).

166 Philipp to Friedrich Stadion, 21 April 1809, in Rössler, *Oesterreichs Kampf*, vol. I, p. 422.

167 The treaties were signed on 25 February (Braunschweig) and 20 March 1809 (Hesse-Kassel); they are printed in Ernstberger, *Freikorps*, pp. 407–14.

168 Memorandum attributed to Friedrich Stadion: 'Allgemeine Gesichtspunkte über den bevorstehenden Krieg in Beziehung auf Deutschland' (printed in August Fournier, 'Oesterreichs Kriegsziele im Jahre 1809', *Beiträge zur neueren Geschichte Oesterreichs*, vol IV (December 1908)). Parts in Rössler, *Oesterreichs Kampf*, vol. I, p. 507.

169 Rudolf von Katte, 'Der Streifzug des Friedrich Karl von Katte auf Magdeburg im April 1809', *Geschichts-Blätter für Stadt und Land Magdeburg*, vol 70/71 (1935/6), pp. 17, 22. Non-Prussians also heartily mistrusted Königsberg's intentions (Thimme, 'Hannoverschen', p. 309).

170 For the efforts of Prussian and other German patriots to enlist English support, see PRO/FO 64/80; Thimme, 'Hannoverschen'; and Alfred Stern's excellent piece, 'Gneisenau's Reise nach London im Jahre 1809 und ihre Vorgeschichte', *Historische Zeitschrift*, vol. 85 (1900). Kleist was dedicated and persistent but also unreliable and passionately furtive; old General Blücher called him 'a complete joker', histrionic, egoistic, untrustworthy and deeply in debt. He seems to have enjoyed the hugger-mugger of clandestine activity at high levels—as a British observer commented, his meetings with Canning 'had made him giddy' (Stern, 18).

171 General von Hüser, quoted in August Fournier, 'Zur Geschichte des Tugendbundes', *Historische Studien und Skizzen*, 1st series (1885), p. 328.

172 Wohlfeil in Groote, pp. 121–2. Thimme, 'Hannoverschen', especially p. 301.

173 Heinrich Zschokke, *Der Krieg Oesterreichs gegen Frankreich und den rheinischen Bund im Jahre 1809*, Aarau: Remigius, 1810, p. 29. Other contemporaries made similar observations; for example: 'Despite the dissatisfaction with which most Germans bore the yoke which the turbulent times had laid upon them, the expectations of the Austrian court were far too premature' (Johann Gottfried von Pahl, a Württemberger writing under the pseudonym Alethinos, *Der Krieg in Deutschland im Jahre 1809 und dessen Resultate politisch und militärisch betrachtet*, Munich: Lentner, 1810, p. 131). Even writing three decades later when he could give

vent to his anti-Napoleon sentiments, Pahl conceded that the reliance on German insurrection was 'not well chosen', though he differentiated between two types of possible German reaction: 'Those German subjects, however, who had not suffered the misfortune of losing their old regimes, rather had retained their old dynasties, were completely unreceptive to calls for rebellion' (*Denkwürdigkeiten aus meinem Leben und aus meiner Zeit*, Tübingen: Fues, 1840, p. 605).

174 Quoted from an anonymous memoir in the Austrian military archives; published in Criste, *Carl*, vol. II, p. 615ff. Among other unflattering references, the angry author referred to Stadion as '... the petty minister, who calculated so poorly ...'

175 *Beobachtungen und historische Sammlung wichtiger Ereignisse aus dem Kriege zwischen Frankreich, dessen Verbündeten und Oesterreich im Jahr 1809*, Weimar: Landes-Industrie Comptoir, 1809, p. 34. The anonymous author also confirms the Austrian officer's assessment: 'The Austrian statesmen still seemed incapable of coping with the human character of the Germans ... how could one hope that the ruling families of Bavaria, Württemberg, Baden, etc., who were tied to the Napoleonic dynasty by the interests of state and by family bonds, would suddenly rise up in hostility against this? Why did they delude themselves, their army and their people with this vain hope, and what did they hope to achieve thereby?'

176 *Krieg*, vol. I, p. 64. This portion of the Austrian official history was written by Oskar Criste, an admirer of Archduke Charles (he authored, for example, the fine three-volume biography cited above); on the other hand, another contributor to this history, Max Ritter von Hoen, drew the opposite conclusion: 'One cannot argue that the diplomacy of Minister Stadion provided insufficient preparation for the war' (in '1809. Ein Gedenkblatt zur Jahrhundertfeier des grossen Krieges', *Streffleurs österreichische militärische Zeitschrift* [hereafter ÖMZ], vol. I, no. 1 (January 1909)). See also Münchow-Pohl's insightful comments, pp. 83–8, 143–5.

177 It is useful to turn once more to Prince de Ligne for a cogent observation made during the days immediately prior to the war: 'What nonsense at my meals every day! They say Napoleon is frightened; counter-revolution in France; rebellion throughout the empire; English landings everywhere; rise of 30,000 Hessians; neutrality or alliance with Russia will choke both emperors [meaning that some believed Austria would also take on Russia if it did not ally with Vienna]; junction with Karageorge [Serbian patriot]; battle of the Turks; the Prussians with us ... who knows what! All of this supported by fools and by a single man of spirit who, abhorring Napoleon, wants all of Europe to be his infernal machine even at the risk of overturning it' (*Fragments*, vol. II, pp. 174–5).

CHAPTER 2: WHAT DO THEY INTEND?

1 The title and some of this chapter are drawn from a paper presented to the Consortium on Revolutionary Europe in 1996: John H. Gill 'What Do They Intend? Austrian War Aims in 1809', Consortium on Revolutionary Europe, *Selected Papers 1996*, ed. Charles Crouch, Kyle O. Eidahl and Donald D. Horward, Tallahassee: Florida State University, 1996, pp. 295–302.

2 Gräfin Lulu Thürheim, diary entry for 27 January 1809, quoted in Criste, *Carl*, vol. II, p. 456. Eduard Wertheimer presents much evidence for the enthusiasm

in Vienna; the Papal nuncio, for example, reported to the Vatican on 28 January 1809 that 'The aspect of this capital is now totally military' (in his article: 'Zur Geschichte Wiens im Jahre 1809', *Archiv für österreichische Geschichte*, vol. 47 (1889), pp. 170–3).

3   Claude Dodun to Champagny, no. 6/2, 18 March 1809, AE, vol. 382 (note that there are two reports from Dodun bearing the number 6; one dated 15 March and another dated 18 March, I have chosen unilaterally to refer to them as 6/1 and 6/2). See also Andréossy's reports of 6 and 8 February 1809; and Dodun's reports of 1, 6, 8, 11 and 23 March 1809 (AE, vol. 382). In the 23 March letter, Dodun commented:'I do not know how to portray for you, my lord, the extraordinary tableau this capital presents.'

4   Carl Friedrich Freiherr Kübeck von Kübau, diary entry for 23 March 1809, in his *Tagebücher*, ed. Max Freiherr von Kübeck, Vienna: Gerold, 1909, vol. I, p. 264. See also the journal of Roger de Damas for 9 March 1809: 'The harangues, the sermons, the blessing of flags, the departure of the Landwehr, all these exalt the minds of Vienna these days and offer the appearance of enthusiasm and devotion' (vol. II, p. 84).

5   The 'cry for war' quote is from 'Mémoire sur la Guerre éclatée en 1809', MOL, P300/1/100. The popularity of 'Oesterreich über Alles' is from Langsam, p. 100. Dodun repeatedly reported the profusion of 'patriotic élan' as manifested in song, theatre, and other public displays. See also the reminiscences of the patriotic writer Karoline Pichler in Friedrich M. Kircheisen (ed.), *Feldzugserinnerungen aus dem Kriegsjahre 1809*, Hamburg: Gutenberg, 1909. Karen Hagemann places the 1809 patriotic writings in the context of gender history in '"Be Proud and Firm, Citizens of Austria!" Patriotism and Masculinity in Texts of the "Political Romantics" Written During Austria's Anti-Napoleonic Wars', *German Studies Review*, vol. XXIX, no. 1 (February 2006).

6   Grünne letter to Prince de Ligne, 23 September 1809 in AN, AF/IV/1639: Campagne d'Autriche, and printed in Joseph von Hormayr, *Das Heer von Inneröstreich*, Leipzig: Brockhaus, 1817, pp. 391–3. Commenting on the army's morale several years later, a Prussian military journal noted: 'Despite being composed of the most contradictory elements, the Austrian army was inspired by the highest esprit du corps', in 'Über den Volkskrieg mit Bezug auf den Tyroler Krieg 1809', *Militair-Wochenblatt*, no. 107 (11 July 1818).

7   Finckenstein's 23 March 1809 report quoted in Rössler, *Oesterreichs Kampf*, vol. I, p. 428. See also his reports of 9 and 30 July 1808 in Hassel, pp. 521, 523. One of the members of the Liechtenstein clan reportedly believed that 'the conquest of Bavaria will be as easy as a promenade through the Prater' (Dodun to Champagny, no. 4, 11 March 1809, AE, vol. 382).

8   *Beobachtungen*, p. 29.

9   Dodun to Champagny, no. 6/2, 18 March 1809 (AE, vol. 382).

10   Andréossy to Champagny, no. 7, 13 February 1809 (AE, vol. 382).

11   Alexander to Rumiantsev, 14 February 1809 (*VPR*, vol. IV, p. 493).

12   Anstett report of 14 February 1809 in Martens, vol. III, p. 32. Napoleon had indeed made a statement like this to Rumiantsev and Kurakin (Kurakin to Alexander, 30 January 1809, *VPR*, vol. IV, p. 469), but Stadion, wilfully or through ignorance, took the phrase out of context; it is clear from Kurakin's report, that Napoleon

was making a *conditional* threat: *if* Austria attacked, *then* the French would be in Vienna in forty days. Stadion apparently learned of Napoleon's comment from Metternich's reporting of his discussion with the Russian diplomats (such as Metternich to Stadion, 2 February 1809, Metternich, *Memoirs*, vol. II, p. 319, which mentioned similar French threats).

13 Austrian finance minister O'Donnell told the French ambassador that 'For me, *in my department, I have been on a war footing for a long time; the army devours everything; and this cannot continue*' (recounted in Andréossy to Champagny, no. 7, 13 February 1809, AE, vol. 382, emphasis in the original).

14 Charles to Mayer according to the latter's recollections (Mayer, 'Journal für das Jahr 1809', Nachl., Nachlass Mayer von Heldensfeld, B/857, no. 111). The 8 February 1809 meeting is discussed in *Krieg*, vol. I, p. 179; and Rothenberg, *Adversaries*, p. 124.

15 The following is drawn primarily from *Krieg*, vol. I, pp. 178–80. In addition to the actions listed here, some minor military measures had been ordered on 2 February: the departure of some troops from particularly distant garrisons (one infantry regiment, two cuirassier regiments, and seven Grenz regiments), the departure of some 12,000 Hungarian recruits, and the establishment of reserve formations and Landbataillone (militia battalions) along the Military Border regions.

16 These were to ease the burden on the Habsburg hereditary lands in Austria (Erbländer). As Palatine of Hungary, Joseph was essentially Kaiser Franz's viceroy. As a result, all instructions for Hungarian military activity had to pass through him directly from the Kaiser (i.e. not from Charles); a cumbersome mechanism at best and one that would hamper operations as the war entered Hungary in May and June. The need for men and horses had been raised in November 1808, causing Joseph to protest that this measure would be disruptive to mobilisation of the Insurrection and alarming to the populace (to Franz, 22 January 1809, in Domanovszky, vol. IV, pp. 354–9).

17 Rothenberg, *Adversaries*, p. 124. Albert Eusebius von Wallenstein (1583–1634) left a legacy—a powerful military leader of independent means, beyond the control of the reigning emperor, a challenge to the dynasty—that haunted Habsburgs for three centuries. See Gordon A. Craig, 'Command and Staff Problems in the Austrian Army, 1740–1866', in his *War, Politics, and Diplomacy*, New York: Praeger, 1966.

18 These were the artillery *Handlanger* ('rude mechanicals' to perform manual, non-technical labour in artillery batteries) and the train personnel quota from the hereditary lands.

19 Stadion's 23 December 1808 instructions for Metternich are printed in Beer, pp. 536–9.

20 The following draws heavily on Botzenhart, pp. 284–92. Stadion's quote is from his 12 March 1809 instructions for Metternich in Grunwald, 'La Fin d'une Ambassade' (nos. 19 and 20). Metternich's change in tone was prompted by a 21 February 1809 letter from Stadion in the wake of the 8 February conference (Grunwald, 'La Fin d'une Ambassade'); three days later, Kaiser Franz remarked that he wanted Metternich to 'put the knife to his [Napoleon's] throat' (imperial comments on Stadion's 24 February 1809 memorandum in Wertheimer, *Geschichte*, vol. II, p. 300).

21 Botzenhart, pp. 291–2.

22 Stadion to Metternich, 12 March 1809, in Grunwald, 'La Fin d'une Ambassade'; Stadion to Metternich, 31 March 1809 (enciphered), HHStA.

23 In Metternich's reports of 31 January 1809 and 11 January (no. 1/I) respectively (HHStA, *Frankreich: Berichte 1809*, Kart. 205). Metternich's apparent ignorance is based on my reading of his reports from this period, for example, 17 January 1809 (no. 3) and 20 March 1809 (no. 15/A). This was similar to the ambassador's position in the autumn of 1808 as noted in Chapter 1.

24 Kraehe, pp. 73–4. This despite Metternich's warning that Napoleon wanted Austria to be 'the first to take hostile measures' (in his 20 March 1809 report, no. 15/A). As late as 1 February 1809, Archduke Joseph was still arguing against Austria assuming the aggressor's role (letter to the Kaiser in Domanovszky, vol. IV, pp. 366–70).

25 War aims for an offensive venture had been discussed in December 1808 when the decision for war was made (Friedrich von Gentz had drafted a concept for Germany's political future and much of the wording in later documents came from Stadion's 4 December briefing), and they were certainly in Stadion's mind as early as September, but it seems that the leap from defensive to offensive war was made without a clear definition of the presumed war's purpose. See Rössler's chapters in *Oesterreichs Kampf*: 'Das Reformjahr 1808' for details of Stadion's presentations to the Kaiser in the latter part of 1808, and 'Das Kriegsziel Oesterreichs 1809' for Gentz's memoir; see also Archduke Charles, 'Vortrag an den Kaiser, ob ein Krieg gegen Frankreich im gegenwärtigen Momente zweckmässig wäre' in *Ausgewählte Schriften*, Vienna, 1893, vol. VI, p. 300ff.

26 Quoted in Dodun to Champagny, no. 6/2, 18 March 1809 (AE, vol. 382). Also in Criste, *Carl*, vol. II, p. 457.

27 Instructions for Leutnant Wagner in Fedorowicz, p. 69. This analysis relies primarily on the following key documents relating to Austrian war aims: 4 December 1808 briefing to the Kaiser (P. Stadion); 22 January 1809 briefing to the Kaiser (P. Stadion); 28 January 1809 instructions for Wallmoden and Wagner (P. Stadion); 3 March 1809 instructions for de La Tour (P. Stadion); 'Bemerkungen über den Marsch der Kays. Königl. Armeen nach Deutschland' (attributed to P. Stadion); 'Allgemeine Gesichtspunkte über den bevorstehenden Krieg in Beziehung auf Deutschland' (attributed to F. Stadion, printed in Fournier, 'Oesterreichs Kriegsziele'); Wagner's 12 March 1809 note to the British government. See notes for exact citations. Evidently, these goals were no secret; Dodun neatly summarised them in report no. 4, 11 March 1809 (AE, vol. 382).

28 Stadion's briefing of 22 January 1809 in Rössler, *Oesterreichs Kampf*, vol. I, p. 533.

29 'Allgemeine Gesichtspunkt über die bevorstehenden Krieg in Beziehung auf Deutschland' (attributed to Friedrich Stadion) in Fournier, 'Oesterreichs Kriegsziele', p. 223.

30 Undated and unsigned memorandum attributed to Stadion: 'Bemerkungen über den Marsch der Kays. Königl. Armeen nach Deutschland', quoted in Rössler, *Oesterreichs Kampf*, vol. I, pp. 503, 505.

31 'Allgemeine Gesichtspunkt über die bevorstehenden Krieg in Beziehung auf Deutschland' (attributed to Friedrich Stadion) in Fournier, 'Oesterreichs Kriegsziele', p. 223.

32 Stadion's briefing of 22 January 1809 in Rössler, *Oesterreichs Kampf*, vol. I, p. 535.

33 The key figures were Franz's brother Archduke Ferdinand, Grand Duke of Würzburg (and a member of the Rheinbund!) who supposedly received only partial compensation for his former possessions around Salzburg; another brother, Archduke Anton, the Grand Master of the Teutonic Order, who had lost his German lands to Württemberg; and Franz's uncle, Ferdinand, who never took possession of the territories in Baden he was supposed to have acquired as compensation for the loss of the Duchy of Modena in Italy. See Fournier's footnote in 'Oesterreichs Kriegsziele', p. 216.

34 Instructions for Leutnant Wagner in Fedorowicz, pp. 69–70; Stadion's 4 December 1808 briefing (HHStA); Wagner's 12 March 1809 note to the British government (PRO/FO 7/90).

35 Stadion's 4 December 1808 briefing (HHStA).

36 The authors of *Krieg 1809* discuss the theoretical requirement to carry the war into France on p. 167 of vol. I.

37 Stadion's 23 December 1808 instructions for Metternich in Beer, p. 538; although Napoleon's personal future and France's role in Europe were decidedly ambiguous in Austrian planning, there is no evidence to indicate that Stadion considered this war a crusade to restore the Bourbons (see Botzenhart, p. 278; and Rössler, *Oesterreichs Kampf*, vol. I, p. 526).

38 Discussing Napoleon's view of such wars of limited objectives, Peter Paret argues that 'Napoleon excluded limited wars for circumscribed goals from his political and military system' (in *Makers of Modern Strategy*, Princeton: Princeton University Press, 1986, p. 136). See also Schroeder/Kagan.

39 Kraehe, p. 80.

40 Charles certainly believed a revived Reich ('the wish for the old order') to be the goal of some his contemporaries and one that they believed could be attained 'with force and without great difficulty'; he specifically named the Stadion brothers as harbouring these desires (he also mistakenly attributed them to Metternich). See 'Denkschrift', *Ausgewählte Schriften*, vol. VI, pp. 319–49 (quote from p. 326). Charles's own musings about the defence of Germany more than hint at a return to an Austrian-led Reich (Grünne to Stadion, 1 April 1809, quoted in Rössler, *Oesterreichs Kampf*, vol. I, pp. 520–2).

41 Former Russian ambassador, Andrei Kyrillovich Razumovsky, quoted in Dodun to Champagny, no. 4, 11 March 1809, AE, vol. 382. Towards the end of the month, Dodun reported that Gentz was preparing a work that would 'prove Kaiser Franz's rights to the former German union' ('l'ancien Corps Germanique'), Dodun to Champagny, no. 7, 23 March 1809 (AE, vol. 382).

42 Austria refused to 'guarantee the conquests granted to France since the Revolution by the various peace treaties that preceded the Peace of Pressburg' (Instructions for Wallmoden, 29 January 1809, HHStA, *Russland III/36*, extracts in Fournier, 'Oesterreichs Kriegsziele', p. 218).

43 Stuart to Canning, 12 April 1809, no. 1 (PRO/FO 342/2).

44 Stadion's 22 January 1809 briefing quoted in Rössler, *Oesterreichs Kampf*, vol. I, p. 528.

45 Quote from Stadion's 22 January 1809 briefing, Rössler, *Oesterreichs Kampf*, vol. I, p. 533.

46 Rössler, *Stadion*, vol. II, p. 19. See also Rössler, *Oesterreichs Kampf*, vol. I, p. 535ff.

47 Charles's 26 November 1808 note quoted in Rössler, *Oesterreichs Kampf*, vol. I, p. 424. Stadion held similar views: 'The military operations must agree with this political viewpoint' (27 September 1808 briefing in Rössler, *Oesterreichs Kampf*, vol. I, p. 380).

48 Rauchensteiner, *Franz*, p. 94.

49 Johann lamented that Austria 'counted on much assistance which was by no means assured' (*Feldzugserzählungen*, p. 45).

50 Stadion to Major Goltz, 28 January 1809 according to Goltz's report cited in Rössler, *Oesterreichs Kampf*, vol. I, p. 424.

51 From one of Stadion's February 1809 memoranda (Rössler, *Oesterreichs Kampf*, vol. I, p. 425).

52 First quote from Stadion's 4 December 1808 briefing (HHStA, parts in Rössler, *Oesterreichs Kampf*, vol. I, p. 398); Stadion thus happily assumed that several months would pass before 'France can oppose us with substantial reinforcements'. Second quote from 'Bemerkungen über den Marsch der Kays. Königl. Armeen nach Deutschland' (in Rössler, *Oesterreichs Kampf*, vol. I, p. 506). In addition to these two documents from Stadion himself, I have incorporated Charles's impracticable concept for the defence of Germany against France (described in a letter from Grünne to Stadion, 1 April 1809, quoted in Rössler, *Oesterreichs Kampf*, vol. I, pp. 520–2) to arrive at this construct. The 4 December briefing reveals some of the shallowness of Stadion's thinking on war aims. Once Germany and northern Italy were secure, he commented, Austria could view the next events 'with confidence', or, if all was proceeding particularly well, Vienna could consider giving its plans 'broader scope'; he did not trouble to develop the phrase 'broader scope' in any detail.

53 Schroeder calls Austria's political goals 'hazy' and its military strategy 'crazy' (p. 363). Hertenberger and Wiltschek write that 'The conditions which Stadion named for the maintenance of peace were simply ridiculous' (p. 208). Broers comments that the Austrians 'failed to grasp the organizational powers of the Napoleonic state' (p. 165).

54 Charles, 'Vortrag an den Kaiser, ob ein Krieg gegen Frankreich im gegenwärtigen Momente zweckmässig wäre' in *Ausgewählte Schriften*, vol. VI, p. 300ff. The date of this presentation is open to question: the editors of Charles's writings suggest January 1809, but Rössler argues persuasively that it was written before the Erfurt meeting between Napoleon and the tsar, thus placing it in September or early October 1808. In either case, it reflects the core of the archduke's thinking on this question, an attitude that changed little—and then only temporarily—in the first months of 1809.

55 For example, Grünne to Stadion, 1 April 1809, quoted in Rössler, *Oesterreichs Kampf*, vol. I, pp. 520–2.

56 Charles, 'Denkschrift', *Ausgewählte Schriften*, vol. VI, p. 326.

57 Radetzky to Liechtenstein, 1 December 1809, published in 'Ein Memoire Radetzky's, das Heerwesen Oesterreichs beleuchtend, aus dem Jahre 1809', *Mittheilungen des k. k. Kriegsarchivs*, vol. VIII (1884), p. 362ff.

58 The initial operational plan for the war had only one corps on the Italian frontier. There was also, however, a personality factor in the decision to strengthen the force intended for this front: the Archduke Johann, pleased to be in command, lobbied for more troops to give his position greater importance and enhance his independence from his brother Charles's orders. See below.

59 For Stadion's mistrust of the army, see quotes in Chapter 1. See also Grünne to de Ligne, 23 September 1809 (AN AF/IV/1639) and Rössler, *Oesterreichs Kampf*, vol. I, p. 425, and vol. II, pp. 11, 79–84.

60 Johann maintained that Mayer was equally pessimistic (*Feldzugserzählungen*, p. 15); Rauchensteiner disagrees (Rauchensteiner, *Franz*, p. 89).

61 Josef Radetzky, 'Erinnerungen aus dem Leben des FM. Grafen Radetzky', *Mittheilungen des k. k. Kriegsarchivs*, new series I (1887), p. 64.

62 Mayer's journal quoted in Rauchensteiner, *Franz*, p. 95.

63 'The Austrian Main Army could hardly have any other aim than that of defeating Davout' from Charles's instructions to Mayer, 2 February 1809, quoted in Ernst Zehetbauer, *Landwehr gegen Napoleon*, Vienna: öbv & hpt, 1999, p. 227. Strictly speaking, there were two French commands in Germany in early 1809: Davout's Army of the Rhine and Marshal Jean-Baptiste Bernadotte's small Corps of the Government of the Hanseatic Towns (*corps de troupes du gouvernement des villes hanséatiques*). These had been formed in October 1808 upon the dissolution of the Grande Armée (Decree of 12 October 1808, *Correspondence*, no. 14376).

64 Annex to Stadion's instructions for Wagner, 29 January 1809 (Fedorowicz, p. 71).

65 Charles's instructions to Mayer quoted in *Krieg*, vol. II, p. 6 (quotation from this source); and Mayer's Operations Plan, 8 February 1809, Kriegsarchiv, Alte Feldakten [hereafter KAFA], 1809/Hauptarmee/Deutschland/2/27).

66 See Mayer's 'Journal' (Nachl.); *Krieg*, vol. I, pp. 168–72; Rauchensteiner, *Franz*, 94; Moritz Edlen von Angeli, *Erzherzog Carl*, Vienna: Braumüller, 1897, vol. IV, pp. 12–20. Zehetbauer includes extensive quotes from Charles's instructions, pp. 210–11. In addition to being disappointed at Prussia's demurral, Charles reportedly complained that he had been deceived regarding Russia's stance: while others continued to hold out hope for assistance from the tsar, as Schwarzenberg's couriers began to reach Vienna, the generalissimus lamented that all of his plans had been calculated on the certitude that Russia would remain neutral (Dodun to Champagny, no. 4, 11 March 1809, AE, vol. 382).

67 According to Mayer's estimate, the French had 15,000 in Dalmatia and 62,800 French, Italians and Neapolitans in the Italian peninsula (Operations Plan, 8 February 1809, KAFA). The intelligence estimate upon which the plan was based is in 'Completter Stand der Franzosen in Deutschland und Italien, und ihrer Allierten, die Conscription vom Jahr 1810 mitgerechnet', 7 February 1809 in KAFA, Kart. 1450.

68 Operations Plan, 8 February 1809 (KAFA). See also *Krieg*, vol. I, 171–4; Angeli, vol. IV, pp. 21–4; and Criste, *Carl*, vol. III, p. 4. In reality, potential French strength in Germany was about 176,000 in early January: 92,000 under Davout and

Bernadotte and the prospect of some 84,000 Rheinbund troops (which were only in the very initial stages of mobilisation in January and February). An additional 27,000–30,000 (the four infantry divisions and cavalry brigade that eventually became Massena's Corps) were in France (see Charles Saski, *Campagne de 1809*, Paris: Berger-Levrault, 1899–1902, vol. I, Annexes 2 and 3).

69 Insurrection numbers from *Krieg*, vol. I, p. 88. Although the Hungarian Diet had granted Franz the authority to call up 80,000 Insurrection troops in a national emergency, only some 35,000 were actually raised in the early phases of the conflict. The Croatian levy was to supply 13,000 men, the Slovenian 5,000. Not until 15 June 1809 did the Transylvanian Diet approve an Insurrection force (to be 8,500 strong). Mayer placed no great reliance on these forces.

70 Metternich's 4 December 1808 memorandum entitled 'Armée française: Guerre d'Espagne', printed in Beer, pp. 529–35. Emphasis in original. Metternich estimated French forces able to oppose Austria at 206,000, of whom only 107,000 would be French, the remainder being 'confederates and allies'. He repeated his assessment of French troop quality as he described unit movements in March: 'They are nothing but conscripts' (Metternich to Stadion, 17 March 1809, no. 14/A, HHStA).

71 Operations Plan, 8 February 1809 (KAFA). Johann remarked bitterly that 'The enemy in Italy is completely ignored!' and 'No one ever wanted to believe the [enemy] strengths that the archduke [Johann] provided; there could be at most 30,000 total there; that was the opinion' (Johann, *Feldzugserzählungen*, pp. 38–9).

72 'In an offensive war, the principal aim of a general must be to exploit the advantages of the situation ... as quickly as possible and, through decisive operations from the very outset, to thwart the intentions of the enemy and to render him incapable of gaining any superiority. To this end, the campaign must be opened with all strength at the decisive point, all other borders of the state are occupied by only as many troops as are absolutely necessary to cover these provinces against enemy raids ...' (from *Grundsätze der höheren Kriegskunst für die Generäle der österreichischen Armee*, in *Ausgewählte Schriften*, vol. I, p. 7). The authors of *Krieg 1809* imply that Charles only undertook these divergent operations against his will for political reasons (vol. I, p. 172); I am not convinced.

73 The selection of Bohemia was evidently congruent with Charles's thinking in early February; not only did he approve Mayer's plan for the deployment of the Main Army, his own vague concept (handed to a much piqued Mayer on 8 February when the general arrived to present *his* plan—unfortunately this brief draft is lost to history) also pointed to a concentration in Bohemia (Mayer's 'Journal', Nachl.; and Rauchensteiner, *Franz*, p. 95). Based on unspecified 'indications', the authors of the official history suggest that the Main Army would have deployed in the Danube valley from the outset had it not been for 'the fiction of a Prussian alliance' (*Krieg*, vol. I, p. 170).

74 The Austrian strength figure is my gross estimate for illustrative purposes only. It is based on strengths of the various corps of the Main Army on 20 March 1809 (from *Krieg*, vol. I, p. 664): I (25,500), II (26,100), III (20,400), IV (13,500), V (23,500), VI (28,500), IR (13,700), IIR (3,900). Note that all of the corps were still awaiting considerable reinforcements on this date. The strength of VIII Corps (21,300) is for late March (from Johann, *Feldzugserzählungen*, p. 33); it also

received reinforcements before the campaign opened (see Hans von Zwiedineck-Südenhorst, *Erzherzog Johann von Oesterreich im Feldzuge von 1809*, Graz: Styria, 1892, p. 1). This total figure could increase from 176,000 to approximately 200,000 if strength returns from early April are used.

75 Compared to Mayer's figure of some 200,000 French in Germany with another 16,000 or so relatively close in France, the nine Austrian corps could muster only 176,000–200,000 as indicated above. The 40,000 Prussians would provide at best a limited numerical advantage, thus the importance of concentration and speed.

76 Mayer's Operations Plan, 8 February 1809 (KAFA); *Krieg*, vol. I, p. 177; Johann, *Feldzugserzählungen*, p. 27; and an undated post-war letter from Mayer to Prince de Ligne, in Joseph von Hormayr, *Das Heer von Inneröstreich*, Leipzig: Brockhaus, 1817, p. 409.

77 Orders issued on 11 February 1809, see *Krieg*, vol. II, p. 7. IX Corps was now to concentrate at Laibach.

78 For Johann's influence, see *Krieg*, vol. I, p. 184 and vol. II, p. 7; he makes no reference to these specifics in his memoirs. Stadion's exact role (if any) in these military decisions is not clear, but his desire for an invasion of northern Italy was certainly well established (see, among other statements, his 4 December 1808 Vortrag, HHStA). Johann's expectation that Italy would be an important theatre for offensive operations is evident from his memoirs of the campaign (*Feldzugserzählungen*, pp. 17–21).

79 *Krieg*, vol. II, pp. 14–15; Johann, *Feldzugserzählungen*, p. 30.

80 Charles's note and Johann's acerbic marginalia are in Johann, *Feldzugserzählungen*, pp. 36–41.

81 *Krieg*, vol. I, p. 185.

82 *Krieg*, vol. I, pp. 185–89; and Stadion's 4 December 1808 memo (HHStA).

83 *Krieg*, vol. I, pp. 189–91 and Appendix XVI.

84 *Krieg*, vol. I, p. 190.

85 Such as reports from Hauptmann Ludwig Freiherr von Welden in Bavaria. The French knew of Welden's espionage mission:'An officer of the General Staff, Baron von Velden [sic], has established himself in Munich, where, under the pretext of family matters, he observes what is happening in the Tyrol and in Wirtemberg [sic]' (Andréossy to Champagny, no. 8, 14 February 1809, AE, vol. 382). Welden would later make an historical contribution to the campaign, completing the account of the war begun by fellow participant GM Karl von Stutterheim. Curiously, some of this intelligence was not shared with Mayer, who was 'astounded' to learn on 15 February that Charles believed Davout and Bernadotte had already set their troops in motion (Mayer's 'Journal', Nachl.).

86 This paragraph is drawn from *Krieg*, vol. I, pp. 190, 192; Metternich's reports of 12 January (no. 2C), 17 January (no. 3), 31 January (enciphered), and 7 March 1809 (nos. 12B and 12C) (HHStA); [Karl von Stutterheim], *La Guerre de l'An 1809 entre l'Autriche et la France*, Vienna: Strauss, 1811, pp. XLI–XLIII; Heller von Hellwald, pp. 164–70. Dodun specifically reported that news of French movements (Legrand, Carra Saint-Cyr, Molitor and Boudet) had caused Austria to change its plans (Dodun to Champagny, no. 7, 23 March 1809, AE, vol. 382). See also Moritz Edlen von Angeli, *Erzherzog Carl von Oesterreich als Feldherr und Heeresorganisator*, Vienna: Braumüller, 1897, vol. IV, pp. 33–4.

87 Criste sees Prussia as the most important factor in the change of plans, *Carl*, vol. III, p. 14.

88 The advantages and disadvantages of the two courses of action are discussed in 'Beitrag', *Ausgewählte Schriften*, vol. VI, pp. 358–9; *Krieg*, vol. I, p. 193–5; Rothenberg, *Adversaries*, pp. 130–1; Grünne to de Ligne, 23 September 1809 (AN AF/IV/1639); and Lindenau's 'Ausweis', MOL, P300/1/98. See especially a 9 March 1809 memorandum drawn up by Stutterheim wherein he compared the two plans (in KAFA, Kart. 1389 under the archivist's title 'Gutachten über die Frage; ob die Hauptarmee aus Böhmen oder aus dem Donau-Thal ausbrechen solle?'; extract published in Christian Freiherr Binder von Kriegelstein, *Der Krieg Napoleons gegen Oesterreich 1809*, ed. Maximilian Ritter von Hoen, Berlin: Voss, 1906, vol. I, p. 95). Stutterheim was a close associate of Stadion's and participated in the debate during February and March. Quote is from this memorandum as transcribed in Binder.

89 Binder, vol. I, pp. 95–7. For Charles's attitude toward 'the great clumsiness' of his army, see 'Denkschrift', *Ausgewählte Schriften*, vol. VI, pp. 333–4. Lindenau's condemnation of the Bohemian plan may have also helped to change Charles's mind. Shown a copy of the plan in February, the archduke's old military tutor irritated His Imperial Highness by exclaiming 'That is no plan at all!' (Lindenau, 'Ausweis', P300/1/98). Lindenau, on the other hand, was one of those who thought that the Danube option would allow Austria to knock Bavaria out of the war, while other contemporaries observed that Austria would forfeit important opportunities to rouse German populations against Napoleon by opening the war with an invasion of staunchly pro-French and anti-Austrian Bavaria (Marcel Dunan, *Napoléon et l'Allemagne*, Paris: Plon, 1942, p. 243).

90 For example: Adolf von Horsetzky, *Kriegsgeschichtliche Uebersicht der wichtigsten Feldzüge der letzten 100 Jahre*, Vienna: Seidel & Sohn, 1894, p. 135; and Siegfried Fielder, *Kriegswesen und Kriegführung im Zeitalter der Revolutionskriege*, Koblenz: Bernhard & Graefe, 1988, p. 238. Francis Loraine Petre also refers to earlier commentators in his fine work: *Napoleon and the Archduke Charles*, London: John Lane, 1909, p. 73. One of the most provocative analyses of a possible early Austrian advance is offered by Hauptmann Walter von Breman in 'Die Tage von Regensburg', *Beiheft zum Militär-Wochenblatt*, Berlin, 1891: he argues that the Hauptarmee could have started its approach to the border in Bohemia on 17 March (minus IV and V Corps) and thus could have deployed along the general line of Mosbach to Regen in Bavaria by 25 March with 95,000 men. He further states that the two corps in the Danube valley could have been on the Isar by 26 March 30,000 strong. Unfortunately, Bremen was writing without the benefit of much of the later scholarship, especially the Austrian official history, so he was unaware of some of the Hauptarmee's other problems; moreover, he presupposes dramatic changes in the Austrian high command's outlook.

91 Binder, vol. I, p. 97 (the average march distances were calculated including rest days); *Krieg*, vol. I, Appendix XVI (march tables). Radetzky was enormously frustrated by the move, 'Erinnerungen', p. 65. FML Johann von Hiller was appalled and called the move 'a scandal of the first order', estimating that it cost the Austrian army ten days: Manfried Rauchensteiner, *Feldzeugmeister Johann Freiherr von Hiller*, Vienna: Notring, 1972, pp. 119–20. Mayer was another participant who regretted the shift.

92   Charles, 'Beitrag', *Ausgewählte Schriften*, vol. VI, p. 359.

93   Quotes from *Krieg*, vol. I, pp. 194–8. Hess, who later became a Feldmarschall, was attached to the Generalquartiermeisterstab in 1809 and wrote his commentary in 1810. First quote is from the author of this portion of *Krieg*, Eberhard Mayerhoffer von Vedropolje. One scholar suggests an additional motive behind the shift: Charles and other members of the Austrian military hierarchy may have recalled the successful operations against the French in 1796, which were based on the Danube approach (Heinrich Ommen, *Die Kriegsführung des Erzherzogs Carl*, Vaduz: Kraus Reprints, 1965, p. 112).

94   Johann, *Feldzugserzählungen*, p. 28; Mayer quoted in Binder, vol. I, p. 92. Johann also commented that 'Unfortunately one had delayed so long and lost valuable time in the endless vacillation over decisions' (*Feldzugserzählungen*, p. 23).

95   In his more optimistic moments, Charles made light of the time lost; asked if Austrian slowness would not allow France more time to prepare, he replied 'the French may have sent 25,000 men to Germany since learning of our armaments: very well! just 25,000 more men for us to gobble up' (Dodun to Champagny, no. 7, 23 March 1809, AE, vol. 382).

96   See John H. Gill, 'Decision in Bavaria: The Austrian Invasion of 1809' in Jonathan North (ed.), *The Napoleon Options*, London: Greenhill, 2000, for a speculative examination of how an Austrian attack might have unfolded had it been launched in late March. It is important to note that Berthier was in Paris with Napoleon until 31 March. Therefore an earlier Austrian offensive would probably have brought the emperor himself to the battlefield immediately, there would have been no Berthier interregnum to cause confusion and dispersion in the French forces.

97   This discussion is drawn from *Krieg*, vol. I, pp. 196–8; and Binder, vol. I, pp. 97–8.

98   For an exhaustively detailed look at the artillery's situation, see Major Semek, 'Die Artillerie im Jahre 1809', *Mittheilungen des K. und K. Kriegsarchivs*, vol. III (1904). Many units were not fully manned and equipped until mid-April.

99   Quoted in Binder, vol. I, p. 98. In a 29 March 1809 note to Oberst Franz Brusch von Neuburg (VII Corps Chief of Staff), GM Prochaska wrote: 'The Main Army has not been so fortunate as to gather in all its manpower requirements and unit fillers before the beginning of operations. We thus march with considerably less infantry than we had hoped to have' (in *Krieg*, vol. I, p. 199).

100 In January, the French ambassador reported rumours that Austria would attack 'at the beginning of March', but commented cogently that 'the beginning of March seems too soon to me' (Andréossy to Champagny, no. 1, 15 January 1809, AE, vol. 382).

101 Damas, diary entry for 3 March 1809, vol. I, p. 82.

102 Some contemporaries agreed; indeed, some suggested that Vienna should have attacked *months* earlier, that is, in late 1808 (see, for example, Pahl, *Krieg*, p. 143; and his subsequent *Denkwürdigkeiten aus meinem Leben und aus meiner Zeit*, Tübingen, 1840, pp. 611–12). The Austrian army, of course, was in no condition to launch an offensive in 1808.

103 Johann, *Feldzugserzählungen*, p. 28. Johann and Radetzky saw Prochaska as nothing more than a 'puppet' controlled by Grünne and Wimpffen (p. 28, and Radetzky, 'Erinnerungen', p. 65).

104 The apparent cause of his relief was that he had supposedly chattered about Austria's plans for the coming war while inebriated and that he was a frequent guest of the French ambassador, GD Andréossy.

105 Quote from Rauchensteiner, *Franz*, p. 92.

106 The best sources for this affair are: Criste, *Carl*, vol. II, pp. 8–13; Hertenberger/Wiltschek, pp. 211–12; and especially Rauchensteiner, *Franz*, pp. 90–8. See also *Krieg*, vol. I, p. 183; and Binder, vol. I. pp. 92–5. Although it seems unlikely, it is important to note that both Grünne and Radetzky claimed that Mayer had *not* supported the Bohemian option, but rather pushed for the shift to the Danube valley: Grünne in his letter to Prince de Ligne, 23 September 1809 (AN, AF/IV/1639), and Radetzky in his *Erinnerungen*, p. 64.

107 The Grenzer (literally 'borderers') were raised along the monarchy's borders with the turbulent Ottoman Empire. A strange and complex institution, Austria's 'Military Border' is best covered in Gunther E. Rothenberg, *The Military Border in Croatia 1740–1881*, Chicago: University of Chicago Press, 1966.

108 Figures drawn from *Krieg*, vol. I, Appendices III and XII; and Angeli, vol. IV, pp. 14–16. Note that the formal authorised strength of these forces was well above the figures listed here, but 'these numbers were never attained' (Angeli, vol. IV, p. 14).

109 This section draws principally on *Krieg*, vol. I, pp. 74–115; and Rothenberg, *Adversaries*, pp. 103–30.

110 Semek, p. 87, 104–9, Anton Dolleczek, *Geschichte der Oesterreichischen Artillerie*, Vienna: Kreisel & Gröger, 1887, p. 451.

111 *Krieg*, vol. I, p. 102.

112 The focus was on target practice and those activities associated with service in advance and rear guards (Karl Kandelsdorfer, *Geschichte des k. u. k. Feld-Jäger-Bataillons Nr. 3*, Vienna: Vergani, 1899, vol. I, p. 36).

113 Austrian practice invites comparison with French tactical norms and the British use of rifle units, a comparison that does not show Austria in a very favourable light.

114 Georg Freiherr von Valentini, *Versuch einer Geschichte des Feldzugs von 1809 an der Donau*, 2nd edn, Berlin: Nikolai, 1818, pp. 282–3. Valentini's analysis of Austrian tactical difficulties is excellent.

115 Valentini, pp. 277, 280.

116 Rothenberg, *Adversaries*, p. 111.

117 Semek, pp. 99, 102. Semek highlights (p. 77) a tactical peculiarity of the Austrian mounted artillery: according to regulations, the mobile batteries were not intended to support the cavalry. Instead, they were to serve as a mobile reserve for the local commander and to operate with advance guard detachments, seizing and dominating key terrain features until the rest of the advance guard could arrive. To emphasise this distinction, the batteries were deliberately designated as 'Kavallerie-Geschütz-Batterien' or 'cavalry gun batteries' rather than simply 'cavalry batteries'. In the event, however, this regulation was often ignored.

118 *Dienst-Reglement für die kaiserlich-königliche Infanterie*, Vienna: k.u.k. Hof- und Staats-Druckerey, 1807–8.

119 *Beobachtungen*, pp. 33–4.

120 Radetzky, 'Erinnerungen', p. 63.

121 Karl Johann Ritter von Grueber, *Lebenserinnerungen eines Reiteroffiziers vor Hundert Jahren*, Vienna: Seidel und Sohn, 1906, p. 62.

122 Information drawn from *Krieg*, vol. I, pp. 185–7; the history of the 9th Jäger Battalion; and the histories of the following infantry regiments: 2, 30, 34, 47, 51, 58, 59, 60, 62, 63 (the latter covered in the history of Infantry Regiment No. 55). See bibliography for complete citations of unit histories. The quote reference III/ *Stain* is from Binder, vol. I, p. 181, citing the record of V Corps on 18 April when this battalion had to be left behind owing to its poor level of readiness. Note that our Bavarian observer commented favourably on the drill and 'martial bearing' of the regiments he encountered in Munich, especially the O'Reilly Chevaulegers (*Beobachtungen*, p. 33).

123 Reminiscences of Franz Gräffer quoted in Alfred Plischnack, *Vive l'Empereur, weil's sein muss*, Vienna: Amalthea, 1999, p. 65.

124 'Eipeldauer', quoted in Zehetbauer, p. 227 (also pp. 108, 231–2).

125 Quoted in Binder, vol. I, p. 52.

126 Zehetbauer, pp. 222, 233, 287, 296.

127 Report of GM Graf Kinsky, 4 May 1809, quoted in Binder, vol. I, p. 52. There were two Landwehr brigade commanders with the name Kinsky (Karl and Franz); unfortunately, Binder does not specify which one wrote this report, so it is difficult to know which exact battalions are being described. Binder states that he found almost no favourable references to the Landwehr in searching through the archives in Vienna. For some of the innumerable complaints about equipment, see Zehetbauer, pp. 233–47, 250, 254, 269, 282, 293, 305, and note 559. See also comments from two contemporary Austrian reports in Friedrich Reschounig, 'Das Jahr 1809 im Urtheile der Zeitgenossen', dissertation, University of Vienna, 1939, p. 23.

128 For desertions and disturbances, see Zehetbauer, pp. 242, 247, 249, 250, 268–70, 273. According to Strobl von Ravelsberg, the 1st Budweis and the 1st Chrudim also mutinied; he, however, only mentions four Bohemian battalions as actually indulging in mutiny (these two plus the 2nd Chrudim and 1st Prachin). See Ferdinand Strobl von Ravelsberg, *Die Landwehr von Anno Neun*, Vienna: Stern, 1909. Note that the 3rd Iglau was planned but never formed.

129 Charles, 'Denkschrift', *Ausgewählte Schriften*, vol. VI, p. 332. See also *Krieg*, vol. I, pp. 85, 188–9.

130 According to Zehetbauer (note 500), the Vienna Volunteers were 'regular Landwehr of the City of Vienna' not Freibataillone, which enlisted only for the duration of a specific conflict. Wrede, however, classes them as free battalions but also says that they were filled out with volunteers (Alphons Freiherr von Wrede, *Geschichte der K. und K. Wehrmacht*, Vienna: Seidel & Sohn, 1898, vol. II, pp. 459–60). Ferdinand Strobl von Ravelsberg does little to clarify the question (*Die Landwehr Anno Neun*, Vienna: Stern, 1909).

131 In the case of the Vienna Volunteers, the equipment situation posed a peculiar social and logistical problem. The volunteer units were not routinely issued with rucksacks, instead each battalion was to have several mules to carry underwear and other necessities heaped together in large communal panniers. The Viennese battalions, formed of men from widely varying social classes, asked for individual

packs so that the soldiers from more elevated backgrounds would not have to mix their undergarments with those of the lower classes, whom they saw as less attentive to personal hygiene and often literally lousy. Zehetbauer, p. 238.

132 *Krieg*, vol. I, pp. 85–6.

133 Joseph initially detected little enthusiasm for the coming war in Hungary, and told the Kaiser in a 1 February letter that 'the general attitude here is against the war'; further, he argued that an offensive war would have a 'very disadvantageous' effect on 'popular opinion and defensive preparations' (*Krieg*, vol. III, p. 368). The French ambassador was also sceptical of Hungarian upper-class support for the Habsburg cause, asking in January: 'will the noble of Hungary serve as a simple hussar?' (Andréossy to Champagny, no. 1, 15 January 1809, AE, vol. 382).

134 Joseph repeatedly recounted his woes in his correspondence with Kaiser Franz, such as his letters of 17 March and 4 April 1809, in Domanovszky, vol. III, p. 408ff. By March, his impression of sympathy and support for the Kaiser had improved over his impressions from January, but this transitory improvement in spirit did nothing to ameliorate the gross material deficiencies: Joseph to Franz, 3, 4, and 8 March 1809, Domanovszky, vol. III, pp. 392–96. See Domokos Kosáry, *Napoléon et la Hongrie*, Budapest: Akademiai Kiado, 1979, for a discussion of Hungarian elite attitudes.

135 With the exception of the Neutra Insurrection Cavalry Regiment, the horse and foot of the Insurrection were not mustered until mid-May. Joseph to Franz, 17 March 1809, Domanovszky, vol. III, pp. 408–15. Mustering table in Alexander (Sandor) Kisfaludy, 'Auszug aus der Geschichte der Insurrection des Adels von Ungarn im Jahre 1809 und 1810', manuscript, Országos Szechényi Könyvtár. Kisfaludy also details many of the resource problems that plagued the Insurrection.

136 Quoted from an anonymous 1810 memorandum entitled 'Bemerkungen über die französische Armee und unsere Lage' and cited extensively in 'Die Armee Napoleon I. im Jahre 1809', in *Mittheilungen des k. k. Kriegs-Archivs*, Vienna, 1881, p. 389. Prince de Ligne recounted in early 1809 a conversation he had held with a French soldier during 1805: 'You are always defeated, you Austrians, because when one of your generals is attacked, the one who is supposed to support him waits for orders, loses time, and then marches too slowly and too late' (de Ligne, *Fragments*, vol. II, p. 184). Many of these deficiencies are remarkably similar to those that hampered Maria Theresa's military during the previous century, see Christopher Duffy's excellent study of the Austrian Army of that period: *Instrument of War*, Rosemont: The Emperor's Press, 2000.

137 Rauchensteiner, *Hiller*, p. 41.

138 Charles, 'Denkschrift', *Ausgewählte Schriften*, vol. VI, p. 331.

139 See Charles, 'Denkschrift', *Ausgewählte Schriften*, vol. VI, pp. 330–3; *Krieg*, vol. I, pp. 98–9; and 'Die Armee Napoleon I. im Jahre 1809', in *Mittheilungen des k. k. Kriegs-Archivs*, Vienna, 1881.

140 The Austrian official history tries to exculpate Charles by arguing that lack of funds forced him to rely on books and theory rather than actual training (*Krieg*, vol. I, p. 116).

141 *Krieg*, vol. I, pp. 89–90.

142 Charles, 'Denkschrift', *Ausgewählte Schriften*, vol. VI, p. 330.

143 Napoleon, January 1821, quoted in Henri Gatien Bertrand, *Cahiers de Sainte-Hélène*, Paris: Flammarion, 1949, vol. II, p. 29. For other comments from Napoleon denigrating Austrian employment of cavalry, see *Correspondence*, vol. XXXI, p. 428. GD Drouet made similar remarks to Napoleon in March 1809: 'You know, Sire, that I have always fought in Germany: I have noted that the Austrians do not know how to use their numerous and splendid cavalry' (Jean Baptiste Drouet d'Erlon, *Vie Militaire*, Paris: Barba, 1844, pp. 52–3).

144 American scholar Gunther Rothenberg once commented that he had 'never seen an Austrian field order less than six pages long'. Discussion on 'Education and the Commander' at the 1983 conference of the Consortium on Revolutionary Europe in Clarence B. Davis (ed.), *Proceedings of the Consortium on Revolutionary Europe 1983*, Athens, GA: Consortium on Revolutionary Europe, 1985, p. 113.

145 Rothenberg, p. 333. See also Damas, diary entries for 3 March and 2 August 1809, vol. II, pp. 82, 131.

146 Damas, diary entry for 4 February 1809, vol. II, p. 81.

147 Charles once wrote: 'the plans of those men must always fail, who with no knowledge of war do not know how to assess the scope and worth of operations, just as those recommendations which are formed away from the theater of war no longer fit the prevailing circumstances when they come to be executed' (in Gerd Holler, . . . *für Kaiser und Vaterland*, Vienna: Amalthea, 1990, p. 143).

148 Charles to Bellegarde, 27 March 1809, KAFA, 1809/Hauptarmee/Deutschland/3/136.

149 Quoted in Binder, vol. I, p. 92.

150 Quotation from Charles's late March note to Johann in *Feldzugserzählungen*, p. 36.

151 This figure reflects regular soldiers actually with the armies when hostilities opened and thus does not encompass the battalions still on the road to join the Main Army. Note that for this listing (only) garrison battalions and reserve Grenz battalions are included under the rubric 'regulars'. Troop strengths for the following section are drawn from *Krieg*, vols I and II; Johann, *Feldzugserzählungen*, pp. 50–3; and Gustav Just, 'Das Herzogthum Warschau', *Mitteilungen des K. und K. Kriegsarchivs*, vol. IV (1906), Appendix XVII.

152 The actual number of regulars allotted to the Main Army was closer to 177,000, but 5,800 of them were detached for border duty in Bohemia or to support the blockade of the Bavarian fortress of Oberhaus at Passau. The effective field force thus numbered about 171,000.

153 Quotation from Charles's late March note to Johann in *Feldzugserzählungen*, p. 37.

154 After the war, Charles regretted that he had committed two corps to the thrust out of Bohemia 'when one would have sufficed' (Charles, 'Beitrag zur Geschichte', p. 365).

155 'Allgemeine Dispositionen für die Vorrückung der k. k. Armee', 27 March 1809, in *Krieg*, vol. II, p. 17.

156 From a memorandum Johann submitted on 15 February 1809, cited in *Feldzugserzählungen*, p. 23.

157 The total of Landwehr troops should have been around 34,000, but in Johann's opinion some 6,800 were so unprepared that they could not be committed to any sort of operations whatsoever (*Feldzugserzählungen*, p. 51; and *Krieg*, vol. II, p. 10). See discussion in volume II of this work.

158 Johann's thoughts on his operational planning from *Feldzugserzählungen*, p. 44. His formal plan was submitted on 28 March 1809 (in *Krieg*, vol. II, p. 449–50).

159 Johann's operations plan, 28 March 1809 (in *Krieg*, vol. II, p. 449).

160 Johann's operations plan, 28 March 1809 (in *Krieg*, vol. II, p. 450).

161 Johann, *Feldzugserzählungen*, p. 43.

162 Johann, *Feldzugserzählungen*, p. 23. Based on Johann's comment and the repeated Austrian appeals to Britain to block movement of GD Auguste Marmont's troops from Dalmatia to Italy by sea, historian Emil von Woinovich's assertion that Austria *expected* Marmont to strike north overland seems mistaken (in *Kämpfe in der Lika in Kroatien und Dalmatien 1809*, volume 6 of *Das Kriegsjahr 1809 in Einzeldarstellungen*, ed. Alois Veltzé, Vienna: Stern, 1906, p. 9).

163 The optimistic in Austria hoped that Ferdinand would drive Polish, French, or Saxon troops towards the Prussian frontier where Prussian troops would be forced to engage them and thus drag the reluctant Friedrich Wilhelm into war with Napoleon. Some Prussians shared this dream: in mid-April, the enthusiastic Oberst Goetzen wrote secretly to Ferdinand to tell the Austrian archduke that Prussian troops in the number of 19,000 infantry and 2,000 cavalry would 'energetically oppose' the entry of French or Polish troops into Prussian territory (Ferdinand to Charles, 22 April 1809, in Bronislaw Pawlowski, *Historja Wojny Polsko-Austrajackiej 1809 Roku*, Warsaw, 1935, p. 167).

164 Charles to Ferdinand, 28 March 1809, printed in Gustav Just, *Politik oder Strategie? Kritische Studien über den Warschauer Feldzug Oesterreichs und die Haltung Russlands 1809*, Vienna: Seidel & Sohn, 1909, pp. 71–2. See also Stadion to Archduke Franz d'Este, 21 April 1809 (Fedorowicz, pp. 321–3).

165 Oswald Graf Kielmansegg, *Schwarzenberg Uhlanen 1790–1887*, Tarnow, 1887, p. 110.

166 These were 7,500 men in thirty-six depot companies and two depot squadrons under FML Friedrich Karl Wilhelm Fürst Hohenlohe-Ingelfingen; they were scattered as garrisons among Lemberg, Cracow, Tarnow, and Sandomierz. The depot troops were supplemented by border guards. Angeli, vol. IV, Appendix 4.

167 Information on the sedentary forces is drawn from *Krieg*, vol. I, pp. 82–4, 202–5 and Appendix XIX.

CHAPTER 3: AUSTRIA WOULD NOT BE SO FOOLISH

1 The tsar and his foreign minister certainly saw no imminent threat to Austria. Foreign minister Rumiantsev wrote to the Russian ambassador in Vienna (Kurakin) on 14 August 1808 asking why Austria was arming in 'an extraordinary manner . . . If it is to defend the state which he [Franz] believes to be in extreme peril, the present time offers nothing which would legitimise such an apprehension.' Also Alexander to Kurakin, same date, both in *VPR*, vol. IV, pp. 316–18. Throughout 1808 Metternich repeatedly emphasised that Austria faced no *immediate* peril from France. He was convinced that Napoleon was a long-term threat, but that he would not turn on Austria until the Iberian situation was under control and Russian support assured. Metternich's comments along these lines appear in reports to Stadion from 27 April, 23 June, and 25 July 1808 among others (in Metternich, *Memoirs*, vol. II, pp. 205, 213, 217, 229).

2   Austria's perhaps willful ignoring of Napoleon's strategic goals from Broers, p. 165. The tsar's quote is from Alexander to Rumiantsev, 14 February 1809, *VPR*, vol. IV, p. 493.

3   Drawn partly from Vandal, vol. II, pp. 4–5.

4   Printed in Bittard des Portes, p. 135. In a 16 August 1808 letter to Andréossy, Champagny explained that Napoleon wanted neither 'to abandon it [Spain] to the English nor to the horrible anarchy that menaces it' (AE, vol. 381). Caulaincourt's account of the Erfurt event repeatedly touches on the importance of Great Britain in Napoleon's strategic calculations (Armand de Caulaincourt, *Memoirs of General de Caulaincourt*, London: Cassell, 1935, vol. I, pp. 21–39, 47–9).

5   Schroeder (p. 353) suggests that 'the fragile personal basis of the Empire' was also important to Napoleon. Without an heir, he might not have wanted to hazard the chance of death in another campaign.

6   Andréossy to Champagny, 27 April, 6 May, and 20 May 1808, AE, vol. 381.

7   Champagny to Andréossy, 22 May 1808, AE, vol. 381.

8   Champagny to Andréossy, 22 and 29 May 1808, AE, vol. 381.

9   Andréossy to Champagny, no. 34, 18 July 1808, AE, vol. 381.

10 Champagny to Andréossy, 29 June 1808, AE, vol. 381. Champagny placed almost all of Andréossy's reports 'sous les yeux' of Napoleon (for example: Champagny to Andréossy, 24 June 1808).

11 The wealth of intelligence is reflected in, among other places, AE, vol. 381. For example: extracts from Bavarian reports of 24 and 26 May 1808; Legrand to Berthier, 12 June 1808; Otto to Champagny, 14 June 1808; Andréossy's reports of 22 June, 29 June, and 18 July 1808, nos. 25, 27, 34; and Mortier to Berthier, 12 August 1808. In his 10 August letter (no. 39), Andréossy wrote: 'Austria has never been so war-like'. Andréossy supplied very detailed estimates of Austrian troop strengths and dispositions such as the tables accompanying his reports of 18 July and 6 September 1808.

12 Eberhard Mayerhoffer von Vedropolje, '1809. Aufmarsch des Heeres Napoleon I', *Organ der Militärwissenschaftlichen Vereine*, vol. LXVII (1903), pp. 16–17. For Austrian worries: Stadion to Metternich, 12 June 1808, in Botzenhart, p. 230; and Metternich to Stadion, 23 June 1808, in Metternich, *Memoirs*, vol. II, p. 215.

13 Napoleon to Champagny, 11 July 1808, *Correspondance*, no. 14177. Andréossy reported that Austria appeared 'disconcerted' by the mobilisation of the Rheinbund contingents (Andréossy to Champagny, no. 41, 24 August 1808, AE, vol. 381).

14 Rheinbund mobilisation directed by Napoleon's letters to the respective princes (25 July 1808, *Correspondance*, no. 14230, and 7 September 1808, no. 14302). The conscripts were raised by two imperial decisions on 10 and 12 September 1808, each calling for 80,000 men (Alain Pigeard, *L'Armée Napoléonienne*, Paris: Curandéra, 1993, p. 304).

15 Champagny to Metternich, 30 July 1808, quoted in Botzenhart, p. 236. For a time, Napoleon was undecided about removing Mortier's corps from Germany: Napoleon to Soult, 23 August 1808, *Lettres Inédites de Napoléon Ier*, ed. Léon Lecestre, Paris: Plon, 1897, vol. I, pp. 234–5.

16 Metternich to Stadion, 23 June 1808, Metternich, *Memoirs*, vol. II, p. 209. The Russian ambassador in Paris reported that 'the anxious public believes war is

inevitable' (Tolstoi to Rumiantsev, 18 August 1808, quoted in Botzenhart, p. 241, referring to popular opinion in Paris). Likewise, the Prussian ambassador declared that 'People speak generally and decidedly about a war against Austria' (Brockhausen to Friedrich Wilhelm, 1 June 1808 in Hassel, p. 175); the American minister discussed 'the approaching storm' (John Armstrong to James Madison, 28 August 1808, US National Archives [hereafter NA], Dispatches from US Ministers to France, vol. 11, M34/roll 14, Record Group 59). The view from Vienna was similar and the Bavarian ambassador reported that 'all the elements of a war have been, so to speak, piled up, and lack only a spark for a great part of the continent to be set ablaze again' (Rechberg letter of 3 August 1808 quoted in Dunan, note 92, p. 632).

17 Champagny to Andréossy, 27 July 1808 (AE, vol. 381) and Champagny to Metternich, 30 July 1808 in Botzenhart, 236. Napoleon to Champagny, 28 May 1808, *Correspondance*, no. 14003.

18 The American minister's report on the interview in Armstrong to Madison, 28 August 1808, NA, vol. 11, M34/roll 14, Record Group 59.

19 Quote from Champagny's report on the interview to Andréossy, 16 August 1808 in AE, vol. 381, major extracts printed in *Correspondance*, no. 14254. It is this quote that is featured in the Preface to the present volume.

20 Quote from the Prussian ambassador's report on the Napoleon–Metternich exchange, Brockhausen to Friedrich Wilhelm, 18 August 1808, in Hassel, p. 507. Metternich's account contains a similar phrase, Metternich to Stadion, 17 August 1808, in Oncken, pp. 599–605. Oncken also has the Saxon ambassador's 16 August 1808 report. The best analysis of this famous interchange is Botzenhart, pp. 237–43, drawing on French, Austrian, Russian, Prussian, and various German reports.

21 Armstrong to Madison, 28 August 1808, NA, Dispatches from U.S. Ministers to France, vol. 11, M34/roll 14, Record Group 59.

22 Stadion to Metternich, 16 August 1808 (reached Metternich on 23 August), in Beer, p. 325. Metternich was also told that Stadion wanted to avoid anything that France might use to 'justify an attack against Austria'. Stadion's sense of life-or-death desperation, however, was also evident in this letter: 'If peace can only be preserved by us voluntarily and immediately consenting to our own political annihilation, then we will face the unfortunate necessity of taking our chances with events as they present themselves' (in Beer, p. 321).

23 Napoleon to Daru, 26 August 1808, *Dernières Lettres Inédites de Napoléon Ier*, ed. Léonce de Brotonne, Paris: Champion, 1903, pp. 348–9. Champagny informed Andréossy and adjured the ambassador to confirm execution of Metternich's promises (letter of 26 August 1808 in AE, vol. 381).

24 Napoleon to Jerome, 7 September 1808, *Correspondance*, no. 14302. The reassuring letter is Napoleon to Jerome, 12 October 1808 in *Lettres Inédites*, vol. I, p. 246–7.

25 Schroeder argues that Napoleon never developed a policy for Austria but attempted to 'exploit victories for the moment and leave all possibilities open for the future' (p. 281).

26 Driault, *Tilsit*, p. 345. In July 1808, Sultan Mustapha IV was overthrown and killed in a complex tangle of intrigues and violence that left the Ottoman capital in chaos for months.

27 Napoleon to Alexander, 8 July 1808 (*Correspondance*, no. 14170) and Napoleon to Caulaincourt, 9 July 1808 (*Lettres Inédites*, vol. I, pp. 214–15). Champagny reinforced this theme several weeks later: '. . . we cannot penetrate its intentions, we cannot divine the motives for its actions. The emperor has ignored its military movements for a long time, but the disquiet manifested by the courts of Germany bordering on Austria has finally forced him to give these some attention' (Champagny to Caulaincourt, 30 July 1808, in Bittard des Portes, p. 127).

28 Caulaincourt, vol. I, p. 21. The ambassador records that he argued with Napoleon, attempting to persuade the emperor that a harsh approach to Austria would be detrimental and that Europe's attitude towards France resulted from its fear of him as exemplified by Vienna's sense that it was embarking on a 'war of desperation' (pp. 21–9).

29 Napoleon to Champagny, 10 August 1808, *Correspondance*, no. 14248.

30 For Talleyrand's curious role in the Erfurt negotiations (which he considered his greatest achievement) and his larger efforts to limit Napoleon's expansion, see Georges Lacour-Gayet, *Talleyrand*, Paris: Payot, 1930, vol. II, pp. 238–54; and Emile Dard, *Napoleon and Talleyrand*, London: Philip Allan, 1937, pp. 181–94.

31 Conversation with Caulaincourt in Caulaincourt, vol. I, p. 26.

32 Article 10 of the 'Convention d'alliance' signed at Erfurt on 12 October 1808 in M. de Clercq, *Recueil des Traités de la France*, Paris: Amyot, 1864, vol. II, pp. 284–6. As André Fugier points out, a solid Russian guarantee against Austrian aggression was 'essential' for France: *La Révolution Française et l'Empire Napoléonien*, Paris: Hachette, 1954, p. 250.

33 First quote from Napoleon to Soult, 10 September 1808 (*Correspondance*, no. 14309); second from Champagny to Caulaincourt, 30 July 1808 in Bittard des Portes, p. 127. Other examples are Napoleon to Eugene, 10 August 1808 (*Correspondance*, no. 14249), and Napoleon to Davout, 23 August 1808 (*Correspondance*, no. 14269). The conciliatory gesture was the forthcoming removal of French troops from Silesia as Napoleon withdrew men from Prussia in accordance with undertakings he was about to sign with that state (Napoleon to Caulaincourt, 23 and 26 August 1808 in *Lettres Inédites*, vol. I, pp. 233–6).

34 Décret portant organisation de l'Armée du Rhin, 12 October 1808, *Correspondance*, no. 14376.

35 Andréossy to Champagny, no. 48, 22 September 1808, AE, vol. 381. Napoleon himself pointed to the similarity between the 15 August (with Metternich in Paris) and 1 October (with Vincent in Erfurt) audiences: Napoleon to Caulaincourt, 6 March 1809 in *Lettres Inédites*, vol. I, pp. 288–90.

36 Caulaincourt, vol. I, p. 36.

37 Champagny to Andréossy, 1 October 1808, AE, vol. 381, parts printed in Vandal, vol. I, p. 484–5. The foreign minister expressed 'astonishment' at what the French perceived as Austrian repudiation of a promise made by Metternich to recognise Joseph.

38 Vincent to Stadion, 1 October 1808, in Hassel, p. 280.

39 First quote: Alexander to Franz, 12 October 1808 in Beer, p. 477; parts cited in Vandal, vol. I, p. 486. Second quote: Alexander to Kurakin, 16 October 1808, *VPR*, vol. IV, pp. 364–5.

40 Napoleon to Franz, 14 October 1808, *Correspondance*, no. 14380.

41 G. Paulus, 'Bayerische Kriegsvorbereitungen, Mobilmachung und Einleitung zum Feldzuge 1809', *Darstellungen aus der Bayerischen Kriegs- und Heeresgeschichte*, vol. 2, Munich: Lindauer, 1893, pp. 98–100. The invasion of mice is from [Max von Prielmeyer], *Geschichte des k. b. I. Infanterie-Regiments König*, Munich: Huttler, 1881, p. 139. See also histories of the Bavarian 3rd, 7th, 8th, 10th, and 11th Infantry Regiments. For Württemberg: *Geschichte des 3. Württ. Infanterie-Regiments No. 121 1716–1891*, Stuttgart: Kohlhammer, 1891, pp. 216–17. Saxony: O. Schuster and F. A. Francke, *Geschichte der Sächsischen Armee von deren Errichtung bis auf die neueste Zeit*, Leipzig: Duncker & Humblot, 1885, vol. II, p. 270. For Baden: Karl von Zech and Friedrich von Porbeck, *Geschichte der Badischen Truppen 1809*, Heidelberg: Winter, 1909, pp. 6–8. Westphalia was also directed to mobilise its army, but seems to have done nothing along these lines, probably owing to the primitive state of the army's organisation.

42 Caulaincourt notes that the letter to George III was especially important to Napoleon because it 'tinged the interior of the [Franco-Russian] alliance with a marked anti-English colour' (Caulaincourt, vol. I, p. 37).

43 Lettre aux princes de la Confédération, 12–14 October 1808, *Correspondance*, no. 14382. Napoleon to Jerome, 12 October 1808 in *Lettres Inédites*, vol. I, pp. 246–7.

44 Caulaincourt, vol. I, p. 42.

45 Alexander to Kurakin, 7 November 1808, *VPR*, vol. IV, pp. 385–6. Vandal (vol. I, pp. 493–5) makes much of Talleyrand's role and grants him rather too much importance here; as noted earlier, Stadion by this time was 'already captive of his war policy' (Botzenhart) and placed little trust in Talleyrand anyway.

46 Napoleon to Davout, 25 October 1808, *Correspondance*, no. 14410. Champagny told Andréossy that the conference had 'fulfilled expectations' (Champagny to Andréossy, 12 October 1808, AE, vol. 381).

47 Napoleon to Josephine, 5 November 1808, *Correspondance*, no. 14441.

48 Some of the material in this section is taken from a paper presented to the Consortium on Revolutionary Europe in 1997: John H. Gill, 'The Strategic Setting in 1809: Intelligence and Operational Decisions on the Road to War', Consortium on Revolutionary Europe, *Selected Papers 1997*, ed. Kyle O. Eidahl, Donald D. Horward and John Severn, Tallahassee: Florida State University, 1997, pp. 485–94.

49 For example, Napoleon to Berthier, 1 July 1808, *Correspondance*, no. 14147, directing Daru and Davout to send agents into Bohemia to observe 'les mouvements réel des Autrichiens'. Champagny to Andréossy, 24 June 1808, AE, vol. 381.

50 Reports from Andréossy in Vienna and, after Andréossy departed in February, from chargé Dodun were excellent. Those for January through April 1809 are in AE, vol. 382.

51 Jean Tulard (ed.), *Dictionnaire Napoléon*, Paris: Fayard, 1987, 'Espionnage', by Alain Montarras. Napoleon detailed Lagrange's mission (even to the extent of how he should keep his files of regiments and commanders) in a letter to Berthier dated 3 March 1806 (*Correspondance*, no. 9919); apparently Lagrange was still at the legation

in Vienna in 1809. List of units passing through Vienna in Dodun to Champagny, no. 2, 6 March 1809 AE, vol. 382.

52　Metternich to Stadion, 12 January 1809, no. 2/A, HHStA.

53　Some examples of Davout's intelligence role: Davout to Napoleon, 27 December 1808, to Clarke, 30 January 1809, to Friant, 20 March 1809, and to Napoleon, 24 March 1809 in Louis-Nicolas Davout, *Correspondance du Maréchal Davout*, ed. Charles de Mazade, Paris: Plon, 1885, vol. II, pp. 337, 367, 407, 439; Davout to Bourgoing, 8 January 1809, to Saunier, 28 January 1809, and Bourgoing to Davout, 12 March 1809 in Fedorowicz, pp. 42–3, 74, 155; and report of Colonel André Méda, 17 February 1809 in Delphin C. Oré, *1er Régiment de Chasseurs*, Chateaudun: Laussedat, 1903, pp. 117–18. Light cavalry operations along the Bohemian frontier are covered in detail in A. Ledru, *Montbrun 1809*, Paris: Fournier, 1913, pp. 36–47; while C. P. V. Pajol, *Pajol, Général en Chef*, Paris: Didot, 1874, pp. 442–5, provides that general's reports to Davout. Also useful is John R. Elting, *Swords Around a Throne*, New York: The Free Press, 1988, p. 118. Details of collars, cuffs, turnbacks and shakos, today often relegated to the arcana of uniformology, provided key intelligence in Napoleon's time.

54　Among many examples: Napoleon to Champagny, 25 June 1808, *Correspondance*, no. 14128; to Berthier, 1 July 1808, *Correspondance*, no. 14147; to Champagny, 14 January 1809, *Correspondance*, no. 14700; to Champagny, 23 February 1809 in *Lettres Inédites*, vol. I, p. 284; and to Eugene, 16 March 1809, *Correspondance*, no. 14909. Also Champagny to Andréossy, 17 and 25 January 1809, AE, vol. 382.

55　See S. J. Watson, *By Command of the Emperor*, Cambridge: Trotman, 1988, p. 108, and Edward A. Whitcomb, *Napoleon's Diplomatic Service*, Durham, NC: Duke University Press, 1979, p. 30. With thanks to the late John Elting for reminding me of these two sources.

56　Paulus provides a detailed account of Bavarian intelligence collection during the months leading up to war in 'Bayerische Kriegsvorbereitungen, Mobilmachung und Einleitung zum Feldzuge 1809'. Also: Alfred Döderlein, *Geschichte des Königlich Bayerischen 8. Infanterie-Regiments (Pranckh)*, Landshut: Rietsch, 1898, pp. 106–7.

57　For example: Davout to Napoleon, 23 November, 20 December, and 21 December 1808 in *Correspondance du Maréchal Davout*, vol. II, pp. 318, 332–35.

58　Rechberg letters of 21 October and 15 October (respectively) 1808 quoted in Dunan, note 92, p. 632.

59　Napoleon to Champagny, 14 January 1809, *Correspondance*, no. 14700.

60　Described in Louis Garros, *Quel Roman que ma vie! Itinéraire de Napoléon Bonaparte*, Paris: Editions de l'Encyclopédie Française, 1947, pp. 309–10. Also the new edition of this classic, reissued under the editorship of Jean Tulard as *Itinéraire de Napoléon au Jour le Jour*, Saint-Estève, 1992 and 1998, p. 304. According to a member of the imperial household, 'the snow fell in large and continued flakes' that day (Louis François Joseph de Bausset, *Private Memoirs of the Court of Napoleon*, Philadelphia: Carey, Lea & Carey, 1828, p. 241).

61　Jean-Jacques-Régis Cambacérès, *Mémoires Inédits*, Paris: Perrin, 1999, vol. II, p. 250; Jean-Jacques Pelet, *Mémoires sur la Guerre de 1809 en Allemagne*, Paris: Roret, 1824–26, vol. I, pp. 46–8; Etienne-Denis Pasquier, *Memoirs of Chancellor Pasquier*, New York: Scribner's Sons, 1893, vol. I, pp. 372–9; Savary, vol. II, pp. 17–18; Dard, pp. 196–9; Lacour-Gayet, vol. II, pp. 266–71. Fouché's curious memoirs, even if authored by one of his agents, speak distinctly of his concern that Napoleon might be killed in battle or by assassination; he may even have communicated something of this concern to Napoleon given the wording of the Emperor's reply to him, 7 December 1808 in *Lettres Inédites*, vol. I, p. 257: 'Vous avez tort de craindre pour moi'. Fouché's book also protests complete innocence for himself and for Talleyrand against the accusation of plotting to prepare a successor to Napoleon without the emperor's permission (Joseph Fouché, *Memoirs Relating to Fouché*, New York: Sturgis & Walton, 1912, pp. 250–61). On Fouché, see Louis Madelin, *Fouché*, Paris: Plon, 1930, vol. II, pp. 74–90; and Hubert Cole, *Fouché: The Unprincipled Patriot*, New York: McCall, 1971, pp. 181–5. A tidy summary is in Jean de Bourgoing, *1809*, Vienna: Bergland, 1959, pp. 9–10. Also very useful is Adolphe Thiers, *Histoire du Consulat et de l'Empire*, Paris: Paulin, 1851, vol. X, pp. 13–17.

62 This conclusion is based primarily on the recollections of GD Anne-Jean-Marie-René Savary in his *Mémoires du Duc de Rovigo*, Paris: Bossange, 1828, vol. IV, p. 25. Hughes-Bernard Maret, with Napoleon at the time as his state secretary (more or less his civil chief of staff), also recorded that the emperor had received disturbing news from Paris while at Astorga regarding 'a plot hatched in the capital by the same hands that accomplished the deed in 1814'. Maret, however, mistakenly placed the incident on 6 January (quoted in Alfred Auguste Ernouf, *Maret Duc de Bassano*, Paris: Perrin, 1884, pp. 252–3). Pelet notes that previous news concerning 'the men of March 1814' had arrived on 24 December. Moreover, it is logical to assume that the several letters written to the emperor by different correspondents concerning Talleyrand and Fouché did not arrive in the same packet.

63 Bausset, p. 241.

64 Balagny, Dominique E.P., *Campagne de l'Empereur Napoléon en Espagne (1808-1809)*, Paris: Berger-Levrault, 1902–7, vol. V, pp. 345–75.

65 Savary, vol. IV, p. 26.

66 This is the notorious scene in which Napoleon referred to Talleyrand rather indelicately as 'so much filth in a silk stocking'.

67 Metternich to Stadion, 31 January 1809 (enciphered), HHStA, Frankreich, Berichte 1809/I, Kart. 205. Talleyrand's favourite themes were that 'Napoleon definitely wants war' and that the emperor was weak on the domestic front.

68 Most of these are in vol. XVIII of Napoleon's *Correspondance*; others are in vol. I of *Lettres Inédites* and in vol. II of *Unpublished Correspondence of Napoleon I Preserved in the War Archives*, ed. Ernest Picard and Louis Tuetey, New York: Duffield, 1913 [hereafter Napoleon, *War Archives*].

69 Napoleon to Clarke, 1 January 1809, *Correspondance*, no. 14634. Davout to Clarke, 8 January 1809: 'It is a fact that the armaments continue and that the war party is very active, but . . . I do not believe that anything will commence here before two or three months have passed' (Saski, vol. I. pp. 29). Also Andréossy to Champagny, 15 January 1809, no. 1, AE, vol. 382.

70 Andréossy to Champagny, 3 and 7 December 1808, nos. 54 and 55, AE, vol. 381.

71 Napoleon to Otto, 15 January 1809, *Correspondance*, no. 14710. Other references to the shift of Oudinot's corps: Napoleon to Champagny, 9 January 1809, *Correspondance*, no. 14668; Napoleon to Davout, 15 January 1809, *Correspondance*, no. 14711; and

Napoleon to Maximilian Joseph, 15 January 1809, *Correspondance*, no. 14720. He also referred to the impact of his return to Paris in a letter to Joseph: 'In any event, my simple presence in Paris will neutralise Austria' (15 January 1809, *Correspondance*, no. 14717).

72 Metternich to Stadion, 20 January 1809, (enciphered), HHStA, Frankreich, Berichte 1809/I, Kart. 205. In an earlier, unenciphered, report, Metternich had drawn on other sources to reach the same conclusion (Metternich to Stadion, 17 January 1809, no. 3).

73 Napoleon, redaction of draft newspaper article, January 1809, in *Inédits Napoléoniens*, ed. Arthur Chuquet, Paris: de Boccard, 1914–19, vol. II, p. 34. The emperor also reduced the strength figures attributed to the Austrian forces, doubtless to make them appear less formidable. Similar media themes were promoted for the press in Westphalia specifically to counter Austrian journal articles (Champagny to Reinhard, 21 January 1809 in Albert du Casse, *Les Rois Frères de Napoléon Ier*, Paris: Baillière, 1883, p. 225). Among many other examples in the *Correspondance*: Napoleon to Clarke and to Fouché, 13 January 1809, nos. 14691 and 14694; Napoleon to King Friedrich Wilhelm, 15 January, no. 14722 and to Louis, 21 February 1809, no. 14799. Reschounig provides several interesting examples from the *Moniteur* and the *Journal de l'Empire*, pp. 30–4. Pahl recalled an article in a Paris newspaper dated 21 January 1809 in which rumors of war were declared groundless and previous opprobrium against Austria was muted (Pahl, *Denkwürdigkeiten*, p. 597).

74 Instructions for halting the two divisions at Metz and Nancy are in Napoleon to Clarke, 14 January 1809, in Napoleon, *War Archives*, vol. II, p. 624; reference in Saski, vol. I, p. 36. Napoleon's letter to Cambacérès is dated 8 January 1809, *Correspondance*, no. 14663. At the same time, articles in the *Moniteur* spoke soothingly of Austria's 'purely defensive' actions: *Moniteur*, 13 January 1809, quoted in Reschounig, p. 31.

75 Napoleon to Eugene, 15 January, 26 January, and 27 February 1809, *Correspondance*, nos. 14715, 14741, and 14820. Eugene was careful to observe these restrictions, even though he appears to have been somewhat more nervous than his step-father: Eugene to Napoleon, 8 March 1809, Eugene de Beauharnais, *Mémoires et Correspondance*, ed. Albert du Casse, Paris: Lévy, 1858–60 [hereafter du Casse, *Eugène*], vol. IV, p. 365. The troops in Germany had similar instructions; for example, Friant to Davout, 2 March 1809, and Berthier to Davout, 11 March 1809, both in Saski, vol. I, pp. 95, 230–2.

76 Napoleon to Louis X, 15 January 1809, *Correspondance*, no. 14719. The other letters relevant to the Rheinbund are 14718, 14720, 14721, 14722, 14723, 14724, 14725, all dated 15 January 1809 from Valladolid.

77 Napoleon to Caulaincourt, 14 January 1809, *Lettres Inédites*, vol. I, pp. 269–71. A second letter to Caulaincourt, same date, is on pages 271–3, followed by the brief note to Alexander. The letter to Alexander was originally published in Serge Tatistcheff, *Alexandre Ier et Napoléon*, Paris: Perrin, 1891, p. 467.

78 Champagny to Andréossy, 17 and 25 January 1809, AE, vol. 382.

79 Dodun to Champagny, no. 1, 1 March 1809, AE, vol. 382. Here again, Talleyrand betrayed Napoleon, this time by providing advance warning that Andréossy would

be recalled (Metternich to Stadion, 20 January 1809, (enciphered), HHStA, Frankreich, Berichte 1809/I, Kart. 205). The diplomatic community in Vienna interpreted the public rationale for Andréossy's departure as a pretence: Arthur Kleinschmidt, *Bayern und Hessen 1799–1816*, Berlin: Räde, 1900, p. 46, citing communications from Westphalia to the Bavarian ambassador in March 1809.

80 Attachment to Dodun to Champagny, no. 2, 6 March 1809, AE, vol. 382.

81 Metternich to Stadion, 25 January 1809, (enciphered), in Grunwald, 'La Fin d'une Ambassade', pp. 841–2. It is interesting to note that in late January Talleyrand, through Metternich, had urged Vienna to use recent French actions 'as a pretext' to place its forces on a war footing. Stadion, however, would have needed no external advice to recognise and exploit this opportunity (Metternich to Stadion, 31 January 1809, (enciphered), HHStA, Frankreich, Berichte 1809/I, Kart. 205).

82 Stadion to Metternich, 21 February 1809, Grunwald, 'La Fin d'une Ambassade', p. 842.

83 Champagny to Napoleon, 2 March 1809, in *Correspondance*, vol. XVIII, pp. 303–6.

84 Lefebvre, vol. IV, p. 100.

85 Alexander to Kurakin, 10 July 1808, Vandal, vol. I, pp. 375–6.

86 Champagny to Andréossy, 17 and 25 January 1809, AE, vol. 382. Also Andréossy's report to Champagny during his trip: Andréossy to Champagny, 3 March 1809, and Champagny to Napoleon, 13 March 1809, both in Saski, vol. I, pp. 257–9, 281–2. Andréossy reached Paris on 13 March and reported to the foreign minister immediately.

87 For example, Charles Reinhard, Napoleon's minister in Westphalia, reported information from the Westphalian ambassador in Vienna and other confidential contacts (Reinhard to Champagny, 3 and 28 February 1809 in du Casse, *Les Rois Frères*, pp. 227, 241). Some Bavarian reporting is in Saski, vol. I, pp. 95, 122–3.

88 Eugene's efforts in Italy included sending GB Louis Gareau across the border disguised as a farmer in early March, and dispatching an engineer captain named Poussin in the habit of a wine merchant. Another officer was sent on a spurious mission to Vienna as a courier to learn what he could of Austrian activity. From *Krieg*, vol. II, p. 43; and du Casse, *Eugène*, vol. IV, pp. 277–82.

89 Note, for example, the tracking of the *Czartoryski* Infantry Regiment: Davout to Poniatowski, 28 January 1809; Poniatowski to Davout, 4 February and 4 March 1809. Or, more generally, Davout to Colonel Saunier, 28 January 1809. All in Fedorowicz, pp. 73, 74, 88, 116.

90 Space limitations prohibit an exhaustive list of the Saxon intelligence reports and sources Davout, Daru and others employed, but some examples will illustrate their depth and utility. On 1 January 1809, the French ambassador's secretary wrote to Davout from Dresden to report that his intelligence network was established and to promise that he would soon forward a table with the locations of the Austrian forces in Bohemia (Saski, vol. I, pp. 41–2). A thick file in the Saxon War Archives contains a host of intelligence reports on Austrian activity, such as an unsigned report dated 26 February 1809 noting that regiments were being filled with recruits and reservists, that officers were to receive their *Kriegsgehalt* as of 1 March, and that Austria had six corps in Bohemia, each of approximately 30,000 men. All from Sächsisches Hauptstaatsarchiv Dresden [hereafter SächsHStA], Geheimes

Kriegs-Kollegium, D1481, *Eingegange Nachrichten über die Truppenbewegungen in Böhmen.* Much of the Saxon reporting came through the French legation in Dresden, examples in Saski, vol. I, pp. 93–4, 126–8.

91 Fedorowicz contains many reports from Polish sources, for example: Poniatowski to Davout, 29 December 1808 (p. 25); Romeuf to Davout, 7 January 1809 (p. 35f.); Bourgoing to Clarke, 24 February 1809 forwarding a report from a Polish officer who had travelled to Cracow; Rozniecki to Davout, 5 March 1809 (p. 116f.); Sokolnicki to Davout, 11 March 1809 (pp. 150–3); Zajoncek to Davout, 11 March 1809 (p. 154).

92 Sample reports can be found in Dodun to Champagny, no. 2, 6 March 1809 and no. 4, 11 March 1809 in AE, vol. 382; Eugene to Napoleon, 8 March 1809 in du Casse, *Eugène*, vol. IV, p. 365; Poniatowski to Davout, 4 and 8 March 1809 in *Correspondance du Prince Joseph Poniatowski avec la France*, Posen, 1921–3, vol. II, pp. 43–5; Oré, pp. 117–19; unsigned letters to Berthier from Vienna, 4 and 11 March 1809, SächsHStA, Geheimes Kriegs-Kollegium, D1475, *Briefe, Befehle und anderes dem Feldzug 1809 betreffend.*

93 Napoleon to Champagny, 23 February 1809, *Lettres Inédites*, vol. I, pp. 284–5.

94 These examples are from: Napoleon to Champagny, 14 March 1809 (newspapers from Vienna, Cracow, and Pressburg), *Correspondance*, no. 14894; Napoleon to Clarke, 14 March 1809 (maps), *Correspondance*, no. 14895; Napoleon to Eugene, 16 March 1809 (reconnaissance in Italy), *Correspondance*, no. 14909; Eugene to Marmont, 14 March 1809, in Auguste-Frédéric-Louis Viesse de Marmont, *Mémoires du Maréchal Duc de Raguse de 1792 à 1832*, Paris: Perrotin, 1857, vol. III, p. 195.

94 Percentage based on comparing the French estimate of Austrian forces on 7 April 1809 with the complete planned order of battle of the Austrian Main Army as presented in *Krieg*, vol. I, Appendix XIII: of 182 battalions and 164 squadrons, the French correctly identified 176 and 156 respectively. *Actual* Austrian strength was somewhat less on this date as many battalions were still on the road when the war opened. Earlier French estimates of Austrian forces in Bohemia (equally accurate) were dated 20 February and (?) March 1809, Archives de la guerre, Service historique de la armée de terre [hereafter AG], *Armée d'Allemagne: Armées prussiennes et autrichiennes*, Kart. C2/520. French assessments of Austrian forces facing Italy and Poland were also fairly accurate: Eugene to Napoleon, 20 March and 3 April 1809, in Eugene, *Mémoires et Correspondance*, vol. IV, pp. 392, 421; and Napoleon to Eugene, 15 March 1809, *Correspondance*, no. 14903. See the intelligence reports in Fedorowicz for Poland. Much of this intelligence was collated and analysed by Claude Mounier, a secretary in the imperial cabinet (Saski, vol. I, pp. 124–6).

96 Napoleon to Caulaincourt, 9 July 1808, *Lettres Inédites*, vol. I, p. 214.

97 'Insolent' and 'ridiculous' in Napoleon to Caulaincourt, 6 August 1808, *Lettres Inédites*, vol. I, p. 229. 'Panicky fear' from Napoleon to Joseph, 14 July 1808, *Lettres Inédites*, vol. I, p. 216. 'Far from wanting war' in Napoleon to Soult, 10 September 1808, *Correspondance*, no. 14309.

98 Lefebvre, vol. IV, p. 85 and Champagny to Andréossy, 29 June 1808, AE, vol. 381.

414 ~ NOTES TO PAGES 88–90

99 'Excessive dread' in Napoleon to Soult, 10 September 1808, *Correspondance*, no. 14309. 'Nothing to fear' in Napoleon to Eugene, 10 August 1808, *Correspondance*, no. 14249. 'Everything will return' in Napoleon to Caulaincourt, 26 August 1808, *Lettres Inédites*, vol. I, p. 235.

100 Napoleon to King Friedrich of Württemberg, 21 February 1809, *Correspondance*, no. 14800.

101 Letters to the Rheinbund princes, 15 January 1809, *Correspondance*, nos. 14710 and 14715 through 14725. Specific quotes from Napoleon to King Friedrich-August of Saxony, 15 January 1809, *Correspondance*, no. 14721; to King Friedrich of Württemberg, 15 January 1809, *Correspondance*, no. 14722; to King Friedrich-August of Saxony, 6 March 1809, *Correspondance*, no. 14864. Napoleon repeatedly described Vienna as 'seized' with 'deluded recklessness' or 'giddiness' (*vertige*).

102 Napoleon to Caulaincourt, 6 and 23 February 1809, *Lettres Inédites*, vol. I, pp. 280, 286. 'The diversion Austria is making in favour of England' in Napoleon to King Friedrich of Württemberg, 14 February 1809, *Correspondance*, no. 14779.

103 Napoleon to Dalberg, 15 January 1809, *Correspondance*, no. 14725.

104 Napoleon to Otto, 4 March 1809, *Correspondance*, no. 14849.

105 'Rushing to its ruin' in Napoleon to Louis, 21 March 1809, *Correspondance*, no. 14937 among many other locations. 'Sound its last hour' in Napoleon to Cambacérès, 8 January 1809, *Correspondance*, no. 14663. 'Cease to reign' in Napoleon to Jerome, 16 January 1809, *Correspondance*, no. 14731. 'Be in Vienna quickly' in Napoleon to Caulaincourt, 6 March 1809, *Lettres Inédites*, vol. I, p. 288. In addition to many other quotes already cited, his desire to avoid war is clear in correspondence among his subordinates such as Davout to Oudinot, 3 March 1809, and Berthier to Davout, 11 March 1809, both in Saski, vol. I, pp. 80–1, 230–2.

106 Napoleon to Eugene, 22 March 1809, *Correspondance*, no. 14945; Napoleon to Eugene, 27 March 1809, du Casse, *Eugène*, vol. IV, p. 409. Also Berthier to Massena and Davout, 16 March 1809, both in Saski, vol. I, pp. 280–1.

107 Napoleon to Clarke, 13 and 21 February 1809, *Correspondance*, nos. 14772 and 14794. The light cavalry regiments were the 11th, 12th, and 16th Chasseurs. The 16th Chasseurs are not mentioned in these two orders; their movement dates and destinations are taken from: Lieutenant Chevillotte, '16eme Chasseurs à Cheval: Historique', manuscript, AG, 1887, pp. 101–2.

108 Guard: Napoleon to Bessières, 15 February 1809, *Correspondance*, no. 14780. Massena's corps: Napoleon to Clarke, 21 and 23 February 1809, *Correspondance*, nos. 14795 and 14806.

109 Curiously, Dupas remained under Bernadotte's orders. That meant that the marshal would eventually have nominal command of the Dupas at Hanover, the Saxon army at Dresden and the Polish forces gathering around Warsaw. Napoleon to Berthier, 5 and 7 March 1809, Saski, vol. I, pp. 156, 185.

110 For Davout, Poland, and Bernadotte: Napoleon to Davout, 4 March 1809, *Correspondance*, no. 14848; Berthier to Davout, 4 March 1809, Saski, vol. I, p. 144. For Massena: Napoleon to Clarke, 4 March 1809, *Correspondance*, no. 14844. For Berthier's appointment: Napoleon to Clarke, 4 March 1809, Saski, vol. I, p. 129. This imperial order of 4 March designated Berthier as the major general for all the separate constituent elements of Napoleon's forces in Germany; when these

were amalgamated into the Army of Germany a new order was issued confirming Berthier as major general of this new entity (Saski, vol. I, p. 129). Detailed expansions of Napoleon's initial instructions came in letters from Berthier to Davout, Oudinot, and Massena on 11 March 1809, Saski, vol. I, pp. 230–5. Davout received lengthy additional instructions in a 17 March 1809 letter, *Correspondance*, no. 14915. See also an excellent review of Saski in *Revue de Cavalerie*, March 1899.

111   The infantry shifted north to Eugene was: two battalions of the 22nd Léger (III, IV), two battalions of the 3rd Italian Line (I, III), and all four battalions of the 23rd Léger, 52nd Ligne, 62nd Ligne, and 102nd Ligne. Cavalry was: the 9th and 25th Chasseurs and the 23rd, 28th, 29th and 30th Dragoons. A battery of six guns also joined Eugene from Naples via Rome. Not all of these troops reached northern Italy before the opening of hostilities. Miollis was left so depleted that two Neapolitan battalions (I and II of 1st Light Infantry), two squadrons of the 1st Neapolitan Chasseurs, and the 3rd Battalion of the Tour d'Auvergne Regiment were sent to him from the Army of Naples. He also received a Corsican light infantry battalion: IV/Corsican Chasseurs. Still, this seems a scanty force to guard and maintain order in Rome, in Tuscany, and along the Adriatic coast. Details are comprehensively laid out in *Krieg*, vol. II, pp. 31–8. Note, however, that the authors of this work missed the renaming of the 'Dalmatian Legion' into the 'Dalmatian Regiment'; they believed that there were two Dalmatian units and thereby credit the French with four extra battalions.

112   Thiers, vol. X, p. 37.

113   Most of this guidance is contained in three letters from Napoleon to Eugene, all dated 14 January 1809, and 'Notes sur la Défense de l'Italie', also dated 14 January 1809, all in *Correspondance*, nos. 14704 to 14707. For analysis of these instructions and others, see Robert M. Epstein, *Prince Eugene at War 1809*, Arlington: Texas: Empire Games Press, 1984; and Albert Pingaud, 'Napoléon et la Défense de l'Italie sur la Piave', *Revue des Études Napoléoniennes*, vol. XIX (July–December 1922).

114   One often encounters confusion regarding the designation of Marmont's command, which began the campaign as the Army of Dalmatia, but which became 11th Corps in mid-July. This work follows the historical designation, using 'Army of Dalmatia' for the active phase of the campaign and introducing '11th Corps' at the historical point.

115   Napoleon to Eugene, 14 and 16 March 1809, Napoleon, *Correspondance*, nos. 14900 and 14909. Compare Frederick C. Schneid, *Napoleon's Italian Campaigns 1805–1815*, Westport, CT: Praeger, 2002, pp. 66–8, and Epstein, p. 40.

116   Napoleon to Louis, 11 March 1809, Napoleon, *Correspondance*, no. 14886.

117   Napoleon to Jerome, 17 March 1809, Napoleon, *Correspondance*, no. 14918.

118   Berthier to Max Joseph, 21 March 1809, cited in Oskar Bezzel, 'Die Massnahmen Bayerns zum Grenzschutze im Feldzuge 1809', *Darstellungen aus der Bayerischen Kriegs- und Heeresgeschichte*, vol. 14, Munich: Lindauer, 1905, p. 79.

119   Napoleon to Clarke, 3 and 13 March 1809, Napoleon, *Correspondance*, nos. 14838 and 14891. Also Napoleon to Clarke, 23 March 1809 in Napoleon, *War Archives*, vol. II, p. 802. These notes and some of Clarke's replies are in chapter IX of Saski, vol. I. Decree of 23 March 1809 in Saski, vol. I, p. 549ff. The order to form the two reserve divisions is Napoleon to Clarke, 3 April 1809, in Saski, vol. II, p. 10. Napoleon initially calculated that the total strength of the reserve demi-brigades

would be approximately 45,500, but Clarke believed that they would number nearly 55,000.

120 Napoleon to Clarke, 19 March 1809, *Correspondance*, no. 14929.
121 Napoleon to Clarke, 14 January 1809 in Napoleon, *War Archives*, vol. II, p. 628.
122 The director general of reviews and conscription was GD Jean Gérard Lacuée. GD Jean François Aimé Dejean was minister of war administration. For two examples of the emperor's astonishing attention to detail, see his meticulous instructions on sappers, miners, pioneers, and the tools of their trades in Napoleon to Bertrand, 22 March 1809 and Imperial Order, 23 March 1809, Saski, vol. I, pp. 340–2, 350–3. See also Mathieu Dumas, *Memoirs of His Own Time*, Philadelphia, Lea & Blanchard, 1839, vol. II, pp. 188–9.
123 Napoleon's marginal notes dated 6 March 1809 in 'Situation de l'Armée d'Italie', 1 March 1809, AN, AF*/IV/1377, *Livrets des armées: Situations des troupes en Italie*. Note that the figure 94,600 includes *all* troops on the Army of Italy's rolls in northern *and* central Italy (active, depot, fortress garrison) and is highlighted here simply to indicate Napoleon's focus on detail; the number of mobile, field troops immediately available for combat operations in northern Italy when hostilities began in April was 72,300 (based on the 1 April 1809 'Situation').
124 Noret, 'Historique du 2e Régiment d'Infanterie de Ligne', manuscript, AG, 1875, vol. I, pp. 169–70, 185.
125 Other examples: IV/1st Léger was with the Army of Italy, while the regiment's other three battalions were in Spain; the 16th Ligne was the opposite, its first three battalions were in Massena's corps, while the fourth was in the Army of Spain's order of battle (Maurice Alexandre Poitevin, *Historique du 16e Régiment d'Infanterie*, Paris: Baudoin, 1888). Seven of the eight regiments in the Army of Dalmatia had only their first and second battalions at hand under Marmont, the third and fourth battalions were in Italy.
126 Napoleon to Lacuée, 5 December 1808, *Correspondance*, no. 14535. Napoleon to Clarke, 1 January 1809, *Correspondance*, no. 14634.
127 Two orders from Napoleon to Clarke, 13 February 1809, Saski, vol. I, pp. 53–5, 61–5. Clarke to Napoleon, 15 February 1809, Saski, vol. I, pp. 65–8. Oudinot was allotted twelve march battalions in February and two more in March: Imperial Orders to Clarke, 8 and 15 March 1809, Saski, vol. I, pp. 210–12, 266.
128 Imperial Decree, 23 February 1809, Saski, vol. I, pp. 101–3.
129 Boyeldieu's notes in L. Loÿ, 'Le Général de Division Baron Boyeldieu', *Carnet de la Sabretache*, No. 264 (August 1914–May 1919), p. 488.
130 Imperial Order to Clarke, 6 March 1809, Saski, vol. I, pp. 167–70. Clarke to Massena, 10 March 1809, Saski, vol. I, pp. 222–4. Massena announced the arrival of these men in an order of the day dated 22 March 1809 (GLA 48/4276).
131 Joachim Joseph Delmarche, *Les Soirées du Grenadier or Mémoires de Joachim Delmarche*, Philippeville: Musée de Cerfontaine, 1980, pp. 20–1. Enrolled in the 14th Ligne, Delmarche and some other replacements departed Sedan for Spain after six months of training, but 'on arrival in Metz, we received counter-orders. We were incorporated in the 18th Ligne'. In all, the line regiments of the corps were to receive 1,900 men in this fashion during the first half of April.

132 The Portuguese comprised approximately 1,700 men in a two-squadron cavalry regiment and a three-battalion infantry regiment: Napoleon to Clarke, 7 March 1809, *Correspondance*, no. 14867; Saski, vol. I, Annex 13; Paul Boppe, *La Légion Portugaise 1807–1813*, Paris: Berger-Levrault, 1897. A decree dated 16 January 1809 reorganised the Guard and created one regiment each of Tirailleurs-Grenadiers and Tirailleurs-Chasseurs; decrees for the four new Guard conscript battalions (two each of Conscript-Grenadiers and Conscript-Chasseurs) were dated 29 and 31 March 1809: Saski, vol. I, Annexes 5, 7, 20 and 20*bis*. Also L. Fallou, *La Garde Impériale*, Paris: La Giberne, 1901, pp. 132, 135, 166, 168. The Provisional Chasseur Regiment was ordered into existence on 16 March 1809, Saski, vol. I, p. 277–9.

133 Napoleon initially called for three (Imperial Order, 6 March 1809, Saski, vol. I, pp. 160–2), then four of these provisional regiments (to Clarke, 12 March 1809, *Correspondance*, no. 14889), but finally increased the number to six several days later (Imperial Decree, 17 March 1809, Saski, vol. I, Appendix 17).

134 Bavarian ambassador to Westphalia, Graf Emmanuel Johann von Lerchenfeld-Köfering, to Max Joseph, 26 March 1809 in Kleinschmidt, *Bayern und Hessen*, p. 47.

135 Marmont's command in Dalmatia had not had a major combat role since 1805 and is not considered here.

136 Letter from Lieutenant Charles A. Faré, 9 October 1808, in *Lettres d'un Jeune Officier a sa Mère*, Paris: Delgrave, 1889, p. 192.

137 As used here, 'veteran' merely indicates soldiers who joined the army prior to 1808; some of the men I have termed 'veterans' therefore may have been completely innocent of combat experience. These approximate percentages were calculated by comparing the number of conscripts assigned to each infantry regiment from the February and September 1808 drafts with the nominal total of 3,360 officers and men on the rolls of a standard five-battalion regiment (four field battalions and one depot battalion). Conscription data drawn from Lacuée's reports dated 14 May, 11 June, 12 July and 1 August 1808 (AN, AF/IV/1375, *Pièces Diverses: Rapports à l'Empereur de Lacuée*); and summary conscription reports from September (AN, AF/IV/1373, *Pièces Diverses: Rapports et pièces diverses concernant la conscription*). These figures, of course, represent the intentions of the ministers in Paris and do not necessarily reflect the number of conscripts who actually arrived at each regimental depot, or made it from the depots to the field units. Nonetheless, it is reasonable to assume that the figures are generally correct even if they are not precise in every individual case. Likewise, although new recruits went first to the depots, because the depots were largely emptied during this period, it makes sense to assume that many new recruits ended up in the field battalions.

138 Eberhard Mayerhoffer von Vedropolje, 'Die französische "Armee in Deutschland" bei Ausbruch des Krieges im Jahre 1809', *Organ der militär-wissenschaftliche Vereine*, vol. LXV (1902), p. 285; Thiers, vol. X, pp. 29–30.

139 Letter of 26 March 1809 in Alexander Coudreux, *Lettres du Commandant Coudreux a Son Frère 1804–1815*, ed. Gustave Schlumberger, Paris: Plon, 1908, p. 147.

140 Raymond-Aimery-Philippe-Joseph de Montesquiou-Fezensac, *Souvenirs Militaires de 1804 à 1814*, Paris: Dumaine, 1870, p. 129. See also the discussion in Hugo Friedrich Philipp Johann Freiherr von Freytag-Loringhoven, 'Die Armeen des

ersten Kaiserreichs', *Vierteljahrsheft für Truppenführung und Heereskunde*, vol. V, Berlin, 1908, p. 218.

141 From an Austrian memorandum from 1810 entitled 'Bemerkungen über die französische Armee und unsere Lage' extensively quoted in 'Die Armee Napoleon I. im Jahre 1809', *Mittheilungen des K. K. Kriegsarchiv*, Vienna, 1881, p. 393. See also Charles, 'Beitrag', *Ausgewählte Schriften*, vol. VI, p. 356.

142 Carl von Clausewitz, *On War*, ed. and trans. Michael Howard and Peter Paret, Princeton: Princeton University Press, 1984, p. 170.

143 This rather famous quote is from Napoleon to Massena, 18 April 1809, *Correspondance*, no. 15087.

144 Berthier to Lefebvre, 21 April 1809, Saski, vol. II, p. 302.

145 Napoleon to Clarke, 25 April 1809, *Correspondance*, no. 15113.

146 Austrian sources contend that the French artillery in 1809 was not up to the qualitative standard of earlier years. This is difficult to quantify, but seems a reasonable assumption, in particular if one compares the slightly degraded French artillery arm with its much improved Austrian counterpart. As noted in the text, however, the French retained their battlefield mobility and organisational flexibility. See: Mayerhoffer, 'Die französische "Armee in Deutschland"', pp. 238–49; and 'Die Armee Napoleon I. im Jahre 1809', pp. 374–5.

147 Songis to Berthier, 21 and 24 March in Saski, vol. I, pp. 337–40, 373–4.

148 Songis to Berthier, 29 March 1809, in Saski, vol. I, p. 416. Also Songis to Berthier, 6 April 1809 in Saski, vol. II, pp. 38–9.

149 Massena, for example, complained of shortages in a 28 March 1809 letter to Songis (Saski, vol. I, pp. 410–11). Oudinot worried that his 12-pounders had to march with four-horse teams (Mayerhoffer, 'Die französische "Armee in Deutschland"', p. 241).

150 Hauptmann Karl von Freydorf, letter of 16 April 1809, quoted in Zech/Porbeck, p. 17.

151 For example, two transportation battalions were barely beginning to form, leaving the army short some 300 caissons (Daru to Napoleon, 25 March 1809, Saski, vol. I, pp. 446–7).

152 In French: *44e bataillon de la flottille* and *bataillon d'ouvriers militaires de la marine*. Correspondence, decree, and history in 'Les Marins de la Flottille et les Ouvriers Militaires de la Marine pendant la Campagne de 1809 en Autriche', *Carnet de la Sabretache*, 1895, pp. 145–55. Good synopsis in Elting, *Swords*, p. 308.

153 Louis Saveur François Sherlock, a retired adjutant-général (he had served as Augereau's chief of staff in 1797) and member of the Council of 500, who had been living in Vienna for two years after having been implicated in the Moreau conspiracy. Though convinced that Napoleon hated him, he had refused offers to spy against France and departed Vienna on 15 March carrying dispatches for Otto from chargé Dodun. Arriving in Munich on 24 March, he wrote to Davout and Massena to apprise them of his situation and to pass on impressions and intelligence about Austrian war preparations. Biographic note and the 24 March letter from Sherlock to Davout are in Saski, vol. I, pp. 356–7; see also pp. 370, 376–7. His letter to Massena is in *Carnet de la Sabretache*, no. 198 (June 1909). Intelligence provided to Massena and other biographic details in Eduard Gachot, *1809: Napoléon en*

Allemagne, Paris: Plon, 1913, pp. 16–19; and Jean Baptiste Koch (ed.), *Mémoires de Massena*, Paris: Paulin et Lechevalier, 1850, vol. VI, pp. 59–61, 68.

154 Napoleon to Berthier, 23 March 1809, Saski, vol. I, pp. 356–7.

155 Napoleon to Eugene, 27 March 1809, du Casse, *Eugène*, vol. IV, p. 409.

156 One line of the French optical telegraph system ran from Paris to Strasbourg, but terminated there.

157 Berthier to Vignolle and Monthion, 21 March 1809 in Saski, vol. I, pp. 327–8; quote from the instructions for Monthion. His order to Bertrand, also dated 21 March, is on pp. 326–7.

158 Victor Bernard Derrécagaix, *Le Maréchal Berthier*, Paris: Chapelot, 1905, vol. II, p. 299.

159 Text in several locations: Saski, vol. I, pp. 421–35; *Correspondance*, 30 March 1809, no. 14975; Pelet, vol. II, pp. 343–63.

160 Saski, vol. I, p. 425 (all quotes from the 30 March 'Instructions' are taken from this source). Note that the two heavy cavalry divisions Napoleon envisaged were to be formed by dividing Nansouty's division in half.

161 Saski, vol. I, p. 425.

162 Saski, vol. I, p. 427. Another example is in a letter he sent to Eugene shortly before departing for Germany: 'if the Austrians attack before the 15th, we will retire behind the Lech' (Napoleon to Eugene, 12 April 1809, du Casse, *Eugène*, vol. IV, p. 444).

163 Napoleon to Daru, 24 March 1809, Saski, vol. I, pp. 442–3. Saski's chapter XIV in vol. I (pp. 442–70), and pp. 48–84 in vol. II cover administrative measures in great detail from 25 March.

164 Saski, vol. I, pp. 422–33.

165 The search for guns to arm the fortresses and bridgeheads affords one of those remarkable examples of Napoleon's prodigious memory: Writing to Berthier on 8 April 1809: 'I recall that there are many and very good ones [guns] near Kronach' (Saski, vol. II, p. 30).

166 Passau had already garnered a great deal of attention. See Napoleon to Clarke, 1 March 1809, in which the Emperor ordered a special reconnaissance of the city and 'Note sur Passau', 1 March 1809. Both in Saski, vol. I, pp. 76–80.

167 Colonel Hubert Camon referred to Napoleon's deployment as '*en attente strategique, à l'affût*' in *La Guerre Napoléonienne: Précis des Campagnes*, Paris: Teissèdre, 1999, p. 237.

168 Saski, vol. I, p. 426.

169 Napoleon to Berthier, 8 April 1809, Saski, vol. II, p. 31. See also Berthier to Max Joseph, 21 March 1809 in [Petit] *Histoire des Campagnes de l'Empereur Napoléon dans la Bavière et l'Autriche en 1805, dans la Prusse et la Pologne en 1806 et 1807, dans la Bavière et l'Autriche en 1809*, Paris: Piquet, 1843, p. 319.

170 For French military analyst General Henry Bonnal, followed by British historian F. Lorraine Petre, Napoleon's attention to Passau and the Danube suggests that his strategy was dominated by 'the preconceived idea of a march on Vienna' and that he thereby lost the opportunity for 'a decisive battle that could have finished the war at the end of April'. This is an overwrought interpretation in my view. Henry Bonnal, *La Manoeuvre de Landshut*, Paris: Chapelot, 1905, pp. 28–9; Petre, pp. 65–71.

171 According to Saski (vol. I, p. 420), it is almost certain that Napoleon dictated the 'Instructions' to Berthier, and then corrected the text with him. Bonnal indicates a similar conclusion (p. 49). Note, however, that Bonnal mistakenly has Berthier *arriving* in Strasbourg on 31 March (p. 48); in fact, he *departed* Paris that day to reach the latter city on 4 April (Berthier's telegraphic message to Napoleon, 4 April 1809, Saski, vol. II, p. 16).

172 Napoleon to Berthier, 5 April 1809, Saski, vol. II, pp. 20–1. Note that Napoleon expected to obtain approximately 4,000 Saxon troops by recalling those in Poland; in fact the number was only some 1,800 to 2,000 in General Dyherrn's detachment at Warsaw. The *Zastrow* Cuirassiers (659 men) had been called back to Saxony from Danzig prior to Napoleon's 5 April order (based on an order from GD Rapp dated 31 March 1809 in SächsHStA, Geheimes Kriegs-Kollegium, D1475, *Briefe, Befehle und Anderes dem Feldzug 1809 betreffend*); *Zastrow* strength from the situation report of the Danzig garrison, 15 January 1809, AG, *Armée d'Allemagne: Garnisons françaises*, Carton C2/511. The cuirassiers are not included in my accounting of Bernadotte's or Dyherrn's manpower strengths. Significant Saxon infantry and artillery detachments remained in Danzig, Stettin, and Glogau; see John H. Gill, *With Eagles to Glory*, London: Greenhill, 1992, pp. 279–82.

173 Napoleon to Berthier, 1 and 6 April 1809, Saski, vol. II, pp. 2–4 and 22–3.

174 *Krieg*, vol. I, p. 156.

175 Mayerhoffer von Vedropolje burdens these letters of 1 and 6 April with rather too much significance in my view (*Krieg*, vol. I, pp. 155–6). They certainly passed through Berthier to Davout – as did almost all of the Emperor's operational correspondence with his marshals – but their influence likely did no more than tint his thinking during the first days of the war.

176 The initial concept is in the 30 March 'Instructions', but much more detail is provided in a 10 April 1809 letter from Berthier to Clarke (Saski, vol. II, pp. 43–7).

177 Wilhelm Freiherr von Schauroth, *Im Rheinbund-Regiment der Herzoglich Sächsischen Kontingente Koburg-Hildburghausen-Gotha-Weimar während der Feldzüge in Tirol, Spanien und Russland 1809–1813*, Berlin: Mittler, 1905, p. 2.

178 Jean-Pierre Bial, *Souvenirs des Guerres de la Révolution et de l'Empire*, Paris: Pensée Latine, 1927, pp. 214–15.

179 Coudreux, 26 March 1809 letter, p. 147.

180 Quoted in Alain Pigeard, *Les Etoiles de Napoléon*, Paris: Quatuor, 1996, pp. 493–4.

181 Quote from General Mouton, Pigeard, p. 383. Excellent biographical material on all three of Davout's 'original' division commanders is in Georges Rivollet, *Général de Bataille Charles Antoine Louis Morand, Comte de l'Empire (1771–1835)*, *Généraux Friant et Gudin du 3e Corps d'Armée*, Paris: Peyronnet, 1963.

182 Quotes from contemporaries cited in Pigeard, *Etoiles*, p. 554.

183 'Tough nut' (*un dur à cuire*) from Bial, p. 214. The best biography is John G. Gallaher, *The Iron Marshal*, Carbondale: Southern Illinois University Press, 1976. For English sources, see also Elting, *Swords*, pp. 132–3; and David Chandler's chapter in David G. Chandler (ed.), *Napoleon's Marshals*, New York: Macmillan, 1987. French biographies include F. G. Hourtoulle, *Davout le Terrible*, Paris: Maloine, 1975; Henri Vigier, *Davout Maréchal de l'Empire*, Paris: Ollendorf, 1898; and L-J. Gabriel de Chenier, *Histoire de la Vie Politique, Militaire et Administrative*

du Maréchal Davout, Paris: Cosse, Marchal et Cie., 1866, but none of these rise above the ordinary. Unfortunately, Daniel Reichel's excellent *Davout et l'Art de la Guerre*, Paris: Delachaux et Niestlé, 1975, does not cover the 1809 conflict.

184 The commander of the 10th Léger, Colonel Pierre Berthezène, relates such an inspirational incident on 19 April 1809: Pierre Berthezène, *Souvenirs Militaires de la République et de l'Empire*, Paris: Dumaine, 1855, pp. 195–6. The incident is also told in Adélaïde-Louise de Blocqueville, *Le Maréchal Davout Prince d'Eckmühl*, Paris: Didier, 1879, pp. 345–7. Marie Théodore Gueulluy, comte de Rumigny, a sous-lieutenant in the 12th Ligne, provides an excellent portrait of Davout in his *Souvenirs*, Paris: Emile-Paul, 1921, pp. 51–2.

185 Davout, ever careful and watchful, employed different deception techniques to keep the Austrians from learning of his movements. To mask the departure of most of the French troops from the fortresses, for instance, his staff issued march orders to the foreign troops indicating destinations in Swedish Pomerania; they only learned of their true missions when they arrived in their new garrison locations, thinking that they were simply to pass through. Similarly, he delayed divulging the shift of his headquarters from Erfurt to Würzburg as long as possible to deny this key intelligence to Austrian spies. Mayerhoffer ,'Aufmarsch', pp. 23, 31.

186 Gallaher, pp. 213–14.

187 3rd Corps 'Situation' of 15 April 1809, Saski, vol. II. The artillery figures are from pp. 18, 382. A further 8,080 men were on detached service or in the hospitals. For this and other corps orders of battle, see also Mayerhoffer, 'Die französische "Armee in Deutschland"', pp. 271–84.

188 The light cavalry were: 12th Chasseurs (Jacquinot) and GB Piré's brigade (8th Hussars and 16th Chasseurs). Pajol's and Piré's troopers were to form a division of the Cavalry Reserve under GD Louis-Pierre Montbrun.

189 Gill, *Eagles*, pp. 385–93. The regiments were the 2nd, 4th, 5th and 6th Rheinbund.

190 An unnamed general quoted in Charles Thomas, *Les Grands Cavaliers du Premier Empire*, Paris: Berger-Levrault, 1890–1909, vol. II, pp. 28–9. References to Nansouty's mordant nature are remarkable in their consistency.

191 Possibly as many as 5,340. See Appendix.

192 Koch, *Massena*, vol. VI, pp. 55–6; also Saski, vol. II, 329. See also letters from GB Ledru des Essarts to his sister, 7 and 17 April 1809 in Jean-Louis Bonnéry, *Ledru des Essarts: Un Grand Patriote Sarthois Méconnu*, Le Mans: Imprimerie Maine Libre, 1988, pp. 61, 66.

193 Johann von Borcke, *Kriegerleben*, ed. Stanislaus von Leszczynski, Berlin: Mittler, 1888, p. 128.

194 Borcke, p. 51.

195 Quote from a letter written by Hauptmann Karl von Freydorf, 11 April 1809 in Zech/Porbeck, p. 19. French concerns about the Hessian and Baden muskets as well as Massena's desire to replace the muskets with French versions are in Koch, *Mémoires de Massena*, vol. VI, pp. 68–9.

196 Ernest Picard, *Préceptes et Jugements de Napoléon*, Paris: Berger-Levrault, 1913, p. 465.

197 Picard, *Préceptes et Jugements*, p. 482. Marshall Cornwall has written a fine, readable biography in English: *Marshal Massena*, London: Oxford University Press, 1965; see

also his chapter in Chandler, *Napoleon's Marshals*. Important French biographies include Gachot's and Koch's works. See also Donald D. Horward's contributions to the Consortium on Revolutionary Europe annual papers, such as 'Massena: Napoleon's Great Competitor', Consortium on Revolutionary Europe, *Selected Papers 1997*, ed. Kyle O. Eidahl, Donald D. Horward and John Severn, Tallahassee: Florida State University, 1997, pp. 289–98.

198 A. Augustin-Thierry, *Massena, L'Enfant Gâte de la Victoire*, Paris: Albin Michel, 1947, pp. 252–4, 257. Madame Le Berton was the wife of Colonel Jacques Le Berton, chief of staff to Carra Saint-Cyr and the sister of Lieutenant Renique, one of Massena's staff officers.

199 French strength figures from the 4th Corps 15 April 1809 situation report in Saski, vol. II. Hessians from Saski and Carl Christian Freiherr von Röder von Diersburg, *Geschichte des 1. Grossherzoglich Hessischen Infanterie- (Leibgarde-) Regiments Nr. 115*, ed. Fritz Beck, Berlin: Mittler & Sohn, 1899, p. 145. Baden figures from Zech/Porbeck, pp. 16–17. A summary campaign report in the Baden archives gives the contingent's strength as 5,669 infantry, 475 cavalry and 369 artillerymen at the start of the war: Generallandesarchiv Karlsruhe [hereafter GLA], 48/4285, 'Rapport historique de la campagne contre l'Autriche l'an 1809'. This latter report is used for the Baden Light Dragoons based on the addition of detachments noted in Saski.

200 There were some exceptions: 24th and 26th Léger as well as 4th and 18th Ligne were regiments of Massena's corps, as was the 46th Ligne. This latter battalion (IV/46th Ligne) never joined Oudinot; it was diverted to rear area security duties en route to the corps.

201 The force in the Tyrol, under GL Georg von Kinkel, was based on the 11th Infantry Regiment, the 2nd Light Infantry Battalion (*Wreden*) and one artillery battery. Reinforcements from 7th Corps were the 3rd and 4th Light Battalions and two squadrons of the 1st Dragoon Regiment (Gill, *Eagles*, pp. 68–71).

202 See, for example, the anti-Austrian comments of a Bavarian artillery corporal from the 1st Division in Christian Schaller, *Fragmente aus dem Feldzuge gegen Oestreich im Jahr 1809*, Augsburg: Bürglen, 1810, pp. 7–17.

203 Napoleon to Max Joseph, 14 March 1809, *Correspondance*, no. 14901.

204 Quote from Eugen Zoellner, *Geschichte des K. B. 11. Infanterie-Regiments 'von der Tann' 1805–1905*, Munich: Lindauer, 1905, p. 56. Wrede received reports from the civil commissioner in Passau every day, and sometimes several times a day. His biographer, Johann von Heilmann, portrays a daily report in the morning full of urgent alarms followed by an afternoon message that retracted the previous missive (*Feldmarschall Fürst Wrede*, Leipzig: Duncker & Humblot, 1881, p. 119).

205 Picard, *Préceptes et Jugements*, p. 464.

206 Friedrich Mändler, *Erinnerungen aus meinen Feldzügen*, Nürnberg: Lotzbeck, 1854, p. 2.

207 Bezzel, 'Grenzschutze', pp. 78–82.

208 Quote from Friedrich to Napoleon, 23 March 1809, in August von Schlossberger (ed.), *Politische und Militärische Correspondenz König Friedrichs von Württemberg mit Kaiser Napoleon I. 1805–1813*, Stuttgart: Kohlhammer, 1889, pp. 142–3. Other indignant correspondence from Friedrich is dated 1 and 6 April 1809, Schlossberger,

pp. 148–50. Also Heinz Kraft, *Die Württemberger in den Napoleonischen Kriegen*, Stuttgart: Kohlhammer, 1953, pp. 143–6.

209   Napoleon to Friedrich, 17 March, 31 March, and 5 April 1809, *Correspondance*, nos. 14920, 14986, and 15019.

210   Napoleon to Friedrich, 17 March 1809, *Correspondance*, no. 14920; 'Instructions for the Major General', 30 March 1809, *Correspondance*, no. 14975; Napoleon to Berthier, 8 April 1809, *Correspondance*, no. 15029. The Württemberg contingent was to detach one cavalry regiment for service with Lasalle's light cavalry division of the Cavalry Reserve (but this did not occur).

211   Strength figures from Saski, vol. II, annexe. The entire saga of Dupas and Rouyer, their peregrinations and chain of command, is exceedingly confused. This information was culled from Ferdinand Dubouloz-Dupas and André Folliet, *Le Général Dupas*, Paris: Chapelot, 1899, pp. 203–5 (which source, however, misses the temporary assignment to Vandamme); Rouyer was placed under Vandamme's orders according to Berthier to Vandamme, 17 April 1809 in Saski, vol. II, pp. 212–13. Rouyer was *technically* under Dupas' command and both *technically*, at least, came under Vandamme for a brief time. Dupas and his two regiments with Rouyer's Rheinbund troops attached are only listed on one 8th Corps 'Situation'—that of 1 May 1809 ('Situation' for 8th Corps, AG, *Armée d'Allemagne*, Kart. C2/508). It is not clear that Vandamme ever exercised any real command authority over Dupas or that Dupas ever had very much to do with Rouyer's day-to-day activities even during this brief period.

212   In one of his first Orders of the Day to the corps, Vandamme especially praised 'the fine appearance and instruction' of the Light Brigade: Vandamme, Order of the Day, 8 April 1809, Hauptstaatsarchiv Stuttgart [hereafter HStAS], *Kabinet, Geheimer Rat, Ministerien 1806–1945, Oesterreicher Feldzug 1809*, E289aBü72. On training see Johann Gottlob Herre, *Erinnerungen eines Schlossaufsehers: aus den Feldzügen der Jahren 1806, 1809, 1813, 1814 und 1815*, Mergentheim, 1847, p. 12: 'the horse artillery achieved ever higher levels of training'. Also Ferdinand Fromm, *Geschichte des Infanterie-Regiments König Wilhelm I (6. Württ.) Nr. 124*, Weingarten: regimental, 1901, 36. On tactical developments, see Fromm (pp. 34–6) and Albert von Pfister, *Das Infanterieregiment Kaiser Wilhelm, König von Preussen (2. Württ.) No. 120*, Stuttgart: Metzler, 1881, pp. 168–9.

213   Leo Ignaz Stadlinger, a lieutenant in the *Neubronn* Fusilier Regiment, quoted in Paul Dorsch (ed.), *Kriegszüge der Württemberger im 19. Jahrhundert*, Calw: Vereinsbuchhandlung, 1913, p. 43. Jäger Schäffer's 5 April 1809 letter is quoted in *Baden und Württemberg im Napoleonischen Zeitalter*, Stuttgart: Cantz, 1987, vol. I, p. 430.

214   Jean-Roche Coignet, *The Note-Books of Captain Coignet*, London: Greenhill, 1989, p. 170.

215   Scheltens, *Souvenirs d'un Grognard Belge*, Brussels: Dessart, n.d., p. 92.

216   Dupas also had command of Rouyer's German division. Dupas's strength from *Krieg*, vol. I, p. 649. Beaumont's strength from his report of 13 April 1809: 'Etat Sommaire des Détachments de Dragons arrivé jusqu'a à ce jour à Strasbourg pour former les 6 Régiments provisoires de Dragons', AG, *Armée d'Allemagne: Réserve général de cavalerie; divisions de cavalerie*, Kart. C2/510.

217 Saxon strength at this point is variously reported as 14,030 (*Etat Sommaire des Troupes Saxonnes*, April 1809, AG, *Armée d'Allemagne: Armées prussiennes et autrichiennes*, Kart. C2/520), and 14,550 (undated report from late March or early April, AG, *Armée d'Allemagne*, Kart. C2/509). Based on later strength reports, the latter seems more likely. See order of battle appendix for discussion of the strength figure (19,096) given in Moritz Exner, *Die Antheilnahme der Königlich Sächsischen Armee am Feldzug gegen Oesterreich und die kriegerischen Ereignisse in Sachsen im Jahre 1809*, Dresden: Baensch, 1894, pp. 16–21.

218 Clarke to Mortier, 2 April 1809 in Pelet, vol. II, p. 364. See also Thiers, vol. X, p. 105; and Charles Oman, *A History of the Peninsular War*, London: Greenhill, 1995, vol. II, pp. 410–11.

219 By early April, 10th Corps had approximately 7,320 Westphalians, 5,580 Dutch, and 1,090 Berg troops on hand in various locations, not counting fortress garrisons or the ad hoc battalion of 750 Frenchmen en route from the border. An additional 1,500 Westphalian recruits were on hand but not yet even uniformed. Sources: report of troops stationed in Westphalia, 10 April 1809, AG, *Armée d'Allemagne*, Kart. C2/509 for the Westphalians; 10th Corps situation report, 31 May 1809, AG, *Armée d'Allemagne*, Kart. C2/509 for the Dutch and Berg troops; 26th Military Division, 'Situation du Bataillon commandée par M. le Colonel Chabert', 29 March 1809, AG, *Armée d'Allemagne*, Kart. C2/511 for the French.

220 Napoleon to Jerome, 9 April 1809, *Correspondance*, No. 15042.

221 Quote from the 30 March 'Instructions' in Saski, vol. I, p. 425.

222 Bonnal, p. 48.

223 March 'Instructions' in Saski, vol. I, p. 428.

224 Another anomaly of the Army of Germany was the numbering of its constituent corps. Where the corps of the Grande Armée had traditionally been numbered sequentially, the new organisation left the numbers 1, 5, and 6 vacant. They remained unused throughout the conflict, and even when the Army of Dalmatia was redesignated as a corps later in the war, it received the number 11 rather than one of the empty positions. It is not clear why Napoleon selected the numbers as he did for his new Army of Germany, but his decision is perhaps explained by considering that the vacant numbers represented those corps that had retained their original Grande Armée numbers when they crossed the Pyrenees to become part of the Army of Spain. See brief footnote in [Petit] *Histoire des Campagnes de l'Empereur Napoléon*, p. 431.

225 Curiously, Napoleon did *not* call upon the 2nd Westphalian Division, which was passing through Metz on its way to Spain. The 7,900 men of the division could have easily marched east and joined Jerome in the defence of his new kingdom, but the emperor had them continue their journey to Catalonia, where the division would be destroyed in the siege of Gerona.

226 Polish strength from Duchy of Warsaw 'Situation' of 6 April 1809 in Joseph Poniatowski, *Correspondance du Prince Joseph Poniatowski avec la France*, Posen, 1921–3, pp. 84–5; the figure includes 2,000 Saxons. Marmont's strength from 'Situation' of 15 April 1809, AG, *Armée de Dalmatie: Situations minutes*, Kart. C6/15. Troops in Italy from 'Situation de l'Armée d'Italie', 1 April 1809, AN, AF*/IV/1377, *Livrets des armées: Situations des troupes en Italie*; note that the 72,000 figure

includes neither the 12,000 men of the army's 6th Division in Tuscany and Rome nor some 16,000 in garrisons and depot units (all numbers are for those 'present under arms'). For troops in Germany see earlier discussion in this chapter.

CHAPTER 4: IT IS WAR

1   There being limited utility in using the following narrative to trace the complex movements of the two armies between 10 and 15 April, readers are directed to the accompanying maps for general locations of major formations.

2   See appropriate appendices for strength, detachments, missing units, and sourcing. Note that figures in the main text do not include artillerymen, nor are absent units included.

3   Oscar Criste, *Erzherzog Karl und die Armee*, vol. V of *Das Kriegsjahr 1809 in Einzeldarstellungen*, ed. Emil von Woinovich, Vienna: Stern, 1906, p. 47; Alexander Kirchhammer, 'Zur offiziellen "Relation" über die Schlacht von Aspern 1809', *Beilage des Fremden-Blatt*, 26 July 1902.

4   On Hiller: Rauchensteiner, *Hiller*, especially pp. 118–21; Rothenberg, *Adversaries*, pp. 120–1, 156.

5   Quote from Hans von Zwiedineck-Südenhorst, 'Die Ostalpen in den Franzosenkriegen', *Zeitschrift des Deutschen und Oesterreichischen Alpenvereins* (1899), pp. 82–3. Similarly, Rothenberg calls him 'a remarkably unlucky and inept general', *Adversaries*, p. 145.

6   Hiller pleaded with Charles to be allowed to keep Jellacic under his direct command. Manfried Rauchensteiner (ed.), 'Das sechste österr. Armeekorps im Krieg 1809. Nach den Aufzeichnungen des FZM Johann Freiherr v. Hiller (1748–1819)', in *Mitteilungen des österr. Staatsarchivs*, 1964/5 [hereafter Hiller], p. 152. Strength of Jellacic's command is for 2 April, from '6tes Armee-Corps: Journal über die Operationen der detachierten Division des Bn. Fr. Jellachich', KAFA, *Journale der Hauptarmee und Korps*, Kart. 5; see also Criste, *Carl*, vol. III, p. 16.

7   For brief biographic sketches of most of the key Austrian leaders, see Criste, *Erzherzog Karl und die Armee*. Although most of these sketches are decidedly hagiographic, there is no mention of Archduke Ludwig whatsoever (other than a rather unflattering portrait of him in an aged state). Nor do several other corps commanders receive any mention: namely Kolowrat and the Gyulai brothers.

8   The six companies were: two from the 1st Innviertel and four from the 4th Traunviertel.

9   The dispositions and designations of the Landwehr battalions from Sinzendorf to the south are drawn from Zehetbauer, p. 242; they are consistent with the map at Beilage 7 of *Krieg*, vol. I.

10 The status of the Landwehr battalions under Richter and Oberdorf is not very clear; this description is shown in *Krieg*, vol. I, Appendix XIX and the map at Beilage 7. The cavalry squadron was III/*Schwarzenberg* Uhlans No. 3.

11 Landwehr under Am Ende: 2nd, 3rd, and 5th Leitmeritz, 1st and 2nd Rakonitz, 1st Saaz. The regular battalions were III/*Anton Mittrowsky* No. 10 and III/*Erbach* No. 42.

12 *Krieg*, vol. I, p. 215.

13 Errors in Stadion's description include: there were only two corps in Bohemia, not three; Bellegarde was headed for Bayreuth with Kolowrat, not Dresden by himself; Rosenberg was south of the Danube; Charles was aiming the Hauptarmee at the Regensburg area, not Munich.

14 Stuart to Canning, 12 April 1809, no. 1 (PRO/FO 342/2). The interview with Stadion upon which Stuart's dispatch was founded occurred on the evening of 6 April. Writing on the 12th, Stuart reported that the Austrian Army had crossed the frontier on 9 April.

15 The various proclamations mentioned here are printed in *Krieg*, vol. I, Appendices XXI, XXIV, XXV, and XXVI. The 6 April Order of the Day became an indelible part of the mythos of the Austrian imperial army; nearly every regimental history includes the entire text in the section devoted to the 1809 war.

16 Binder, vol. I, p. 101.

17 *Krieg*, vol. I, p. 217. From Braunau on the 10th, for instance, Charles altered the march goals he had previously set for the 11th and 12th. The intelligence that reached headquarters on the 10th was contradictory and confusing, but painted a general picture of Allied strength on the Lech (where at least 50,000 men were reported) and weakness towards Regensburg (reportedly garrisoned by only 3,000). Additionally, there seemed to be Bavarian divisions at Munich and either Freising or Landshut (in addition to Wrede at Straubing). There was no new information on Davout. Evidently on this basis, Charles seems to have concluded that there was no immediate danger of a major encounter and that the greatest threat to the Hauptarmee lay in the French forces along the Lech. He therefore shifted the southern column (V, VI, and II Reserve Corps) to the left (west) toward Marktl and Neuötting. The northern column (III, IV, and I Reserve Corps) was to continue as before. See *Krieg*, vol. I, p. 226. On Charles's apparent assumption that the bulk of the Allied forces were to be found on the Lech, see *Krieg*, vol. I, pp. 233, 303.

18 Hiller's account of this meeting is in Hiller, pp. 152–3. His lingering resentment is evident on pp. 157 and 158. See also Hiller, pp. 120–1. The logistical challenge of supplying such a large force in a land of limited roads and resources is another major argument against Hiller's concept. The authors of *Krieg* ridicule the notion in vol. I, p. 220.

19 The detachment consisted of four squadrons of *Liechtenstein* Hussars, a battalion of W*arasdin-St George* Grenzers and two guns. This scene is taken from Hiller's journal and may be more than a little self-serving, but the fact of VI Corps crossing the river in the late afternoon of 9 April with a small detachment remains. The account in *Krieg* (vol. I, p. 224) is more modest. Composition of the detachment is from Cajetan Pizzighelli, *Geschichte des k. u. k. Husaren-Regimentes Wilhelm II. König von Württemberg Nr. 6*, Rzeszow: regimental, 1897, p. 218.

20 August Netoliczka, *Geschichte des k. k. 9. Infanterie-Regiments Graf Hartmann-Clarstein*, Comorn: Siegler, 1866, p. 157; and Alfred Ritter von Sypniewski, *Geschichte des k. und k. Infanterie-Regimentes Feldmarschall Carl Joseph Graf Clerfayt de Croix*, Jaroslau: regimental, 1894, p. 205.

21 Charles to Albert, 8 April 1809, in Criste, *Carl*, vol. III, p. 475.

22 Kübeck, vol. I, p. 264. Others, of course, also used this rubric, see *Beobachtungen*, p. 90.

23 This detachment consisted of: two (possibly three) companies of III/*de Vaux* Infantry No. 45, four companies of the 2nd Inner Austrian Volunteers (Salzburger Jäger), one company of the 2nd Salzburg Landwehr, a company of local Tyrolian militia Schützen and one *Zug* (platoon) of *O'Reilly* Chevaulegers No. 3. Taxis received his orders on 9 April ('6tes Armee-Corps: Journal über der Operationen der detachierten Division des Bn Fr. Jellachich', KAFA, Kart. 1385; also *Krieg*, vol. III, p. 81 and Stutterheim, p. 51). A second detachment (the remaining four companies of III/*de Vaux* under Oberstleutnant Samuel Reissenfels) was detached on 11 April to blockade Kufstein.

24 Pierre-Martin Pirquet, *Journal de Campagne*, Liege: Société des Bibliophiles, 1970, vol. I, p. 78.

25 The authors of *Krieg* are especially critical of the manner in which artillery was intermingled with the infantry and cavalry.

26 Grueber, *Reiteroffiziers vor Hundert Jahren*, p. 63.

27 Eberhard Mayerhoffer von Vedropolje, *Oesterreichs Krieg mit Napoleon I. 1809*, Vienna: Seidel & Sohn, 1904, p. 18. This slender volume is a model of military history and analysis.

28 Binder, vol. I, p. 102. The same day (11 April), Charles allowed limited quartering in towns and villages as long as the troops remained within easy recall of their units.

29 'Diabolical weather' is from a letter Charles sent to Herzog Albert, 12 April 1809, in Wertheimer, vol. II, p. 302.

30 *Krieg*, vol. I, p. 236.

31 Charles, 'Denkschrift', *Ausgewählte Schriften*, vol. VI, p. 335. He complained that 'even on the Inn the Austrians lacked intelligence from the far side'.

32 Oberleutnant Heinrich von Hess quoted in *Krieg*, vol. I, p. 218. See also Angeli, vol. IV, pp. 43–50.

33 *Krieg*, vol. I, p. 223.

34 'It was generally believed in the Austrian army that the enemy had the intention of uniting behind the Lech, and the news that Davout was directing himself toward Ingolstadt fortified this opinion' (Stutterheim, pp. 81–2).

35 I have used conditional phrasing here ('seems' and 'apparently'), because the published evidence does not support more conclusive statements (as noted in *Krieg*, vol. I, pp. 231–5). The author of the first volume of *Krieg*, Mayerhoffer von Vedropolje was more specific in his article '1809: Die Konzentrierungsbewegungen der Armee Napoleon I. in der Zeit vom 10. bis 17. April', *Organ der Militärwissenschaftlichen Vereine*, vol. LXIX (1904), p. 192 (in reference to the situation on 16 April): 'The army had crossed the Isar, but the headquarters of the generalissimus was not yet clear about what should happen next'. Criste offers a picture of definitive information and intentions that seems unrealistic (*Carl*, vol. III, pp. 24–6). Angeli depicts some of the uncertainty by providing extracts and summaries of some of the Austrian intelligence on 11 April (vol. IV, pp. 52–5).

36 *Krieg*, vol. I, pp. 232–3.

37 Sources: E. Heinze, *Geschichte des Kgl. Bayer. 6. Chevaulegers-Regiments*, Leipzig: Klinkhardt, 1898, pp. 328–9; *Krieg*, vol. I, p. 244. According to the latter, only a half-

squadron of hussars took part in the skirmish; the Austrians losing two horses and the Bavarians three prisoners and four horses.

38 Sources: Emil Buxbaum, *Das Königlich Bayerische 3. Chevaulegers-Regiment*, Munich: Oldenbourg, 1884, p. 122 (the author mistakenly places the action on 15 April); Pizzighelli, *Husaren-Regimentes Wilhelm II*, p. 219; *Krieg*, vol. I, pp. 244–5. The Bavarians were from I/1st Chevaulegers; the 1st and 2nd Squadrons of *Liechtenstein* were engaged. Austrian losses were a few wounded.

39 *Krieg*, vol. I, pp. 242–5. Also: Pizzighelli, *Husaren-Regimentes Nr. 6*, p. 219; Gustav Ritter Amon von Treuenfest, *Geschichte des kaiserl. und königl. Husaren-Regimentes Nr. 10 Friedrich Wilhelm III. König von Preussen*, Vienna: regimental, 1892, p. 242; and *Geschichte des k. k. achten Uhlanen-Regimentes Erzherzog Ferdinand Maximilian*, Vienna: Hof- und Staatsdruckerei, 1860, p. 98; Erich Freiherr Riedl von Riedenau, *Geschichte des k. und k. Uhlanen-Regimentes Erzherzog Karl Nr. 3*, Vienna: Hof- und Staatsdruckerei, 1901, pp. 43–4.

40 *Krieg*, vol. I, pp. 247–9; Treuenfest, *Husaren-Regimentes Nr. 10*, p. 242.

41 Scheibler's detachment consisted of II/*Klebek*, two squadrons of *Rosenberg* Chevaulegers (Scheibler's own regiment), and two companies of *St Georg* Grenzer. This detachment had been formed on 12 April, but the two Grenzer companies did not join until the 13th. *Krieg*, vol. I, pp. 244, 250; Victor Grois, *Geschichte des k. k. Infanterie-Regiments Nr. 14*, Linz: Feichtinger, 1876, p. 217.

42 *Krieg*, vol. I, p. 230.

43 Dedovich had some 4,000 regulars and 4,300 Landwehr (counting all companies of all battalions). For Oberhaus, see *Krieg*, vol. I, p. 246, and vol. III, pp. 91–3.

44 Bellegarde note to the commander of the French outposts, 9 April 1809, in Saski, vol. II, p. 95. Colonel Méda did not hesitate to report this key development, sending copies of the declaration to Davout and Friant at 7 p.m. on the evening of 9 April: 'I have the honour to send you a non-commissioned officer carrying the declaration of war' (Méda to Davout and Friant, 9 April 1809, 7 p.m., in Saski, vol. II, p. 97).

45 Comment on camping in the snow is from Ludwig Rona, *Geschichte des k. u. k. Infanterie-Regimentes Adolf Grossherzog von Luxemburg, Herzog zu Nassau Nr. 15*, Prague: Bellmann, 1901, p. 408.

46 Kandelsdorfer, *Feld-Jäger-Bataillons Nr. 3*, p. 60.

47 Méda to Friant, 10 April 1809, 2.30 p.m., in Saski, vol. II, p. 101.

48 Charles Henri Lejeune, 'Souvenirs', *Carnet de la Sabretache*, September 1910.

49 'The march of the 2nd Division was not disturbed today', Friant's papers quoted in Saski, vol. II, p. 119.

50 Davout to Berthier, 13 April 1809, 6 a.m., in Saski, vol. II, p. 126.

51 Hippolyte d'Espinchal, *Souvenirs Militaires*, Paris: Ollendorf, 1901, vol. I, p. 227; Coudreux, p. 147.

52 Sources for the 11 April skirmish: *Krieg*, vol. I, pp. 256–7; Karl Anton Ritter von Jedina, *Geschichte des kaiserlich königlich österreichischen ersten Uhlanen-Regimentes*, Vienna: Schmid, 1845, p. 103; Karl Kandelsdorfer, *Geschichte des K. und K. Feld-Jäger-Bataillons Nr. 7*, Bruck an der Mur, battalion, 1896, pp. 28–32; General Friant's papers quoted in Saski, vol. II, p. 111; Jean François Friant, *Vie Militaire du Lieutenant-Général Comte Friant*, Paris: Dentu, 1857, pp. 156–7; Oré, p. 121; Lt. Sommervogel, 'Historique du 33eme Régiment d'Infanterie', manuscript, AG, 1891,

pp. 83–4; A. Adam, *Historique du 111e Régiment d'Infanterie*, Bastia: Ollagnier, 1890, pp. 57–8. There is some confusion in French reporting of events in his area on 10 and 11 April. Davout reported a skirmish between Hirschau and 'Hambach' (Hahnbach) on 10 April between the 111th Ligne and a large Austrian detachment (Davout to Berthier, 13 April 1809, 6 a.m., in Saski, vol. II, p. 126); Adam's detailed history of the 111th Ligne also mentions a similar skirmish at 'Ambach' (again Hahnbach) on 10 April. I suspect that Davout's report simply erred in giving the wrong date for the skirmish as his report mentions nothing for 11 April. Adam, however, relates a fairly detailed account of a small action in 'Ambach' (sic) on the 10th and the Hirschau action on the 11th. The most likely explication is that Adam mistakenly describes one action (11 April) as taking place over two days (10 and 11 April). No other source even puts the 111th Ligne at Hahnbach until the 11 April. There is no mention of such an engagement on 10 April in any Austrian sources; indeed, the Austrians would have been delighted to have marched as far Hahnbach on the first day of their invasion.

53 Casualties from *Krieg*, vol. I, Appendix XXX.
54 Quoted in Kandelsdorfer, *Feld-Jäger-Bataillons Nr. 7*, p. 31.
55 Mensdorff must have overestimated French numbers as the two sides should have been fairly even in overall strength. Indeed, on 12 April, Mensdorff had been joined by Rittmeister Wilhelm Freiherr von Mengen with one and one-half squadrons of *Merveldt* from Steffanini's detachment. It is not clear where Mengen was on the 13th, but Mensdorff should have had considerably more cavalry than Méda on the field.
56 A detachment from I Corps arrived too late to join the fray: two companies of 3rd Jägers and a squadron of *Blankenstein* Hussars No. 6 under Major Georg Wieland.
57 Sources for the skirmish at Amberg: *Krieg*, vol. I, pp. 264–6; Baxa, pp. 22–4 (Jäger Hauptmann Peter Tailleur's report on the skirmish); Jedina, pp. 103–5; Saski, vol. II, p. 140 (Méda's report); Oré, pp. 122–3; Adam, *111e Régiment*, pp. 58–60. Méda described the tangled cavalry melee as 'long and very hot, the men were so close that they could neither cut nor thrust and the lances were practically useless'.
58 Friant to Davout, 14 April 1809, noon, in Saski, vol. II, p. 154. Friant wrote this brief note on the spot just as he was ordering his men to advance.
59 The 15th Léger went into action with only two of its three battalions at Ursensollen as indicated in Friant's 15 April report reproduced in Saski (vol. II, pp. 156–7); the other battalion was with GB Piré's brigade near Nuremberg (as shown in *Krieg*, vol. I, Beilage 9). In this, Friant's biography, which in most cases closely follows the archival record, seems to be mistaken when it specifically states three (Friant, p. 159).
60 Kandelsdorfer, *Feld-Jäger-Bataillons Nr. 3*, p. 61.
61 Davout to Berthier, 14 April 1809, in Saski, vol. II, pp. 143–5.
62 Friant had placed the 108th Ligne at Kastl in reserve and had the 111th Ligne echeloned further back on the Neumarkt road. The 108th Ligne's three voltigeur companies also took part in the combat, probably toward the end of the action (Friant, p. 159).
63 Friant to Davout, 15 April 1809, in Saski, vol. II, pp. 154–8. Montbrun, with his two hussars regiments and three companies of the 13th Léger, rode up from Velburg

to take the Austrians in the flank, but returned to his starting point on reaching Pfaffenhofen, where he learned from Jacquinot that the combat was over (Ledru, *Montbrun*, pp. 58–9).

64 Sources for the engagement at Ursensollen: *Krieg*, vol. I, pp. 268–70; Kandelsdorfer, *Feld-Jäger-Bataillons Nr. 3*, pp. 61–3 (including Fresnel's report of the engagement); Pizzighelli, *Husaren-Regimentes Nr. 6*, p. 565; Josef May, *Geschichte des kaiserlich und königlich Infanterie-Regimentes No. 35*, Pilsen: Maasch, 1901, p. 145; Friant's reports in Saski, vol. II, pp. 154–9; Oré, 124; Victor Louis Jean François Belhomme, *Historique du 90e Régiment d'Infanterie de Ligne ex–15e Léger*, Paris: Tanera, 1875, pp. 74–5.

65 Casualties from *Krieg*, vol. I, Appendix XXX and Friant's report quoted in Friant, p. 160.

66 *Krieg*, vol. I, 270.

67 The cavalry platoon was also from the *Merveldt* Uhlans.

68 *Krieg*, vol. I, pp. 262–3.

69 *Krieg*, vol. I, pp. 240, 323.

70 Leutnant Hess quoted in *Krieg*, vol. I, p. 264.

71 Lefebvre to Oudinot, 9 April 1809, and Oudinot to Berthier, 5 p.m., 9 April 1809, both in Saski, vol. II, pp. 93–4.

72 Berthier to Napoleon, 11 April 1809, 5.30 a.m., in Saski, vol. II, p. 112.

73 Reports of Austrian activity along the Inn had become increasingly insistent during the first week of April and there had been a number of false alarms. Multiple Bavarian reports, for instance, insisted that the Austrians would invade on the night of 6/7 April. The often-hectic Bavarian correspondence for this period is in the Bayerisches Haupstaatsarchiv, Abt. IV, Kriegsarchiv [hereafter BKA], B442; with many thanks to that institution's Dr A. Fuchs for his invaluable assistance. Published sources for the issue of the false reports include: *Krieg*, vol. I, pp. 275–6; Binder, vol. I, pp. 110–15; Heilmann, *Wrede*, pp. 119–20; Wrede to St Hilaire, 9 April 1809, in Saski, vol. II, p. 94.

74 Ludwig to Max Joseph, 9 April 1809, BKA/B442.

75 Lefebvre to Ludwig, 9 April 1809, BKA/B442. For Lefebvre, this was an early example of what he came to see as a chronic Bavarian incapacity in reconnaissance and outpost duties. Although he praised many qualities in his Bavarian troops, he repeatedly asked for French light cavalry and infantry to perform reconnaissance and outpost duties, being convinced that the Bavarians were not up to meeting these demanding tasks. See his request to Berthier on 15 April 1809: 'It is a matter of the greatest urgency to have a regiment of French light troops with the army that I command' (Saski, vol. II, p. 172).

76 For Lefebvre, of course, it meant the second alarm in twenty-four hours and once again putting his corps in motion. Recall that Charles's adjutant arrived in Munich on the night of the 9th and that the delivery of official notices to Allied outposts took place on the morning of the 10th.

77 Tulard/Garros, *Itinéraire*, p. 310. Weather apparently precluded use of the optical telegraph from Strasbourg to Paris, so Berthier's message to Napoleon had to be sent by courier (*Krieg*, vol. I, p. 275).

78 *Krieg*, vol. I, p. 275.

79 See, for example, Ludwig von Madroux, 'August von Floret', *Archiv für Offiziere aller Waffen*, vol. 3, no. 2 (1846), p. 162; and F. von Fabrice, *Das Königlich Bayerische 6. Infanterie-Regiment*, Munich: Oldenbourg, 1896, vol. II, p. 168.

80 Some samples of the rush of orders issued by 4th Corps headquarters on 10 April are in Saski, vol. II, pp. 102–4.

81 Ledru des Essarts to his sister, 17 April 1809, in Ledru, *Ledru des Essarts*, p. 66.

82 Philippe Réne Girault, *Mes Campagnes sous la Révolution et l'Empire*, Paris: Le Sycomore, 1983, p. 154. Young Markgraf Wilhelm of Baden remembered that 'The weather was always most inclement, it snowed heavily and the ground was frozen' (*Denkwürdigkeiten des Markgrafen Wilhelm von Baden*, ed. Karl Obser, Heidelberg: Winter, 1906, vol. I, p. 66).

83 Vandamme to Neubronn, 11 April (first quote) and 13 April 1809 (second quote), HStAS, E289aBü73, Mobile Kommandobehörden I, *Weisungen Generals Vandamme und anderer französischer Stabsoffiziere an Generalleutnant von Neubronn*.

84 Lefebvre to Crown Prince Ludwig, 7 April 1809, BKA/B442. This order detailed a host of measures to enhance his command's readiness to react quickly when the Austrians attacked. Other measures are contained in the 7 April Order of the Day. In response, Ludwig sent two letters on 8 April 1809: one supplied the latest intelligence from an officer opposite Schärding, the other reported that 1st Division had complied with orders to increase readiness; Deroy sent a similar report on 8 April 1809 (all BKA/B442).

85 Even Wrede's sympathetic biographer Heilmann blames the general in this instance, calling his withdrawal 'completely unjustified' (*Wrede*, p. 120). See Berthier to Lefebvre, 13 April 1809 (Saski, vol. II, p. 128) and Berthier to Wrede, 14 April 1809 (Saski, vol. II, p. 161).

86 Mändler, p. 2.

87 Wrede to Max Joseph, 11 April 1809, BKA/B442.

88 Davout to Berthier, 13 April, 6 a.m., in Saski, vol. II, pp. 126–7.

89 Instructions to Davout were contained in several messages, but the foundation was Berthier to Davout, 11 March 1809 in Saski, vol. I, 230–2. The 11 March signal stressed the necessity of uniting with Massena and Oudinot on the Danube 'either at Ingolstadt or at Donauwörth'. The next major order was that issued by the Major General from Strasbourg when he learned of the Austrian invasion: Berthier to Davout, 11 April 1809, 8. a.m. (received 13 April) in Saski, vol. II, pp. 114–15.

90 Piré's force consisted of his brigade (8th Hussars and 16th Chasseurs), plus the 12th Chasseurs and a battalion of the 15th Léger. Jacquinot had only one regiment of his brigade (2nd Chasseurs) as the 1st and 12th were detached elsewhere. Montbrun had one light infantry regiment (13th Léger) and most of Pajol's brigade minus Pajol (5th Hussars, 7th Hussars, one squadron of 11th Chasseurs). Pajol himself was at Regensburg with the remaining two squadrons of the 11th, the 10th Léger and two guns; St Hilaire sent the 57th Ligne to reinforce Pajol on 14 April.

91 Davout to Berthier, 13 April, 6 a.m., in Saski, vol. II, p. 126–7. Eberhard Mayerhoffer von Vedropolje observes that 'Napoleon, had he arrived in the theatre of war on the 13th, would have found the army's situation well suited to begin operations immediately', in '1809: Die Konzentrierungsbewegungen der Armee Napoleon I.

in der Zeit vom 10. bis 17. April', *Organ der Militärwissenschaftlichen Vereine*, vol. LXIX (1904), p. 166.

92 Berthier to Davout and Berthier to Wrede, both 13 April 1809, 11.30 p.m., in Saski, vol. II, pp. 137–9. Davout apparently acquired other details verbally from the 3rd Corps staff officer who brought the dispatches from Berthier.

93 In accordance with the organisation of the Army of Germany, St Hilaire was to join Oudinot's two divisions to form 2nd Corps, while Montbrun and Nansouty would come under the Cavalry Reserve.

94 Berthier to Oudinot, Wrede, Massena, Lefebvre, Davout, and Napoleon, 13 April, between 8 p.m. and 9 p.m., in Saski, vol. II, pp. 133–7. Berthier's previous instructions for Davout were for 3rd Corps to concentrate between Ingolstadt and Regensburg (11 April 1809, 8 a.m., in Saski, vol. II, pp. 114–15).

95 Napoleon to Berthier, 10 April 1809, noon, *Correspondance*, no. 15048. Subsequent quotations are from this note.

96 Napoleon to Berthier, 10 April 1809 (telegram), *Correspondance*, no. 15047.

97 Binder completely misreads this aspect of the Berthier–Napoleon correspondance (vol. I, p. 131).

98 Binder, vol. I, p. 128. Binder's actual phrase is '*im dunklen Drang etwas zu thun*'.

99 This quote, the previous quote and the reference to 40,000 Austrians marching into the Tyrol are from Berthier to Napoleon, 13 April 1809, 9 p.m., in Saski, vol. II, pp. 135–6.

100 Napoleon had designated Berthier as commander of the Army of the Reserve in 1800 prior to the Marengo campaign, but this was a mere ruse and Berthier never had to exercise command in any real sense. Note that several commentators lend Berthier considerable sympathy arguing, as Mayerhoffer von Vedropolje does, that 'it would never occur to Berthier to view himself as the army's commander' owing to the smothering domination he was accustomed to enduring in Napoleon's presence ('Konzentrierungsbewegungen', p. 173). This is an important and valid point not to be overlooked. Without attempting long-distance psychoanalysis, however, it is also crucial to note that Berthier occasionally slipped into a semblance of the commander role very much on his own accord. As Binder points out (vol. I, p. 150), one example of Berthier's clumsy attempt to fit into his commander role is his use of the word 'chat' (*jaser*) in describing his intention to meet with Davout: 'I believe it to be indispensable that I go to see the state of things myself and chat with the Duke of Auerstädt' (Berthier to Massena, 15 April 1809, 4 a.m., in Saski, vol. II, p. 166). Such usages, though not consistent, seem to belie the notion that he was constantly oppressed and unable to thrust himself forward as a true interim commander. Note, however, that Berthier only used this informal and potentially demeaning term in a missive to Massena, not to Davout himself.

101 Berthier to Davout, 13 April 1809, 8.30 p.m., in Saski, vol. II, p. 135.

102 Binder, vol. I, pp. 123–8. Berthier could have satisfied his urge to 'do something' and matched Napoleon's intentions, for instance, by pulling the army back to the Lech, even leaving Davout around Ingolstadt, thus both gathering the Allied forces and allowing time for Austrians dispositions and intentions to manifest themselves.

103 Berthier to Napoleon, 14 April 1809, midnight, in Saski, vol. II, pp. 162–3. I have taken the English translation in part from Petre's rendering (p. 82). Binder correctly

observes that Berthier expected Napoleon to arrive at any moment and did not want to make any errors that might incur imperial wrath; moreover, believing that Napoleon's arrival was imminent, Berthier did not expect to retain his command function for very long (Binder, vol. I, p. 138).

104 Louis François Lejeune, *Memoirs of Baron Lejeune*, Felling: Worley reprint, 1987, vol. I, pp. 215–16. Parts of this insightful passage are in many books on the campaign: Petre, p. 83, for example.

105 Berthezène, p. 188.

106 Sous-Lieutenant Jean Marie Putigny in *Putigny: Grognard d'Empire*, Paris: Gallimard, 1950, p. 180. Note that Jean Tulard suspects Putigny's memoirs of considerable embellishment (see his invaluable *Nouvelle Bibliographie Critique des Mémoires sur l'Époque Napoléonienne Écrits ou Traduits en Français*, Paris: Droz, 1991, pp. 242–3); they are used here keeping this caution in mind, but with the sense that Putigny's words, even if heavily embroidered over the years, convey the general impressions and emotions of young soldiers and officers of the period.

107 All quotes in this paragraph from Davout to Berthier, 14 April 1809, 1.15 p.m., in Saski, vol. II, pp. 145–7. Reviewing the campaign, Alexandre de Laborde writes of Davout at this stage: 'For two days he refused to implement a disposition that subsequent events could have rendered very dangerous; but finally, receiving an order more definitive than its predecessors, he put himself on the march for Hemau from Ingolstadt' (*Précis Historique de la Guerre entre la France et l'Autriche en 1809*, Paris: Didot, 1822, p. 20). Laborde overstates the time (it would be more accurate to say that Davout delayed for one day, not two), but he captures the moment well.

108 All preceding quotes in the paragraph except one ('I have no doubt') from Berthier to Davout, 14 April 1809, noon in Saski, vol. II, p. 151; Binder claims this note was sent at 10 a.m. rather than noon (vol. I, p. 137). The other three letters of 14 April are marked as noon, 4 p.m., and 10 p.m. All are in Saski, vol. II, pp. 150–1, 153–4, 160–1. Berthier thus sent two at midday before he had received Davout's note and two thereafter.

109 Quote ('I have no doubt') is from Berthier to Davout, 14 April 1809, 4 p.m., in Saski, vol. II, p. 153.

110 In a summary report to Napoleon that night, Berthier did not miss the chance to make a snide and petty remark about Davout's initial concentration at Ingolstadt: 'The Duke of Auerstädt made a premature movement . . .' See Berthier to Napoleon, 14 April 1809, midnight, in Saski, vol. II, pp. 162–3.

111 Quoted from Davout's 'Registre d'Ordres' in Binder, vol. I, p. 135.

112 Davout's description of the roads north of the Danube in his message to Berthier, 14 April, 1.15 p.m., in Saski, vol. II, p. 147.

113 Joseph Dauer, *Das königlich Bayerische 10. Infanterie-Regiment Prinz Ludwig*, Ingolstadt: Ganghofer, 1901, p. 221.

114 'Tagebuch eines bayerischen Artillerieoffiziers aus dem Jahre 1809', *Das Bayernland*, Munich, 1908, p. 436.

115 The composition of these two detachments is not entirely clear. Sources agree that there were two infantry battalions: I/8th Infantry at Allershausen and 1st Light at Attenkirchen. The maps in *Krieg* show two squadrons at each location, but

Völderndorff is not specific and the relevant regimental histories do not illuminate the matter; there may have been only two squadrons total. The detachments were under French Chef d'Escadron Gabriel Montélégier. Döderlein, pp. 117–18; Völderndorff und Waradein, Eduard Freiherr von, *Kriegsgeschichte von Bayern unter König Maximilian Jospeh I.*, Munchen: 1826, pp. 61–3. Note that the 7th Corps Reserve Artillery had been marching with the 1st Division and stopped in Rudertshausen west of Au on the evening of 15 April (Rudolf von Xylander, *Geschichte des 1. Feld-Artillerie-Regiments*, Berlin: Mittler & Sohn, 1909, vol. II, p. 138).

116 Lefevbre to Berthier, 15 April, 11 p.m., and Berthier to Lefebvre, 16 April 1809, 5 a.m., in Saski, vol. II, pp. 172 and 180.

117 Massena, for instance, having assumed responsibility for Oudinot's corps as directed in Berthier's 11 April instructions, was puzzled and troubled when a 15 April message incongruously informed Massena that 'these are the circumstances where you should give orders to General Oudinot'. Had Berthier forgotten that Oudinot had already been under Massena's command for several days? This was hardly a minor detail. Berthier to Massena, 11 April 1809, 6 a.m., and Berthier to Massena, 15 April 1809, 4 a.m., in Saski, vol. II, pp. 113 and 166.

118 Berthier directed St Hilaire to march to Augsburg via Freising 'to put yourself in line with the army' as long as Lefebvre held Munich; if Munich had been evacuated, St Hilaire was to move directly to Augsburg as soon as Davout's men were in Regensburg (Berthier to St Hilaire, 14 April 1809, noon, in Saski, vol. II, p. 152).

119 The observations here are developed from Binder, vol. I, pp. 143–9; and *Krieg*, vol. I, pp. 306–7.

120 Eight hours later, Berthier seemed to have forgotten this change because his summary report to Napoleon on the night of the 14th mistakenly informed the emperor that St Hilaire was still under orders to move to Landshut or Freising! Berthier to Davout, 14 April 1809, 4 p.m., and Berthier to Napoleon, 14 April, midnight, in Saski, vol. II, pp. 153 and 162–64.

121 Rudolf von Xylander, 'Zum Gedächtnis des Feldzugs 1809', *Darstellungen aus der Bayerischen Kriegs- und Heeresgeschichte*, vol. 18 (1909), p. 12; *Krieg*, vol. I, pp. 306–7. On the evening of the 15th, Lefebvre, in the belief that he was following orders, wrote to Berthier to report that Deroy 'is in position before Landshut and will remain there until the arrival of St Hilaire's division' (Lefebvre to Berthier, 15 April 1809, evening, and Lefebvre to Berthier, 16 April 1809, 1 p.m., in Saski, vol. II, pp. 174, 190; also Lefebvre to Massena, 16 April 1809, 1 p.m. in Binder, vol. I, pp. 162–3).

122 Michel Molières, *La Campagne de 1809*, Paris: Le Livre Chez Vous, 2003, pp. 101–6.

123 Quotes: 'terrible blunders' is from Petre, (p. 79); 'clear and precise' as well as 'nothing to desire' are from Pelet, vol. II, pp. 214, 216. A French army instructional manual from the 1930s acidly notes that Berthier had decided to unite the Army of Germany at a location (Regensburg) that was closer to the enemy than it was to the rest of the Allied army (Ecole Supérieure de Guerre, *Campagne de 1809*, Paris, 1931, vol. I, p. 18). See also Maximilian Yorck von Wartenburg, who asks: 'was it indeed possible to misunderstand' Napoleon's instructions? (*Napoleon as*

a General, Carlisle: US Army War College, Art of War Colloquium, 1983, pp. 139–40); Antoine Henri Jomini, *The Art of War,* Westport, CT: Greenwood, n.d.; reprint of 1862 edition, p. 242. Henri Lachouque is also critical, but milder, in his *Napoleon's Battles,* London: George Allen & Unwin, 1964, pp. 233–5. Elting and Esposito are more forgiving of Berthier: *A Military Atlas of the Napoleonic Wars,* New York: Praeger, 1964, p. 93.

124 Quotes:'detailed but imprecise'is from Derrécagaix, vol. II, p. 305;'very ambiguous' from Thiers, vol. X, p. 420. Prussian historian Hugo Friedrich Philipp Johann Freiherr von Freytag-Loringhoven also criticises the'lack of clarity' in Napoleon's orders (*Napoleonische Initiaitive 1809 und 1814,* Berlin: Mittler und Sohn, 1896, p. 8). Thiers writes (p. 421) that after going through the relevant correspondance 'day by day and hour by hour', he cannot accept the blame placed on Berthier: 'Could Berthier have taken upon himself a decision as daring as concentrating the army by a double movement on the flanks in the presence of the enemy? We can hardly imagine it.' My reading of the dispatch record is less lenient than that of Thiers.

125 Bonnal, pp. 49, 73. See also Petre (p. 82) and Chandler (p. 732), who follow Bonnal in this judgement.

126 Derrécagaix, vol. II, pp. 295–319; Thiers, vol. X, pp. 420–1; S. J. Watson, *By Command of the Emperor,* London: Trotman reprint, 1988, pp. 162–8; Bremen,'Die Tage von Regensburg', pp. 273–5. In apparently unconscious irony, Derrécagaix implies in the early portion of his chapter on 1809 that many of the concepts for the army's initial dispositions sprang from Berthier's mind, as if the chief of staff were the author rather than the executor of the plans.

127 'Difficult to comprehend' is from Massena's biographer, Koch, in vol. VI, p. 100. Saski's contention is in vol. I, p. 420.

128 Drouet, pp. 52–3.

129 Bonnal, pp. 77–9. Ségur comments that Berthier 'misunderstood the essence of his instructions' and 'instead of assembling everything, he dispersed everything!' (Philippe-Paul Ségur, *Histoire et Mémoires,* Paris: Didot, 1873, p. 320).

130 Hauptmann Rudolf von Xylander, an instructor at the Bavarian War Academy, proffers Berthier's memory some sympathy in his analysis, but shares the assessment that Napoleon's 10 April instructions, clearly distinguishing between the two broad contingencies, were difficult to misunderstand ('Zum Gedächtnis des Feldzugs 1809', p. 11).

131 Quotes: 'tool' and 'nullity' ('in seiner Nichtigkeit') are from *Krieg,* vol. I, p. 286; 'fear of responsibility' is from Lt. Col. de Philipp, *Le Service d'Etat-Major pendant les Guerres du Premier Empire,* Paris: Teissèdre, 2002, p. 134. Binder repeatedly condemns Berthier's hastiness and ill-considered capitulation to the 'urge to act' (vol. I, pp. 128–9); he concludes that Berthier was not the sort of person who could make wise decisions rapidly (vol. I, pp. 159–61).

132 Koch, vol. VI, p. 102.

133 The number of marches is from Petre, p. 90; and Breman, p. 274. See Appendix for strength calculations.

134 Guillaume de Latrille, Comte de Lorencez, 'Etat Raisonné de Mes Services', *Le Carnet Historique & Littéraire,* vol. X (1901), p. 415.

CHAPTER 5: EIGHT DAYS IN APRIL, I:
THE WAR OPENS AND THE TIDE TURNS

1 The description of Napoleon's ride to Donauwörth in these two paragraphs is based predominantly on the detailed portrayal in Edouard Gachot, *1809 Napoléon en Allemagne*, vol. VI of *Histoire Militaire de Massena*, Paris: Plon, 1913, pp. 43–50. See also Savary, pp. 67–70.

2 Quote from young Leutnant Karl von Suckow, a Prussian who had just taken service in the Württemberg Guard Jäger; the visit afforded him his first glimpse of Napoleon. See his *Aus meinem Soldatenleben*, Stuttgart: Krabbe, 1862, pp. 114–18.

3 Alexandre Bellot de Kergorre, *Journal d'un Commissaire des Guerres pendant le Premier Empire (1806–1821)*, Paris: La Vouivre, 1997, p. 31.

4 According to Gachot (pp. 48–9), the emperor's staff also selected the Dillingen route because they thought it would be more secure. The more direct road from Aalen to Donauwörth passed through Nördlingen, but, knowing little of Austrian dispositions, Lauriston and Savary thought travel through Nördlingen would take Napoleon and his small escort too close to the frontier and possibly leave him subject to interception if the Austrians had already reached Regensburg.

5 The exact hour of Napoleon's arrival in Donauwörth is impossible to state with precision: Saski gives 5 a.m., but Gachot, relying on records in Donauwörth, says 6 a.m. It may have been earlier. Whatever the specific hour, the emperor clearly appeared unannounced in the town around daybreak. The quality of timekeeping in the early nineteenth century makes the quest for such exactitude a fairly otiose endeavour in any case.

6 Napoleon to Otto, 4 March 1809, *Correspondance*, no. 14849. Kergorre used the same term, writing that Napoleon 'arrived in Strasbourg like a lightning bolt' (p. 31).

7 Alois Staudenraus, *Chronik der Stadt Landshut in Bayern*, Landshut: Thomann, 1832, p. 30.

8 Recall that Radetzky's command consisted of the *Gradiska* Grenzer (two battalions of six companies each), two squadrons of *Kienmayer* Hussars, two squadrons of *Karl* Uhlans, and a cavalry battery. Of these, four Grenzer companies and most of the uhlans (the lone platoon or 'Zug' excepted) had deployed to Landshut and its environs on the 15th.

9 Note that the names 'Seligenthal' and 'St Nikolaus' are rendered in a variety of ways (Seelingthal, Nikolai, etc.): 'Seligenthal' is the current spelling for the cloister, but the modern name for the other suburb is 'Nikola'.

10 Additional details: the cavalry with 1st Brigade was one squadron of the 2nd Dragoons and two from the 4th Chevaulegers; the infantry on the heights was 14th Infantry, II/5 (minus the detached Schützen), and two 7th Light companies; the squadron at Bruckberg was from 4th Chevaulegers; Preysing's other four squadrons were on the heights as were one foot and one light battery. The foot battery at the river was that of Hauptmann Peters: two of his guns were placed near a large farm not far from the Lendbrücke (see text) and two were near the paper mill; the location of the other two is not clear, many sources put them with the 5th Light battalion at the Spitalbrücke, but the history of the Bavarian artillery specifically states that this

is incorrect. The reserve battery had not yet joined 3rd Division, so Deroy only had three batteries for eighteen pieces. Recall that one company of 10th Infantry and a gun had been left at Moosburg and were in the process of withdrawing to Furth on the 16th. This portrayal is a correction to that in Gill, *Eagles* at pp. 73–4.

11 Quote from *Krieg*, vol. I, p. 310.

12 The times here are approximate, but it is clear that the final efforts at negotiation took place between 10 and 10.30, with the firing starting between 10.30 and 11 on the morning of the 16th.

13 Radetzky's strength on 16 April: *Gradiska* Grenzer (2,328), *Kienmayer* Hussars (280), *Karl* Uhlans (270). From *Krieg*, vol. I, p. 310.

14 Details of the Austrian pioneers in action are from Wilhelm Brinner, *Geschichte des k. k. Pionnier-Regimentes*, Vienna: Seidel & Sohn, 1878, pp. 49–53. All accounts of the action on 16 April focus on the repair of the Lendbrücke and the 5th Light's defence of the Spitalbrücke site. What transpired at the Spitalbrücke *after* the Lendbrücke had been repaired is unclear, but the available material suggests that the 5th Light withdrew in good order (the Austrians say that it was driven off) and that the Austrian pioneers did not complete their repairs to the Spitalbrücke until later in the afternoon.

15 This, of course, was only Scheibler's little detachment; Deroy did not know that Hiller's main body was still many kilometres to the rear. Nor could he know that Hiller did *not* receive instructions to turn downstream to Landshut until late in the afternoon. It is not clear when Deroy learned of the much more dangerous threat posed to his left flank by Rosenberg, who *did* have orders to march towards Landshut.

16 Deroy to Wrede in Edmund Höfler, *Der Feldzug des Jahres 1809 in Deutschland und Tyrol*, Augsburg: Rieger, 1858, pp. 27–8. See also Deroy's report to Lefebvre in Saski, vol. II, p. 222.

17 *Krieg*, vol. I, p. 321; Madroux, 'August von Floret', p. 162.

18 Some sources state that there were only one and one-half uhlan squadrons.

19 The 5th Infantry's history states that the battalion rejoined Deroy at Arth, but, for tactical and topographical reasons, this must be an error in an otherwise excellent work: the battalion clearly crossed the stream at Aich and could not come to Arth without passing through Pfettrach and the division's rear guard position in that town. Possibly, Metzen did not meet up with Deroy in person until he reached Arth. See Gerneth and Kiesling, *Geschichte des Königlich Bayerischen 5. Infanterie-Regiments*, Berlin: Mittler & Sohn, 1893, pp. 197–8.

20 The detachment detailed to Gammelsdorf found Austrians already in the village (probably Scheibler's men) and returned to Furth only to learn that their comrades had already marched off to rejoin the division. The two detachments evidently linked up with their division later during the evening. The history of the 5th Infantry provides these details on the 7th Light's peregrinations on 16 April (see citation below).

21 The division had halted at Arth to await the successful disengagement of the rear guard. During the retirement from Pfettrach, Austrian cavalry briefly discomfited Seydewitz's men with a sudden charge as the Bavarians rode around the eastern edge of the village to avoid the flames.

22 Distance measured from Seligenthal to Siegenburg.

23 Quoted in Johann Heilmann, *Leben des Grafen Bernhard Erasmus v. Deroy*, Augsburg: Rieger, 1855, p. 54.

24 This insight from Binder, vol. I, pp. 166–7.

25 Sources for the engagement at Landshut on 16 April in addition to those mentioned above (Höfler, Reithofer, Staudenraus): *Krieg*, vol. I, pp. 303–21; Franz Berg, *Geschichte des Königl. Bayer. 4. Jäger-Bataillons*, Landshut: Rietsch, 1887, pp. 212–15; Franz Christoph, 'Die Isar-Uebergänge der Oesterreicher bei Landshut am 16. und 21. April 1809', *Verhandlungen des Historischen Vereins für Niederbayern*, pp. 209–24; Dauer, vol. IV, pp. 220–4; Ferdinand Ebhardt, *Geschichte des k. k. 33. Infanterie-Regiments, Ung. Weisskirchen*: Wunder, 1888, pp. 500–1; Gerneth/Kiesling, pp. 194–201; Heilmann, *Deroy*, pp. 47–55; Heinze, pp. 329–32; Josef Obpacher, *Das k. b. 2. Chevaulegers-Regiment*, Munich: Bayerisches Kriegsarchiv, 1926, pp. 179–82; Riedl, pp. 44–7; M. Ruith, *Das k. bayerische 10. Infanterie-Regiment "Prinz Ludwig"*, Ingolstadt: Ganghofer, 1882, pp. 147–8; Johann Baptist Schels, 'Das Gefecht an der Isar bei Landshut am 16. April 1809', *ÖMZ*, vol. 5 (1845); Franz Schubert and Hans Vara, *Geschichte des K. B. 13. Infanterie-Regiments*, Munich: Lindau, 1906, vol. I, pp. 134–8; Julius Stanka, *Geschichte des K. und K. Infanterie-Regimentes Erzherzog Karl Nr. 3*, Vienna: regimental, 1894, pp. 421–2; Stutterheim, pp. 96–102; Völderndorff, pp. 55–8; Gustav Ritter Amon von Treuenfest, *Geschichte des k. k. Huszaren-Regimentes Alexander Freiherr v. Koller Nr. 8*, Vienna: Mayer, 1880, pp. 446–8; Xylander, *Geschichte des 1. Feld-Artillerie-Regiments*, vol. II, pp. 138–40.

26 From H. Sommerrock, 'Kriegserlebnisse im Jahre 1805 und 1809 bei und in Landshut und insbesondere zu Berg ob Landshut', *Verhandlungen des Historischen Vereins für Niederbayern*, no. 47 (1911).

27 The Austrians (Stipsicz Hussars No. 10) had nine casualties in this scuffle, the Bavarian two (*Krieg*, vol. I, Appendix XXX; and Oskar von Sichlern, *Geschichte des königlich bayerischen 5. Chevaulegers-Regiments "Prinz Otto"*, Munich: regimental, 1876, p. 73).

28 Quote from Schels, 'Das Gefecht an der Isar bei Landshut'.

29 Unfortunately for Hiller, two battalions of *Splényi* Infantry No. 51 marched off to the wrong Buch, reaching Buch am Buchrain west of Isen, nearly thirty kilometres south of their actual destination.

30 Best had four companies each in Thonstetten and Bruckberg. The other battalion of his regiment, II/*Klebek*, was assigned to Scheibler and moved from Moosburg to Bruckberg when Best arrived in the former town.

31 The authors of *Krieg* (vol. I, p. 325) mention a skirmish near Dietldorf on the 16th between some of Crenneville's troops (a platoon each of Jäger and uhlans) and French hussars, but gives no details. I have not been able to locate any other reference to this incident.

32 This paragraph is based on *Krieg*, vol. I, pp. 323–5, both quotes being from p. 324. For a flattering picture of Bellegarde, see Karl Freiherr von Smola, *Das Leben des Feldmarschalls Heinrich Grafen von Bellegarde*, Vienna: Heubner, 1847.

33 Davout unfairly displayed a deep distrust of the Bavarians at this stage of the campaign. He had evidently been harbouring doubts for some days when an officer arrived from Deroy to report on the engagement at Landshut. Unfortunately for

Franco-Bavarian amity, this officer's performance brought the marshal's suspicions into the open. Apparently tongue-tied in the face of Davout's inquisitorial questioning, the young Bavarian left Davout with the impression that either the Bavarians were in full rout to the rear or that the fight at Landshut had been a sham and that the Bavarians might be preparing to defect to Austria (it is easy to imagine that language problems may have contributed to the Bavarian's predicament). Writing to Berthier just after midnight on the 17th, he recalled Wrede's hasty evacuation of Straubing on 9 April and speculated that 'some black treason' might be afoot. Knowing that the Bavarians were to retire to the north bank of the Danube via Ingolstadt, he became concerned for the safety of the vital bridge there and sent strict orders to Demont (whose division was in Ingolstadt) to assume all responsibility for its remaining under French control. If Bavarian troops arrived in the town, Demont was to insist politely but firmly that the Bavarians pass through and continue their retreat to Rain as per their instructions from the major general. Davout's letters to Berthier and Demont, both dated 17 April, 1 a.m., are in Saski, vol. II, pp. 213–14.

34 Albrecht Adam, *Aus dem Leben eines Schlachtenmalers*, Stuttgart: Cotta, 1886, pp. 55–6. Adam was an artist attached to the suite of a staff officer in 7th Corps headquarters.

35 Berthier to Napoleon, postscript to report of 16 April 1809, 8 a.m., in Saski, vol. II, p. 182.

36 *Krieg*, vol. I, p. 328–29.

37 See *Krieg*, vol. I, pp. 325–29.

38 *Krieg*, vol. I, p. 330.

39 The *Levenehr* Dragoons (from II Reserve Corps) were attached to III Corps to make up for the continued absence of the *Hessen-Homburg* Hussars from the III Corps order of battle (Stutterheim, p. 124). The hussars did not reach Landshut until 21 April.

40 Reinwald's detachment consisted of Infantry Regiment No. 40 (formerly *Josef Mittrowsky*), four platoons of *Stipsicz* Hussars, and four guns. Note that III/*J. Mittrowsky* only had four of its six companies; the other two were still en route to the army. The detachment totaled approximately 2,800 infantry and cavalry.

41 The following description of advance guard activity on 17 April largely follows *Krieg*, vol. I, pp. 330–5.

42 There is considerable variance in casualty reporting for the engagement at Schweinbach: the Austrians claim a loss of only twenty-three while inflicting sixty-six on the Bavarians (although approximately fifteen of these were prisoners who had to be left behind when the Austrians retreated); Wrede's report does not list Bavarian losses, but claims sixty-two uhlans captured; Leutnant Madroux of the *König* Chevaulegers, a participant, states that his regiment lost 'a few dead and many wounded' while capturing thirty uhlans, but mentions no Bavarian prisoners. Sources: *Krieg*, vol. I, pp. 333–5 and Appendix XXX; M. H., *Kurze Darstellung der Geschichte des Königlich Bayerischen 4. Chevaulegers-Regiment "König"*, Berlin: Mittler & Sohn, 1895, p. 19; Madroux, 'August von Floret', pp. 162–5; Riedl, pp. 47–8; Stutterheim, p. 125; Völderndorff, p. 64; Wrede, 'Rapport sur les differentes affaires qu'a eues la 2e division bavaroise sous les ordres du lieutenant-général

baron de Wrède, depuis le commencement des hostilitiés', 4 May 1809, in Pelet, vol. II, pp. 439–40. Radetzky did report that evening that Wrede was withdrawing to Neustadt, but this information probably did not come from this skirmish (and would soon be turned on its head in any event).

43 The bridge had been demolished by winter ice (Laborde, p. 27).

44 According to Austrian accounts, there were two separate engagements in the same general area on the 17th. The first was between a squadron of *Klenau* under Rittmeister Johann Freiherr Wasseige and elements of the 11th Chasseurs. As Wasseige was withdrawing, Rittmeister Franz Ritter von Böhm arrived with a separate *Klenau* detachment and skirmished briefly with the French. French sources make almost no mention of this small clash (or pair of clashes); it receives passing comment in Ledru's study of Montbrun, but no recognition in Pajol's biography or in the history of the 11th Chasseurs. Davout noted it in a report to Berthier at 8 a.m., 18 April 1809, in Saski, vol. II, p. 233. The narrative here is condensed from *Krieg*, vol. I, p. 332.

45 An interesting side note on tactical deception: to confuse any French or Bavarian observers, VI Corps temporarily added a squadron of *Liechtenstein* Hussars to Scheibler's command on the 17th (*Krieg*, vol. I, p. 335).

46 L. A. Unger, *Histoire Critique des Exploits et Vicissitudes de la Cavallerie*, Paris: Corréard, 1848, vol. I, pp. 9–13.

47 The description of Austrian deliberations is taken from *Krieg*, vol. I, pp. 336–40. The observations are my own.

48 Charles to Bellegarde, 17 April 1809, in *Krieg*, vol. I, p. 337.

49 *Krieg*, vol. I, p. 337.

50 Order to FML Hiller, 17 April 1809, in *Krieg*, vol. I, pp. 338–9.

51 Deroy marched at about 9 p.m.; Wrede at approximately 10 (Nicolaus Stark, *Erinnerungs-Blätter an die Schlachttage bei Abensberg*, Abensberg, 1908, p. 40).

52 Other than the specific units listed, it is not clear what other troops (if any) Klenau may have had on hand or nearby. At least one battery had been added to his command at some point, as he brought two into play on the 17th.

53 Some sources state that Klenau had two batteries on the heights for a total of three in action on the 17th.

54 'Kurze Beschreibung der hitzigen Schlacht und des fürchterlichen Brandes am 23. April 1809 in Regensburg und Stadtamhof', by an eyewitness, in Julius Wackenreiter, *Die Erstürmung von Regensburg*, Regensburg: Bösenecker, 1865, p. 197.

55 Sources: *Krieg*, vol. I, pp. 344–6; Emile Espérandieu, *Histoire Abrégée des Campagnes du 61me Régiment d'Infanterie*, Marseilles: Aubertin, 1897; Capitaine Froidevaux, 'Notice Historique sur le 30e Régiment d'Infanterie et les Régiments qui l'ont précédé', manuscript, AG, 1887; Johann Hiederer, *Die Schreckenstage von Stadtamhof*, Regensburg: Habbel, 1899, pp. 13–14; Kandelsdorfer, *Feld-Jäger-Bataillons Nr. 7*, p. 33; Capitaine Pagès Xartart, 'Historique du 17e Régiment d'Infanterie de Ligne', manuscript, AG, 1894; Wackenreiter, pp. 5, 59. Davout reported the skirmish in a letter to Berthier, 11 p.m., 17 April 1809, Saski, vol. II, pp. 216–17; St Hilaire's account is also on this page. According to their regimental histories, the 30th and 61st Ligne also played small parts in this engagement. The Austrian dragoons seem to have

had no role in the fight (J. Strack, *Geschichte des Sechsten Dragoner-Regimentes Carl Ludwig Graf Ficquelmont*, Vienna: Hof- und Staatsdruckerei, 1856).

56 Paraphrased from Binder, vol. I, p. 175. The authors of the Austrian official history observe that Napoleon arrived in Donauwörth with the thought that his army might have to fight a 'Battle of Augsburg' somewhere east of that city (*Krieg*, vol. I, pp. 348–9), but this notion evaporated quickly as he pored over the correspondence at headquarters.

57 Ségur, who recounts this incident, states that he heard it from Monthion 'many times' (Ségur, *Histoires et Mémoires*, vol. III, p. 322).

58 The original instructions are Napoleon to Davout, 17 April 1809, 10 a.m. (sent by four different couriers between 10 and 11 .m. on the 17th). A 1 p.m. message from Berthier has been lost to history (Davout referred to it in Davout to Berthier, 18 April 1809, 8 .m., in Saski, vol. II, p. 232), and Napoleon sent another at 6 p.m. (Saski, vol. II, pp. 209–11). The letters to Lefebvre and Wrede were sent at 11 a.m. and noon respectively (Saski, vol. II, pp. 199–206).

59 Napoleon, with little detailed information on Davout's deployments, was operating under the false assumption that Friant was on or close to the Altmühl; in fact, he was along the Regensburg–Nuremberg road with orders to march for Regensburg. In my view, the emperor expected Friant to fall back along the north bank of the Danube in the general direction of Ingolstadt more or less independent of the movement of the rest of 3rd Corps south of the great river. The authors of the Austrian history take a similar view (*Krieg*, vol. I, p. 353). Petre (p. 94), following Bonnal (pp. 115–16), concludes that Napoleon wanted, indeed ordered, Friant to join Davout at Neustadt on the 18th, a requirement that would have left Friant no option but to cross the Danube at Kehlheim where the bridge was destroyed. There is no specific evidence to support this rather tormented interpretation and it seems far more reasonable to conclude that Napoleon simply wanted Friant at Ingolstadt with the rest of 3rd Corps by the quickest and safest route: whether north or south of the river, whether with or separate from Davout, were minor considerations.

60 Bonnal (pp. 114–15) and Petre (p. 93) argue that Napoleon greatly underestimated the strength of the 'corps from Landshut' on 17 April, thinking it only one army corps and not recognising that it represented the Main Army under the archduke's personal command. It is entirely possible that Napoleon did not appreciate the strength of the Austrian force marching north from Landshut, but Bonnal and Petre place too much emphasis on the term 'corps d'armée autrichien' that Napoleon uses once in his 17 April, 10 a.m. letter to Davout and repeated in the 11 a.m. note to Lefebvre. In those same messages and elsewhere (to Davout, Lefebvre, Wrede, Massena) he also uses the phrases 'corps de Landshut', 'colonne de Landshut', 'les colonnes', 'la colonne ennemie', and (by evening when he had the initial reports from Deroy's fight on the 16th) 'les corps ennemies qui ont débouché par Freising et Landshut'. The essential point, however, is not whether Napoleon correctly gauged the force debouching from Landshut, rather that he clearly perceived, as early as midmorning on 17 April, that a major Austrian force was approaching from the Isar, that this was probably the location of the principal enemy army, and that he had a chance to crush it if he could retrieve Davout and bring up Massena.

61 This and all quotes in this paragraph are from Napoleon to Davout, 17 April 1809, 10 a.m., and Napoleon to Lefebvre, 17 April 1809, 11 a.m., in Saski, vol. II, pp. 199–200. Napoleon knew that Wrede's division was in contact with the Austrians: Wrede to Berthier, 16 April 1809, 11 a.m. (approx.), and 16 April 1809, 6 p.m., in Saski, vol. II, pp. 191–2.

62 Readers should note that Napoleon's messages on the 17th do *not* contain these explicit statements, but they clearly imply that he did not expect to find major Austrian forces at Munich, that Bellegarde was not an immediate threat (Davout was to 'mask' Bellegarde), and that the Army of Germany could surprise and defeat a significant enemy force between the Isar and the Danube north of Landshut. By a process of elimination, we can infer that Napoleon thought that this was likely to be the principal Austrian army, but he does not make a specific statement to this effect in these 17 April missives.

63 Lefebvre's and Wrede's reports (five and two respectively) for 17 April are in Saski, vol. II, pp. 220–5. Particularly important were Deroy's account of the engagement at Landshut (Lefebvre included this in a message at 4 p.m.) and a superbly detailed intelligence report from Wrede sent at 9 a.m.

64 Berthier to Moulin, 18 April 1809, and Massena to Moulin, 18 April 1809, in Saski, vol. II, pp. 218–19.

65 Napoleon's proclamation makes an interesting contrast with the famous but lengthy order of the day that Charles issued on 6 April and the ponderous language the Austrian leaders employed to importune the people of Bavaria and to exhilarate their own population.

66 Proclamation and letter to Otto, 17 April 1809, in Saski, vol. II, p. 201.

67 Napoleon to Davout, 17 April 1809, 6 p.m., in Saski, vol. II, pp. 210–11. Note that Napoleon used the word 'communication' here to mean his ability to issue orders promptly and securely, something he could not do reliably when he dictated this missive on the evening of the 17th. He made a similar prediction in a 17 April letter to Max Joseph of Bavaria: 'Everything leads to the conclusion that Wednesday or Thursday we will have some action' (Saski, vol. II, p. 208).

68 One can argue that Massena might have taken steps to assemble his divisions more tightly on the 16th or 17th, but in the prevailing uncertainty on the Allied side under Berthier's command, he preferred to ease his logistical burden by dispersing his men until he knew that they actually would be called upon to march. Bonnal quote from p.122.

69 Massena to Napoleon, 8.15 p.m., 17 April 1809, in Saski, vol. II, pp. 217–19; Davout to Berthier, 8 a.m., 18 April 1809, in Saski, vol. II, pp. 232–3.

70 Drouet to Deroy, 17 April 1809, 8 p.m., BKA/B442. Deroy's expectation that 'we will evidently not be able to stay in Ingolstadt, rather will probably have to march on to Neuburg' and his hope to rest his men there were based on a chance meeting with one of Lefebvre's staff officers, Chef de Bataillon Jean Maingranaud, on the road near Vohburg; they are in a letter (apparently to Wrede), dated 17 April 1809, 10.30 p.m., BKA/B442.

71 Quote from Wrede's account of operations in Pelet, vol. II, p. 440. Wrede's summary leaves the impression that he had received direct orders from Napoleon. Such direct communication *was* a frequent occurrence, but on this occasion it

seems that the orders came from 7th Corps headquarters: Drouet to Wrede, 17 April 1809, 9 p.m., BKA/B442.

72 Quotes from Drouet to Ludwig, 17 April 1809, 9 p.m. (received at 1 a.m.), BKA/ B442. The decision to march the 1st Division on the north bank of the Danube added eleven kilometres to their route; it was probably the result of French concerns about the possibility of Austrian forces being in the Dürnbucher Forst.

73 Napoleon expected the 2nd and 3rd Divisions to be in place by 9 a.m. on the 18th and hoped that the 1st would arrive by 11 a.m. Napoleon to Lefebvre, 18 April 1809, 4 a.m., in Saski, vol. II, pp. 228–9.

74 The 3rd Division reached Neustadt at 3 p.m., the 1st at 4 p.m. This summary of the convoluted Bavarian movements on 17 and 18 April is drawn primarily from Gerneth/Kiesling, pp. 201–2; supplemented by Dauer, p. 224; Fabrice, pp. 170–1; Schubert/Vara, p. 138; and the correspondence in BKA/B442.

75 Napoleon to Lefebvre, 18 April 1809, 4 a.m., in Saski, vol. II, pp. 228–9.

76 This skirmish cost the Austrians forty-eight men, the Bavarians twenty-four. Sources: *Krieg*, vol. I, p. 364 and Annex XXX; Gill, *Eagles*, p. 81; Riedl, p. 49. The Bavarians again made use of their Schützen, but the weight of the engagement was carried by their artillery and cavalry, 'no real infantry combat occurred' (Eugen Zoellner, *Geschichte des K. B. 11. Infanterie-Regiments 'von der Tann' 1805–1905*, Munich: Lindauer, 1905, p. 58). Note that many sources refer to the Bavarian '12th Infantry' in this skirmish: there was no 12th Infantry Regiment in the Bavarian army in 1809. The regiment of that number had been disbanded in 1806 for mutiny. The mistake arises from Wrede's combat history of his division as published in Pelet. In what was doubtless an error of transcription, which Pelet and the French editors would not notice, this published report refers to the 12th Line on 18 April.

77 Heinrich von Roos, *Mit Napoleon in Russland*, Stuttgart: Lutz, 1911, p. 243. A surgeon with the Württemberg contingent, Roos added several vivid anecdotes from 1809 to his memoir of the Russian campaign. Lodged in a rude hut in Ingolstadt on the 18th, he states that he observed Napoleon and several senior officers in a small nearby house as they conversed with three men in peasants' clothing. The men came to the house, had brief conversations with the French, and departed with serious expressions; Roos and his colleagues concluded that they were French spies delivering news and receiving new tasks from Napoleon.

78 The 'Saxon Duchies' were a collection of five monarchies located in central Germany (what is now the German state of Thüringen): Gotha, Hildburghausen, Koburg, Meiningen, and Weimar. Their Rheinbund contingents were combined into a single regiment.

79 Schauroth, p. 6. This sort of escort duty was exhausting for the light cavalry units involved: seventy of the 511 horses belonging to the Württemberg *Herzog Louis* Jäger-zu-Pferd were incapacitated following the day's ride with Napoleon (R. Starklof, *Geschichte des Königlich Württembergischen Zweiten Reiter-Regiments ehemaligen Jäger-Regiments zu Pferde Herzog Louis*, Darmstadt and Leipzig: Zernin, 1862, p. 98).

80 'Le Centenaire des Cuirassiers', *Carnet de la Sabretache* (1904); also Elting, p. 233.

81 Coming upon this detachment, an artillery drummer noted two guns 'loaded and masked, that is, covered with branches in front so that the enemy would not see

them' (N. Reichold, *Soldaten-Sohn und das Kriegsleben von 1805 bis 1815*, Munich, 1851, p. 90).

82 Lorencez, p. 415.

83 Berthezène, p. 189.

84 Putigny, p. 181.

85 Mändler, p. 3.

86 Adam, *Aus dem Leben*, p. 59; similarly: Völderndorff, p. 67.

87 There is an interesting historiographical aspect to this little engagement, in that French regimental histories give us what one might term 'routine prominence' (that is, it is treated as one of many successful small combats in the regiment's background), where the normally voluble Austrian official history barely covers it. If the French accounts are correct, their casualties came to forty or fifty: the 17th Ligne claims to have lost two officers wounded and twenty-two men killed or wounded, and Armand Coutard, the battalion commander in the 65th speaks of fifteen dead and some twenty wounded in his report. The history of Austrian Infantry Regiment No. 25 also spends a page on this fight (but does not mention casualties). There is no reference to the 18th in the otherwise precise history of the 7th Jäger Battalion. Curiously, in *Krieg*, where paragraphs are spent on firefights with far fewer casualties, this one does not even find a mention in the detailed appendix of losses. See Pages Xartart (17th Ligne); Armand Coutard's battle report in Henry de Riancey, *Le Général Comte de Coutard*, Paris: Dentu, 1857, p. 57; and *Geschichte des k. k. 25. Infanterie-Regiments FZM, Freiherr Lazarus von Mamula*, Prague: regimental, 1875, p. 424.

88 Pajol's report is published in Pajol, pp. 329–31. See also Ledru, *Montbrun*, p. 63. According to the history of the 11th Chasseurs, the regiment had twenty-four wounded and five killed (Moine de Margon, pp. 102–3). As with the 18 April engagement at Reinhausen, Pajol's fight on the 18th receives only passing mention in *Krieg*, vol. I, p. 368; it is not mentioned at all in the history of the *Klenau* Chevaulegers (Cajetan Pizzighelli, *Geschichte des K. und K. Dragoner-Regimentes Johannes Josef Fürst von und zu Liechtenstein Nr. 10 1631–1903*, Vienna: regimental, 1903).

89 Napoleon to Massena, 18 April 1809, in Saski, vol. II, pp. 240–2. It is important to note here that Napoleon, after only twenty-four hours in the theatre of war, already had a reasonably accurate, if unspecific, assessment of Austrian strength and intentions. He also clearly recognised those areas where information was lacking and accounted for these uncertainties in his thinking. This letter to Massena, for instance, speaks not only of the force advancing from Landshut under the archduke's personal command, but also of enemy columns coming from Moosburg and/or Freising (i.e. Hiller, though Napoleon did not yet know this).

90 By just mentioning 'three' divisions, Napoleon indicated acceptance of Massena's concern that Boudet's men could not adhere to the demanding timetable.

91 Massena to Oudinot, 18 April 1809, 2 p.m., in Saski, vol. II, pp. 242–3.

92 Quote from the 18 April entry in the journal of the Baden brigade, GLA, 48/4286, 'Journal des Grossherzoglich Badischen General-Staab'.

93 An anonymous Hessian account published as 'Feldzug der 2ten Division 4ten Armeecorps der Armee von Teutschland im Jahr 1809', *Pallas*, vol. VI (1810), p. 615. The author was a member of the contingent.

94 'Trailing stragglers' is my assumption; unfortunately, we have no figures for how many men actually stayed with the colours for this march.

95 Quote from the 18 April entry in the journal of the Baden brigade, GLA, 48/4286.

96 Prussian commentator, Hugo Freiherr von Freytag-Loringhoven, provides an excellent summary of accomplishments in 1806, but is too ready to write off the French and their German allies in 1809 ('Marschanordnungen und Marschleistungen unter Napoleon', *Beiheft zum Militär-Wochenblatt*, (1893), pp. 237–50).

97 This account draws heavily on *Krieg*, vol. I, pp. 363–74; Angeli, vol. IV, pp. 79–86; Stutterheim, pp. 126–31.

98 Vécsey report, 17 April 1809, quoted in Binder, vol. I, p. 180. Binder also quotes part of Rosenberg's cover letter sent the following morning.

99 Rosenberg to Charles, 18 April 1809, 6 a.m., quoted extensively in *Krieg*, vol. I, pp. 357–8.

100 Stutterheim, p. 127.

101 *Krieg 1809*, vol. I, p. 360, gives the Austrian strength at this stage as 71,300. The book offers no details, so it is impossible to tell how they reached this substantially higher figure; perhaps they included artillerymen along with infantry and cavalry. The figure here is taken from the order of battle appendix and includes III Corps with the attached *Levenehr* Dragoons (24,480), IV Corps (17,591), and I Reserve Corps with Lindenau's division (24,569). Stutterheim's advance guard, though not actually at Rohr, is included in this figure; the three missing battalions of Lindenau's division are not.

102 Mesko had one battalion of *Brod* Grenz Infantry No. 7 and a squadron of *Kienmayer* Hussars. The force in Mainburg consisted of two *Brod* companies, a platoon of *Kienmayer* Hussars from V Corps and a separate detachment from II Reserve Corps (two squadrons of *Knesevich* Dragoons). A total of eight companies of *Brod* Grenzer were thus deployed south away from the corps, leaving four companies with the corps main body.

103 Klier, p. 31.

104 Instructions for Hiller, 18 April 1809, quoted in *Krieg*, vol. I, pp. 361–2.

105 *Krieg*, vol. I, pp. 361–2.

106 In addition, FML Karl Freiherr von Vincent had six squadrons at Mauern. See *Krieg*, vol. I, p. 369.

107 Hiller, p. 158.

108 Charles to Kolowrat, 18 April 1809, in *Krieg*, vol. I, p. 361, and in Binder, vol. I, p. 181. Kolowrat was to inform Bellegarde of the change in Austrian plans.

109 Bellegarde's planned move was in response to an order from Charles that he received at midday on the 18th. Even though he should have clearly understood by then that Davout was already in the process of crossing the Danube to the south, Bellegarde did not take the initiative to adjust his movements according to the prevailing situation, instead, he simply obeyed orders that were clearly out of date. The authors of *Krieg* criticise him severely on this and other occasions (vol. I, pp. 372–4).

110 Angeli (vol. IV, p. 86) arrives at the strange conclusion that Charles initially wanted to deal with Lefebvre before tackling Davout; Binder scornfully dismisses

this judgement (vol. I, p. 181) and the Austrian official history does not even raise it.

111 Binder, vol. I, p. 191. At least one of the officers in attendance during the conference in Rohr concluded that the purpose of this initial disposition was to await a major battle in a supposedly favourable position: Oberst Karl von Quasdanovich, the IV Corps chief of staff, wrote that 'The advance to the heights above Abensberg and the acceptance of a general engagement there was the goal of the orders resulting from this disposition' (Quasdanovich to Franz, 20 April 1810, in Angeli, vol. IV, p. 86).

112 Lefebvre to Davout, 18 April 1809, 4 p.m., in Stutterheim, p. 131; and Angeli, vol. IV, p. 87. Note that the version in *Krieg*, printed as 'Siegenburg et Vohburg' [rather than Biburg], is clearly in error (vol. I, pp. 375–6). Binder (vol. I, p. 190) states that the Austrians also recovered a copy of Davout's march order. This stunning good fortune is mentioned in no other source, French or Austrian. It thus seems highly unlikely that the Austrians had this information in hand on the morning of 19 April 1809. It is possible that Binder was referring to a French document that fell into Austrian hands some time after 19 April or was acquired by a subsequent Austrian researcher (Welden collected a number of French and German materials that he left in the Austrian Kriegsarchiv).

113 A probe into Abbach during the night of 18/19 April by the *Vincent* Chevaulegers will be discussed below. This information (that Davout was planning to evacuate Regensburg) seems to have reached army headquarters some time after 6 a.m. (*Krieg*, vol. I, p. 381), probably close to 7 a.m. Binder, on the other hand, states that the timing of this intelligence is not clear, that is, whether it arrived before or after the issuance of the second disposition for 19 April (Binder, vol. I, p. 190). See also Stutterheim, pp. 130–1.

114 Stutterheim, pp. 132–3.

115 The strength figures in this paragraph differ from those presented on p. 377 of the first volume of *Krieg*. My figures, in line with the standard adopted for this work, include only infantry and cavalry. Although not specifically stated, it appears that those in the Austrian history are higher because they include artillery, train, and other troops.

116 Note that Lindenau only had nine of his assigned twelve battalions: two battalions of *EH Karl* No. 3 had been left in Furth on 18 April to protect the passage of the army's trains against a fictitious enemy threat from Mainburg and had not yet rejoined their division, while III/Stain No. 50, too inexperienced to commit to a fight, had remained in the rear of V Corps.

117 As quoted in Stutterheim, p. 133. Note that I include III/*Stain* (approximately 1,000 men) here in the figure for V Corps and II Reserve Corps, thus the disparity with the 18,800 cited in *Krieg*.

118 The figure for Hiller includes all of his local detachments (such as Scheibler), but does not include Jellacic.

119 Davout's march order is in Saski, vol. II, pp. 237–8. Details follow: Colonel Jean Nicolas Eloi Mathis of the 2nd Chasseurs was responsible for the escort of the trains with his regiment and I/30th Ligne (picked up en route); the 8th Hussars rode with the centre column, two squadrons ahead and one as rear

guard; GB Clément's cuirassier brigade (and GD St Sulpice personally) also accompanied the centre column; the 1st Chasseurs (and presumably GB Jacquinot) rode with the Gudin/Friant column, as did Guiton's cuirassiers. Davout placed himself with the left column where contact was most likely. Davout's orders as printed in Saski and elsewhere do not mention the 16th Chasseurs. Bonnal (p. 145) places them on Gudin's left under GB Piré and some of the battle reporting suggests that they did perform a screening role on the corps' left flank between Saalhaupt, Schneidhart, and Teugn. As far as cavalry was concerned, however, only Montbrun's squadrons played any significant role on the 19th, the other troopers (Jacquinot's, Piré's, the cuirassiers) were spectators to a quintessential infantry battle.

120 Note that the strength Saski gives (vol. II, p. 255) is slightly lower because he does not include I/30 Ligne, which had been sent to guard the defile at Abbach and which subsequently accompanied the baggage train. I think it appropriate to include this battalion. Not included here are Demont's division, the 65th Ligne in Regensburg, and Guyon's detachment on the Altmühl (12th Chasseurs, I/111th Ligne and two companies of III/15th Léger). Apparently through an oversight, Saski only counts the cuirassier regiments as having three squadrons each; they should each have four squadrons.

121 General sources for the fight with Davout's corps on the 19th include: *Krieg*, vol. I, pp. 380–401; Angeli, vol. IV, pp. 90–7; Binder, vol. I, pp. 193–208; Pelet, vol. I, pp. 293–300; Stutterheim, pp. 138–58; Ian Castle, *Eggmühl 1809*, Osprey Campaign Series No. 56, London: Osprey, 1998, pp. 23–37 (some good terrain maps).

122 Gudin had also dispatched four companies of the 12th Ligne to secure his flank towards Dünzling. These do not seem to have engaged in any combat. From Gudin's report in Saski, vol. II, p. 254.

123 Note that many contemporary reports refer to 'Post-Saal'. This was the old post-house between Obersaal and Untersaal. To assist readers with modern maps, I have used Obersaal.

124 Stutterheim was authorised to call upon *Erzherzog Ludwig* No. 8 and *Koburg* No. 22 for support (*Krieg*, vol. I, p. 382).

125 Quotes from Stutterheim, pp. 146–7. There is some confusion about the disposition of the *Vincent* Chevaulegers on the 19th: Stutterheim started with four squadrons, but *Krieg*, vol. I, p. 383 indicates that he had only three after IV Corps moved out for Dünzling; according to this source, two stayed with Steyrer and three rode with Rosenberg. Late in the day, however, Stutterheim took four squadrons to support Hohenzollern's right flank. The regimental history is unclear on this point (Gustav Ritter Amon von Treuenfest, *Geschichte des k. k. Dragoner-Regimentes Nr. 14*, Vienna: Brzezowsky, 1886, p. 395).

126 This, too, is not unlike McClellan at Antietam.

127 Steyrer was the commander of the *Chasteler* Infantry Regiment. As part of the confusion regarding the whereabouts of the various elements of the *Vincent* Chevaulegers during the day, *Krieg* (vol. I, p. 383) places two squadrons with Steyrer, but other sources only indicate one.

128 The engagement between Hausen and Teugn is called 'the Battle of Thann' in some sources, even though that village played no role in the fighting.

129 Hohenzollern claimed that cannon fire from the direction of Abensberg sparked his concern. If his hearing was correct, this must have been some desultory and insignificant exchange as the actual fighting along the Abens lay some hours in the future (*Krieg*, vol. I, p. 384).

130 Approximately 1,090 Grenzer and 260 hussars. Third Corps also placed a hussar picket at Reissing.

131 Oberst Johann Mayer von Heldensfeld, his chief of staff, urged Hohenzollern to shift the corps to the right and co-ordinate its advance with Rosenberg, but the commander held to his instructions to march on Abbach. Mayer was partially wrong: shifting to the right would have taken III Corps away from the Regensburg–Abensberg road and thus away from the link it was supposed to break between Davout and Lefebvre (*Krieg*, vol. I, p. 386). On the other hand, Mayer was absolutely correct in recommending close co-ordination with IV Corps; Austrian actions throughout the day were marked by astonishing ignorance of neighbouring unit locations and intentions.

132 Quote from *Krieg*, vol. I, p. 386.

133 Quote from Berthezène's account of the action (p. 193); he was watching with the 10th Léger on the hillside to the north. Comments on the 3rd Ligne's condition as it reached the top of the hill are paraphrased from the 3rd Corps account of the battle in Saski, vol. II, pp. 255–6.

134 Lorencez, p. 418.

135 Quote from the battle report of St Hilaire's division in Saski, vol. II, p. 257.

136 *Krieg*, vol. I, p. 389.

137 Berthezène, p. 194.

138 This is my best estimate of the sequence of action here in the centre of the French line. As noted elsewhere, the entire action is confused owing to the rugged, obscuring terrain and the intermixing of units and detachments of units. However, it seems likely St Hilaire was in the process of pulling out his two much-used regiments and replacing them with fresh troops as Liechtenstein attacked. Berthezène reports that Davout's chief of staff, GD Jean Dominique Compans, brought up the 72nd just as an Austrian advance was underway; he states that Compans launched the 72nd in a telling counterattack that contributed to the enemy's repulse (Berthezène, p. 195); this could be consistent with an effort to relieve the weary elements in contact. The 72nd took the place of the 3rd Ligne on the French right, while the 105th relieved the 57th on the left (Thiers, vol. X, p. 136).

139 This is the result of my analysis. According to the authors of *Krieg* (vol. I, pp. 380–2, 389–91), Stutterheim's Grenzer evicted Petit from the woods and were in the process of pursuing him when Friant appeared. This seems unlikely, especially as Petit and III/7th Light were almost immediately thrown into the fight with Hohenzollern's command.

140 Two additional points are useful here. First, from the French accounts published in Saski, it seems that the 48th Ligne and I/108th Ligne may have been involved in supporting Sarraire for a time. Even if they were involved north of Schneidhart for part of the battle, however, I conclude that both of these units eventually found themselves committed to the fight between Hausen and Teugn. See Friant's report and the 108th Ligne's account in Saski, vol. II, pp. 260–1. Second, it is possible

that Sarraire's men drifted far to their right after repulsing the Grenzer towards Schneidhart. Friant's account (Friant, p. 163) suggests that these companies may have been in action north of Hausen. With no map and in the heat of battle in a tangled, wooded countryside, this is certainly plausible that Sarraire may have ended up some distance from Schneidhart, but like so many other details of this battle, we cannot be certain.

141 For the 111th Ligne, see Adam, *111e Régiment*, pp. 62–4. Thiers made a valiant and diligent effort to unravel the fighting at Hausen–Teugn, and he presents some important aspects of the fighting, but the published version mistakenly mixes the 33rd Ligne of Friant's division with the 3rd Ligne of St Hilaire's. Unfortunately, the regimental history of the 33rd follows Thiers uncritically and thus offers an erroneous version of the regiment's limited role in the battle (Lieutenant Sommervogel, 'Historique du 33e Régiment d'Infanterie', manuscript, AG, 1891).

142 This is the point at which the 72nd Ligne, led into action by Compans, may have played a key role.

143 'Geschichte des kaiserlich-österreichischen 7. Infanterie-Regiments Grossherzog Toskano', *Oesterreichische Militärische Zeitschrift* (1824).

144 Gustav Ritter Amon von Treuenfest, *Geschichte des k. k. Infanterie-Regiments Nr. 20*, Vienna: Mayer, 1878, p. 338.

145 This may have been as little as three of the regiment's twelve companies; parts remained behind to support the batteries north of Hausen (*Geschichte des kaiserlichen und königlichen Infanterie-Regimentes Freiherr von Mollinary Nr. 38*, Budapest, regimental, 1892, pp. 170–1).

146 Other than the 48th Ligne, I/108, and the voltigeurs from 33rd, 108th, and 111th Regiments, it is impossible to tell exactly which units of Friant's division fought in the woods north of Hausen. It seems clear that the 33rd, most of the 108th (2nd and 3rd Battalions), and II/111th saw little, if any, battle on the 19th. The actions of the 15th Léger, however, are also uncertain. As will be seen later in this section, parts of the regiment and III/111th were engaged in very heavy fighting near Dünzling; and Sarraire (at a minimum) contested the hills with Stutterheim's Grenzer, later supported by four companies of the 108th, but the details are imprecise and contradictory.

147 According to the historical account submitted by 3rd Corps, Davout ordered two regiments of the 3rd Division to 'retrace their steps through the woods' to form west of Teugn (Saski, vol. II, p. 256). It is not clear which regiments received this mission, nor when they arrived or how long they remained near Teugn. Whatever their identity, they do not seem to have been involved in any of the fighting (note: Binder states that the 12th Ligne lost 312 men on the 19th, indicating the regiment's involvement in serious combat, but I suspect that his calculations are in error).

148 The authors of *Krieg* (vol. I, pp. 389–90) contend that one of GB Gilly's accomplishments was to prevent Stutterheim from interfering in the Battle of Hausen–Teugn earlier in the day, implying that Stutterheim's presence might have been tactically significant. This is a fatuous suggestion incongruent with the intelligence, objectivity, and thoughtfulness that characterise the first volume of the Austrian official history. Stutterheim's command was small: one battalion (*c*.1,100

bayonets) and three or four squadrons (perhaps 400 to 500 sabres). His infantry was vastly outnumbered by Friant alone and his chevaulegers had little role to play in the chaotic skirmishing among the trees near Hausen. Even if they had found a way to cross the wooded hills in reasonable order, they would have faced at least eight squadrons of French cuirassiers at Saalhaupt and perhaps one or two regiments of light cavalry as well (8th Hussars and 16th Chasseurs). With great luck, the psychological impact might have been important, but it likely would have been transitory. Stutterheim was highly competent and his troops did very well for their numbers, but it serves no purpose to exaggerate their potential effect on the battle.

149 The number of grenadier battalions is from Stutterheim (p. 154); *Krieg* does not offer a specific number, but lists five as suffering losses on the 19th (though only *Leiningen* lost more than two).

150 It is worth noting that Montbrun, in his report to Davout that evening, correctly assessed the approximate size of Rosenberg's force at 18,000 and correctly identified both of the Austrian cavalry regiments and three of the infantry regiments. On the other hand, the battle history prepared by his chief of staff (date unknown) mistakenly includes Habsburg dragoons and uhlans among the foes encountered on the 19th. Both items are in Saski, vol. II, pp. 262–3.

151 A company of *Koburg* had already cleared French skirmishers out of the woods north of Paring.

152 The four companies from the 12th Ligne may still have been in this vicinity when the engagement began, but none of the few French accounts mention them. As with all other actions on this day, the details of Gilly's battles are difficult to piece together at this remove in time. However, it is likely that he had to shift most of his men to his left (north) flank; that is, from the area opposite Schneidhart to the area towards Moosholzen. See Friant, p. 164.

153 Quote from the 2nd Division battle report in Saski, vol. II, p. 261. Two companies of the 7th Léger were sent to Montbrun's right flank and may have participated in repelling the Austrian advances toward the wood.

154 Friant's report in Saski, vol. II, pp. 260–1.

155 Espinchal, p. 231.

156 Even from this regiment, the skirmishers of the 1st Battalion went to support *Koburg* (Franz von Branko, *Geschichte des k. k. Infanterie-Regimentes Nr. 44*, Vienna: Hof- und Staatsdruckerei, 1875, p. 163).

157 Rosenberg reported 'the enemy left wing defeated' and claimed that he 'had reached his objective' (quoted in Binder, vol. I, p. 197).

158 According to Espinchal, a battalion of the 7th Léger was placed in Peising while the rest of the command retired to Abbach (Espinchal, p. 232).

159 Pajol's wound from Espinchal (p. 232); Montbrun's report said that Pajol had suffered a contusion.

160 The four companies were from *Hiller* Infantry No. 2, the two squadrons were from Oberst Mayer's regiment, the *Klenau* Chevaulegers. Oberst Josef von Mayer should not be confused with GM Josef Georg von Mayer, a brigadier in Lindenau's division.

161 Additionally, a detachment of four companies of *Hiller* Infantry and two squadrons of *Klenau* Chevaulegers were posted in Obersanding under Oberst Josef Mayer.

162 Quotes from 'Tagebuch über die Vorfallenheiten, während dem Krieg, den das Kaiserthum Frankreich mit Einschluss des rheinischen Bundes gegen den Kaiser von Oesterreich führet; ausgezeichnet bei der Marsch Station Alteglofsheim im Jahre 1809', in C. Will, 'Beitrage zur Geschichte des französisch-österreichischen Kriegs im Jahre 1809', *Verhandlungen des historischen Vereines von Oberpfalz und Regensburg*, vol. 31 (1875), p. 170.

163 Quote from *Krieg*, vol. I, p. 398.

164 This paragraph and the one preceding are based almost entirely on the account in *Krieg*, vol. I, pp. 397–8; the authors' disdain is palpable. Criste, Liechtenstein's biographer, passes over this day with bland statements of fact (Oskar Criste, *Feldmarschall Johannes Fürst von Liechtenstein*, Vienna: Seidel & Sohn, 1905, p. 105).

165 Stutterheim does not give casualty figures, but states that III Corps only had 9,000 men(!) capable of combat operations on the morning of 20 April (p. 172).

166 Austrian casualties are taken from *Krieg*, vol. I, Appendix XXX (including the reference to III Corps wounded being taken prisoner). The number of Austrian prisoners in *Krieg* (at least 689) ties up well with that recorded in *Victoires,Conquêtes, Désastres, Revers et Guerres Civiles des Français, de 1792 a 1815*, Paris: Panckoucke, 1818–1822, vol. XIX, p. 74. As for Davout's losses, French sources, relying mostly on the post-war 'Registre des opérations du 3eme corps' it seems, give: 1,700 for St Hilaire, 377 (or 300 or 370) for Friant, and 200 or 215 for Montbrun. For example: Gachot, p. 73; Laborde, p. 31; Thiers, vol. X, p. 138. Binder (vol. I, pp. 206–7) gives a total of 1,818 for St Hilaire, 2,016 for Friant, 349 for Gudin, 42 for the 7th Léger, and 215 for Montbrun. He based his assessment on a comparison of the 3rd Corps strength returns for 15 and 20 April. This could be close to the truth, but French strength returns must be read with great attention to detail, more attention than Binder sometimes lavishes upon his topic (he can be excellent, trenchant, and even exhilarating to read, but he is sometimes sloppy and his facts often must be checked for precision). Moreover, his figures sometimes seem illogical: the officer casualties differ considerably from Martinien, for instance, 312 men lost seems far too high for Gudin's 12th Ligne (unless it engaged in extensive, unreported combat), and it seems at least worth questioning whether the 15th Léger (1,400 men) truly lost 586 on 19 April alone. He does not even mention the losses in the 17th Ligne. Having not had the chance to review these particular returns myself, I am reluctant to accept Binder's estimates without caveat. *Krieg* follows Binder in a general sense but adds the officer figures from Martinien to arrive at a total loss of 4,247 for the French. Sadly, the authors of *Krieg* did not list their source(s) for these calculations. It is worth noting that the French were protected by the woods for much of the fighting near Hausen and may have suffered fewer casualties on this account.

167 Laborde, p. 29. The frequency with which one encounters such comments, regardless of source, is remarkable.

168 'Rapport du 3e Corps sur les Opérations de la Journée du 19 Avril', in Saski, vol. II, pp. 252–4.

169   Curiously, Pelet dismisses Davout's operation on the 19th as 'more difficult in appearance than in reality'. He contends that 'the circumstances have been distorted abroad and in France' with the Austrians wanting to disguise their errors and Davout's partisans seeking to exaggerate his capabilities. See vol. I, pp. 295–6. Even if we admit a certain degree of mythologising about Davout's performance that day, we must be careful not to obscure either his competent, and at times inspiring, performance or the very real possibility that the Austrians might have intercepted his march effectively and might have inflicted serious injury on 3rd Corps.

170   Davout to Napoleon, 19 April 1809, in Saski, vol. II, pp. 264–5. The authors of *Krieg* aver that Davout's language in this report is subdued and 'very dry' (vol. I, p. 442). I disagree.

171   Vincent Bertrand, *Mémoires: Grande Armée 1805–1815*, Paris: Librairie des Deux Empires, 1998, p. 73.

172   Binder (using Oberst Mayer's personal account), vol. I, p. 193.

173   Hans von Zwiedineck-Südenhorst, 'Die Brigade Thierry im Gefechte von Abensberg am 19. und 20. April 1809', *Mittheilungen des Instituts für österreichische Geschichtsforschung*, Innsbruck, 1896–1903.

174   Charles to Thierry, 19 April 1809, Zwiedineck-Südenhorst, 'Die Brigade Thierry'.

175   Many sources claim that Thierry brought four squadrons of dragoons north of the Seeholz. I believe it was only two, based on Thierry's after-action report (in Zwiedineck-Südenhorst, 'Die Brigade Thierry') and *Krieg*, vol. I, pp. 424–45. A reasonable explanation for the discrepancy could be that two squadrons joined Hardegg north of the Seeholz later in the day after Thierry had called forward his reserves from Bruckhof.

176   Charles quote from 'Beitrag', *Ausgewählte Schriften*, vol. VI, p. 331; see Chapter 2 for an earlier part of this quote. See Thierry's 'Bekenntnuss über das gefecht bey biburg und abendsberg am 19. und 20. april 1809' in Zwiedineck-Südenhorst, 'Die Brigade Thierry', p. 180.

177   Note that I am using the name 'Seeholz' here to designate the entire wooded area east of Abensberg as a matter of convenience and clarity. In fact, the various parts of the wood had different names, which would be both tedious and pointless to utilise.

178   Berthier to Lefebvre, 3 a.m., 19 April 1809, in Saski, vol. II, p. 265. Lefebvre's report of the action is in Lefebvre to Napoleon, 19 April 1809, in Saski, vol. II, p. 269. The marshal communicated this urgency to his divisional commanders in terms such as these: 'Use, general, great celerity in all movements as such is necessary in the circumstances in which we find ourselves' (Drouet to Deroy, 19 April 1809, BKA/ B442).

179   Thierry's 'Bekenntnuss' in Zwiedineck-Südenhorst, 'Die Brigade Thierry', p. 180.

180   Adam, *Aus dem Leben*, pp. 62–3. The Bavarian who first encountered the unfortunate Austrian dragoon was a servant of a local pastor, Franz Xaver Stoll, as related in: Franz Xaver Stoll, 'Treue Beschreibung der zwei Schlachten bei Abensberg und Biburg, geliefert zwischen den Bayern und Oesterreichern und dann zwischen den Bayern und Franzosen gegen die Hauptmacht der Oesterreicher im April 1809', in

'Kriegs-Berichte aus den Jahren 1800 und 1809', ed. J. R. Schuegraf, *Verhandlungen des historischen Vereins für Niederbayern*, vol. 7 (1860), p. 189 (also in Stark, p. 73).

181 Reichold, pp. 90–1; also Schaller, p. 25.

182 II/1st Infantry was in Vohburg guarding the town and Bavarian artillery park. Ludwig's 2nd Brigade remained near Abensberg in reserve.

183 Xylander, *Feld-Artillerie*, vol. II, p. 143. Quote from Regnier's professional account in 'Auszug aus dem Tagebuch eines k. bayerischen Stabsoffiziers', *Archiv für Offiziere aller Waffen*, vol II, 1844, pp. 255–9 (see also Gill, *Eagles*, p. 84).

184 Adam, *Aus dem Leben*, p. 63.

185 Thierry's 'Bekenntnuss' in Zwiedineck-Südenhorst, 'Die Brigade Thierry', p. 183.

186 Quote from Thierry to Charles, 8 p.m., 19 April 1809, in Zwiedineck-Südenhorst, 'Die Brigade Thierry', p. 188.

187 This was Oberleutnant Graf Chotek. Ludwig had sent an officer to Thierry shortly before Chotek's appearance. Note that Binder errs in his depiction of the sequence of events here.

188 Paraphrased from *Krieg*, vol. I, p. 431.

189 Friedrich Anton Heller von Hellwald, *Friedrich Freiherr von Bianchi*, Vienna: Sommer, 1857, p. 236. Lindenau had been performing this duty and Reuss took his place when Lindenau's division was detached to Liechtenstein.

190 At first, only half of Caspar's battery crossed the stream, the other half only joined after the withdrawal of the 3rd Infantry Regiment troops (Xylander, *Feld-Artillerie*, vol. II, pp. 144–5). Exactly how many men of the 3rd Infantry were involved is unclear. Based on the regimental history (Max Ruith and Emil Ball, *Kurze Geschichte des K. B. 3. Infanterie-Regiments Prinz Karl von Bayern*, Ingolstadt, 1890, pp. 155–6), it seems most likely that 2nd Battalion's Schützen and probably all of II/3rd got across the little river. The First Battalion apparently remained at Siegenburg. Given Wrede's conception of their mission as a diversion, it is also likely that they were only intended to alarm the Austrians while protecting Caspar's guns (Höfler, pp. 75–6). The regimental history states that II/3 lost thirty wounded and many killed on 19 April, while I/3 lost only four dead and nine wounded as it endured the Austrian bombardment near Siegenburg. However, it is possible that the entire regiment was involved as stated in Heilmann's Wrede biography (p. 126), the Bavarian General Staff history (pp. 41, 49), and *Krieg* (vol. I, pp. 431–2). Wrede's report of his division's actions makes no mention at all of the 3rd Infantry on 19 April, but specifically states Wrede's desire to draw Thierry's attention (in Pelet, vol. II, pp. 439–40).

191 Xylander, *Feld-Artillerie*, vol. II, pp. 144–5.

192 Quoted in Binder, vol. I, p. 218.

193 Stoll, 'Treue Beschreibung', p. 189. Stark (p. 73) attributes a near-identical quote to Major Krafft of the 6th Bavarian Infantry.

194 I have used regimental accounts for Bavarian losses in the 3rd and 13th Regiments and *Krieg* for the 6th Light.

195 Principal sources for the Engagement at Arnhofen and the skirmishing along the Abens: *Krieg*, vol. I, pp. 419–33; Binder, vol. I, pp. 209–19; Gill, *Eagles*, pp. 81–6; Stutterheim, pp. 158–64; Zwiedineck-Südenhorst, 'Die Brigade Thierry'; Bavarian

General Staff, 'Der Feldzug von 1809 in Bayern', 1865, BKA, Fasz. 652/4; Austrian and Bavarian regimental histories.

196   Austrian losses at Biburg and Siegenburg are hard to explain: *Krieg* only mentions *Duka* and the *Gradiska* Grenzer as taking casualties; this agrees with the *Duka* regimental history, but it would be odd if this regiment lost no more than the Grenzer as indicated by comparing its casualties with the total shown in the text (the *Duka* history gives dead/wounded/missing as ten/fourteen/seventy-three). It is not clear how many (if any) *Gyulai* No. 60 suffered.

197   A cavalry battery was sent to support Scheibler, but the major, concerned that it would only delay him on the poor roads, ordered it to return to Au (*Krieg*, vol. I, p. 435).

198   Sources: *Krieg*, vol. I, pp. 433–5; Oudinot's report as quoted in *Historique du 7e Régiment de Chasseurs*, Valence: Céas, 1891, pp. 36–7; Angeli, vol. IV, pp. 104–5; Grois, pp. 219–20; Saski, vol. II, pp. 248–9. Austrian losses are from *Krieg*, Appendix XXX, but Oudinot reported that his men had captured 260 Austrians and killed sixty. The *Klebek* regimental history (Grois) states that Jamez's battalion lost eighty men dead and wounded. Claparède's losses are likewise from *Krieg*, the casualties for the 7th Chasseurs are given in the regimental history.

199   Quoted in Koch, vol. VI, p. 137.

200   Oudinot to Massena, 19 April 1809, Massena to Napoleon, 9 a.m., 19 April 1809, and Napoleon to Massena, noon, 19 April 1809, all in Saski, vol. II, pp. 248–50. An earlier report from Massena to Napoleon (6 a.m.) is not included in Saski or the Massena biographies (Koch, Gachot). Pelet, who should have known better, repeats the false figures in his history of the campaign (vol. I, p. 302). This canard even appears in some modern histories. Related to the inflated reports on the engagement at Pfaffenhofen is the oft-repeated story proffered by Baden's young Markgraf Wilhelm, then serving as an officer on Massena's staff. Wilhelm, generally a very reliable witness, was to carry Massena's report of the Pfaffenhofen engagement to Napoleon. He tells how Massena bluntly instructed him to exaggerate: when Wilhelm said that he planned to report fifty enemy prisoners in the brief fight, Massena objected and insisted that he claim 400 Austrians had been captured. 'I learned here how one was supposed to draft bulletins', Wilhelm, *Denkwürdigkeiten*, p. 67.

201   Napoleon to Massena, noon, 19 April 1809, all in Saski, vol. II, p. 251.

202   The instructions are published in Coutard, pp. 52–3 and in both editions of the regimental history.

203   Details on Austrians' order of battle (per *Krieg*, vol. I, p. 403) follow. Crenneville: *Frelich* No. 28 (three battalions), three squadrons *Merveldt* Uhlans No. 1, one company of 8th Jägers, one half brigade battery. Weber: *Stuart* No. 18, two position batteries. Rottermund: former *Zedtwitz* No. 25 (minus two companies), 7th Jägers, one squadron *Merveldt*, Erzherzog Johann Dragoons No. 1 (six squadrons), one cavalry battery, one and a half brigade batteries. Kolowrat's main body: Infantry Regiments *Zach* No. 15, *Froon* No. 54 (three battalions each) and *Josef Colloredo* (two battalions), two companies of Infantry Regiment No. 25 former *Zedtwitz*, 8th Jägers (four companies), four squadrons *Merveldt*, *Riesch* Dragoons (six

squadrons), one brigade battery, one cavalry battery, two position batteries. Note that one company of the 8th Jägers is unaccountably missing from this list.

204 In at least one case, a local resident helped the French find a knot of fleeing Austrians. There were also widespread but contested stories that several inhabitants fired on the Austrians during the engagement (Wackenreiter, *Erstürmung*, pp. 62–3). Local historian Johann Hiederer, however, vehemently insists that these tales were fabrications: *Die Schreckenstage von Stadtamhof im April 1809*, Regensburg: Habbel, 1899.

205 The number of Austrians captured is unclear. Austrian sources (*Krieg* and the regimental history) claim seventy-two, but Colonel Coutard reported 400 prisoners and his nephew Armand Coutard gave a figure of 600. Note that eight *Froon* soldiers received awards or official praise for their efforts to defend the battalion's colours (Victor Ritter von Neuwirth, *Geschichte des K. u. K. Infanterie-Regimentes Alt-Starhemberg Nr. 54*, Olmütz: Hölzel, 1894, p. 223).

206 *Krieg*, vol. I, p. 405.

207 Lieutenant Georges Geoffrey Eissen to his father, 26 April 1809 from Regensburg, in 'La Défense et la Capitulation de Ratisbonne en Avril 1809', *Carnet de la Sabretache*, No. 198 (June 1909).

208 Austrian casualty figures taken from *Krieg*, Appendix XXX; using the *Froon* regimental history, I have added those listed in *Krieg* as 'missing' to the rolls of prisoners. The extant figures for the 8th Jägers only list those killed (eight or ten), thus the range of possible losses indicated here is intended to account for a probable twenty to fifty wounded, captured, or missing from the battalion.

209 French losses are based on the Austrian calculation indicating a difference of ninety-eight between the 65th Ligne's strength before the battle (2,086) and the number of men who surrendered on 20 April (1,988). Additional stray Frenchmen in Regensburg could account for a few more casualties and the figure of 100 does not include wounded (who would have been encompassed in the number of prisoners on the 20th). Strangely, Coutard reported that his casualties numbered 800! This seems far too high, even if one includes lightly wounded.

210 Trobriand himself escaped into the city. Sources: *Krieg*, vol. I, pp. 402–6; Riancey, pp. 52–9 (including Armand Coutard's very detailed report); regimental/battalion histories.

211 The Austrian force was a column led by Oberst Josef von Mayer of the *Klenau* Chevaulegers: three squadrons from *Klenau*, two Jäger companies, two battalions of the *Rohan* Infantry Regiment No. 21. From Pizzighelli, *Dragoner-Regimentes Nr. 10*, pp. 251–2.

212 Principal sources for the surrender of the 65th Ligne are: *Krieg*, vol. I, pp. 502–5; Coutard, pp. 59–67; Arvers, Paul, *Historique du 82e Régiment d'Infanterie de Ligne*, Paris: Lahure, 1876, p. 192.

213 Quote from Mändler, p. 7.

214 Crenneville commanded *Frelich* Infantry No. 28 (three battalions), 2nd *Erzherzog Karl* Legion, one company of the 8th Jägers (possibly two), three squadrons of *Merveldt* Uhlans, and a half-battery. Of this force, all were at Etterzhausen except a Jäger company and an uhlan platoon at Kallmünz.

215 Additional detachments included: Oberst Josef von Mayer from Liechtenstein's command at Obersanding with four companies of *Hiller* No. 2 and two squadrons of *Klenau* Chevaulegers No. 5; and Oberst Steyrer at Paring with I/*Chasteler* and two squadrons of *Vincent* Chevaulegers. Stutterheim had joined Rosenberg's main body at Dünzling by the morning of the 20th.

216 According to local lore in Paring, a French cavalry patrol broke into Paring late on the 19th and demanded the whereabouts of 'Kaiser Karl', but rode away on being told by the vicar that 'Kaiser Karl' was not in the area. This anecdote is not recorded elsewhere and seems unlikely (see the delightful collection of local tales in Fritz Angrüner, *Die Schlacht von Abensberg 19./20. April 1809*, Abensberg: Aventinus-Mueum, 1989).

217 Mesko had one battalion and two companies of *Brod* Grenzer and one squadron plus one platoon of *Kienmayer* Hussars. These troops rejoined V Corps east of Siegenburg on the morning of the 20th (the other four *Brod* Grenzer companies and two and three-quarters squadrons of *Kienmayer* were already there). Shortly after Mesko's arrival, eight companies of *Brod* were dispatched to reinforce Schustekh.

218 Hiller's deployments on the evening of the 19th were complicated. At Mainburg (main body): Weissenwolff's brigade (including the three Vienna Volunteer battalions), Hoffmeister's brigade, five squadrons of *Rosenberg* Chevaulegers (four of these under FML Vincent). GM Hohenfeld (Au with two battalions near Hirnkirchen): *Klebek* Infantry (2nd Battalion rejoined from Scheibler), *Jordis* Infantry, three squadrons of *Liechtenstein* Hussars. GM Nordmann (Au): one battalion of *Warasdin-St Georg* Grenzer, three squadrons of *Liechtenstein* Hussars, one cavalry battery. Maj. Scheibler (en route to Mainburg from Hirnkirchen): two companies of *Warasdin-St Georg* Grenzer, one squadron each of *Rosenberg* Chevaulegers and *Liechtenstein* Hussars. Rittmeister Spannagel (at Attenhofen): two companies of *Benjovszky* Infantry Regiment No. 31, one squadron of *Liechtenstein* Hussars. En route to Pfeffenhausen from Scheibler to join the main body: one squadron of *Rosenberg* Chevaulegers. En route to Pfeffenhausen from Nordmann to join the main body: four companies of *Warasdin-St. Georg* Grenzer, two companies of *Benjovszky* Infantry, one squadron of *Rosenberg* Chevaulegers, one-half cavalry battery.

219 Charles to Ludwig, 3.30 p.m., 19 April 1809, in Angeli, vol. IV, p. 106.

220 Napoleon to Massena, noon, 19 April 1809, in Saski, vol. II, p. 250.

221 Counting for the French Davout, Lannes, 7th Corps, 8th Corps, Demont's division, and Nansouty's cavalry division (Massena, Oudinot, Coutard, Guyon, Rouyer not included); counting for the Austrians III, IV, V, and II Reserve Corps, Liechtenstein's command, Thierry's brigade (4,000 to 5,000 men), and the grenadiers (not counting Hiller, the three V Corps Vienna Volunteer battalions, or any Austrian forces north of the Danube).

222 The gap would be at least eight kilometres (measuring from Kirchdorf to the Laaber, even further if measured from Siegenburg) covered by minimal forces (presumably Thierry).

223 'Taint of unreality' is from a work of fiction: Jack Vance, *The Green Pearl*, New York: Berkley, 1985, p. 248.

224 'Have no worries about Vohburg' in Berthier to Lefebvre, 3 a.m., 19 April 1809, in Saski, vol. II, pp. 265–6. See Pelet (vol. I, p. 283) regarding Napoleon's decision

to remain in Ingolstadt during the morning. The authors of *Krieg* (vol. I, p. 420) suggest the possiblity that Napoleon remained in Ingolstadt because he feared that Davout might suffer a disaster and did not want his name associated with defeat; this is a canard.

225 Franz Augustin Klier, *Oesterreichs letzter Krieg im Jahre 1809 gegen Frankreich, Baiern, und die Rheinischen Bundes-Staaten*, Munich: Lentner, 1810, p. 26.

226 Davout to Napoleon, 19 April 1809, and Lefebvre to Napoleon, 19 April 1809, in Saski, vol. II, pp. 264–5, 269–70.

227 Lefebvre to Napoleon, 10 p.m., 19 April 1809, in Saski, vol. II, p. 270.

228 *Krieg*, vol. I, p. 440.

229 Quote from Schauroth, p. 7. By the 20th, the elements of the division were disposed as follows: 5th Rheinbund in Donauwörth (incomplete, awaiting the arrival of half of the Anhalt contingent from Strasbourg), I/6th Rheinbund at Rain, 2nd Rheinbund (Nassau) at Neuburg, II/6th in Gerolfing, and 4th Regiment in Ingolstadt. See Gill, *Eagles*, p. 391.

230 Quote from Donald D. Horward, 'Lannes: Roland of the Army', in David G Chandler (ed.), *Napoleon's Marshals*, New York: Macmillan, 1987, p. 196. See also, Elting, *Swords*, pp. 136–7.

231 This scene, including the dialogue and the quote from Lannes's 20 April letter to Louise, is depicted in Ronald Zins, *Le Maréchal Lannes: Favori de Napoléon*, Entremont le Vieux: Le Temps Traversé, 1994, pp. 247–8.

232 Berthier to Massena, midnight, 19 April 1809, in Saski, vol. II, p. 273.

233 Bonnnal, pp. 163–5. Petre provides a tidy summary of this argument and finds 'strong reason to believe in this theory' given his faith in Bonnal's analysis (pp. 127–8).

234 Quotes from Napoleon to Davout, Lefebvre, and Massena, all on 17 April 1809, published in Saski, vol. II, pp. 199–207. There are any number of similar examples, such as the 18 April 1809 'I regard the enemy as lost' passage to Massena quoted earlier (in Saski, vol. II, p. 242).

235 Berthier to Lefebvre, 3 a.m., 19 April 1809, in Saski, vol. II, p. 265.

236 Stoll, p. 190.

237 At Arnhofen, Thierry had approximately 3,800 infantry and 670 cavalry by the afternoon to hold off some 4,770 Bavarian infantry (2nd and 6th Infantry Regiments, I/1st Infantry, and 1st Light) and Zandt's cavalry brigade of 730; the only area where the Bavarians had a significant advantage was in the number of guns (twelve against four Austrian). The fighting at Hausen-Teugn saw approximately 16,500 Austrian infantry struggling against 16,200 French foot soldiers at the height of the action; in the early phases, a good case can be made that the Austrians considerably outnumbered the French locally. French troops considered for this comparison include all of St Hilaire's division, III/7th Léger (from 3rd Division), and the following from Friant's 2nd Division: 33rd, 48th, I/108th, all voltigeurs of the line regiments (the remaining troops of the 108th and II/111th numbered perhaps 1,800 men). In neither of these cases was the French numerical superiority overwhelming.

238 'Utterly incomprehensible' in Hellmuth von Moltke's trenchant words, 'Der Feldzug 1809 in Bayern', *Moltkes Kriegsgeschichtlche Arbeiten*, Berlin: Mittler, 1899, p. 21. Pelet is similarly puzzled: 'It is difficult to give valid reasons that explicate

the sequence of operations by the Austrian army and the particular motives that determined the archduke's conduct during that day' (vol. I, p. 307).

239 He had, for instance, prohibited the corps commanders from changing their internal orders of battle without his approval in his 9 April order of the day (published in 'Beiträge zur Geschichte des österreichischen Heerwesens 1809', *Oesterreichische Militärische Zeitschrift*, vol. 3 (1869)).

240 At the tactical level, Scheibler complained that 'companies were capriciously detached left and right, so that the entire infantry was soon dispersed by companies and platoons' (Scheibler's report on Pfaffenhofen in Binder, vol. I, p. 221).

241 Rosenberg quoted in Binder, vol. I, p. 197.

242 See the severe criticism in *Krieg*, vol. I, pp. 398–400.

243 Berthezène, p. 196. Lorencez, on the other hand, avers that Davout only appeared at the end of the action and then claimed all credit for himself at the expense of St Hilaire (p. 419).

244 The local situation was very uncertain and Davout may have overestimated the enemy's strength; he reported to Napoleon that afternoon that his men had overcome 80,000 Austrians (Davout to Napoleon, 19 April 1809, in Saski, vol. II, pp. 264–5).

245 Oudinot to Massena, 19 April 1809, and Davout to Napoleon, 19 April 1809, both in Saski, vol. II, pp. 248–9, 264–5.

246 Friant's report. Most of this report is printed in Saski, vol. II, pp. 260–1, but Friant, pp. 161–6, brings the entire text, including the line about the voltigeur officers.

247 Stutterheim, p. 137.

248 Yorck von Wartenburg, p. 143.

249 Heinrich Zchokke, *Der Krieg Oesterreichs gegen Frankreich und den rheinischen Bund im Jahre 1809*, Aarau: Remigius, 1810, p. 31.

CHAPTER 6: EIGHT DAYS IN APRIL, II: FOUR MORE VICTORIES

1 'Dreary, raw, and rainy' from Binder, vol. I, p. 237.

2 Adam, *Aus dem Leben*, p. 64.

3 Schaller, pp. 26–7. Another eyewitness, Eduard von Völderndorff und Waradein on the 1st Division staff, described Napoleon's unexpected appearance in similar terms: 'a general cheer of joy along the entire line announced an extraordinary event. Napoleon, escorted by his most renowned commanders, appeared in the middle of the cheering Bavarians' (p. 77).

4 Adam, *Aus dem Leben*, 65.

5 This version of this famous speech is translated from the rendition in Marcus Junkelmann, *Napoleon und Bayern*, Regensburg: Pustet, 1985, pp. 13–14. On Bavarian enthusiasm, see [Johann von Heilmann] 'Das "Bayerische Corps der grossen Armée" im Aprilfeldzuge von 1809', *Jahrbücher für die Deutsche Armee und Marine*, vol. XXI (1876), p. 25.

6 Reichold, pp. 96–7. Reichold also noted that 'To that date we had not seen any French'.

7 Adam, *Aus dem Leben*, p. 65.

8 Binder, from his reading of the material in the Austrian War Archives, suggests that this meeting was rather acrimonious, with Ludwig anxious to withdraw and Hiller haughty and disdainful that the V Corps commander had not found the means within his own resources to support Schustekh (vol. I, p. 246).

9 Extract from Hiller's report to Charles, noon, 20 April 1809, in Angeli, vol. IV, p. 120. This report, however, never made it to Charles; as with several others sent from the left wing that day, the couriers were either captured or forced to turn back.

10 This summary drawn from *Krieg*, vol. I, pp. 445–7.

11 Hiller, p. 160.

12 The following description reflects my assessment that the sequence of the Battle of Abensberg, at the broadest level, was the result of Napoleon's planning and orders, specifically that he initially held back Wrede and the right flank to allow the left flank attack (Crown Prince Ludwig and Lannes) to develop. Contemporary remarks by a Bavarian officer confirm Napoleon's efforts to orchestrate the attacks by Lannes and the Bavarian 1st Division (F. A. Bran, 'Bemerkungen über den gegenwärtigen Krieg', *Minerva*, vol. II (1809)).

13 The four reserve artillery batteries of 7th Corps were distributed to the divisions on the 20th: Ludwig thus had Hauptmann Graf Leiningen's 12-pounder battery in support as he attacked Thierry. In the event, however, only Hofstetten's 6-pounders played any role in the fight: Thierry's defence collapsed before any of the other batteries came into action. The Bavarians here, as in many occasions during this war, made extensive use of their Schützen; see, for instance, Oberleutnant Frankl's (I/2) report of his actions on the 20th leading the regiment's Schützen (BKA/B442).

14 It is possible that the first cavalry engagement took place north of Rohr as is related in some accounts, and that the Austrian cavalry fled to the ridge south of town only to be attacked a second time.

15 Dezydery (Désiré) Chlapowski, *Mémoires sur les Guerres de Napoléon 1806–1813*, Paris: Plon, 1908, p. 117.

16 This description of the fight at Bachl and Rohr is assembled from *Krieg*, vol. I, pp. 449–53, 458–60; Buxbaum, p. 123; Espérandieu; Froidevaux; François Gay de Vernon, *Historique du 2e Régt. de Chasseurs à Cheval*, Paris: Librairie Militaire, 1865, p. 115 (Lion's exploit); Hödl, p. 253; Hutter, pp. 192–3; Oré, pp. 125–6; Pages Xartart; Pizzighelli, *Infanterie-Regiment No. 1*, pp. 357–8. Note that there are extensive quotes from Morand's midnight report to Davout in the three French infantry regimentals. It is not clear whose flags Lion captured or where: his victims were probably parts of the *Brod* Grenzer at Rohr or the two companies of *Peterwardein* Grenzer at Bachl. The best information on this aspect of the Battle of Abensberg is in the French infantry regimentals.

17 It is not clear when VI Corps began its march to Rottenburg. Hiller departed with his staff shortly after noon and the lead elements of the corps may have marched at about the same time. However, Binder reports (vol. I, p. 247) that Weissenwolff's brigade did not leave the bivouac until 4 p.m. Of course, it would have taken several hours for the entire force to march, but it seems to me logical that the troops did not get on the road until some time into the afternoon as the road distance from Niederhornbach to Rottenburg is only some ten kilometres.

18 According to *Krieg*, vol. I, p. 461, Hiller's horse apparently threw a shoe and, incredibly, he halted to have it re-shod, rather than take one of his staff officers' mounts and continue on his way. The authors state that this is a 'peculiar excuse for the delayed arrival of a corps commander on the battlefield' and attribute it to Hiller's official account, but this aspect does not appear in the version as published by Rauchensteiner (Hiller, p. 160).

19 Hiller, p. 160. I have used 'disorganised, retreating soldiers' for the handy German word 'Versprengter'.

20 Hiller added the note to a noon dispatch from Schustekh to Ludwig that passed through his hands on its way to the archduke (*Krieg*, vol. I, p. 461). He does not mention this in his subsequent account.

21 Some Austrian accounts (such as the history of the *Deutschmeister* Regiment) claim that this attack resulted in the capture of 300 or so Bavarian prisoners. Gachot also states that Bavarians were present. There are two errors in these claims. First, although some Bavarian cavalry had arrived on the banks of the Laaber near Rottenburg in the pursuit from Rohr, there was no Bavarian infantry in the area. Second, it is unlikely that *Deutschmeister* captured 300 enemy troops, French or Bavarian; even if they did, I suspect that the captivity was brief and that most prisoners (if there were any) were freed almost immediately thanks to the French counter-attack.

22 Quotes in this and the previous sentence from Hiller, pp. 160–1.

23 There is some question as to the exact composition of this force. The Bavarian components are clear: Seydewitz with his two regiments and Colonel Louis François Elie Pelletier, Comte de Montmarie commanding the 5th and 7th Light Battalions with three guns. It is also clear that at least one brigade of French heavy cavalry was present. Most likely, this was, as Bonnal (pp. 178–9, 180–1) states, St Germain's cuirassiers; it is possible, though much less likely, as Binder writes, that the cuirassier brigade was Guiton's. Bonnal also states that the entire 'expedition' was commanded by Nansouty. Note that the Bavarian General Staff study proffers the unlikely notion that the force included two Bavarian batteries rather than three guns. I have used the 7th Corps after-action report and other material in Saski (vol. II, pp. 287–9) as well as Bavarian regimental histories for this assessment.

24 Mändler, p. 9. The soldiers were very conscious of Napoleon's presence. One Bavarian unit went so far as to entitle its after-action report 'Relation of the Battle that Occurred on the Morning of 20 April near Abensberg under the Eyes of the Emperor Napoleon' (BKA/B442).

25 This is my assessment, almost all of Napoleon's battlefield orders were verbal and thus left no written record.

26 From the memoirs of battalion surgeon H. von Gross in Paul Dorsch, *Kriegszüge der Württemberger im 19. Jahrhundert: Erinnerungen von Mitkämpfer*, Calw: Vereinsbuchhandlung, 1913, p. 49.

27 Heinz Kraft, *Die Württemberger in den Napoleonischen Kriegen*, Stuttgart: Kohlhammer, 1953, pp. 190–1.

28 Gross in Dorsch, p. 50. It seems likely that Napoleon gave several inspirational speeches such as this to various elements of the Württemberg contingent.

29   Recall that the other eight companies of *Brod* Grenzer had marched off to Rohr
     that morning to join the four squadrons of *Kienmayer* Hussars under Schustekh;
     the other two hussar squadrons were probably still covering the heights south of
     Siegenburg.

30   Binder comments that Bianchi 'was world-wise' and 'knew well enough that any
     sort of heroism' leading to an entangling engagement would be 'undesirable' (vol. I,
     p. 251). Use of battalion mass formation is from Heller, *Bianchi*, p. 236.

31   Wrede's 12-pounder battery (Dobl), attached to the division as of the 19 April,
     apparently took no part in the day's action; but seems to have followed Wrede to
     Schweinbach.

32   Quote from the Bavarian General Staff history, p. 74. This account speculates that
     the 6th Infantry was probably following the remnants of Hammer's force but its
     route is unknown. The 2nd Battalion of the 3rd Infantry, on the other hand, tracked
     after parts of Radetzky's brigade that retreated up the valley of the Perkabach.

33   On the Austrian side, this includes: V Corps minus Schustekh's detachment
     (11,870), II Reserve Corps (4,550), Hammer's remnants (1,600). This does not
     include the three Vienna Volunteer battalions assigned to V Corps or any of the
     VI Corps troops that had made their way to Pfeffenhausen by evening. For the
     Allies: Wrede (7,900), Hügel (3,440 including five cavalry squadrons), and the rest
     of 8th Corps (7,700). All figures are my estimates.

34   The Austrian forces included: three companies of *Brod* Grenzer, two companies of
     Gradiska Grenzer, and two squadrons of *EH Karl* Uhlans. Resting nearby was a
     battalion of *Gyulai* Infantry. *Krieg*, vol. I, p. 474.

35   Binder states that Ludwig was thinking of retreat as early as 9 a.m. when he talked
     with Hiller in Pürkwang and was looking for an excuse (vol. I, p. 246, 252).

36   The Austrian forces Ludwig found in and around Pfeffenhausen that evening
     included the three battalions of Vienna Volunteers belonging to V Corps and a
     substantial number of VI Corps troops: Hohenfeld's brigade (six battalions), the
     three VI Corps Vienna Volunteer battalions, four companies of *St Georg* Grenzer,
     two companies of *Benjovszky* Infantry, three squadrons of *Liechtenstein* Hussars,
     and one squadron of *Rosenberg* Chevaulegers (another *Rosenberg* squadron may
     also have been on hand). Based on *Krieg*, vol. I, p. 458, and my own calculations.

37   Extracts from Ludwig to Hiller, 10.30 and 11 p.m., 20 April 1809, in Angeli, vol. IV,
     p. 128.

38   Bianchi, for instance, had been forgotten in the chaos and was lucky to notice the
     retreating V Corps column as he sat sleeplessly near a campfire (Heller, *Bianchi*, p.
     236).

39   The description of the attack on Pfeffenhausen is adapted from Gill, *Eagles*, p. 92.
     Note that my previous conclusion regarding the Army of Germany's parole for 21
     April appears to have been incorrect. In *Eagles* (p. 92), I mention that Napoleon
     chose 'Bravoure et Bavière' as the challenge and password for 21 April in recognition
     of the Bavarian contribution to the victory on the 20th. Further research in
     the Bavarian War Archives shows, however, that these two words had been
     disseminated on the 19th before the Battle of Abensberg. The parole was thus not
     selected as a reward for the Bavarian performance on 20 April, but still illustrates

Napoleon's leadership skills, especially his ability to nurture the honour and pride of the units under his command regardless of nationality.

40   Hiller to Charles, 10.45 p.m., 20 April 1809, in *Krieg*, vol. I, p. 476. This was another report that never reached Archduke Charles.

41   Theobald to Friedrich, 21 April 1809, HStAS, E270aBü83. Theobald was the king's personal observer, reporting to Friedrich only and not under French command.

42   Figures are taken from *Krieg*, vol. I, Appendix XXX. This source gives the Austrian losses as 6,883 officers and men for the two days among the units of the left wing including Thierry. I have added 384 from Pfanzelter for a grand total of 7,267. However, the figure may have been several hundred higher as the Austrian calculation does not seem to account for all of the losses of the *Lindenau* Infantry Regiment. Four of the lost Austrian guns also came from Pfanzelter's command. As noted earlier, numbers for Thierry are incomplete and cannot be disaggregated between 19 and 20 April.

43   Figures are taken from *Krieg*, vol. I, Appendix XXX. The Austrian figures are generally in accord with those from Bavarian, Württemberg, and French sources. The Austrians estimated 200 total losses for the French, but Morand only reported some sixty-six casualties on the 20th. Thiry gives a figure of 215 for Lannes's corps (Jean Thiry, *Wagram*, Paris, Berger-Levrault, 1966, p. 68). Most of the Allied losses came from the 1st and 2nd Bavarian Divisions: 439 and 235 respectively for the two days.

44   Kübeck, p. 265.

45   Pirquet, diary entry 21 April, p. 80.

46   Vukassovich was left at Hausen with II/*Peterwardein* and four squadrons of *Ferdinand* Hussars; he withdrew at approximately 3 p.m. according to Austrian accounts on the approach of French forces. GM Kayser with the *W. Colloredo* infantry remained at Dietenhofen to cover Vukassovich's withdrawal. Both detachments were united with III Corps by 6 p.m., Kayser south of the river and Vukassovich on the high ground immediately north of Leierndorf.

47   Moltke, p. 31.

48   Charles to Franz, 8 a.m., 20 April 1809, in *Krieg*, vol. I, p. 498.

49   Davout to Napoleon, 4.30 p.m., 20 April 1809, in Saski, vol. II, p. 293.

50   Pelet states that Davout had orders to 'harass' and 'contain' the enemy (vol. II, p. 7); Saski makes a similar assertion (vol. II, p. 284), but neither authority provides any written documentation and Davout's 4.30 p.m. letter to Napoleon certainly suggests that his corps had been left without orders through either an error on Napoleon's part or a failure of Berthier and his staff to communicate the Emperor's intentions. Binder claims that there are no orders in the archival record (vol. I, p. 227). As to Morand, Gudin, and St Sulpice, Bonnal (p. 174) says that these generals received orders, but these are nowhere evident and it seems likely that they got their instructions verbally from Lannes when he arrived to assume command. Gudin, at least, seems to have been in the dark during the early morning hours (from a letter cited in Binder, vol. I, p. 227).

51   According to my calculations, 3rd Corps was now reduced to some 20,000 infantry and 2,800 horse (deducting approximately 500 cavalry for the one or two squadrons of the 8th Hussars detached with Jacquinot). The Austrian history,

evidently assuming higher losses on the 19th, credits Davout with 17,800 infantry, 3,200 cavalry, and thirty guns (*Krieg*, vol. I, p. 502).

52 *Krieg*, vol. I, p. 500.

53 Binder, vol. I, p. 229.

54 According to *Krieg*, vol. I, p. 504: 1,933 soldiers, 105 noncombatants, and fifty-five officers; the men were marched off to Austria, but the officers remained in Regensburg. Note that 591 Austrians prisoners gained their freedom through the fall of the city. Riancey, though obviously canted in favour of his subject, gives much interesting detail (pp. 59–65). See also the 26 April 1809 letter from Lieutenant Eissen to his father in *Carnet de la Sabretache*, No. 198 (June 1909). Pelet (vol. II, p. 30) and Koch (pp. 153–4), on the other hand, rather unfairly excoriate Coutard for the surrender and the failure to destroy the bridge.

55 *Krieg*, vol. I, p. 506. Also Herzog Albert, 'Mémoire sur la Guerre éclatée en 1809', MOL/P300/1/100.

56 In accordance with his earlier orders, Kolowrat initially left two regiments (*Froon* and *Zedtwitz*) and several batteries opposite Stadtamhof, but set the bulk of his corps on the road that evening before speaking with Charles. He brought Crenneville's detachment further west as well. *Krieg*, vol. I, pp. 504–5.

57 This is the third member of the Hardegg family mentioned in this volume, all three were cavalrymen, two of them with uhlan regiments; the other two were: Oberst Anton Leonhard (*Levenehr* Dragoons) and Oberstleutnant Heinrich (*EH Karl* Uhlans). Note that most of the Hardegg male offspring were given Johann as their first name, for the sake of clarity and convenience I follow the Austrian practice of leaving this out.

58 Adam, *111e Régiment* , pp. 73–4; *Krieg*, vol. I, p. 507 and Appendix XXX. Note that the authors of *Krieg* repeatedly refer to the 15th Léger when discussing Guyon's detachment, evidently mistaking the two companies for an entire battalion and neglecting I/111 Ligne; Adam's detailed history clarifies the order of battle.

59 Capitaine Lemaitre, 'Historique du 56e Régiment d'Infanterie de Ligne', manuscript, AG, 1869, p. 158.

60 Recall that the French 9th Hussars of Colbert's brigade and the Baden Light Dragoons were with Claparède while the Hessian Chevaulegers had joined Marulaz.

61 'Feldzug der 2ten Division', p. 615.

62 The four musketeer companies of Baden II/1st Infantry had been detached to guard the 4th Corps artillery park under Major Karl von Brandt, a duty they would retain for the entire war. Their battalion thus took the field in each engagement with an actual combat strength of only two companies (one each of grenadiers and voltigeurs).

63 Principal source for Massena's march on the 20th is *Krieg*, vol. I, pp. 464–7.

64 Petre (p. 129) observes that this sort of command flexibility would have been completely alien to an Austrian general. Petre perhaps exaggerates this point, but the basic idea is valid.

65 A plaque on the side of this nondescript structure, more recently known as the 'Gasthof zur Post', reminds the modern visitor that: 'In 1809 this house was honoured by the presence of the Archduke Charles coming from the east on 18

April, and the Emperor Napoleon coming from the west on 20 April'. With appreciation to Herr Karl Gorbunov, 1. Bürgermeister of Rohr for background information that this was the 'Posthalterei und Gaststätte zur Post'. According to Angrüner, however, this was the 'Bräuhaus Weinzierl' in 1809 (p. 13).

66 Binder (vol. I, p. 232) states that the epilepsy idea was first asserted by Joseph von Hormayr in a work published in 1848, *Kaiser Franz und Metternich*. *Krieg* quickly dismisses the controversy (vol. I, p. 500); Criste states that 'it is not necessary to seek the sources of the Archduke Charles's mistakes in his illness', but avers that his physical problems 'seem to have actually made themselves evident in the time between 17 and 20 April' (*Carl*, vol. III, pp. 69–70). Unfortunately, the most recent biography (Hertenberger/Wiltschek) makes no mention at all of his whereabouts on 20 April. Neither Angeli nor Stutterheim raises the issue.

67 According to Binder (vol. I, pp. 228–9), Hohenzollern reported at least twice, once shortly after noon and again in the early evening. To his credit, Hohenzollern had sent a staff officer to Rohr and thus learned that Schustekh was gone and the town was in French hands. Criste, on the other hand, states that no additional messages came to army headquarters after those sent in the morning (*Carl*, vol. III, p. 52); perhaps Criste was (disingenuously) referring solely to reports from Hiller's command.

68 Klier, p. 32.

69 Strength estimates from *Krieg*, vol. I, pp. 463–4.

70 The other two squadrons did not join the regiment until early May when it was in Bohemia.

71 Hiller, p. 161.

72 Ludwig to Franz, 22 April 1809, in *Krieg*, vol. III, pp. 648–9.

73 Hiller, p. 162.

74 Brentano quoted in *Krieg*, vol. I, pp. 483–4.

75 Klier, p. 32.

76 Clarification on the *Hessen-Homburg* Hussars: only four squadrons took part in this fighting; the other two (of the six in the Landshut area) were escorting the headquarters baggage of the army towards Straubing. Recall that the final two joined the regiment in early May in Bohemia.

77 Napoleon to Davout, 21 April 1809, 5 a.m., in Saski, vol. II, p. 304. Berthier, doubtless using Napoleon's words, had written the same phrase to Davout the previous evening (Berthier to Davout, 20 April 1809, 8 p.m., in Saski, vol. II, p. 295).

78 Berthier to Davout, 20 April 1809, 8 p.m., in Saski, vol. II, pp. 295–6. Savary reported on the evening of the 20th that Austrian prisoners claimed to have seen Archduke Charles during the morning, information that probably contributed to Napoleon's impression that the principal Habsburg host was retreating towards Landshut (his report is in Binder, vol. I, p. 350).

79 See *Krieg*, vol. II, pp. 468–70; and Camon, *Précis des Campagnes*, pp. 254–5.

80 The word 'purge' appears in Napoleon to Davout, 21 April 1809, 5 a.m., in Saski, vol. II, p. 304. The orders to the other commanders, issued between 4 and 5 a.m., are also in Saski, vol. II, pp. 301–3.

81 Nübling, *Geschichte des Grenadier-Regiments König Karl (5. Württembergischen) Nr. 123*, Berlin: Eisenschmidt, 1911, p. 91. The Allied order of march on the Pfeffenhausen axis that morning is not clear. Although the Württemberg cavalry engaged with the Austrian rear guard, none of the other elements of the corps participated in combat until the storming of the city, and then it was only a few light infantry companies.

82 Herre, p. 13.

83 Pirquet, diary entry for 21 April, pp. 80–1. Note that *Krieg* describes the crossing as being conducted in relatively good order (vol. I, p. 480).

84 The Austrian count includes *Karl* Uhlans (eight squadrons), *Hessen-Homburg* Hussars (four squadrons), *Kienmayer* Hussars (four squadrons), *Liechtenstein* Hussars (probably four squadrons); some additional *Kienmayer* elements may have played a role as well. It does not include the cavalry that came in with Nordmann and Scheibler. On the Allied side: Nansouty (16 squadrons), St Sulpice (16 squadrons), Jacquinot (six squadrons), Zandt (six squadrons), Preysing (eight squadrons). Note, however, that it is by no means clear that all of these Allied squadrons were actually engaged. The Württemberg cavalry (twelve to sixteen squadrons) is not included as it remained out of the fight.

85 Nordmann: five companies of *St Georg* Grenzer and two and one-half squadrons of *Liechtenstein* Hussars. Scheibler had only one squadron each of *Liechtenstein* and *Rosenberg*; he had left his two Grenzer companies at Pfeffenhausen during the night where they had joined Ludwig's column. *Krieg*, vol. I, 480–81.

86 Bianchi left III/*Duka* and III/*Gyulai* with Oberst Emerich Freiherr von Bakonyi of *Duka* in command of both.

87 A. Albert, *Le Manuscrit des Carabiniers*, Paris: Bruno Sepulchre, 1989, p. 181.

88 The Württemberg light infantry had been deploying to attack St Nikolas when they were ordered to halt. Only two companies, one each from *Neuffer* and *Brüsselle*, participated in the attack on the suburbs and Landshut itself. [Roessler], *Tagebücher aus den zehen Feldzügen der Württemberger unter der Regierung König Friedrichs*, Ludwigsburg: Nast, 1820, vol. I, pp. 138–9.

89 The two *Benjovszky* companies had ended up in Zwischen den Brücken as the battalion withdrew from its earlier position in the plains supporting Vincent. As far as the pioneers are concerned: eighty men would have represented between 20 and 30 per cent of the pioneer division. At the same time, the soldiers of the 5th Pioneer Division successfully dismantled a bridge upstream; though not specifically stated in Brinner, this was probably the Lendbrücke, which otherwise hardly figures in accounts of this battle. The information on the pioneers is from Brinner, p. 55.

90 *Prise de Landshut* by Louis Hersent. When Mouton ordered a copy made for each of his three children, the artist gave the saddle blanket on Mouton's horse a different colour for each child. Laurent Goergler, *Georges Mouton, Comte de Lobau*, Drulingen: Scheuer, 1998, p. 51. Note that the famous spy, Charles Louis Schulmeister, was apparently present at Landshut in the company of Savary, and may have a played a subsidiary role in the battle, but the notion that he led the charge over the main bridge is farfetched, likely nothing more than a local legend in his home city, Strasbourg (see Paul Muller, *L'Espionnage Miliaire sous Napoléon*, Paris: Berger-Levrault, 1896, p. 144; also L. Ferdinand Dieffenbach, *Karl Ludwig*

Schulmeister, Leipzig: Webel, 1879, p. 61; Abel Douay and Gérard Hertault, *Schulmeister*, Paris: Nouveau Monde, 2002, p. 138).

91 Morand to Davout, 21 April 1809, midnight, in Saski, vol. II, p. 324; Pages Xartart; Etienne Béniton [known as 'Capitaine Gervais'], *A la Conquête de l'Europe: Souvenirs d'un Soldat de l'Empire*, ed. Michael Legat, Paris: Editions du Grenadier, 2002, pp. 204–5. Where we know little about how the Austrians captured the Spitalbrücke on 16 April, the reverse applies for 21 April: it is not clear what, if anything, happened at the Lendbrücke. Except as suggested in Brinner, both sides are silent in their accounts.

92 The two Württemberg companies have already been mentioned. The three Bavarian battalions were the two of the 7th Infantry (led by the regiment's grenadiers) and I/3 (possibly only the battalion's Schützen at first).

93 Although the attackers can be detailed with fair accuracy, it is nearly impossible to specify which Austrian units participated in the defence of Landshut. In part this is owing to the confusion in the town, but it also results from repeated instances of Austrian regiments dropping off one battalion or one 'division' (two companies) to fight in the town while the rest withdrew.

94 The losses here were small: five to twelve Austrians and a few Frenchmen. At Moosburg, on the other hand, the French inflicted some forty or fifty casualties on the Austrians; French losses are unknown, but were evidently minimal.

95 Pelet, vol. II, p. 44; Koch, p. 159. Marulaz: 9th Hussars, Hessians, 3rd, 14th, 19th, and 23rd Chasseurs.

96 Though partially exercises in exculpation, accounts from both Hiller and Ludwig stressed the threat posed by Massena's advance as the prime rationale for their retreat. See their 22 April reports in *Krieg*, vol. III, pp. 645–9.

97 A small detachment was sent as far as Altfraunhofen on the Kleine Vils but only encountered French cavalry patrols (*Krieg*, vol. I, p. 485). As with the fighting in Landshut, it is difficult to know with any certainty which Austrian units were covering the left flank at any particular point in the battle. Kienmayer was there first with three of his grenadier battalions and his dragoon regiment. *Krieg* (vol. I, p. 486) states that Nordmann occupied this position with his Grenzer, the *Liechtenstein* Hussars, I/*Klebek*, and I/*Jordis* when Marulaz and Claparède arrived, but it is not clear whether Kienmayer had departed or was still present at that time.

98 Pirquet, diary entry for 21 April, p. 81.

99 Austrian reports quoted in Binder, vol. I, p. 264.

100 Summarising the withdrawal the following year, Hiller bitterly criticised Ludwig and his staff for departing Vilsbiburg 'for what reason I do not know' and ignoring his instructions, so that he found 'such alarm in Vilsbiburg that more or less all of the drivers had ridden off with their horses, pushed over the wagons, and caused such chaos that order could not be restored despite all of my exertions up to 9 p.m.' (Hiller, pp. 162–3).

101 Radetzky, as usual, had the *Gradiska* Grenzer and *Karl* Uhlans; Vincent commanded seven squadrons of *Rosenberg* Chevaulegers and a remnant 'squadron' (thirty men) of *Liechtenstein* Hussars (*Krieg*, vol. I, p. 489).

102 As noted in Chapter 5, Reinwald's detachment consisted of Infantry Regiment No. 40 (formerly *Josef Mittrowsky*), four platoons of *Stipsicz* Hussars and four guns. The

3rd Battalion of *J. Mittrowsky* only had four of its six companies. The detachment totalled approximately 2,800 infantry and cavalry.

103   'Tagebuch eines bayerischen Artillerieoffiziers'.

104   As is often the case, French casualties can only be estimated. The Austrian official history suggests that 1,500 'would not be too high' (*Krieg*, vol. I, Appendix XXX) and Binder believes the number was between 1,500 and 2,000 (vol. I, p. 267). The generally reliable histories of the 30th and 61st Ligne, however, state that Morand's division overall lost only 159 dead and wounded, with perhaps a handful captured, per Morand's report of the battle. Adding 100 cavalry casualties (probably too many as the Austrians only lost 176 cavalry total) and some 50 to 100 for Claparède, would give a figure of only 300 to 350. Gachot (p. 89) and Thiry (p. 71) give the total casualties (without breakdown) as 774. This does not seem an unreasonable figure, though one might use 700 to 1,000 as a compromise between 350 and 1,500 to account for possible under-reporting by the French. According to Martinien, French officer losses at Landshut numbered only ten from Morand's infantry (none from Claparède) and two from the heavy cavalry.

105   This figure, taken from Appendix XXX in *Krieg*, vol. I, includes losses during the retreat on the 22nd, but the authors of *Krieg* note that casualties in several VI Corps regiments may have been even higher, raising the total losses by as much as another 2,757 men (10,760 total).

106   'Geschichte des k. k. 49. Linien-Infanterie-Regiments Baron Kerpen in den Feldzügen von 1809, 1813, 1814 und 1815', *Oesterreichische militärische Zeitschrift*, vol. 10 (1821). This is a published version of the regimental history O'Brien (by then an Oberst) wrote in 1818 (manuscript in the Austrian War Archive); as the authors of *Krieg* note, however, someone other than O'Brien apparently edited the manuscript before it was published (vol. IV, p. 300).

107   *Krieg*, vol. I, p. 495. Recall that one of these guns had been lost on 19 April. In addition, Pfanzelter lost four on the 20th, so a total of twenty-three cannon fell into Allied hands from 19 to 21 April from units associated with the left wing.

108   Hiller, p. 163. In a 22 April report to Charles, Hiller specifically praised the *Scharlach* and *Kirchenbetter* Grenadier Battalions (in *Krieg*, vol. III, p. 646), but the official history discusses *Scharlach* and *Scovaud* at the Landshut bridges and in the early parts of the retreat and makes no mention of *Kirchenbetter*. It seems likely that these three battalions and *Puteany* were involved in the rear guard actions. The *Brzezinski* Grenadiers took over some of the rear guard duties as the retreat passed through Geisenhausen (where Kienmayer had sent the battalion on learning of Massena's approach); the two squadrons of *Knesevich* Dragoons also contributed to the defence at this point.

109   Berthier to Davout, 8 p.m., 20 April 1809, in Saski, vol. II, p. 296.

110   Napoleon to Davout, 5 a.m., 21 April 1809, in Saski, vol. II, pp. 304–5.

111   The best description of this bold bit of bravado is Binder (vol. II, p. 270), who terms it a 'Husarenstück'. The chronicle of Davout's 3rd Corps refers to Hundt's 'imprudent' remarks and the key intelligence he thereby provided to Davout (in Saski, vol. II, p. 306).

112   Davout to Napoleon (sent between 7 and 8 a.m.), 21 April 1809, in Saski, vol. II, pp. 306–8.

113 According to Binder's research, the 1st *Erzherzog Karl* Legion 'literally disintegrated' during this withdrawal (vol. I, p. 217).

114 Steyrer had I/*Chasteler* and two squadrons of *Vincent* Chevaulegers. Stutterheim brought a battalion of *Reuss-Greitz*, four more squadons of *Vincent* and a cavalry battery. Steyrer left his cavalry with Stutterheim, so that the latter fought his action with one battalion, six squadrons and one battery. Additionally, a Rittmeister named Kaiser from Rosenberg's staff led two companies of II/*Chasteler* and some cavalry towards Schneidhart, but it is not clear that they were involved in any action.

115 Rosenberg's account quoted in Binder, vol. II, p. 272.

116 This and previous quote from Berthier to Lefebvre, 5 a.m., 21 April 1809, in Saski, vol. II, pp. 302–3.

117 Strength figures are my approximations of infantry and cavalry numbers taking into account estimated losses from the fighting on 19 April. Davout's strength here does not include Montbrun (3,500).

118 This outline is drawn from *Krieg*, vol. I, pp. 514–17.

119 Charles had intended that III Corps hold the left of the Austrian line from the Laaber to the Laichlings, with IV Corps on its right around the Sandings, Lindenau and Vecsey from thence to the Danube and the reserves (grenadiers and heavy cavalry) in a large triangle generally defined by Alteglofsheim–Haus–Einhausen.

120 Use of the designation 'Hill 402' is my shorthand for the knoll between Schierling and Unterlaichling (based on its height in metres); contemporary sources only refer to it in relation to the two villages.

121 Sources for this remarkable sequence are *Krieg*, vol. I, p. 528; and Binder, vol. I, pp. 273–4.

122 Quoted in Binder, vol. I, p. 274.

123 'Outmoded' in that the absence of the corps structure and other echelons above brigade was characteristic of armies of the previous century.

124 St Hilaire attacked Unterlaichling with a battalion of the 57th Ligne and a voltigeur company from the 10th Léger; the French after-action report claims that 400 prisoners were taken, clearly an exaggeration (French 3rd Corps account in Saski, vol. II, pp. 312–14). Other elements from the division attacked or demonstrated towards Oberlaichling.

125 French 3rd Corps account in Saski, vol. II, pp. 312–14; Binder, vol. I, pp. 276–7; *Krieg*, vol. I, pp. 525–6.

126 Simon Duneau, *Historique du 48e Régiment d'Infanterie*, Paris: Rouff, 1878, p. 57.

127 Coudreux, letter to his brother, 28 April 1809, p. 148.

128 Approximate losses: 1,100 from Friant, 400 from St Hilaire, 350 Bavarians. See *Krieg*, vol. II, Appendix XXX; and Binder, vol. I, p. 278.

129 Pelet, vol. II, pp. 60–1.

130 'A happy mixture of audacity and prudence' in the words of Pelet, vol. II, p. 57.

131 Pelet, vol. II, p. 50.

132 Davout to Napoleon, 21 April 1809, 11 p.m., and Berthier to Davout, 21 April 1809, in Saski, vol. II, pp. 317–18. Note that Ludwig's cavalry brigade was at Landshut.

133 Alfons Freiherr von Wrede, *Geschichte des K. u. K. mährischen Dragoner-Regimentes Albrecht Prinz von Preussen*, Brunn: Rohrer, 1906, p. 417. It is not clear whether Klehe was formally 'attached' to Hohenzollern or not.

134 In Will, 'Beitrage zur Geschichte', p. 171.

135 Quote from a letter to Feldmarschall Herzog Albert von Sachsen-Teschen, 21 April 1809, in *Krieg*, vol. I, p. 536.

136 According to my calculations, Vukassovich should have had approximately 1,700 infantry and 500 cavalry in his four squadrons of *Erzherzog Ferdinand* Hussars and two battalions of *Peterwardein* Grenzer; Bieber's infantry strength should have been approximately 3,600 in the *Kaunitz* (2,100) and *Württemberg* (1,500) Infantry Regiments. *Krieg* (vol. I, p. 538), however, lists 4,300 infantry for *both* brigades; this seems far too low even after subtracting battle casualties for the 19th (these battalions were not seriously engaged on the 20th or 21st). If the official history is correct, the infantry in these two brigades must have suffered fairly severe march attrition (some 17 per cent) during two days of unexceptional marching.

137 *Krieg*, vol. I, p. 538.

138 Montbrun's dispositions: three companies and one squadron of the 11th Chasseurs at Abbach, a similar force at Peising under GB Pajol, the remaining squadron of the 11th Chasseurs and one light infantry company forward of Dünzling, and both hussar regiments with five companies of the 7th Léger in reserve at Eiglstetten (1,800 metres north-east of Saalhaupt). See Bonnal, pp. 245–6. Writing after the war, Charles claimed that he was fully aware of Davout's efforts to conceal the French numerical inferiority. Although the archduke then chastises himself for inactivity, what we know of his actions and orders at the time does not suggest that he saw through Davout's deceptions or that he understood French dispositions as well as he states in his post-war work (Charles, 'Beitrag zur Geschichte', p. 366).

139 *Krieg*, vol. I, p. 535.

140 Savary, vol. IV, p. 83.

141 Napoleon to St Sulpice, 7.30 p.m., 21 April 1809; and Berthier to Vandamme, 21 April 1809, both in Saski, vol. II, pp. 329–30.

142 Charles Eugène Montesquiou was 27 years old; his younger brother, with the artfully alliterative name Ambroise Anatole Augustin, was also an imperial staff officer. According to *Krieg* (vol. I, pp. 491–2) the cavalry that accompanied Montesquiou was a squadron of the 1st Bavarian Chevaulegers, but the regimental history does not mention this action.

143 Davout's initial notes to Napoleon were sent (1) between 7 and 8 a.m., (2) between 10 and 11 a.m., (3) at approximately 2.30 p.m., and (4) at 5 p.m. Each of these forwarded a report from Montbrun: 6 a.m., 7 a.m., 1 p.m., and 3.30 p.m respectively. All of this correspondence is in Saski, vol. II, pp. 306–10.

144 Davout to Napoleon, between 10 and 11 a.m., 21 April 1809, in Saski, vol. II, p. 308.

145 Lefebvre to Napoleon, 9 a.m., 21 April 1809, in Saski, vol. II, p. 319.

146 Joseph Szymanowski, *Mémoires*, Paris: Lavauzelle, 1900, pp. 34–5.

147 The timing of Szymanowski's travels and Napoleon's decisions is approximate and is based on my calculations. 'Scales from his eyes' is from Petre, p. 167.

148 Napoleon to Lannes and Bessières, Berthier to Massena, all sent at 3 a.m., 22 April 1809, in Saski, vol. II, pp. 337–8.

149 Berthier to Moulin, 3 a.m., 22 April 1809, in Saski, vol. II, p. 330; and Napoleon to Rouyer, 22 April 1809, in Saski, vol. II, p. 339. Note that both Saski and Pelet (vol.

II, p. 65) give 21 April as the date of the letter to Moulin, but this makes no sense as the gist of the letter is based on French possession of Landshut which, as we have just seen, was not secured until the afternoon of the 21st. I therefore speculate that it was incorrectly dated when sent.

150 Calculated in round numbers as follows: 8,500 (Morand), 9,100 (Gudin), 2,700 (Hügel) for 20,300 infantry in the lead with 5,500 horse (St Sulpice 3,240, Wöllwarth 2,200, one squadron of the Bavarian 1st Chevaulegers 120). These to be followed by Nansouty (3,300), the rest of the Bavarian 1st Cavalry Brigade (610), Massena's light horse (1,600), Massena's three infantry divisions (25,500), and Espagne (2,900). Four of the Württemberg infantry regiments (minus *Neubronn* in Landshut) were also potentially available (4,700) as well as II/*Camrer* (650), which did make an appearance on the battlefield. The Württemberg artillery histories state that the kingdom's large foot artillery battery also fought at Eggmühl; if so, its impact was not significant.

151 Napoleon to Lannes, 3 a.m., 22 April 1809, in Saski, vol. II, p. 337.

152 Napoleon to Davout, 2.30 a.m. and 4 a.m., 22 April 1809, in Saski, vol. II, pp. 334–7.

153 Montesquiou to Napoleon, 22 April 1809, in Saski, vol. II, p. 336. Intelligence of this nature came from all manner of sources. For example, the French questioned a peasant named Georg Hutmann whose wagon had been requisitioned by the Austrians. Hutmann reported large Austrian troop concentrations south of Regensburg and assured the French that Charles was gathering a major force in the area (Kraft, p. 157).

154 François Dumonceau cited in Pigeard, *Les Etoiles*, p. 279.

155 Roos, pp. 243–4.

156 At some point during the day, II/*Camrer* joined the battle from Ingolstadt, but there are no details regarding its actual involvement. See Roessler, *Tagebücher*, p. 139; and R. M. Felder, *Der schwarze Jäger oder Württembergs Krieger in den Jahren 1805–1816*, Cannstatt: Ruckhäberle, 1839, vol. II, p. 17.

157 Herre, pp. 13–14.

158 Roos, p. 244.

159 These figures include all of the Austrian attack 'columns' and the French forces on the immediate battlefield during the fighting: Davout, Lefebvre, Lannes, the heavy cavalry, the Württemberg light troops (and II/*Camrer*), the cavalry of the 1st Bavarian Division, the 14th Chasseurs, and the Baden Light Dragoons. These numbers do not include the Austrian garrison troops in Regensburg or the following Allies: Boudet, Tharreau, Colbert, Massena, the Württemberg line infantry.

160 Deducting some 3,500 for Montbrun.

161 This figure includes those Allied units that followed the advance, but were not actually engaged: Morand, 1st Bavarian Division, and Demont. This calculation leaves a force of some 48,300 against Rosenberg. One could further reduce this figure to 43,300 by deducting most of Deroy's infantry (5,000) as only the 14th Line and the division's Schützen actually took part in the fighting.

162 Deroy's report quoted in Gerneth/Kiesling, vol. II, p. 209. Deroy took advantage of the lull to write a report summarising his division's actions over the preceding several days (22 April 1809 report in BKA/B442).

163 Kolowrat, for example, rode towards Abbach, but only gained a superficial impression of the French position and did not see that Montbrun was badly outnumbered (*Krieg*, vol. I, p. 547).

164 Stutterheim, p. 241.

165 Binder, vol. I, p. 287. Vukassovich's first report was sent at noon. Binder notes that the order for Bieber to retire north of the Laaber probably came from Rosenberg.

166 Binder (vol. I, p. 288) is bitingly critical of Rosenberg, commenting that the Austrian commander's first thought was retreat.

167 In German: 'sich so gut wie möglich aus dem Gefecht zu ziehen' (quoted in *Krieg*, vol. I, p. 563). See also Binder, vol. I, p. 290.

168 Almost every account of the battle notes Napoleon's presence 'on the heights above Lindach' or 'near Lindach'. However, there is a higher hill above Zaitzkofen and Unterdeggenbach that today bears the name 'Napoleonshöhe'. We cannot know whether Napoleon actually bestrode this piece of turf in 1809 (it is certainly possible that he rode to this prominent hill to get a view of his right flank), but the modern visitor will find it an accessible vantage point where he/she may pull off the road for a magnificent view of the battlefield (although in my most recent stop the former historical plaque was missing—2006).

169 Pelet, vol. II, pp. 77–9.

170 Bial, p. 215.

171 It is not completely clear where Ludwig's division stood in reserve. Most likely it was north of the Laaber, north-west of Schierling (as shown on the map), but some accounts place it on the heights south of the little river.

172 Roos, p. 244.

173 'Feldzug der 2ten Division', pp. 616–17.

174 Charles, 'Denkschrift', *Ausgewählte Schriften*, vol. VI, p. 338.

175 Pelet, vol. II, pp. 78–9.

176 Roos, p. 245.

177 Pelet, vol. II, pp. 79–80.

178 Kraft, p. 158.

179 Roos, p. 246.

180 Roos, p. 246. The fact that Roos included this vivid description of the struggle at Eggmühl in his memoirs of the 1812 campaign is a testament to the impact these events of 1809 had on him.

181 Details of the attack on Eggmühl are from Felder, *Der schwarze Jäger*, pp. 16–19; Karl Muff and Adolf Wenscher, *Geschichte des Grenadier-Regiments König Karl (5. Württembergischen) Nro. 123.*, Stuttgart: Metzler, 1889, p. 19; and Nübling, *Geschichte des Grenadier-Regiments König Karl (5. Württembergischen Nr. 123*, Berlin: Eisenschmidt, 1911, pp. 94–7; Württemberg artillery regimentals.

182 Bial, p. 216.

183 At Napoleon's direction, Lefebvre had detached one and one-half squadrons of the 4th Chevaulegers *Bubenhofen* and one squadron of *Taxis* Dragoons to gather information and to establish liaison with the column marching up from Landshut. The dragoons returned to their regiment in time to participate in the attack on the Austrian guns at Eggmühl, but the light horse squadron (initially sent to

Langquaid) and the half-squadron (sent to scout towards the Landshut road) were absent when the famous charge took place (Gill, *Eagles*, p. 97).

184 Units involved included: Nansouty's 1st Heavy Cavalry Division (twenty-four squadrons), St Sulpice's 2nd Heavy Cavalry Division (sixteen squadrons), French 14th Chasseurs (two squadrons), Seydewitz's brigade (six and one-half squadrons), Württemberg light cavalry (ten squadrons). This made a total of up to 10,500 cavalry (using early April order of battle figures minus estimated casualties) or at least 8,600 if one deducts 20 per cent for march attrition. Missing from the Württemberg cavalry division were six squadrons scouting and screening along the army's right flank: the Leib Chevaulegers (left at Essenbach) and two squadrons of *Herzog Louis* sent to reconnoitre towards the Danube before the engagement at Eggmühl. St. Sulpice's men bore the brunt of the fight for the French. The 14th Chasseurs and the two *Herzog Louis* squadrons apparently remained in support during the struggle.

185 Roos, p. 246.

186 Wilhelm, *Denkwürdigkeiten*, p. 72.

187 Lejeune, vol. I, p. 228.

188 Schaller, p. 34.

189 Roos, p. 246; Pelet, vol. II, p. 84.

190 R. de Place, *Historique du 12e Cuirassiers*, Paris: Lahure, 1889, p. 96.

191 Savary, vol. IV, p. 86.

192 Stutterheim, p. 254.

193 Stutterheim, p. 255.

194 *Krieg*, vol. I, p. 561 (the Austrian official history refers to the 'Stärke und überlegenen Gefechtsweise des Gegners').

195 Pelet, vol. II, pp. 81–2. Pelet had ridden to the front of the immense French march column with his corps commander, Marshal Massena, but with 4th Corps still many kilometres to the south, he had literally nothing to do; noting the importance of the Rogging heights, he rode over to the Stanglmühle to encourage the French skirmishers to advance.

196 *Infanterie-Regimentes Freiherr von Mollinary Nr. 38*, p. 173.

197 *Krieg*, vol. I, p. 556; Saski, vol. II, p. 352.

198 The history of the *Koburg* Infantry, however, states that the regiment held off the French pursuit near Höhenberg for a time (Faust, Fr., *Geschichte des k. k. Infanteire-Regiments von Plüschau, nun Prinz Leopold beider Sicilien*, Wein, 1841, p. 91).

199 'Neunter Tagesbericht von der Kaiserl. Königl. Armee', Vienna, 25 April 1809 in 'Proclamationen, Circularien, summarischer Ausweis und Verzeichnis 1809', MOL/P300/1/104.

200 'I do not know if the report made by the archuke's aide-de-camp may have given a false idea of matters or if it [the report] was poorly composed', wrote Albert ('Mémoire sur la Guerre éclatée en 1809', MOL/P300/1/100).

201 Charles, 'Beitrag', *Ausgewählte Schriften*, vol. VI, p. 363.

202 From an account by Major François Louis Boudin de Roville, one of St Hilaire's staff officers, in Saski, vol. II, pp. 347–8.

203 The Württemberg *Herzog Heinrich* Chevaulegers probably fought in this combat. Napoleon had sent the regiment to support Davout after the capture of the battery

at Kraxenhöfen and it was involved in a serious encounter late in the day, losing its commander in the process.

204 Deroy praised his men for 'manoeuvring as on the exercise field' and reserved especial commendation for the Schützen ('Rapport über die Operationen der 3ten Armee Division', 26 April 1809, BKA/B442).

205 The timing is my guess. Fourth Corps seems to have been in full retreat at approximately 4 p.m. and the cavalry fight at Alteglofsheim apparently began near 7 p.m.

206 In Will, 'Beitrage zur Geschichte', pp. 159–60.

207 First quote from an anonymous grenadier officer cited in Oskar Posselt, *Geschichte des k. und k. Infanterieregiments Ritter v. Pino Nr. 40*, Rzeszow: Gerold, 1913, p. 344. The second quote is from Oberst Johann Mayer von Heldensfeld cited in Binder, vol. I, p. 298. The absence of the army's elite reserve is remarkable and I follow Binder's conclusion that the majority were caught in Rosenberg's retreat and swept away. A Bavarian soldier recalled that 'An imperial grenadier said in my presence that seven battalions of his fellows had laid down their arms in this battle'; this was clearly a gross exaggeration, but suggests the degree of disorder in the grenadiers that afternoon and evening ('Tagebuch eines bayerischen Artillerieoffiziers', p. 447).

208 Cuirassiers (ten squadrons), *Vincent* Chevaulegers (8 squadrons), *Stipsicz* Hussars (seven squadrons), *Ferdinand* Hussars (four squadrons) according to *Krieg*, vol. I, p. 568. Recall that each cuirassier regiment had one squadron detached under Klehe. Stutterheim (p. 260) writes that he had only two squadrons of *Ferdinand* Hussars, but perhaps he was referring to effective strength rather than the nominal number of squadrons.

209 Cuirassiers (forty squadrons), Württemberg *König* Jägers (four squadrons), Württemberg *Herzog Louis* Jägers (two squadrons), French 14th Chasseurs (two squadrons), Bavarian 1st Chevaulegers *Kronprinz* (four squadrons), Seydewitz's Bavarian brigade (six and one-half squadrons), Baden Light Dragoons (four squadrons). Note that *Krieg*, vol. I, p. 568 credits the Allies with sixty-five and one-half squadrons without a detailed breakdown. It is not clear how many Austrian horsemen were on the field; Stutterheim gives 'no more than 2,000' (p. 260), and *Krieg* (vol. I, p. 568) merely says that the light horse was probably at half strength, which would leave a total of perhaps some 2,200.

210 Binder, vol. I, p. 300. There were four cuirassier regiments north of the Pfatter (twenty-four squadrons); the other four squadrons of *Ferdinand* Hussars might also have been summoned, but these and Major Klehe's troopers were quite busy holding off Davout's advance. Whether any or all of these might have arrived in time is open to question, but Binder's principal point is that no effort was expended to even the odds when the Austrians might have fielded an approximately equal number of squadrons against the Allies.

211 Stutterheim, p. 261. Pelet likewise felt that Schneller 'should have limited himself to gaining time' (vol. II, p. 91). Other contemporary authorities highlighted Schneller's dicey situation and the challenge of finding any 'correct' tactical solution: F. R. von Canitz and C. W. E. von Dallwitz, *Nachrichten und Betrachtungen über die Thaten und Schicksale der Reuterei*, Berlin and Posen: Mittler, 1824, vol. II, pp. 146–9; Unger, vol. I, pp. 22–5.

212 I have used the French spelling here (from Six). Wurzbach spells the name 'Rousseles'.

213 Lejeune, vol. I, p. 231. The sun set at 7.13 p.m. on 22 April 1809; the moon was already up and about 44 per cent visible (data from the US Naval Observatory, http://aa.usno.navy.mil).

214 Pelet, vol. II, p. 91.

215 Pelet, vol. II, p. 92.

216 For many contemporary commentators, this battle proved the value of the full cuirass as compared to the half-cuirass: Friedrich Wilhelm Graf von Bismark, *Ideen-Taktik der Reuterei*, Karlsruhe: Müller, 1829, p. 220; Jean Baptiste Antoine Marcellin Marbot, *The Memoirs of Baron de Marbot*, London: Longmans, Green, and Co., 1905, vol. I, p. 300 (also Marbot's analysis, cited in Canitz/Dallwitz, vol. II, pp. 149–50); Pelet, vol. II, pp. 92–3. It is particularly important to note Pelet's observation that the inferiority of the half-cuirass was evident not only, as usually asserted, during the pursuit because pursuing cavalry could stab fleeing troopers in the back, but rather during a tight melee such as Alteglofsheim.

217 Quote from St Sulpice's after-action report as cited in H. de Fontenaille, 'Histoire Militaire: 5eme de Cuirassiers', manuscript, AG, 1890.

218 It is important to note that our sources for the cavalry battle at Alteglofsheim are limited and very many (including *Krieg* and Petre) are, or seem to be, based on the description provided by a Württemberg cavalry officer named Friedrich Wilhelm von Bismark in his *Ideen-Taktik der Reuterei* published in 1829 (pp. 207–27). Bismark was a bold and competent leader and a cavalry expert who later rose to become a general-leutnant and a well-known commentator on cavalry tactics. However, he was a squadron commander in the Württemberg Leib Chevaulegers in 1809 with the rank of Rittmeister. As we have seen, this regiment was screening the Allied flank well south of Alteglofsheim at the time of the battle, so while we cannot be sure that he was not present, it is highly *unlikely* that Bismark personally witnessed what he so vividly described. He no doubt discussed the battle in detail with countrymen who were there and with French officers after the fact, and he probably read relevant after-action reports, but we must bear his likely absence from the battlefield in mind when assessing his account.

219 Charles, 'Denkschrift', *Ausgewählte Schriften*, vol. VI, p. 339.

220 Marbot, vol. I, p. 300.

221 In Will, 'Beitrage zur Geschichte', p. 161.

222 Maximilian Ritter von Thielen, *Erinnerungen aus dem Kriegerleben eines 82jährigen Veteranen der österreichischen Armee*, Vienna: Braumüller, 1863, p. 45.

223 Treuenfest, *Infanterie-Regiments Nr. 20*, p. 340.

224 Binder, vol. I, pp. 301–2.

225 Only 131 men escaped the disaster. The story of Nissel's battalion is told in some detail (but not with the greatest consistency) in Rona, pp. 410–11; and Emil Schmedes, *Geschichte des k. k. 28. Infanterie-Regimentes*, Vienna: Seidel & Sohn, 1878, pp. 148–9.

226 *Krieg*, vol. I, 575–76; Binder, vol. I, 301-02; Gustav Ritter Amon von Treuenfest, *Geschichte des Kärnthnerischen Infanterie-Regiments Nr. 7*, Vienna: St. Norbertus, 1891, p. 485; Treuenfest, *Infanterie-Regiments Nr. 20*, pp. 340–1. The regimental

histories paint a somewhat rosy picture compared to *Krieg* and Binder, but even they cannot completely disguise the prevailing disorder. There may have been other instances of Austrian cavalry overrunning its own infantry during this wild retreat.

227 Hohenzollern's phrase from his after-action report as quoted in Binder, vol. I, p. 301.

228 'Civil twilight', the period when terrestrial objects can be clearly distinguished under good weather conditions, had ended at approximately 7.47 p.m. (data and definition from the US Naval Observatory, http://aa.usno.navy.mil/faq/docs/RST_defs).

229 Grueber, p. 65.

230 The quote is also from the memoirs of Oberleutnant Grueber of the *Albert* Cuirassiers, p. 64. Siegenthal's brigade was north/north-east of Egglfing, west of the post road.

231 Four squadrons of the *EH Franz* Cuirassiers followed behind their sister regiment, while the regiment's other two squadrons attempted to get behind the French. The latter effort apparently did not succeed, but *EH Franz*, usually forgotten in histories of this fight, was sufficiently engaged to suffer a loss of thirty-nine men and fifty-two horses (*Geschichte des k. und k. Dragoner-Regiments Graf Paar Nr. 2*, Olmütz, 1895, p. 377). See also Grueber, p. 65. Austrian accounts of the engagements on the 22nd often refer to French 'guard' cavalry, especially 'grenadiers à cheval', because the two French line carabinier regiments wore a uniform that was almost indistinguishable from that of the Guard Horse Grenadiers.

232 Sources for this brief discussion include: Koch, vol. VI, p. 174; Marbot, vol. I, pp. 300–1; Pelet, vol. II, pp. 93–4, Zins, p. 251. As Petre points out, 'it would seem hardly justifiable to accuse Napoleon of want of energy in not pursuing in the night after Eggmühl' (p. 202). Yorck von Wartenburg, on the other hand, considers Napoleon's decison to pause 'an obvious strategical error' (p. 147).

233 Strack, *Geschichte des Sechsten Dragoner-Regimentes*, p. 42; and Strobl von Ravelsberg, *Geschichte des k. und k. 12. Dragoner-Regiments*, p. 118.

234 The Austrian official history (*Krieg*, vol. I, p. 579) states that the Baden Light Dragoons conducted a reconnaissance towards Geiselhöring on the night of the 22nd, but there is no mention of such an action in the Baden archival records.

235 For Montbrun's actions, see Ledru, pp. 73–6; and Pajol, pp. 340–2.

236 Espinchal states that 'Boudet's brigade' came up during the day, p. 233. Boudet's exact movements during the period from 20 to 23 April are unclear.

237 First quote from Meier, p. 34. Second quote from a Bavarian eyewitness cited in Gerneth/Kiesling, p. 213.

238 Benedikt Peter, *Wachtmeister Peter*, Stuttgart: Steinkopf, 1980, p. 14.

239 According to Beilage 18 of *Krieg*, GL Neubronn was at Oberlindhart with two battalions and four squadrons, three battalions were in Ergoldsbach, and one battalion each in Essenbach and Altheim. Regiment *Neubronn* was serving as the Landshut garrison and cavalry outposted the roads leading to Straubing. Precise designations are not clear.

240 Rouyer's battalions were posted as follows: Donauwörth (5th Rheinbund), Rain (I/6th Rheinbund), Neuburg (2nd Rheinbund), Gerolfing (II/6th Rheinbund), Ingolstadt (4th Rheinbund). See Gill, *Eagles*, p. 391.

241 Will, 'Beitrage zur Geschichte', pp. 157, 161–2, 173.

242 'Tagebuch eines bayerischen Artillerieoffiziers', p. 447.

243 Völderndorff (p. 103) claims that Bavaria's Crown Prince Ludwig had installed himself in a nearby house, but had to evacuate suddenly when the fire threatened to trap him; the village chronicle, on the other hand, states that he slept in the Schloss (Will, 'Beitrage zur Geschichte', p. 173).

244 A contemporary report cited in Wackenreiter, p. 74.

245 Bellegarde had left two battalions and one squadron behind at Neumarkt and Amberg; another detachment was in Nürnberg.

246 In addition to the regimental histories and memoirs cited above, the principal sources used for the Battle of Eggmühl are: Binder, vol. I, pp. 282–307; *Krieg*, vol. I, pp. 542–79; Pelet, vol. II, pp. 65–97; Saski, vol. II, pp. 332–56; Stutterheim, pp. 232–67.

247 Moreover, Binder (vol. I, pp. 303–4) points out that the available casualty figures were calculated several days later when some, perhaps many, stragglers had returned to their regiments. He thus speculates that the number actually missing on 23 April was considerably higher than the 10,700 figure. On the Austrian guns, twenty-six were from IV Corps, the rest from III Corps; note that eight of those mentioned as part of III Corps were probably Bieber's brigade battery, meaning that Rosenberg's initial command lost thirty-four guns total.

248 Casualties from *Krieg*, vol. I, Appendix XXX. Other than the two batteries taken north of Eggmühl near Kraxenhöfen and five guns lost in Köfering, this work does not detail how the other pieces were lost. It seems likely that Bieber's brigade battery was captured, but that still leaves ten guns whose histories we do not know.

249 *Krieg*, vol. I, p. 580.

250 *Krieg*, vol. I, p. 580.

251 *Krieg*, vol. I, pp. 580–1.

252 *Krieg*, vol. I, p. 580.

253 *Krieg*, vol. I. pp. 581–2 (emphasis in original).

254 Rona, p. 412.

255 Each gate was also known by the major city to which its road led: Straubing, Landshut, and Ingolstadt respectively.

256 Hohenzollern had parts of *W. Colloredo*, *Schröder*, and two battalions (I and II) of *EH Karl* as far as combat troops were concerned (*Krieg*, vol. I, p. 583).

257 The comment on disorder during the retreat is from Binder, vol. I, p. 312.

258 St Julien marched with several companies of *W. Colloredo* and *Schröder*, as well as *Manfredini* and *Würzburg* (*Krieg*, vol. I, p. 584). Schneller's men disappear from the records on the 23rd, so the authors of *Krieg* assume that the brigade crossed the pontoon bridge some time before 9 a.m.

259 Adam, *Aus dem Leben*, p. 70; Wilhelm, *Denkwürdigkeiten*, p. 73.

260 Wilhelm, *Denkwürdigkeiten*, p. 73.

261 This figure includes: Lannes, Davout, Massena, Lefebvre, Oudinot, Nansouty, St. Sulpice, Tharreau, Boudet, ten Württemberg cavalry squadrons, and the Württemberg Light Brigade; it does not include the Württemberg line infantry or the detached six cavalry squadrons.

262 Napoleon to Massena, 23 April 1809, Saski, vol. II, pp. 361–2. Massena commanded the same troops that he had brought north from Landshut: Legrand, Carra Saint-

Cyr, Claparède, and Espagne. For light cavalry, he had the Baden Light Dragoons. The 9th Hussars rejoined Colbert's brigade.

263 The light horsemen served as Napoleon's bodyguard; they returned to the division on 25 April. In addition, one infantry battalion (II/8) was detailed to escort 3,000 Austrian captives to Landshut; 1st Light assumed this duty on the 24th and marched its charges to Augsburg; it would not rejoin its division until 6 May at Wasserburg.

264 This number would grow to something over 80,000 with the arrival of the remaining Württemberg troops late in the day.

265 It is not clear how many 12-pounder position batteries were covering the bridging site. The official history speaks of one battery (*Krieg*, vol. I, p. 590), but Binder states that there were three 12-pounder batteries and four brigade batteries (vol. I, p. 313).

266 Vécsey had all eight squadrons of *Klenau* Chevaulegers, I/*Rohan*, three Jäger battalions (5th, 6th, and 7th), and his cavalry battery.

267 Stutterheim, p. 270.

268 On the French side this counts Nansouty (*c.*4,500), St Sulpice (*c.*3,000), and the 14th Chasseurs (*c.*350). Montbrun and Piré totalled approximately 3,400 additional sabres.

269 The presence of French light cavalry is from Fontenaille; given the disposition of French light cavalry that day, these men were almost certainly the 14th Chasseurs. The somewhat scattered nature of the initial pursuit and the emperor's urgency are from Albert, *Carabiniers*, p. 182.

270 J. W. Ridler, 'Rückerinnerung an Österreichische Helden', *Archiv für Geographie, Historie, Staats- und Kriegskunst*, nos. 45 and 46 (April 1811); Stanka, p. 428.

271 The 7th Jägers evidently moved from Hemau to Regensburg late on 22 April or during the night of 22/3 April. This would have left Crenneville with only the 8th Jägers and two uhlan squadrons. The battalion histories and *Krieg* (vol. I, pp. 533, 594) do not clarify the confusion in this instance.

272 Adjutant-Commandant Noël Petit-Pressigny, 'Relation historque du combat de Ratisbonne', in Saski, vol. II, p. 365.

273 Both Espinchal (p. 234) and Charles Henri Lejeune (p. 522) mention this problem.

274 Both quotes from Espinchal, p. 235.

275 Mansuet Padewieth, *Geschichte des kaiserl. königl. 18. Linien-Infanterie-Regimentes*, Vienna: Hof- und Staatsdruckerei, 1859, p. 172.

276 Vécsey: one cavalry battery plus 5th, 6th, 7th Jägers, and I/*Rohan*; Montbrun: two battalions of 7th Léger, no artillery.

277 Losses in both cases are taken from *Krieg*, vol. I, Appendix XXX. The Austrian official history does not describe this fighting in any detail and does not specify that the losses were prisoners and missing (that is my conclusion), but the large number of casualties suggests considerable disorder and discouragement.

278 The story of cuirassiers swimming the Danube is from Grueber, p. 68. With considerable detail, he writes that Siegenthal marched the regiment to the riverbank and plunged in, the regiment following almost as if on parade. Thielen, on the other hand, makes no mention of aquatic adventures, but says that his regiment

(*Kronprinz*) withdrew over the stone bridge in Regensburg (p. 46). *Krieg* simply states that all four regiments 'seem to have used the pontoon bridge' (vol. I, p. 588).

279 There was a small gap in the wall near the Danube on the upstream (west) side of the city, but the French did not notice this vulnerability (*Krieg*, vol. I, p. 591).

280 3rd Division report in Saski, vol. II, p. 366 (note that the report refers to I/7th Léger; this is a reporting error as the 1st and 2nd Battalions were with Montbrun).

281 Wackenreiter, pp. 75–6.

282 Ségur, *Histoire et Mémoires*, vol. III, p. 329.

283 Lorencez, p. 423.

284 Berthezène, p. 212.

285 Report of Major Baron Bourgignon, commander of III/*Zach* in Rona, p. 413.

286 Marbot, vol. I, p. 305.

287 According to Colonel Blein (see below), this was II/25th Ligne.

288 Major Bourgignon, commanding III/*Zach*, at first did not believe that the French had entered the city (Rona, p. 413). It is most interesting to compare his official report with those in Saski and with Marbot's lively account as they describe the same events from opposite sides. Rather surprisingly, they are fairly close in most respects.

289 The precise details of the storm are clouded in confusion. For instance, different reports give different officers credit for being the first up the ladders: an engineer officer named Beaulieu or François Joseph de Viry (another of Lannes's staff officers) with La Bédoyère instead of Marbot. In addition to Marbot and Lejuene (see below), key sources include: the 3rd Corps after-action report and a 24 April 1809 account by engineer Colonel Ange François Blein (both in Saski, vol. II, pp. 366–8); as well as a 26 April 1809 report and sketches by engineer Chef de Bataillon Feraudy in 'Prise de Ratisbonne', *Carnet de la Sabretache* (1895), pp. 227–32. The history of the 85th Ligne provides some detail (E. Sage, 'Historique du 85e Régiment d'Infanterie de Ligne et du 10e Régiment d'Infanterie Légère', manuscript, AG, 1877), but the 25th's account sheds no additional light (Capitaine Adjutant-Major de Fraguier, 'Historique du 25e Régiment de Ligne', manuscript, AG, 1886). The famous scene with Lannes and his staff officers, described in vivid detail many years later by Marbot (vol. I, pp. 304–8), may have been embellished over time, but its basic elements seem accurate. The impetuosity and determination are entirely consistent with Lannes's character and leadership style; and other sources give similar details (e.g., Lejeune, vol. I, p. 236; Pelet, vol. II, pp. 106–8). Marcel Doher's biography of La Bédoyère basically repeats Marbot's account (*Charles de La Bédoyère*, Paris: Peyronnet, 1963, pp. 43–5).

290 Morand's men began to enter Regensburg via the breach at approximately 5 p.m. (see his report in Saski, vol. II, p. 366).

291 Blein to Bertrand, 24 April 1809. Most of this report is in Saski, vol. II, pp. 367–8; but this portion is only found in the full report as printed in *Carnet* (1895), p. 230.

292 Kolowrat's corps remained on the Trinity Heights until approximately 10 p.m., when Crenneville's small command (coming from Hemau) took its place. Crenneville (8th Jägers and two squadrons of *Merveldt* Uhlans reinforced by the 7th Jägers) withdrew to the east some time after midnight. See *Krieg*, vol. I, p. 594; vol. IV, p. 6. Chief Austrian accounts for the fall of Regensburg are *Krieg*, vol. I, pp. 591–4; Rona, pp. 411–14; *Geschichte des k. k. 25. Infanterie-Regiments*, pp. 426–9;

Stutterheim, pp. 278–83. Stutterheim and some others place the French entry into Regensburg at 6 or 7 p.m.; I have followed *Krieg* and French accounts to locate the assault at approximtely 4 p.m. or shortly thereafter.

293 French and Austrian casualties from *Krieg*, vol. I, Appendix XXX; and Binder, vol. I, p. 314; there are scattered details in some of the French regimental histories. French casualties may have been as high as 1,500 or so. Note that Austrian losses here include those suffered by the *Karl* Infantry on 22 April and the 118 officers and men lost when the Württemberg *Louis* Jägers surprised a squadron of *Riesch* Dragoons on the night of 22/3 April.

294 This is the story as told in Coutard's biography (pp. 65–7). Szymanowski's account is similar, though less detailed (p. 35). The 65th apparently had one of its three eagles at Regensburg because Coutard's report to Davout at 10 p.m. on the night of the 20th specifically states 'my two eagles are with the regiment's grand baggage'; Davout would have known that the regiment had one other eagle, and the statement would serve to put the Austrians off the scent (report in *Historique du 65e Régiment d'Infanterie de Ligne*, Paris: Tanera, 1875, p. 14; and Bissey, Lafond and Durand, *Historique du 65e Régiment d'Infanterie de Ligne*, Nantes, regimental, 1888, pp. 46–7). See also Jean Regnault, who seems to overlook some of this detail in his work: *Les Aigles Impériales et le Drapeau Tricolore 1804–1815*, Paris: Peyronnet, 1967, p. 120.

295 These were *Herzog Heinrich* and Leib Chevaulegers.

296 Operations journal quoted in Binder, vol. I, p. 315. Binder expresses astonishment that the headquarters engaged in such laborious staff work during a crisis in combat.

297 St Julien's force consisted of *Würzburg* and *Manfredini* as well as a few companies from *Schröder* and *Wenzel Colloredo*. It is indicative of the army's dreadful state that this command totalled only some 2,600 men. *Krieg*, vol. I, p. 594.

298 This regiment's activities between 21 and 24 April are, as the official historians note (*Krieg*, vol. IV, p. 15), 'shrouded in considerable darkness'. A total of six squadrons arrived in Landshut on 21 April. Four of these fought at Landshut with Hiller, but separated from Hiller's column during the retreat and somehow made their way over the Danube to end up in Cham late on the 23rd or early on the 24th. Two squadrons escorted the army headquarters baggage train: one of these apparently crossed the Danube at Straubing with the baggage and came to Cham; the other split away at Straubing and rode to Deggendorf to destroy the bridge there after the *Riesch* Dragoon squadron tasked with this mission had been destroyed by the Baden Light Dragoons. This latter squadron stayed on the north bank after completing its assignment. The remaining two squadrons joined the regiment in early May.

299 In Neumarkt: Oberst Franz Chevalier Rousseau with one battalion and four companies of *Erbach* Infantry and a squadron of *Schwarzenberg* Uhlans. In Amberg: 4th *EH Karl* Legion and the other two *Erbach* companies (III/*Erbach* was detached in Bohemia). In Nuremberg: an uhlan detachment under Major Johann Metzger Freiherr von Hackenthal. See *Krieg*, vol. I, p. 595, and vol. IV, p. 5.

300 This depiction of Austrian deployments is taken from *Krieg*, vol. I, pp. 594–5; vol. IV, pp. 3–5. Nostitz had the 1st and 2nd Battalions of *Anton Mittrowsky*, 1st Jäger Battalion, one squadron of *Schwarzenberg* Uhlans, and a 3-pounder battery (III/*A. Mittrowsky* was detached in Bohemia). The three detachments mentioned above also belonged to Nostitz's 'reserve brigade' of I Corps.

301 GM Provenchères was at Hohenlinden: one battalion of *Esterhazy* Infantry No. 32, two squadrons of *O'Reilly* Chevaulegers, one-half 3-pounder battery. Oberstleutnant Taxis covered the exits from the Tyrol: two (possibly three) companies of III/*de Vaux* Infantry, four companies of the 2nd Inner Austrian Volunteers (Salzburger Jäger), one company of 2nd Salzburg Landwehr, a company of local Tyrolian militia Schützen and one platoon of *O'Reilly* Chevaulegers. The 1st Hausruck Landwehr was at Wasserburg, the 2nd Hausruck at Rosenheim. Jellacic apparently did not know that the 3rd Innviertel had two companies inside Bavaria (one and one-half in Traunstein, one-half in Reichenhall); its other two companies were in Strasswalchen. All from *Krieg*, vol. III, pp. 80–5.

302 Losses from *Krieg*, vol. I, Appendix XXX.

303 Moltke, p. 46.

304 Pelet, vol. II, p. 134.

305 Moltke, p. 46. See also two excellent pieces written by Bavarian officers: Rudolf von Xylander, 'Zum Gedächtnis des Feldzugs 1809 in Bayern', *Darstellungen aus der Bayerischen Kriegs- und Heeresgeschichte*, vol. 18 (1909); and Herman Hutter, 'Die Operationen Napoleons in den Tagen vom 16. bis 24. April 1809', *Neue militärische Blätter*, vol. XX (1882).

306 This remark is taken from his 'Notes sur le manuscrit venu de Sainte-Hélène', *Correspondance*, vol. XXXI, p. 235. Similar quotations abound: 'Notes sur l'ouvrage intitulé Considerations sur l'Art de la Guerre', *Correspondance*, vol. XXXI, p. 359; Bertrand, *Cahiers*, vol. II, pp. 93–4; Gaspard Gourgaud, *Talks of Napoleon at St. Helena*, Chicago: McClurg, 1904, p. 143. See also Jomini, *Art of War*, p. 115.

307 Bonnal, pp. 353–4.

308 Bonnal offers a decidedly more skeptical analysis stressing his belief that Napoleon lost several opportunities to destroy the Austrian army, see pp. 343–51.

309 Charles, 'Beitrag', *Ausgewählte Schriften*, vol. VI, pp. 364–5.

310 Espinchal, p. 234.

311 Pelet, vol. II, p. 61.

312 Petre (p. 201) attributes 'a natural tendency to indolence' to Charles, a rather harsh judgment; but the word certainly applies to any number of lesser Austrian generals and Charles himself cannot escape censure for lassitude at several points during the campaign.

313 Grünne to Prince de Ligne, 28 September 1809, published in Joseph Hormayr, *Das Heer von Innerösterreich unter den Befehlen des Erzherzogs Johann im Kriege von 1809 in Italien, Tyrol und Ungarn*, Leipzig & Altenburg: Brockhaus, 1817, pp. 394–7.

314 Criste, *Carl*, vol. III, p. 64.

315 For example, Charles to Franz, 27 April 1809, in Criste, *Carl*, vol. III, p. 77.

316 See his two key analyses on 1809: 'Denkschrift', *Ausgewählte Schriften*, vol. VI, pp. 331–4; and 'Beitrag', *Ausgewählte Schriften*, vol. VI, pp. 364–6 (quote from p. 365).

INTERMEZZO: THE FIRST CAMPAIGN

1 Stutterheim, p. 283 (keep in mind that Stutterheim was writing in 1810/11). Napoleon agreed: 'Eggmühl decided the fate of a war' (August 1816, Emmanuel Las

Cases, *Journal of the Private Life and Conversations of the Emperor Napoleon at Saint Helena*, London: Colburn, 1823, vol. VI, p. 7).

2   Vincent Bertrand, *Mémoires*, p. 75.

3   Ségur, vol. III, p. 324.

APPENDICES

1   Cited in Philipp, *Le Service d'Etat-Major*, p. 66.

2   Order of battle and strength taken from *Krieg*, vol. I, Appendices XIII, XVIII, XXVII.

3   Basic composition and strength as of 6 April taken from '2tes Armee-Corps: Operations-Journal', KAFA, *Operations-Journale der Hauptarmee und Korps*, Kart. 1382; supplemented by *Krieg*, vol. I, Appendices XIII and XVIII; and Stutterheim, p. xlviii. Strength of *Zach* (three battalions) taken from Rona, p. 408; the archival reference only lists two battalions at 2,033 men. Strength of *Stuart* computed by subtracting that of the 3rd Battalion (1,235 according to *Krieg*, vol. III, pp. 92–3) from the total of 3,700 in the archival record (which is dated 6 April, thus three days before the 3rd Battalion was detached). Note that this computation for the infantry is 279 men less than that given in *Krieg*, vol. I, Appendix XIII for 10 April (21,090); the source of the discrepancy is not clear, but it is small enough to be explained by changes in the numbers of sick or of small detachments. The archival and *Krieg* figures for the cavalry are identical.

4   Binder (vol. I, p. 286) gives this battalion a strength of 827 (not including officers, musicians, etc. who would account for perhaps another twenty or so) as of 15 April. It is possible that a filler detachment arrived just before or after hostilities opened to bring the 7th Jägers up to strength. On the other hand, the battalion's history (Kandelsdorfer, p. 26) states that it mustered 952 men when gathered in Bohemia in mid-March.

5   Basic composition and strength as of 16 April taken from 'Operations-Journal des 3ten Armee-Corps', KAFA, *Operations-Journale der Hauptarmee und Korps*, Kart. 1382; supplemented by *Krieg*, vol. I, Appendices XIII and XVIII; and Stutterheim, p. xlviii. Note that this computation for the infantry is 124 men more than that given in *Krieg*, vol. I, Appendix XIII for 10 April (22,555); the source of the discrepancy is not clear, but it is small enough to be explained by changes in the numbers of sick or of small detachments. The archival and *Krieg* figures for the cavalry are identical. The third battalions of *Würzburg* and *Württemberg* reached the Inn on approximately 24 April and were incorporated into Hiller's command.

6   Four of these companies (those of *Schröder* and *Lindenau*) joined Hiller's command on the Inn in late April. Those of *Kaiser* and *Kaunitz* met their battalions in Bohemia in late April or early May. There is no clear information on the missing companies from *Manfredini* and the one from *W. Colloredo*, but it seems reasonable to conclude that they also rejoined their home battalions in Bohemia during late April or early May, thus after the first campaign. Information from regimental histories and *Krieg*, vol. III, 71-77.

7 Basic composition and strength taken from *Krieg*, vol. I, Appendices XIII and XVIII, order of battle modified as indicated in Stutterheim, p. XLVIII and Treuenfest, *Husaren-Regimentes No. 10*, pp. 240–3. While III/*Bellegarde* united with its regiment in Bohemia during the retreat, the third battalions of *Czartoryski* and *Chasteler* reached the Inn on approximately 24 April and were incorporated into Hiller's command. The *Reuss-Greitz* battalion marched into Moosbach on the 27th and was sent to join Jellacic's division.

8 Basic composition and strength as of 12 April taken from 'Vtes Armee-Corps: dessen Geschichte von der Zusammensetzung angefangen bis zur Auflösung 1809', KAFA, *Operations-Journale der Hauptarmee und Korps*, Kart. 1383; supplemented by *Krieg*, vol. I, Appendices XIII and XVIII; and Stutterheim, p. xlviii. Reaching Braunau on approximately 23 April, III/*Beaulieu* was incorporated into the regiment during Hiller's retreat from Bavaria.

9 *Krieg*, vol. I, Appendices XIII and XVIII. Regimental strengths for Jellacic were for 2 April from '6tes Armee-Corps: Journal über die Operationen der detachierten Division des Bn. Fr. Jellachich', KAFA, *Operations-Journale der Hauptarmee und Korps*, Kart. 1385.

10 *Krieg*, vol. I, Appendices XIII and XVIII.

11 *Krieg*, vol. I, Appendices XIII and XVIII.

12 *Krieg*, vol. III, pp. 85–97. Landwehr strengths from two March 1809 (not further dated) reports: 'Ausweis über die Landwehr Bataillons und die Depots in Böhmen' and 'Ausweis über die Landwehr Bataillons und die Depots im Oesterreich Ob- und Unter der Enns dann im Salzburgischen' both in KAFA, Kart. 1451.

13 Sources: principally Saski, vol. I, pp. 532–3, and vol. II, pp. 18, 380–2, annexes. Supplemented by 'Livret de Situation', May 1809, AG, *Armée d'Allemagne—Livrets*, C2/674; *Krieg*, vol. I, Appendix IX; and Mayerhoffer, 'Armee in Deutschland'.

14 Sources as for 2nd Corps. The assignment of brigade commanders in 3rd Corps is a best guess for approximately 15 April based on biographies of the generals and Binder, vol. I. pp. 351–2. Davout made a number of changes immediately before and shortly after the start of hostilities: apparently on 30 March, 9 April, 17 April, and 19 April with some généraux de brigade moving from the three organic line divisions of his corps to Demont's reserve division (e.g. GB Girard) and others shifting among divisions (GB Barbanègre) or moving to the corps staff (GB Hervo). GB Jean Baptiste Boyer, mentioned in some sources, was not promoted to that rank until 5 June 1809.

15 Sources for French troops: principally Saski, vol. I, pp. 532–3, and vol. II, pp. 18, 380–2, and annexes. Supplemented by 'Livret de Situation', May 1809, AG, *Armée d'Allemagne—Livrets*, C2/674; *Krieg*, vol. I, Appendix IX; and Mayerhoffer, 'Armee in Deutschland'. For Baden troops: Zech/Porbeck, pp. 16–17; Söllner, pp. 74, 107–8, 143; and GLA, 48/4285, 'Rapport historique de la campagne contre l'Autriche l'an 1809'. For Hessian troops: Röder von Diersburg, *Geschichte des 1. Grossherzoglich Hessischen Infanterie*, p. 145.

16 Sources: Saski, vol. II, annex; and Gill, *Eagles*, pp. 66–70.

17 Sources: Saski, vol. II, annex; and Gill, *Eagles*, pp. 131–4.

18 Sources: AG, situation report for the Saxon contingent (undated, late March or early April), *Armée d'Allemagne*, C2/509; and Exner, pp. 16–21. Also: April 'Etat

Sommaire' in AG, *Armée d'Allemagne*, C2/508 and 20 May 'Etat Sommaire' in C2/520. Major Becker, 'Auszüge über die Aufstellung, Eintheilung und Stärke der königlich Sächsischen Armee während des Feldzugs im Jahr 1809', SächsHStA, Generalstab (bezw. Generalkommando), D4097.

19 Sources for Westphalian troops: Situation report for troops stationed in Westphalia, 10 April 1809, AG, *Armée d'Allemagne*, C2/509. For Dutch troops: 10th Corps 'Situation', 31 May 1809, AG, *Armée d'Allemagne*, C2/509. For Chabert's battalion: 26th Military Division, 'Situation du bataillon commandé par M. le Colonel Chabert', 29 March 1809, AG, *Armée d'Allemagne*, C2/511.

20 Saski, vol. I, Annex 8. Information is dated 28 March 1809, so it is possible that several of the replacement detachments already en route could have reached the division before 10 April bringing the total strength to 5,337 as indicted in Mayerhoffer, 'Armee in Deutschland', p. 284.

21 Gill, *Eagles*, p. 392. Note that many French 'situations' simply list the full, authorised manpower for the various German units, so that it is frequently difficult to arrive at a good estimate of their strength.

22 Dupas arrived in Würzburg on 21 April. These figures are from information dated 28 March 1809 and presented in Saski, vol. I, Annex 11. Note that an additional 700 replacements for the 19th Ligne were to be picked up in Würzburg, but were not yet with the division on 10 April. The number of guns is from Mayerhoffer, 'Armee in Deutschland', p. 235; and Ferdinand Dubouloz-Dupas and André Folliet, *Le Général Dupas*, Paris: Chapelot, 1899, p. 207. The extraordinarily large number of artillerymen is explained by the number of train personnel (524); Dupas initially referred to his artillery component as a 'park', which was reorganised as 'divisional artillery' in May (still with 12 guns). See Dubouloz-Dupas.

23 Bruyère arrived in Bamberg on 18 April and reached Donauwörth on the 23rd. These figures are from information dated 28 March 1809 and presented in Saski, vol. I, Annex 11. Note that the 3rd Squadron of the 24th was serving with Marmont's army. The 13th Chasseurs had their first three squadrons on hand; the fourth was being formed in the depot and would join the regiment in several tranches during the campaign.

24 Strength and organisation from 'Situation' dated 18 May 1809 in Saski, vol. III, Annex 8. In April, the Guard was still moving east from Spain and France to join the Army of Germany.

25 GD Beaumont, 'Etat des Détachments de Dragons', 13 April 1809, AG, *Armée d'Allemagne*, C2/510.

26 Gill, *Eagles*, p. 388.

27 Strength is from 'Livret de Situation' dated 1 June 1809, AG, *Armée d'Allemagne—Livrets*, C2/675.

28 'Livret de Situation' dated 1 June 1809, AG, *Armée d'Allemagne—Livrets*, C2/675. An additional 119 men were en route to join the battalion.

29 Napoleon wanted to provide light cavalry *companies d'ordonnances* (translated here as 'staff hussars' to avoid misleading terms such as 'adjutant companies' or 'ordnance companies') for the army to perform staff duties, thereby relieving combat regiments of these wearing and demanding tasks; he designated 202 men of a regiment currently in Spain, the 10th Hussars, for this purpose. By using

the hussars in this manner, he also intended to avoid an unpalatable mixing of uniforms in organizations such as in the 1st Provisional Chasseur Regiment. From information dated 1 March 1809 and presented in Saski, vol. I, Annex 19.

30 'Les Marins de la Flottille et les Ouvriers Militaires de la Marine pendant la Campagne de 1809 en Autriche', *Carnet de la Sabretache* (1895).

31 II Corps 'Situation', 1 June 1809, AG, *Armée d'Allemagne*, C2/506; Paul Boppe, *La Légion Portugaise 1807–1813*, Paris: Berger-Levrault, 1897. Eventually, the Portuguese cavalry component would refer to itself as two 'regiments', the 1st of two squadrons and the 2nd with only one, but the combined strength would barely approximate a single regiment.

32 Unless otherwise noted, all information here is derived from sources as for 10 April order of battle, supplemented by relevant sections of *Krieg*, vol. I.

33 Sources as for 10 April order of battle; *Krieg*, vol. I, p. 403. Binder gives figures for the corps' early report of 15 April: these are generally the same as those for 6 April with the exception of the 7th Jäger Battalion, which Binder lists as 827 NCO's and men (not including officers or musicians); I have thus used the higher strength for this battalion on 19–20 April, but have subtracted losses for the battles north of Regensburg (117 officers and men). On the other hand, note that Binder mistakenly states that III/*J. Colloredo* reached II Corps on 17 April; in fact, the battalion had been detached to suppress a Landwehr mutiny in Bohemia early in April and did not rejoin its regiment until 26 June (Pillersdorf, p. 361).

34 Sources as for 10 April order of battle; *Krieg*, vol. I, pp. 427–9, 442–4.

35 Sources as for 10 April order of battle; *Krieg*, vol. I, p. 445.

36 Strength here based on estimates of 1,000 casualties on the 19th and 135 for the preceding engagements. As mentioned in the text, Friant's losses at Hausen-Teugn could vary from 377 to 2,016 giving a strength on the following day of anywhere between 9,500 and 8,000.

37 Strength derived by subtracting 1,700 casualties on 19 April from previous figures.

38 Subtracts losses from 19 April and rounds down.

39 Assumes approximately fifty casualties for III/7th Léger on 19 April.

40 Subtracts estimated losses from 11, 13, and 14 April.

41 Brigade composition taken from Ian Castle, *Eggmühl 1809*, Oxford: Osprey, 1998, p. 69.

42 Saski, vol. I, Annex 8 (as for 10 April order of battle). Information is dated 28 March 1809, so it is possible that several of the replacement detachments already en route could have reached the division before 10 April bringing the total strength to 5,337 as indicted in Mayerhoffer, 'Armee in Deutschland', p. 284.

43 Gill, *Eagles*, p. 392.

44 Unless otherwise noted, all information here is derived from sources as the previous orders of battle, supplemented by relevant sections of *Krieg*, vol. I and other sources as indicated.

45 The 7th Jägers evidently marched to Regensburg late on the 22nd or during the night of 22/3 April. The battalion was not present for the Battle of Eggmühl, but arrived in time to suffer heavy losses in the fighting on the 23rd.

46 Sources as for the previous orders of battle; *Krieg*, vol. I, p. 403. Binder gives figures for the corps' early report of 15 April: these are generally the same as those for

6 April with the exception of the 7th Jäger Battalion, which Binder lists as 827 NCO's and men (not including officers or musicians); I have thus used the higher strength Binder gives for this battalion on 19–20 April, but have subtracted losses for the battles north of Regensburg (117 officers and men). On the other hand, note that Binder mistakenly states that III/J. *Colloredo* reached II Corps on 17 April; in fact, the battalion had been detached to suppress a Landwehr mutiny in Bohemia early in April and did not rejoin its regiment until 26 June (Pillersdorf, p. 361). Total infantry strength here agrees with the official history (*Krieg*, vol. I, p. 536), but is lower than the 24,000 in Angeli (vol. IV, p. 155) and Stutterheim (p. 237) because the latter two sources include the two battalions left north of the Danube and because they evidently overestimated the strengths of the available battalions.

47 The strengths of the two groups of *Klenau* Chevaulegers are taken from *Krieg*, vol. I, pp. 536–7; the source does not explain the discrepancy: that is, why one group of four squadrons should be 200 troopers stronger than the other. The regimental history states that the 1st and 2nd 'Columns' each had three squadrons, while two other squadrons had been on outpost duty and were reassembling themselves on the morning of 22 April (Pizzighelli, *Dragoner-Regimentes Nr. 10*, p. 42).

48 This depiction of the Regensburg garrison follows the two relevant regimental histories: *Geschichte des K. K. 25. Infanterie-Regiments*, p. 425, and Rona, p. 410. *Krieg*, vol. I, p. 536, places only one (unspecified) battalion in the city.

49 Total infantry strength here agrees with the official history (*Krieg*, vol. I, p. 537), but is lower than the 12,000 in Angeli (vol. IV, p. 155) and Stutterheim (p. 237) probably because they overestimated the strengths of the available battalions.

50 Note that *Krieg* (vol. I, p. 537) gives Hohenzollern 14,640 men. This seems far too many. Even 10,000 men may be generous: Stutterheim (p. 237) and Angeli (vol. IV, p. 155) both list 8,000, the latter indicating a quote from the operations order.

51 Saski, vol. III, p. 25.

52 The division suffered an unknown number of losses on 21 April; to account for this, I deducted approximately 700 from the total strength of Lannes' command (making estimated changes to the individual regimental numbers based on officer casualties from Martinien).

53 Figures do not reflect any losses for 21 April (there were not many).

54 Saski, vol. I, Annex 8 (as for 10 April order of battle), and Mayerhoffer, 'Armee in Deutschland', p. 284. Figures do not reflect any losses for 21 April (there were not many).

55 Gill, *Eagles*, p. 392.

Bibliographic Note

The third volume of this study is slated to bear the load of an extensive bibliography to supply readers with a complete catalogue of the sources consulted and to serve as a comprehensive thematic starting point for future researchers on the war. Readers of the present volume will find full citations in the endnotes, but it seems useful to expend a few words on some of the principal sources for the political background to the conflict and the first campaign.

Select archival material from Paris, Vienna, and London informs the discussion of Austria's approach to the question of war (especially the instructions for Schwarzenberg and the British replies to Austrian importunities) and French appraisals of Habsburg thinking as reflected in the thorough reporting from the embassy in Vienna. Much of the key material, however, is also available in published form. In addition to the various editions of Napoleon's correspondence, several important Russian and Prussian sources are noted below, as are excellent studies by authors such as Beer, Fournier, Gaede, Lefebvre, Pertz, Thiers, and Wertheimer. Though wariness is advised in using Hellmuth Rössler owing to his political leanings (his first volume was published in Nazi Germany), his two works on Stadion are fundamental and contain much crucial material.

On the operational side, the most important Austrian work is the semi-official *Krieg 1809*, a superb analysis remarkably free, in most cases, of national bias. The authors drew on German archives, but it is important to note that they did not use French archival material except where it had already appeared in print. One of the team of contributors, Mayerhofer von Vedropolje, also produced a slender but superb single-volume summary of the war. To these must be added Stutterheim's fine account, which has the added benefit of drawing on his personal experiences as a general in the war. Charles himself wrote two fairly honest, if often self-deprecating, assessments. Likewise, from the French perspective, Pelet's fine history is enriched by his experiences as a staff officer for Massena. Saski's conscientious work provides the modern reader with an enormous amount of primary source material for the opening stages of the war. Binder von Kriegelstein presents excellent analysis enlivened by his mordant writing style. I also culled material from Austrian, German, and French archives to complete the orders of battle.

I have made extensive use of memoirs in this volume. All of the normal cautions concerning 'remembering with advantages' apply, but many of these works offer unique insights and images if used carefully. Similarly, I have found a wealth of detail in regimental and contingent histories. These run the gamut of quality from hagiographic overviews to detailed, scholarly studies, but judiciously employed, they can bridge the gap between memoirs and secondary accounts.

Angeli, Moritz Edlen von, *Erzherzog Carl von Oesterreich als Feldherr und Heeresorganisator*, Vienna: Braumüller, 1897.

'Die Armee Napoleon I. im Jahre 1809', *Mittheilungen des k. k. Kriegs-Archivs*, Vienna, 1881.

Arneth, Alfred Ritter von, *Johann Freiherr von Wessenberg*, Vienna: Braumüller, 1898.

Bailleu, Paul (ed.), *Briefwechsel König Friedrich Wilhelm's III und der Königin Luise mit Kaiser Alexander I.*, Leipzig: Hirzel, 1900.

Bavaria, Generalstabssektion des königlichen bayerischen Generalquartiermeister-stabes, *Der Feldzug von 1809 in Bayern*, manuscript, Bayerisches Kriegsarchiv, 1865.

Beer, Adolf, *Zehn Jahre österreichischer Politik 1801–1810*, Leipzig: Brockhaus, 1877.

'Beiträge zur Geschichte des österreichischen Heerwesens 1809', *Oesterreichische Militärische Zeitschrift*, vol. 3 (1869).

Beobachtungen und historische Sammlung wichtiger Ereignisse aus dem Kriege zwischen Frankreich, dessen Verbündeten und Oesterreich im Jahr 1809, Weimar: Landes-Industrie Comptoir, 1809.

Binder von Kriegelstein, Christian Freiherr, *Der Krieg Napoleons gegen Oesterreich 1809*, ed. Maximilian Ritter von Hoen, Berlin: Voss, 1906.

Bonnal, Henry, *La Manœuvre de Landshut*, Paris: Chapelot, 1905.

Botzenhart, Manfred, *Metternichs Pariser Botschafterzeit*, Münster: Aschendorff, 1967.

Broers, Michael, *Europe Under Napoleon 1799–1815*, London: Arnold, 1996.

Castle, Ian, *Eggmühl 1809*, London: Osprey, 1998.

Chandler, David G., *The Campaigns of Napoleon*, New York: Macmillan, 1966.

Charles, Archduke of Austria, *Ausgewählte Schriften*, Vienna: Braumüller, 1893–4.

Criste, Oskar, *Erzherzog Carl von Oesterreich: Ein Lebensbild*, Vienna: Braumüller, 1912.

Duncker, Max, 'Friedrich Wilhelm III. im Jahre 1809', *Preussischer Jahrbücher*, vol. 41 (1878).

Elting, John R., *Swords Around a Throne*, New York: Free Press, 1988.

Fedorowicz, Wladyslaw de, *1809: Campagne de Pologne*, Paris: Plon, 1911.

Fournier, August, 'Oesterreichs Kriegsziele im Jahre 1809', *Beiträge zur neueren Geschichte Oesterreichs*, vol. IV (December 1908).

Gaede, Udo, *Preussens Stellung zur Kriegsfrage im Jahre 1809*, Hannover and Leipzig: Hahn, 1897.

Gill, John H., *With Eagles to Glory*, London: Greenhill, 1992.

—— 'What Do They Intend? Austrian War Aims in 1809', in The Consortium on Revolutionary Europe, *Selected Papers 1996*, ed. Charles Crouch, Kyle O. Eidahl and Donald D. Horward, Tallahassee: Florida State University, 1996.

—— 'The Strategic Setting in 1809: Intelligence and Operational Decisions on the Road to War', in The Consortium on Revolutionary Europe, *Selected Papers 1997*, ed. Kyle O. Eidahl, Donald D. Horward and John Severn, Tallahassee: Florida State University, 1997.

—— 'Decision in Bavaria: The Austrian Invasion of 1809', in Jonathan North (ed.), *The Napoleon Options*, London: Greenhill, 2000.

Granier, Herman (ed.), *Berichte aus der Berliner Franzosenzeit 1807–1809*, Leipzig: Hirzel, 1913.

Grunwald, Constantin de, 'La Fin d'une Ambassade: Metternich à Paris en 1808–1809', *Revue de Paris*, 1 and 15 October 1937.

Hassel, Paul, *Geschichte der Preussischen Politik*, Leipzig: Hirzel, 1881.

Hertenberger, Helmut and Franz Wiltschek, *Erzherzog Karl: Der Sieger von Aspern*, Graz: Styria, 1983.

Hutter, Herman, 'Die Operationen Napoleons in den Tagen vom 16. bis 24. April 1809', *Neue Militärische Blätter*, vol. XX (1882).

Johann, Archduke of Austria, *Erzherzog Johanns 'Feldzugserzählung' 1809*, ed. Alois Veltzé, *Supplement zu den Mitteilungen des k. u. k. Kriegsarchivs*, Vienna: Seidel & Sohn, 1909.

Koch, Jean Baptiste, *Mémoires d'André Massena*, Paris: Bonnot, 1967 (reprint of 1850 edition).

Kraehe, Enno E., *Metternich's German Policy*, Princeton: Princeton University Press, 1963.

Krieg 1809, Vienna: Seidel & Sohn, 1907–10.

Lefebvre, Armand and Eduard Lefebvre de Béhaine, *Histoire des Cabinets de l'Europe pendant le Consulat et l'Empire*, Paris: Amyot, 1867–8.

Lehmann, Max, *Scharnhorst*, Leipzig, 1887.

Martens, Fedor, *Recueil des Traités et Conventions Conclus par la Russie avec les Puissances Etrangères*, St Petersburg, 1876–1908.

Mayerhoffer von Vedropolje, Eberhard, *Oesterreichs Krieg mit Napoleon I*, Vienna: Seidel & Sohn, 1904.

Metternich-Winneburg, Prince Clemens Lothar Wenzel von, *Memoirs of Prince Metternich*, New York: Fertig, 1970.

Mikhaïlowitch, Grand Duke Nicolas (ed.), *Les Relations Diplomatiques de la Russie et de la France d'aprés les Rapports des Ambassadeurs d'Alexandre et de Napoléon*, St Petersburg, 1905.

Moltke, Hellmuth von, 'Der Feldzug 1809 in Bayern', in *Moltkes Kriegsgeschichtliche Arbeiten*, Berlin: Mittler, 1899.

Muir, Rory, *Britain and the Defeat of Napoleon 1807–1815*, New Haven, CT: Yale University Press, 1996.

Münchow-Pohl, Bernd von, *Zwischen Reform und Krieg: Untersuchungen zur Bewusstseinlage in Preussen 1809–1812*, Göttingen: Vandenhoeck & Ruprecht, 1987.

Napoléon I, *Correspondance de Napoléon Ier publiée par ordre de l'Empereur Napoléon III*, Paris: Imprimerie Impériale, 1858–70.

—— *Supplément à la Correspondance de Napoléon Ier*, Paris: Dentu, 1887.

—— *Lettres Inédites de Napoléon Ier*, ed. Léon Lecestre, Paris: Plon, 1897.

—— *Lettres Inédites de Napoléon Ier*, ed. Léonce de Brotonne, Paris: Champion, 1898.

—— *Dernières Lettres Inédites de Napoléon Ier*, ed. Léonce de Brotonne, Paris: Champion, 1903.

——*Unpublished Correspondence of Napoleon I Preserved in the War Archives*, ed. Ernest Picard and Louis Tuetey, New York: Duffield, 1913.

Oncken, Wilhelm, *Oesterreich und Preussen im Befreiungskriege*, Berlin: Grote, 1879.

Pelet, Jean-Jacques, *Mémoires sur la guerre de 1809 en Allemagne*, Paris: Roret, 1824–6.

Pertz, Georg Heinrich, *Das Leben des Ministers Freiherrn vom Stein*, Berlin: Reimer, 1851.

—— *Das Leben des Feldmarschalls Grafen Neithardt von Gneisenau*, Berlin: Reimer, 1864.

Petre, Francis Loraine, *Napoleon and the Archduke Charles*, London: John Lane, 1909.

Rauchensteiner, Manfried, *Kaiser Franz und Erzherzog Karl*, Vienna: Verlag für Geschichte und Politik, 1972.

—— *Feldzeugmeister Johann Freiherr von Hiller*, Vienna: Notring, 1972.

Rössler, Hellmuth, *Oesterreichs Kampf um Deutschlands Befreiung*, Hamburg: Hanseatische Verlagsanstalt, 1940.

—— *Graf Johann Philipp Stadion: Napoleons deutscher Gegenspieler*, Vienna: Herold, 1966.

Rothenberg, Gunther E. *Napoleon's Great Adversaries: The Archduke Charles and the Austrian Army 1792–1814*, Bloomington: Indiana University Press, 1982.

Russia, Ministerstvo Inostrannykh del, *Vneshniaia Politika Rossii XIX i nachala XX veka: dokumenti rossiiskogo Ministersva Inostrannykh del*, Moscow: Foreign Ministry, 1965.

Saski, Charles, *Campagne de 1809 en Allemagne et en Autriche*, Paris: Berger-Levrault, 1899–1902.

Schroeder, Paul W. *The Transformation of European Politics*, Oxford: Clarendon Press, 1994.

Stamm-Kuhlmann, Thomas, *König in Preussens grosser Zeit: Friedrich Wilhelm III., der Melancholiker auf dem Thron*, Berlin: Siedler, 1992.

Stern, Alfred, *Abhandlungen und Aktenstücke*, Leipzig: Duncker, 1885.

[Stutterheim, Karl Freiherr von], *La Guerre de l'An 1809 entre l'Autriche et la France*, Vienna: Strauss, 1811.

Tatistcheff, Serge, *Alexandre Ier et Napoléon d'après leur Correspondance Inédite*, Paris: Perrin, 1891.

Thiers, Adolphe, *Histoire du Consulat et de l'Empire*, Paris: Paulin, 1845–69.

Thimme, Friedrich. 'Die hannoverschen Aufstandspläne im Jahre 1809 und England', *Zeitschrift des Historischen Vereins für Niedersachsen*, 1897.

Thimme, Friedrich, 'Zu den Erhebungsplänen der preussischen Patrioten im Sommer 1808', *Historische Zeitschrift*, 86, 1901.

Vandal, Albert, *Napoléon et Alexandre Ier*, Paris: Plon, 1918.

Vann, James Allen, 'Habsburg Policy and the Austrian War of 1809', *Central European History*, VII, 4, December 1974.

Vaupel, Rudolf ed., *Das Preussische Heer von Tilsiter Frieden bis zur Befreiung*, Leipzig: Hirzel, 1938.

Wertheimer, Eduard, 'Berichte des Grafen Friedrich Lothar Stadion ueber die Beziehungen zwischen Oesterreich und Baiern (1807–1809)', *Archiv für Oesterreichische Geschichte*, 63, 1882.

—— *Geschichte Oesterreichs und Ungarns im ersten Jahrzehnt des 19. Jahrhunderts*, Leipzig: Duncker & Humblot, 1890.

Xylander, Rudolf von, 'Zum Gedächtnis des Feldzugs 1809 in Bayern', *Darstellungen aus der Bayerischen Kriegs- und Heeresgeschichte*, 18, Munich: Lindauer, 1909.

Zehetbauer, Ernst, *Landwehr gegen Napoleon: Oesterreichs erste Miliz und der Nationalkrieg von 1809*, Vienna: öbv & hpt, 1999.

Index